Introduction to Automata Theory, Languages, and Computation

SECOND EDITION

JOHN E. HOPCROFT
Cornell University

RAJEEV MOTWANI
Stanford University

JEFFREY D. ULLMAN
Stanford University

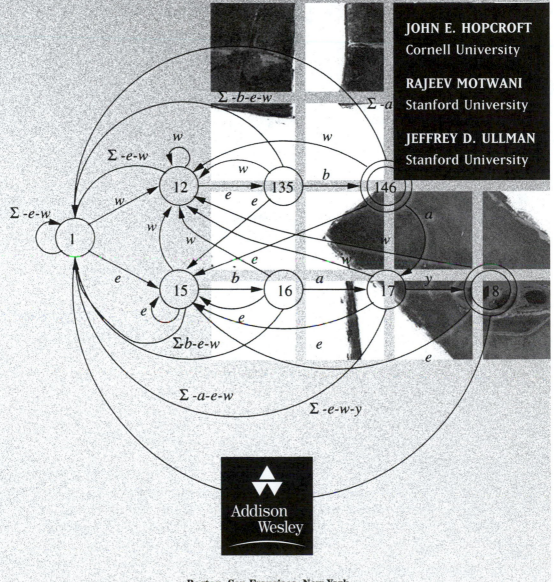

Addison
Wesley

Boston San Francisco New York
London Toronto Sydney Tokyo Singapore Madrid
Mexico City Munich Paris Cape Town Hong Kong Montreal

Senior Acquisitions Editor	*Maite Suarez-Rivas*
Project Editor	*Katherine Harutunian*
Executive Marketing Manager	*Michael Hirsch*
Cover Design	*Leslie Haimes*
Art Direction	*Regina Hagen*
Prepress and Manufacturing	*Caroline Fell*

Access the latest information about Addison-Wesley titles from our World Wide Web site: http://www.awl.com

The programs and applications presented in this book have been included for their instructional value. They have been tested with care, but are not guaranteed for any particular purpose. The publisher does not offer any warranties or representations, not does it accept any liabilities with respect to the programs or applications.

Library of Congress Cataloging-in-Publication Data

Hopcroft, John E., 1939-
    Introduction to automata theory, languages, and computation / John E.
    Hopcroft, Rajeev Motwani, Jeffrey D. Ullman.—2nd ed.
       p. cm.
    ISBN 0-201-44124-1
       1. Machine theory. 2. Formal languages. 3. Computational complexity.
       I. Motwani, Rajeev. II. Ullman, Jeffrey D., 1942-.

QA267 .H56 2001
511.3—dc21   00-064608

12345678910-MA-0403020100

Preface

In the preface from the 1979 predecessor to this book, Hopcroft and Ullman marveled at the fact that the subject of automata had exploded, compared with its state at the time they wrote their first book, in 1969. Truly, the 1979 book contained many topics not found in the earlier work and was about twice its size. If you compare this book with the 1979 book, you will find that, like the automobiles of the 1970's, this book is "larger on the outside, but smaller on the inside." That sounds like a retrograde step, but we are happy with the changes for several reasons.

First, in 1979, automata and language theory was still an area of active research. A purpose of that book was to encourage mathematically inclined students to make new contributions to the field. Today, there is little direct research in automata theory (as opposed to its applications), and thus little motivation for us to retain the succinct, highly mathematical tone of the 1979 book.

Second, the role of automata and language theory has changed over the past two decades. In 1979, automata was largely a graduate-level subject, and we imagined our reader was an advanced graduate student, especially those using the later chapters of the book. Today, the subject is a staple of the undergraduate curriculum. As such, the content of the book must assume less in the way of prerequisites from the student, and therefore must provide more of the background and details of arguments than did the earlier book.

A third change in the environment is that Computer Science has grown to an almost unimaginable degree in the past two decades. While in 1979 it was often a challenge to fill up a curriculum with material that we felt would survive the next wave of technology, today very many subdisciplines compete for the limited amount of space in the undergraduate curriculum.

Fourthly, CS has become a more vocational subject, and there is a severe pragmatism among many of its students. We continue to believe that aspects of automata theory are essential tools in a variety of new disciplines, and we believe that the theoretical, mind-expanding exercises embodied in the typical automata course retain their value, no matter how much the student prefers to learn only the most immediately monetizable technology. However, to assure a continued place for the subject on the menu of topics available to the computer science student, we believe it is necessary to emphasize the applications along with the mathematics. Thus, we have replaced a number of the more abstruse topics in the earlier book with examples of how the ideas are used today. While applications of automata and language theory to compilers are now so well understood that they are normally covered in a compiler course, there are a variety of more recent uses, including model-checking algorithms to verify protocols and document-description languages that are patterned on context-free grammars.

A final explanation for the simultaneous growth and shrinkage of the book is that we were today able to take advantage of the $\TeX$ and $\LaTeX$ typesetting systems developed by Don Knuth and Les Lamport. The latter, especially, encourages the "open" style of typesetting that makes books larger, but easier to read. We appreciate the efforts of both men.

Use of the Book

This book is suitable for a quarter or semester course at the Junior level or above. At Stanford, we have used the notes in CS154, the course in automata and language theory. It is a one-quarter course, which both Rajeev and Jeff have taught. Because of the limited time available, Chapter 11 is not covered, and some of the later material, such as the more difficult polynomial-time reductions in Section 10.4 are omitted as well. The book's Web site (see below) includes notes and syllabi for several offerings of CS154.

Some years ago, we found that many graduate students came to Stanford with a course in automata theory that did not include the theory of intractability. As the Stanford faculty believes that these ideas are essential for every computer scientist to know at more than the level of "NP-complete means it takes too long," there is another course, CS154N, that students may take to cover only Chapters 8, 9, and 10. They actually participate in roughly the last third of CS154 to fulfill the CS154N requirement. Even today, we find several students each quarter availing themselves of this option. Since it requires little extra effort, we recommend the approach.

Prerequisites

To make best use of this book, students should have taken previously a course covering discrete mathematics, e.g., graphs, trees, logic, and proof techniques. We assume also that they have had several courses in programming, and are familiar with common data structures, recursion, and the role of major system components such as compilers. These prerequisites should be obtained in a typical freshman-sophomore CS program.

Exercises

The book contains extensive exercises, with some for almost every section. We indicate harder exercises or parts of exercises with an exclamation point. The hardest exercises have a double exclamation point.

Some of the exercises or parts are marked with a star. For these exercises, we shall endeavor to maintain solutions accessible through the book's Web page. These solutions are publicly available and should be used for self-testing. Note that in a few cases, one exercise B asks for modification or adaptation of your solution to another exercise A. If certain parts of A have solutions, then you should expect the corresponding parts of B to have solutions as well.

Support on the World Wide Web

The book's home page is

```
http://www-db.stanford.edu/~ullman/ialc.html
```

Here are solutions to starred exercises, errata as we learn of them, and backup materials. We hope to make available the notes for each offering of CS154 as we teach it, including homeworks, solutions, and exams.

Acknowledgements

A handout on "how to do proofs" by Craig Silverstein influenced some of the material in Chapter 1. Comments and errata on drafts of this book were received from: Zoe Abrams, George Candea, Haowen Chen, Byong-Gun Chun, Jeffrey Shallit, Bret Taylor, Jason Townsend, and Erik Uzureau. They are gratefully acknowledged. Remaining errors are ours, of course.

> J. E. H.
> R. M.
> J. D. U.
> Ithaca NY and Stanford CA
> September, 2000

Table of Contents

Chapter 1

Automata: The Methods and the Madness

Automata theory is the study of abstract computing devices, or "machines." Before there were computers, in the 1930's, A. Turing studied an abstract machine that had all the capabilities of today's computers, at least as far as in what they could compute. Turing's goal was to describe precisely the boundary between what a computing machine could do and what it could not do; his conclusions apply not only to his abstract *Turing machines*, but to today's real machines.

In the 1940's and 1950's, simpler kinds of machines, which we today call "finite automata," were studied by a number of researchers. These automata, originally proposed to model brain function, turned out to be extremely useful for a variety of other purposes, which we shall mention in Section 1.1. Also in the late 1950's, the linguist N. Chomsky begun the study of formal "grammars." While not strictly machines, these grammars have close relationships to abstract automata and serve today as the basis of some important software components, including parts of compilers.

In 1969, S. Cook extended Turing's study of what could and what could not be computed. Cook was able to separate those problems that can be solved efficiently by computer from those problems that can in principle be solved, but in practice take so much time that computers are useless for all but very small instances of the problem. The latter class of problems is called "intractable," or "NP-hard." It is highly unlikely that even the exponential improvement in computing speed that computer hardware has been following ("Moore's Law") will have significant impact on our ability to solve large instances of intractable problems.

All of these theoretical developments bear directly on what computer scientists do today. Some of the concepts, like finite automata and certain kinds of formal grammars, are used in the design and construction of important kinds of software. Other concepts, like the Turing machine, help us understand what we can expect from our software. Especially, the theory of intractable problems lets us deduce whether we are likely to be able to meet a problem "head-on" and write a program to solve it (because it is not in the intractable class), or whether we have to find some way to work around the intractable problem: find an approximation, use a heuristic, or use some other method to limit the amount of time the program will spend solving the problem.

In this introductory chapter, we begin with a very high-level view of what automata theory is about, and what its uses are. Much of the chapter is devoted to a survey of proof techniques and tricks for discovering proofs. We cover deductive proofs, reformulating statements, proofs by contradiction, proofs by induction, and other important concepts. A final section introduces the concepts that pervade automata theory: alphabets, strings, and languages.

1.1   Why Study Automata Theory?

There are several reasons why the study of automata and complexity is an important part of the core of Computer Science. This section serves to introduce the reader to the principal motivation and also outlines the major topics covered in this book.

1.1.1   Introduction to Finite Automata

Finite automata are a useful model for many important kinds of hardware and software. We shall see, starting in Chapter 2, examples of how the concepts are used. For the moment, let us just list some of the most important kinds:

1. Software for designing and checking the behavior of digital circuits.

2. The "lexical analyzer" of a typical compiler, that is, the compiler component that breaks the input text into logical units, such as identifiers, keywords, and punctuation.

3. Software for scanning large bodies of text, such as collections of Web pages, to find occurrences of words, phrases, or other patterns.

4. Software for verifying systems of all types that have a finite number of distinct states, such as communications protocols or protocols for secure exchange of information.

While we shall soon meet a precise definition of automata of various types, let us begin our informal introduction with a sketch of what a finite automaton is and does. There are many systems or components, such as those enumerated above, that may be viewed as being at all times in one of a finite number of "states." The purpose of a state is to remember the relevant portion of the system's history. Since there are only a finite number of states, the entire history generally cannot be remembered, so the system must be designed carefully, to remember what is important and forget what is not. The advantage of having only a finite number of states is that we can implement the system with a fixed set of resources. For example, we could implement it in hardware as a circuit, or as a simple form of program that can make decisions looking only at a limited amount of data or using the position in the code itself to make the decision.

Example 1.1: Perhaps the simplest nontrivial finite automaton is an on/off switch. The device remembers whether it is in the "on" state or the "off" state, and it allows the user to press a button whose effect is different, depending on the state of the switch. That is, if the switch is in the off state, then pressing the button changes it to the on state, and if the switch is in the on state, then pressing the same button turns it to the off state.

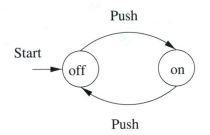

Figure 1.1: A finite automaton modeling an on/off switch

The finite-automaton model for the switch is shown in Fig. 1.1. As for all finite automata, the states are represented by circles; in this example, we have named the states *on* and *off*. Arcs between states are labeled by "inputs," which represent external influences on the system. Here, both arcs are labeled by the input *Push*, which represents a user pushing the button. The intent of the two arcs is that whichever state the system is in, when the *Push* input is received it goes to the other state.

One of the states is designated the "start state," the state in which the system is placed initially. In our example, the start state is *off*, and we conventionally indicate the start state by the word *Start* and an arrow leading to that state.

It is often necessary to indicate one or more states as "final" or "accepting" states. Entering one of these states after a sequence of inputs indicates that the input sequence is good in some way. For instance, we could have regarded the state *on* in Fig. 1.1 as accepting, because in that state, the device being controlled by the switch will operate. It is conventional to designate accepting states by a double circle, although we have not made any such designation in Fig. 1.1. □

Example 1.2: Sometimes, what is remembered by a state can be much more complex than an on/off choice. Figure 1.2 shows another finite automaton that could be part of a lexical analyzer. The job of this automaton is to recognize the keyword then. It thus needs five states, each of which represents a different position in the word then that has been reached so far. These positions correspond to the prefixes of the word, ranging from the empty string (i.e., nothing of the word has been seen so far) to the complete word.

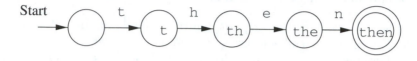

Figure 1.2: A finite automaton modeling recognition of then

In Fig. 1.2, the five states are named by the prefix of then seen so far. Inputs correspond to letters. We may imagine that the lexical analyzer examines one character of the program that it is compiling at a time, and the next character to be examined is the input to the automaton. The start state corresponds to the empty string, and each state has a transition on the next letter of then to the state that corresponds to the next-larger prefix. The state named then is entered when the input has spelled the word then. Since it is the job of this automaton to recognize when then has been seen, we could consider that state the lone accepting state.   □

1.1.2   Structural Representations

There are two important notations that are not automaton-like, but play an important role in the study of automata and their applications.

1. *Grammars* are useful models when designing software that processes data with a recursive structure. The best-known example is a "parser," the component of a compiler that deals with the recursively nested features of the typical programming language, such as expressions — arithmetic, conditional, and so on. For instance, a grammatical rule like $E \Rightarrow E + E$ states that an expression can be formed by taking any two expressions and connecting them by a plus sign; this rule is typical of how expressions of real programming languages are formed. We introduce context-free grammars, as they are usually called, in Chapter 5.

2. *Regular Expressions* also denote the structure of data, especially text strings. As we shall see in Chapter 3, the patterns of strings they describe are exactly the same as what can be described by finite automata. The style of these expressions differs significantly from that of grammars, and we shall content ourselves with a simple example here. The UNIX-style regular expression '[A-Z][a-z]*[ ][A-Z][A-Z]' represents capitalized words followed by a space and two capital letters. This expression represents patterns in text that could be a city and state, e.g., Ithaca NY. It misses multiword city names, such as Palo Alto CA, which could be captured by the more complex expression

'([A-Z][a-z]*[ ])*[ ][A-Z][A-Z]'

When interpreting such expressions, we only need to know that [A-Z] represents a range of characters from capital "A" to capital "Z" (i.e., any capital letter), and [ ] is used to represent the blank character alone. Also, the symbol * represents "any number of" the preceding expression. Parentheses are used to group components of the expression; they do not represent characters of the text described.

1.1.3 Automata and Complexity

Automata are essential for the study of the limits of computation. As we mentioned in the introduction to the chapter, there are two important issues:

1. What can a computer do at all? This study is called "decidability," and the problems that can be solved by computer are called "decidable." This topic is addressed in Chapter 9.

2. What can a computer do efficiently? This study is called "intractability," and the problems that can be solved by a computer using no more time than some slowly growing function of the size of the input are called "tractable." Often, we take all polynomial functions to be "slowly growing," while functions that grow faster than any polynomial are deemed to grow too fast. The subject is studied in Chapter 10.

1.2 Introduction to Formal Proof

If you studied plane geometry in high school any time before the 1990's, you most likely had to do some detailed "deductive proofs," where you showed the truth of a statement by a detailed sequence of steps and reasons. While geometry has its practical side (e.g., you need to know the rule for computing the area of a rectangle if you need to buy the correct amount of carpet for a room), the study of formal proof methodologies was at least as important a reason for covering this branch of mathematics in high school.

In the USA of the 1990's it became popular to teach proof as a matter of personal feelings about the statement. While it is good to feel the truth of a statement you need to use, important techniques of proof are no longer mastered in high school. Yet proof is something that every computer scientist needs to understand. Some computer scientists take the extreme view that a formal proof of the correctness of a program should go hand-in-hand with the writing of the program itself. We doubt that doing so is productive. On the other hand, there are those who say that proof has no place in the discipline of programming. The slogan "if you are not sure your program is correct, run it and see" is commonly offered by this camp.

Our position is between these two extremes. Testing programs is surely essential. However, testing goes only so far, since you cannot try your program on every input. More importantly, if your program is complex — say a tricky recursion or iteration — then if you don't understand what is going on as you go around a loop or call a function recursively, it is unlikely that you will write the code correctly. When your testing tells you the code is incorrect, you still need to get it right.

To make your iteration or recursion correct, you need to set up an inductive hypothesis, and it is helpful to reason, formally or informally, that the hypothesis is consistent with the iteration or recursion. This process of understanding the workings of a correct program is essentially the same as the process of proving theorems by induction. Thus, in addition to giving you models that are useful for certain types of software, it has become traditional for a course on automata theory to cover methodologies of formal proof. Perhaps more than other core subjects of computer science, automata theory lends itself to natural and interesting proofs, both of the *deductive* kind (a sequence of justified steps) and the *inductive* kind (recursive proofs of a parameterized statement that use the statement itself with "lower" values of the parameter).

1.2.1   Deductive Proofs

As mentioned above, a deductive proof consists of a sequence of statements whose truth leads us from some initial statement, called the *hypothesis* or the *given statement(s)*, to a *conclusion* statement. Each step in the proof must follow, by some accepted logical principle, from either the given facts, or some of the previous statements in the deductive proof, or a combination of these.

The hypothesis may be true or false, typically depending on values of its parameters. Often, the hypothesis consists of several independent statements connected by a logical AND. In those cases, we talk of each of these statements as a hypothesis, or as a given statement.

The theorem that is proved when we go from a hypothesis H to a conclusion C is the statement "if H then C." We say that C is *deduced* from H. An example theorem of the form "if H then C" will illustrate these points.

Theorem 1.3: If $x \geq 4$, then $2^x \geq x^2$. □

It is not hard to convince ourselves informally that Theorem 1.3 is true, although a formal proof requires induction and will be left for Example 1.17. First, notice that the hypothesis H is "$x \geq 4$." This hypothesis has a parameter, x, and thus is neither true nor false. Rather, its truth depends on the value of the parameter x; e.g., H is true for $x = 6$ and false for $x = 2$.

Likewise, the conclusion C is "$2^x \geq x^2$." This statement also uses parameter x and is true for certain values of x and not others. For example, C is false for $x = 3$, since $2^3 = 8$, which is not as large as $3^2 = 9$. On the other hand, C is true for $x = 4$, since $2^4 = 4^2 = 16$. For $x = 5$, the statement is also true, since $2^5 = 32$ is at least as large as $5^2 = 25$.

Perhaps you can see the intuitive argument that tells us the conclusion $2^x \geq x^2$ will be true whenever $x \geq 4$. We already saw that it is true for $x = 4$. As x grows larger than 4, the left side, 2^x doubles each time x increases by 1. However, the right side, x^2, grows by the ratio $\left(\frac{x+1}{x}\right)^2$. If $x \geq 4$, then $(x + 1)/x$ cannot be greater than 1.25, and therefore $\left(\frac{x+1}{x}\right)^2$ cannot be bigger than 1.5625. Since $1.5625 < 2$, each time x increases above 4 the left side 2^x grows more than the right side x^2. Thus, as long as we start from a value like $x = 4$ where the inequality $2^x \geq x^2$ is already satisfied, we can increase x as much as we like, and the inequality will still be satisfied.

We have now completed an informal but accurate proof of Theorem 1.3. We shall return to the proof and make it more precise in Example 1.17, after we introduce "inductive" proofs.

Theorem 1.3, like all interesting theorems, involves an infinite number of related facts, in this case the statement "if $x \geq 4$ then $2^x \geq x^2$" for all integers x. In fact, we do not need to assume x is an integer, but the proof talked about repeatedly increasing x by 1, starting at $x = 4$, so we really addressed only the situation where x is an integer.

Theorem 1.3 can be used to help deduce other theorems. In the next example, we consider a complete deductive proof of a simple theorem that uses Theorem 1.3.

Theorem 1.4: If x is the sum of the squares of four positive integers, then $2^x \geq x^2$.

PROOF: The intuitive idea of the proof is that if the hypothesis is true for x, that is, x is the sum of the squares of four positive integers, then x must be at least 4. Therefore, the hypothesis of Theorem 1.3 holds, and since we believe that theorem, we may state that its conclusion is also true for x. The reasoning can be expressed as a sequence of steps. Each step is either the hypothesis of the theorem to be proved, part of that hypothesis, or a statement that follows from one or more previous statements.

By "follows" we mean that if the hypothesis of some theorem is a previous statement, then the conclusion of that theorem is true, and can be written down as a statement of our proof. This logical rule is often called *modus ponens*; i.e., if we know H is true, and we know "if H then C" is true, we may conclude that C is true. We also allow certain other logical steps to be used in creating a statement that follows from one or more previous statements. For instance, if A and B are two previous statements, then we can deduce and write down the statement "A and B."

Figure 1.3 shows the sequence of statements we need to prove Theorem 1.4. While we shall not generally prove theorems in such a stylized form, it helps to think of proofs as very explicit lists of statements, each with a precise justification. In step (1), we have repeated one of the given statements of the theorem: that x is the sum of the squares of four integers. It often helps in proofs if we name quantities that are referred to but not named, and we have done so here, giving the four integers the names a, b, c, and d.

	Statement	Justification
1.	$x = a^2 + b^2 + c^2 + d^2$	Given
2.	$a \geq 1; b \geq 1; c \geq 1; d \geq 1$	Given
3.	$a^2 \geq 1; b^2 \geq 1; c^2 \geq 1; d^2 \geq 1$	(2) and properties of arithmetic
4.	$x \geq 4$	(1), (3), and properties of arithmetic
5.	$2^x \geq x^2$	(4) and Theorem 1.3

Figure 1.3: A formal proof of Theorem 1.4

In step (2), we put down the other part of the hypothesis of the theorem: that the values being squared are each at least 1. Technically, this statement represents four distinct statements, one for each of the four integers involved. Then, in step (3) we observe that if a number is at least 1, then its square is also at least 1. We use as a justification the fact that statement (2) holds, and "properties of arithmetic." That is, we assume the reader knows, or can prove simple statements about how inequalities work, such as the statement "if $y \geq 1$, then $y^2 \geq 1$."

Step (4) uses statements (1) and (3). The first statement tells us that x is the sum of the four squares in question, and statement (3) tells us that each of the squares is at least 1. Again using well-known properties of arithmetic, we conclude that x is at least $1 + 1 + 1 + 1$, or 4.

At the final step (5), we use statement (4), which is the hypothesis of Theorem 1.3. The theorem itself is the justification for writing down its conclusion, since its hypothesis is a previous statement. Since the statement (5) that is the conclusion of Theorem 1.3 is also the conclusion of Theorem 1.4, we have now proved Theorem 1.4. That is, we have started with the hypothesis of that theorem, and have managed to deduce its conclusion.   □

1.2.2   Reduction to Definitions

In the previous two theorems, the hypotheses used terms that should have been familiar: integers, addition, and multiplication, for instance. In many other theorems, including many from automata theory, the terms used in the statement may have implications that are less obvious. A useful way to proceed in many proofs is:

- If you are not sure how to start a proof, convert all terms in the hypothesis to their definitions.

Here is an example of a theorem that is simple to prove once we have expressed its statement in elementary terms. It uses the following two definitions:

1. A set S is *finite* if there exists an integer n such that S has exactly n elements. We write $\|S\| = n$, where $\|S\|$ is used to denote the number

of elements in a set S. If the set S is not finite, we say S is *infinite*. Intuitively, an infinite set is a set that contains more than any integer number of elements.

2. If S and T are both subsets of some set U, then T is the *complement* of S (with respect to U) if $S \cup T = U$ and $S \cap T = \emptyset$. That is, each element of U is in exactly one of S and T; put another way, T consists of exactly those elements of U that are not in S.

Theorem 1.5: Let S be a finite subset of some infinite set U. Let T be the complement of S with respect to U. Then T is infinite.

PROOF: Intuitively, this theorem says that if you have an infinite supply of something (U), and you take a finite amount away (S), then you still have an infinite amount left. Let us begin by restating the facts of the theorem as in Fig. 1.4.

Original Statement	New Statement
S is finite	There is a integer n such that $\|S\| = n$
U is infinite	For no integer p is $\|U\| = p$
T is the complement of S	$S \cup T = U$ and $S \cap T = \emptyset$

Figure 1.4: Restating the givens of Theorem 1.5

We are still stuck, so we need to use a common proof technique called "proof by contradiction." In this proof method, to be discussed further in Section 1.3.3, we assume that the conclusion is false. We then use that assumption, together with parts of the hypothesis, to prove the opposite of one of the given statements of the hypothesis. We have then shown that it is impossible for all parts of the hypothesis to be true and for the conclusion to be false at the same time. The only possibility that remains is for the conclusion to be true whenever the hypothesis is true. That is, the theorem is true.

In the case of Theorem 1.5, the contradiction of the conclusion is "T is finite." Let us assume T is finite, along with the statement of the hypothesis that says S is finite; i.e., $\|S\| = n$ for some integer n. Similarly, we can restate the assumption that T is finite as $\|T\| = m$ for some integer m.

Now one of the given statements tells us that $S \cup T = U$, and $S \cap T = \emptyset$. That is, the elements of U are exactly the elements of S and T. Thus, there must be $n + m$ elements of U. Since $n + m$ is an integer, and we have shown $\|U\| = n + m$, it follows that U is finite. More precisely, we showed the number of elements in U is some integer, which is the definition of "finite." But the statement that U is finite contradicts the given statement that U is infinite. We have thus used the contradiction of our conclusion to prove the contradiction of one of the given statements of the hypothesis, and by the principle of "proof by contradiction" we may conclude the theorem is true. □

Proofs do not have to be so wordy. Having seen the ideas behind the proof, let us reprove the theorem in a few lines.

PROOF: (of Theorem 1.5) We know that $S \cup T = U$ and S and T are disjoint, so $\|S\| + \|T\| = \|U\|$. Since S is finite, $\|S\| = n$ for some integer n, and since U is infinite, there is no integer p such that $\|U\| = p$. So assume that T is finite; that is, $\|T\| = m$ for some integer m. Then $\|U\| = \|S\| + \|T\| = n + m$, which contradicts the given statement that there is no integer p equal to $\|U\|$. □

1.2.3   Other Theorem Forms

The "if-then" form of theorem is most common in typical areas of mathematics. However, we see other kinds of statements proved as theorems also. In this section, we shall examine the most common forms of statement and what we usually need to do to prove them.

Ways of Saying "If-Then"

First, there are a number of kinds of theorem statements that look different from a simple "if H then C" form, but are in fact saying the same thing: if hypothesis H is true for a given value of the parameter(s), then the conclusion C is true for the same value. Here are some of the other ways in which "if H then C" might appear.

1. H implies C.

2. H only if C.

3. C if H.

4. Whenever H holds, C follows.

We also see many variants of form (4), such as "if H holds, then C follows," or "whenever H holds, C holds."

Example 1.6: The statement of Theorem 1.3 would appear in these four forms as:

1. $x \geq 4$ implies $2^x \geq x^2$.

2. $x \geq 4$ only if $2^x \geq x^2$.

3. $2^x \geq x^2$ if $x \geq 4$.

4. Whenever $x \geq 4$, $2^x \geq x^2$ follows.

□

Statements With Quantifiers

Many theorems involve statements that use the *quantifiers* "for all" and "there exists," or similar variations, such as "for every" instead of "for all." The order in which these quantifiers appear affects what the statement means. It is often helpful to see statements with more than one quantifier as a "game" between two players — for-all and there-exists — who take turns specifying values for the parameters mentioned in the theorem. "For-all" must consider all possible choices, so for-all's choices are generally left as variables. However, "there-exists" only has to pick one value, which may depend on the values picked by the players previously. The order in which the quantifiers appear in the statement determines who goes first. If the last player to make a choice can always find some allowable value, then the statement is true.

For example, consider an alternative definition of "infinite set": set S is *infinite* if and only if for all integers n, there exists a subset T of S with exactly n members. Here, "for-all" precedes "there-exists," so we must consider an arbitrary integer n. Now, "there-exists" gets to pick a subset T, and may use the knowledge of n to do so. For instance, if S were the set of integers, "there-exists" could pick the subset $T = \{1, 2, \ldots, n\}$ and thereby succeed regardless of n. That is a proof that the set of integers is infinite.

The following statement looks like the definition of "infinite," but is *incorrect* because it reverses the order of the quantifiers: "there exists a subset T of set S such that for all n, set T has exactly n members." Now, given a set S such as the integers, player "there-exists" can pick any set T; say $\{1, 2, 5\}$ is picked. For this choice, player "for-all" must show that T has n members for *every* possible n. However, "for-all" cannot do so. For instance, it is false for $n = 4$, or in fact for any $n \neq 3$.

In addition, in formal logic one often sees the operator $\rightarrow$ in place of "if-then." That is, the statement "if H then C" could appear as $H \rightarrow C$ in some mathematical literature; we shall not use it here.

If-And-Only-If Statements

Sometimes, we find a statement of the form "A if and only if B." Other forms of this statement are "A iff B,"[1] "A is equivalent to B," or "A exactly when B." This statement is actually two if-then statements: "if A then B," and "if B then A." We prove "A if and only if B" by proving these two statements:

---

[1] Iff, short for "if and only if," is a non-word that is used in some mathematical treatises for succinctness.

How Formal Do Proofs Have to Be?

The answer to this question is not easy. The bottom line regarding proofs is that their purpose is to convince someone, whether it is a grader of your classwork or yourself, about the correctness of a strategy you are using in your code. If it is convincing, then it is enough; if it fails to convince the "consumer" of the proof, then the proof has left out too much.

Part of the uncertainty regarding proofs comes from the different knowledge that the consumer may have. Thus, in Theorem 1.4, we assumed you knew all about arithmetic, and would believe a statement like "if $y \geq 1$ then $y^2 \geq 1$." If you were not familiar with arithmetic, we would have to prove that statement by some steps in our deductive proof.

However, there are certain things that are required in proofs, and omitting them surely makes the proof inadequate. For instance, any deductive proof that uses statements which are not justified by the given or previous statements, cannot be adequate. When doing a proof of an "if and only if" statement, we must surely have one proof for the "if" part and another proof for the "only-if" part. As an additional example, inductive proofs (discussed in Section 1.4) require proofs of the basis and induction parts.

---

1. The *if part*: "if B then A," and

2. The *only-if part*: "if A then B," which is often stated in the equivalent form "A only if B."

The proofs can be presented in either order. In many theorems, one part is decidedly easier than the other, and it is customary to present the easy direction first and get it out of the way.

In formal logic, one may see the operator $\leftrightarrow$ or $\equiv$ to denote an "if-and-only-if" statement. That is, $A \equiv B$ and $A \leftrightarrow B$ mean the same as "A if and only if B."

When proving an if-and-only-if statement, it is important to remember that you must prove both the "if" and "only-if" parts. Sometimes, you will find it helpful to break an if-and-only-if into a succession of several equivalences. That is, to prove "A if and only if B," you might first prove "A if and only if C," and then prove "C if and only if B." That method works, as long as you remember that each if-and-only-if step must be proved in both directions. Proving any one step in only one of the directions invalidates the entire proof.

The following is an example of a simple if-and-only-if proof. It uses the notations:

1. $\lfloor x \rfloor$, the *floor* of real number x, is the greatest integer equal to or less than x.

2. $\lceil x \rceil$, the *ceiling* of real number x, is the least integer equal to or greater than x.

Theorem 1.7: Let x be a real number. Then $\lfloor x \rfloor = \lceil x \rceil$ if and only if x is an integer.

PROOF: (Only-if part) In this part, we assume $\lfloor x \rfloor = \lceil x \rceil$ and try to prove x is an integer. Using the definitions of the floor and ceiling, we notice that $\lfloor x \rfloor \leq x$, and $\lceil x \rceil \geq x$. However, we are given that $\lfloor x \rfloor = \lceil x \rceil$. Thus, we may substitute the floor for the ceiling in the first inequality to conclude $\lceil x \rceil \leq x$. Since both $\lceil x \rceil \leq x$ and $\lceil x \rceil \geq x$ hold, we may conclude by properties of arithmetic inequalities that $\lceil x \rceil = x$. Since $\lceil x \rceil$ is always an integer, x must also be an integer in this case.

(If part) Now, we assume x is an integer and try to prove $\lfloor x \rfloor = \lceil x \rceil$. This part is easy. By the definitions of floor and ceiling, when x is an integer, both $\lfloor x \rfloor$ and $\lceil x \rceil$ are equal to x, and therefore equal to each other.   □

1.2.4   Theorems That Appear Not to Be If-Then Statements

Sometimes, we encounter a theorem that appears not to have a hypothesis. An example is the well-known fact from trigonometry:

Theorem 1.8: $\sin^2 \theta + \cos^2 \theta = 1$.   □

Actually, this statement *does* have a hypothesis, and the hypothesis consists of all the statements you need to know to interpret the statement. In particular, the hidden hypothesis is that θ is an angle, and therefore the functions sine and cosine have their usual meaning for angles. From the definitions of these terms, and the Pythagorean Theorem (in a right triangle, the square of the hypotenuse equals the sum of the squares of the other two sides), you could prove the theorem. In essence, the if-then form of the theorem is really: "if θ is an angle, then $\sin^2 \theta + \cos^2 \theta = 1$."

1.3   Additional Forms of Proof

In this section, we take up several additional topics concerning how to construct proofs:

1. Proofs about sets.

2. Proofs by contradiction.

3. Proofs by counterexample.

1.3.1 Proving Equivalences About Sets

In automata theory, we are frequently asked to prove a theorem which says that the sets constructed in two different ways are the same sets. Often, these sets are sets of character strings, and the sets are called "languages," but in this section the nature of the sets is unimportant. If E and F are two expressions representing sets, the statement $E = F$ means that the two sets represented are the same. More precisely, every element in the set represented by E is in the set represented by F, and every element in the set represented by F is in the set represented by E.

Example 1.9: The *commutative law of union* says that we can take the union of two sets R and S in either order. That is, $R \cup S = S \cup R$. In this case, E is the expression $R \cup S$ and F is the expression $S \cup R$. The commutative law of union says that $E = F$. □

We can write a set-equality $E = F$ as an if-and-only-if statement: an element x is in E if and only if x is in F. As a consequence, we see the outline of a proof of any statement that asserts the equality of two sets $E = F$; it follows the form of any if-and-only-if proof:

1. Proof that if x is in E, then x is in F.

2. Prove that if x is in F, then x is in E.

As an example of this proof process, let us prove the *distributive law of union over intersection*:

Theorem 1.10: $R \cup (S \cap T) = (R \cap S) \cup (R \cap T)$.

PROOF: The two set-expressions involved are $E = R \cup (S \cap T)$ and

$$F = (R \cap S) \cup (R \cap T)$$

We shall prove the two parts of the theorem in turn. In the "if" part we assume element x is in E and show it is in F. This part, summarized in Fig. 1.5, uses the definitions of union and intersection, with which we assume you are familiar.

Then, we must prove the "only-if" part of the theorem. Here, we assume x is in F and show it is in E. The steps are summarized in Fig. 1.6. Since we have now proved both parts of the if-and-only-if statement, the distributive law of union over intersection is proved. □

1.3.2 The Contrapositive

Every if-then statement has an equivalent form that in some circumstances is easier to prove. The *contrapositive* of the statement "if H then C" is "if not C then not H." A statement and its contrapositive are either both true or both false, so we can prove either to prove the other.

To see why "if H then C" and "if not C then not H" are logically equivalent, first observe that there are four cases to consider:

	Statement	Justification
1.	x is in $R \cup (S \cap T)$	Given
2.	x is in R or x is in $S \cap T$	(1) and definition of union
3.	x is in R or x is in both S and T	(2) and definition of intersection
4.	x is in $R \cup S$	(3) and definition of union
5.	x is in $R \cup T$	(3) and definition of union
6.	x is in $(R \cup S) \cap (R \cup T)$	(4), (5), and definition of intersection

Figure 1.5: Steps in the "if" part of Theorem 1.10

	Statement	Justification
1.	x is in $(R \cup S) \cap (R \cup T)$	Given
2.	x is in $R \cup S$	(1) and definition of intersection
3.	x is in $R \cup T$	(1) and definition of intersection
4.	x is in R or x is in both S and T	(2), (3), and reasoning about unions
5.	x is in R or x is in $S \cap T$	(4) and definition of intersection
6.	x is in $R \cup (S \cap T)$	(5) and definition of union

Figure 1.6: Steps in the "only-if" part of Theorem 1.10

1. H and C both true.

2. H true and C false.

3. C true and H false.

4. H and C both false.

There is only one way to make an if-then statement false; the hypothesis must be true and the conclusion false, as in case (2). For the other three cases, including case (4) where the conclusion is false, the if-then statement itself is true.

Now, consider for which cases the contrapositive "if not C then not H" is false. In order for this statement to be false, its hypothesis (which is "not C") must be true, and its conclusion (which is "not H") must be false. But "not C" is true exactly when C is false, and "not H" is false exactly when H is true. These two conditions are again case (2), which shows that in each of the four cases, the original statement and its contrapositive are either both true or both false; i.e., they are logically equivalent.

Saying "If-And-Only-If" for Sets

As we mentioned, theorems that state equivalences of expressions about sets are if-and-only-if statements. Thus, Theorem 1.10 could have been stated: an element x is in $R \cup (S \cap T)$ if and only if x is in

$$(R \cup S) \cap (R \cup T)$$

Another common expression of a set-equivalence is with the locution "all-and-only." For instance, Theorem 1.10 could as well have been stated "the elements of $R \cup (S \cap T)$ are all and only the elements of

$$(R \cup S) \cap (R \cup T)$$

The Converse

Do not confuse the terms "contrapositive" and "converse." The *converse* of an if-then statement is the "other direction"; that is, the converse of "if H then C" is "if C then H." Unlike the contrapositive, which is logically equivalent to the original, the converse is *not* equivalent to the original statement. In fact, the two parts of an if-and-only-if proof are always some statement and its converse.

Example 1.11 : Recall Theorem 1.3, whose statement was: "if $x \geq 4$, then $2^x \geq x^2$." The contrapositive of this statement is "if not $2^x \geq x^2$ then not $x \geq 4$." In more colloquial terms, making use of the fact that "not $a \geq b$" is the same as $a < b$, the contrapositive is "if $2^x < x^2$ then $x < 4$."   □

When we are asked to prove an if-and-only-if theorem, the use of the contrapositive in one of the parts allows us several options. For instance, suppose we want to prove the set equivalence $E = F$. Instead of proving "if x is in E then x is in F and if x is in F then x is in E," we could also put one direction in the contrapositive. One equivalent proof form is:

- If x is in E then x is in F, and if x is not in E then x is not in F.

We could also interchange E and F in the statement above.

1.3.3   Proof by Contradiction

Another way to prove a statement of the form "if H then C" is to prove the statement

- "*H* and not *C* implies falsehood."

That is, start by assuming both the hypothesis *H* and the negation of the conclusion *C*. Complete the proof by showing that something known to be false follows logically from *H* and *C*. This form of proof is called *proof by contradiction*.

Example 1.12: Recall Theorem 1.5, where we proved the if-then statement with hypothesis *H* = "*U* is an infinite set, *S* is a finite subset of *U*, and *T* is the complement of *S* with respect to *U*." The conclusion *C* was "*T* is infinite." We proceeded to prove this theorem by contradiction. We assumed "not *C*"; that is, we assumed *T* was finite.

Our proof was to derive a falsehood from *H* and not *C*. We first showed from the assumptions that *S* and *T* are both finite, that *U* also must be finite. But since *U* is stated in the hypothesis *H* to be infinite, and a set cannot be both finite and infinite, we have proved the logical statement "false." In logical terms, we have both a proposition *p* (*U* is finite) and its negation, not *p* (*U* is infinite). We then use the fact that "*p* and not *p*" is logically equivalent to "false." □

To see why proofs by contradiction are logically correct, recall from Section 1.3.2 that there are four combinations of truth values for *H* and *C*. Only the second case, *H* true and *C* false, makes the statement "if *H* then *C*" false. By showing that *H* and not *C* leads to falsehood, we are showing that case 2 cannot occur. Thus, the only possible combinations of truth values for *H* and *C* are the three combinations that make "if *H* then *C*" true.

1.3.4 Counterexamples

In real life, we are not told to prove a theorem. Rather, we are faced with something that seems true — a strategy for implementing a program for example — and we need to decide whether or not the "theorem" is true. To resolve the question, we may alternately try to prove the theorem, and if we cannot, try to prove that its statement is false.

Theorems generally are statements about an infinite number of cases, perhaps all values of its parameters. Indeed, strict mathematical convention will only dignify a statement with the title "theorem" if it has an infinite number of cases; statements that have no parameters, or that apply to only a finite number of values of its parameter(s) are called *observations*. It is sufficient to show that an alleged theorem is false in any one case in order to show it is not a theorem. The situation is analogous to programs, since a program is generally considered to have a bug if it fails to operate correctly for even one input on which it was expected to work.

It often is easier to prove that a statement is not a theorem than to prove it *is* a theorem. As we mentioned, if *S* is any statement, then the statement "*S* is not a theorem" is itself a statement without parameters, and thus can be regarded as an observation rather than a theorem. The following are two examples, first of an obvious nontheorem, and the second a statement that just misses being a theorem and that requires some investigation before resolving the question of whether it is a theorem or not.

Alleged Theorem 1.13: All primes are odd. (More formally, we might say: if integer x is a prime, then x is odd.)

DISPROOF: The integer 2 is a prime, but 2 is even.   □

Now, let us discuss a "theorem" involving modular arithmetic. There is an essential definition that we must first establish. If a and b are positive integers, then $a \bmod b$ is the remainder when a is divided by b, that is, the unique integer r between 0 and $b - 1$ such that $a = qb + r$ for some integer q. For example, $8 \bmod 3 = 2$, and $9 \bmod 3 = 0$. Our first proposed theorem, which we shall determine to be false, is:

Alleged Theorem 1.14: There is no pair of integers a and b such that

$$a \bmod b = b \bmod a$$

□

When asked to do things with pairs of objects, such as a and b here, it is often possible to simplify the relationship between the two by taking advantage of symmetry. In this case, we can focus on the case where $a < b$, since if $b < a$ we can swap a and b and get the same equation as in Alleged Theorem 1.14. we must be careful, however, not to forget the third case, where $a = b$. This case turns out to be fatal to our proof attempts.

Let us assume $a < b$. Then $a \bmod b = a$, since in the definition of $a \bmod b$ we have $q = 0$ and $r = a$. That is, when $a < b$ we have $a = 0 \times b + a$. But $b \bmod a < a$, since anything mod a is between 0 and $a - 1$. Thus, when $a < b$, $b \bmod a < a \bmod b$, so $a \bmod b = b \bmod a$ is impossible. Using the argument of symmetry above, we also know that $a \bmod b \neq b \bmod a$ when $b < a$.

However, consider the third case: $a = b$. Since $x \bmod x = 0$ for any integer x, we *do* have $a \bmod b = b \bmod a$ if $a = b$. We thus have a disproof of the alleged theorem:

DISPROOF: (of Alleged Theorem 1.14) Let $a = b = 2$. Then

$$a \bmod b = b \bmod a = 0$$

□

In the process of finding the counterexample, we have in fact discovered the exact conditions under which the alleged theorem holds. Here is the correct version of the theorem, and its proof.

Theorem 1.15: $a \bmod b = b \bmod a$ if and only if $a = b$.

PROOF: (If part) Assume $a = b$. Then as we observed above, $x \bmod x = 0$ for any integer x. Thus, $a \bmod b = b \bmod a = 0$ whenever $a = b$.

(Only-if part) Now, assume $a \bmod b = b \bmod a$. The best technique is a proof by contradiction, so assume in addition the negation of the conclusion; that is, assume $a \neq b$. Then since $a = b$ is eliminated, we have only to consider the cases $a < b$ and $b < a$.

We already observed above that when $a < b$, we have $a \bmod b = a$ and $b \bmod a < a$. Thus, these statements, in conjunction with the hypothesis $a \bmod b = b \bmod a$ lets us derive a contradiction.

By symmetry, if $b < a$ then $b \bmod a = b$ and $a \bmod b < b$. We again derive a contradiction of the hypothesis, and conclude the only-if part is also true. We have now proved both directions and conclude that the theorem is true. $\square$

1.4 Inductive Proofs

There is a special form of proof, called "inductive," that is essential when dealing with recursively defined objects. Many of the most familiar inductive proofs deal with integers, but in automata theory, we also need inductive proofs about such recursively defined concepts as trees and expressions of various sorts, such as the regular expressions that were mentioned briefly in Section 1.1.2. In this section, we shall introduce the subject of inductive proofs first with "simple" inductions on integers. Then, we show how to perform "structural" inductions on any recursively defined concept.

1.4.1 Inductions on Integers

Suppose we are given a statement $S(n)$, about an integer n, to prove. One common approach is to prove two things:

1. The *basis*, where we show $S(i)$ for a particular integer i. Usually, $i = 0$ or $i = 1$, but there are examples where we want to start at some higher i, perhaps because the statement S is false for a few small integers.

2. The *inductive step*, where we assume $n \geq i$, where i is the basis integer, and we show that "if $S(n)$ then $S(n + 1)$."

Intuitively, these two parts should convince us that $S(n)$ is true for every integer n that is equal to or greater than the basis integer i. We can argue as follows. Suppose $S(n)$ were false for one or more of those integers. Then there would have to be a smallest value of n, say j, for which $S(j)$ is false, and yet $j \geq i$. Now j could not be i, because we prove in the basis part that $S(i)$ is true. Thus, j must be greater than i. We now know that $j - 1 \geq i$, and $S(j - 1)$ is true.

However, we proved in the inductive part that if $n \geq i$, then $S(n)$ implies $S(n + 1)$. Suppose we let $n = j - 1$. Then we know from the inductive step that $S(j - 1)$ implies $S(j)$. Since we also know $S(j - 1)$, we can conclude $S(j)$.

We have assumed the negation of what we wanted to prove; that is, we assumed $S(j)$ was false for some $j \geq i$. In each case, we derived a contradiction, so we have a "proof by contradiction" that $S(n)$ is true for all $n \geq i$.

Unfortunately, there is a subtle logical flaw in the above reasoning. Our assumption that we can pick a least $j \geq i$ for which $S(j)$ is false depends on our believing the principle of induction in the first place. That is, the only way to prove that we can find such a j is to prove it by a method that is essentially an inductive proof. However, the "proof" discussed above makes good intuitive sense, and matches our understanding of the real world. Thus, we generally take as an integral part of our logical reasoning system:

- *The Induction Principle*: If we prove $S(i)$ and we prove that for all $n \geq i$, $S(n)$ implies $S(n+1)$, then we may conclude $S(n)$ for all $n \geq i$.

The following two examples illustrate the use of the induction principle to prove theorems about integers.

Theorem 1.16: For all $n \geq 0$:

$$\sum_{i=1}^{n} i^2 = \frac{n(n+1)(2n+1)}{6} \tag{1.1}$$

PROOF: The proof is in two parts: the basis and the inductive step; we prove each in turn.

BASIS: For the basis, we pick $n = 0$. it might seem surprising that the theorem even makes sense for $n = 0$, since the left side of Equation (1.1) is $\sum_{i=1}^{0}$ when $n = 0$. However, there is a general principle that when the upper limit of a sum (0 in this case) is less than the lower limit (1 here), the sum is over no terms and therefore the sum is 0. That is, $\sum_{i=1}^{0} i^2 = 0$.

The right side of Equation (1.1) is also 0, since $0 \times (0+1) \times (2 \times 0+1)/6 = 0$. Thus, Equation (1.1) is true when $n = 0$.

INDUCTION: Now, assume $n \geq 0$. We must prove the inductive step, that Equation (1.1) implies the same formula with $n + 1$ substituted for n. The latter formula is

$$\sum_{i=1}^{[n+1]} i^2 = \frac{[n+1]([n+1]+1)(2[n+1]+1)}{6} \tag{1.2}$$

We may simplify Equations (1.1) and (1.2) by expanding the sums and products on the right sides. These equations become:

$$\sum_{i=1}^{n} i^2 = (2n^3 + 3n^2 + n)/6 \tag{1.3}$$

$$\sum_{i=1}^{n+1} i^2 = (2n^3 + 9n^2 + 13n + 6)/6 \qquad (1.4)$$

We need to prove (1.4) using (1.3), since in the induction principle, these are statements $S(n + 1)$ and $S(n)$, respectively. The "trick" is to break the sum to $n + 1$ on the right of (1.4) into a sum to n plus the $(n + 1)$st term. In that way, we can replace the sum to n by the left side of (1.3) and show that (1.4) is true. These steps are as follows:

$$\left(\sum_{i=1}^{n} i^2\right) + (n + 1)^2 = (2n^3 + 9n^2 + 13n + 6)/6 \qquad (1.5)$$

$$(2n^3 + 3n^2 + n)/6 + (n^2 + 2n + 1) = (2n^3 + 9n^2 + 13n + 6)/6 \qquad (1.6)$$

The final verification that (1.6) is true requires only simple polynomial algebra on the left side to show it is identical to the right side. $\square$

Example 1.17: In the next example, we prove Theorem 1.3 from Section 1.2.1. Recall this theorem states that if $x \geq 4$, then $2^x \geq x^2$. We gave an informal proof based on the idea that the ratio $x^2/2^x$ shrinks as x grows above 4. We can make the idea precise if we prove the statement $2^x \geq x^2$ by induction on x, starting with a basis of $x = 4$. Note that the statement is actually false for $x < 4$.

BASIS: If $x = 4$, then 2^x and x^2 are both 16. Thus, $2^4 \geq 4^2$ holds.

INDUCTION: Suppose for some $x \geq 4$ that $2^x \geq x^2$. With this statement as the hypothesis, we need to prove the same statement, with $x + 1$ in place of x, that is, $2^{[x+1]} \geq [x + 1]^2$. These are the statements $S(x)$ and $S(x + 1)$ in the induction principle; the fact that we are using x instead of n as the parameter should not be of concern; x or n is just a local variable.

As in Theorem 1.16, we should rewrite $S(x + 1)$ so it can make use of $S(x)$. In this case, we can write $2^{[x+1]}$ as 2×2^x. Since $S(x)$ tells us that $2^x \geq x^2$, we can conclude that $2^{x+1} = 2 \times 2^x \geq 2x^2$.

But we need something different; we need to show that $2^{x+1} \geq (x + 1)^2$. One way to prove this statement is to prove that $2x^2 \geq (x + 1)^2$ and then use the transitivity of $\geq$ to show $2^{x+1} \geq 2x^2 \geq (x + 1)^2$. In our proof that

$$2x^2 \geq (x + 1)^2 \qquad (1.7)$$

we may use the assumption that $x \geq 4$. Begin by simplifying (1.7):

$$x^2 \geq 2x + 1 \qquad (1.8)$$

Divide (1.8) by x, to get:

Integers as Recursively Defined Concepts

We mentioned that inductive proofs are useful when the subject matter is recursively defined. However, our first examples were inductions on integers, which we do not normally think of as "recursively defined." However, there is a natural, recursive definition of when a number is a nonnegative integer, and this definition does indeed match the way inductions on integers proceed: from objects defined first, to those defined later.

BASIS: 0 is an integer.

INDUCTION: If n is an integer, then so is $n + 1$.

$$x \geq 2 + \frac{1}{x} \tag{1.9}$$

Since $x \geq 4$, we know $1/x \leq 1/4$. Thus, the left side of (1.9) is at least 4, and the right side is at most 2.25. We have thus proved the truth of (1.9). Therefore, Equations (1.8) and (1.7) are also true. Equation (1.7) in turn gives us $2x^2 \geq (x+1)^2$ for $x \geq 4$ and lets us prove statement $S(x + 1)$, which we recall was $2^{x+1} \geq (x+1)^2$. □

1.4.2   More General Forms of Integer Inductions

Sometimes an inductive proof is made possible only by using a more general scheme than the one proposed in Section 1.4.1, where we proved a statement S for one basis value and then proved that "if $S(n)$ then $S(n+1)$." Two important generalizations of this scheme are:

1. We can use several basis cases. That is, we prove $S(i), S(i + 1), \ldots, S(j)$ for some $j > i$.

2. In proving $S(n + 1)$, we can use the truth of all the statements

$$S(i), S(i + 1), \ldots, S(n)$$

rather than just using $S(n)$. Moreover, if we have proved basis cases up to $S(j)$, then we can assume $n \geq j$, rather than just $n \geq i$.

The conclusion to be made from this basis and inductive step is that $S(n)$ is true for all $n \geq i$.

Example 1.18: The following example will illustrate the potential of both principles. The statement $S(n)$ we would like to prove is that if $n \geq 8$, then n can be written as a sum of 3's and 5's. Notice, incidentally, that 7 cannot be written as a sum of 3's and 5's.

BASIS: The basis cases are $S(8)$, $S(9)$, and $S(10)$. The proofs are $8 = 3 + 5$, $9 = 3 + 3 + 3$, and $10 = 5 + 5$, respectively.

INDUCTION: Assume that $n \geq 10$ and that $S(8), S(9), \ldots, S(n)$ are true. We must prove $S(n+1)$ from these given facts. Our strategy is to subtract 3 from $n + 1$, observe that this number must be writable as a sum of 3's and 5's, and add one more 3 to the sum to get a way to write $n + 1$.

More formally, observe that $n - 2 \geq 8$, so we may assume $S(n - 2)$. That is, $n - 2 = 3a + 5b$ for some integers a and b. Then $n + 1 = 3 + 3a + 5b$, so $n + 1$ can be written as the sum of $a + 1$ 3's and b 5's. That proves $S(n + 1)$ and concludes the inductive step. □

1.4.3   Structural Inductions

In automata theory, there are several recursively defined structures about which we need to prove statements. The familiar notions of trees and expressions are important examples. Like inductions, all recursive definitions have a basis case, where one or more elementary structures are defined, and an inductive step, where more complex structures are defined in terms of previously defined structures.

Example 1.19 : Here is the recursive definition of a tree:

BASIS: A single node is a tree, and that node is the *root* of the tree.

INDUCTION: If $T_1, T_2, \ldots, T_k$ are trees, then we can form a new tree as follows:

1. Begin with a new node N, which is the root of the tree.

2. Add copies of all the trees $T_1, T_2, \ldots, T_k$.

3. Add edges from node N to the roots of each of the trees $T_1, T_2, \ldots, T_k$.

Figure 1.7 shows the inductive construction of a tree with root N from k smaller trees. □

Example 1.20 : Here is another recursive definition. This time we define *expressions* using the arithmetic operators $+$ and $*$, with both numbers and variables allowed as operands.

BASIS: Any number or letter (i.e., a variable) is an expression.

INDUCTION: If E and F are expressions, then so are $E + F$, $E * F$, and (E).

For example, both 2 and x are expressions by the basis. The inductive step tells us $x + 2$, $(x + 2)$, and $2 * (x + 2)$ are all expressions. Notice how each of these expressions depends on the previous ones being expressions. □

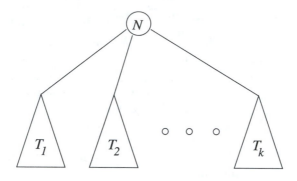

Figure 1.7: Inductive construction of a tree

Intuition Behind Structural Induction

We can suggest informally why structural induction is a valid proof method. Imagine the recursive definition establishing, one at a time, that certain structures $X_1, X_2, \ldots$ meet the definition. The basis elements come first, and the fact that X_i is in the defined set of structures can only depend on the membership in the defined set of structures that precede X_i on the list. Viewed this way, a structural induction is nothing but an induction on integer n of the statement $S(X_n)$. This induction may be of the generalized form discussed in Section 1.4.2, with multiple basis cases and an inductive step that uses all previous instances of the statement. However, we should remember, as explained in Section 1.4.1, that this intuition is not a formal proof, and in fact we must assume the validity this induction principle as we did the validity of the original induction principle of that section.

When we have a recursive definition, we can prove theorems about it using the following proof form, which is called *structural induction*. Let $S(X)$ be a statement about the structures X that are defined by some particular recursive definition.

1. As a basis, prove $S(X)$ for the basis structure(s) X.

2. For the inductive step, take a structure X that the recursive definition says is formed from $Y_1, Y_2, \ldots, Y_k$. Assume that the statements $S(Y_1), S(Y_2), \ldots, S(Y_k)$, and use these to prove $S(X)$.

Our conclusion is that $S(X)$ is true for all X. The next two theorems are examples of facts that can be proved about trees and expressions.

Theorem 1.21: Every tree has one more node than it has edges.

PROOF: The formal statement $S(T)$ we need to prove by structural induction is: "if T is a tree, and T has n nodes and e edges, then $n = e + 1$."

BASIS: The basis case is when T is a single node. Then $n = 1$ and $e = 0$, so the relationship $n = e + 1$ holds.

INDUCTION: Let T be a tree built by the inductive step of the definition, from root node N and k smaller trees $T_1, T_2, \ldots, T_k$. We may assume that the statements $S(T_i)$ hold for $i = 1, 2, \ldots, k$. That is, let T_i have n_i nodes and e_i edges; then $n_i = e_i + 1$.

The nodes of T are node N and all the nodes of the T_i's. There are thus $1 + n_1 + n_2 + \cdots + n_k$ nodes in T. The edges of T are the k edges we added explicitly in the inductive definition step, plus the edges of the T_i's. Hence, T has

$$k + e_1 + e_2 + \cdots + e_k \tag{1.10}$$

edges. If we substitute $e_i + 1$ for n_i in the count of the number of nodes of T we find that T has

$$1 + [e_1 + 1] + [e_2 + 1] + \cdots + [e_k + 1] \tag{1.11}$$

nodes. Since there are k of the "+1" terms in (1.10), we can regroup (1.11) as

$$k + 1 + e_1 + e_2 + \cdots + e_k \tag{1.12}$$

This expression is exactly 1 more than the expression of (1.10) that was given for the number of edges of T. Thus, T has one more node than it has edges. □

Theorem 1.22: Every expression has an equal number of left and right parentheses.

PROOF: Formally, we prove the statement $S(G)$ about any expression G that is defined by the recursion of Example 1.20: the numbers of left and right parentheses in G are the same.

BASIS: If G is defined by the basis, then G is a number or variable. These expressions have 0 left parentheses and 0 right parentheses, so the numbers are equal.

INDUCTION: There are three rules whereby expression G may have been constructed according to the inductive step in the definition:

1. $G = E + F$.

2. $G = E * F$.

3. $G = (E)$.

We may assume that $S(E)$ and $S(F)$ are true; that is, E has the same number of left and right parentheses, say n of each, and F likewise has the same number of left and right parentheses, say m of each. Then we can compute the numbers of left and right parentheses in G for each of the three cases, as follows:

1. If $G = E + F$, then G has $n + m$ left parentheses and $n + m$ right parentheses; n of each come from E and m of each come from F.

2. If $G = E * F$, the count of parentheses for G is again $n + m$ of each, for the same reason as in case (1).

3. If $G = (E)$, then there are $n+1$ left parentheses in G — one left parenthesis is explicitly shown, and the other n are present in E. Likewise, there are $n + 1$ right parentheses in G; one is explicit and the other n are in E.

In each of the three cases, we see that the numbers of left and right parentheses in G are the same. This observation completes the inductive step and completes the proof. $\square$

1.4.4   Mutual Inductions

Sometimes, we cannot prove a single statement by induction, but rather need to prove a group of statements $S_1(n), S_2(n), \ldots, S_k(n)$ together by induction on n. Automata theory provides many such situations. In Example 1.23 we sample the common situation where we need to explain what an automaton does by proving a group of statements, one for each state. These statements tell under what sequences of inputs the automaton gets into each of the states.

Strictly speaking, proving a group of statements is no different from proving the *conjunction* (logical AND) of all the statements. For instance, the group of statements $S_1(n), S_2(n), \ldots, S_k(n)$ could be replaced by the single statement $S_1(n)$ AND $S_2(n)$ AND $\cdots$ AND $S_k(n)$. However, when there are really several independent statements to prove, it is generally less confusing to keep the statements separate and to prove them all in their own parts of the basis and inductive steps. We call this sort of proof *mutual induction*. An example will illustrate the necessary steps for a mutual recursion.

Example 1.23 : Let us revisit the on/off switch, which we represented as an automaton in Example 1.1. The automaton itself is reproduced as Fig. 1.8. Since pushing the button switches the state between *on* and *off*, and the switch starts out in the *off* state, we expect that the following statements will together explain the operation of the switch:

$S_1(n)$: The automaton is in state *off* after n pushes if and only if n is even.

$S_2(n)$: The automaton is in state *on* after n pushes if and only if n is odd.

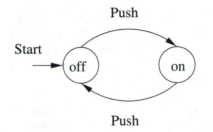

Figure 1.8: Repeat of the automaton of Fig. 1.1

We might suppose that S_1 implies S_2 and vice-versa, since we know that a number n cannot be both even and odd. However, what is not always true about an automaton is that it is in one and only one state. It happens that the automaton of Fig. 1.8 is always in exactly one state, but that fact must be proved as part of the mutual induction.

We give the basis and inductive parts of the proofs of statements $S_1(n)$ and $S_2(n)$ below. The proofs depend on several facts about odd and even integers: if we add or subtract 1 from an even integer, we get an odd integer, and if we add or subtract 1 from an odd integer we get an even integer.

BASIS: For the basis, we choose $n = 0$. Since there are two statements, each of which must be proved in both directions (because S_1 and S_2 are each "if-and-only-if" statements), there are actually four cases to the basis, and four cases to the induction as well.

1. $[S_1;$ If] Since 0 is in fact even, we must show that after 0 pushes, the automaton of Fig. 1.8 is in state *off*. Since that is the start state, the automaton is indeed in state *off* after 0 pushes.

2. $[S_1;$ Only-if] The automaton is in state *off* after 0 pushes, so we must show that 0 is even. But 0 is even by definition of "even," so there is nothing more to prove.

3. $[S_2;$ If] The hypothesis of the "if" part of S_2 is that 0 is odd. Since this hypothesis H is false, any statement of the form "if H then C" is true, as we discussed in Section 1.3.2. Thus, this part of the basis also holds.

4. $[S_2;$ Only-if] The hypothesis, that the automaton is in state *on* after 0 pushes, is also false, since the only way to get to state *on* is by following an arc labeled *Push*, which requires that the button be pushed at least once. Since the hypothesis is false, we can again conclude that the if-then statement is true.

INDUCTION: Now, we assume that $S_1(n)$ and $S_2(n)$ are true, and try to prove $S_1(n+1)$ and $S_2(n+1)$. Again, the proof separates into four parts.

1. $[S_1(n+1);$ If] The hypothesis for this part is that $n+1$ is even. Thus, n is odd. The "if" part of statement $S(n)$ says that after n pushes, the automaton is in state *off*. The arc from *off* to *on* labeled *Push* tells us that the $(n+1)$st push will cause the automaton to enter state *on*. That completes the proof of the "if" part of S_1.

2. $[S_1(n+1);$ Only-if] The hypothesis is that the automaton is in state *on* after $n+1$ pushes. Inspecting the automaton of Fig. 1.8 tells us that the only way to get to state *on* is to be in state *off* and receive an input *Push*. Thus, if we are in state *on* after $n+1$ pushes, we must have been in state *off* after n pushes. Then, we may use the "only-if" part of statement $S_2(n)$ to conclude that n is even. Consequently, $n+1$ is odd, which is the desired conclusion for the only-if portion of $S_1(n+1)$.

3. $[S_2(n+1);$ If] This part is essentially the same as part (1), with the roles of statements S_1 and S_2 exchanged, and with the roles of "odd" and "even" exchanged. The reader should be able to construct this part of the proof easily.

4. $[S_2(n+1);$ Only-if] This part is essentially the same as part (2), with the roles of statements S_1 and S_2 exchanged, and with the roles of "odd" and "even" exchanged.

□

We can abstract from Example 1.23 the pattern for all mutual inductions:

- Each of the statements must be proved separately in the basis and in the inductive step.

- If the statements are "if-and-only-if," then both directions of each statement must be proved, both in the basis and in the induction.

1.5 The Central Concepts of Automata Theory

In this section we shall introduce the most important definitions of terms that pervade the theory of automata. These concepts include the "alphabet" (a set of symbols), "strings" (a list of symbols from an alphabet), and "language" (a set of strings from the same alphabet).

1.5.1 Alphabets

An *alphabet* is a finite, nonempty set of symbols. Conventionally, we use the symbol Σ for an alphabet. Common alphabets include:

1. $\Sigma = \{0, 1\}$, the *binary* alphabet.

2. $\Sigma = \{a, b, \ldots, z\}$, the set of all lower-case letters.

3. The set of all ASCII characters, or the set of all printable ASCII characters.

1.5.2 Strings

A *string* (or sometimes *word*) is a finite sequence of symbols chosen from some alphabet. For example, 01101 is a string from the binary alphabet $\Sigma = \{0, 1\}$. The string 111 is another string chosen from this alphabet.

The Empty String

The *empty string* is the string with zero occurrences of symbols. This string, denoted ϵ, is a string that may be chosen from any alphabet whatsoever.

Length of a String

It is often useful to classify strings by their *length*, that is, the number of positions for symbols in the string. For instance, 01101 has length 5. It is common to say that the length of a string is "the number of symbols" in the string; this statement is colloquially accepted but not strictly correct. Thus, there are only two symbols, 0 and 1, in the string 01101, but there are five *positions* for symbols, and its length is 5. However, you should generally expect that "the number of symbols" can be used when "number of positions" is meant.

The standard notation for the length of a string w is $|w|$. For example, $|011| = 3$ and $|\epsilon| = 0$.

Powers of an Alphabet

If Σ is an alphabet, we can express the set of all strings of a certain length from that alphabet by using an exponential notation. We define Σ^k to be the set of strings of length k, each of whose symbols is in Σ.

Example 1.24: Note that $\Sigma^0 = \{\epsilon\}$, regardless of what alphabet Σ is. That is, ϵ is the only string whose length is 0.

If $\Sigma = \{0, 1\}$, then $\Sigma^1 = \{0, 1\}$, $\Sigma^2 = \{00, 01, 10, 11\}$,

$$\Sigma^3 = \{000, 001, 010, 011, 100, 101, 110, 111\}$$

and so on. Note that there is a slight confusion between Σ and Σ^1. The former is an alphabet; its members 0 and 1 are symbols. The latter is a set of strings; its members are the strings 0 and 1, each of which is of length 1. We shall not try to use separate notations for the two sets, relying on context to make it clear whether $\{0, 1\}$ or similar sets are alphabets or sets of strings. □

Type Convention for Symbols and Strings

Commonly, we shall use lower-case letters at the beginning of the alphabet (or digits) to denote symbols, and lower-case letters near the end of the alphabet, typically w, x, y, and z, to denote strings. You should try to get used to this convention, to help remind you of the types of the elements being discussed.

The set of all strings over an alphabet Σ is conventionally denoted Σ^*. For instance, $\{0,1\}^* = \{\epsilon, 0, 1, 00, 01, 10, 11, 000, \ldots\}$. Put another way,

$$\Sigma^* = \Sigma^0 \cup \Sigma^1 \cup \Sigma^2 \cup \cdots$$

Sometimes, we wish to exclude the empty string from the set of strings. The set of nonempty strings from alphabet Σ is denoted Σ^+. Thus, two appropriate equivalences are:

- $\Sigma^+ = \Sigma^1 \cup \Sigma^2 \cup \Sigma^3 \cup \cdots$.

- $\Sigma^* = \Sigma^+ \cup \{\epsilon\}$.

Concatenation of Strings

Let x and y be strings. Then xy denotes the *concatenation* of x and y, that is, the string formed by making a copy of x and following it by a copy of y. More precisely, if x is the string composed of i symbols $x = a_1 a_2 \cdots a_i$ and y is the string composed of j symbols $y = b_1 b_2 \cdots b_j$, then xy is the string of length $i + j$: $xy = a_1 a_2 \cdots a_i b_1 b_2 \cdots b_j$.

Example 1.25: Let $x = 01101$ and $y = 110$. Then $xy = 01101110$ and $yx = 11001101$. For any string w, the equations $\epsilon w = w\epsilon = w$ hold. That is, ϵ is the *identity for concatenation*, since when concatenated with any string it yields the other string as a result (analogously to the way 0, the identity for addition, can be added to any number x and yields x as a result). $\square$

1.5.3   Languages

A set of strings all of which are chosen from some Σ^*, where Σ is a particular alphabet, is called a *language*. If Σ is an alphabet, and $L \subseteq \Sigma^*$, then L is a *language over* Σ. Notice that a language over Σ need not include strings with all the symbols of Σ, so once we have established that L is a language over Σ, we also know it is a language over any alphabet that is a superset of Σ.

The choice of the term "language" may seem strange. However, common languages can be viewed as sets of strings. An example is English, where the collection of legal English words is a set of strings over the alphabet that consists of all the letters. Another example is C, or any other programming language, where the legal programs are a subset of the possible strings that can be formed from the alphabet of the language. This alphabet is a subset of the ASCII characters. The exact alphabet may differ slightly among different programming languages, but generally includes the upper- and lower-case letters, the digits, punctuation, and mathematical symbols.

However, there are also many other languages that appear when we study automata. Some are abstract examples, such as:

1. The language of all strings consisting of n 0's followed by n 1's, for some $n \geq 0$: $\{\epsilon, 01, 0011, 000111, \ldots\}$.

2. The set of strings of 0's and 1's with an equal number of each:

$$\{\epsilon, 01, 10, 0011, 0101, 1001, \ldots\}$$

3. The set of binary numbers whose value is a prime:

$$\{10, 11, 101, 111, 1011, \ldots\}$$

4. Σ^* is a language for any alphabet Σ.

5. $\emptyset$, the empty language, is a language over any alphabet.

6. $\{\epsilon\}$, the language consisting of only the empty string, is also a language over any alphabet. Notice that $\emptyset \neq \{\epsilon\}$; the former has no strings and the latter has one string.

The only important constraint on what can be a language is that all alphabets are finite. Thus languages, although they can have an infinite number of strings, are restricted to consist of strings drawn from one fixed, finite alphabet.

1.5.4 Problems

In automata theory, a *problem* is the question of deciding whether a given string is a member of some particular language. It turns out, as we shall see, that anything we more colloquially call a "problem" can be expressed as membership in a language. More precisely, if Σ is an alphabet, and L is a language over Σ, then the problem L is:

- Given a string w in Σ^*, decide whether or not w is in L.

Example 1.26: The problem of testing primality can be expressed by the language L_p consisting of all binary strings whose value as a binary number is a prime. That is, given a string of 0's and 1's, say "yes" if the string is the binary representation of a prime and say "no" if not. For some strings, this

---

Set-Formers as a Way to Define Languages

It is common to describe a language using a "set-former":

$$\{w \mid \text{something about } w\}$$

This expression is read "the set of words w such that (whatever is said about w to the right of the vertical bar)." Examples are:

1. $\{w \mid w$ consists of an equal number of 0's and 1's $\}$.

2. $\{w \mid w$ is a binary integer that is prime $\}$.

3. $\{w \mid w$ is a syntactically correct C program $\}$.

It is also common to replace w by some expression with parameters and describe the strings in the language by stating conditions on the parameters. Here are some examples; the first with parameter n, the second with parameters i and j:

1. $\{0^n 1^n \mid n \geq 1\}$. Read "the set of 0 to the n 1 to the n such that n is greater than or equal to 1," this language consists of the strings $\{01, 0011, 000111, \ldots\}$. Notice that, as with alphabets, we can raise a single symbol to a power n in order to represent n copies of that symbol.

2. $\{0^i 1^j \mid 0 \leq i \leq j\}$. This language consists of strings with some 0's (possibly none) followed by at least as many 1's.

---

decision is easy. For instance, 0011101 cannot be the representation of a prime, for the simple reason that every integer except 0 has a binary representation that begins with 1. However, it is less obvious whether the string 11101 belongs to L_p, so any solution to this problem will have to use significant computational resources of some kind: time and/or space, for example. □

One potentially unsatisfactory aspect of our definition of "problem" is that one commonly thinks of problems not as decision questions (is or is not the following true?) but as requests to compute or transform some input (find the best way to do this task). For instance, the task of the parser in a C compiler can be thought of as a problem in our formal sense, where one is given an ASCII string and asked to decide whether or not the string is a member of L_c, the set of valid C programs. However, the parser does more than decide. It produces a parse tree, entries in a symbol table and perhaps more. Worse, the compiler as a whole solves the problem of turning a C program into object code for some

---

Is It a Language or a Problem?

Languages and problems are really the same thing. Which term we prefer to use depends on our point of view. When we care only about strings for their own sake, e.g., in the set $\{0^n1^n \mid n \geq 1\}$, then we tend to think of the set of strings as a language. In the last chapters of this book, we shall tend to assign "semantics" to the strings, e.g., think of strings as coding graphs, logical expressions, or even integers. In those cases, where we care more about the thing represented by the string than the string itself, we shall tend to think of a set of strings as a problem.

---

machine, which is far from simply answering "yes" or "no" about the validity of a program.

Nevertheless, the definition of "problems" as languages has stood the test of time as the appropriate way to deal with the important questions of complexity theory. In this theory, we are interested in proving lower bounds on the complexity of certain problems. Especially important are techniques for proving that certain problems cannot be solved in an amount of time that is less than exponential in the size of their input. It turns out that the yes/no or language-based version of known problems are just as hard in this sense, as their "solve this" versions.

That is, if we can prove it is hard to decide whether a given string belongs to the language L_X of valid strings in programming language X, then it stands to reason that it will not be easier to translate programs in language X to object code. For if it were easy to generate code, then we could run the translator, and conclude that the input was a valid member of L_X exactly when the translator succeeded in producing object code. Since the final step of determining whether object code has been produced cannot be hard, we can use the fast algorithm for generating the object code to decide membership in L_X efficiently. We thus contradict the assumption that testing membership in L_X is hard. We have a proof by contradiction of the statement "if testing membership in L_X is hard, then compiling programs in programming language X is hard."

This technique, showing one problem hard by using its supposed efficient algorithm to solve efficiently another problem that is already known to be hard, is called a "reduction" of the second problem to the first. It is an essential tool in the study of the complexity of problems, and it is facilitated greatly by our notion that problems are questions about membership in a language, rather than more general kinds of questions.

1.6   Summary of Chapter 1

✦ *Finite Automata*: Finite automata involve states and transitions among states in response to inputs. They are useful for building several different kinds of software, including the lexical analysis component of a compiler and systems for verifying the correctness of circuits or protocols, for example.

✦ *Regular Expressions*: These are a structural notation for describing the same patterns that can be represented by finite automata. They are used in many common types of software, including tools to search for patterns in text or in file names, for instance.

✦ *Context-Free Grammars*: These are an important notation for describing the structure of programming languages and related sets of strings; they are used to build the parser component of a compiler.

✦ *Turing Machines*: These are automata that model the power of real computers. They allow us to study decidabilty, the question of what can or cannot be done by a computer. They also let us distinguish tractable problems — those that can be solved in polynomial time — from the intractable problems — those that cannot.

✦ *Deductive Proofs*: This basic method of proof proceeds by listing statements that are either given to be true, or that follow logically from some of the previous statements.

✦ *Proving If-Then Statements*: Many theorems are of the form "if (something) then (something else)." The statement or statements following the "if" are the hypothesis, and what follows "then" is the conclusion. Deductive proofs of if-then statements begin with the hypothesis, and continue with statements that follow logically from the hypothesis and previous statements, until the conclusion is proved as one of the statements.

✦ *Proving If-And-Only-If Statements*: There are other theorems of the form "(something) if and only if (something else)." They are proved by showing if-then statements in both directions. A similar kind of theorem claims the equality of the sets described in two different ways; these are proved by showing that each of the two sets is contained in the other.

✦ *Proving the Contrapositive*: Sometimes, it is easier to prove a statement of the form "if H then C" by proving the equivalent statement: "if not C then not H." The latter is called the contrapositive of the former.

✦ *Proof by Contradiction*: Other times, it is more convenient to prove the statement "if H then C" by proving "if H and not C then (something known to be false)." A proof of this type is called proof by contradiction.

✦ *Counterexamples*: Sometimes we are asked to show that a certain statement is not true. If the statement has one or more parameters, then we can show it is false as a generality by providing just one counterexample, that is, one assignment of values to the parameters that makes the statement false.

✦ *Inductive Proofs*: A statement that has an integer parameter n can often by proved by induction on n. We prove the statement is true for the basis, a finite number of cases for particular values of n, and then prove the inductive step: that if the statement is true for values up to n, then it is true for $n + 1$.

✦ *Structural Inductions*: In some situations, including many in this book, the theorem to be proved inductively is about some recursively defined construct, such as trees. We may prove a theorem about the constructed objects by induction on the number of steps used in its construction. This type of induction is referred to as structural.

✦ *Alphabets*: An alphabet is any finite set of symbols.

✦ *Strings*: A string is a finite-length sequence of symbols.

✦ *Languages and Problems*: A language is a (possibly infinite) set of strings, all of which choose their symbols from some one alphabet. When the strings of a language are to be interpreted in some way, the question of whether a string is in the language is sometimes called a problem.

1.7   References for Chapter 1

For extended coverage of the material of this chapter, including mathematical concepts underlying Computer Science, we recommend [1].

1. A. V. Aho and J. D. Ullman, *Foundations of Computer Science*, Computer Science Press, New York, 1994.

Chapter 2

Finite Automata

This chapter introduces the class of languages known as "regular languages." These languages are exactly the ones that can be described by finite automata, which we sampled briefly in Section 1.1.1. After an extended example that will provide motivation for the study to follow, we define finite automata formally.

As was mentioned earlier, a finite automaton has a set of states, and its "control" moves from state to state in response to external "inputs." One of the crucial distinctions among classes of finite automata is whether that control is "deterministic," meaning that the automaton cannot be in more than one state at any one time, or "nondeterministic," meaning that it may be in several states at once. We shall discover that adding nondeterminism does not let us define any language that cannot be defined by a deterministic finite automaton, but there can be substantial efficiency in describing an application using a nondeterministic automaton. In effect, nondeterminism allows us to "program" solutions to problems using a higher-level language. The nondeterministic finite automaton is then "compiled," by an algorithm we shall learn in this chapter, into a deterministic automaton that can be "executed" on a conventional computer.

We conclude the chapter with a study of an extended nondeterministic automaton that has the additional choice of making a transition from one state to another spontaneously, i.e., on the empty string as "input." These automata also accept nothing but the regular languages. However, we shall find them quite important in Chapter 3, when we study regular expressions and their equivalence to automata.

The study of the regular languages continues in Chapter 3. There, we introduce another important way to describe regular languages: the algebraic notation known as regular expressions. After discussing regular expressions, and showing their equivalence to finite automata, we use both automata and regular expressions as tools in Chapter 4 to show certain important properties of the regular languages. Examples of such properties are the "closure" properties, which allow us to claim that one language is regular because one or more other languages are known to be regular, and "decision" properties. The latter are algorithms to answer questions about automata or regular expressions, e.g., whether two automata or expressions represent the same language.

2.1   An Informal Picture of Finite Automata

In this section, we shall study an extended example of a real-world problem whose solution uses finite automata in an important role. We investigate protocols that support "electronic money" — files that a customer can use to pay for goods on the internet, and that the seller can receive with assurance that the "money" is real. The seller must know that the file has not been forged, nor has it been copied and sent to the seller, while the customer retains a copy of the same file to spend again.

The nonforgeability of the file is something that must be assured by a bank and by a cryptography policy. That is, a third player, the bank, must issue and encrypt the "money" files, so that forgery is not a problem. However, the bank has a second important job: it must keep a database of all the valid money that it has issued, so that it can verify to a store that the file it has received represents real money and can be credited to the store's account. We shall not address the cryptographic aspects of the problem, nor shall we worry about how the bank can store and retrieve what could be billions of "electronic dollar bills." These problems are not likely to represent long-term impediments to the concept of electronic money, and examples of its small-scale use have existed since the late 1990's.

However, in order to use electronic money, protocols need to be devised to allow the manipulation of the money in a variety of ways that the users want. Because monetary systems always invite fraud, we must verify whatever policy we adopt regarding how money is used. That is, we need to prove the only things that can happen are things we intend to happen — things that do not allow an unscrupulous user to steal from others or to "manufacture" money. In the balance of this section, we shall introduce a very simple example of a (bad) electronic-money protocol, model it with finite automata, and show how constructions on automata can be used to verify protocols (or, in this case, to discover that the protocol has a bug).

2.1.1   The Ground Rules

There are three participants: the customer, the store, and the bank. We assume for simplicity that there is only one "money" file in existence. The customer may decide to transfer this money file to the store, which will then redeem the file from the bank (i.e., get the bank to issue a new money file belonging to the store rather than the customer) and ship goods to the customer. In addition, the customer has the option to cancel the file. That is, the customer may ask the bank to place the money back in the customer's account, making the money no longer spendable. Interaction among the three participants is thus limited to five events:

1. The customer may decide to *pay*. That is, the customer sends the money to the store.

2. The customer may decide to *cancel*. The money is sent to the bank with a message that the value of the money is to be added to the customer's bank account.

3. The store may *ship* goods to the customer.

4. The store may *redeem* the money. That is, the money is sent to the bank with a request that its value be given to the store.

5. The bank may *transfer* the money by creating a new, suitably encrypted money file and sending it to the store.

2.1.2 The Protocol

The three participants must design their behaviors carefully, or the wrong things may happen. In our example, we make the reasonable assumption that the customer cannot be relied upon to act responsibly. In particular, the customer may try to copy the money file, use it to pay several times, or both pay and cancel the money, thus getting the goods "for free."

The bank must behave responsibly, or it cannot be a bank. In particular, it must make sure that two stores cannot both redeem the same money file, and it must not allow money to be both canceled and redeemed. The store should be careful as well. In particular, it should not ship goods until it is sure it has been given valid money for the goods.

Protocols of this type can be represented as finite automata. Each state represents a situation that one of the participants could be in. That is, the state "remembers" that certain important events have happened and that others have not yet happened. Transitions between states occur when one of the five events described above occur. We shall think of these events as "external" to the automata representing the three participants, even though each participant is responsible for initiating one or more of the events. It turns out that what is important about the problem is what sequences of events can happen, not who is allowed to initiate them.

Figure 2.1 represents the three participants by automata. In that diagram, we show only the events that affect a participant. For example, the action *pay* affects only the customer and store. The bank does not know that the money has been sent by the customer to the store; it discovers that fact only when the store executes the action *redeem*.

Let us examine first the automaton (c) for the bank. The start state is state 1; it represents the situation where the bank has issued the money file in question but has not been requested either to redeem it or to cancel it. If a

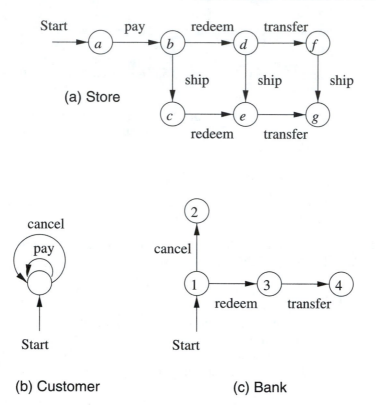

Figure 2.1: Finite automata representing a customer, a store, and a bank

cancel request is sent to the bank by the customer, then the bank restores the money to the customer's account and enters state 2. The latter state represents the situation where the money has been cancelled. The bank, being responsible, will not leave state 2 once it is entered, since the bank must not allow the same money to be cancelled again or spent by the customer.[1]

Alternatively, when in state 1 the bank may receive a *redeem* request from the store. If so, it goes to state 3, and shortly sends the store a *transfer* message, with a new money file that now belongs to the store. After sending the transfer message, the bank goes to state 4. In that state, it will neither accept *cancel* or *redeem* requests nor will it perform any other actions regarding this particular money file.

Now, let us consider Fig. 2.1(a), the automaton representing the actions of the store. While the bank always does the right thing, the store's system has some defects. Imagine that the shipping and financial operations are done by

---

[1]You should remember that this entire discussion is about one single money file. The bank will in fact be running the same protocol with a large number of electronic pieces of money, but the workings of the protocol are the same for each of them, so we can discuss the problem as if there were only one piece of electronic money in existence.

separate processes, so there is the opportunity for the *ship* action to be done either before, after, or during the redemption of the electronic money. That policy allows the store to get into a situation where it has already shipped the goods and then finds out the money was bogus.

The store starts out in state *a*. When the customer orders the goods by performing the *pay* action, the store enters state *b*. In this state, the store begins both the shipping and redemption processes. If the goods are shipped first, then the store enters state *c*, where it must still redeem the money from the bank and receive the *transfer* of an equivalent money file from the bank. Alternatively, the store may send the *redeem* message first, entering state *d*. From state *d*, the store might next ship, entering state *e*, or it might next receive the transfer of money from the bank, entering state *f*. From state *f*, we expect that the store will eventually ship, putting the store in state *g*, where the transaction is complete and nothing more will happen. In state *e*, the store is waiting for the *transfer* from the bank. Unfortunately, the goods have already been shipped, and if the *transfer* never occurs, the store is out of luck.

Last, observe the automaton for the customer, Fig. 2.1(b). This automaton has only one state, reflecting the fact that the customer "can do anything." The customer can perform the *pay* and *cancel* actions any number of times, in any order, and stays in the lone state after each action.

2.1.3 Enabling the Automata to Ignore Actions

While the three automata of Fig. 2.1 reflect the behaviors of the three participants independently, there are certain transitions that are missing. For example, the store is not affected by a *cancel* message, so if the *cancel* action is performed by the customer, the store should remain in whatever state it is in. However, in the formal definition of a finite automaton, which we shall study in Section 2.2, whenever an input X is received by an automaton, the automaton must follow an arc labeled X from the state it is in to some new state. Thus, the automaton for the store needs an additional arc from each state to itself, labeled *cancel*. Then, whenever the *cancel* action is executed, the store automaton can make a "transition" on that input, with the effect that it stays in the same state it was in. Without these additional arcs, whenever the *cancel* action was executed the store automaton would "die"; that is, the automaton would be in no state at all, and further actions by that automaton would be impossible.

Another potential problem is that one of the participants may, intentionally or erroneously, send an unexpected message, and we do not want this action to cause one of the automata to die. For instance, suppose the customer decided to execute the *pay* action a second time, while the store was in state *e*. Since that state has no arc out with label *pay*, the store's automaton would die before it could receive the transfer from the bank. In summary, we must add to the automata of Fig. 2.1 loops on certain states, with labels for all those actions that must be ignored when in that state; the complete automata are shown in Fig. 2.2. To save space, we combine the labels onto one arc, rather than

showing several arcs with the same heads and tails but different labels. The
two kinds of actions that must be ignored are:

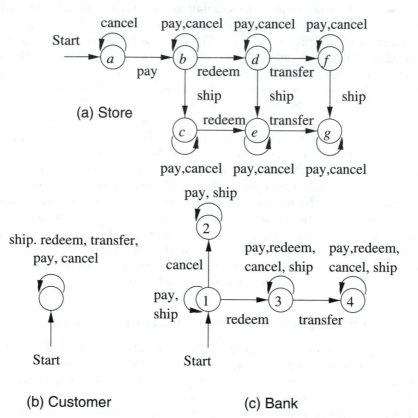

(a) Store

(b) Customer   (c) Bank

Figure 2.2: The complete sets of transitions for the three automata

1. *Actions that are irrelevant to the participant involved.* As we saw, the
   only irrelevant action for the store is *cancel*, so each of its seven states
   has a loop labeled *cancel*. For the bank, both *pay* and *ship* are irrelevant,
   so we have put at each of the bank's states an arc labeled *pay, ship*. For
   the customer, *ship*, *redeem* and *transfer* are all irrelevant, so we add arcs
   with these labels. In effect, it stays in its one state on any sequence of
   inputs, so the customer automaton has no effect on the operation of the
   overall system. Of course, the customer is still a participant, since it is
   the customer who initiates the *pay* and *cancel* actions. However, as we
   mentioned, the matter of who initiates actions has nothing to do with the
   behavior of the automata.

2. *Actions that must not be allowed to kill an automaton.* As mentioned, we
   must not allow the customer to kill the store's automaton by executing *pay*

again, so we have added loops with label *pay* to all but state *a* (where the *pay* action is expected and relevant). We have also added loops with labels *cancel* to states 3 and 4 of the bank, in order to prevent the customer from killing the bank's automaton by trying to cancel money that has already been redeemed. The bank properly ignores such a request. Likewise, states 3 and 4 have loops on *redeem*. The store should not try to redeem the same money twice, but if it does, the bank properly ignores the second request.

2.1.4 The Entire System as an Automaton

While we now have models for how the three participants behave, we do not yet have a representation for the interaction of the three participants. As mentioned, because the customer has no constraints on behavior, that automaton has only one state, and any sequence of events lets it stay in that state; i.e., it is not possible for the system as a whole to "die" because the customer automaton has no response to an action. However, both the store and bank behave in a complex way, and it is not immediately obvious in what combinations of states these two automata can be.

The normal way to explore the interaction of automata such as these is to construct the *product* automaton. That automaton's states represent a pair of states, one from the store and one from the bank. For instance, the state $(3, d)$ of the product automaton represents the situation where the bank is in state 3, and the store is in state d. Since the bank has four states and the store has seven, the product automaton has $4 \times 7 = 28$ states.

We show the product automaton in Fig. 2.3. For clarity, we have arranged the 28 states in an array. The row corresponds to the state of the bank and the column to the state of the store. To save space, we have also abbreviated the labels on the arcs, with P, S, C, R, and T standing for pay, ship, cancel, redeem, and transfer, respectively.

To construct the arcs of the product automaton, we need to run the bank and store automata "in parallel." Each of the two components of the product automaton independently makes transitions on the various inputs. However, it is important to notice that if an input action is received, and one of the two automata has no state to go to on that input, then the product automaton "dies"; it has no state to go to.

To make this rule for state transitions precise, suppose the product automaton is in state (i, x). That state corresponds to the situation where the bank is in state i and the store in state x. Let Z be one of the input actions. We look at the automaton for the bank, and see whether there is a transition out of state i with label Z. Suppose there is, and it leads to state j (which might be the same as i if the bank loops on input Z). Then, we look at the store and see if there is an arc labeled Z leading to some state y. If both j and y exist, then the product automaton has an arc from state (i, x) to state (j, y), labeled Z. If either of states j or y do not exist (because the bank or store has no arc

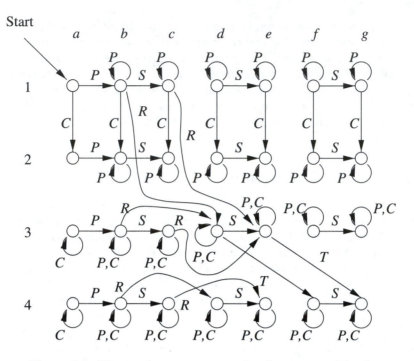

Figure 2.3: The product automaton for the store and bank

out of i or x, respectively, for input Z), then there is no arc out of (i, x) labeled Z.

We can now see how the arcs of Fig. 2.3 were selected. For instance, on input *pay*, the store goes from state a to b, but stays put if it is in any other state besides a. The bank stays in whatever state it is in when the input is *pay*, because that action is irrelevant to the bank. This observation explains the four arcs labeled P at the left ends of the four rows in Fig. 2.3, and the loops labeled P on other states.

For another example of how the arcs are selected, consider the input *redeem*. If the bank receives a *redeem* message when in state 1, it goes to state 3. If in states 3 or 4, it stays there, while in state 2 the bank automaton dies; i.e., it has nowhere to go. The store, on the other hand, can make transitions from state b to d or from c to e when the *redeem* input is received. In Fig. 2.3, we see six arcs labeled *redeem*, corresponding to the six combinations of three bank states and two store states that have outward-bound arcs labeled R. For example, in state $(1, b)$, the arc labeled R takes the automaton to state $(3, d)$, since *redeem* takes the bank from state 1 to 3 and the store from b to d. As another example, there is an arc labeled R from $(4, c)$ to $(4, e)$, since *redeem* takes the bank from state 4 back to state 4, while it takes the store from state c to state e.

2.1.5 Using the Product Automaton to Validate the Protocol

Figure 2.3 tells us some interesting things. For instance, of the 28 states, only ten of them can be reached from the start state, which is $(1, a)$ — the combination of the start states of the bank and store automata. Notice that states like $(2, e)$ and $(4, d)$ are not *accessible*, that is, there is no path to them from the start state. Inaccessible states need not be included in the automaton, and we did so in this example just to be systematic.

However, the real purpose of analyzing a protocol such as this one using automata is to ask and answer questions that mean "can the following type of error occur?" In the example at hand, we might ask whether it is possible that the store can ship goods and never get paid. That is, can the product automaton get into a state in which the store has shipped (that is, the state is in column c, e, or g), and yet no transition on input T was ever made or will be made?

For instance, in state $(3, e)$, the goods have shipped, but there will eventually be a transition on input T to state $(4, g)$. In terms of what the bank is doing, once it has gotten to state 3, it has received the *redeem* request and processed it. That means it must have been in state 1 before receiving the *redeem* and therefore the *cancel* message had not been received and will be ignored if received in the future. Thus, the bank will eventually perform the transfer of money to the store.

However, state $(2, c)$ is a problem. The state is accessible, but the only arc out leads back to that state. This state corresponds to a situation where the bank received a *cancel* message before a *redeem* message. However, the store received a *pay* message; i.e., the customer was being duplicitous and has both spent and canceled the same money. The store foolishly shipped before trying to redeem the money, and when the store does execute the *redeem* action, the bank will not even acknowledge the message, because it is in state 2, where it has canceled the money and will not process a *redeem* request.

2.2 Deterministic Finite Automata

Now it is time to present the formal notion of a finite automaton, so that we may start to make precise some of the informal arguments and descriptions that we saw in Sections 1.1.1 and 2.1. We begin by introducing the formalism of a deterministic finite automaton, one that is in a single state after reading any sequence of inputs. The term "deterministic" refers to the fact that on each input there is one and only one state to which the automaton can transition from its current state. In contrast, "nondeterministic" finite automata, the subject of Section 2.3, can be in several states at once. The term "finite automaton" will refer to the deterministic variety, although we shall use "deterministic" or the abbreviation *DFA* normally, to remind the reader of which kind of automaton we are talking about.

2.2.1   Definition of a Deterministic Finite Automaton

A *deterministic finite automaton* consists of:

1. A finite set of *states*, often denoted Q.

2. A finite set of *input symbols*, often denoted Σ.

3. A *transition function* that takes as arguments a state and an input symbol and returns a state. The transition function will commonly be denoted δ. In our informal graph representation of automata, δ was represented by arcs between states and the labels on the arcs. If q is a state, and a is an input symbol, then $\delta(q, a)$ is that state p such that there is an arc labeled a from q to p.[2]

4. A *start state*, one of the states in Q.

5. A set of *final* or *accepting* states F. The set F is a subset of Q.

A deterministic finite automaton will often be referred to by its acronym: *DFA*. The most succinct representation of a DFA is a listing of the five components above. In proofs we often talk about a DFA in "five-tuple" notation:

$$A = (Q, \Sigma, \delta, q_0, F)$$

where A is the name of the DFA, Q is its set of states, Σ its input symbols, δ its transition function, q_0 its start state, and F its set of accepting states.

2.2.2   How a DFA Processes Strings

The first thing we need to understand about a DFA is how the DFA decides whether or not to "accept" a sequence of input symbols. The "language" of the DFA is the set of all strings that the DFA accepts. Suppose $a_1 a_2 \cdots a_n$ is a sequence of input symbols. We start out with the DFA in its start state, q_0. We consult the transition function δ, say $\delta(q_0, a_1) = q_1$ to find the state that the DFA A enters after processing the first input symbol a_1. We process the next input symbol, a_2, by evaluating $\delta(q_1, a_2)$; let us suppose this state is q_2. We continue in this manner, finding states $q_3, q_4, \ldots, q_n$ such that $\delta(q_{i-1}, a_i) = q_i$ for each i. If q_n is a member of F, then the input $a_1 a_2 \cdots a_n$ is accepted, and if not then it is "rejected."

Example 2.1: Let us formally specify a DFA that accepts all and only the strings of 0's and 1's that have the sequence 01 somewhere in the string. We can write this language L as:

$$\{w \mid w \text{ is of the form } x01y \text{ for some strings}$$
$$x \text{ and } y \text{ consisting of 0's and 1's only}\}$$

---

[2] More accurately, the graph is a picture of some transition function δ, and the arcs of the graph are constructed to reflect the transitions specified by δ.

Another equivalent description, using parameters x and y to the left of the vertical bar, is:

$$\{x01y \mid x \text{ and } y \text{ are any strings of 0's and 1's}\}$$

Examples of strings in the language include 01, 11010, and 100011. Examples of strings *not* in the language include ϵ, 0, and 111000.

What do we know about an automaton that can accept this language L? First, its input alphabet is $\Sigma = \{0, 1\}$. It has some set of states, Q, of which one, say q_0, is the start state. This automaton has to remember the important facts about what inputs it has seen so far. To decide whether 01 is a substring of the input, A needs to remember:

1. Has it already seen 01? If so, then it accepts every sequence of further inputs; i.e., it will only be in accepting states from now on.

2. Has it never seen 01, but its most recent input was 0, so if it now sees a 1, it will have seen 01 and can accept everything it sees from here on?

3. Has it never seen 01, but its last input was either nonexistent (it just started) or it last saw a 1? In this case, A cannot accept until it first sees a 0 and then sees a 1 immediately after.

These three conditions can each be represented by a state. Condition (3) is represented by the start state, q_0. Surely, when just starting, we need to see a 0 and then a 1. But if in state q_0 we next see a 1, then we are no closer to seeing 01, and so we must stay in state q_0. That is, $\delta(q_0, 1) = q_0$.

However, if we are in state q_0 and we next see a 0, we are in condition (2). That is, we have never seen 01, but we have our 0. Thus, let us use q_2 to represent condition (2). Our transition from q_0 on input 0 is $\delta(q_0, 0) = q_2$.

Now, let us consider the transitions from state q_2. If we see a 0, we are no better off than we were, but no worse either. We have not seen 01, but 0 was the last symbol, so we are still waiting for a 1. State q_2 describes this situation perfectly, so we want $\delta(q_2, 0) = q_2$. If we are in state q_2 and we see a 1 input, we now know there is a 0 followed by a 1. We can go to an accepting state, which we shall call q_1, and which corresponds to condition (1) above. That is, $\delta(q_2, 1) = q_1$.

Finally, we must design the transitions for state q_1. In this state, we have already seen a 01 sequence, so regardless of what happens, we shall still be in a situation where we've seen 01. That is, $\delta(q_1, 0) = \delta(q_1, 1) = q_1$.

Thus, $Q = \{q_0, q_1, q_2\}$. As we said, q_0 is the start state, and the only accepting state is q_1; that is, $F = \{q_1\}$. The complete specification of the automaton A that accepts the language L of strings that have a 01 substring, is

$$A = (\{q_0, q_1, q_2\}, \{0, 1\}, \delta, q_0, \{q_1\})$$

where δ is the transition function described above. $\square$

2.2.3   Simpler Notations for DFA's

Specifying a DFA as a five-tuple with a detailed description of the δ transition function is both tedious and hard to read. There are two preferred notations for describing automata:

1. A *transition diagram*, which is a graph such as the ones we saw in Section 2.1.

2. A *transition table*, which is a tabular listing of the δ function, which by implication tells us the set of states and the input alphabet.

Transition Diagrams

A *transition diagram* for a DFA $A = (Q, \Sigma, \delta, q_0, F)$ is a graph defined as follows:

a) For each state in Q there is a node.

b) For each state q in Q and each input symbol a in Σ, let $\delta(q, a) = p$. Then the transition diagram has an arc from node q to node p, labeled a. If there are several input symbols that cause transitions from q to p, then the transition diagram can have one arc, labeled by the list of these symbols.

c) There is an arrow into the start state q_0, labeled *Start*. This arrow does not originate at any node.

d) Nodes corresponding to accepting states (those in F) are marked by a double circle. States not in F have a single circle.

Example 2.2: Figure 2.4 shows the transition diagram for the DFA that we designed in Example 2.1. We see in that diagram the three nodes that correspond to the three states. There is a *Start* arrow entering the start state, q_0, and the one accepting state, q_1, is represented by a double circle. Out of each state is one arc labeled 0 and one arc labeled 1 (although the two arcs are combined into one with a double label in the case of q_1). The arcs each correspond to one of the δ facts developed in Example 2.1.   □

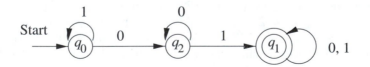

Figure 2.4: The transition diagram for the DFA accepting all strings with a substring 01

Transition Tables

A *transition table* is a conventional, tabular representation of a function like δ that takes two arguments and returns a value. The rows of the table correspond to the states, and the columns correspond to the inputs. The entry for the row corresponding to state q and the column corresponding to input a is the state $\delta(q, a)$.

Example 2.3: The transition table corresponding to the function δ of Example 2.1 is shown in Fig. 2.5. We have also shown two other features of a transition table. The start state is marked with an arrow, and the accepting states are marked with a star. Since we can deduce the sets of states and input symbols by looking at the row and column heads, we can now read from the transition table all the information we need to specify the finite automaton uniquely. □

	0	1
→ q_0	q_2	q_0
* q_1	q_1	q_1
q_2	q_2	q_1

Figure 2.5: Transition table for the DFA of Example 2.1

2.2.4 Extending the Transition Function to Strings

We have explained informally that the DFA defines a language: the set of all strings that result in a sequence of state transitions from the start state to an accepting state. In terms of the transition diagram, the language of a DFA is the set of labels along all the paths that lead from the start state to any accepting state.

Now, we need to make the notion of the language of a DFA precise. To do so, we define an *extended transition function* that describes what happens when we start in any state and follow any sequence of inputs. If δ is our transition function, then the extended transition function constructed from δ will be called $\hat{\delta}$. The extended transition function is a function that takes a state q and a string w and returns a state p — the state that the automaton reaches when starting in state q and processing the sequence of inputs w. We define $\hat{\delta}$ by induction on the length of the input string, as follows:

BASIS: $\hat{\delta}(q, \epsilon) = q$. That is, if we are in state q and read no inputs, then we are still in state q.

INDUCTION: Suppose w is a string of the form xa; that is, a is the last symbol of w, and x is the string consisting of all but the last symbol.[3] For example, $w = 1101$ is broken into $x = 110$ and $a = 1$. Then

$$\hat{\delta}(q, w) = \delta\big(\hat{\delta}(q, x), a\big) \tag{2.1}$$

Now (2.1) may seem like a lot to take in, but the idea is simple. To compute $\hat{\delta}(q, w)$, first compute $\hat{\delta}(q, x)$, the state that the automaton is in after processing all but the last symbol of w. Suppose this state is p; that is, $\hat{\delta}(q, x) = p$. Then $\hat{\delta}(q, w)$ is what we get by making a transition from state p on input a, the last symbol of w. That is, $\hat{\delta}(q, w) = \delta(p, a)$.

Example 2.4: Let us design a DFA to accept the language

$$L = \{w \mid w \text{ has both an even number of 0's and an even number of 1's}\}$$

It should not be surprising that the job of the states of this DFA is to count both the number of 0's and the number of 1's, but count them modulo 2. That is, the state is used to remember whether the number of 0's seen so far is even or odd, and also to remember whether the number of 1's seen so far is even or odd. There are thus four states, which can be given the following interpretations:

q_0: Both the number of 0's seen so far and the number of 1's seen so far are even.

q_1: The number of 0's seen so far is even, but the number of 1's seen so far is odd.

q_2: The number of 1's seen so far is even, but the number of 0's seen so far is odd.

q_3: Both the number of 0's seen so far and the number of 1's seen so far are odd.

State q_0 is both the start state and the lone accepting state. It is the start state, because before reading any inputs, the numbers of 0's and 1's seen so far are both zero, and zero is even. It is the only accepting state, because it describes exactly the condition for a sequence of 0's and 1's to be in language L.

We now know almost how to specify the DFA for language L. It is

$$A = (\{q_0, q_1, q_2, q_3\}, \{0, 1\}, \delta, q_0, \{q_0\})$$

---

[3]Recall our convention that letters at the beginning of the alphabet are symbols, and those near the end of the alphabet are strings. We need that convention to make sense of the phrase "of the form xa."

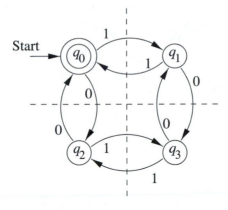

Figure 2.6: Transition diagram for the DFA of Example 2.4

where the transition function δ is described by the transition diagram of Fig. 2.6. Notice how each input 0 causes the state to cross the horizontal, dashed line. Thus, after seeing an even number of 0's we are always above the line, in state q_0 or q_1 while after seeing an odd number of 0's we are always below the line, in state q_2 or q_3. Likewise, every 1 causes the state to cross the vertical, dashed line. Thus, after seeing an even number of 1's, we are always to the left, in state q_0 or q_2, while after seeing an odd number of 1's we are to the right, in state q_1 or q_3. These observations are an informal proof that the four states have the interpretations attributed to them. However, one could prove the correctness of our claims about the states formally, by a mutual induction in the spirit of Example 1.23.

We can also represent this DFA by a transition table. Figure 2.7 shows this table. However, we are not just concerned with the design of this DFA; we want to use it to illustrate the construction of $\hat{\delta}$ from its transition function δ. Suppose the input is 110101. Since this string has even numbers of 0's and 1's both, we expect it is in the language. Thus, we expect that $\hat{\delta}(q_0, 110101) = q_0$, since q_0 is the only accepting state. Let us now verify that claim.

	0	1
$* \rightarrow q_0$	q_2	q_1
q_1	q_3	q_0
q_2	q_0	q_3
q_3	q_1	q_2

Figure 2.7: Transition table for the DFA of Example 2.4

The check involves computing $\hat{\delta}(q_0, w)$ for each prefix w of 110101, starting at ϵ and going in increasing size. The summary of this calculation is:

Standard Notation and Local Variables

After reading this section, you might imagine that our customary notation is required; that is, you *must* use δ for the transition function, use A for the name of a DFA, and so on. We tend to use the same variables to denote the same thing across all examples, because it helps to remind you of the types of variables, much the way a variable i in a program is almost always of integer type. However, we are free to call the components of an automaton, or anything else, anything we wish. Thus, you are free to call a DFA M and its transition function T if you like.

Moreover, you should not be surprised that the same variable means different things in different contexts. For example, the DFA's of Examples 2.1 and 2.4 both were given a transition function called δ. However, the two transition functions are each local variables, belonging only to their examples. These two transition functions are very different and bear no relationship to one another.

- $\hat{\delta}(q_0, \epsilon) = q_0$.

- $\hat{\delta}(q_0, 1) = \delta\big(\hat{\delta}(q_0, \epsilon), 1\big) = \delta(q_0, 1) = q_1$.

- $\hat{\delta}(q_0, 11) = \delta\big(\hat{\delta}(q_0, 1), 1\big) = \delta(q_1, 1) = q_0$.

- $\hat{\delta}(q_0, 110) = \delta\big(\hat{\delta}(q_0, 11), 0\big) = \delta(q_0, 0) = q_2$.

- $\hat{\delta}(q_0, 1101) = \delta\big(\hat{\delta}(q_0, 110), 1\big) = \delta(q_2, 1) = q_3$.

- $\hat{\delta}(q_0, 11010) = \delta\big(\hat{\delta}(q_0, 1101), 0\big) = \delta(q_3, 0) = q_1$.

- $\hat{\delta}(q_0, 110101) = \delta\big(\hat{\delta}(q_0, 11010), 1\big) = \delta(q_1, 1) = q_0$.

$\square$

2.2.5   The Language of a DFA

Now, we can define the *language* of a DFA $A = (Q, \Sigma, \delta, q_0, F)$. This language is denoted $L(A)$, and is defined by

$$L(A) = \{w \mid \hat{\delta}(q_0, w) \text{ is in } F\}$$

That is, the language of A is the set of strings w that take the start state q_0 to one of the accepting states. If L is $L(A)$ for some DFA A, then we say L is a *regular language*.

Example 2.5: As we mentioned earlier, if A is the DFA of Example 2.1, then $L(A)$ is the set of all strings of 0's and 1's that contain a substring 01. If A is instead the DFA of Example 2.4, then $L(A)$ is the set of all strings of 0's and 1's whose numbers of 0's and 1's are both even. □

2.2.6 Exercises for Section 2.2

Exercise 2.2.1: In Fig. 2.8 is a marble-rolling toy. A marble is dropped at A or B. Levers x_1, x_2, and x_3 cause the marble to fall either to the left or to the right. Whenever a marble encounters a lever, it causes the lever to reverse after the marble passes, so the next marble will take the opposite branch.

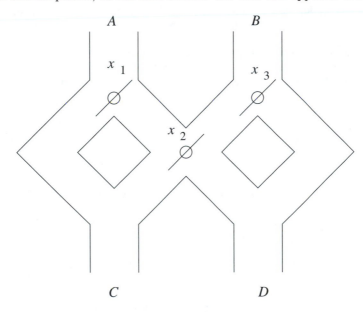

Figure 2.8: A marble-rolling toy

* a) Model this toy by a finite automaton. Let the inputs A and B represent the input into which the marble is dropped. Let acceptance correspond to the marble exiting at D; nonacceptance represents a marble exiting at C.

! b) Informally describe the language of the automaton.

c) Suppose that instead the levers switched *before* allowing the marble to pass. How would your answers to parts (a) and (b) change?

*! **Exercise 2.2.2:** We defined $\hat{\delta}$ by breaking the input string into any string followed by a single symbol (in the inductive part, Equation 2.1). However, we informally think of $\hat{\delta}$ as describing what happens along a path with a certain

string of labels, and if so, then it should not matter how we break the input
string in the definition of $\hat{\delta}$. Show that in fact, $\hat{\delta}(q, xy) = \hat{\delta}(\hat{\delta}(q, x), y)$ for any
state q and strings x and y. *Hint*: Perform an induction on $|y|$.

! **Exercise 2.2.3:** Show that for any state q, string x, and input symbol a,
$\hat{\delta}(q, ax) = \hat{\delta}(\delta(q, a), x)$. *Hint*: Use Exercise 2.2.2.

Exercise 2.2.4: Give DFA's accepting the following languages over the alphabet $\{0, 1\}$:

* a) The set of all strings ending in 00.

 b) The set of all strings with three consecutive 0's (not necessarily at the
    end).

 c) The set of strings with 011 as a substring.

! **Exercise 2.2.5:** Give DFA's accepting the following languages over the alphabet $\{0, 1\}$:

 a) The set of all strings such that each block of five consecutive symbols
    contains at least two 0's.

 b) The set of all strings whose tenth symbol from the right end is a 1.

 c) The set of strings that either begin or end (or both) with 01.

 d) The set of strings such that the number of 0's is divisible by five, and the
    number of 1's is divisible by 3.

!! **Exercise 2.2.6:** Give DFA's accepting the following languages over the alphabet $\{0, 1\}$:

* a) The set of all strings beginning with a 1 that, when interpreted as a binary
    integer, is a multiple of 5. For example, strings 101, 1010, and 1111 are
    in the language; 0, 100, and 111 are not.

 b) The set of all strings that, when interpreted *in reverse* as a binary inte-
    ger, is divisible by 5. Examples of strings in the language are 0, 10011,
    1001100, and 0101.

Exercise 2.2.7: Let A be a DFA and q a particular state of A, such that
$\delta(q, a) = q$ for all input symbols a. Show by induction on the length of the
input that for all input strings w, $\hat{\delta}(q, w) = q$.

Exercise 2.2.8: Let A be a DFA and a a particular input symbol of A, such
that for all states q of A we have $\delta(q, a) = q$.

 a) Show by induction on n that for all $n \geq 0$, $\hat{\delta}(q, a^n) = q$, where a^n is the
    string consisting of n a's.

b) Show that either $\{a\}^* \subseteq L(A)$ or $\{a\}^* \cap L(A) = \emptyset$.

*! **Exercise 2.2.9:** Let $A = (Q, \Sigma, \delta, q_0, \{q_f\})$ be a DFA, and suppose that for all a in Σ we have $\delta(q_0, a) = \delta(q_f, a)$.

a) Show that for all $w \neq \epsilon$ we have $\hat{\delta}(q_0, w) = \hat{\delta}(q_f, w)$.

b) Show that if x is a nonempty string in $L(A)$, then for all $k > 0$, x^k (i.e., x written k times) is also in $L(A)$.

*! **Exercise 2.2.10:** Consider the DFA with the following transition table:

	0	1
$\to A$	A	B
$*B$	B	A

Informally describe the language accepted by this DFA, and prove by induction on the length of an input string that your description is correct. *Hint:* When setting up the inductive hypothesis, it is wise to make a statement about what inputs get you to each state, not just what inputs get you to the accepting state.

! **Exercise 2.2.11:** Repeat Exercise 2.2.10 for the following transition table:

	0	1
$\to *A$	B	A
$*B$	C	A
C	C	C

2.3 Nondeterministic Finite Automata

A "nondeterministic" finite automaton (*NFA*) has the power to be in several states at once. This ability is often expressed as an ability to "guess" something about its input. For instance, when the automaton is used to search for certain sequences of characters (e.g., keywords) in a long text string, it is helpful to "guess" that we are at the beginning of one of those strings and use a sequence of states to do nothing but check that the string appears, character by character. We shall see an example of this type of application in Section 2.4.

Before examining applications, we need to define nondeterministic finite automata and show that each one accepts a language that is also accepted by some DFA. That is, the NFA's accept exactly the regular languages, just as DFA's do. However, there are reasons to think about NFA's. They are often more succinct and easier to design than DFA's. Moreover, while we can always convert an NFA to a DFA, the latter may have exponentially more states than the NFA; fortunately, cases of this type are rare.

2.3.1 An Informal View of Nondeterministic Finite Automata

Like the DFA, an NFA has a finite set of states, a finite set of input symbols, one start state and a set of accepting states. It also has a transition function, which we shall commonly call δ. The difference between the DFA and the NFA is in the type of δ. For the NFA, δ is a function that takes a state and input symbol as arguments (like the DFA's transition function), but returns a set of zero, one, or more states (rather than returning exactly one state, as the DFA must). We shall start with an example of an NFA, and then make the definitions precise.

Example 2.6: Figure 2.9 shows a nondeterministic finite automaton, whose job is to accept all and only the strings of 0's and 1's that end in 01. State q_0 is the start state, and we can think of the automaton as being in state q_0 (perhaps among other states) whenever it has not yet "guessed" that the final 01 has begun. It is always possible that the next symbol does not begin the final 01, even if that symbol is 0. Thus, state q_0 may transition to itself on both 0 and 1.

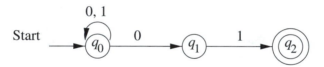

Figure 2.9: An NFA accepting all strings that end in 01

However, if the next symbol is 0, this NFA also guesses that the final 01 has begun. An arc labeled 0 thus leads from q_0 to state q_1. Notice that there are two arcs labeled 0 out of q_0. The NFA has the option of going either to q_0 or to q_1, and in fact it does both, as we shall see when we make the definitions precise. In state q_1, the NFA checks that the next symbol is 1, and if so, it goes to state q_2 and accepts.

Notice that there is no arc out of q_1 labeled 0, and there are no arcs at all out of q_2. In these situations, the thread of the NFA's existence corresponding to those states simply "dies," although other threads may continue to exist. While a DFA has exactly one arc out of each state for each input symbol, an NFA has no such constraint; we have seen in Fig. 2.9 cases where the number of arcs is zero, one, and two, for example.

Figure 2.10 suggests how an NFA processes inputs. We have shown what happens when the automaton of Fig. 2.9 receives the input sequence 00101. It starts in only its start state, q_0. When the first 0 is read, the NFA may go to either state q_0 or state q_1, so it does both. These two threads are suggested by the second column in Fig. 2.10.

Then, the second 0 is read. State q_0 may again go to both q_0 and q_1. However, state q_1 has no transition on 0, so it "dies." When the third input, a

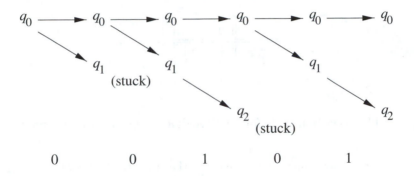

Figure 2.10: The states an NFA is in during the processing of input sequence 00101

1, occurs, we must consider transitions from both q_0 and q_1. We find that q_0 goes only to q_0 on 1, while q_1 goes only to q_2. Thus, after reading 001, the NFA is in states q_0 and q_2. Since q_2 is an accepting state, the NFA accepts 001.

However, the input is not finished. The fourth input, a 0, causes q_2's thread to die, while q_0 goes to both q_0 and q_1. The last input, a 1, sends q_0 to q_0 and q_1 to q_2. Since we are again in an accepting state, 00101 is accepted. □

2.3.2 Definition of Nondeterministic Finite Automata

Now, let us introduce the formal notions associated with nondeterministic finite automata. The differences between DFA's and NFA's will be pointed out as we do. An NFA is represented essentially like a DFA:

$$A = (Q, \Sigma, \delta, q_0, F)$$

where:

1. Q is a finite set of *states*.

2. Σ is a finite set of *input symbols*.

3. q_0, a member of Q, is the *start state*.

4. F, a subset of Q, is the set of *final* (or *accepting*) states.

5. δ, the *transition function* is a function that takes a state in Q and an input symbol in Σ as arguments and returns a subset of Q. Notice that the only difference between an NFA and a DFA is in the type of value that δ returns: a set of states in the case of an NFA and a single state in the case of a DFA.

Example 2.7 : The NFA of Fig. 2.9 can be specified formally as

$$(\{q_0, q_1, q_2\}, \{0, 1\}, \delta, q_0, \{q_2\})$$

	0	1
$\rightarrow q_0$	$\{q_0, q_1\}$	$\{q_0\}$
q_1	$\emptyset$	$\{q_2\}$
$*q_2$	$\emptyset$	$\emptyset$

Figure 2.11: Transition table for an NFA that accepts all strings ending in 01

where the transition function δ is given by the transition table of Fig. 2.11. □

Notice that transition tables can be used to specify the transition function for an NFA as well as for a DFA. The only difference is that each entry in the table for the NFA is a set, even if the set is a *singleton* (has one member). Also notice that when there is no transition at all from a given state on a given input symbol, the proper entry is $\emptyset$, the empty set.

2.3.3   The Extended Transition Function

As for DFA's, we need to extend the transition function δ of an NFA to a function $\hat{\delta}$ that takes a state q and a string of input symbols w, and returns the set of states that the NFA is in if it starts in state q and processes the string w. The idea was suggested by Fig. 2.10; in essence $\hat{\delta}(q, w)$ is the column of states found after reading w, if q is the lone state in the first column. For instance, Fig. 2.10 suggests that $\hat{\delta}(q_0, 001) = \{q_0, q_2\}$. Formally, we define $\hat{\delta}$ for an NFA's transition function δ by:

BASIS: $\hat{\delta}(q, \epsilon) = \{q\}$. That is, without reading any input symbols, we are only in the state we began in.

INDUCTION: Suppose w is of the form $w = xa$, where a is the final symbol of w and x is the rest of w. Also suppose that $\hat{\delta}(q, x) = \{p_1, p_2, \ldots, p_k\}$. Let

$$\bigcup_{i=1}^{k} \delta(p_i, a) = \{r_1, r_2, \ldots, r_m\}$$

Then $\hat{\delta}(q, w) = \{r_1, r_2, \ldots, r_m\}$. Less formally, we compute $\hat{\delta}(q, w)$ by first computing $\hat{\delta}(q, x)$, and by then following any transition from any of these states that is labeled a.

Example 2.8: Let us use $\hat{\delta}$ to describe the processing of input 00101 by the NFA of Fig. 2.9. A summary of the steps is:

1. $\hat{\delta}(q_0, \epsilon) = \{q_0\}$.

2. $\hat{\delta}(q_0, 0) = \delta(q_0, 0) = \{q_0, q_1\}$.

3. $\hat{\delta}(q_0, 00) = \delta(q_0, 0) \cup \delta(q_1, 0) = \{q_0, q_1\} \cup \emptyset = \{q_0, q_1\}$.

4. $\hat{\delta}(q_0, 001) = \delta(q_0, 1) \cup \delta(q_1, 1) = \{q_0\} \cup \{q_2\} = \{q_0, q_2\}$.

5. $\hat{\delta}(q_0, 0010) = \delta(q_0, 0) \cup \delta(q_2, 0) = \{q_0, q_1\} \cup \emptyset = \{q_0, q_1\}$.

6. $\hat{\delta}(q_0, 00101) = \delta(q_0, 1) \cup \delta(q_1, 1) = \{q_0\} \cup \{q_2\} = \{q_0, q_2\}$.

Line (1) is the basis rule. We obtain line (2) by applying δ to the lone state, q_0, that is in the previous set, and get $\{q_0, q_1\}$ as a result. Line (3) is obtained by taking the union over the two states in the previous set of what we get when we apply δ to them with input 0. That is, $\delta(q_0, 0) = \{q_0, q_1\}$, while $\delta(q_1, 0) = \emptyset$. For line (4), we take the union of $\delta(q_0, 1) = \{q_0\}$ and $\delta(q_1, 1) = \{q_2\}$. Lines (5) and (6) are similar to lines (3) and (4). □

2.3.4 The Language of an NFA

As we have suggested, an NFA accepts a string w if it is possible to make any sequence of choices of next state, while reading the characters of w, and go from the start state to any accepting state. The fact that other choices using the input symbols of w lead to a nonaccepting state, or do not lead to any state at all (i.e., the sequence of states "dies"), does not prevent w from being accepted by the NFA as a whole. Formally, if $A = (Q, \Sigma, \delta, q_0, F)$ is an NFA, then

$$L(A) = \{w \mid \hat{\delta}(q_0, w) \cap F \neq \emptyset\}$$

That is, $L(A)$ is the set of strings w in Σ^* such that $\hat{\delta}(q_0, w)$ contains at least one accepting state.

Example 2.9: As an example, let us prove formally that the NFA of Fig. 2.9 accepts the language $L = \{w \mid w$ ends in $01\}$. The proof is a mutual induction of the following three statements that characterize the three states:

1. $\hat{\delta}(q_0, w)$ contains q_0 for every w.

2. $\hat{\delta}(q_0, w)$ contains q_1 if and only if w ends in 0.

3. $\hat{\delta}(q_0, w)$ contains q_2 if and only if w ends in 01.

To prove these statements, we need to consider how A can reach each state; i.e., what was the last input symbol, and in what state was A just before reading that symbol?

Since the language of this automaton is the set of strings w such that $\hat{\delta}(q_0, w)$ contains q_2 (because q_2 is the only accepting state), the proof of these three statements, in particular the proof of (3), guarantees that the language of this NFA is the set of strings ending in 01. The proof of the theorem is an induction on $|w|$, the length of w, starting with length 0.

BASIS: If $|w| = 0$, then $w = \epsilon$. Statement (1) says that $\hat{\delta}(q_0, \epsilon)$ contains q_0, which it does by the basis part of the definition of $\hat{\delta}$. For statement (2), we know that ϵ does not end in 0, and we also know that $\hat{\delta}(q_0, \epsilon)$ does not contain q_1, again by the basis part of the definition of $\hat{\delta}$. Thus, the hypotheses of both directions of the if-and-only-if statement are false, and therefore both directions of the statement are true. The proof of statement (3) for $w = \epsilon$ is essentially the same as the above proof for statement (2).

INDUCTION: Assume that $w = xa$, where a is a symbol, either 0 or 1. We may assume statements (1) through (3) hold for x, and we need to prove them for w. That is, we assume $|w| = n + 1$, so $|x| = n$. We assume the inductive hypothesis for n and prove it for $n + 1$.

1. We know that $\hat{\delta}(q_0, x)$ contains q_0. Since there are transitions on both 0 and 1 from q_0 to itself, it follows that $\hat{\delta}(q_0, w)$ also contains q_0, so statement (1) is proved for w.

2. (If) Assume that w ends in 0; i.e., $a = 0$. By statement (1) applied to x, we know that $\hat{\delta}(q_0, x)$ contains q_0. Since there is a transition from q_0 to q_1 on input 0, we conclude that $\hat{\delta}(q_0, w)$ contains q_1.

   (Only-if) Suppose $\hat{\delta}(q_0, w)$ contains q_1. If we look at the diagram of Fig. 2.9, we see that the only way to get into state q_1 is if the input sequence w is of the form $x0$. That is enough to prove the "only-if" portion of statement (2).

3. (If) Assume that w ends in 01. Then if $w = xa$, we know that $a = 1$ and x ends in 0. By statement (2) applied to x, we know that $\hat{\delta}(q_0, x)$ contains q_1. Since there is a transition from q_1 to q_2 on input 1, we conclude that $\hat{\delta}(q_0, w)$ contains q_2.

   (Only-if) Suppose $\hat{\delta}(q_0, w)$ contains q_2. Looking at the diagram of Fig. 2.9, we discover that the only way to get to state q_2 is for w to be of the form $x1$, where $\hat{\delta}(q_0, x)$ contains q_1. By statement (2) applied to x, we know that x ends in 0. Thus, w ends in 01, and we have proved statement (3).

□

2.3.5   Equivalence of Deterministic and Nondeterministic Finite Automata

Although there are many languages for which an NFA is easier to construct than a DFA, such as the language (Example 2.6) of strings that end in 01, it is a surprising fact that every language that can be described by some NFA can also be described by some DFA. Moreover, the DFA in practice has about as many states as the NFA, although it often has more transitions. In the worst case, however, the smallest DFA can have 2^n states while the smallest NFA for the same language has only n states.

The proof that DFA's can do whatever NFA's can do involves an important "construction" called the *subset construction* because it involves constructing all subsets of the set of states of the NFA. In general, many proofs about automata involve constructing one automaton from another. It is important for us to observe the subset construction as an example of how one formally describes one automaton in terms of the states and transitions of another, without knowing the specifics of the latter automaton.

The subset construction starts from an NFA $N = (Q_N, \Sigma, \delta_N, q_0, F_N)$. Its goal is the description of a DFA $D = (Q_D, \Sigma, \delta_D, \{q_0\}, F_D)$ such that $L(D) = L(N)$. Notice that the input alphabets of the two automata are the same, and the start state of D is the set containing only the start state of N. The other components of D are constructed as follows.

- Q_D is the set of subsets of Q_N; i.e., Q_D is the *power set* of Q_N. Note that if Q_N has n states, then Q_D will have 2^n states. Often, not all these states are accessible from the start state of Q_D. Inaccessible states can be "thrown away," so effectively, the number of states of D may be much smaller than 2^n.

- F_D is the set of subsets S of Q_N such that $S \cap F_N \neq \emptyset$. That is, F_D is all sets of N's states that include at least one accepting state of N.

- For each set $S \subseteq Q_N$ and for each input symbol a in Σ,

$$\delta_D(S, a) = \bigcup_{p \text{ in } S} \delta_N(p, a)$$

That is, to compute $\delta_D(S, a)$ we look at all the states p in S, see what states N goes to from p on input a, and take the union of all those states.

	0	1
$\emptyset$	$\emptyset$	$\emptyset$
$\rightarrow \{q_0\}$	$\{q_0, q_1\}$	$\{q_0\}$
$\{q_1\}$	$\emptyset$	$\{q_2\}$
$*\{q_2\}$	$\emptyset$	$\emptyset$
$\{q_0, q_1\}$	$\{q_0, q_1\}$	$\{q_0, q_2\}$
$*\{q_0, q_2\}$	$\{q_0, q_1\}$	$\{q_0\}$
$*\{q_1, q_2\}$	$\emptyset$	$\{q_2\}$
$*\{q_0, q_1, q_2\}$	$\{q_0, q_1\}$	$\{q_0, q_2\}$

Figure 2.12: The complete subset construction from Fig. 2.9

Example 2.10: Let N be the automaton of Fig. 2.9 that accepts all strings that end in 01. Since N's set of states is $\{q_0, q_1, q_2\}$, the subset construction produces a DFA with $2^3 = 8$ states, corresponding to all the subsets of these three states. Figure 2.12 shows the transition table for these eight states; we shall show shortly the details of how some of these entries are computed.

Notice that this transition table belongs to a deterministic finite automaton. Even though the entries in the table are sets, the states of the constructed DFA *are* sets. To make the point clearer, we can invent new names for these states, e.g., A for $\emptyset$, B for $\{q_0\}$, and so on. The DFA transition table of Fig 2.13 defines exactly the same automaton as Fig. 2.12, but makes clear the point that the entries in the table are single states of the DFA.

	0	1
A	A	A
$\rightarrow B$	E	B
C	A	D
$*D$	A	A
E	E	F
$*F$	E	B
$*G$	A	D
$*H$	E	F

Figure 2.13: Renaming the states of Fig. 2.12

Of the eight states in Fig. 2.13, starting in the start state B, we can only reach states B, E, and F. The other five states are inaccessible from the start state and may as well not be there. We often can avoid the exponential-time step of constructing transition-table entries for every subset of states if we perform "lazy evaluation" on the subsets, as follows.

BASIS: We know for certain that the singleton set consisting only of N's start state is accessible.

INDUCTION: Suppose we have determined that set S of states is accessible. Then for each input symbol a, compute the set of states $\delta_D(S, a)$; we know that these sets of states will also be accessible.

For the example at hand, we know that $\{q_0\}$ is a state of the DFA D. We find that $\delta_D(\{q_0\}, 0) = \{q_0, q_1\}$ and $\delta_D(\{q_0\}, 1) = \{q_0\}$. Both these facts are established by looking at the transition diagram of Fig. 2.9 and observing that on 0 there are arcs out of q_0 to both q_0 and q_1, while on 1 there is an arc only to q_0. We thus have one row of the transition table for the DFA: the second row in Fig. 2.12.

One of the two sets we computed is "old"; $\{q_0\}$ has already been considered. However, the other — $\{q_0, q_1\}$ — is new and its transitions must be computed. We find $\delta_D(\{q_0, q_1\}, 0) = \{q_0, q_1\}$ and $\delta_D(\{q_0, q_1\}, 1) = \{q_0, q_2\}$. For instance, to see the latter calculation, we know that

$$\delta_D(\{q_0, q_1\}, 1) = \delta_N(q_0, 1) \cup \delta_N(q_1, 1) = \{q_0\} \cup \{q_2\} = \{q_0, q_2\}$$

We now have the fifth row of Fig. 2.12, and we have discovered one new state of D, which is $\{q_0, q_2\}$. A similar calculation tells us

$$\delta_D(\{q_0, q_2\}, 0) = \delta_N(q_0, 0) \cup \delta_N(q_2, 0) = \{q_0, q_1\} \cup \emptyset = \{q_0, q_1\}$$
$$\delta_D(\{q_0, q_2\}, 1) = \delta_N(q_0, 1) \cup \delta_N(q_2, 1) = \{q_0\} \cup \emptyset = \{q_0\}$$

These calculations give us the sixth row of Fig. 2.12, but it gives us only sets of states that we have already seen.

Thus, the subset construction has converged; we know all the accessible states and their transitions. The entire DFA is shown in Fig. 2.14. Notice that it has only three states, which is, by coincidence, exactly the same number of states as the NFA of Fig. 2.9, from which it was constructed. However, the DFA of Fig. 2.14 has six transitions, compared with the four transitions in Fig. 2.9. □

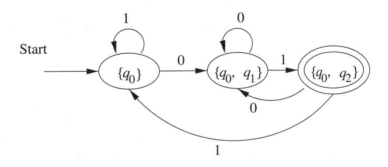

Figure 2.14: The DFA constructed from the NFA of Fig 2.9

We need to show formally that the subset construction works, although the intuition was suggested by the examples. After reading sequence of input symbols w, the constructed DFA is in one state that is the set of NFA states that the NFA would be in after reading w. Since the accepting states of the DFA are those sets that include at least one accepting state of the NFA, and the NFA also accepts if it gets into at least one of its accepting states, we may then conclude that the DFA and NFA accept exactly the same strings, and therefore accept the same language.

Theorem 2.11: If $D = (Q_D, \Sigma, \delta_D, \{q_0\}, F_D)$ is the DFA constructed from NFA $N = (Q_N, \Sigma, \delta_N, q_0, F_N)$ by the subset construction, then $L(D) = L(N)$.

PROOF: What we actually prove first, by induction on $|w|$, is that

$$\hat{\delta}_D(\{q_0\}, w) = \hat{\delta}_N(q_0, w)$$

Notice that each of the $\hat{\delta}$ functions returns a set of states from Q_N, but $\hat{\delta}_D$ interprets this set as one of the states of Q_D (which is the power set of Q_N), while $\hat{\delta}_N$ interprets this set as a subset of Q_N.

BASIS: Let $|w| = 0$; that is, $w = \epsilon$. By the basis definitions of $\hat{\delta}$ for DFA's and NFA's, both $\hat{\delta}_D(\{q_0\}, \epsilon)$ and $\hat{\delta}_N(q_0, \epsilon)$ are $\{q_0\}$.

INDUCTION: Let w be of length $n + 1$, and assume the statement for length n. Break w up as $w = xa$, where a is the final symbol of w. By the inductive hypothesis, $\hat{\delta}_D(\{q_0\}, x) = \hat{\delta}_N(q_0, x)$. Let both these sets of N's states be $\{p_1, p_2, \ldots, p_k\}$.

The inductive part of the definition of $\hat{\delta}$ for NFA's tells us

$$\hat{\delta}_N(q_0, w) = \bigcup_{i=1}^{k} \delta_N(p_i, a) \tag{2.2}$$

The subset construction, on the other hand, tells us that

$$\delta_D(\{p_1, p_2, \ldots, p_k\}, a) = \bigcup_{i=1}^{k} \delta_N(p_i, a) \tag{2.3}$$

Now, let us use (2.3) and the fact that $\hat{\delta}_D(\{q_0\}, x) = \{p_1, p_2, \ldots, p_k\}$ in the inductive part of the definition of $\hat{\delta}$ for DFA's:

$$\hat{\delta}_D(\{q_0\}, w) = \delta_D\left(\hat{\delta}_D(\{q_0\}, x), a\right) = \delta_D(\{p_1, p_2, \ldots, p_k\}, a) = \bigcup_{i=1}^{k} \delta_N(p_i, a) \tag{2.4}$$

Thus, Equations (2.2) and (2.4) demonstrate that $\hat{\delta}_D(\{q_0\}, w) = \hat{\delta}_N(q_0, w)$. When we observe that D and N both accept w if and only if $\hat{\delta}_D(\{q_0\}, w)$ or $\hat{\delta}_N(q_0, w)$, respectively, contain a state in F_N, we have a complete proof that $L(D) = L(N)$. $\square$

Theorem 2.12: A language L is accepted by some DFA if and only if L is accepted by some NFA.

PROOF: (If) The "if" part is the subset construction and Theorem 2.11.

(Only-if) This part is easy; we have only to convert a DFA into an identical NFA. Put intuitively, if we have the transition diagram for a DFA, we can also interpret it as the transition diagram of an NFA, which happens to have exactly one choice of transition in any situation. More formally, let $D = (Q, \Sigma, \delta_D, q_0, F)$ be a DFA. Define $N = (Q, \Sigma, \delta_N, q_0, F)$ to be the equivalent NFA, where δ_N is defined by the rule:

- If $\delta_D(q, a) = p$, then $\delta_N(q, a) = \{p\}$.

It is then easy to show by induction on $|w|$, that if $\hat{\delta}_D(q_0, w) = p$ then

$$\hat{\delta}_N(q_0, w) = \{p\}$$

We leave the proof to the reader. As a consequence, w is accepted by D if and only if it is accepted by N; i.e., $L(D) = L(N)$. $\square$

2.3.6 A Bad Case for the Subset Construction

In Example 2.10 we found that the DFA had no more states than the NFA. As we mentioned, it is quite common in practice for the DFA to have roughly the same number of states as the NFA from which it is constructed. However, exponential growth in the number of states is possible; all the 2^n DFA states that we could construct from an n-state NFA may turn out to be accessible. The following example does not quite reach that bound, but it is an understandable way to reach 2^n states in the smallest DFA that is equivalent to an $n+1$-state NFA.

Example 2.13: Consider the NFA N of Fig. 2.15. $L(N)$ is the set of all strings of 0's and 1's such that the nth symbol from the end is 1. Intuitively, a DFA D that accepts this language must remember the last n symbols it has read. Since any of 2^n subsets of the last n symbols could have been 1, if D has fewer than 2^n states, then there would be some state q such that D can be in state q after reading two different sequences of n bits, say $a_1 a_2 \cdots a_n$ and $b_1 b_2 \cdots b_n$.

Since the sequences are different, they must differ in some position, say $a_i \neq b_i$. Suppose (by symmetry) that $a_i = 1$ and $b_i = 0$. If $i = 1$, then q must be both an accepting state and a nonaccepting state, since $a_1 a_2 \cdots a_n$ is accepted (the nth symbol from the end is 1) and $b_1 b_2 \cdots b_n$ is not. If $i > 1$, then consider the state p that D enters after reading $i - 1$ 0's. Then p must be both accepting and nonaccepting, since $a_i a_{i+1} \cdots a_n 00 \cdots 0$ is accepted and $b_i b_{i+1} \cdots b_n 00 \cdots 0$ is not.

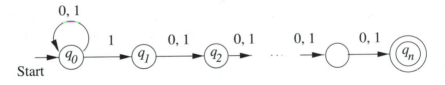

Figure 2.15: This NFA has no equivalent DFA with fewer than 2^n states

Now, let us see how the NFA N of Fig. 2.15 works. There is a state q_0 that the NFA is always in, regardless of what inputs have been read. If the next input is 1, N may also "guess" that this 1 will be the nth symbol from the end, so it goes to state q_1 as well as q_0. From state q_1, any input takes N to q_2, the next input takes it to q_3, and so on, until $n - 1$ inputs later, it is in the accepting state q_n. The formal statement of what the states of N do is:

1. N is in state q_0 after reading any sequence of inputs w.

2. N is in state q_i, for $i = 1, 2, \ldots, n$, after reading input sequence w if and only if the ith symbol from the end of w is 1; that is, w is of the form $x 1 a_1 a_2 \cdots a_{i-1}$, where the a_j's are each input symbols.

We shall not prove these statements formally; the proof is an easy induction on $|w|$, mimicking Example 2.9. To complete the proof that the automaton

---

The Pigeonhole Principle

In Example 2.13 we used an important reasoning technique called the *pigeonhole principle*. Colloquially, if you have more pigeons than pigeonholes, and each pigeon flies into some pigeonhole, then there must be at least one hole that has more than one pigeon. In our example, the "pigeons" are the sequences of n bits, and the "pigeonholes" are the states. Since there are fewer states than sequences, one state must be assigned two sequences.

The pigeonhole principle may appear obvious, but it actually depends on the number of pigeonholes being finite. Thus, it works for finite-state automata, with the states as pigeonholes, but does not apply to other kinds of automata that have an infinite number of states.

To see why the finiteness of the number of pigeonholes is essential, consider the infinite situation where the pigeonholes correspond to integers $1, 2, \ldots$. Number the pigeons $0, 1, 2, \ldots$, so there is one more pigeon than there are pigeonholes. However, we can send pigeon i to hole $i + 1$ for all $i \geq 0$. Then each of the infinite number of pigeons gets a pigeonhole, and no two pigeons have to share a pigeonhole.

---

accepts exactly those strings with a 1 in the nth position from the end, we consider statement (2) with $i = n$. That says N is in state q_n if and only if the nth symbol from the end is 1. But q_n is the only accepting state, so that condition also characterizes exactly the set of strings accepted by N. □

2.3.7 Exercises for Section 2.3

* **Exercise 2.3.1:** Convert to a DFA the following NFA:

		0	1
---------------		----------	-------
$\rightarrow p$		$\{p, q\}$	$\{p\}$
q		$\{r\}$	$\{r\}$
r		$\{s\}$	$\emptyset$
$*s$		$\{s\}$	$\{s\}$

Exercise 2.3.2: Convert to a DFA the following NFA:

		0	1
---------------		----------	----------
$\rightarrow p$		$\{q, s\}$	$\{q\}$
$*q$		$\{r\}$	$\{q, r\}$
r		$\{s\}$	$\{p\}$
$*s$		$\emptyset$	$\{p\}$

Dead States and DFA's Missing Some Transitions

We have formally defined a DFA to have a transition from any state, on any input symbol, to exactly one state. However, sometimes, it is more convenient to design the DFA to "die" in situations where we know it is impossible for any extension of the input sequence to be accepted. For instance, observe the automaton of Fig. 1.2, which did its job by recognizing a single keyword, then, and nothing else. Technically, this automaton is not a DFA, because it lacks transitions on most symbols from each of its states.

However, such an automaton is an NFA. If we use the subset construction to convert it to a DFA, the automaton looks almost the same, but it includes a *dead state*, that is, a nonaccepting state that goes to itself on every possible input symbol. The dead state corresponds to $\emptyset$, the empty set of states of the automaton of Fig. 1.2.

In general, we can add a dead state to any automaton that has *no more* than one transition for any state and input symbol. Then, add a transition to the dead state from each other state q, on all input symbols for which q has no other transition. The result will be a DFA in the strict sense. Thus, we shall sometimes refer to an automaton as a DFA if it has *at most* one transition out of any state on any symbol, rather than if it has *exactly one* transition.

! **Exercise 2.3.3:** Convert the following NFA to a DFA and informally describe the language it accepts.

	0	1
$\to p$	$\{p, q\}$	$\{p\}$
q	$\{r, s\}$	$\{t\}$
r	$\{p, r\}$	$\{t\}$
$*s$	$\emptyset$	$\emptyset$
$*t$	$\emptyset$	$\emptyset$

! **Exercise 2.3.4:** Give nondeterministic finite automata to accept the following languages. Try to take advantage of nondeterminism as much as possible.

* a) The set of strings over alphabet $\{0, 1, \ldots, 9\}$ such that the final digit has appeared before.

  b) The set of strings over alphabet $\{0, 1, \ldots, 9\}$ such that the final digit has *not* appeared before.

  c) The set of strings of 0's and 1's such that there are two 0's separated by a number of positions that is a multiple of 4. Note that 0 is an allowable multiple of 4.

Exercise 2.3.5: In the only-if portion of Theorem 2.12 we omitted the proof by induction on $|w|$ that if $\hat{\delta}_D(q_0, w) = p$ then $\hat{\delta}_N(q_0, w) = \{p\}$. Supply this proof.

! **Exercise 2.3.6:** In the box on "Dead States and DFA's Missing Some Transitions," we claim that if N is an NFA that has at most one choice of state for any state and input symbol (i.e., $\delta(q, a)$ never has size greater than 1), then the DFA D constructed from N by the subset construction has exactly the states and transitions of N plus transitions to a new dead state whenever N is missing a transition for a given state and input symbol. Prove this contention.

Exercise 2.3.7: In Example 2.13 we claimed that the NFA N is in state q_i, for $i = 1, 2, \ldots, n$, after reading input sequence w if and only if the ith symbol from the end of w is 1. Prove this claim.

2.4 An Application: Text Search

In this section, we shall see that the abstract study of the previous section, where we considered the "problem" of deciding whether a sequence of bits ends in 01, is actually an excellent model for several real problems that appear in applications such as Web search and extraction of information from text.

2.4.1 Finding Strings in Text

A common problem in the age of the Web and other on-line text repositories is the following. Given a set of words, find all documents that contain one (or all) of those words. A search engine is a popular example of this process. The search engine uses a particular technology, called *inverted indexes*, where for each word appearing on the Web (there are 100,000,000 different words), a list of all the places where that word occurs is stored. Machines with very large amounts of main memory keep the most common of these lists available, allowing many people to search for documents at once.

Inverted-index techniques do not make use of finite automata, but they also take very large amounts of time for crawlers to copy the Web and set up the indexes. There are a number of related applications that are unsuited for inverted indexes, but are good applications for automaton-based techniques. The characteristics that make an application suitable for searches that use automata are:

1. The repository on which the search is conducted is rapidly changing. For example:

    (a) Every day, news analysts want to search the day's on-line news articles for relevant topics. For example, a financial analyst might search for certain stock ticker symbols or names of companies.

(b) A "shopping robot" wants to search for the current prices charged for the items that its clients request. The robot will retrieve current catalog pages from the Web and then search those pages for words that suggest a price for a particular item.

2. The documents to be searched cannot be cataloged. For example, Amazon.com does not make it easy for crawlers to find all the pages for all the books that the company sells. Rather, these pages are generated "on the fly" in response to queries. However, we could send a query for books on a certain topic, say "finite automata," and then search the pages retrieved for certain words, e.g., "excellent" in a review portion.

2.4.2 Nondeterministic Finite Automata for Text Search

Suppose we are given a set of words, which we shall call the *keywords*, and we want to find occurrences of any of these words. In applications such as these, a useful way to proceed is to design a nondeterministic finite automaton, which signals, by entering an accepting state, that it has seen one of the keywords. The text of a document is fed, one character at a time to this NFA, which then recognizes occurrences of the keywords in this text. There is a simple form to an NFA that recognizes a set of keywords.

1. There is a start state with a transition to itself on every input symbol, e.g. every printable ASCII character if we are examining text. Intuitively, the start state represents a "guess" that we have not yet begun to see one of the keywords, even if we have seen some letters of one of these words.

2. For each keyword $a_1 a_2 \cdots a_k$, there are k states, say $q_1, q_2, \ldots, q_k$. There is a transition from the start state to q_1 on symbol a_1, a transition from q_1 to q_2 on symbol a_2, and so on. The state q_k is an accepting state and indicates that the keyword $a_1 a_2 \cdots a_k$ has been found.

Example 2.14: Suppose we want to design an NFA to recognize occurrences of the words web and ebay. The transition diagram for the NFA designed using the rules above is in Fig. 2.16. State 1 is the start state, and we use Σ to stand for the set of all printable ASCII characters. States 2 through 4 have the job of recognizing web, while states 5 through 8 recognize ebay. □

Of course the NFA is not a program. We have two major choices for an implementation of this NFA.

1. Write a program that simulates this NFA by computing the set of states it is in after reading each input symbol. The simulation was suggested in Fig. 2.10.

2. Convert the NFA to an equivalent DFA using the subset construction. Then simulate the DFA directly.

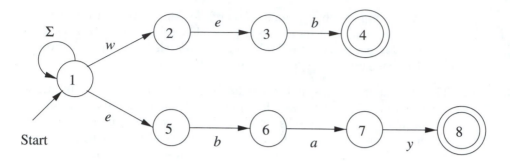

Figure 2.16: An NFA that searches for the words web and ebay

Some text-processing programs, such as advanced forms of the UNIX grep command (egrep and fgrep) actually use a mixture of these two approaches. However, for our purposes, conversion to a DFA is easy and is guaranteed not to increase the number of states.

2.4.3   A DFA to Recognize a Set of Keywords

We can apply the subset construction to any NFA. However, when we apply that construction to an NFA that was designed from a set of keywords, according to the strategy of Section 2.4.2, we find that the number of states of the DFA is never greater than the number of states of the NFA. Since in the worst case the number of states exponentiates as we go to the DFA, this observation is good news and explains why the method of designing an NFA for keywords and then constructing a DFA from it is used frequently. The rules for constructing the set of DFA states is as follows.

a) If q_0 is the start state of the NFA, then $\{q_0\}$ is one of the states of the DFA.

b) Suppose p is one of the NFA states, and it is reached from the start state along a path whose symbols are $a_1 a_2 \cdots a_m$. Then one of the DFA states is the set of NFA states consisting of:

   1. q_0.

   2. p.

   3. Every other state of the NFA that is reachable from q_0 by following a path whose labels are a suffix of $a_1 a_2 \cdots a_m$, that is, any sequence of symbols of the form $a_j a_{j+1} \cdots a_m$.

Note that in general, there will be one DFA state for each NFA state p. However, in step (b), two states may actually yield the same set of NFA states, and thus become one state of the DFA. For example, if two of the keywords begin with the same letter, say a, then the two NFA states that are reached from q_0 by an arc labeled a will yield the same set of NFA states and thus get merged in the DFA.

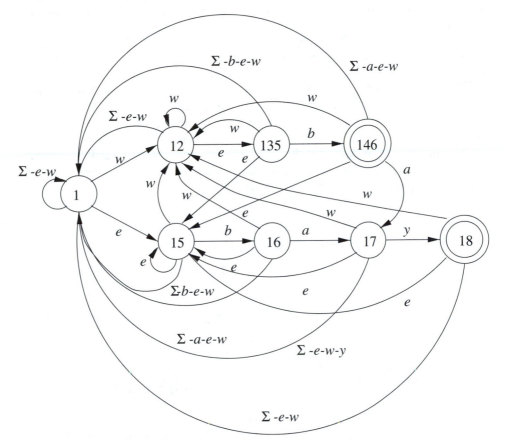

Figure 2.17: Conversion of the NFA from Fig. 2.16 to a DFA

Example 2.15: The construction of a DFA from the NFA of Fig. 2.16 is shown in Fig. 2.17. Each of the states of the DFA is located in the same position as the state p from which it is derived using rule (b) above. For example, consider the state 135, which is our shorthand for $\{1, 3, 5\}$. This state was constructed from state 3. It includes the start state, 1, because every set of the DFA states does. It also includes state 5 because that state is reached from state 1 by a suffix, e, of the string we that reaches state 3 in Fig. 2.16.

The transitions for each of the DFA states may be calculated according to the subset construction. However, the rule is simple. From any set of states that includes the start state q_0 and some other states $\{p_1, p_2, \ldots, p_n\}$, determine, for each symbol x, where the p_i's go in the NFA, and let this DFA state have a transition labeled x to the DFA state consisting of q_0 and all the targets of the

p_i's on symbol x. On all symbols x such that there are no transitions out of any of the p_i's on symbol x, let this DFA state have a transition on x to that state of the DFA consisting of q_0 and all states that are reached from q_0 in the NFA following an arc labeled x.

For instance, consider state 135 of Fig. 2.17. The NFA of Fig. 2.16 has transitions on symbol b from states 3 and 5 to states 4 and 6, respectively. Therefore, on symbol b, 135 goes to 146. On symbol e, there are no transitions of the NFA out of 3 or 5, but there is a transition from 1 to 5. Thus, in the DFA, 135 goes to 15 on input e. Similarly, on input w, 135 goes to 12.

On every other symbol x, there are no transitions out or 3 or 5, and state 1 goes only to itself. Thus, there are transitions from 135 to 1 on every symbol in Σ other than b, e, and w. We use the notation $\Sigma - b - e - w$ to represent this set, and use similar representations of other sets in which a few symbols are removed from Σ. □

2.4.4   Exercises for Section 2.4

Exercise 2.4.1: Design NFA's to recognize the following sets of strings.

* a) abc, abd, and aacd. Assume the alphabet is $\{a, b, c, d\}$.

  b) 0101, 101, and 011.

  c) ab, bc, and ca. Assume the alphabet is $\{a, b, c\}$.

Exercise 2.4.2: Convert each of your NFA's from Exercise 2.4.1 to DFA's.

2.5   Finite Automata With Epsilon-Transitions

We shall now introduce another extension of the finite automaton. The new "feature" is that we allow a transition on ϵ, the empty string. In effect, an NFA is allowed to make a transition spontaneously, without receiving an input symbol. Like the nondeterminism added in Section 2.3, this new capability does not expand the class of languages that can be accepted by finite automata, but it does give us some added "programming convenience." We shall also see, when we take up regular expressions in Section 3.1, how NFA's with ϵ-transitions, which we call ϵ-NFA's, are closely related to regular expressions and useful in proving the equivalence between the classes of languages accepted by finite automata and by regular expressions.

2.5.1   Uses of ϵ-Transitions

We shall begin with an informal treatment of ϵ-NFA's, using transition diagrams with ϵ allowed as a label. In the examples to follow, think of the automaton as accepting those sequences of labels along paths from the start state to an accepting state. However, each ϵ along a path is "invisible"; i.e., it contributes nothing to the string along the path.

Example 2.16: In Fig. 2.18 is an ϵ-NFA that accepts decimal numbers consisting of:

1. An optional $+$ or $-$ sign,

2. A string of digits,

3. A decimal point, and

4. Another string of digits. Either this string of digits, or the string (2) can be empty, but at least one of the two strings of digits must be nonempty.

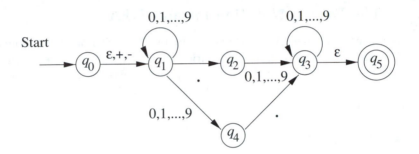

Figure 2.18: An ϵ-NFA accepting decimal numbers

Of particular interest is the transition from q_0 to q_1 on any of ϵ, $+$, or $-$. Thus, state q_1 represents the situation in which we have seen the sign if there is one, but none of the digits or decimal point. State q_2 represents the situation where we have just seen the decimal point, and may or may not have seen prior digits. In q_4 we have definitely seen at least one digit, but not the decimal point. Thus, the interpretation of q_3 is that we have seen a decimal point and at least one digit, either before or after the decimal point. We may stay in q_3 reading whatever digits there are, and also have the option of "guessing" the string of digits is complete and going spontaneously to q_5, the accepting state. □

Example 2.17: The strategy we outlined in Example 2.14 for building an NFA that recognizes a set of keywords can be simplified further if we allow ϵ-transitions. For instance, the NFA recognizing the keywords web and ebay, which we saw in Fig. 2.16, can also be implemented with ϵ-transitions as in Fig. 2.19. In general, we construct a complete sequence of states for each keyword, as if it were the only word the automaton needed to recognize. Then, we add a new start state (state 9 in Fig. 2.19), with ϵ-transitions to the start-states of the automata for each of the keywords. □

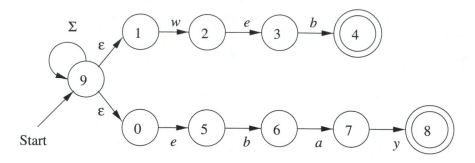

Figure 2.19: Using ϵ-transitions to help recognize keywords

2.5.2   The Formal Notation for an ϵ-NFA

We may represent an ϵ-NFA exactly as we do an NFA, with one exception: the transition function must include information about transitions on ϵ. Formally, we represent an ϵ-NFA A by $A = (Q, \Sigma, \delta, q_0, F)$, where all components have their same interpretation as for an NFA, except that δ is now a function that takes as arguments:

1. A state in Q, and

2. A member of $\Sigma \cup \{\epsilon\}$, that is, either an input symbol, or the symbol ϵ. We require that ϵ, the symbol for the empty string, cannot be a member of the alphabet Σ, so no confusion results.

Example 2.18 : The ϵ-NFA of Fig. 2.18 is represented formally as

$$E = (\{q_0, q_1, \ldots, q_5\}, \{., +, -, 0, 1, \ldots, 9\}, \delta, q_0, \{q_5\})$$

where δ is defined by the transition table in Fig. 2.20.   □

	ϵ	$+,-$	$.$	$0, 1, \ldots, 9$
q_0	$\{q_1\}$	$\{q_1\}$	$\emptyset$	$\emptyset$
q_1	$\emptyset$	$\emptyset$	$\{q_2\}$	$\{q_1, q_4\}$
q_2	$\emptyset$	$\emptyset$	$\emptyset$	$\{q_3\}$
q_3	$\{q_5\}$	$\emptyset$	$\emptyset$	$\{q_3\}$
q_4	$\emptyset$	$\emptyset$	$\{q_3\}$	$\emptyset$
q_5	$\emptyset$	$\emptyset$	$\emptyset$	$\emptyset$

Figure 2.20: Transition table for Fig. 2.18

2.5.3   Epsilon-Closures

We shall proceed to give formal definitions of an extended transition function for ϵ-NFA's, which leads to the definition of acceptance of strings and languages by these automata, and eventually lets us explain why ϵ-NFA's can be simulated by DFA's. However, we first need to learn a central definition, called the ϵ-*closure* of a state. Informally, we ϵ-close a state q by following all transitions out of q that are labeled ϵ. However, when we get to other states by following ϵ, we follow the ϵ-transitions out of those states, and so on, eventually finding every state that can be reached from q along any path whose arcs are all labeled ϵ. Formally, we define the ϵ-closure ECLOSE(q) recursively, as follows:

BASIS: State q is in ECLOSE(q).

INDUCTION: If state p is in ECLOSE(q), and there is a transition from state p to state r labeled ϵ, then r is in ECLOSE(q). More precisely, if δ is the transition function of the ϵ-NFA involved, and p is in ECLOSE(q), then ECLOSE(q) also contains all the states in $\delta(p, \epsilon)$.

Example 2.19: For the automaton of Fig. 2.18, each state is its own ϵ-closure, with two exceptions: ECLOSE$(q_0) = \{q_0, q_1\}$ and ECLOSE$(q_3) = \{q_3, q_5\}$. The reason is that there are only two ϵ-transitions, one that adds q_1 to ECLOSE(q_0) and the other that adds q_5 to ECLOSE(q_3).

A more complex example is given in Fig. 2.21. For this collection of states, which may be part of some ϵ-NFA, we can conclude that

$$\text{ECLOSE}(1) = \{1, 2, 3, 4, 6\}$$

Each of these states can be reached from state 1 along a path exclusively labeled ϵ. For example, state 6 is reached by the path $1 \rightarrow 2 \rightarrow 3 \rightarrow 6$. State 7 is not in ECLOSE(1), since although it is reachable from state 1, the path must use the arc $4 \rightarrow 5$ that is not labeled ϵ. The fact that state 6 is also reached from state 1 along a path $1 \rightarrow 4 \rightarrow 5 \rightarrow 6$ that has non-ϵ transitions is unimportant. The existence of one path with all labels ϵ is sufficient to show state 6 is in ECLOSE(1). □

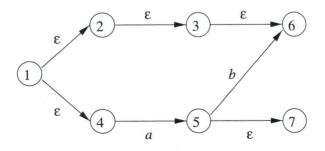

Figure 2.21: Some states and transitions

2.5.4 Extended Transitions and Languages for ϵ-NFA's

The ϵ-closure allows us to explain easily what the transitions of an ϵ-NFA look like when given a sequence of (non-ϵ) inputs. From there, we can define what it means for an ϵ-NFA to accept its input.

Suppose that $E = (Q, \Sigma, \delta, q_0, F)$ is an ϵ-NFA. We first define $\hat{\delta}$, the extended transition function, to reflect what happens on a sequence of inputs. The intent is that $\hat{\delta}(q, w)$ is the set of states that can be reached along a path whose labels, when concatenated, form the string w. As always, ϵ's along this path do not contribute to w. The appropriate recursive definition of $\hat{\delta}$ is:

BASIS: $\hat{\delta}(q, \epsilon) = \text{ECLOSE}(q)$. That is, if the label of the path is ϵ, then we can follow only ϵ-labeled arcs extending from state q; that is exactly what ECLOSE does.

INDUCTION: Suppose w is of the form xa, where a is the last symbol of w. Note that a is a member of Σ; it cannot be ϵ, which is not in Σ. We compute $\hat{\delta}(q, w)$ as follows:

1. Let $\{p_1, p_2, \ldots, p_k\}$ be $\hat{\delta}(q, x)$. That is, the p_i's are all and only the states that we can reach from q following a path labeled x. This path may end with one or more transitions labeled ϵ, and may have other ϵ-transitions, as well.

2. Let $\bigcup_{i=1}^{k} \delta(p_i, a)$ be the set $\{r_1, r_2, \ldots, r_m\}$. That is, follow all transitions labeled a from states we can reach from q along paths labeled x. The r_j's are *some* of the states we can reach from q along paths labeled w. The additional states we can reach are found from the r_j's by following ϵ-labeled arcs in step (3), below.

3. Then $\hat{\delta}(q, w) = \bigcup_{j=1}^{m} \text{ECLOSE}(r_j)$. This additional closure step includes all the paths from q labeled w, by considering the possibility that there are additional ϵ-labeled arcs that we can follow after making a transition on the final "real" symbol, a.

Example 2.20: Let us compute $\hat{\delta}(q_0, 5.6)$ for the ϵ-NFA of Fig. 2.18. A summary of the steps needed are as follows:

- $\hat{\delta}(q_0, \epsilon) = \text{ECLOSE}(q_0) = \{q_0, q_1\}$.

- Compute $\hat{\delta}(q_0, 5)$ as follows:

  1. First compute the transitions on input 5 from the states q_0 and q_1 that we obtained in the calculation of $\hat{\delta}(q_0, \epsilon)$, above. That is, we compute $\delta(q_0, 5) \cup \delta(q_1, 5) = \{q_1, q_4\}$.

  2. Next, ϵ-close the members of the set computed in step (1). We get $\text{ECLOSE}(q_1) \cup \text{ECLOSE}(q_4) = \{q_1\} \cup \{q_4\} = \{q_1, q_4\}$. That set is $\hat{\delta}(q_0, 5)$. This two-step pattern repeats for the next two symbols.

- Compute $\hat{\delta}(q_0, 5.)$ as follows:

  1. First compute $\delta(q_1, .) \cup \delta(q_4, .) = \{q_2\} \cup \{q_3\} = \{q_2, q_3\}$.
  2. Then compute

  $$\hat{\delta}(q_0, 5.) = \text{ECLOSE}(q_2) \cup \text{ECLOSE}(q_3) = \{q_2\} \cup \{q_3, q_5\} = \{q_2, q_3, q_5\}$$

- Compute $\hat{\delta}(q_0, 5.6)$ as follows:

  1. First compute $\delta(q_2, 6) \cup \delta(q_3, 6) \cup \delta(q_5, 6) = \{q_3\} \cup \{q_3\} \cup \emptyset = \{q_3\}$.
  2. Then compute $\hat{\delta}(q_0, 5.6) = \text{ECLOSE}(q_3) = \{q_3, q_5\}$.

□

Now, we can define the language of an ϵ-NFA $E = (Q, \Sigma, \delta, q_0, F)$ in the expected way: $L(E) = \{w \mid \hat{\delta}(q_0, w) \cap F \neq \emptyset\}$. That is, the language of E is the set of strings w that take the start state to at least one accepting state. For instance, we saw in Example 2.20 that $\hat{\delta}(q_0, 5.6)$ contains the accepting state q_5, so the string 5.6 is in the language of that ϵ-NFA.

2.5.5 Eliminating ϵ-Transitions

Given any ϵ-NFA E, we can find a DFA D that accepts the same language as E. The construction we use is very close to the subset construction, as the states of D are subsets of the states of E. The only difference is that we must incorporate ϵ-transitions of E, which we do through the mechanism of the ϵ-closure.

Let $E = (Q_E, \Sigma, \delta_E, q_0, F_E)$. Then the equivalent DFA

$$D = (Q_D, \Sigma, \delta_D, q_D, F_D)$$

is defined as follows:

1. Q_D is the set of subsets of Q_E. More precisely, we shall find that the only accessible states of D are the ϵ-*closed* subsets of Q_E, that is, those sets $S \subseteq Q_E$ such that $S = \text{ECLOSE}(S)$. Put another way, the ϵ-closed sets of states S are those such that any ϵ-transitions out of one of the states in S lead to a state that is also in S. Note that $\emptyset$ is an ϵ-closed set.

2. $q_D = \text{ECLOSE}(q_0)$; that is, we get the start state of D by closing the set consisting of only the start state of E. Note that this rule differs from the original subset construction, where the start state of the constructed automaton was just the set containing the start state of the given NFA.

3. F_D is those sets of states that contain at least one accepting state of E. That is, $F_D = \{S \mid S \text{ is in } Q_D \text{ and } S \cap F_E \neq \emptyset\}$.

4. $\delta_D(S, a)$ is computed, for all a in Σ and sets S in Q_D by:

(a) Let $S = \{p_1, p_2, \ldots, p_k\}$.

(b) Compute $\bigcup_{i=1}^{k} \delta(p_i, a)$; let this set be $\{r_1, r_2, \ldots, r_m\}$.

(c) Then $\delta_D(S, a) = \bigcup_{j=1}^{m} \text{ECLOSE}(r_j)$.

Example 2.21: Let us eliminate ϵ-transitions from the ϵ-NFA of Fig. 2.18, which we shall call E in what follows. From E, we construct an DFA D, which is shown in Fig. 2.22. However, to avoid clutter, we omitted from Fig. 2.22 the dead state $\emptyset$ and all transitions to the dead state. You should imagine that for each state shown in Fig. 2.22 there are additional transitions from any state to $\emptyset$ on any input symbols for which a transition is not indicated. Also, the state $\emptyset$ has transitions to itself on all input symbols.

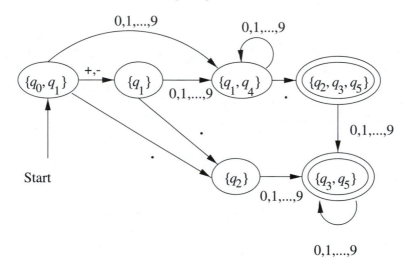

Figure 2.22: The DFA D that eliminates ϵ-transitions from Fig. 2.18

Since the start state of E is q_0, the start state of D is $\text{ECLOSE}(q_0)$, which is $\{q_0, q_1\}$. Our first job is to find the successors of q_0 and q_1 on the various symbols in Σ; note that these symbols are the plus and minus signs, the dot, and the digits 0 through 9. On $+$ and $-$, q_1 goes nowhere in Fig. 2.18, while q_0 goes to q_1. Thus, to compute $\delta_D(\{q_0, q_1\}, +)$ we start with $\{q_1\}$ and ϵ-close it. Since there are no ϵ-transitions out of q_1, we have $\delta_D(\{q_0, q_1\}, +) = \{q_1\}$. Similarly, $\delta_D(\{q_0, q_1\}, -) = \{q_1\}$. These two transitions are shown by one arc in Fig. 2.22.

Next, we need to compute $\delta_D(\{q_0, q_1\}, \cdot)$. Since q_0 goes nowhere on the dot, and q_1 goes to q_2 in Fig. 2.18, we must ϵ-close $\{q_2\}$. As there are no ϵ-transitions out of q_2, this state is its own closure, so $\delta_D(\{q_0, q_1\}, \cdot) = \{q_2\}$.

Finally, we must compute $\delta_D(\{q_0, q_1\}, 0)$, as an example of the transitions from $\{q_0, q_1\}$ on all the digits. We find that q_0 goes nowhere on the digits, but q_1 goes to both q_1 and q_4. Since neither of those states have ϵ-transitions out, we conclude $\delta_D(\{q_0, q_1\}, 0) = \{q_1, q_4\}$, and likewise for the other digits.

We have now explained the arcs out of $\{q_0, q_1\}$ in Fig. 2.22. The other transitions are computed similarly, and we leave them for you to check. Since q_5 is the only accepting state of E, the accepting states of D are those accessible states that contain q_5. We see these two sets $\{q_3, q_5\}$ and $\{q_2, q_3, q_5\}$ indicated by double circles in Fig. 2.22. $\square$

Theorem 2.22: A language L is accepted by some ϵ-NFA if and only if L is accepted by some DFA.

PROOF: (If) This direction is easy. Suppose $L = L(D)$ for some DFA. Turn D into an ϵ-DFA E by adding transitions $\delta(q, \epsilon) = \emptyset$ for all states q of D. Technically, we must also convert the transitions of D on input symbols, e.g., $\delta_D(q, a) = p$ into an NFA-transition to the set containing only p, that is $\delta_E(q, a) = \{p\}$. Thus, the transitions of E and D are the same, but E explicitly states that there are no transitions out of any state on ϵ.

(Only-if) Let $E = (Q_E, \Sigma, \delta_E, q_0, F_E)$ be an ϵ-NFA. Apply the modified subset construction described above to produce the DFA

$$D = (Q_D, \Sigma, \delta_D, q_D, F_D)$$

We need to show that $L(D) = L(E)$, and we do so by showing that the extended transition functions of E and D are the same. Formally, we show $\hat{\delta}_E(q_0, w) = \hat{\delta}_D(q_D, w)$ by induction on the length of w.

BASIS: If $|w| = 0$, then $w = \epsilon$. We know $\hat{\delta}_E(q_0, \epsilon) = \text{ECLOSE}(q_0)$. We also know that $q_D = \text{ECLOSE}(q_0)$, because that is how the start state of D is defined. Finally, for a DFA, we know that $\hat{\delta}(p, \epsilon) = p$ for any state p, so in particular, $\hat{\delta}_D(q_D, \epsilon) = \text{ECLOSE}(q_0)$. We have thus proved that $\hat{\delta}_E(q_0, \epsilon) = \hat{\delta}_D(q_D, \epsilon)$.

INDUCTION: Suppose $w = xa$, where a is the final symbol of w, and assume that the statement holds for x. That is, $\hat{\delta}_E(q_0, x) = \hat{\delta}_D(q_D, x)$. Let both these sets of states be $\{p_1, p_2, \ldots, p_k\}$.

By the definition of $\hat{\delta}$ for ϵ-NFA's, we compute $\hat{\delta}_E(q_0, w)$ by:

1. Let $\{r_1, r_2, \ldots, r_m\}$ be $\bigcup_{i=1}^{k} \delta_E(p_i, a)$.

2. Then $\hat{\delta}_E(q_0, w) = \bigcup_{j=1}^{m} \text{ECLOSE}(r_j)$.

If we examine the construction of DFA D in the modified subset construction above, we see that $\delta_D(\{p_1, p_2, \ldots, p_k\}, a)$ is constructed by the same two steps (1) and (2) above. Thus, $\hat{\delta}_D(q_D, w)$, which is $\delta_D(\{p_1, p_2, \ldots, p_k\}, a)$ is the same set as $\hat{\delta}_E(q_0, w)$. we have now proved that $\hat{\delta}_E(q_0, w) = \hat{\delta}_D(q_D, w)$ and completed the inductive part. $\square$

2.5.6   Exercises for Section 2.5

* **Exercise 2.5.1:** Consider the following ϵ-NFA.

	ϵ	a	b	c
$\to p$	$\emptyset$	$\{p\}$	$\{q\}$	$\{r\}$
q	$\{p\}$	$\{q\}$	$\{r\}$	$\emptyset$
$*r$	$\{q\}$	$\{r\}$	$\emptyset$	$\{p\}$

a) Compute the ϵ-closure of each state.

b) Give all the strings of length three or less accepted by the automaton.

c) Convert the automaton to a DFA.

Exercise 2.5.2: Repeat Exercise 2.5.1 for the following ϵ-NFA:

	ϵ	a	b	c
$\to p$	$\{q, r\}$	$\emptyset$	$\{q\}$	$\{r\}$
q	$\emptyset$	$\{p\}$	$\{r\}$	$\{p, q\}$
$*r$	$\emptyset$	$\emptyset$	$\emptyset$	$\emptyset$

Exercise 2.5.3: Design ϵ-NFA's for the following languages. Try to use ϵ-transitions to simplify your design.

a) The set of strings consisting of zero or more a's followed by zero or more b's, followed by zero or more c's.

! b) The set of strings that consist of either 01 repeated one or more times or 010 repeated one or more times.

! c) The set of strings of 0's and 1's such that at least one of the last ten positions is a 1.

2.6   Summary of Chapter 2

✦ *Deterministic Finite Automata*: A DFA has a finite set of states and a finite set of input symbols. One state is designated the start state, and zero or more states are accepting states. A transition function determines how the state changes each time an input symbol is processed.

✦ *Transition Diagrams*: It is convenient to represent automata by a graph in which the nodes are the states, and arcs are labeled by input symbols, indicating the transitions of that automaton. The start state is designated by an arrow, and the accepting states by double circles.

✦ *Language of an Automaton*: The automaton accepts strings. A string is accepted if, starting in the start state, the transitions caused by processing the symbols of that string one-at-a-time lead to an accepting state. In terms of the transition diagram, a string is accepted if it is the label of a path from the start state to some accepting state.

✦ *Nondeterministic Finite Automata*: The NFA differs from the DFA in that the NFA can have any number of transitions (including zero) to next states from a given state on a given input symbol.

✦ *The Subset Construction*: By treating sets of states of an NFA as states of a DFA, it is possible to convert any NFA to a DFA that accepts the same language.

✦ *ϵ-Transitions*: We can extend the NFA by allowing transitions on an empty input, i.e., no input symbol at all. These extended NFA's can be converted to DFA's accepting the same language.

✦ *Text-Searching Applications*: Nondeterministic finite automata are a useful way to represent a pattern matcher that scans a large body of text for one or more keywords. These automata are either simulated directly in software or are first converted to a DFA, which is then simulated.

2.7 References for Chapter 2

The formal study of finite-state systems is generally regarded as originating with [2]. However, this work was based on a "neural nets" model of computing, rather than the finite automaton we know today. The conventional DFA was independently proposed, in several similar variations, by [1], [3], and [4]. The nondeterministic finite automaton and the subset construction are from [5].

1. D. A. Huffman, "The synthesis of sequential switching circuits," *J. Franklin Inst.* **257**:3-4 (1954), pp. 161–190 and 275–303.

2. W. S. McCulloch and W. Pitts, "A logical calculus of the ideas immanent in nervous activity," *Bull. Math. Biophysics* **5** (1943), pp. 115–133.

3. G. H. Mealy, "A method for synthesizing sequential circuits," *Bell System Technical Journal* **34**:5 (1955), pp. 1045–1079.

4. E. F. Moore, "Gedanken experiments on sequential machines," in [6], pp. 129–153.

5. M. O. Rabin and D. Scott, "Finite automata and their decision problems," *IBM J. Research and Development* **3**:2 (1959), pp. 115–125.

6. C. E. Shannon and J. McCarthy, *Automata Studies*, Princeton Univ. Press, 1956.

Chapter 3

Regular Expressions and Languages

We begin this chapter by introducing the notation called "regular expressions." These expressions are another type of language-defining notation, which we sampled briefly in Section 1.1.2. Regular expressions also may be thought of as a "programming language," in which we express some important applications, such as text-search applications or compiler components. Regular expressions are closely related to nondeterministic finite automata and can be thought of as a "user-friendly" alternative to the NFA notation for describing software components.

In this chapter, after defining regular expressions, we show that they are capable of defining all and only the regular languages. We discuss the way that regular expressions are used in several software systems. Then, we examine the algebraic laws that apply to regular expressions. They have significant resemblance to the algebraic laws of arithmetic, yet there are also some important differences between the algebras of regular expressions and arithmetic expressions.

3.1 Regular Expressions

Now, we switch our attention from machine-like descriptions of languages — deterministic and nondeterministic finite automata — to an algebraic description: the "regular expression." We shall find that regular expressions can define exactly the same languages that the various forms of automata describe: the regular languages. However, regular expressions offer something that automata do not: a declarative way to express the strings we want to accept. Thus, regular expressions serve as the input language for many systems that process strings. Examples include:

1. Search commands such as the UNIX `grep` or equivalent commands for finding strings that one sees in Web browsers or text-formatting systems. These systems use a regular-expression-like notation for describing patterns that the user wants to find in a file. Different search systems convert the regular expression into either a DFA or an NFA, and simulate that automaton on the file being searched.

2. Lexical-analyzer generators, such as Lex or Flex. Recall that a lexical analyzer is the component of a compiler that breaks the source program into logical units (called *tokens*) of one or more characters that have a shared significance. Examples of tokens include keywords (e.g., `while`), identifiers (e.g., any letter followed by zero or more letters and/or digits), and signs, such as `+` or `<=`. A lexical-analyzer generator accepts descriptions of the forms of tokens, which are essentially regular expressions, and produces a DFA that recognizes which token appears next on the input.

3.1.1   The Operators of Regular Expressions

Regular expressions denote languages. For a simple example, the regular expression $01^* + 10^*$ denotes the language consisting of all strings that are either a single 0 followed by any number of 1's or a single 1 followed by any number of 0's. We do not expect you to know at this point how to interpret regular expressions, so our statement about the language of this expression must be accepted on faith for the moment. We shortly shall define all the symbols used in this expression, so you can see why our interpretation of this regular expression is the correct one. Before describing the regular-expression notation, we need to learn the three operations on languages that the operators of regular expressions represent. These operations are:

1. The *union* of two languages L and M, denoted $L \cup M$, is the set of strings that are in either L or M, or both. For example, if $L = \{001, 10, 111\}$ and $M = \{\epsilon, 001\}$, then $L \cup M = \{\epsilon, 10, 001, 111\}$.

2. The *concatenation* of languages L and M is the set of strings that can be formed by taking any string in L and concatenating it with any string in M. Recall Section 1.5.2, where we defined the concatenation of a pair of strings; one string is followed by the other to form the result of the concatenation. We denote concatenation of languages either with a dot or with no operator at all, although the concatenation operator is frequently called "dot." For example, if $L = \{001, 10, 111\}$ and $M = \{\epsilon, 001\}$, then $L.M$, or just LM, is $\{001, 10, 111, 001001, 10001, 111001\}$. The first three strings in LM are the strings in L concatenated with ϵ. Since ϵ is the identity for concatenation, the resulting strings are the same as the strings of L. However, the last three strings in LM are formed by taking each string in L and concatenating it with the second string in M, which is 001. For instance, 10 from L concatenated with 001 from M gives us 10001 for LM.

3. The *closure* (or *star*, or *Kleene closure*)[1] of a language L is denoted L^* and represents the set of those strings that can be formed by taking any number of strings from L, possibly with repetitions (i.e., the same string may be selected more than once) and concatenating all of them. For instance, if $L = \{0, 1\}$, then L^* is all strings of 0's and 1's. If $L = \{0, 11\}$, then L^* consists of those strings of 0's and 1's such that the 1's come in pairs, e.g., 011, 11110, and ϵ, but not 01011 or 101. More formally, L^* is the infinite union $\cup_{i \geq 0} L^i$, where $L^0 = \{\epsilon\}$, $L^1 = L$, and L^i, for $i > 1$ is $LL \cdots L$ (the concatenation of i copies of L.

Example 3.1: Since the idea of the closure of a language is somewhat tricky, let us study a few examples. First, let $L = \{0, 11\}$. $L^0 = \{\epsilon\}$, independent of what language L is; the 0th power represents the selection of zero strings from L. $L^1 = L$, which represents the choice of one string from L. Thus, the first two terms in the expansion of L^* give us $\{\epsilon, 0, 11\}$.

Next, consider L^2. We pick two strings from L, with repetitions allowed, so there are four choices. These four selections give us $L^2 = \{00, 011, 110, 1111\}$. Similarly, L^3 is the set of strings that may be formed by making three choices of the two strings in L and gives us

$$\{000, 0011, 0110, 1100, 01111, 11011, 11110, 111111\}$$

To compute L^*, we must compute L^i for each i, and take the union of all these languages. L^i has 2^i members. Although each L^i is finite, the union of the infinite number of terms L^i is generally an infinite language, as it is in our example.

Now, let L be the set of all strings of 0's. Note that L is infinite, unlike our previous example, which is a finite language. However, it is not hard to discover what L^* is. $L^0 = \{\epsilon\}$, as always. $L^1 = L$. L^2 is the set of strings that can be formed by taking one string of 0's and concatenating it with another string of 0's. The result is still a string of 0's. In fact, every string of 0's can be written as the concatenation of two strings of 0's (don't forget that ϵ is a "string of 0's"; this string can always be one of the two strings that we concatenate). Thus, $L^2 = L$. Likewise, $L^3 = L$, and so on. Thus, the infinite union $L^* = L^0 \cup L^1 \cup L^2 \cup \cdots$ is L in the particular case that the language L the set of all strings of 0's.

For a final example, $\emptyset^* = \{\epsilon\}$. Note that $\emptyset^0 = \{\epsilon\}$, while $\emptyset^i$, for any $i \geq 1$, is empty, since we can't select any strings from the empty set. In fact, $\emptyset$ is one of only two languages whose closure is *not* infinite. □

3.1.2 Building Regular Expressions

Algebras of all kinds start with some elementary expressions, usually constants and/or variables. Algebras then allow us to construct more expressions by

---

[1]The term "Kleene closure" refers to S. C. Kleene, who originated the regular expression notation and this operator.

Use of the Star Operator

We saw the star operator first in Section 1.5.2, where we applied it to an alphabet, e.g., Σ^*. That operator formed all strings whose symbols were chosen from alphabet Σ. The closure operator is essentially the same, although there is a subtle distinction of types.

Suppose L is the language containing strings of length 1, and for each symbol a in Σ there is a string a in L. Then, although L and Σ "look" the same, they are of different types; L is a set of strings, and Σ is a set of symbols. On the other hand, L^* denotes the same language as Σ^*.

---

applying a certain set of operators to these elementary expressions and to previously constructed expressions. Usually, some method of grouping operators with their operands, such as parentheses, is required as well. For instance, the familiar arithmetic algebra starts with constants such as integers and real numbers, plus variables, and builds more complex expressions with arithmetic operators such as $+$ and $\times$.

The algebra of regular expressions follows this pattern, using constants and variables that denote languages, and operators for the three operations of Section 3.1.1 —union, dot, and star. We can describe the regular expressions recursively, as follows. In this definition, we not only describe what the legal regular expressions are, but for each regular expression E, we describe the language it represents, which we denote $L(E)$.

BASIS: The basis consists of three parts:

1. The constants ϵ and $\emptyset$ are regular expressions, denoting the languages $\{\epsilon\}$ and $\emptyset$, respectively. That is, $L(\epsilon) = \{\epsilon\}$, and $L(\emptyset) = \emptyset$.

2. If a is any symbol, then **a** is a regular expression. This expression denotes the language $\{a\}$. That is, $L(\mathbf{a}) = \{a\}$. Note that we use boldface font to denote an expression corresponding to a symbol. The correspondence, e.g. that **a** refers to a, should be obvious.

3. A variable, usually capitalized and italic such as L, is a variable, representing any language.

INDUCTION: There are four parts to the inductive step, one for each of the three operators and one for the introduction of parentheses.

1. If E and F are regular expressions, then $E + F$ is a regular expression denoting the union of $L(E)$ and $L(F)$. That is, $L(E+F) = L(E) \cup L(F)$.

2. If E and F are regular expressions, then EF is a regular expression denoting the concatenation of $L(E)$ and $L(F)$. That is, $L(EF) = L(E)L(F)$.

Expressions and Their Languages

Strictly speaking, a regular expression E is just an expression, not a language. We should use $L(E)$ when we want to refer to the language that E denotes. However, it is common usage to refer to say "E" when we really mean "$L(E)$." We shall use this convention as long as it is clear we are talking about a language and not about a regular expression.

Note that the dot can optionally be used to denote the concatenation operator, either as an operation on languages or as the operator in a regular expression. For instance, **0.1** is a regular expression meaning the same as **01** and representing the language $\{01\}$. However, we shall avoid the dot as concatenation in regular expressions.[2]

3. If E is a regular expression, then E^* is a regular expression, denoting the closure of $L(E)$. That is, $L(E^*) = \big(L(E)\big)^*$.

4. If E is a regular expression, then (E), a parenthesized E, is also a regular expression, denoting the same language as E. Formally; $L\big((E)\big) = L(E)$.

Example 3.2 : Let us write a regular expression for the set of strings that consist of alternating 0's and 1's. First, let us develop a regular expression for the language consisting of the single string 01. We can then use the star operator to get an expression for all strings of the form $0101 \cdots 01$.

The basis rule for regular expressions tells us that **0** and **1** are expressions denoting the languages $\{0\}$ and $\{1\}$, respectively. If we concatenate the two expressions, we get a regular expression for the language $\{01\}$; this expression is **01**. As a general rule, if we want a regular expression for the language consisting of only the string w, we use w itself as the regular expression. Note that in the regular expression, the symbols of w will normally we written in boldface, but the change of font is only to help you distinguish expressions from strings and should not be taken as significant.

Now, to get all strings consisting of zero or more occurrences of 01, we use the regular expression $(\mathbf{01})^*$. Note that we first put parentheses around **01**, to avoid confusing with the expression $\mathbf{01}^*$, whose language is all strings consisting of a 0 and any number of 1's. The reason for this interpretation is explained in Section 3.1.3, but briefly, star takes precedence over dot, and therefore the argument of the star is selected before performing any concatenations.

However, $L\big((\mathbf{01})^*\big)$ is not exactly the language that we want. It includes only those strings of alternating 0's and 1's that begin with 0 and end with 1. We also need to consider the possibility that there is a 1 at the beginning and/or

---

[2]In fact, UNIX regular expressions use the dot for an entirely different purpose: representing any ASCII character.

a 0 at the end. One approach is to construct three more regular expressions that handle the other three possibilities. That is, $(\mathbf{10})^*$ represents those alternating strings that begin with 1 and end with 0, while $\mathbf{0}(\mathbf{10})^*$ can be used for strings that both begin and end with 0 and $\mathbf{1}(\mathbf{01})^*$ serves for strings that begin and end with 1. The entire regular expression is

$$(\mathbf{01})^* + (\mathbf{10})^* + \mathbf{0}(\mathbf{10})^* + \mathbf{1}(\mathbf{01})^*$$

Notice that we use the $+$ operator to take the union of the four languages that together give us all the strings with alternating 0's and 1's.

However, there is another approach that yields a regular expression that looks rather different and is also somewhat more succinct. Start again with the expression $(\mathbf{01})^*$. We can add an optional 1 at the beginning if we concatenate on the left with the expression $\epsilon + \mathbf{1}$. Likewise, we add an optional 0 at the end with the expression $\epsilon + \mathbf{0}$. For instance, using the definition of the $+$ operator:

$$L(\epsilon + \mathbf{1}) = L(\epsilon) \cup L(\mathbf{1}) = \{\epsilon\} \cup \{1\} = \{\epsilon, 1\}$$

If we concatenate this language with any other language L, the ϵ choice gives us all the strings in L, while the 1 choice gives us $1w$ for every string w in L. Thus, another expression for the set of strings that alternate 0's and 1's is:

$$(\epsilon + \mathbf{1})(\mathbf{01})^*(\epsilon + \mathbf{0})$$

Note that we need parentheses around each of the added expressions, to make sure the operators group properly. □

3.1.3   Precedence of Regular-Expression Operators

Like other algebras, the regular-expression operators have an assumed order of "precedence," which means that operators are associated with their operands in a particular order. We are familiar with the notion of precedence from ordinary arithmetic expressions. For instance, we know that $xy+z$ groups the product xy before the sum, so it is equivalent to the parenthesized expression $(xy) + z$ and not to the expression $x(y + z)$. Similarly, we group two of the same operators from the left in arithmetic, so $x - y - z$ is equivalent to $(x - y) - z$, and not to $x - (y - z)$. For regular expressions, the following is the order of precedence for the operators:

1. The star operator is of highest precedence. That is, it applies only to the smallest sequence of symbols to its left that is a well-formed regular expression.

2. Next in precedence comes the concatenation or "dot" operator. After grouping all stars to their operands, we group concatenation operators to their operands. That is, all expressions that are *juxtaposed* (adjacent, with no intervening operator) are grouped together. Since concatenation

is an associative operator it does not matter in what order we group consecutive concatenations, although if there is a choice to be made, you should group them from the left. For instance, **012** is grouped **(01)2**.

3. Finally, all unions (+ operators) are grouped with their operands. Since union is also associative, it again matters little in which order consecutive unions are grouped, but we shall assume grouping from the left.

Of course, sometimes we do not want the grouping in a regular expression to be as required by the precedence of the operators. If so, we are free to use parentheses to group operands exactly as we choose. In addition, there is never anything wrong with putting parentheses around operands that you want to group, even if the desired grouping is implied by the rules of precedence.

Example 3.3: The expression **01* + 1** is grouped $(0(1^*)) + 1$. The star operator is grouped first. Since the symbol **1** immediately to its left is a legal regular expression, that alone is the operand of the star. Next, we group the concatenation between **0** and **(1*)**, giving us the expression **(0(1*))**. Finally, the union operator connects the latter expression and the expression to its right, which is **1**.

Notice that the language of the given expression, grouped according to the precedence rules, is the string 1 plus all strings consisting of a 0 followed by any number of 1's (including none). Had we chosen to group the dot before the star, we could have used parentheses, as **(01)* + 1**. The language of this expression is the string 1 and all strings that repeat 01, zero or more times. Had we wished to group the union first, we could have added parentheses around the union to make the expression **0(1* + 1)**. That expression's language is the set of strings that begin with 0 and have any number of 1's following. □

3.1.4 Exercises for Section 3.1

Exercise 3.1.1: Write regular expressions for the following languages:

* * a) The set of strings over alphabet $\{a, b, c\}$ containing at least one a and at least one b.

  b) The set of strings of 0's and 1's whose tenth symbol from the right end is 1.

  c) The set of strings of 0's and 1's with at most one pair of consecutive 1's.

! Exercise 3.1.2: Write regular expressions for the following languages:

* * a) The set of all strings of 0's and 1's such that every pair of adjacent 0's appears before any pair of adjacent 1's.

  b) The set of strings of 0's and 1's whose number of 0's is divisible by five.

!! **Exercise 3.1.3 :** Write regular expressions for the following languages:

   a) The set of all strings of 0's and 1's not containing 101 as a substring.

   b) The set of all strings with an equal number of 0's and 1's, such that no prefix has two more 0's than 1's, nor two more 1's than 0's.

   c) The set of strings of 0's and 1's whose number of 0's is divisible by five and whose number of 1's is even.

! **Exercise 3.1.4 :** Give English descriptions of the languages of the following regular expressions:

* a) $(1 + \epsilon)(00^*1)^*0^*$.

   b) $(0^*1^*)^*000(0 + 1)^*$.

   c) $(0 + 10)^*1^*$.

*! **Exercise 3.1.5 :** In Example 3.1 we pointed out that $\emptyset$ is one of two languages whose closure is finite. What is the other?

3.2   Finite Automata and Regular Expressions

While the regular-expression approach to describing languages is fundamentally different from the finite-automaton approach, these two notations turn out to represent exactly the same set of languages, which we have termed the "regular languages." We have already shown that deterministic finite automata, and the two kinds of nondeterministic finite automata — with and without ϵ-transitions — accept the same class of languages. In order to show that the regular expressions define the same class, we must show that:

   1. Every language defined by one of these automata is also defined by a regular expression. For this proof, we can assume the language is accepted by some DFA.

   2. Every language defined by a regular expression is defined by one of these automata. For this part of the proof, the easiest is to show that there is an NFA with ϵ-transitions accepting the same language.

Figure 3.1 shows all the equivalences we have proved or will prove. An arc from class X to class Y means that we prove every language defined by class X is also defined by class Y. Since the graph is strongly connected (i.e., we can get from each of the four nodes to any other node) we see that all four classes are really the same.

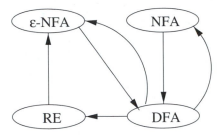

Figure 3.1: Plan for showing the equivalence of four different notations for regular languages

3.2.1 From DFA's to Regular Expressions

The construction of a regular expression to define the language of any DFA is surprisingly tricky. Roughly, we build expressions that describe sets of strings that label certain paths in the DFA's transition diagram. However, the paths are allowed to pass through only a limited subset of the states. In an inductive definition of these expressions, we start with the simplest expressions that describe paths that are not allowed to pass through *any* states (i.e., they are single nodes or single arcs), and indictively build the expressions that let the paths go through progressively larger sets of states. Finally, the paths are allowed to go through any state; i.e., the expressions we generate at the end represent all possible paths. These ideas appear in the proof of the following theorem.

Theorem 3.4 : If $L = L(A)$ for some DFA A, then there is a regular expression R such that $L = L(R)$.

PROOF: Let us suppose that A's states are $\{1, 2, \ldots, n\}$ for some integer n. No matter what the states of A actually are, there will be n of them for some finite n, and by renaming the states, we can refer to the states in this manner, as if they were the first n positive integers. Our first, and most difficult, task is to construct a collection of regular expressions that describe progressively broader sets of paths in the transition diagram of A.

Let us use $R_{ij}^{(k)}$ as the name of a regular expression whose language is the set of strings w such that w is the label of a path from state i to state j in A, and that path has no intermediate node whose number is greater than k. Note that the beginning and end points of the path are not "intermediate," so there is no constraint that i and/or j be less than or equal to k.

Figure 3.2 suggests the requirement on the paths represented by $R_{ij}^{(k)}$. There, the vertical dimension represents the state, from 1 at the bottom to n at the top, and the horizontal dimension represents travel along the path. Notice that in this diagram we have shown both i and j to be greater than k, but either or both could be k or less. Also notice that the path passes through node k twice, but never goes through a state higher than k, except at the endpoints.

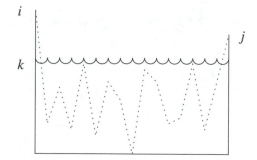

Figure 3.2: A path whose label is in the language of regular expression $R_{ij}^{(k)}$

To construct the expressions $R_{ij}^{(k)}$, we use the following inductive definition, starting at $k = 0$ and finally reaching $k = n$. Notice that when $k = n$, there is no restriction at all on the paths represented, since there *are* no states greater than n.

BASIS: The basis is $k = 0$. Since all states are numbered 1 or above, the restriction on paths is that the path must have no intermediate states at all. There are only two kinds of paths that meet such a condition:

1. An arc from node (state) i to node j.

2. A path of length 0 that consists of only some node i.

If $i \neq j$, then only case (1) is possible. We must examine the DFA A and find those input symbols a such that there is a transition from state i to state j on symbol a.

a) If there is no such symbol a, then $R_{ij}^{(0)} = \emptyset$.

b) If there is exactly one such symbol a, then $R_{ij}^{(0)} = \mathbf{a}$.

c) If there are symbols $a_1, a_2, \ldots, a_k$ that label arcs from state i to state j, then $R_{ij}^{(0)} = \mathbf{a_1} + \mathbf{a_2} + \cdots + \mathbf{a_k}$.

However, if $i = j$, then the legal paths are the path of length 0 and all loops from i to itself. The path of length 0 is represented by the regular expression ϵ, since that path has no symbols along it. Thus, we add ϵ to the various expressions devised in (a) through (c) above. That is, in case (a) [no symbol a] the expression becomes ϵ, in case (b) [one symbol a] the expression becomes $\epsilon + \mathbf{a}$, and in case (c) [multiple symbols] the expression becomes $\epsilon + \mathbf{a_1} + \mathbf{a_2} + \cdots + \mathbf{a_k}$.

INDUCTION: Suppose there is a path from state i to state j that goes through no state higher than k. There are two possible cases to consider:

1. The path does not go through state k at all. In this case, the label of the path is in the language of $R_{ij}^{(k-1)}$.

2. The path goes through state k at least once. Then we can break the path into several pieces, as suggested by Fig. 3.3. The first goes from state i to state k without passing through k, the last piece goes from k to j without passing through k, and all the pieces in the middle go from k to itself, without passing through k. Note that if the path goes through state k only once, then there are no "middle" pieces, just a path from i to k and a path from k to j. The set of labels for all paths of this type is represented by the regular expression $R_{ik}^{(k-1)}(R_{kk}^{(k-1)})^*R_{kj}^{(k-1)}$. That is, the first expression represents the part of the path that gets to state k the first time, the second represents the portion that goes from k to itself, zero times, once, or more than once, and the third expression represents the part of the path that leaves k for the last time and goes to state j.

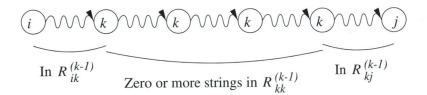

In $R_{ik}^{(k-1)}$ Zero or more strings in $R_{kk}^{(k-1)}$ In $R_{kj}^{(k-1)}$

Figure 3.3: A path from i to j can be broken into segments at each point where it goes through state k

When we combine the expressions for the paths of the two types above, we have the expression

$$R_{ij}^{(k)} = R_{ij}^{(k-1)} + R_{ik}^{(k-1)}(R_{kk}^{(k-1)})^*R_{kj}^{(k-1)}$$

for the labels of all paths from state i to state j that go through no state higher than k. If we construct these expressions in order of increasing superscript, then since each $R_{ij}^{(k)}$ depends only on expressions with a smaller superscript, then all expressions are available when we need them.

Eventually, we have $R_{ij}^{(n)}$ for all i and j. We may assume that state 1 is the start state, although the accepting states could be any set of the states. The regular expression for the language of the automaton is then the sum (union) of all expressions $R_{1j}^{(n)}$ such that state j is an accepting state. $\square$

Example 3.5 : Let us convert the DFA of Fig. 3.4 to a regular expression. This DFA accepts all strings that have at least one 0 in them. To see why, note that the automaton goes from the start state 1 to accepting state 2 as soon as it sees an input 0. The automaton then stays in state 2 on all input sequences. Below are the basis expressions in the construction of Theorem 3.4.

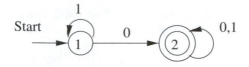

Figure 3.4: A DFA accepting all strings that have at least one 0

$R_{11}^{(0)}$	$\epsilon + 1$
$R_{12}^{(0)}$	0
$R_{21}^{(0)}$	$\emptyset$
$R_{22}^{(0)}$	$(\epsilon + 0 + 1)$

For instance, $R_{11}^{(0)}$ has the term ϵ because the beginning and ending states are the same, state 1. It has the term 1 because there is an arc from state 1 to state 1 on input 1. As another example, $R_{12}^{(0)}$ is 0 because there is an arc labeled 0 from state 1 to state 2. There is no ϵ term because the beginning and ending states are different. For a third example, $R_{21}^{(0)} = \emptyset$, because there is no arc from state 2 to state 1.

Now, we must do the induction part, building more complex expressions that first take into account paths that go through state 1, and then paths that can go through states 1 and 2, i.e., any path. The rule for computing the expressions $R_{ij}^{(1)}$ are instances of the general rule given in the inductive part of Theorem 3.4:

$$R_{ij}^{(1)} = R_{ij}^{(0)} + R_{i1}^{(0)}(R_{11}^{(0)})^* R_{1j}^{(0)} \tag{3.1}$$

The table in Fig. 3.5 gives first the expressions computed by direct substitution into the above formula, and then a simplified expression that we can show, by ad-hoc reasoning, to represent the same language as the more complex expression.

	By direct substitution	Simplified
$R_{11}^{(1)}$	$\epsilon + 1 + (\epsilon + 1)(\epsilon + 1)^*(\epsilon + 1)$	1^*
$R_{12}^{(1)}$	$0 + (\epsilon + 1)(\epsilon + 1)^*0$	1^*0
$R_{21}^{(1)}$	$\emptyset + \emptyset(\epsilon + 1)^*(\epsilon + 1)$	$\emptyset$
$R_{22}^{(1)}$	$\epsilon + 0 + 1 + \emptyset(\epsilon + 1)^*0$	$\epsilon + 0 + 1$

Figure 3.5: Regular expressions for paths that can go through only state 1

For example, consider $R_{12}^{(1)}$. Its expression is $R_{12}^{(0)} + R_{11}^{(0)}(R_{11}^{(0)})^* R_{12}^{(0)}$, which we get from (3.1) by substituting $i = 1$ and $j = 2$.

To understand the simplification, note the general principle that if R is any regular expression, then $(\epsilon + R)^* = R^*$. The justification is that both sides of the equation describe the language consisting of any concatenation of zero or more strings from $L(R)$. In our case, we have $(\epsilon + 1)^* = 1^*$; notice that both expressions denote any number of 1's. Further, $(\epsilon + 1)1^* = 1^*$. Again, it can be observed that both expressions denote "any number of 1's." Thus, the original expression $R_{12}^{(1)}$ is equivalent to $\mathbf{0} + \mathbf{1}^*\mathbf{0}$. This expression denotes the language containing the string 0 and all strings consisting of a 0 preceded by any number of 1's. This language is also expressed by the simpler expression $\mathbf{1}^*\mathbf{0}$.

The simplification of $R_{11}^{(1)}$ is similar to the simplification of $R_{12}^{(1)}$ that we just considered. The simplification of $R_{21}^{(1)}$ and $R_{22}^{(1)}$ depends on two rules about how $\emptyset$ operates. For any regular expression R:

1. $\emptyset R = R\emptyset = \emptyset$. That is, $\emptyset$ is an *annihilator* for concatenation; it results in itself when concatenated, either on the left or right, with any expression. This rule makes sense, because for a string to be in the result of a concatenation, we must find strings from both arguments of the concatenation. Whenever one of the arguments is $\emptyset$, it will be impossible to find a string from that argument.

2. $\emptyset + R = R + \emptyset = R$. That is, $\emptyset$ is the identity for union; it results in the other expression whenever it appears in a union.

As a result, an expression like $\emptyset(\epsilon + \mathbf{1})^*(\epsilon + \mathbf{1})$ can be replaced by $\emptyset$. The last two simplifications should now be clear.

Now, let us compute the expressions $R_{ij}^{(2)}$. The inductive rule applied with $k = 2$ gives us:

$$R_{ij}^{(2)} = R_{ij}^{(1)} + R_{i2}^{(1)}(R_{22}^{(1)})^* R_{2j}^{(1)} \tag{3.2}$$

If we substitute the simplified expressions from Fig. 3.5 into (3.2), we get the expressions of Fig. 3.6. That figure also shows simplifications following the same principles that we described for Fig. 3.5.

	By direct substitution	Simplified
$R_{11}^{(2)}$	$\mathbf{1}^* + \mathbf{1}^*\mathbf{0}(\epsilon + \mathbf{0} + \mathbf{1})^*\emptyset$	$\mathbf{1}^*$
$R_{12}^{(2)}$	$\mathbf{1}^*\mathbf{0} + \mathbf{1}^*\mathbf{0}(\epsilon + \mathbf{0} + \mathbf{1})^*(\epsilon + \mathbf{0} + \mathbf{1})$	$\mathbf{1}^*\mathbf{0}(\mathbf{0} + \mathbf{1})^*$
$R_{21}^{(2)}$	$\emptyset + (\epsilon + \mathbf{0} + \mathbf{1})(\epsilon + \mathbf{0} + \mathbf{1})^*\emptyset$	$\emptyset$
$R_{22}^{(2)}$	$\epsilon + \mathbf{0} + \mathbf{1} + (\epsilon + \mathbf{0} + \mathbf{1})(\epsilon + \mathbf{0} + \mathbf{1})^*(\epsilon + \mathbf{0} + \mathbf{1})$	$(\mathbf{0} + \mathbf{1})^*$

Figure 3.6: Regular expressions for paths that can go through any state

The final regular expression equivalent to the automaton of Fig. 3.4 is constructed by taking the union of all the expressions where the first state is the start state and the second state is accepting. In this example, with 1 as the start state and 2 as the only accepting state, we need only the expression $R_{12}^{(2)}$.

This expression is $\mathbf{1^*0(0+1)^*}$. It is simple to interpret this expression. Its language consists of all strings that begin with zero or more 1's, then have a 0, and then any string of 0's and 1's. Put another way, the language is all strings of 0's and 1's with at least one 0. □

3.2.2   Converting DFA's to Regular Expressions by Eliminating States

The method of Section 3.2.1 for converting a DFA to a regular expression always works. In fact, as you may have noticed, it doesn't really depend on the automaton being deterministic, and could just as well have been applied to an NFA or even an ϵ-NFA. However, the construction of the regular expression is expensive. Not only do we have to construct about n^3 expressions for an n-state automaton, but the length of the expression can grow by a factor of 4 on the average, with each of the n inductive steps, if there is no simplification of the expressions. Thus, the expressions themselves could reach on the order of 4^n symbols.

There is a similar approach that avoids duplicating work at some points. For example, all of the expressions with superscript $(k+1)$ in the construction of Theorem 3.4 use the same subexpression $(R_{kk}^{(k)})^*$; the work of writing that expression is therefore repeated n^2 times.

The approach to constructing regular expressions that we shall now learn involves eliminating states. When we eliminate a state s, all the paths that went through s no longer exist in the automaton. If the language of the automaton is not to change, we must include, on an arc that goes directly from q to p, the labels of paths that went from some state q to state p, through s. Since the label of this arc may now involve strings, rather than single symbols, and there may even be an infinite number of such strings, we cannot simply list the strings as a label. Fortunately, there is a simple, finite way to represent all such strings: use a regular expression.

Thus, we are led to consider automata that have regular expressions as labels. The language of the automaton is the union over all paths from the start state to an accepting state of the language formed by concatenating the languages of the regular expressions along that path. Note that this rule is consistent with the definition of the language for any of the varieties of automata we have considered so far. Each symbol a, or ϵ if it is allowed, can be thought of as a regular expression whose language is a single string, either $\{a\}$ or $\{\epsilon\}$. We may regard this observation as the basis of a state-elimination procedure, which we describe next.

Figure 3.7 shows a generic state s about to be eliminated. We suppose that the automaton of which s is a state has predecessor states $q_1, q_2, \ldots, q_k$ for s and successor states $p_1, p_2, \ldots, p_m$ for s. It is possible that some of the q's are also p's, but we assume that s is not among the q's or p's, even if there is a loop from s to itself, as suggested by Fig. 3.7. We also show a regular expression on each arc from one of the q's to s; expression Q_i labels the arc from q_i. Likewise,

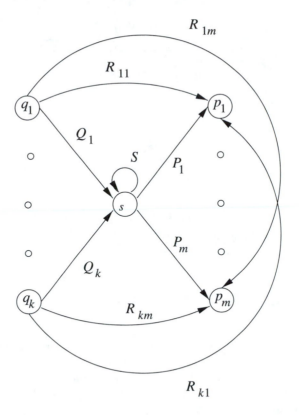

Figure 3.7: A state s about to be eliminated

we show a regular expression P_j labeling the arc from s to p_i, for all i. We show a loop on s with label S. Finally, there is a regular expression R_{ij} on the arc from q_i to p_j, for all i and j. Note that some of these arcs may not exist in the automaton, in which case we take the expression on that arc to be $\emptyset$.

Figure 3.8 shows what happens when we eliminate state s. All arcs involving state s are deleted. To compensate, we introduce, for each predecessor q_i of s and each successor p_j of s, a regular expression that represents all the paths that start at q_i, go to s, perhaps loop around s zero or more times, and finally go to p_j. The expression for these paths is $Q_i S^* P_j$. This expression is added (with the union operator) to the arc from q_i to p_j. If there was no arc $q_i \rightarrow p_j$, then first introduce one with regular expression $\emptyset$.

The strategy for constructing a regular expression from a finite automaton is as follows:

1. For each accepting state q, apply the above reduction process to produce an equivalent automaton with regular-expression labels on the arcs. Eliminate all states except q and the start state q_0.

2. If $q \neq q_0$, then we shall be left with a two-state automaton that looks like

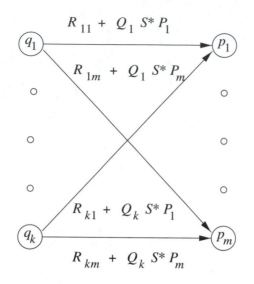

Figure 3.8: Result of eliminating state s from Fig. 3.7

Fig. 3.9. The regular expression for the accepted strings can be described in various ways. One is $(R + SU^*T)^*SU^*$. In explanation, we can go from the start state to itself any number of times, by following a sequence of paths whose labels are in either $L(R)$ or $L(SU^*T)$. The expression SU^*T represents paths that go to the accepting state via a path in $L(S)$, perhaps return to the accepting state several times using a sequence of paths with labels in $L(U)$, and then return to the start state with a path whose label is in $L(T)$. Then we must go to the accepting state, never to return to the start state, by following a path with a label in $L(S)$. Once in the accepting state, we can return to it as many times as we like, by following a path whose label is in $L(U)$.

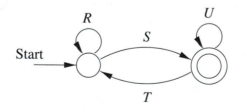

Figure 3.9: A generic two-state automaton

3. If the start state is also an accepting state, then we must also perform a state-elimination from the original automaton that gets rid of every state but the start state. When we do so, we are left with a one-state automaton that looks like Fig. 3.10. The regular expression denoting the

strings that it accepts is R^*.

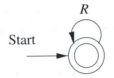

Figure 3.10: A generic one-state automaton

4. The desired regular expression is the sum (union) of all the expressions derived from the reduced automata for each accepting state, by rules (2) and (3).

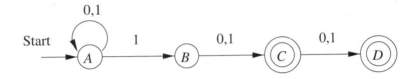

Figure 3.11: An NFA accepting strings that have a 1 either two or three positions from the end

Example 3.6: Let us consider the NFA in Fig. 3.11 that accepts all strings of 0's and 1's such that either the second or third position from the end has a 1. Our first step is to convert it to an automaton with regular expression labels. Since no state elimination has been performed, all we have to do is replace the labels "0,1" with the equivalent regular expression $0 + 1$. The result is shown in Fig. 3.12.

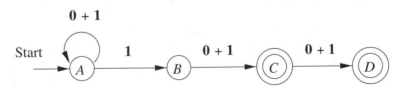

Figure 3.12: The automaton of Fig. 3.11 with regular-expression labels

Let us first eliminate state B. Since this state is neither accepting nor the start state, it will not be in any of the reduced automata. Thus, we save work if we eliminate it first, before developing the two reduced automata that correspond to the two accepting states.

State B has one predecessor, A, and one successor, C. In terms of the regular expressions in the diagram of Fig. 3.7: $Q_1 = 1$, $P_1 = 0 + 1$, $R_{11} = \emptyset$ (since the arc from A to C does not exist), and $S = \emptyset$ (because there is no loop at state B). As a result, the expression on the new arc from A to C is $\emptyset + \mathbf{1}\emptyset^*(\mathbf{0} + \mathbf{1})$.

To simplify, we first eliminate the initial $\emptyset$, which may be ignored in a union. The expression thus becomes $\mathbf{1}\emptyset^*(\mathbf{0} + \mathbf{1})$. Note that the regular expression $\emptyset^*$ is equivalent to the regular expression ϵ, since

$$L(\emptyset^*) = \{\epsilon\} \cup L(\emptyset) \cup L(\emptyset)L(\emptyset) \cup \cdots$$

Since all the terms but the first are empty, we see that $L(\emptyset) = \{\epsilon\}$, which is the same as $L(\epsilon)$. Thus, $\mathbf{1}\emptyset^*(\mathbf{0}+\mathbf{1})$ is equivalent to $\mathbf{1}(\mathbf{0}+\mathbf{1})$, which is the expression we use for the arc $A \to C$ in Fig. 3.13.

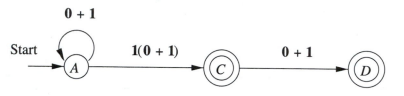

Figure 3.13: Eliminating state B

Now, we must branch, eliminating states C and D in separate reductions. To eliminate state C, the mechanics are similar to those we performed above to eliminate state B, and the resulting automaton is shown in Fig. 3.14.

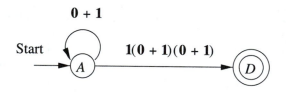

Figure 3.14: A two-state automaton with states A and D

In terms of the generic two-state automaton of Fig. 3.9, the regular expressions from Fig. 3.14 are: $R = \mathbf{0} + \mathbf{1}$, $S = \mathbf{1}(\mathbf{0}+\mathbf{1})(\mathbf{0}+\mathbf{1})$, $T = \emptyset$, and $U = \emptyset$. The expression U^* can be replaced by ϵ, i.e., eliminated in a concatenation; the justification is that $\emptyset^* = \epsilon$, as we discussed above. Also, the expression SU^*T is equivalent to $\emptyset$, since T, one of the terms of the concatenation, is $\emptyset$. The generic expression $(R + SU^*T)^*SU^*$ thus simplifies in this case to R^*S, or $(\mathbf{0}+\mathbf{1})^*\mathbf{1}(\mathbf{0}+\mathbf{1})(\mathbf{0}+\mathbf{1})$. In informal terms, the language of this expression is any string ending in 1, followed by two symbols that are each either 0 or 1. That language is one portion of the strings accepted by the automaton of Fig. 3.11: those strings whose third position from the end has a 1.

Now, we must start again at Fig. 3.13 and eliminate state D instead of C. Since D has no successors, an inspection of Fig. 3.7 tells us that there will be no changes to arcs, and the arc from C to D is eliminated, along with state D. The resulting two-state automaton is shown in Fig. 3.15.

Ordering the Elimination of States

As we observed in Example 3.6, when a state is neither the start state nor an accepting state, it gets eliminated in all the derived automata. Thus, one of the advantages of the state-elimination process compared with the mechanical generation of regular expressions that we described in Section 3.2.1 is that we can start by eliminating all the states that are neither start nor accepting, once and for all. We only have to begin duplicating the reduction effort when we need to eliminate some accepting states.

Even there, we can combine some of the effort. For instance, if there are three accepting states p, q, and r, we can eliminate p and then branch to eliminate either q or r, thus producing the automata for accepting states r and q, respectively. We then start again with all three accepting states and eliminate both q and r to get the automaton for p.

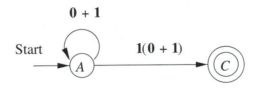
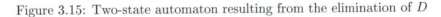

Figure 3.15: Two-state automaton resulting from the elimination of D

This automaton is very much like that of Fig. 3.14; only the label on the arc from the start state to the accepting state is different. Thus, we can apply the rule for two-state automata and simplify the expression to get $(0+1)^*1(0+1)$. This expression represents the other type of string the automaton accepts: those with a 1 in the second position from the end.

All that remains is to sum the two expressions to get the expression for the entire automaton of Fig. 3.11. This expression is

$$(0+1)^*1(0+1) + (0+1)^*1(0+1)(0+1)$$

□

3.2.3 Converting Regular Expressions to Automata

We shall now complete the plan of Fig. 3.1 by showing that every language L that is $L(R)$ for some regular expression R, is also $L(E)$ for some ϵ-NFA E. The proof is a structural induction on the expression R. We start by showing how to construct automata for the basis expressions: single symbols, ϵ, and $\emptyset$. We then show how to combine these automata into larger automata that accept the union, concatenation, or closure of the language accepted by smaller automata.

All of the automata we construct are ϵ-NFA's with a single accepting state.

Theorem 3.7 : Every language defined by a regular expression is also defined by a finite automaton.

PROOF: Suppose $L = L(R)$ for a regular expression R. We show that $L = L(E)$ for some ϵ-NFA E with:

1. Exactly one accepting state.

2. No arcs into the initial state.

3. No arcs out of the accepting state.

The proof is by structural induction on R, following the recursive definition of regular expressions that we had in Section 3.1.2.

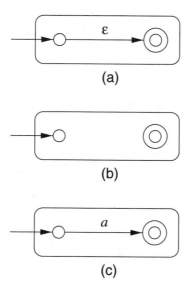

Figure 3.16: The basis of the construction of an automaton from a regular expression

BASIS: There are three parts to the basis, shown in Fig. 3.16. In part (a) we see how to handle the expression ϵ. The language of the automaton is easily seen to be $\{\epsilon\}$, since the only path from the start state to an accepting state is labeled ϵ. Part (b) shows the construction for $\emptyset$. Clearly there are no paths from start state to accepting state, so $\emptyset$ is the language of this automaton. Finally, part (c) gives the automaton for a regular expression **a**. The language of this automaton evidently consists of the one string a, which is also $L(\mathbf{a})$. It is easy to check that these automata all satisfy conditions (1), (2), and (3) of the inductive hypothesis.

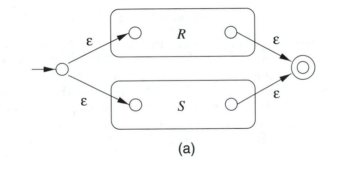

(a)

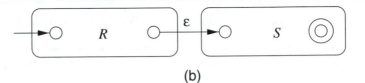

(b)

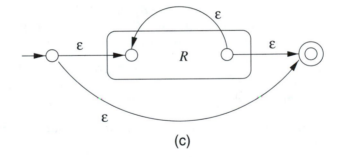

(c)

Figure 3.17: The inductive step in the regular-expression-to-ϵ-NFA construction

INDUCTION: The three parts of the induction are shown in Fig. 3.17. We assume that the statement of the theorem is true for the immediate subexpressions of a given regular expression; that is, the languages of these subexpressions are also the languages of ϵ-NFA's with a single accepting state. The four cases are:

1. The expression is $R + S$ for some smaller expressions R and S. Then the automaton of Fig. 3.17(a) serves. That is, starting at the new start state, we can go to the start state of either the automaton for R or the automaton for S. We then reach the accepting state of one of these automata, following a path labeled by some string in $L(R)$ or $L(S)$, respectively. Once we reach the accepting state of the automaton for R or S, we can follow one of the ϵ-arcs to the accepting state of the new automaton.

Thus, the language of the automaton in Fig. 3.17(a) is $L(R) \cup L(S)$.

2. The expression is RS for some smaller expressions R and S. The automaton for the concatenation is shown in Fig. 3.17(b). Note that the start state of the first automaton becomes the start state of the whole, and the accepting state of the second automaton becomes the accepting state of the whole. The idea is that the only paths from start to accepting state go first through the automaton for R, where it must follow a path labeled by a string in $L(R)$, and then through the automaton for S, where it follows a path labeled by a string in $L(S)$. Thus, the paths in the automaton of Fig. 3.17(b) are all and only those labeled by strings in $L(R)L(S)$.

3. The expression is R^* for some smaller expression R. Then we use the automaton of Fig. 3.17(c). That automaton allows us to go either:

   (a) Directly from the start state to the accepting state along a path labeled ϵ. That path lets us accept ϵ, which is in $L(R^*)$ no matter what expression R is.

   (b) To the start state of the automaton for R, through that automaton one or more times, and then to the accepting state. This set of paths allows us to accept strings in $L(R)$, $L(R)L(R)$, $L(R)L(R)L(R)$, and so on, thus covering all strings in $L(R^*)$ except perhaps ϵ, which was covered by the direct arc to the accepting state mentioned in (3a).

4. The expression is (R) for some smaller expression R. The automaton for R also serves as the automaton for (R), since the parentheses do not change the language defined by the expression.

It is a simple observation that the constructed automata satisfy the three conditions given in the inductive hypothesis — one accepting state, with no arcs into the initial state or out of the accepting state.   □

Example 3.8: Let us convert the regular expression $(\mathbf{0} + \mathbf{1})^*\mathbf{1}(\mathbf{0} + \mathbf{1})$ to an ϵ-NFA. Our first step is to construct an automaton for $\mathbf{0} + \mathbf{1}$. We use two automata constructed according to Fig. 3.16(c), one with label $\mathbf{0}$ on the arc and one with label $\mathbf{1}$. These two automata are then combined using the union construction of Fig. 3.17(a). The result is shown in Fig. 3.18(a).

Next, we apply to Fig. 3.18(a) the star construction of Fig. 3.17(c). This automaton is shown in Fig. 3.18(b). The last two steps involve applying the concatenation construction of Fig. 3.17(b). First, we connect the automaton of Fig. 3.18(b) to another automaton designed to accept only the string 1. This automaton is another application of the basis construction of Fig. 3.16(c) with label $\mathbf{1}$ on the arc. Note that we must create a *new* automaton to recognize 1; we must not use the automaton for 1 that was part of Fig. 3.18(a). The third automaton in the concatenation is another automaton for $\mathbf{0} + \mathbf{1}$. Again, we must create a copy of the automaton of Fig. 3.18(a); we must not use the same copy that became part of Fig. 3.18(b). The complete automaton is shown in

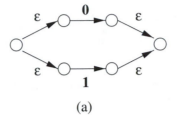

(a)

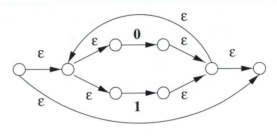

(b)

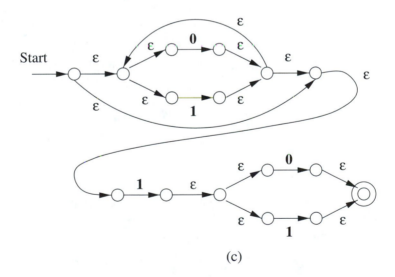

(c)

Figure 3.18: Automata constructed for Example 3.8

Fig. 3.18(c). Note that this ϵ-NFA, when ϵ-transitions are removed, looks just like the much simpler automaton of Fig. 3.15 that also accepts the strings that have a 1 in their next-to-last position. □

3.2.4 Exercises for Section 3.2

Exercise 3.2.1: Here is a transition table for a DFA:

	0	1
→ q_1	q_2	q_1
q_2	q_3	q_1
*q_3	q_3	q_2

* a) Give all the regular expressions $R_{ij}^{(0)}$. *Note*: Think of state q_i as if it were the state with integer number i.

* b) Give all the regular expressions $R_{ij}^{(1)}$. Try to simplify the expressions as much as possible.

  c) Give all the regular expressions $R_{ij}^{(2)}$. Try to simplify the expressions as much as possible.

  d) Give a regular expression for the language of the automaton.

* e) Construct the transition diagram for the DFA and give a regular expression for its language by eliminating state q_2.

Exercise 3.2.2: Repeat Exercise 3.2.1 for the following DFA:

	0	1
→ q_1	q_2	q_3
q_2	q_1	q_3
*q_3	q_2	q_1

Note that solutions to parts (a), (b) and (e) are *not* available for this exercise.

Exercise 3.2.3: Convert the following DFA to a regular expression, using the state-elimination technique of Section 3.2.2.

	0	1
→ *p	s	p
q	p	s
r	r	q
s	q	r

Exercise 3.2.4: Convert the following regular expressions to NFA's with ϵ-transitions.

* a) **01***.

b) **(0 + 1)01**.

c) **00(0 + 1)***.

Exercise 3.2.5: Eliminate ϵ-transitions from your ϵ-NFA's of Exercise 3.2.4. A solution to part (a) appears in the book's Web pages.

! **Exercise 3.2.6:** Let $A = (Q, \Sigma, \delta, q_0, \{q_f\})$ be an ϵ-NFA such that there are no transitions into q_0 and no transitions out of q_f. Describe the language accepted by each of the following modifications of A, in terms of $L = L(A)$:

* a) The automaton constructed from A by adding an ϵ-transition from q_f to q_0.

* b) The automaton constructed from A by adding an ϵ-transition from q_0 to every state reachable from q_0 (along a path whose labels may include symbols of Σ as well as ϵ).

c) The automaton constructed from A by adding an ϵ-transition to q_f from every state that can reach q_f along some path.

d) The automaton constructed from A by doing both (b) and (c).

!! **Exercise 3.2.7:** There are some simplifications to the constructions of Theorem 3.7, where we converted a regular expression to an ϵ-NFA. Here are three:

1. For the union operator, instead of creating new start and accepting states, merge the two start states into one state with all the transitions of both start states. Likewise, merge the two accepting states, having all transitions to either go to the merged state instead.

2. For the concatenation operator, merge the accepting state of the first automaton with the start state of the second.

3. For the closure operator, simply add ϵ-transitions from the accepting state to the start state and vice-versa.

Each of these simplifications, by themselves, still yield a correct construction; that is, the resulting ϵ-NFA for any regular expression accepts the language of the expression. Which subsets of changes (1), (2), and (3) may be made to the construction together, while still yielding a correct automaton for every regular expression?

*!! **Exercise 3.2.8:** Give an algorithm that takes a DFA A and computes the number of strings of length n (for some given n, not related to the number of states of A) accepted by A. Your algorithm should be polynomial in both n and the number of states of A. *Hint:* Use the technique suggested by the construction of Theorem 3.4.

3.3   Applications of Regular Expressions

A regular expression that gives a "picture" of the pattern we want to recognize is the medium of choice for applications that search for patterns in text. The regular expressions are then compiled, behind the scenes, into deterministic or nondeterministic automata, which are then simulated to produce a program that recognizes patterns in text. In this section, we shall consider two important classes of regular-expression-based applications: lexical analyzers and text search.

3.3.1   Regular Expressions in UNIX

Before seeing the applications, we shall introduce the UNIX notation for extended regular expressions. This notation gives us a number of additional capabilities. In fact, the UNIX extensions include certain features, especially the ability to name and refer to previous strings that have matched a pattern, that actually allow nonregular languages to be recognized. We shall not consider these features here; rather we shall only introduce the shorthands that allow complex regular expressions to be written succinctly.

The first enhancement to the regular-expression notation concerns the fact that most real applications deal with the ASCII character set. Our examples have typically used a small alphabet, such as $\{0, 1\}$. The existence of only two symbols allowed us to write succinct expressions like $\mathbf{0} + \mathbf{1}$ for "any character." However, if there were 128 characters, say, the same expression would involve listing them all, and would be highly inconvenient to write. Thus, UNIX regular expressions allow us to write *character classes* to represent large sets of characters as succinctly as possible. The rules for character classes are:

- The symbol . (dot) stands for "any character."

- The sequence $[a_1 a_2 \cdots a_k]$ stands for the regular expression

$$a_1 + a_2 + \cdots + a_k$$

    This notation saves about half the characters, since we don't have to write the +-signs. For example, we could express the four characters used in C comparison operators by [<>=!].

- Between the square braces we can put a range of the form $x\text{-}y$ to mean all the characters from x to y in the ASCII sequence. Since the digits have codes in order, as do the upper-case letters and the lower-case letters, we can express many of the classes of characters that we really care about with just a few keystrokes. For example, the digits can be expressed [0-9], the upper-case letters can be expressed [A-Z], and the set of all letters and digits can be expressed [A-Za-z0-9]. If we want to include a minus sign among a list of characters, we can place it first or last, so it is not confused with its use to form a character range. For example, the set of digits, plus the dot, plus, and minus signs that are used to form signed decimal numbers may be expressed `[-+.0-9]`. Square brackets, or other characters that have special meanings in UNIX regular expressions can be represented as characters by preceding them with a backslash (\).

- There are special notations for several of the most common classes of characters. For instance:

  a) `[:digit:]` is the set of ten digits, the same as `[0-9]`.[3]

  b) `[:alpha:]` stands for any alphabetic character, as does `[A-Za-z]`.

  c) `[:alnum:]` stands for the digits and letters (alphabetic and numeric characters), as does `[A-Za-z0-9]`.

In addition, there are several operators that are used in UNIX regular expressions that we have not encountered previously. None of these operators extend what languages can be expressed, but they sometimes make it easier to express what we want.

1. The operator | is used in place of + to denote union.

2. The operator ? means "zero or one of." Thus, $R?$ in UNIX is the same as $\epsilon + R$ in this book's regular-expression notation.

3. The operator + means "one or more of." Thus, $R+$ in UNIX is shorthand for RR^* in our notation.

4. The operator $\{n\}$ means "n copies of." Thus, $R\{5\}$ in UNIX is shorthand for $RRRRR$.

Note that UNIX regular expressions allow parentheses to group subexpressions, just as for the regular expressions described in Section 3.1.2, and the same operator precedence is used (with ?, + and $\{n\}$ treated like $*$ as far as precedence is concerned). The star operator $*$ is used in UNIX (without being a superscript, of course) with the same meaning as we have used.

3.3.2 Lexical Analysis

One of the oldest applications of regular expressions was in specifying the component of a compiler called a "lexical analyzer." This component scans the source program and recognizes all *tokens*, those substrings of consecutive characters that belong together logically. Keywords and identifiers are common examples of tokens, but there are many others.

---

[3]The notation `[:digit:]` has the advantage that should some code other than ASCII be used, including a code where the digits did not have consecutive codes, `[:digit:]` would still represent `[0123456789]`, while `[0-9]` would represent whatever characters had codes between the codes for 0 and 9, inclusive.

The Complete Story for UNIX Regular Expressions

The reader who wants to get the complete list of operators and short-hands available in the UNIX regular-expression notation can find them in the manual pages for various commands. There are some differences among the various versions of UNIX, but a command like man grep will get you the notation used for the grep command, which is fundamental. "Grep" stands for "Global (search for) Regular Expression and Print," incidentally.

The UNIX command lex and its GNU version flex, accept as input a list of regular expressions, in the UNIX style, each followed by a bracketed section of code that indicates what the lexical analyzer is to do when it finds an instance of that token. Such a facility is called a *lexical-analyzer generator*, because it takes as input a high-level description of a lexical analyzer and produces from it a function that is a working lexical analyzer.

Commands such as lex and flex have been found extremely useful because the regular-expression notation is exactly as powerful as we need to describe tokens. These commands are able to use the regular-expression-to-DFA conversion process to generate an efficient function that breaks source programs into tokens. They make the implementation of a lexical analyzer an afternoon's work, while before the development of these regular-expression-based tools, the hand-generation of the lexical analyzer could take months. Further, if we need to modify the lexical analyzer for any reason, it is often a simple matter to change a regular expression or two, instead of having to go into mysterious code to fix a bug.

Example 3.9: In Fig. 3.19 is an example of partial input to the lex command, describing some of the tokens that are found in the language C. The first line handles the keyword else and the action is to return a symbolic constant (ELSE in this example) to the parser for further processing. The second line contains a regular expression describing identifiers: a letter followed by zero or more letters and/or digits. The action is first to enter that identifier in the symbol table if not already there; lex isolates the token found in a buffer, so this piece of code knows exactly what identifier was found. Finally, the lexical analyzer returns the symbolic constant ID, which has been chosen in this example to represent identifiers.

The third entry in Fig. 3.19 is for the sign >=, a two-character operator. The last example we show is for the sign =, a one-character operator. There would in practice appear expressions describing each of the keywords, each of the signs and punctuation symbols like commas and parentheses, and families of constants such as numbers and strings. Many of these are very simple, just a sequence of one or more specific characters. However, some have more

```
else                     {return(ELSE);}

[A-Za-z][A-Za-z0-9]*     {code to enter the found identifier
                          in the symbol table;
                          return(ID);
                         }

>=                       {return(GE);}

=                        {return(EQ);}

...
```

Figure 3.19: A sample of lex input

of the flavor of identifiers, requiring the full power of the regular-expression notation to describe. The integers, floating-point numbers, character strings, and comments are other examples of sets of strings that profit from the regular-expression capabilities of commands like lex. □

The conversion of a collection of expressions, such as those suggested in Fig. 3.19, to an automaton proceeds approximately as we have described formally in the preceding sections. We start by building an automaton for the union of all the expressions. This automaton in principle tells us only that *some* token has been recognized. However, if we follow the construction of Theorem 3.7 for the union of expressions, the ϵ-NFA state tells us exactly which token has been recognized.

The only problem is that more than one token may be recognized at once; for instance, the string else matches not only the regular expression **else** but also the expression for identifiers. The standard resolution is for the lexical-analyzer generator to give priority to the first expression listed. Thus, if we want keywords like else to be *reserved* (not usable as identifiers), we simply list them ahead of the expression for identifiers.

3.3.3 Finding Patterns in Text

In Section 2.4.1 we introduced the notion that automata could be used to search efficiently for a set of words in a large repository such as the Web. While the tools and technology for doing so are not so well developed as that for lexical analyzers, the regular-expression notation is valuable for describing searches for interesting patterns. As for lexical analyzers, the capability to go from the natural, descriptive regular-expression notation to an efficient (automaton-based) implementation offers substantial intellectual leverage.

The general problem for which regular-expression technology has been found useful is the description of a vaguely defined class of patterns in text. The vagueness of the description virtually guarantees that we shall not describe the pattern correctly at first — perhaps we can never get exactly the right description. By using regular-expression notation, it becomes easy to describe the patterns at a high level, with little effort, and to modify the description quickly when things go wrong. A "compiler" for regular expressions is useful to turn the expressions we write into executable code.

Let us explore an extended example of the sort of problem that arises in many Web applications. Suppose that we want to scan a very large number of Web pages and detect addresses. We might simply want to create a mailing list. Or, perhaps we are trying to classify businesses by their location so that we can answer queries like "find me a restaurant within 10 minutes drive of where I am now."

We shall focus on recognizing street addresses in particular. What is a street address? We'll have to figure that out, and if, while testing the software, we find we miss some cases, we'll have to modify the expressions to capture what we were missing. To begin, a street address will probably end in "Street" or its abbreviation, "St." However, some people live on "Avenues" or "Roads," and these might be abbreviated in the address as well. Thus, we might use as the ending for our regular expression something like:

Street|St\.|Avenue|Ave\.|Road|Rd\.

In the above expression, we have used UNIX-style notation, with the vertical bar, rather than +, as the union operator. Note also that the dots are *escaped* with a preceding backslash, since dot has the special meaning of "any character" in UNIX expressions, and in this case we really want only the period or "dot" character to end the three abbreviations.

The designation such as Street must be preceded by the name of the street. Usually, the name is a capital letter followed by some lower-case letters. We can describe this pattern by the UNIX expression [A-Z][a-z]*. However, some streets have a name consisting of more than one word, such as Rhode Island Avenue in Washington DC. Thus, after discovering that we were missing addresses of this form, we could revise our description of street names to be

'[A-Z][a-z]*([A-Z][a-z]*)*'

The expression above starts with a group consisting of a capital and zero or more lower-case letters. There follow zero or more groups consisting of a blank, another capital letter, and zero or more lower-case letters. The blank is an ordinary character in UNIX expressions, but to avoid having the above expression look like two expressions separated by a blank in a UNIX command line, we are required to place quotation marks around the whole expression. The quotes are not part of the expression itself.

Now, we need to include the house number as part of the address. Most house numbers are a string of digits. However, some will have a letter following, as in "123A Main St." Thus, the expression we use for numbers has an optional capital letter following: [0-9]+[A-Z]?. Notice that we use the UNIX + operator for "one or more" digits and the ? operator for "zero or one" capital letter. The entire expression we have developed for street addresses is:

```
'[0-9]+[A-Z]? [A-Z][a-z]*( [A-Z][a-z]*)*
(Street|St\.|Avenue|Ave\.|Road|Rd\.)'
```

If we work with this expression, we shall do fairly well. However, we shall eventually discover that we are missing:

1. Streets that are called something other than a street, avenue, or road. For example, we shall miss "Boulevard," "Place," "Way," and their abbreviations.

2. Street names that are numbers, or partially numbers, like "42nd Street."

3. Post-Office boxes and rural-delivery routes.

4. Street names that don't end in anything like "Street." An example is El Camino Real in Silicon Valley. Being Spanish for "the royal road," saying "El Camino Real Road" would be redundant, so one has to deal with complete addresses like "2000 El Camino Real."

5. All sorts of strange things we can't even imagine. Can you?

Thus, having a regular-expression compiler can make the process of slow convergence to the complete recognizer for addresses much easier than if we had to recode every change directly in a conventional programming language.

3.3.4 Exercises for Section 3.3

! **Exercise 3.3.1:** Give a regular expression to describe phone numbers in all the various forms you can think of. Consider international numbers as well as the fact that different countries have different numbers of digits in area codes and in local phone numbers.

!! **Exercise 3.3.2:** Give a regular expression to represent salaries as they might appear in employment advertising. Consider that salaries might be given on a per hour, week, month, or year basis. They may or may not appear with a dollar sign, or other unit such as "K" following. There may be a word or words nearby that identify a salary. Suggestion: look at classified ads in a newspaper, or on-line jobs listings to get an idea of what patterns might be useful.

! **Exercise 3.3.3:** At the end of Section 3.3.3 we gave some examples of improvements that could be possible for the regular expression that describes addresses. Modify the expression developed there to include all the mentioned options.

3.4   Algebraic Laws for Regular Expressions

In Example 3.5, we saw the need for simplifying regular expressions, in order to keep the size of expressions manageable. There, we gave some ad-hoc arguments why one expression could be replaced by another. In all cases, the basic issue was that the two expressions were *equivalent*, in the sense that they defined the same languages. In this section, we shall offer a collection of algebraic laws that bring to a higher level the issue of when two regular expressions are equivalent. Instead of examining specific regular expressions, we shall consider pairs of regular expressions with variables as arguments. Two expressions with variables are *equivalent* if whatever languages we substitute for the variables, the results of the two expressions are the same language.

An example of this process in the algebra of arithmetic is as follows. It is one matter to say that $1+2 = 2+1$. That is an example of the commutative law of addition, and it is easy to check by applying the addition operator on both sides and getting $3 = 3$. However, the *commutative law of addition* says more; it says that $x + y = y + x$, where x and y are variables that can be replaced by any two numbers. That is, no matter what two numbers we add, we get the same result regardless of the order in which we sum them.

Like arithmetic expressions, the regular expressions have a number of laws that work for them. Many of these are similar to the laws for arithmetic, if we think of union as addition and concatenation as multiplication. However, there are a few places where the analogy breaks down, and there are also some laws that apply to regular expressions but have no analog for arithmetic, especially when the closure operator is involved. The next sections form a catalog of the major laws. We conclude with a discussion of how one can check whether a proposed law for regular expressions is indeed a law; i.e., it will hold for any languages that we may substitute for the variables.

3.4.1   Associativity and Commutativity

Commutativity is the property of an operator that says we can switch the order of its operands and get the same result. An example for arithmetic was given above: $x + y = y + x$. *Associativity* is the property of an operator that allows us to regroup the operands when the operator is applied twice. For example, the associative law of multiplication is $(x \times y) \times z = x \times (y \times z)$. Here are three laws of these types that hold for regular expressions:

- $L + M = M + L$. This law, the *commutative law for union*, says that we may take the union of two languages in either order.

- $(L + M) + N = L + (M + N)$. This law, the *associative law for union*, says that we may take the union of three languages either by taking the union of the first two initially, or taking the union of the last two initially. Note that, together with the commutative law for union, we conclude that we can take the union of any collection of languages with any order and grouping, and the result will be the same. Intuitively, a string is in $L_1 \cup L_2 \cup \cdots \cup L_k$ if and only if it is in one or more of the L_i's.

- $(LM)N = L(MN)$. This law, the *associative law for concatenation*, says that we can concatenate three languages by concatenating either the first two or the last two initially.

Missing from this list is the "law" $LM = ML$, which would say that concatenation is commutative. However, this law is false.

Example 3.10: Consider the regular expressions **01** and **10**. These expressions denote the languages $\{01\}$ and $\{10\}$, respectively. Since the languages are different the general law $LM = ML$ cannot hold. If it did, we could substitute the regular expression **0** for L and **1** for M and conclude falsely that **01** = **10**.
□

3.4.2 Identities and Annihilators

An *identity* for an operator is a value such that when the operator is applied to the identity and some other value, the result is the other value. For instance, 0 is the identity for addition, since $0 + x = x + 0 = x$, and 1 is the identity for multiplication, since $1 \times x = x \times 1 = x$. An *annihilator* for an operator is a value such that when the operator is applied to the annihilator and some other value, the result is the annihilator. For instance, 0 is an annihilator for multiplication, since $0 \times x = x \times 0 = 0$. There is no annihilator for addition.

There are three laws for regular expressions involving these concepts; we list them below.

- $\emptyset + L = L + \emptyset = L$. This law asserts that $\emptyset$ is the identity for union.

- $\epsilon L = L\epsilon = L$. This law asserts that ϵ is the identity for concatenation.

- $\emptyset L = L\emptyset = \emptyset$. This law asserts that $\emptyset$ is the annihilator for concatenation.

These laws are powerful tools in simplifications. For example, if we have a union of several expressions, some of which are, or have been simplified to $\emptyset$, then the $\emptyset$'s can be dropped from the union. Likewise, if we have a concatenation of several expressions, some of which are, or have been simplified to ϵ, we can drop the ϵ's from the concatenation. Finally, if we have a concatenation of any number of expressions, and even one of them is $\emptyset$, then the entire concatenation can be replaced by $\emptyset$.

3.4.3 Distributive Laws

A *distributive law* involves two operators, and asserts that one operator can be pushed down to be applied to each argument of the other operator individually. The most common example from arithmetic is the distributive law of multiplication over addition, that is, $x \times (y + z) = x \times y + x \times z$. Since multiplication is commutative, it doesn't matter whether the multiplication is on the left or right of the sum. However, there is an analogous law for regular expressions, that we must state in two forms, since concatenation is not commutative. These laws are:

- $L(M + N) = LM + LN$. This law, is the *left distributive law of concatenation over union.*

- $(M + N)L = ML + NL$. This law, is the *right distributive law of concatenation over union.*

Let us prove the left distributive law; the other is proved similarly. The proof will refer to languages only; it does not depend on the languages having regular expressions.

Theorem 3.11: If L, M, and N are any languages, then

$$L(M \cup N) = LM \cup LN$$

PROOF: The proof is similar to another proof about a distributive law that we saw in Theorem 1.10. We need first to show that a string w is in $L(M \cup N)$ if and only if it is in $LM \cup LN$.

(Only if) If w is in $L(M \cup N)$, then $w = xy$, where x is in L and y is in either M or N. If y is in M, then xy is in LM, and therefore in $LM \cup LN$. Likewise, if y is in N, then xy is in LN and therefore in $LM \cup LN$.

(If) Suppose w is in $LM \cup LN$. Then w is in either LM or in LN. Suppose first that w is in LM. Then $w = xy$, where x is in L and y is in M. As y is in M, it is also in $M \cup N$. Thus, xy is in $L(M \cup N)$. If w is not in LM, then it is surely in LN, and a similar argument shows it is in $L(M \cup N)$. □

Example 3.12: Consider the regular expression $0 + 01^*$. We can "factor out a **0**" from the union, but first we have to recognize that the expression **0** by itself is actually the concatenation of **0** with something, namely ϵ. That is, we use the identity law for concatenation to replace **0** by 0ϵ, giving us the expression $0\epsilon + 01^*$. Now, we can apply the left distributive law to replace this expression by $0(\epsilon + 1^*)$. If we further recognize that ϵ is in $L(1^*)$, then we observe that $\epsilon + 1^* = 1^*$, and can simplify to 01^*. □

3.4.4   The Idempotent Law

An operator is said to be *idempotent* if the result of applying it to two of the same values as arguments is that value. The common arithmetic operators are not idempotent; $x + x \neq x$ in general and $x \times x \neq x$ in general (although there are *some* values of x for which the equality holds, such as $0 + 0 = 0$). However, union and intersection are common examples of idempotent operators. Thus, for regular expressions, we may assert the following law:

- $L + L = L$. This law, the *idempotence law for union*, states that if we take the union of two identical expressions, we can replace them by one copy of the expression.

3.4.5 Laws Involving Closures

There are a number of laws involving the closure operators and its UNIX-style variants $+$ and ?. We shall list them here, and give some explanation for why they are true.

- $(L^*)^* = L^*$. This law says that closing an expression that is already closed does not change the language. The language of $(L^*)^*$ is all strings created by concatenating strings in the language of L^*. But those strings are themselves composed of strings from L. Thus, the string in $(L^*)^*$ is also a concatenation of strings from L and is therefore in the language of L^*.

- $\emptyset^* = \epsilon$. The closure of $\emptyset$ contains only the string ϵ, as we discussed in Example 3.6.

- $\epsilon^* = \epsilon$. It is easy to check that the only string that can be formed by concatenating any number of copies of the empty string is the empty string itself.

- $L^+ = LL^* = L^*L$. Recall that L^+ is defined to be $L + LL + LLL + \cdots$. Also, $L^* = \epsilon + L + LL + LLL + \cdots$. Thus,

$$LL^* = L\epsilon + LL + LLL + LLLL + \cdots$$

When we remember that $L\epsilon = L$, we see that the infinite expansions for LL^* and for L^+ are the same. That proves $L^+ = LL^*$. The proof that $L^+ = L^*L$ is similar.[4]

- $L^* = L^+ + \epsilon$. The proof is easy, since the expansion of L^+ includes every term in the expansion of L^* except ϵ. Note that if the language L contains the string ϵ, then the additional "$+\epsilon$ term is not needed; that is, $L^+ = L^*$ in this special case.

- $L? = \epsilon + L$. This rule is really the definition of the ? operator.

3.4.6 Discovering Laws for Regular Expressions

Each of the laws above was proved, formally or informally. However, there is an infinite variety of laws about regular expressions that might be proposed. Is there a general methodology that will make our proofs of the correct laws

---

[4]Notice that, as a consequence, any language L commutes (under concatenation) with its own closure; $LL^* = L^*L$. That rule does not contradict the fact that, in general, concatenation is not commutative.

easy? It turns out that the truth of a law reduces to a question of the equality of two specific languages. Interestingly, the technique is closely tied to the regular-expression operators, and cannot be extended to expressions involving some other operators, such as intersection.

To see how this test works, let us consider a proposed law, such as

$$(L + M)^* = (L^*M^*)^*$$

This law says that if we have any two languages L and M, and we close their union, we get the same language as if we take the language L^*M^*, that is, all strings composed of zero or more choices from L followed by zero or more choices from M, and close that language.

To prove this law, suppose first that string w is in the language of $(L+M)^*$.[5] Then we can write $w = w_1w_2 \cdots w_k$ for some k, where each w_i is in either L or M. It follows that each w_i is in the language of L^*M^*. To see why, if w is in L, pick one string, w_i, from L; this string is also in L^*. Pick no strings from M; that is, pick ϵ from M^*. If w_i is in M, the argument is similar. Once every w_i is seen to be in L^*M^*, it follows that w is in the closure of this language.

To complete the proof, we also have to prove the converse: that strings in $(L^*M^*)^*$ are also in $(L + M)^*$. We omit this part of the proof, since our objective is not to prove the law, but to notice the following important property of regular expressions.

Any regular expression with variables can be thought of as a *concrete* regular expression, one that has no variables, by thinking of each variable as if it were a distinct symbol. For example, the expression $(L+M)^*$ can have variables L and M replaced by symbols a and b, respectively, giving us the regular expression $(\mathbf{a} + \mathbf{b})^*$.

The language of the concrete expression guides us regarding the form of strings in any language that is formed from the original expression when we replace the variables by languages. Thus, in our analysis of $(L + M)^*$, we observed that any string w composed of a sequence of choices from either L or M, would be in the language of $(L + M)^*$. We can arrive at that conclusion by looking at the language of the concrete expression, $L((\mathbf{a} + \mathbf{b})^*)$, which is evidently the set of all strings of a's and b's. We could substitute any string in L for any occurrence of a in one of those strings, and we could substitute any string in M for any occurrence of b, with possibly different choices of strings for different occurrences of a or b. Those substitutions, applied to all the strings in $(\mathbf{a} + \mathbf{b})^*$, gives us all strings formed by concatenating strings from L and/or M, in any order.

The above statement may seem obvious, but as is pointed out in the box on "Extensions of the Test Beyond Regular Expressions May Fail," it is not even true when some other operators are added to the three regular-expression operators. We prove the general principle for regular expressions in the next theorem.

---

[5]For simplicity, we shall identify the regular expressions and their languages, and avoid saying "the language of" in front of every regular expression.

Theorem 3.13: Let E be a regular expression with variables $L_1, L_2, \ldots, L_m$. Form concrete regular expression C by replacing each occurrence of L_i by the symbol a_i, for $i = 1, 2, \ldots, m$. Then for any languages $L_1, L_2, \ldots, L_m$, every string w in $L(E)$ can be written $w = w_1 w_2 \cdots w_k$, where each w_i is in one of the languages, say L_{j_i}, and the string $a_{j_1} a_{j_2} \cdots a_{j_k}$ is in the language $L(C)$. Less formally, we can construct $L(E)$ by starting with each string in $L(C)$, say $a_{j_1} a_{j_2} \cdots a_{j_k}$, and substituting for each of the a_{j_i}'s any string from the corresponding language L_{j_i}.

PROOF: The proof is a structural induction on the expression E.

BASIS: The basis cases are where E is ϵ, $\emptyset$, or a variable L. In the first two cases, there is nothing to prove, since the concrete expression C is the same as E. If E is a variable L, then $L(E) = L$. The concrete expression C is just $\mathbf{a}$, where a is the symbol corresponding to L. Thus, $L(C) = \{a\}$. If we substitute any string in L for the symbol a in this one string, we get the language L, which is also $L(E)$.

INDUCTION: There are three cases, depending on the final operator of E. First, suppose that $E = F + G$; i.e., a union is the final operator. Let C and D be the concrete expressions formed from F and G, respectively, by substituting concrete symbols for the language-variables in these expressions. Note that the same symbol must be substituted for all occurrences of the same variable, in both F and G. Then the concrete expression that we get from E is $C + D$, and $L(C + D) = L(C) + L(D)$.

Suppose that w is a string in $L(E)$, when the language variables of E are replaced by specific languages. Then w is in either $L(F)$ or $L(G)$. By the inductive hypothesis, w is obtained by starting with a concrete string in $L(C)$ or $L(D)$, respectively, and substituting for the symbols strings in the corresponding languages. Thus, in either case, the string w can be constructed by starting with a concrete string in $L(C+D)$, and making the same substitutions of strings for symbols.

We must also consider the cases where E is FG or F^*. However, the arguments are similar to the union case above, and we leave them for you to complete. $\square$

3.4.7 The Test for a Regular-Expression Algebraic Law

Now, we can state and prove the test for whether or not a law of regular expressions is true. The test for whether $E = F$ is true, where E and F are two regular expressions with the same set of variables, is:

1. Convert E and F to concrete regular expressions C and D, respectively, by replacing each variable by a concrete symbol.

2. Test whether $L(C) = L(D)$. If so, then $E = F$ is a true law, and if not, then the "law" is false. Note that we shall not see the test for whether two

regular expressions denote the same language until Section 4.4. However, we can use ad-hoc means to decide the equality of the pairs of languages that we actually care about. Recall that if the languages are *not* the same, than it is sufficient to provide one counterexample: a single string that is in one language but not the other.

Theorem 3.14: The above test correctly identifies the true laws for regular expressions.

PROOF: We shall show that $L(E) = L(F)$ for any languages in place of the variables of E and F if and only if $L(C) = L(D)$.

(Only if) Suppose $L(E) = L(F)$ for all choices of languages for the variables. In particular, choose for every variable L the concrete symbol a that replaces L in expressions C and D. Then for this choice, $L(C) = L(E)$, and $L(D) = L(F)$. Since $L(E) = L(F)$ is given, it follows that $L(C) = L(D)$.

(If) Suppose $L(C) = L(D)$. By Theorem 3.13, $L(E)$ and $L(F)$ are each constructed by replacing the concrete symbols of strings in $L(C)$ and $L(D)$, respectively, by strings in the languages that correspond to those symbols. If the strings of $L(C)$ and $L(D)$ are the same, then the two languages constructed in this manner will also be the same; that is, $L(E) = L(F)$. □

Example 3.15: Consider the prospective law $(L + M)^* = (L^*M^*)^*$. If we replace variables L and M by concrete symbols a and b respectively, we get the regular expressions $(\mathbf{a} + \mathbf{b})^*$ and $(\mathbf{a}^*\mathbf{b}^*)^*$. It is easy to check that both these expressions denote the language with all strings of a's and b's. Thus, the two concrete expressions denote the same language, and the law holds.

For another example of a law, consider $L^* = L^*L^*$. The concrete languages are $\mathbf{a}^*$ and $\mathbf{a}^*\mathbf{a}^*$, respectively, and each of these is the set of all strings of a's. Again, the law is found to hold; that is, concatenation of a closed language with itself yields that language.

Finally, consider the prospective law $L + ML = (L + M)L$. If we choose symbols a and b for variables L and M, respectively, we have the two concrete regular expressions $\mathbf{a} + \mathbf{ba}$ and $(\mathbf{a} + \mathbf{b})\mathbf{a}$. However, the languages of these expressions are not the same. For example, the string aa is in the second, but not the first. Thus, the prospective law is false. □

3.4.8 Exercises for Section 3.4

Exercise 3.4.1: Verify the following identities involving regular expressions.

* a) $R + S = S + R$.

  b) $(R + S) + T = R + (S + T)$.

  c) $(RS)T = R(ST)$.

Extensions of the Test Beyond Regular Expressions May Fail

Let us consider an extended regular-expression algebra that includes the intersection operator. Interestingly, adding $\cap$ to the three regular-expression operators does not increase the set of languages we can describe, as we shall see in Theorem 4.8. However, it does make the test for algebraic laws invalid.

Consider the "law" $L \cap M \cap N = L \cap M$; that is, the intersection of any three languages is the same as the intersection of the first two of these languages. This "law" is patently false. For example, let $L = M = \{a\}$ and $N = \emptyset$. But the test based on concretizing the variables would fail to see the difference. That is, if we replaced L, M, and N by the symbols a, b, and c, respectively, we would test whether $\{a\} \cap \{b\} \cap \{c\} = \{a\} \cap \{b\}$. Since both sides are the empty set, the equality of languages holds and the test would imply that the "law" is true.

---

d) $R(S + T) = RS + RT$.

e) $(R + S)T = RT + ST$.

* f) $(R^*)^* = R^*$.

g) $(\epsilon + R)^* = R^*$.

h) $(R^*S^*)^* = (R + S)^*$.

! **Exercise 3.4.2:** Prove or disprove each of the following statements about regular expressions.

* a) $(R + S)^* = R^* + S^*$.

b) $(RS + R)^*R = R(SR + R)^*$.

* c) $(RS + R)^*RS = (RR^*S)^*$.

d) $(R + S)^*S = (R^*S)^*$.

e) $S(RS + S)^*R = RR^*S(RR^*S)^*$.

Exercise 3.4.3: In Example 3.6, we developed the regular expression

$$(0 + 1)^*1(0 + 1) + (0 + 1)^*1(0 + 1)(0 + 1)$$

Use the distributive laws to develop two different, simpler, equivalent expressions.

Exercise 3.4.4: At the beginning of Section 3.4.6, we gave part of a proof that $(L^*M^*)^* = (L+M)^*$. Complete the proof by showing that strings in $(L^*M^*)^*$ are also in $(L+M)^*$.

! **Exercise 3.4.5:** Complete the proof of Theorem 3.13 by handling the cases where regular expression E is of the form FG or of the form F^*.

3.5   Summary of Chapter 3

✦ *Regular Expressions*: This algebraic notation describes exactly the same languages as finite automata: the regular languages. The regular-expression operators are union, concatenation (or "dot"), and closure (or "star").

✦ *Regular Expressions in Practice*: Systems such as UNIX and various of its commands use an extended regular-expression language that provides shorthands for many common expressions. Character classes allow the easy expression of sets of symbols, while operators such as one-or-more-of and at-most-one-of augment the usual regular-expression operators.

✦ *Equivalence of Regular Expressions and Finite Automata*: We can convert a DFA to a regular expression by an inductive construction in which expressions for the labels of paths allowed to pass through increasingly larger sets of states are constructed. Alternatively, we can use a state-elimination procedure to build the regular expression for a DFA. In the other direction, we can construct recursively an ϵ-NFA from regular expressions, and then convert the ϵ-NFA to a DFA, if we wish.

✦ *The Algebra of Regular Expressions*: Regular expressions obey many of the algebraic laws of arithmetic, although there are differences. Union and concatenation are associative, but only union is commutative. Concatenation distributes over union. Union is idempotent.

✦ *Testing Algebraic Identities*: We can tell whether a regular-expression equivalence involving variables as arguments is true by replacing the variables by distinct constants and testing whether the resulting languages are the same.

3.6   References for Chapter 3

The idea of regular expressions and the proof of their equivalence to finite automata is the work of S. C. Kleene [3]. However, the construction of an ϵ-NFA from a regular expression, as presented here, is the "McNaughton-Yamada construction," from [4]. The test for regular-expression identities by treating variables as constants was written down by J. Gischer [2]. Although thought to be folklore, this report demonstrated how adding several other operations such as intersection or shuffle (See Exercise 7.3.4) makes the test fail, even though they do not extend the class of languages representable.

Even before developing UNIX, K. Thompson was investigating the use of regular expressions in commands such as `grep`, and his algorithm for processing such commands appears in [5]. The early development of UNIX produced several other commands that make heavy use of the extended regular-expression notation, such as M. Lesk's `lex` command. A description of this command and other regular-expression techniques can be found in [1].

1. A. V. Aho, R. Sethi, and J. D. Ullman, *Compilers: Principles, Techniques, and Tools*, Addison-Wesley, Reading MA, 1986.

2. J. L. Gischer, STAN-CS-TR-84-1033 (1984).

3. S. C. Kleene, "Representation of events in nerve nets and finite automata," In C. E. Shannon and J. McCarthy, *Automata Studies*, Princeton Univ. Press, 1956, pp. 3–42.

4. R. McNaughton and H. Yamada, "Regular expressions and state graphs for automata," *IEEE Trans. Electronic Computers* **9**:1 (Jan., 1960), pp. 39–47.

5. K. Thompson, "Regular expression search algorithm," *Comm. ACM* **11**:6 (June, 1968), pp. 419–422.

Chapter 4

Properties of Regular Languages

The chapter explores the properties of regular languages. Our first tool for this exploration is a way to prove that certain languages are not regular. This theorem, called the "pumping lemma," is introduced in Section 4.1.

One important kind of fact about the regular languages is called a "closure property." These properties let us build recognizers for languages that are constructed from other languages by certain operations. As an example, the intersection of two regular languages is also regular. Thus, given automata that recognize two different regular languages, we can construct mechanically an automaton that recognizes exactly the intersection of these two languages. Since the automaton for the intersection may have many more states than either of the two given automata, this "closure property" can be a useful tool for building complex automata. Section 2.1 used this construction in an essential way.

Some other important facts about regular languages are called "decision properties." Our study of these properties gives us algorithms for answering important questions about automata. A central example is an algorithm for deciding whether two automata define the same language. A consequence of our ability to decide this question is that we can "minimize" automata, that is, find an equivalent to a given automaton that has as few states as possible. This problem has been important in the design of switching circuits for decades, since the cost of the circuit (area of a chip that the circuit occupies) tends to decrease as the number of states of the automaton implemented by the circuit decreases.

4.1   Proving Languages not to be Regular

We have established that the class of languages known as the regular languages has at least four different descriptions. They are the languages accepted by DFA's, by NFA's, and by ϵ-NFA's; they are also the languages defined by regular expressions.

Not every language is a regular language. In this section, we shall introduce a powerful technique, known as the "pumping lemma," for showing certain languages not to be regular. We then give several examples of nonregular languages. In Section 4.2 we shall see how the pumping lemma can be used in tandem with closure properties of the regular languages to prove other languages not to be regular.

4.1.1   The Pumping Lemma for Regular Languages

Let us consider the language $L_{01} = \{0^n1^n \mid n \geq 1\}$. This language contains all strings 01, 0011, 000111, and so on, that consist of one or more 0's followed by an equal number of 1's. We claim that L_{01} is not a regular language. The intuitive argument is that if L_{01} were regular, then L_{01} would be the language of some DFA A. This automaton has some particular number of states, say k states. Imagine this automaton receiving k 0's as input. It is in some state after consuming each of the $k + 1$ prefixes of the input: $\epsilon, 0, 00, \ldots, 0^k$. Since there are only k different states, the pigeonhole principle tells us that after reading two different prefixes, say 0^i and 0^j, A must be in the same state, say state q.

However, suppose instead that after reading i or j 0's, the automaton A starts receiving 1's as input. After receiving i 1's, it must accept if it previously received i 0's, but not if it received j 0's. Since it was in state q when the 1's started, it cannot "remember" whether it received i or j 0's, so we can "fool" A and make it do the wrong thing — accept if it should not, or fail to accept when it should.

The above argument is informal, but can be made precise. However, the same conclusion, that the language L_{01} is not regular, can be reached using a general result, as follows.

Theorem 4.1: (The *pumping lemma for regular languages*) Let L be a regular language. Then there exists a constant n (which depends on L) such that for every string w in L such that $|w| \geq n$, we can break w into three strings, $w = xyz$, such that:

  1. $y \neq \epsilon$.

  2. $|xy| \leq n$.

  3. For all $k \geq 0$, the string xy^kz is also in L.

That is, we can always find a nonempty string y not too far from the beginning of w that can be "pumped"; that is, repeating y any number of times, or deleting it (the case $k = 0$), keeps the resulting string in the language L.

PROOF: Suppose L is regular. Then $L = L(A)$ for some DFA A. Suppose A has n states. Now, consider any string w of length n or more, say $w = a_1 a_2 \cdots a_m$, where $m \geq n$ and each a_i is an input symbol. For $i = 0, 1, \ldots, n$ define state p_i to be $\hat{\delta}(q_0, a_1 a_2 \cdots a_i)$, where δ is the transition function of A, and q_0 is the start state of A. That is, p_i is the state A is in after reading the first i symbols of w. Note that $p_0 = q_0$.

By the pigeonhole principle, it is not possible for the $n+1$ different p_i's for $i = 0, 1, \ldots, n$ to be distinct, since there are only n different states. Thus, we can find two different integers i and j, with $0 \leq i < j \leq n$, such that $p_i = p_j$. Now, we can break $w = xyz$ as follows:

1. $x = a_1 a_2 \cdots a_i$.

2. $y = a_{i+1} a_{i+2} \cdots a_j$.

3. $z = a_{j+1} a_{j+2} \cdots a_m$.

That is, x takes us to p_i once; y takes us from p_i back to p_i (since p_i is also p_j), and z is the balance of w. The relationships among the strings and states are suggested by Fig. 4.1. Note that x may be empty, in the case that $i = 0$. Also, z may be empty if $j = n = m$. However, y can not be empty, since i is strictly less than j.

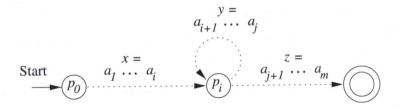

Figure 4.1: Every string longer than the number of states must cause a state to repeat

Now, consider what happens if the automaton A receives the input $xy^k z$ for any $k \geq 0$. If $k = 0$, then the automaton goes from the start state q_0 (which is also p_0) to p_i on input x. Since p_i is also p_j, it must be that A goes from p_i to the accepting state shown in Fig. 4.1 on input z. Thus, A accepts xz.

If $k > 0$, then A goes from q_0 to p_i on input x, circles from p_i to p_i k times on input y^k, and then goes to the accepting state on input z. Thus, for any $k \geq 0$, $xy^k z$ is also accepted by A; that is, $xy^k z$ is in L. $\square$

4.1.2   Applications of the Pumping Lemma

Let us see some examples of how the pumping lemma is used. In each case, we shall propose a language and use the pumping lemma to prove that the language is not regular.

The Pumping Lemma as an Adversarial Game

Recall our discussion from Section 1.2.3 where we pointed out that a theorem whose statement involves several alternations of "for-all" and "there-exists" quantifiers can be thought of as a game between two players. The pumping lemma is an important example of this type of theorem, since it in effect involves four different quantifiers: "**for all** regular languages L **there exists** n such that **for all** w in L with $|w| \geq n$ **there exists** xyz equal to w such that $\cdots$." We can see the application of the pumping lemma as a game, in which:

1. Player 1 picks the language L to be proved nonregular.

2. Player 2 picks n, but doesn't reveal to player 1 what n is; player 1 must devise a play for all possible n's.

3. Player 1 picks w, which may depend on n and which must be of length at least n.

4. Player 2 divides w into x, y, and z, obeying the constraints that are stipulated in the pumping lemma; $y \neq \epsilon$ and $|xy| \leq n$. Again, player 2 does not have to tell player 1 what x, y, and z are, although they must obey the constraints.

5. Player 1 "wins" by picking k, which may be a function of n, x, y, and z, such that $xy^k z$ is not in L.

Example 4.2: Let us show that the language L_{eq} consisting of all strings with an equal number of 0's and 1's (not in any particular order) is not a regular language. In terms of the "two-player game" described in the box on "The Pumping Lemma as an Adversarial Game," we shall be player 1 and we must deal with whatever choices player 2 makes. Suppose n is the constant that must exist if L_{eq} is regular, according to the pumping lemma; i.e., "player 2" picks n. We shall pick $w = 0^n 1^n$, that is, n 0's followed by n 1's, a string that surely is in L_{eq}.

Now, "player 2" breaks our w up into xyz. All we know is that $y \neq \epsilon$, and $|xy| \leq n$. However, that information is very useful, and we "win" as follows. Since $|xy| \leq n$, and xy comes at the front of w, we know that x and y consist only of 0's. The pumping lemma tells us that xz is in L_{eq}, if L_{eq} is regular. This conclusion is the case $k = 0$ in the pumping lemma.[1] However, xz has n 1's, since all the 1's of w are in z. But xz also has fewer than n 0's, because we

---

[1] Observe in what follows that we could have also succeeded by picking $k = 2$, or indeed any value of k other than 1.

lost the 0's of y. Since $y \neq \epsilon$ we know that there can be no more than $n - 1$ 0's among x and z. Thus, after assuming L_{eq} is a regular language, we have proved a fact known to be false, that xz is in L_{eq}. We have a proof by contradiction of the fact that L_{eq} is not regular. □

Example 4.3: Let us show that the language L_{pr} consisting of all strings of 1's whose length is a prime is not a regular language. Suppose it were. Then there would be a constant n satisfying the conditions of the pumping lemma. Consider some prime $p \geq n + 2$; there must be such a p, since there are an infinity of primes. Let $w = 1^p$.

By the pumping lemma, we can break $w = xyz$ such that $y \neq \epsilon$ and $|xy| \leq n$. Let $|y| = m$. Then $|xz| = p - m$. Now consider the string $xy^{p-m}z$, which must be in L_{pr} by the pumping lemma, if L_{pr} really is regular. However,

$$|xy^{p-m}z| = |xz| + (p - m)|y| = p - m + (p - m)m = (m + 1)(p - m)$$

It looks like $|xy^{p-m}z|$ is not a prime, since it has two factors $m + 1$ and $p - m$. However, we must check that neither of these factors are 1, since then $(m + 1)(p - m)$ might be a prime after all. But $m + 1 > 1$, since $y \neq \epsilon$ tells us $m \geq 1$. Also, $p - m > 1$, since $p \geq n + 2$ was chosen, and $m \leq n$ since

$$m = |y| \leq |xy| \leq n$$

Thus, $p - m \geq 2$.

Again we have started by assuming the language in question was regular, and we derived a contradiction by showing that some string not in the language was required by the pumping lemma to be in the language. Thus, we conclude that L_{pr} is not a regular language. □

4.1.3 Exercises for Section 4.1

Exercise 4.1.1: Prove that the following are not regular languages.

a) $\{0^n1^n \mid n \geq 1\}$. This language, consisting of a string of 0's followed by an equal-length string of 1's, is the language L_{01} we considered informally at the beginning of the section. Here, you should apply the pumping lemma in the proof.

b) The set of strings of balanced parentheses. These are the strings of characters "(" and ")" that can appear in a well-formed arithmetic expression.

* c) $\{0^n10^n \mid n \geq 1\}$.

d) $\{0^n1^m2^n \mid n \text{ and } m \text{ are arbitrary integers}\}$.

e) $\{0^n1^m \mid n \leq m\}$.

f) $\{0^n1^{2n} \mid n \geq 1\}$.

! **Exercise 4.1.2:** Prove that the following are not regular languages.

* a) $\{0^n \mid n$ is a perfect square$\}$.

  b) $\{0^n \mid n$ is a perfect cube$\}$.

  c) $\{0^n \mid n$ is a power of 2$\}$.

  d) The set of strings of 0's and 1's whose length is a perfect square.

  e) The set of strings of 0's and 1's that are of the form ww, that is, some string repeated.

  f) The set of strings of 0's and 1's that are of the form ww^R, that is, some string followed by its reverse. (See Section 4.2.2 for a formal definition of the reversal of a string.)

  g) The set of strings of 0's and 1's of the form $w\bar{w}$, where $\bar{w}$ is formed from w by replacing all 0's by 1's, and vice-versa; e.g., $\overline{011} = 100$, and 011100 is an example of a string in the language.

  h) The set of strings of the form $w1^n$, where w is a string of 0's and 1's of length n.

!! **Exercise 4.1.3:** Prove that the following are not regular languages.

  a) The set of strings of 0's and 1's, beginning with a 1, such that when interpreted as an integer, that integer is a prime.

  b) The set of strings of the form 0^i1^j such that the greatest common divisor of i and j is 1.

! **Exercise 4.1.4:** When we try to apply the pumping lemma to a regular language, the "adversary wins," and we cannot complete the proof. Show what goes wrong when we choose L to be one of the following languages:

* a) The empty set.

* b) $\{00, 11\}$.

* c) $(00 + 11)^*$.

  d) 01^*0^*1.

4.2 Closure Properties of Regular Languages

In this section, we shall prove several theorems of the form "if certain languages are regular, and a language L is formed from them by certain operations (e.g., L is the union of two regular languages), then L is also regular. These theorems are often called *closure properties* of the regular languages, since they show that the class of regular languages is closed under the operation mentioned. Closure properties express the idea that when one (or several) languages are regular, then certain related languages are also regular. They also serve as an interesting illustration of how the equivalent representations of the regular languages (automata and regular expressions) reinforce each other in our understanding of the class of languages, since often one representation is far better than the others in supporting a proof of a closure property. Here is a summary of the principal closure properties for regular languages:

1. The union of two regular languages is regular.

2. The intersection of two regular languages is regular.

3. The complement of a regular language is regular.

4. The difference of two regular languages is regular.

5. The reversal of a regular language is regular.

6. The closure (star) of a regular language is regular.

7. The concatenation of regular languages is regular.

8. A homomorphism (substitution of strings for symbols) of a regular language is regular.

9. The inverse homomorphism of a regular language is regular.

4.2.1 Closure of Regular Languages Under Boolean Operations

Our first closure properties are the three boolean operations: union, intersection, and complementation:

1. Let L and M be languages over alphabet Σ. Then $L \cup M$ is the language that contains all strings that are in either or both of L and M.

2. Let L and M be languages over alphabet Σ. Then $L \cap M$ is the language that contains all strings that are in both L and M.

3. Let L be a language over alphabet Σ. Then $\overline{L}$, the *complement* of L, is the set of strings in Σ^* that are not in L.

It turns out that the regular languages are closed under all three of the boolean operations. The proofs take rather different approaches though, as we shall see.

What if Languages Have Different Alphabets?

When we take the union or intersection of two languages L and M, they might have different alphabets. For example, it is possible that $L_1 \subseteq \{a, b\}$ while $L_2 \subseteq \{b, c, d\}$. However, if a language L consists of strings with symbols in Σ, then we can also think of L as a language over any finite alphabet that is a superset of Σ. Thus, for example, we can think of both L_1 and L_2 above as being languages over alphabet $\{a, b, c, d\}$. The fact that none of L_1's strings contain symbols c or d is irrelevant, as is the fact that L_2's strings will not contain a.

Likewise, when taking the complement of a language L that is a subset of Σ_1^* for some alphabet Σ_1, we may choose to take the complement *with respect to* some alphabet Σ_2 that is a superset of Σ_1. If so, then the complement of L will be $\Sigma_2^* - L$; that is, the complement of L with respect to Σ_2 includes (among other strings) all those strings in Σ_2^* that have at least one symbol that is in Σ_2 but not in Σ_1. Had we taken the complement of L with respect to Σ_1, then no string with symbols in $\Sigma_2 - \Sigma_1$ would be in $\overline{L}$. Thus, to be strict, we should always state the alphabet with respect to which a complement is taken. However, often it is obvious which alphabet is meant; e.g., if L is defined by an automaton, then the specification of that automaton includes the alphabet. Thus, we shall often speak of the "complement" without specifying the alphabet.

Closure Under Union

Theorem 4.4: If L and M are regular languages, then so is $L \cup M$.

PROOF: This proof is simple. Since L and M are regular, they have regular expressions; say $L = L(R)$ and $M = L(S)$. Then $L \cup M = L(R + S)$ by the definition of the $+$ operator for regular expressions. $\square$

Closure Under Complementation

The theorem for union was made very easy by the use of the regular-expression representation for the languages. However, let us next consider complementation. Do you see how to take a regular expression and change it into one that defines the complement language? Well neither do we. However, it can be done, because as we shall see in Theorem 4.5, it is easy to start with a DFA and construct a DFA that accepts the complement. Thus, starting with a regular expression, we could find a regular expression for its complement as follows:

1. Convert the regular expression to an ϵ-NFA.

2. Convert that ϵ-NFA to a DFA by the subset construction.

Closure Under Regular Operations

The proof that regular languages are closed under union was exceptionally easy because union is one of the three operations that define the regular expressions. The same idea as Theorem 4.4 applies to concatenation and closure as well. That is:

- If L and M are regular languages, then so is LM.

- If L is a regular language, then so is L^*.

---

3. Complement the accepting states of that DFA.

4. Turn the complement DFA back into a regular expression using the construction of Sections 3.2.1 or 3.2.2.

Theorem 4.5: If L is a regular language over alphabet Σ, then $\overline{L} = \Sigma^* - L$ is also a regular language.

PROOF: Let $L = L(A)$ for some DFA $A = (Q, \Sigma, \delta, q_0, F)$. Then $\overline{L} = L(B)$, where B is the DFA $(Q, \Sigma, \delta, q_0, Q - F)$. That is, B is exactly like A, but the accepting states of A have become nonaccepting states of B, and vice versa. Then w is in $L(B)$ if and only if $\hat{\delta}(q_0, w)$ is in $Q - F$, which occurs if and only if w is not in $L(A)$. $\square$

Notice that it is important for the above proof that $\hat{\delta}(q_0, w)$ is always some state; i.e., there are no missing transitions in A. If there were, then certain strings might lead neither to an accepting nor nonaccepting state of A, and those strings would be missing from both $L(A)$ and $L(B)$. Fortunately, we have defined a DFA to have a transition on every symbol of Σ from every state, so each string leads either to a state in F or a state in $Q - F$.

Example 4.6: Let A be the automaton of Fig. 2.14. Recall that DFA A accepts all and only the strings of 0's and 1's that end in 01; in regular-expression terms, $L(A) = (0 + 1)^*01$. The complement of $L(A)$ is therefore all strings of 0's and 1's that do *not* end in 01. Figure 4.2 shows the automaton for $\{0, 1\}^* - L(A)$. It is the same as Fig. 2.14 but with the accepting state made nonaccepting and the two nonaccepting states made accepting. $\square$

Example 4.7: In this example, we shall apply Theorem 4.5 to show a certain language not to be regular. In Example 4.2 we showed that the language L_{eq} consisting of strings with an equal number of 0's and 1's and is not regular. This proof was a straightforward application of the pumping lemma. Now consider

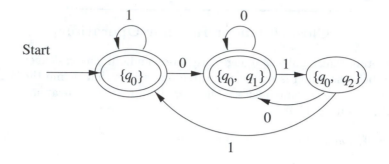

Figure 4.2: DFA accepting the complement of the language $(0 + 1)^*01$

the language M consisting of those strings of 0's and 1's that have an unequal number of 0's and 1's.

It would be hard to use the pumping lemma to show M is not regular. Intuitively, if we start with some string w in M, break it into $w = xyz$, and "pump" y, we might find that y itself was a string like 01 that had an equal number of 0's and 1's. If so, then for no k will xy^kz have an equal number of 0's and 1's, since xyz has an unequal number of 0's and 1's, and the numbers of 0's and 1's change equally as we "pump" y. Thus, we can never use the pumping lemma to contradict the assumption that M is regular.

However, M is still not regular. The reason is that $M = \overline{L}$. Since the complement of the complement is the set we started with, it also follows that $L = \overline{M}$. If M is regular, then by Theorem 4.5, L is regular. But we know L is *not* regular, so we have a proof by contradiction that M is not regular. □

Closure Under Intersection

Now, let us consider the intersection of two regular languages. We actually have little to do, since the three boolean operations are not independent. Once we have ways of performing complementation and union, we can obtain the intersection of languages L and M by the identity

$$L \cap M = \overline{\overline{L} \cup \overline{M}} \tag{4.1}$$

In general, the intersection of two sets is the set of elements that are not in the complement of either set. That observation, which is what Equation (4.1) says, is one of *DeMorgan's laws*. The other law is the same with union and intersection interchanged; that is, $L \cup M = \overline{\overline{L} \cap \overline{M}}$.

However, we can also perform a direct construction of a DFA for the intersection of two regular languages. This construction, which essentially runs two DFA's in parallel, is useful in its own right. For instance, we used it to construct the automaton in Fig. 2.3 that represented the "product" of what two participants — the bank and the store — were doing. We shall make the *product construction* formal in the next theorem.

Theorem 4.8 : If L and M are regular languages, then so is $L \cap M$.

PROOF: Let L and M be the languages of automata $A_L = (Q_L, \Sigma, \delta_L, q_L, F_L)$ and $A_M = (Q_M, \Sigma, \delta_M, q_M, F_M)$. Notice that we are assuming that the alphabets of both automata are the same; that is, Σ is the union of the alphabets of L and M, if those alphabets are different. The product construction actually works for NFA's as well as DFA's, but to make the argument as simple as possible, we assume that A_L and A_M are DFA's.

For $L \cap M$ we shall construct an automaton A that simulates both A_L and A_M. The states of A are pairs of states, the first from A_L and the second from A_M. To design the transitions of A, suppose A is in state (p, q), where p is the state of A_L and q is the state of A_M. If a is the input symbol, we see what A_L does on input a; say it goes to state s. We also see what A_M does on input a; say it makes a transition to state t. Then the next state of A will be (s, t). In that manner, A has simulated the effect of both A_L and A_M. The idea is sketched in Fig. 4.3.

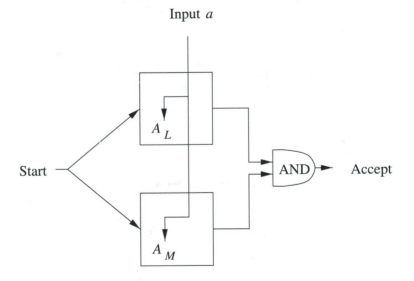

Figure 4.3: An automaton simulating two other automata and accepting if and only if both accept

The remaining details are simple. The start state of A is the pair of start states of A_L and A_M. Since we want to accept if and only if both automata accept, we select as the accepting states of A all those pairs (p, q) such that p is an accepting state of A_L and q is an accepting state of A_M. Formally, we define:

$$A = (Q_L \times Q_M, \Sigma, \delta, (q_L, q_M), F_L \times F_M)$$

where $\delta\big((p, q), a\big) = \big(\delta_L(p, a), \delta_M(q, a)\big)$.

To see why $L(A) = L(A_L) \cap L(A_M)$, first observe that an easy induction on $|w|$ proves that $\hat{\delta}((q_L, q_M), w) = (\hat{\delta}_L(q_L, w), \hat{\delta}_M(q_M, w))$. But A accepts w if and only if $\hat{\delta}((q_L, q_M), w)$ is a pair of accepting states. That is, $\hat{\delta}_L(q_L, w)$ must be in F_L, and $\hat{\delta}_M(q_M, w)$ must be in F_M. Put another way, w is accepted by A if and only if both A_L and A_M accept w. Thus, A accepts the intersection of L and M. $\square$

Example 4.9: In Fig. 4.4 we see two DFA's. The automaton in Fig. 4.4(a) accepts all those strings that have a 0, while the automaton in Fig. 4.4(b) accepts all those strings that have a 1. We show in Fig. 4.4(c) the product of these two automata. Its states are labeled by the pairs of states of the automata in (a) and (b).

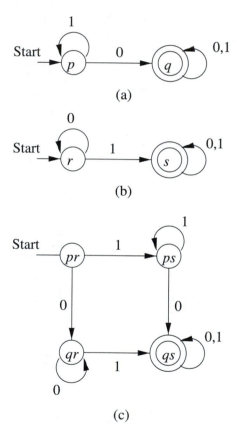

Figure 4.4: The product construction

It is easy to argue that this automaton accepts the intersection of the first two languages: those strings that have both a 0 and a 1. State pr represents only the initial condition, in which we have seen neither 0 nor 1. State qr means that we have seen only 1's, while state ps represents the condition that we have seen only 0's. The accepting state qs represents the condition where we have seen both 0's and 1's. ☐

Closure Under Difference

There is a fourth operation that is often applied to sets and is related to the boolean operations: set difference. In terms of languages, $L - M$, the *difference* of L and M, is the set of strings that are in language L but not in language M. The regular languages are also closed under this operation, and the proof follows easily from the theorems just proven.

Theorem 4.10: If L and M are regular languages, then so is $L - M$.

PROOF: Observe that $L - M = L \cap \overline{M}$. By Theorem 4.5, $\overline{M}$ is regular, and by Theorem 4.8 $L \cap \overline{M}$ is regular. Therefore $L - M$ is regular. ☐

4.2.2   Reversal

The *reversal* of a string $a_1 a_2 \cdots a_n$ is the string written backwards, that is, $a_n a_{n-1} \cdots a_1$. We use w^R for the reversal of string w. Thus, 0010^R is 0100, and $\epsilon^R = \epsilon$.

The reversal of a language L, written L^R, is the language consisting of the reversals of all its strings. For instance, if $L = \{001, 10, 111\}$, then $L^R = \{100, 01, 111\}$.

Reversal is another operation that preserves regular languages; that is, if L is a regular language, so is L^R. There are two simple proofs, one based on automata and one based on regular expressions. We shall give the automaton-based proof informally, and let you fill in the details if you like. We then prove the theorem formally using regular expressions.

Given a language L that is $L(A)$ for some finite automaton, perhaps with nondeterminism and ϵ-transitions, we may construct an automaton for L^R by:

1. Reverse all the arcs in the transition diagram for A.

2. Make the start state of A be the only accepting state for the new automaton.

3. Create a new start state p_0 with transitions on ϵ to all the accepting states of A.

The result is an automaton that simulates A "in reverse," and therefore accepts a string w if and only if A accepts w^R. Now, we prove the reversal theorem formally.

Theorem 4.11: If L is a regular language, so is L^R.

PROOF: Assume L is defined by regular expression E. The proof is a structural induction on the size of E. We show that there is another regular expression E^R such that $L(E^R) = (L(E))^R$; that is, the language of E^R is the reversal of the language of E.

BASIS: If E is ϵ, $\emptyset$, or a, for some symbol a, then E^R is the same as E. That is, we know $\{\epsilon\}^R = \{\epsilon\}$, $\emptyset^R = \emptyset$, and $\{a\}^R = \{a\}$.

INDUCTION: There are three cases, depending on the form of E.

1. $E = E_1 + E_2$. Then $E^R = E_1^R + E_2^R$. The justification is that the reversal of the union of two languages is obtained by computing the reversals of the two languages and taking the union of those languages.

2. $E = E_1 E_2$. Then $E^R = E_2^R E_1^R$. Note that we reverse the order of the two languages, as well as reversing the languages themselves. For instance, if $L(E_1) = \{01, 111\}$ and $L(E_2) = \{00, 10\}$, then $L(E_1 E_2) = \{0100, 0110, 11100, 11110\}$. The reversal of the latter language is

$$\{0010, 0110, 00111, 01111\}$$

If we concatenate the reversals of $L(E_2)$ and $L(E_1)$ in that order, we get

$$\{00, 01\}\{10, 111\} = \{0010, 00111, 0110, 01111\}$$

which is the same language as $\left(L(E_1 E_2)\right)^R$. In general, if a word w in $L(E)$ is the concatenation of w_1 from $L(E_1)$ and w_2 from $L(E_2)$, then $w^R = w_2^R w_1^R$.

3. $E = E_1^*$. Then $E^R = (E_1^R)^*$. The justification is that any string w in $L(E)$ can be written as $w_1 w_2 \cdots w_n$, where each w_i is in $L(E)$. But

$$w^R = w_n^R w_{n-1}^R \cdots w_1^R$$

Each w_i^R is in $L(E^R)$, so w^R is in $(E_1^R)^*$. Conversely, any string in $L\left((E_1^R)^*\right)$ is of the form $w_1 w_2 \cdots w_n$, where each w_i is the reversal of a string in $L(E_1)$. The reversal of this string, $w_n^R w_{n-1}^R \cdots w_1^R$, is therefore a string in $L(E_1^*)$, which is $L(E)$. We have thus shown that a string is in $L(E)$ if and only if its reversal is in $L\left((E_1^R)^*\right)$.

$\square$

Example 4.12 : Let L be defined by the regular expression $(\mathbf{0} + \mathbf{1})\mathbf{0}^*$. Then L^R is the language of $(\mathbf{0}^*)^R(\mathbf{0} + \mathbf{1})^R$, by the rule for concatenation. If we apply the rules for closure and union to the two parts, and then apply the basis rule that says the reversals of $\mathbf{0}$ and $\mathbf{1}$ are unchanged, we find that L^R has regular expression $\mathbf{0}^*(\mathbf{0} + \mathbf{1})$. $\square$

4.2.3 Homomorphisms

A string *homomorphism* is a function on strings that works by substituting a particular string for each symbol.

Example 4.13: The function h defined by $h(0) = ab$ and $h(1) = \epsilon$ is a homomorphism. Given any string of 0's and 1's, it replaces all 0's by the string ab and replaces all 1's by the empty string. For example, h applied to the string 0011 is $abab$. □

Formally, if h is a homomorphism on alphabet Σ, and $w = a_1 a_2 \cdots a_n$ is a string of symbols in Σ, then $h(w) = h(a_1)h(a_2) \cdots h(a_n)$. That is, we apply h to each symbol of w and concatenate the results, in order. For instance, if h is the homomorphism in Example 4.13, and $w = 0011$, then $h(w) = h(0)h(0)h(1)h(1) = (ab)(ab)(\epsilon)(\epsilon) = abab$, as we claimed in that example.

Further, we can apply a homomorphism to a language by applying it to each of the strings in the language. That is, if L is a language over alphabet Σ, and h is a homomorphism on Σ, then $h(L) = \{h(w) \mid w \text{ is in } L\}$. For instance, if L is the language of regular expression **10*1**, i.e., any number of 0's surrounded by single 1's, then $h(L)$ is the language $(\mathbf{ab})^*$. The reason is that h of Example 4.13 effectively drops the 1's, since they are replaced by ϵ, and turns each 0 into ab. The same idea, applying the homomorphism directly to the regular expression, can be used to prove that the regular languages are closed under homomorphisms.

Theorem 4.14: If L is a regular language over alphabet Σ, and h is a homomorphism on Σ, then $h(L)$ is also regular.

PROOF: Let $L = L(R)$ for some regular expression R. In general, if E is a regular expression with symbols in Σ, let $h(E)$ be the expression we obtain by replacing each symbol a of Σ in E by $h(a)$. We claim that $h(R)$ defines the language $h(L)$.

The proof is an easy structural induction that says whenever we take a subexpression E of R and apply h to it to get $h(E)$, the language of $h(E)$ is the same language we get if we apply h to the language $L(E)$. Formally, $L\big(h(E)\big) = h\big(L(E)\big)$.

BASIS: If E is ϵ or $\emptyset$, then $h(E)$ is the same as E, since h does not affect the string ϵ or the language $\emptyset$. Thus, $L\big(h(E)\big) = L(E)$. However, if E is $\emptyset$ or ϵ, then $L(E)$ contains either no strings or a string with no symbols, respectively. Thus $h\big(L(E)\big) = L(E)$ in either case. We conclude $L\big(h(E)\big) = L(E) = h\big(L(E)\big)$.

The only other basis case is if $E = \mathbf{a}$ for some symbol a in Σ. In this case, $L(E) = \{a\}$, so $h\big(L(E)\big) = \{h(a)\}$. Also, $h(E)$ is the regular expression that is the string of symbols $h(a)$. Thus, $L\big(h(E)\big)$ is also $\{h(a)\}$, and we conclude $L\big(h(E)\big) = h\big(L(E)\big)$.

INDUCTION: There are three cases, each of them simple. We shall prove only the union case, where $E = F+G$. The way we apply homomorphisms to regular expressions assures us that $h(E) = h(F + G) = h(F) + h(G)$. We also know that $L(E) = L(F) \cup L(G)$ and

$$L\big(h(E)\big) = L\big(h(F) + h(G)\big) = L\big(h(F)\big) \cup L\big(h(G)\big) \qquad (4.2)$$

by the definition of what "+" means in regular expressions. Finally,

$$h\big(L(E)\big) = h\big(L(F) \cup L(G)\big) = h\big(L(F)\big) \cup h\big(L(G)\big) \qquad (4.3)$$

because h is applied to a language by application to each of its strings individually. Now we may invoke the inductive hypothesis to assert that $L\big(h(F)\big) = h\big(L(F)\big)$ and $L\big(h(G)\big) = h\big(L(G)\big)$. Thus, the final expressions in (4.2) and (4.3) are equivalent, and therefore so are their respective first terms; that is, $L\big(h(E)\big) = h\big(L(E)\big)$.

We shall not prove the cases where expression E is a concatenation or closure; the ideas are similar to the above in both cases. The conclusion is that $L\big(h(R)\big)$ is indeed $h\big(L(R)\big)$; i.e., applying the homomorphism h to the regular expression for language L results in a regular expression that defines the language $h(L)$. □

4.2.4 Inverse Homomorphisms

Homomorphisms may also be applied "backwards," and in this mode they also preserve regular languages. That is, suppose h is a homomorphism from some alphabet Σ to strings in another (possibly the same) alphabet T.[2] Let L be a language over alphabet T. Then $h^{-1}(L)$, read "h inverse of L," is the set of strings w in Σ^* such that $h(w)$ is in L. Figure 4.5 suggests the effect of a homomorphism on a language L in part (a), and the effect of an inverse homomorphism in part (b).

Example 4.15 : Let L be the language of regular expression $(00 + 1)^*$. That is, L consists of all strings of 0's and 1's such that all the 0's occur in adjacent pairs. Thus, 0010011 and 10000111 are in L, but 000 and 10100 are not.

Let h be the homomorphism defined by $h(a) = 01$ and $h(b) = 10$. We claim that $h^{-1}(L)$ is the language of regular expression $(\mathbf{ba})^*$, that is, all strings of repeating ba pairs. We shall prove that $h(w)$ is in L if and only if w is of the form $baba \cdots ba$.

(If) Suppose w is n repetitions of ba for some $n \geq 0$. Note that $h(ba) = 1001$, so $h(w)$ is n repetitions of 1001. Since 1001 is composed of two 1's and a pair of 0's, we know that 1001 is in L. Therefore any repetition of 1001 is also formed from 1 and 00 segments and is in L. Thus, $h(w)$ is in L.

---

[2] That "T" should be thought of as a Greek capital tau, the letter following sigma.

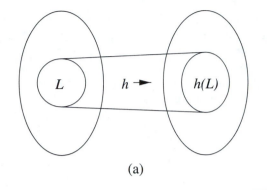

(a)

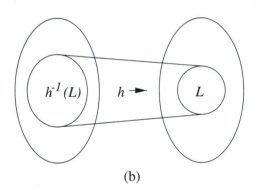

(b)

Figure 4.5: A homomorphism applied in the forward and inverse direction

(Only-if) Now, we must assume that $h(w)$ is in L and show that w is of the form $baba \cdots ba$. There are four conditions under which a string is *not* of that form, and we shall show that if any of them hold then $h(w)$ is not in L. That is, we prove the contrapositive of the statement we set out to prove.

1. If w begins with a, then $h(w)$ begins with 01. It therefore has an isolated 0, and is not in L.

2. If w ends in b, then $h(w)$ ends in 10, and again there is an isolated 0 in $h(w)$.

3. If w has two consecutive a's, then $h(w)$ has a substring 0101. Here too, there is an isolated 0 in w.

4. Likewise, if w has two consecutive b's, then $h(w)$ has substring 1010 and has an isolated 0.

Thus, whenever one of the above cases hold, $h(w)$ is not in L. However, unless at least one of items (1) through (4) hold, then w is of the form $baba \cdots ba$.

To see why, assume none of (1) through (4) hold. Then (1) tells us w must begin with b, and (2) tells us w ends with b. Statements (3) and (4) tell us that a's and b's must alternate in w. Thus, the logical "OR" of (1) through (4) is equivalent to the statement "w is not of the form $baba \cdots ba$." We have proved that the "OR" of (1) through (4) implies $h(w)$ is not in L. That statement is the contrapositive of the statement we wanted: "if $h(w)$ is in L, then w is of the form $baba \cdots ba$. $\square$

We shall next prove that the inverse homomorphism of a regular language is also regular, and then show how the theorem can be used.

Theorem 4.16: If h is a homomorphism from alphabet Σ to alphabet T, and L is a regular language over T, then $h^{-1}(L)$ is also a regular language.

PROOF: The proof starts with a DFA A for L. We construct from A and h a DFA for $h^{-1}(L)$ using the plan suggested by Fig. 4.6. This DFA uses the states of A but translates the input symbol according to h before deciding on the next state.

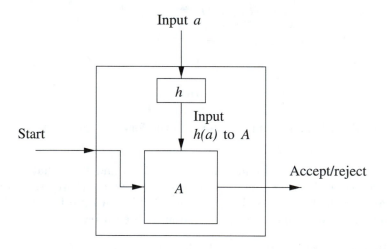

Figure 4.6: The DFA for $h^{-1}(L)$ applies h to its input, and then simulates the DFA for L

Formally, let L be $L(A)$, where DFA $A = (Q, T, \delta, q_0, F)$. Define a DFA

$$B = (Q, \Sigma, \gamma, q_0, F)$$

where transition function γ is constructed by the rule $\gamma(q, a) = \hat{\delta}\big(q, h(a)\big)$. That is, the transition B makes on input a is the result of the sequence of transitions that A makes on the string of symbols $h(a)$. Remember that $h(a)$ could be ϵ, it could be one symbol, or it could be many symbols, but $\hat{\delta}$ is properly defined to take care of all these cases.

It is an easy induction on $|w|$ to show that $\hat{\gamma}(q_0, w) = \hat{\delta}(q_0, h(w))$. Since the accepting states of A and B are the same, B accepts w if and only if A accepts $h(w)$. Put another way, B accepts exactly those strings w that are in $h^{-1}(L)$.
□

Example 4.17 : In this example we shall use inverse homomorphism and several other closure properties of regular sets to prove an odd fact about finite automata. Suppose we required that a DFA visit every state at least once when accepting its input. More precisely, suppose $A = (Q, \Sigma, \delta, q_0, F)$ is a DFA, and we are interested in the language L of all strings w in Σ^* such that $\hat{\delta}(q_0, w)$ is in F, and also for every state q in Q there is some prefix x_q of w such that $\hat{\delta}(q_0, x_q) = q$. Is L regular? We can show it is, but the construction is complex.

First, start with the language M that is $L(A)$, i.e., the set of strings that A accepts in the usual way, without regard to what states it visits during the processing of its input. Note that $L \subseteq M$, since the definition of L puts an additional condition on the strings of $L(A)$. Our proof that L is regular begins by using an inverse homomorphism to, in effect, place the states of A into the input symbols. More precisely, let us define a new alphabet T consisting of symbols that we may think of as triples $[paq]$, where:

1. p and q are states in Q,

2. a is a symbol in Σ, and

3. $\delta(p, a) = q$.

That is, we may think of the symbols in T as representing transitions of the automaton A. It is important to see that the notation $[paq]$ is our way of expressing a single symbol, not the concatenation of three symbols. We could have given it a single letter as a name, but then its relationship to p, q, and a would be hard to describe.

Now, define the homomorphism $h([paq]) = a$ for all p, a, and q. That is, h removes the state components from each of the symbols of T and leaves only the symbol from Σ. Our first step in showing L is regular is to construct the language $L_1 = h^{-1}(M)$. Since M is regular, so is L_1 by Theorem 4.16. The strings of L_1 are just the strings of M with a pair of states, representing a transition, attached to each symbol.

As a very simple illustration, consider the two-state automaton of Fig. 4.4(a). The alphabet Σ is $\{0, 1\}$, and the alphabet T consists of the four symbols $[p0q]$, $[q0q]$, $[p1p]$, and $[q1q]$. For instance, there is a transition from state p to q on input 0, so $[p0q]$ is one of the symbols of T. Since 101 is a string accepted by the automaton, h^{-1} applied to this string will give us $2^3 = 8$ strings, of which $[p1p][p0q][q1q]$ and $[q1q][q0q][p1p]$ are two examples.

We shall now construct L from L_1 by using a series of further operations that preserve regular languages. Our first goal is to eliminate all those strings of L_1 that deal incorrectly with states. That is, we can think of a symbol like

[paq] as saying the automaton was in state p, read input a, and thus entered state q. The sequence of symbols must satisfy three conditions if it is to be deemed an accepting computation of A:

1. The first state in the first symbol must be q_0, the start state of A.

2. Each transition must pick up where the previous one left off. That is, the first state in one symbol must equal the second state of the previous symbol.

3. The second state of the last symbol must be in F. This condition in fact will be guaranteed once we enforce (1) and (2), since we know that every string in L_1 came from a string accepted by A.

The plan of the construction of L is shown in Fig. 4.7.

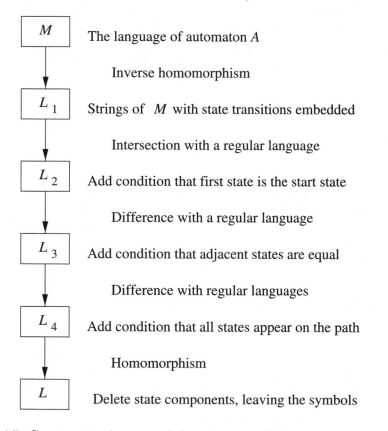

Figure 4.7: Constructing language L from language M by applying operations that preserve regularity of languages

We enforce (1) by intersecting L_1 with the set of strings that begin with a symbol of the form [q_0aq] for some symbol a and state q. That is, let E_1 be the expression $[q_0 a_1 q_1] + [q_0 a_2 q_2] + \cdots$, where the pairs $a_i q_i$ range over all pairs in $\Sigma \times Q$ such that $\delta(q_0, a_i) = q_i$. Then let $L_2 = L_1 \cap L(E_1 T^*)$. Since $E_1 T^*$ is a regular expression denoting all strings in T^* that begin with the start state (treat T in the regular expression as the sum of its symbols), L_2 is all strings that are formed by applying h^{-1} to language M and that have the start state as the first component of its first symbol; i.e., it meets condition (1).

To enforce condition (2), it is easier to subtract from L_2 (using the set-difference operation) all those strings that violate it. Let E_2 be the regular expression consisting of the sum (union) of the concatenation of all pairs of symbols that fail to match; that is, pairs of the form $[paq][rbs]$ where $q \neq r$. Then $T^* E_2 T^*$ is a regular expression denoting all strings that fail to meet condition (2).

We may now define $L_3 = L_2 - L(T^* E_2 T^*)$. The strings of L_3 satisfy condition (1) because strings in L_2 must begin with the start symbol. They satisfy condition (2) because the subtraction of $L(T^* E_2 T^*)$ removes any string that violates that condition. Finally, they satisfy condition (3), that the last state is accepting, because we started with only strings in M, all of which lead to acceptance by A. The effect is that L_3 consists of the strings in M with the states of the accepting computation of that string embedded as part of each symbol. Note that L_3 is regular because it is the result of starting with the regular language M, and applying operations — inverse homomorphism, intersection, and set difference — that yield regular sets when applied to regular sets.

Recall that our goal was to accept only those strings in M that visited every state in their accepting computation. We may enforce this condition by additional applications of the set-difference operator. That is, for each state q, let E_q be the regular expression that is the sum of all the symbols in T such that q appears in neither its first or last position. If we subtract $L(E_q^*)$ from L_3 we have those strings that are an accepting computation of A and that visit state q at least once. If we subtract from L_3 all the languages $L(E_q^*)$ for q in Q, then we have the accepting computations of A that visit all the states. Call this language L_4. By Theorem 4.10 we know L_4 is also regular.

Our final step is to construct L from L_4 by getting rid of the state components. That is, $L = h(L_4)$. Now, L is the set of strings in Σ^* that are accepted by A and that visit each state of A at least once during their acceptance. Since regular languages are closed under homomorphisms, we conclude that L is regular. $\square$

4.2.5 Exercises for Section 4.2

Exercise 4.2.1: Suppose h is the homomorphism from the alphabet $\{0, 1, 2\}$ to the alphabet $\{a, b\}$ defined by: $h(0) = a$; $h(1) = ab$, and $h(2) = ba$.

* a) What is $h(0120)$?

  b) What is $h(21120)$?

* c) If L is the language $L(\mathbf{01^*2})$, what is $h(L)$?

 d) If L is the language $L(\mathbf{0 + 12})$, what is $h(L)$?

* e) Suppose L is the language $\{ababa\}$, that is, the language consisting of only the one string $ababa$. What is $h^{-1}(L)$?

! f) If L is the language $L(\mathbf{a(ba)^*})$, what is $h^{-1}(L)$?

*! **Exercise 4.2.2:** If L is a language, and a is a symbol, then L/a, the *quotient* of L and a, is the set of strings w such that wa is in L. For example, if $L = \{a, aab, baa\}$, then $L/a = \{\epsilon, ba\}$. Prove that if L is regular, so is L/a. *Hint*: Start with a DFA for L and consider the set of accepting states.

! **Exercise 4.2.3:** Lf L is a language, and a is a symbol, then $a\backslash L$ is the set of strings w such that aw is in L. For example, if $L = \{a, aab, baa\}$, then $a\backslash L = \{\epsilon, ab\}$. Prove that if L is regular, so is $a\backslash L$. *Hint*: Remember that the regular languages are closed under reversal and under the quotient operation of Exercise 4.2.2.

! **Exercise 4.2.4:** Which of the following identities are true?

 a) $(L/a)a = L$ (the left side represents the concatenation of the languages L/a and $\{a\}$).

 b) $a(a\backslash L) = L$ (again, concatenation with $\{a\}$, this time on the left, is intended).

 c) $(La)/a = L$.

 d) $a\backslash(aL) = L$.

Exercise 4.2.5: The operation of Exercise 4.2.3 is sometimes viewed as a "derivative," and $a\backslash L$ is written $\frac{dL}{da}$. These derivatives apply to regular expressions in a manner similar to the way ordinary derivatives apply to arithmetic expressions. Thus, if R is a regular expression, we shall use $\frac{dR}{da}$ to mean the same as $\frac{dL}{da}$, if $L = L(R)$.

 a) Show that $\frac{d(R+S)}{da} = \frac{dR}{da} + \frac{dS}{da}$.

*! b) Give the rule for the "derivative" of RS. *Hint*: You need to consider two cases: if $L(R)$ does or does not contain ϵ. This rule is not quite the same as the "product rule" for ordinary derivatives, but is similar.

! c) Give the rule for the "derivative" of a closure, i.e., $\frac{d(R^*)}{da}$.

 d) Use the rules from (a)–(c) to find the "derivative" of regular expression $(\mathbf{0 + 1})^*\mathbf{011}$.

* e) Characterize those languages L for which $\frac{dL}{d0} = \emptyset$.

*! f) Characterize those languages L for which $\frac{dL}{d0} = L$.

! Exercise 4.2.6: Show that the regular languages are closed under the following operations:

    a) $min(L) = \{w \mid w$ is in L, but no proper prefix of w is in $L\}$.

    b) $max(L) = \{w \mid w$ is in L and for no x other than ϵ is wx in $L\}$.

    c) $init(L) = \{w \mid$ for some x, wx is in $L\}$.

Hint: Like Exercise 4.2.2, it is easiest to start with a DFA for L and perform a construction to get the desired language.

! Exercise 4.2.7: If $w = a_1 a_2 \cdots a_n$ and $x = b_1 b_2 \cdots b_m$ are strings of the same length, define $alt(w, x)$ to be the string in which the symbols of w and x alternate, starting with w, that is, $a_1 b_1 a_2 b_2 \cdots a_n b_n$. If L and M are languages, define $alt(L, M)$ to be the set of strings of the form $alt(w, x)$, where w is any string in L and x is any string in M of the same length. Prove that if L and M are regular, so is $alt(L, M)$.

*!! Exercise 4.2.8: Let L be a language. Define $half(L)$ to be the set of first halves of strings in L, that is, $\{w \mid$ for some x such that $|x| = |w|$, we have wx in $L\}$. For example, if $L = \{\epsilon, 0010, 011, 010110\}$ then $half(L) = \{\epsilon, 00, 010\}$. Notice that odd-length strings do not contribute to $half(L)$. Prove that if L is a regular language, so is $half(L)$.

!! Exercise 4.2.9: We can generalize Exercise 4.2.8 to a number of functions that determine how much of the string we take. If f is a function of integers, define $f(L)$ to be $\{w \mid$ for some x, with $|x| = f(|w|)$, we have wx in $L\}$. For instance, the operation $half$ corresponds to f being the identity function $f(n) = n$, since $half(L)$ is defined by having $|x| = |w|$. Show that if L is a regular language, then so is $f(L)$, if f is one of the following functions:

    a) $f(n) = 2n$ (i.e., take the first thirds of strings).

    b) $f(n) = n^2$ (i.e., the amount we take has length equal to the square root of what we do not take).

    c) $f(n) = 2^n$ (i.e., what we take has length equal to the logarithm of what we leave).

!! Exercise 4.2.10: Suppose that L is any language, not necessarily regular, whose alphabet is $\{0\}$; i.e., the strings of L consist of 0's only. Prove that L^* is regular. *Hint*: At first, this theorem sounds preposterous. However, an example will help you see why it is true. Consider the language $L = \{0^i \mid i$ is prime$\}$, which we know is not regular by Example 4.3. Strings 00 and 000 are in L, since 2 and 3 are both primes. Thus, if $j \geq 2$, we can show 0^j is in L^*. If j is even, use $j/2$ copies of 00, and if j is odd, use one copy of 000 and $(j - 3)/2$ copies of 00. Thus, $L^* = 000^*$.

!! **Exercise 4.2.11:** Show that the regular languages are closed under the following operation: $cycle(L) = \{w \mid$ we can write w as $w = xy$, such that yx is in $L\}$. For example, if $L = \{01, 011\}$, then $cycle(L) = \{01, 10, 011, 110, 101\}$. *Hint*: Start with a DFA for L and construct an ϵ-NFA for $cycle(L)$.

!! **Exercise 4.2.12:** Let $w_1 = a_0a_0a_1$, and $w_i = w_{i-1}w_{i-1}a_i$ for all $i > 1$. For instance, $w_3 = a_0a_0a_1a_0a_0a_1a_2a_0a_0a_1a_0a_0a_1a_2a_3$. The shortest regular expression for the language $L_n = \{w_n\}$, i.e., the language consisting of the one string w_n, is the string w_n itself, and the length of this expression is $2^{n+1} - 1$. However, if we allow the intersection operator, we can write an expression for L_n whose length is $O(n^2)$. Find such an expression. *Hint*: Find n languages, each with regular expressions of length $O(n)$, whose intersection is L_n.

! **Exercise 4.2.13:** We can use closure properties to help prove certain languages are not regular. Start with the fact that the language

$$L_{0n1n} = \{0^n1^n \mid n \geq 0\}$$

is not a regular set. Prove the following languages not to be regular by transforming them, using operations known to preserve regularity, to L_{0n1n}:

* a) $\{0^i1^j \mid i \neq j\}$.

  b) $\{0^n1^m2^{n-m} \mid n \geq m \geq 0\}$.

Exercise 4.2.14: In Theorem 4.8, we described the "product construction" that took two DFA's and constructed one DFA whose language is the intersection of the languages of the first two.

  a) Show how to perform the product construction on NFA's (without ϵ-transitions).

  ! b) Show how to perform the product construction on ϵ-NFA's.

  * c) Show how to modify the product construction so the resulting DFA accepts the difference of the languages of the two given DFA's.

  d) Show how to modify the product construction so the resulting DFA accepts the union of the languages of the two given DFA's.

Exercise 4.2.15: In the proof of Theorem 4.8 we claimed that it could be proved by induction on the length of w that

$$\hat{\delta}((q_L, q_M), w) = (\hat{\delta}_L(q_L, w), \hat{\delta}_M(q_M, w))$$

Give this inductive proof.

Exercise 4.2.16: Complete the proof of Theorem 4.14 by considering the cases where expression E is a concatenation of two subexpressions and where E is the closure of an expression.

Exercise 4.2.17: In Theorem 4.16, we omitted a proof by induction on the length of w that $\hat{\gamma}(q_0, w) = \hat{\delta}(q_0, h(w))$. Prove this statement.

4.3   Decision Properties of Regular Languages

In this section we consider how one answers important questions about regular languages. First, we must consider what it means to ask a question about a language. The typical language is infinite, so you cannot present the strings of the language to someone and ask a question that requires them to inspect the infinite set of strings. Rather, we present a language by giving one of the finite representations for it that we have developed: a DFA, an NFA, an ϵ-NFA, or a regular expression.

Of course the language so described will be regular, and in fact there is no way at all to represent completely arbitrary languages. In later chapters we shall see finite ways to represent more than the regular languages, so we can consider questions about languages in these more general classes. However, for many of the questions we ask, algorithms exist only for the class of regular languages. The same questions become "undecidable" (no algorithm to answer them exists) when posed using more "expressive" notations (i.e., notations that can be used to express a larger set of languages) than the representations we have developed for the regular languages.

We begin our study of algorithms for questions about regular languages by reviewing the ways we can convert one representation into another for the same language. In particular, we want to observe the time complexity of the algorithms that perform the conversions. We then consider some of the fundamental questions about languages:

1. Is the language described empty?

2. Is a particular string w in the described language?

3. Do two descriptions of a language actually describe the same language? This question is often called "equivalence" of languages.

4.3.1   Converting Among Representations

We know that we can convert any of the four representations for regular languages to any of the other three representations. Figure 3.1 gave paths from any representation to any of the others. While there are algorithms for any of the conversions, sometimes we are interested not only in the possibility of making a conversion, but in the amount of time it takes. In particular, it is important to distinguish between algorithms that take exponential time (as a function of the size of their input), and therefore can be performed only for relatively small instances, from those that take time that is a linear, quadratic, or some small-degree polynomial of their input size. The latter algorithms are "realistic," in the sense that we expect them to be executable for large instances of the problem. We shall consider the time complexity of each of the conversions we discussed.

Converting NFA's to DFA's

When we start with either an NFA or and ϵ-NFA and convert it to a DFA, the time can be exponential in the number of states of the NFA. First, computing the ϵ-closure of n states takes $O(n^3)$ time. We must search from each of the n states along all arcs labeled ϵ. If there are n states, there can be no more than n^2 arcs. Judicious bookkeeping and well-designed data structures will make sure that we can explore from each state in $O(n^2)$ time. In fact, a transitive closure algorithm such as Warshall's algorithm can be used to compute the entire ϵ-closure at once.[3]

Once the ϵ-closure is computed, we can compute the equivalent DFA by the subset construction. The dominant cost is, in principle, the number of states of the DFA, which can be 2^n. For each state, we can compute the transitions in $O(n^3)$ time by consulting the ϵ-closure information and the NFA's transition table for each of the input symbols. That is, suppose we want to compute $\delta(\{q_1, q_2, \ldots, q_k\}, a)$ for the DFA. There may be as many as n states reachable from each q_i along ϵ-labeled paths, and each of those states may have up to n arcs labeled a. By creating an array indexed by states, we can compute the union of up to n sets of up to n states in time proportional to n^2.

In this way, we can compute, for each q_i, the set of states reachable from q_i along a path labeled a (possibly including ϵ's). Since $k \leq n$, there are at most n states to deal with. We compute the reachable states for each in $O(n^2)$ time. Thus, the total time spent computing reachable states is $O(n^3)$. The union of the sets of reachable states requires only $O(n^2)$ additional time, and we conclude that the computation of one DFA transition takes $O(n^3)$ time.

Note that the number of input symbols is assumed constant, and does not depend on n. Thus, in this and other estimates of running time, we do not consider the number of input symbols as a factor. The size of the input alphabet influences the constant factor that is hidden in the "big-oh" notation, but nothing more.

Our conclusion is that the running time of NFA-to-DFA conversion, including the case where the NFA has ϵ-transitions, is $O(n^3 2^n)$. Of course in practice it is common that the number of states created is much less than 2^n, often only n states. We could state the bound on the running time as $O(n^3 s)$, where s is the number of states the DFA actually has.

DFA-to-NFA Conversion

This conversion is simple, and takes $O(n)$ time on an n-state DFA. All that we need to do is modify the transition table for the DFA by putting set-brackets around states and, if the output is an ϵ-NFA, adding a column for ϵ. Since we treat the number of input symbols (i.e., the width of the transition table) as a constant, copying and processing the table takes $O(n)$ time.

---

[3]For a discussion of transitive closure algorithms, see A. V. Aho, J. E. Hopcroft, and J. D. Ullman, *Data Structures and Algorithms*, Addison-Wesley, 1984.

Automaton-to-Regular-Expression Conversion

If we examine the construction of Section 3.2.1 we observe that at each of n rounds (where n is the number of states of the DFA) we can quadruple the size of the regular expressions constructed, since each is built from four expressions of the previous round. Thus, simply writing down the n^3 expressions can take time $O(n^3 4^n)$. The improved construction of Section 3.2.2 reduces the constant factor, but does not affect the worst-case exponentiality of the problem.

The same construction works in the same running time if the input is an NFA, or even an ϵ-NFA, although we did not prove those facts. It is important to use those constructions for NFA's, however. If we first convert an NFA to a DFA and then convert the DFA to a regular expression, it could take time $O(n^3 4^{n^3 2^n})$, which is doubly exponential.

Regular-Expression-to-Automaton Conversion

Conversion of a regular expression to an ϵ-NFA takes linear time. We need to parse the expression efficiently, using a technique that takes only $O(n)$ time on a regular expression of length n.[4] The result is an expression tree with one node for each symbol of the regular expression (although parentheses do not have to appear in the tree; they just guide the parsing of the expression).

Once we have an expression tree for the regular expression, we can work up the tree, building the ϵ-NFA for each node. The construction rules for the conversion of a regular expression that we saw in Section 3.2.3 never add more than two states and four arcs for any node of the expression tree. Thus, the numbers of states and arcs of the resulting ϵ-NFA are both $O(n)$. Moreover, the work at each node of the parse tree in creating these elements is constant, provided the function that processes each subtree returns pointers to the start and accepting states of its automaton.

We conclude that construction of an ϵ-NFA from a regular expression takes time that is linear in the size of the expression. We can eliminate ϵ-transitions from an n-state ϵ-NFA, to make an ordinary NFA, in $O(n^3)$ time, without increasing the number of states. However, proceeding to a DFA can take exponential time.

4.3.2 Testing Emptiness of Regular Languages

At first glance the answer to the question "is regular language L empty?" is obvious: $\emptyset$ is empty, and all other regular languages are not. However, as we discussed at the beginning of Section 4.3, the problem is not stated with an explicit list of the strings in L. Rather, we are given some representation for L and need to decide whether that representation denotes the language $\emptyset$.

---

[4]Parsing methods capable of doing this task in $O(n)$ time are discussed in A. V. Aho, R. Sethi, and J. D. Ullman, *Compiler Design: Principles, Tools, and Techniques*, Addison-Wesley, 1986.

If our representation is any kind of finite automaton, the emptiness question is whether there is any path whatsoever from the start state to some accepting state. If so, the language is nonempty, while if the accepting states are all separated from the start state, then the language is empty. Deciding whether we can reach an accepting state from the start state is a simple instance of graph-reachability, similar in spirit to the calculation of the ϵ-closure that we discussed in Section 2.5.3. The algorithm can be summarized by this recursive process.

BASIS: The start state is surely reachable from the start state.

INDUCTION: If state q is reachable from the start state, and there is an arc from q to p with any label (an input symbol, or ϵ if the automaton is an ϵ-NFA), then p is reachable.

In that manner we can compute the set of reachable states. If any accepting state is among them, we answer "no" (the language of the automaton is *not* empty), and otherwise we answer "yes." Note that the reachability calculation takes no more time that $O(n^2)$ if the automaton has n states, and in fact it is no worse than proportional to the number of arcs in the automaton's transition diagram, which could be less than n^2 and cannot be more than $O(n^2)$.

If we are given a regular expression representing the language L, rather than an automaton, we could convert the expression to an ϵ-NFA and proceed as above. Since the automaton that results from a regular expression of length n has at most $O(n)$ states and transitions, the algorithm takes $O(n)$ time.

However, we can also inspect the regular expression to decide whether it is empty. Notice first that if the expression has no occurrence of $\emptyset$, then its language is surely not empty. If there are $\emptyset$'s, the language may or may not be empty. The following recursive rules tell whether a regular expression denotes the empty language.

BASIS: $\emptyset$ denotes the empty language; ϵ and **a** for any input symbol a do not.

INDUCTION: Suppose R is a regular expression. There are four cases to consider, corresponding to the ways that R could be constructed.

1. $R = R_1 + R_2$. Then $L(R)$ is empty if and only if both $L(R_1)$ and $L(R_2)$ are empty.

2. $R = R_1 R_2$. Then $L(R)$ is empty if and only if either $L(R_1)$ or $L(R_2)$ is empty.

3. $R = R_1^*$. Then $L(R)$ is not empty; it always includes at least ϵ.

4. $R = (R_1)$. Then $L(R)$ is empty if and only if $L(R_1)$ is empty, since they are the same language.

4.3.3 Testing Membership in a Regular Language

The next question of importance is, given a string w and a regular language L, is w in L. While w is represented explicitly, L is represented by an automaton or regular expression.

If L is represented by a DFA, the algorithm is simple. Simulate the DFA processing the string of input symbols w, beginning in the start state. If the DFA ends in an accepting state, the answer is "yes"; otherwise the answer is "no." This algorithm is extremely fast. If $|w| = n$, and the DFA is represented by a suitable data structure, such as a two-dimensional array that is the transition table, then each transition requires constant time, and the entire test takes $O(n)$ time.

If L has any other representation besides a DFA, we could convert to a DFA and run the test above. That approach could take time that is exponential in the size of the representation, although it is linear in $|w|$. However, if the representation is an NFA or ϵ-NFA, it is simpler and more efficient to simulate the NFA directly. That is, we process symbols of w one at a time, maintaining the set of states the NFA can be in after following any path labeled with that prefix of w. The idea was presented in Fig. 2.10.

If w is of length n, and the NFA has s states, then the running time of this algorithm is $O(ns^2)$. Each input symbol can be processed by taking the previous set of states, which numbers at most s states, and looking at the successors of each of these states. We take the union of at most s sets of at most s states each, which requires $O(s^2)$ time.

If the NFA has ϵ-transitions, then we must compute the ϵ-closure before starting the simulation. Then the processing of each input symbol a has two stages, each of which requires $O(s^2)$ time. First, we take the previous set of states and find their successors on input symbol a. Next, we compute the ϵ-closure of this set of states. The initial set of states for the simulation is the ϵ-closure of the initial state of the NFA.

Lastly, if the representation of L is a regular expression of size s, we can convert to an ϵ-NFA with at most $2s$ states, in $O(s)$ time. We then perform the simulation above, taking $O(ns^2)$ time on an input w of length n.

4.3.4 Exercises for Section 4.3

* **Exercise 4.3.1:** Give an algorithm to tell whether a regular language L is infinite. *Hint*: Use the pumping lemma to show that if the language contains any string whose length is above a certain lower limit, then the language must be infinite.

Exercise 4.3.2: Give an algorithm to tell whether a regular language L contains at least 100 strings.

Exercise 4.3.3: Suppose L is a regular language with alphabet Σ. Give an algorithm to tell whether $L = \Sigma^*$, i.e., all strings over its alphabet.

Exercise 4.3.4: Give an algorithm to tell whether two regular languages L_1 and L_2 have at least one string in common.

Exercise 4.3.5: Give an algorithm to tell, for two regular languages L_1 and L_2 over the same alphabet Σ, whether there is any string in Σ^* that is in neither L_1 nor L_2.

4.4 Equivalence and Minimization of Automata

In contrast to the previous questions — emptiness and membership — whose algorithms were rather simple, the question of whether two descriptions of two regular languages actually define the same language involves considerable intellectual mechanics. In this section we discuss how to test whether two descriptors for regular languages are *equivalent*, in the sense that they define the same language. An important consequence of this test is that there is a way to minimize a DFA. That is, we can take any DFA and find an equivalent DFA that has the minimum number of states. In fact, this DFA is essentially unique: given any two minimum-state DFA's that are equivalent, we can always find a way to rename the states so that the two DFA's become the same.

4.4.1 Testing Equivalence of States

We shall begin by asking a question about the states of a single DFA. Our goal is to understand when two distinct states p and q can be replaced by a single state that behaves like both p and q. We say that states p and q are *equivalent* if:

- For all input strings w, $\hat{\delta}(p, w)$ is an accepting state if and only if $\hat{\delta}(q, w)$ is an accepting state.

Less formally, it is impossible to tell the difference between equivalent states p and q merely by starting in one of the states and asking whether or not a given input string leads to acceptance when the automaton is started in this (unknown) state. Note we do *not* require that $\hat{\delta}(p, w)$ and $\hat{\delta}(q, w)$ are the *same* state, only that either both are accepting or both are nonaccepting.

If two states are not equivalent, then we say they are *distinguishable*. That is, state p is distinguishable from state q if there is at least one string w such that one of $\hat{\delta}(p, w)$ and $\hat{\delta}(q, w)$ is accepting, and the other is not accepting.

Example 4.18: Consider the DFA of Fig. 4.8, whose transition function we shall refer to as δ in this example. Certain pairs of states are obviously not equivalent. For example, C and G are not equivalent because one is accepting and the other is not. That is, the empty string distinguishes these two states, because $\hat{\delta}(C, \epsilon)$ is accepting and $\hat{\delta}(G, \epsilon)$ is not.

Consider states A and G. String ϵ doesn't distinguish them, because they are both nonaccepting states. String 0 doesn't distinguish them because they go to

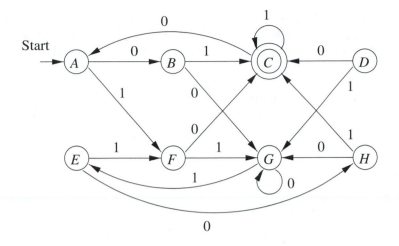

Figure 4.8: An automaton with equivalent states

states B and G, respectively on input 0, and both these states are nonaccepting. Likewise, string 1 doesn't distinguish A from G, because they go to F and E, respectively, and both are nonaccepting. However, 01 distinguishes A from G, because $\hat{\delta}(A, 01) = C$, $\hat{\delta}(G, 01) = E$, C is accepting, and E is not. Any input string that takes A and G to states only one of which is accepting is sufficient to prove that A and G are not equivalent.

In contrast, consider states A and E. Neither is accepting, so ϵ does not distinguish them. On input 1, they both go to state F. Thus, no input string that begins with 1 can distinguish A from E, since for any string x, $\hat{\delta}(A, 1x) = \hat{\delta}(E, 1x)$.

Now consider the behavior of states A and E on inputs that begin with 0. They go to states B and H, respectively. Since neither is accepting, string 0 by itself does not distinguish A from E. However, B and H are no help. On input 1 they both go to C, and on input 0 they both go to G. Thus, all inputs that begin with 0 will fail to distinguish A from E. We conclude that no input string whatsoever will distinguish A from E; i.e., they are equivalent states. $\square$

To find states that are equivalent, we make our best efforts to find pairs of states that are distinguishable. It is perhaps surprising, but true, that if we try our best, according to the algorithm to be described below, then any pair of states that we do not find distinguishable are equivalent. The algorithm, which we refer to as the *table-filling algorithm*, is a recursive discovery of distinguishable pairs in a DFA $A = (Q, \Sigma, \delta, q_0, F)$.

BASIS: If p is an accepting state and q is nonaccepting, then the pair $\{p, q\}$ is distinguishable.

INDUCTION: Let p and q be states such that for some input symbol a, $r = \delta(p, a)$ and $s = \delta(q, a)$ are a pair of states known to be distinguishable. Then

$\{p, q\}$ is a pair of distinguishable states. The reason this rule makes sense is that there must be some string w that distinguishes r from s; that is, exactly one of $\hat{\delta}(r, w)$ and $\hat{\delta}(s, w)$ is accepting. Then string aw must distinguish p from q, since $\hat{\delta}(p, aw)$ and $\hat{\delta}(q, aw)$ is the same pair of states as $\hat{\delta}(r, w)$ and $\hat{\delta}(s, w)$.

Example 4.19: Let us execute the table-filling algorithm on the DFA of Fig 4.8. The final table is shown in Fig. 4.9, where an x indicates pairs of distinguishable states, and the blank squares indicate those pairs that have been found equivalent. Initially, there are no x's in the table.

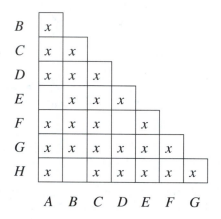

Figure 4.9: Table of state inequivalences

For the basis, since C is the only accepting state, we put x's in each pair that involves C. Now that we know some distinguishable pairs, we can discover others. For instance, since $\{C, H\}$ is distinguishable, and states E and F go to H and C, respectively, on input 0, we know that $\{E, F\}$ is also a distinguishable pair. In fact, all the x's in Fig. 4.9 with the exception of the pair $\{A, G\}$ can be discovered simply by looking at the transitions from the pair of states on either 0 or on 1, and observing that (for one of those inputs) one state goes to C and the other does not. We can show $\{A, G\}$ is distinguishable on the next round, since on input 1 they go to F and E, respectively, and we already established that the pair $\{E, F\}$ is distinguishable.

However, then we can discover no more distinguishable pairs. The three remaining pairs, which are therefore equivalent pairs, are $\{A, E\}$, $\{B, H\}$, and $\{D, F\}$. For example, consider why we can not infer that $\{A, E\}$ is a distinguishable pair. On input 0, A and E go to B and H, respectively, and $\{B, H\}$ has not yet been shown distinguishable. On input 1, A and E both go to F, so there is no hope of distinguishing them that way. The other two pairs, $\{B, H\}$ and $\{D, F\}$ will never be distinguished because they each have identical transitions on 0 and identical transitions on 1. Thus, the table-filling algorithm stops with the table as shown in Fig. 4.9, which is the correct determination of equivalent and distinguishable states. □

Theorem 4.20: If two states are not distinguished by the table-filling algorithm, then the states are equivalent.

PROOF: Let us again assume we are talking of the DFA $A = (Q, \Sigma, \delta, q_0, F)$. Suppose the theorem is false; that is, there is at least one pair of states $\{p, q\}$ such that

1. States p and q are distinguishable, in the sense that there is some string w such that exactly one of $\hat{\delta}(p, w)$ and $\hat{\delta}(q, w)$ is accepting, and yet

2. The table-filling algorithm does not find p and q to be distinguished.

Call such a pair of states a *bad pair*.

If there are bad pairs, then there must be some that are distinguished by the shortest strings among all those strings that distinguish bad pairs. Let $\{p, q\}$ be one such bad pair, and let $w = a_1 a_2 \cdots a_n$ be a string as short as any that distinguishes p from q. Then exactly one of $\hat{\delta}(p, w)$ and $\hat{\delta}(q, w)$ is accepting.

Observe first that w cannot be ϵ, since if ϵ distinguishes a pair of states, then that pair is marked by the basis part of the table-filling algorithm. Thus, $n \geq 1$.

Consider the states $r = \delta(p, a_1)$ and $s = \delta(q, a_1)$. States r and s are distinguished by the string $a_2 a_3 \cdots a_n$, since this string takes r and s to the states $\hat{\delta}(p, w)$ and $\hat{\delta}(q, w)$. However, the string distinguishing r from s is shorter than any string that distinguishes a bad pair. Thus, $\{r, s\}$ cannot be a bad pair. Rather, the table-filling algorithm must have discovered that they are distinguishable.

But the inductive part of the table-filling algorithm will not stop until it has also inferred that p and q are distinguishable, since it finds that $\delta(p, a_1) = r$ is distinguishable from $\delta(q, a_1) = s$. We have contradicted our assumption that bad pairs exist. If there are no bad pairs, then every pair of distinguishable states is distinguished by the table-filling algorithm, and the theorem is true. □

4.4.2 Testing Equivalence of Regular Languages

The table-filling algorithm gives us an easy way to test if two regular languages are the same. Suppose languages L and M are each represented in some way, e.g., one by a regular expression and one by an NFA. Convert each representation to a DFA. Now, imagine one DFA whose states are the union of the states of the DFA's for L and M. Technically, this DFA has two start states, but actually the start state is irrelevant as far as testing state equivalence is concerned, so make any state the lone start state.

Now, test if the start states of the two original DFA's are equivalent, using the table-filling algorithm. If they are equivalent, then $L = M$, and if not, then $L \neq M$.

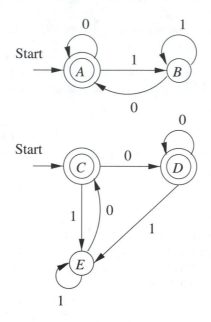

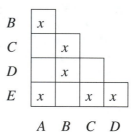

Figure 4.10: Two equivalent DFA's

Example 4.21: Consider the two DFA's in Fig. 4.10. Each DFA accepts the empty string and all strings that end in 0; that is the language of regular expression $\epsilon + (\mathbf{0} + \mathbf{1})^*\mathbf{0}$. We can imagine that Fig. 4.10 represents a single DFA, with five states A through E. If we apply the table-filling algorithm to that automaton, the result is as shown in Fig. 4.11.

B	x			
C		x		
D		x		
E	x		x	x
	A	B	C	D

Figure 4.11: The table of distinguishabilities for Fig. 4.10

To see how the table is filled out, we start by placing x's in all pairs of states where exactly one of the states is accepting. It turns out that there is no more to do. The four remaining pairs, $\{A, C\}$, $\{A, D\}$, $\{C, D\}$, and $\{B, E\}$ are all equivalent pairs. You should check that no more distinguishable pairs are discovered in the inductive part of the table-filling algorithm. For instance, with the table as in Fig. 4.11, we cannot distinguish the pair $\{A, D\}$ because on 0 they go to themselves, and on 1 they go to the pair $\{B, E\}$, which has not yet been distinguished. Since A and C are found equivalent by this test, and those states were the start states of the two original automata, we conclude that these DFA's do accept the same language. □

The time to fill out the table, and thus to decide whether two states are equivalent is polynomial in the number of states. If there are n states, then there are $\binom{n}{2}$, or $n(n-1)/2$ pairs of states. In one round, we consider all pairs of states, to see if one of their successor pairs has been found distinguishable, so a round surely takes no more than $O(n^2)$ time. Moreover, if on some round, no additional x's are placed in the table, then the algorithm ends. Thus, there can be no more than $O(n^2)$ rounds, and $O(n^4)$ is surely an upper bound on the running time of the table-filling algorithm.

However, a more careful algorithm can fill the table in $O(n^2)$ time. The idea is to initialize, for each pair of states $\{r, s\}$, a list of those pairs $\{p, q\}$ that "depend on" $\{r, s\}$. That is, if $\{r, s\}$ is found distinguishable, then $\{p, q\}$ is distinguishable. We create the lists initially by examining each pair of states $\{p, q\}$, and for each of the fixed number of input symbols a, we put $\{p, q\}$ on the list for the pair of states $\{\delta(p, a), \delta(q, a)\}$, which are the successor states for p and q on input a.

If we ever find $\{r, s\}$ to be distinguishable, then we go down the list for $\{r, s\}$. For each pair on that list that is not already distinguishable, we make that pair distinguishable, and we put the pair on a queue of pairs whose lists we must check similarly.

The total work of this algorithm is proportional to the sum of the lengths of the lists, since we are at all times either adding something to the lists (initialization) or examining a member of the list for the first and last time (when we go down the list for a pair that has been found distinguishable). Since the size of the input alphabet is considered a constant, each pair of states is put on $O(1)$ lists. As there are $O(n^2)$ pairs, the total work is $O(n^2)$.

4.4.3 Minimization of DFA's

Another important consequence of the test for equivalence of states is that we can "minimize" DFA's. That is, for each DFA we can find an equivalent DFA that has as few states as any DFA accepting the same language. Moreover, except for our ability to call the states by whatever names we choose, this minimum-state DFA is unique for the language.

The central idea behind the minimization of DFA's is that the notion of state equivalence lets us partition the states into blocks such that:

1. All the states in a block are equivalent.

2. No two states chosen from two different blocks are equivalent.

Example 4.22: Consider the table of Fig. 4.9, where we determined the state equivalences and distinguishabilities for the states of Fig. 4.8. The partition of the states into equivalent blocks is ($\{A, E\}$, $\{B, H\}$, $\{C\}$, $\{D, F\}$, $\{G\}$). Notice that the three pairs of states that are equivalent are each placed in a block together, while the states that are distinguishable from all the other states are each in a block alone.

For the automaton of Fig. 4.10, the partition is ($\{A, C, D\}$, $\{B, E\}$). This example shows that we can have more than two states in a block. It may appear fortuitous that A, C, and D can all live together in a block, because every pair of them is equivalent, and none of them is equivalent to any other state. However, as we shall see in the next theorem to be proved, this situation is guaranteed by our definition of "equivalence" for states. □

Theorem 4.23: The equivalence of states is transitive. That is, if in some DFA $A = (Q, \Sigma, \delta, q_0, F)$ we find that states p and q are equivalent, and we also find that q and r are equivalent, then it must be that p and r are equivalent.

PROOF: Note that transitivity is a property we expect of any relationship called "equivalence." However, simply calling something "equivalence" doesn't make it transitive; we must prove that the name is justified.

Suppose that the pairs $\{p, q\}$ and $\{q, r\}$ are equivalent, but pair $\{p, r\}$ is distinguishable. Then there is some input string w such that exactly one of $\hat{\delta}(p, w)$ and $\hat{\delta}(r, w)$ is an accepting state. Suppose, by symmetry, that $\hat{\delta}(p, w)$ is the accepting state.

Now consider whether $\hat{\delta}(q, w)$ is accepting or not. If it is accepting, then $\{q, r\}$ is distinguishable, since $\hat{\delta}(q, w)$ is accepting, and $\hat{\delta}(r, w)$ is not. If $\hat{\delta}(q, w)$ is nonaccepting, then $\{p, q\}$ is distinguishable for a similar reason. We conclude by contradiction that $\{p, r\}$ was not distinguishable, and therefore this pair is equivalent. □

We can use Theorem 4.23 to justify the obvious algorithm for partitioning states. For each state q, construct a block that consists of q and all the states that are equivalent to q. We must show that the resulting blocks are a partition; that is, no state is in two distinct blocks.

First, observe that all states in any block are mutually equivalent. That is, if p and r are two states in the block of states equivalent to q, then p and r are equivalent to each other, by Theorem 4.23.

Suppose that there are two overlapping, but not identical blocks. That is, there is a block B that includes states p and q, and another block C that includes p but not q. Since p and q are in a block together, they are equivalent. Consider how the block C was formed. If it was the block generated by p, then q would be in C, because those states are equivalent. Thus, it must be that there is some third state s that generated block C; i.e., C is the set of states equivalent to s.

We know that p is equivalent to s, because p is in block C. We also know that p is equivalent to q because they are together in block B. By the transitivity of Theorem 4.23, q is equivalent to s. But then q belongs in block C, a contradiction. We conclude that equivalence of states partitions the states; that is, two states either have the same set of equivalent states (including themselves), or their equivalent states are disjoint. To conclude the above analysis:

Theorem 4.24: If we create for each state q of a DFA a *block* consisting of q and all the states equivalent to q, then the different blocks of states form a *partition* of the set of states.[5] That is, each state is in exactly one block. All members of a block are equivalent, and no pair of states chosen from different blocks are equivalent. □

We are now able to state succinctly the algorithm for minimizing a DFA $A = (Q, \Sigma, \delta, q_0, F)$.

1. Use the table-filling algorithm to find all the pairs of equivalent states.

2. Partition the set of states Q into blocks of mutually equivalent states by the method described above.

3. Construct the minimum-state equivalent DFA B by using the blocks as its states. Let γ be the transition function of B. Suppose S is a set of equivalent states of A, and a is an input symbol. Then there must exist one block T of states such that for all states q in S, $\delta(q, a)$ is a member of block T. For if not, then input symbol a takes two states p and q of S to states in different blocks, and those states are distinguishable by Theorem 4.24. That fact lets us conclude that p and q are not equivalent, and they did not both belong in S. As a consequence, we can let $\gamma(S, a) = T$. In addition:

   (a) The start state of B is the block containing the start state of A.

   (b) The set of accepting states of B is the set of blocks containing accepting states of A. Note that if one state of a block is accepting, then all the states of that block must be accepting. The reason is that any accepting state is distinguishable from any nonexcepting state, so you can't have both accepting and nonaccepting states in one block of equivalent states.

Example 4.25: Let us minimize the DFA from Fig. 4.8. We established the blocks of the state partition in Example 4.22. Figure 4.12 shows the minimum-state automaton. Its five states correspond to the five blocks of equivalent states for the automaton of Fig. 4.8.

The start state is $\{A, E\}$, since A was the start state of Fig. 4.8. The only accepting state is $\{C\}$, since C is the only accepting state of Fig. 4.8. Notice that the transitions of Fig. 4.12 properly reflect the transitions of Fig. 4.8. For instance, Fig. 4.12 has a transition on input 0 from $\{A, E\}$ to $\{B, H\}$. That

---

[5] You should remember that the same block may be formed several times, starting from different states. However, the partition consists of the *different* blocks, so this block appears only once in the partition.

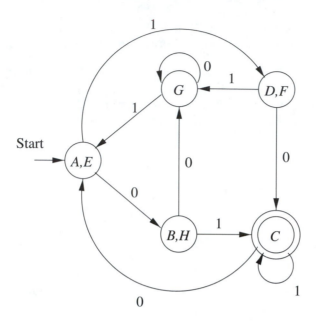

Figure 4.12: Minimum-state DFA equivalent to Fig. 4.8

makes sense, because in Fig. 4.8, A goes to B on input 0, and E goes to H. Likewise, on input 1, $\{A, E\}$ goes to $\{D, F\}$. If we examine Fig. 4.8, we find that both A and E go to F on input 1, so the selection of the successor of $\{A, E\}$ on input 1 is also correct. Note that the fact neither A nor E goes to D on input 1 is not important. You may check that all of the other transitions are also proper.   □

4.4.4   Why the Minimized DFA Can't Be Beaten

Suppose we have a DFA A, and we minimize it to construct a DFA M, using the partitioning method of Theorem 4.24. That theorem shows that we can't group the states of A into fewer groups and still have an equivalent DFA. However, could there be another DFA N, unrelated to A, that accepts the same language as A and M, yet has fewer states than M? We can prove by contradiction that N does not exist.

First, run the state-distinguishability process of Section 4.4.1 on the states of M and N together, as if they were one DFA. We may assume that the states of M and N have no names in common, so the transition function of the combined automaton is the union of the transition rules of M and N, with no interaction. States are accepting in the combined DFA if and only if they are accepting in the DFA from which they come.

The start states of M and N are indistinguishable because $L(M) = L(N)$. Further, if $\{p, q\}$ are indistinguishable, then their successors on any one input

Minimizing the States of an NFA

You might imagine that the same state-partition technique that minimizes the states of a DFA could also be used to find a minimum-state NFA equivalent to a given NFA or DFA. While we can, by a process of exhaustive enumeration, find an NFA with as few states as possible accepting a given regular language, we cannot simply group the states of some given NFA for the language.

An example is in Fig. 4.13. None of the three states are equivalent. Surely accepting state B is distinguishable from nonaccepting states A and C. However, A and C are distinguishable by input 0. The successors of C are A alone, which does not include an accepting state, while the successors of A are $\{A, B\}$, which does include an accepting state. Thus, grouping equivalent states does not reduce the number of states of Fig. 4.13.

However, we can find a smaller NFA for the same language if we simply remove state C. Note that A and B alone accept all strings ending in 0, while adding state C does not allow us to accept any other strings.

symbol are also indistinguishable. The reason is that if we could distinguish the successors, then we could distinguish p from q.

Neither M nor N could have an inaccessible state, or else we could eliminate that state and have an even smaller DFA for the same language. Thus, every state of M is indistinguishable from at least one state of N. To see why, suppose p is a state of M. Then there is some string $a_1 a_2 \cdots a_k$ that takes the start state of M to state p. This string also takes the start state of N to some state q. Since we know the start states are indistinguishable, we also know that their successors under input symbol a_1 are indistinguishable. Then, the successors of those states on input a_2 are indistinguishable, and so on, until we conclude

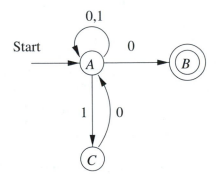

Figure 4.13: An NFA that cannot be minimized by state equivalence

that p and q are indistinguishable.

Since N has fewer states than M, there are two states of M that are indistinguishable from the same state of N, and therefore indistinguishable from each other. But M was designed so that all its states *are* distinguishable from each other. We have a contradiction, so the assumption that N exists is wrong, and M in fact has as few states as any equivalent DFA for A. Formally, we have proved:

Theorem 4.26 : If A is a DFA, and M the DFA constructed from A by the algorithm described in the statement of Theorem 4.24, then M has as few states as any DFA equivalent to A. $\square$

In fact we can say something even stronger than Theorem 4.26. There must be a one-to-one correspondence between the states of any other minimum-state N and the DFA M. The reason is that we argued above how each state of M must be equivalent to one state of N, and no state of M can be equivalent to two states of N. We can similarly argue that no state of N can be equivalent to two states of M, although each state of N must be equivalent to one of M's states. Thus, the minimum-state DFA equivalent to A is unique except for a possible renaming of the states.

	0	1
$\rightarrow A$	B	A
B	A	C
C	D	B
$*D$	D	A
E	D	F
F	G	E
G	F	G
H	G	D

Figure 4.14: A DFA to be minimized

4.4.5   Exercises for Section 4.4

* **Exercise 4.4.1 :** In Fig. 4.14 is the transition table of a DFA.

  a) Draw the table of distinguishabilities for this automaton.

  b) Construct the minimum-state equivalent DFA.

Exercise 4.4.2 : Repeat Exercise 4.4.1 for the DFA of Fig 4.15.

!! **Exercise 4.4.3 :** Suppose that p are q are distinguishable states of a given DFA A with n states. As a function of n, what is the tightest upper bound on how long the shortest string that distinguishes p from q can be?

	0	1
→ A	B	E
B	C	F
*C	D	H
D	E	H
E	F	I
*F	G	B
G	H	B
H	I	C
*I	A	E

Figure 4.15: Another DFA to minimize

4.5 Summary of Chapter 4

✦ *The Pumping Lemma*: If a language is regular, then every sufficiently long string in the language has a nonempty substring that can be "pumped," that is, repeated any number of times while the resulting strings are also in the language. This fact can be used to prove that many different languages are *not* regular.

✦ *Operations That Preserve the Property of Being a Regular Language*: There are many operations that, when applied to regular languages, yield a regular language as a result. Among these are union, concatenation, closure, intersection, complementation, difference, reversal, homomorphism (replacement of each symbol by an associated string), and inverse homomorphism.

✦ *Testing Emptiness of Regular Languages*: There is an algorithm that, given a representation of a regular language, such as an automaton or regular expression, tells whether or not the represented language is the empty set.

✦ *Testing Membership in a Regular Language*: There is an algorithm that, given a string and a representation of a regular language, tells whether or not the string is in the language.

✦ *Testing Distinguishability of States*: Two states of a DFA are distinguishable if there is an input string that takes exactly one of the two states to an accepting state. By starting with only the fact that pairs consisting of one accepting and one nonaccepting state are distinguishable, and trying to discover addition pairs of distinguishable states by finding pairs whose successors on one input symbol are distinguishable, we can discover all pairs of distinguishable states.

✦ *Minimizing Deterministic Finite Automata*: We can partition the states
  of any DFA into groups of mutually indistinguishable states. Members of
  two different groups are always distinguishable. If we replace each group
  by a single state, we get an equivalent DFA that has as few states as any
  DFA for the same language.

4.6   References for Chapter 4

Except for the obvious closure properties of regular expressions — union, concatenation, and star — that were shown by Kleene [6], almost all results about
closure properties of the regular languages mimic similar results about context-
free languages (the class of languages we study in the next chapters). Thus,
the pumping lemma for regular languages is a simplification of a corresponding result for context-free languages by Bar-Hillel, Perles, and Shamir [1]. The
same paper indirectly gives us several of the other closure properties shown
here. However, the closure under inverse homomorphism is from [2].

The quotient operation introduced in Exercise 4.2.2 is from [3]. In fact, that
paper talks about a more general operation where in place of a single symbol a
is any regular language. The series of operations of the "partial removal" type,
starting with Exercise 4.2.8 on the first halves of strings in a regular language,
began with [8]. Seiferas and McNaughton [9] worked out the general case of
when a removal operation preserves regular languages.

The original decision algorithms, such as emptiness, finiteness, and membership for regular languages, are from [7]. Algorithms for minimizing the states
of a DFA appear there and in [5]. The most efficient algorithm for finding the
minimum-state DFA is in [4].

1. Y. Bar-Hillel, M. Perles, and E. Shamir, "On formal properties of simple
   phrase-structure grammars," *Z. Phonetik. Sprachwiss. Kommunikationsforsch.* **14** (1961), pp. 143–172.

2. S. Ginsburg and G. Rose, "Operations which preserve definability in languages," *J. ACM* **10**:2 (1963), pp. 175–195.

3. S. Ginsburg and E. H. Spanier, "Quotients of context-free languages," *J.
   ACM* **10**:4 (1963), pp. 487–492.

4. J. E. Hopcroft, "An $n \log n$ algorithm for minimizing the states in a finite
   automaton," in Z. Kohavi (ed.) *The Theory of Machines and Computations*, Academic Press, New York, pp. 189–196.

5. D. A. Huffman, "The synthesis of sequential switching circuits," *J. Franklin Inst.* **257**:3-4 (1954), pp. 161–190 and 275–303.

6. S. C. Kleene, "Representation of events in nerve nets and finite automata,"
   in C. E. Shannon and J. McCarthy, *Automata Studies*, Princeton Univ.
   Press, 1956, pp. 3–42.

7. E. F. Moore, "Gedanken experiments on sequential machines," in C. E. Shannon and J. McCarthy, *Automata Studies*, Princeton Univ. Press, 1956, pp. 129–153.

8. R. E. Stearns and J. Hartmanis, "Regularity-preserving modifications of regular expressions," *Information and Control* **6**:1 (1963), pp. 55–69.

9. J. I. Seiferas and R. McNaughton, "Regularity-preserving modifications," *Theoretical Computer Science* **2**:2 (1976), pp. 147–154.

Chapter 5

Context-Free Grammars and Languages

We now turn our attention away from the regular languages to a larger class of languages, called the "context-free languages." These languages have a natural, recursive notation, called "context-free grammars." Context-free grammars have played a central role in compiler technology since the 1960's; they turned the implementation of parsers (functions that discover the structure of a program) from a time-consuming, ad-hoc implementation task into a routine job that can be done in an afternoon. More recently, the context-free grammar has been used to describe document formats, via the so-called document-type definition (DTD) that is used in the XML (extensible markup language) community for information exchange on the Web.

In this chapter, we introduce the context-free grammar notation, and show how grammars define languages. We discuss the "parse tree," a picture of the structure that a grammar places on the strings of its language. The parse tree is the product of a parser for a programming language and is the way that the structure of programs is normally captured.

There is an automaton-like notation, called the "pushdown automaton," that also describes all and only the context-free languages; we introduce the pushdown automaton in Chapter 6. While less important than finite automata, we shall find the pushdown automaton, especially its equivalence to context-free grammars as a language-defining mechanism, to be quite useful when we explore the closure and decision properties of the context-free languages in Chapter 7.

5.1 Context-Free Grammars

We shall begin by introducing the context-free grammar notation informally. After seeing some of the important capabilities of these grammars, we offer formal definitions. We show how to define a grammar formally, and introduce the process of "derivation," whereby it is determined which strings are in the language of the grammar.

5.1.1   An Informal Example

Let us consider the language of palindromes. A *palindrome* is a string that reads the same forward and backward, such as `otto` or `madamimadam` ("Madam, I'm Adam," allegedly the first thing Eve heard in the Garden of Eden). Put another way, string w is a palindrome if and only if $w = w^R$. To make things simple, we shall consider describing only the palindromes with alphabet $\{0, 1\}$. This language includes strings like 0110, 11011, and ϵ, but not 011 or 0101.

It is easy to verify that the language L_{pal} of palindromes of 0's and 1's is not a regular language. To do so, we use the pumping lemma. If L_{pal} is a regular language, let n be the associated constant, and consider the palindrome $w = 0^n10^n$. If L_{pal} is regular, then we can break w into $w = xyz$, such that y consists of one or more 0's from the first group. Thus, xz, which would also have to be in L_{pal} if L_{pal} were regular, would have fewer 0's to the left of the lone 1 than there are to the right of the 1. Therefore xz cannot be a palindrome. We have now contradicted the assumption that L_{pal} is a regular language.

There is a natural, recursive definition of when a string of 0's and 1's is in L_{pal}. It starts with a basis saying that a few obvious strings are in L_{pal}, and then exploits the idea that if a string is a palindrome, it must begin and end with the same symbol. Further, when the first and last symbols are removed, the resulting string must also be a palindrome. That is:

BASIS: ϵ, 0, and 1 are palindromes.

INDUCTION: If w is a palindrome, so are $0w0$ and $1w1$. No string is a palindrome of 0's and 1's, unless it follows from this basis and induction rule.

A context-free grammar is a formal notation for expressing such recursive definitions of languages. A grammar consists of one or more variables that represent classes of strings, i.e., languages. In this example we have need for only one variable P, which represents the set of palindromes; that is the class of strings forming the language L_{pal}. There are rules that say how the strings in each class are constructed. The construction can use symbols of the alphabet, strings that are already known to be in one of the classes, or both.

Example 5.1 : The rules that define the palindromes, expressed in the context-free grammar notation, are shown in Fig. 5.1. We shall see in Section 5.1.2 what the rules mean.

The first three rules form the basis. They tell us that the class of palindromes includes the strings ϵ, 0, and 1. None of the right sides of these rules (the portions following the arrows) contains a variable, which is why they form a basis for the definition.

The last two rules form the inductive part of the definition. For instance, rule 4 says that if we take any string w from the class P, then $0w0$ is also in class P. Rule 5 likewise tells us that $1w1$ is also in P.   □

$$
\begin{array}{rccl}
1. & P & \to & \epsilon \\
2. & P & \to & 0 \\
3. & P & \to & 1 \\
4. & P & \to & 0P0 \\
5. & P & \to & 1P1 \\
\end{array}
$$

Figure 5.1: A context-free grammar for palindromes

5.1.2 Definition of Context-Free Grammars

There are four important components in a grammatical description of a language:

1. There is a finite set of symbols that form the strings of the language being defined. This set was $\{0,1\}$ in the palindrome example we just saw. We call this alphabet the *terminals*, or *terminal symbols*.

2. There is a finite set of *variables*, also called sometimes *nonterminals* or *syntactic categories*. Each variable represents a language; i.e., a set of strings. In our example above, there was only one variable, P, which we used to represent the class of palindromes over alphabet $\{0,1\}$.

3. One of the variables represents the language being defined; it is called the *start symbol*. Other variables represent auxiliary classes of strings that are used to help define the language of the start symbol. In our example, P, the only variable, is the start symbol.

4. There is a finite set of *productions* or *rules* that represent the recursive definition of a language. Each production consists of:

   (a) A variable that is being (partially) defined by the production. This variable is often called the *head* of the production.

   (b) The production symbol $\to$.

   (c) A string of zero or more terminals and variables. This string, called the *body* of the production, represents one way to form strings in the language of the variable of the head. In so doing, we leave terminals unchanged and substitute for each variable of the body any string that is known to be in the language of that variable.

   We saw an example of productions in Fig. 5.1.

The four components just described form a *context-free grammar*, or just *grammar*, or *CFG*. We shall represent a CFG G by its four components, that is, $G = (V, T, P, S)$, where V is the set of variables, T the terminals, P the set of productions, and S the start symbol.

Example 5.2: The grammar G_{pal} for the palindromes is represented by

$$G_{pal} = (\{P\}, \{0, 1\}, A, P)$$

where A represents the set of five productions that we saw in Fig. 5.1.   □

Example 5.3: Let us explore a more complex CFG that represents (a simplification of) expressions in a typical programming language. First, we shall limit ourselves to the operators $+$ and $*$, representing addition and multiplication. We shall allow arguments to be identifiers, but instead of allowing the full set of typical identifiers (letters followed by zero or more letters and digits), we shall allow only the letters a and b and the digits 0 and 1. Every identifier must begin with a or b, which may be followed by any string in $\{a, b, 0, 1\}^*$.

We need two variables in this grammar. One, which we call E, represents expressions. It is the start symbol and represents the language of expressions we are defining. The other variable, I, represents identifiers. Its language is actually regular; it is the language of the regular expression

$$\mathbf{(a + b)(a + b + 0 + 1)^*}$$

However, we shall not use regular expressions directly in grammars. Rather, we use a set of productions that say essentially the same thing as this regular expression.

$$
\begin{array}{rlcl}
1. & E & \rightarrow & I \\
2. & E & \rightarrow & E + E \\
3. & E & \rightarrow & E * E \\
4. & E & \rightarrow & (E) \\
\\
5. & I & \rightarrow & a \\
6. & I & \rightarrow & b \\
7. & I & \rightarrow & Ia \\
8. & I & \rightarrow & Ib \\
9. & I & \rightarrow & I0 \\
10. & I & \rightarrow & I1 \\
\end{array}
$$

Figure 5.2: A context-free grammar for simple expressions

The grammar for expressions is stated formally as $G = (\{E, I\}, T, P, E)$, where T is the set of symbols $\{+, *, (,), a, b, 0, 1\}$ and P is the set of productions shown in Fig. 5.2. We interpret the productions as follows.

Rule (1) is the basis rule for expressions. It says that an expression can be a single identifier. Rules (2) through (4) describe the inductive case for expressions. Rule (2) says that an expression can be two expressions connected by a plus sign; rule (3) says the same with a multiplication sign. Rule (4) says

---

Compact Notation for Productions

It is convenient to think of a production as "belonging" to the variable of its head. We shall often use remarks like "the productions for A" or "A-productions" to refer to the productions whose head is variable A. We may write the productions for a grammar by listing each variable once, and then listing all the bodies of the productions for that variable, separated by vertical bars. That is, the productions $A \to \alpha_1$, $A \to \alpha_2, \ldots, A \to \alpha_n$ can be replaced by the notation $A \to \alpha_1|\alpha_2|\cdots|\alpha_n$. For instance, the grammar for palindromes from Fig. 5.1 can be written as $P \to \epsilon \mid 0 \mid 1 \mid 0P0 \mid 1P1$.

---

that if we take any expression and put matching parentheses around it, the result is also an expression.

Rules (5) through (10) describe identifiers I. The basis is rules (5) and (6); they say that a and b are identifiers. The remaining four rules are the inductive case. They say that if we have any identifier, we can follow it by a, b, 0, or 1, and the result will be another identifier. □

5.1.3   Derivations Using a Grammar

We apply the productions of a CFG to infer that certain strings are in the language of a certain variable. There are two approaches to this inference. The more conventional approach is to use the rules from body to head. That is, we take strings known to be in the language of each of the variables of the body, concatenate them, in the proper order, with any terminals appearing in the body, and infer that the resulting string is in the language of the variable in the head. We shall refer to this procedure as *recursive inference*.

There is another approach to defining the language of a grammar, in which we use the productions from head to body. We expand the start symbol using one of its productions (i.e., using a production whose head is the start symbol). We further expand the resulting string by replacing one of the variables by the body of one of its productions, and so on, until we derive a string consisting entirely of terminals. The language of the grammar is all strings of terminals that we can obtain in this way. This use of grammars is called *derivation*.

We shall begin with an example of the first approach — recursive inference. However, it is often more natural to think of grammars as used in derivations, and we shall next develop the notation for describing these derivations.

Example 5.4 : Let us consider some of the inferences we can make using the grammar for expressions in Fig. 5.2. Figure 5.3 summarizes these inferences. For example, line (*i*) says that we can infer string a is in the language for I by using production 5. Lines (*ii*) through (*iv*) say we can infer that $b00$

is an identifier by using production 6 once (to get the b) and then applying production 9 twice (to attach the two 0's).

	String Inferred	For lang-uage of	Production used	String(s) used
(i)	a	I	5	—
(ii)	b	I	6	—
(iii)	$b0$	I	9	(ii)
(iv)	$b00$	I	9	(iii)
(v)	a	E	1	(i)
(vi)	$b00$	E	1	(iv)
(vii)	$a + b00$	E	2	$(v), (vi)$
$(viii)$	$(a + b00)$	E	4	(vii)
(ix)	$a * (a + b00)$	E	3	$(v), (viii)$

Figure 5.3: Inferring strings using the grammar of Fig. 5.2

Lines (v) and (vi) exploit production 1 to infer that, since any identifier is an expression, the strings a and $b00$, which we inferred in lines (i) and (iv) to be identifiers, are also in the language of variable E. Line (vii) uses production 2 to infer that the sum of these identifiers is an expression; line $(viii)$ uses production 4 to infer that the same string with parentheses around it is also an identifier, and line (ix) uses production 3 to multiply the identifier a by the expression we had discovered in line $(viii)$. □

The process of deriving strings by applying productions from head to body requires the definition of a new relation symbol $\Rightarrow$. Suppose $G = (V, T, P, S)$ is a CFG. Let $\alpha A\beta$ be a string of terminals and variables, with A a variable. That is, α and β are strings in $(V \cup T)^*$, and A is in V. Let $A \rightarrow \gamma$ be a production of G. Then we say $\alpha A\beta \underset{G}{\Rightarrow} \alpha\gamma\beta$. If G is understood, we just say $\alpha A\beta \Rightarrow \alpha\gamma\beta$. Notice that one derivation step replaces any variable anywhere in the string by the body of one of its productions.

We may extend the $\Rightarrow$ relationship to represent zero, one, or many derivation steps, much as the transition function δ of a finite automaton was extended to $\hat{\delta}$. For derivations, we use a $*$ to denote "zero or more steps, as follows:

BASIS: For any string α of terminals and variables, we say $\alpha \underset{G}{\overset{*}{\Rightarrow}} \alpha$. That is, any string derives itself.

INDUCTION: If $\alpha \underset{G}{\overset{*}{\Rightarrow}} \beta$ and $\beta \underset{G}{\Rightarrow} \gamma$, then $\alpha \underset{G}{\overset{*}{\Rightarrow}} \gamma$. That is, if α can become β by zero or more steps, and one more step takes β to γ, then α can become γ. Put another way, $\alpha \underset{G}{\overset{*}{\Rightarrow}} \beta$ means that there is a sequence of strings $\gamma_1, \gamma_2, \ldots, \gamma_n$, for some $n \geq 1$, such that

1. $\alpha = \gamma_1$,

2. $\beta = \gamma_n$, and

3. For $i = 1, 2, \ldots, n - 1$, we have $\gamma_i \Rightarrow \gamma_{i+1}$.

If grammar G is understood, then we use $\overset{*}{\Rightarrow}$ in place of $\overset{*}{\underset{G}{\Rightarrow}}$.

Example 5.5: The inference that $a * (a + b00)$ is in the language of variable E can be reflected in a derivation of that string, starting with the string E. Here is one such derivation:

$$E \Rightarrow E * E \Rightarrow I * E \Rightarrow a * E \Rightarrow$$

$$a * (E) \Rightarrow a * (E + E) \Rightarrow a * (I + E) \Rightarrow a * (a + E) \Rightarrow$$

$$a * (a + I) \Rightarrow a * (a + I0) \Rightarrow a * (a + I00) \Rightarrow a * (a + b00)$$

At the first step, E is replaced by the body of production 3 (from Fig. 5.2). At the second step, production 1 is used to replace the first E by I, and so on. Notice that we have systematically adopted the policy of always replacing the leftmost variable in the string. However, at each step we may choose which variable to replace, and we can use any of the productions for that variable. For instance, at the second step, we could have replaced the second E by (E), using production 4. In that case, we would say $E * E \Rightarrow E * (E)$. We could also have chosen to make a replacement that would fail to lead to the same string of terminals. A simple example would be if we used production 2 at the first step, and said $E \Rightarrow E + E$. No replacements for the two E's could ever turn $E + E$ into $a * (a + b00)$.

We can use the $\overset{*}{\Rightarrow}$ relationship to condense the derivation. We know $E \overset{*}{\Rightarrow} E$ by the basis. Repeated use of the inductive part gives us $E \overset{*}{\Rightarrow} E*E$, $E \overset{*}{\Rightarrow} I*E$, and so on, until finally $E \overset{*}{\Rightarrow} a * (a + b00)$.

The two viewpoints — recursive inference and derivation — are equivalent. That is, a string of terminals w is inferred to be in the language of some variable A if and only if $A \overset{*}{\Rightarrow} w$. However, the proof of this fact requires some work, and we leave it to Section 5.2. □

5.1.4 Leftmost and Rightmost Derivations

In order to restrict the number of choices we have in deriving a string, it is often useful to require that at each step we replace the leftmost variable by one of its production bodies. Such a derivation is called a *leftmost derivation*, and we indicate that a derivation is leftmost by using the relations $\underset{lm}{\Rightarrow}$ and $\underset{lm}{\overset{*}{\Rightarrow}}$, for one or many steps, respectively. If the grammar G that is being used is not obvious, we can place the name G below the arrow in either of these symbols.

Similarly, it is possible to require that at each step the rightmost variable is replaced by one of its bodies. If so, we call the derivation *rightmost* and use

---

Notation for CFG Derivations

There are a number of conventions in common use that help us remember the role of the symbols we use when discussing CFG's. Here are the conventions we shall use:

1. Lower-case letters near the beginning of the alphabet, a, b, and so on, are terminal symbols. We shall also assume that digits and other characters such as $+$ or parentheses are terminals.

2. Upper-case letters near the beginning of the alphabet, A, B, and so on, are variables.

3. Lower-case letters near the end of the alphabet, such as w or z, are strings of terminals. This convention reminds us that the terminals are analogous to the input symbols of an automaton.

4. Upper-case letters near the end of the alphabet, such as X or Y, are either terminals or variables.

5. Lower-case Greek letters, such as α and β, are strings consisting of terminals and/or variables.

There is no special notation for strings that consist of variables only, since this concept plays no important role. However, the a string named α or another Greek letter might happen to have only variables.

---

the symbols $\Rightarrow_{rm}$ and $\overset{*}{\Rightarrow}_{rm}$ to indicate one or many rightmost derivation steps, respectively. Again, the name of the grammar may appear below these symbols if it is not clear which grammar is being used.

Example 5.6: The derivation of Example 5.5 was actually a leftmost derivation. Thus, we can describe the same derivation by:

$$E \underset{lm}{\Rightarrow} E * E \underset{lm}{\Rightarrow} I * E \underset{lm}{\Rightarrow} a * E \underset{lm}{\Rightarrow}$$

$$a * (E) \underset{lm}{\Rightarrow} a * (E + E) \underset{lm}{\Rightarrow} a * (I + E) \underset{lm}{\Rightarrow} a * (a + E) \underset{lm}{\Rightarrow}$$

$$a * (a + I) \underset{lm}{\Rightarrow} a * (a + I0) \underset{lm}{\Rightarrow} a * (a + I00) \underset{lm}{\Rightarrow} a * (a + b00)$$

We can also summarize the leftmost derivation by saying $E \overset{*}{\underset{lm}{\Rightarrow}} a * (a + b00)$, or express several steps of the derivation by expressions such as $E * E \overset{*}{\underset{lm}{\Rightarrow}} a * (E)$.

There is a rightmost derivation that uses the same replacements for each variable, although it makes the replacements in different order. This rightmost derivation is:

$$E \underset{rm}{\Rightarrow} E * E \underset{rm}{\Rightarrow} E * (E) \underset{rm}{\Rightarrow} E * (E + E) \underset{rm}{\Rightarrow}$$

$$E * (E + I) \underset{rm}{\Rightarrow} E * (E + I0) \underset{rm}{\Rightarrow} E * (E + I00) \underset{rm}{\Rightarrow} E * (E + b00) \underset{rm}{\Rightarrow}$$

$$E * (I + b00) \underset{rm}{\Rightarrow} E * (a + b00) \underset{rm}{\Rightarrow} I * (a + b00) \underset{rm}{\Rightarrow} a * (a + b00)$$

This derivation allows us to conclude $E \overset{*}{\underset{rm}{\Rightarrow}} a * (a + b00)$. □

Any derivation has an equivalent leftmost and an equivalent rightmost derivation. That is, if w is a terminal string, and A a variable, then $A \overset{*}{\Rightarrow} w$ if and only if $A \overset{*}{\underset{lm}{\Rightarrow}} w$, and $A \overset{*}{\Rightarrow} w$ if and only if $A \overset{*}{\underset{rm}{\Rightarrow}} w$. We shall also prove these claims in Section 5.2.

5.1.5 The Language of a Grammar

If $G(V, T, P, S)$ is a CFG, the *language* of G, denoted $L(G)$, is the set of terminal strings that have derivations from the start symbol. That is,

$$L(G) = \{w \text{ in } T \mid S \overset{*}{\underset{G}{\Rightarrow}} w\}$$

If a language L is the language of some context-free grammar, then L is said to be a *context-free language*, or CFL. For instance, we asserted that the grammar of Fig. 5.1 defined the language of palindromes over alphabet $\{0, 1\}$. Thus, the set of palindromes is a context-free language. We can prove that statement, as follows.

Theorem 5.7: $L(G_{pal})$, where G_{pal} is the grammar of Example 5.1, is the set of palindromes over $\{0, 1\}$.

PROOF: We shall prove that a string w in $\{0, 1\}^*$ is in $L(G_{pal})$ if and only if it is a palindrome; i.e., $w = w^R$.

(If) Suppose w is a palindrome. We show by induction on $|w|$ that w is in $L(G_{pal})$.

BASIS: We use lengths 0 and 1 as the basis. If $|w| = 0$ or $|w| = 1$, then w is ϵ, 0, or 1. Since there are productions $P \to \epsilon$, $P \to 0$, and $P \to 1$, we conclude that $P \overset{*}{\Rightarrow} w$ in any of these basis cases.

INDUCTION: Suppose $|w| \geq 2$. Since $w = w^R$, w must begin and end with the same symbol That is, $w = 0x0$ or $w = 1x1$. Moreover, x must be a palindrome; that is, $x = x^R$. Note that we need the fact that $|w| \geq 2$ to infer that there are two distinct 0's or 1's, at either end of w.

If $w = 0x0$, then we invoke the inductive hypothesis to claim that $P \overset{*}{\Rightarrow} x$. Then there is a derivation of w from P, namely $P \Rightarrow 0P0 \overset{*}{\Rightarrow} 0x0 = w$. If $w = 1x1$, the argument is the same, but we use the production $P \rightarrow 1P1$ at the first step. In either case, we conclude that w is in $L(G_{pal})$ and complete the proof.

(Only if) Now, we assume that w is in $L(G_{pal})$; that is, $P \overset{*}{\Rightarrow} w$. We must conclude that w is a palindrome. The proof is an induction on the number of steps in a derivation of w from P.

BASIS: If the derivation is one step, then it must use one of the three productions that do not have P in the body. That is, the derivation is $P \Rightarrow \epsilon$, $P \Rightarrow 0$, or $P \Rightarrow 1$. Since ϵ, 0, and 1 are all palindromes, the basis is proven.

INDUCTION: Now, suppose that the derivation takes $n+1$ steps, where $n \geq 1$, and the statement is true for all derivations of n steps. That is, if $P \overset{*}{\Rightarrow} x$ in n steps, then x is a palindrome.

Consider an $(n+1)$-step derivation of w, which must be of the form

$$P \Rightarrow 0P0 \overset{*}{\Rightarrow} 0x0 = w$$

or $P \Rightarrow 1P1 \overset{*}{\Rightarrow} 1x1 = w$, since $n+1$ steps is at least two steps, and the productions $P \rightarrow 0P0$ and $P \rightarrow 1P1$ are the only productions whose use allows additional steps of a derivation. Note that in either case, $P \overset{*}{\Rightarrow} x$ in n steps.

By the inductive hypothesis, we know that x is a palindrome; that is, $x = x^R$. But if so, then $0x0$ and $1x1$ are also palindromes. For instance, $(0x0)^R = 0x^R0 = 0x0$. We conclude that w is a palindrome, which completes the proof. $\square$

5.1.6   Sentential Forms

Derivations from the start symbol produce strings that have a special role. We call these "sentential forms." That is, if $G = (V, T, P, S)$ is a CFG, then any string α in $(V \cup T)^*$ such that $S \overset{*}{\Rightarrow} \alpha$ is a *sentential form*. If $S \overset{*}{\underset{lm}{\Rightarrow}} \alpha$, then α is a *left-sentential form*, and if $S \overset{*}{\underset{rm}{\Rightarrow}} \alpha$, then α is a *right-sentential form*. Note that the language $L(G)$ is those sentential forms that are in T^*; i.e., they consist solely of terminals.

Example 5.8 : Consider the grammar for expressions from Fig. 5.2. For example, $E * (I + E)$ is a sentential form, since there is a derivation

$$E \Rightarrow E * E \Rightarrow E * (E) \Rightarrow E * (E + E) \Rightarrow E * (I + E)$$

However this derivation is neither leftmost nor rightmost, since at the last step, the middle E is replaced.

As an example of a left-sentential form, consider $a * E$, with the leftmost derivation

---

The Form of Proofs About Grammars

Theorem 5.7 is typical of proofs that show a grammar defines a particular, informally defined language. We first develop an inductive hypothesis that states what properties the strings derived from each variable have. In this example, there was only one variable, P, so we had only to claim that its strings were palindromes.

We prove the "if" part: that if a string w satisfies the informal statement about the strings of one of the variables A, then $A \stackrel{*}{\Rightarrow} w$. In our example, since P is the start symbol, we stated "$P \stackrel{*}{\Rightarrow} w$" by saying that w is in the language of the grammar. Typically, we prove the "if" part by induction on the length of w. If there are k variables, then the inductive statement to be proved has k parts, which must be proved as a mutual induction.

We must also prove the "only-if" part, that if $A \stackrel{*}{\Rightarrow} w$, then w satisfies the informal statement about the strings derived from variable A. Again, in our example, since we had to deal only with the start symbol P, we assumed that w was in the language of G_{pal} as an equivalent to $P \stackrel{*}{\Rightarrow} w$. The proof of this part is typically by induction on the number of steps in the derivation. If the grammar has productions that allow two or more variables to appear in derived strings, then we shall have to break a derivation of n steps into several parts, one derivation from each of the variables. These derivations may have fewer than n steps, so we have to perform an induction assuming the statement for all values n or less, as discussed in Section 1.4.2.

$$E \underset{lm}{\Rightarrow} E * E \underset{lm}{\Rightarrow} I * E \underset{lm}{\Rightarrow} a * E$$

Additionally, the derivation

$$E \underset{rm}{\Rightarrow} E * E \underset{rm}{\Rightarrow} E * (E) \underset{rm}{\Rightarrow} E * (E + E)$$

shows that $E * (E + E)$ is a right-sentential form. □

5.1.7 Exercises for Section 5.1

Exercise 5.1.1: Design context-free grammars for the following languages:

* a) The set $\{0^n 1^n \mid n \geq 1\}$, that is, the set of all strings of one or more 0's followed by an equal number of 1's.

*! b) The set $\{a^i b^j c^k \mid i \neq j \text{ or } j \neq k\}$, that is, the set of strings of a's followed by b's followed by c's, such that there are either a different number of a's and b's or a different number of b's and c's, or both.

! c) The set of all strings of a's and b's that are *not* of the form ww, that is, not equal to any string repeated.

!! d) The set of all strings with twice as many 0's as 1's.

Exercise 5.1.2: The following grammar generates the language of regular expression $0^*1(0+1)^*$:

$$
\begin{aligned}
S &\rightarrow A1B \\
A &\rightarrow 0A \mid \epsilon \\
B &\rightarrow 0B \mid 1B \mid \epsilon
\end{aligned}
$$

Give leftmost and rightmost derivations of the following strings:

* a) 00101.

  b) 1001.

  c) 00011.

! **Exercise 5.1.3:** Show that every regular language is a context-free language. *Hint*: Construct a CFG by induction on the number of operators in the a regular expression.

! **Exercise 5.1.4:** A CFG is said to be *right-linear* if each production body has at most one variable, and that variable is at the right end. That is, all productions of a right-linear grammar are of the form $A \rightarrow wB$ or $A \rightarrow w$, where A and B are variables and w some string of zero or more terminals.

  a) Show that every right-linear grammar generates a regular language. *Hint*: Construct an ϵ-NFA that simulates leftmost derivations, using its state to represent the lone variable in the current left-sentential form.

  b) Show that every regular language has a right-linear grammar. *Hint*: Start with a DFA and let the variables of the grammar represent states.

*! **Exercise 5.1.5:** Let $T = \{0, 1, (,), +, *, \emptyset, e\}$. We may think of T as the set of symbols used by regular expressions over alphabet $\{0, 1\}$; the only difference is that we use e for symbol ϵ, to avoid potential confusion in what follows. Your task is to design a CFG with set of terminals T that generates exactly the regular expressions with alphabet $\{0, 1\}$.

Exercise 5.1.6: We defined the relation $\overset{*}{\Rightarrow}$ with a basis "$\alpha \Rightarrow \alpha$" and an induction that says "$\alpha \overset{*}{\Rightarrow} \beta$ and $\beta \Rightarrow \gamma$ imply $\alpha \overset{*}{\Rightarrow} \gamma$. There are several other ways to define $\overset{*}{\Rightarrow}$ that also have the effect of saying that "$\overset{*}{\Rightarrow}$ is zero or more $\Rightarrow$ steps." Prove that the following are true:

  a) $\alpha \overset{*}{\Rightarrow} \beta$ if and only if there is a sequence of one or more strings

$$\gamma_1, \gamma_2, \ldots, \gamma_n$$

  such that $\alpha = \gamma_1$, $\beta = \gamma_n$, and for $i = 1, 2, \ldots, n-1$ we have $\gamma_i \Rightarrow \gamma_{i+1}$.

  b) If $\alpha \overset{*}{\Rightarrow} \beta$, and $\beta \overset{*}{\Rightarrow} \gamma$, then $\alpha \overset{*}{\Rightarrow} \gamma$. *Hint*: use induction on the number of steps in the derivation $\beta \overset{*}{\Rightarrow} \gamma$.

! **Exercise 5.1.7:** Consider the CFG G defined by productions:

$$S \rightarrow aS \mid Sb \mid a \mid b$$

  a) Prove by induction on the string length that no string in $L(G)$ has *ba* as a substring.

  b) Describe $L(G)$ informally. Justify your answer using part (a).

!! **Exercise 5.1.8:** Consider the CFG G defined by productions:

$$S \rightarrow aSbS \mid bSaS \mid \epsilon$$

Prove that $L(G)$ is the set of all strings with an equal number of a's and b's.

5.2 Parse Trees

There is a tree representation for derivations that has proved extremely useful. This tree shows us clearly how the symbols of a terminal string are grouped into substrings, each of which belongs to the language of one of the variables of the grammar. But perhaps more importantly, the tree, known as a "parse tree" when used in a compiler, is the data structure of choice to represent the source program. In a compiler, the tree structure of the source program facilitates the translation of the source program into executable code by allowing natural, recursive functions to perform this translation process.

   In this section, we introduce the parse tree and show that the existence of parse trees is tied closely to the existence of derivations and recursive inferences. We shall later study the matter of ambiguity in grammars and languages, which is an important application of parse trees. Certain grammars allow a terminal string to have more than one parse tree. That situation makes the grammar unsuitable for a programming language, since the compiler could not tell the structure of certain source programs, and therefore could not with certainty deduce what the proper executable code for the program was.

5.2.1 Constructing Parse Trees

Let us fix on a grammar $G = (V, T, P, S)$. The *parse trees* for G are trees with the following conditions:

  1. Each interior node is labeled by a variable in V.

  2. Each leaf is labeled by either a variable, a terminal, or ϵ. However, if the leaf is labeled ϵ, then it must be the only child of its parent.

Review of Tree Terminology

We assume you have been introduced to the idea of a tree and are familiar with the commonly used definitions for trees. However, the following will serve as a review.

- Trees are collections of *nodes*, with a *parent-child* relationship. A node has at most one parent, drawn above the node, and zero or more children, drawn below. Lines connect parents to their children. Figures 5.4, 5.5, and 5.6 are examples of trees.

- There is one node, the *root*, that has no parent; this node appears at the top of the tree. Nodes with no children are called *leaves*. Nodes that are not leaves are *interior nodes*.

- A child of a child of a $\cdots$ node is a *descendant* of that node. A parent of a parent of a $\cdots$ is an *ancestor*. Trivially, nodes are ancestors and descendants of themselves.

- The children of a node are ordered "from the left," and drawn so. If node N is to the left of node M, then all the descendants of N are considered to be to the left of all the descendants of M.

---

3. If an interior node is labeled A, and its children are labeled

$$X_1, X_2, \ldots, X_k$$

respectively, from the left, then $A \rightarrow X_1 X_2 \cdots X_k$ is a production in P. Note that the only time one of the X's can be ϵ is if that is the label of the only child, and $A \rightarrow \epsilon$ is a production of G.

Example 5.9 : Figure 5.4 shows a parse tree that uses the expression grammar of Fig. 5.2. The root is labeled with the variable E. We see that the production used at the root is $E \rightarrow E + E$, since the three children of the root have labels E, $+$, and E, respectively, from the left. At the leftmost child of the root, the production $E \rightarrow I$ is used, since there is one child of that node, labeled I. □

Example 5.10 : Figure 5.5 shows a parse tree for the palindrome grammar of Fig. 5.1. The production used at the root is $P \rightarrow 0P0$, and at the middle child of the root it is $P \rightarrow 1P1$. Note that at the bottom is a use of the production $P \rightarrow \epsilon$. That use, where the node labeled by the head has one child, labeled ϵ, is the only time that a node labeled ϵ can appear in a parse tree. □

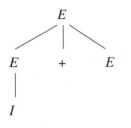

Figure 5.4: A parse tree showing the derivation of $I + E$ from E

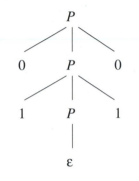

Figure 5.5: A parse tree showing the derivation $P \overset{*}{\Rightarrow} 0110$

5.2.2 The Yield of a Parse Tree

If we look at the leaves of any parse tree and concatenate them from the left, we get a string, called the *yield* of the tree, which is always a string that is derived from the root variable. The fact that the yield is derived from the root will be proved shortly. Of special importance are those parse trees such that:

1. The yield is a terminal string. That is, all leaves are labeled either with a terminal or with ϵ.

2. The root is labeled by the start symbol.

These are the parse trees whose yields are strings in the language of the underlying grammar. We shall also prove shortly that another way to describe the language of a grammar is as the set of yields of those parse trees having the start symbol at the root and a terminal string as yield.

Example 5.11: Figure 5.6 is an example of a tree with a terminal string as yield and the start symbol at the root; it is based on the grammar for expressions that we introduced in Fig. 5.2. This tree's yield is the string $a * (a + b00)$ that was derived in Example 5.5. In fact, as we shall see, this particular parse tree is a representation of that derivation. □

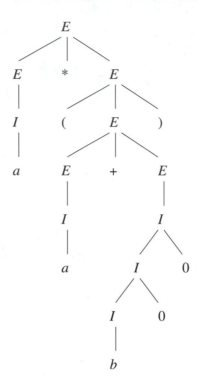

Figure 5.6: Parse tree showing $a*(a+b00)$ is in the language of our expression grammar

5.2.3   Inference, Derivations, and Parse Trees

Each of the ideas that we have introduced so far for describing how a grammar works gives us essentially the same facts about strings. That is, given a grammar $G = (V, T, P, S)$, we shall show that the following are equivalent:

1. The recursive inference procedure determines that terminal string w is in the language of variable A.

2. $A \stackrel{*}{\Rightarrow} w$.

3. $A \stackrel{*}{\underset{lm}{\Rightarrow}} w$.

4. $A \stackrel{*}{\underset{rm}{\Rightarrow}} w$.

5. There is a parse tree with root A and yield w.

In fact, except for the use of recursive inference, which we only defined for terminal strings, all the other conditions — the existence of derivations, leftmost or rightmost derivations, and parse trees — are also equivalent if w is a string that has some variables.

We need to prove these equivalences, and we do so using the plan of Fig. 5.7. That is, each arc in that diagram indicates that we prove a theorem that says if w meets the condition at the tail, then it meets the condition at the head of the arc. For instance, we shall show in Theorem 5.12 that if w is inferred to be in the language of A by recursive inference, then there is a parse tree with root A and yield w.

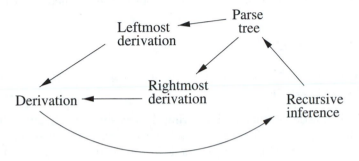

Figure 5.7: Proving the equivalence of certain statements about grammars

Note that two of the arcs are very simple and will not be proved formally. If w has a leftmost derivation from A, then it surely has a derivation from A, since a leftmost derivation *is* a derivation. Likewise, if w has a rightmost derivation, then it surely has a derivation. We now proceed to prove the harder steps of this equivalence.

5.2.4 From Inferences to Trees

Theorem 5.12: Let $G = (V, T, P, S)$ be a CFG. If the recursive inference procedure tells us that terminal string w is in the language of variable A, then there is a parse tree with root A and yield w.

PROOF: The proof is an induction on the number of steps used to infer that w is in the language of A.

BASIS: One step. Then only the basis of the inference procedure must have been used. Thus, there must be a production $A \to w$. The tree of Fig. 5.8, where there is one leaf for each position of w, meets the conditions to be a parse tree for grammar G, and it evidently has yield w and root A. In the special case that $w = \epsilon$, the tree has a single leaf labeled ϵ and is a legal parse tree with root A and yield w.

INDUCTION: Suppose that the fact w is in the language of A is inferred after $n+1$ inference steps, and that the statement of the theorem holds for all strings x and variables B such that the membership of x in the language of B was inferred using n or fewer inference steps. Consider the last step of the inference that w is in the language of A. This inference uses some production for A, say $A \to X_1 X_2 \cdots X_k$, where each X_i is either a variable or a terminal.

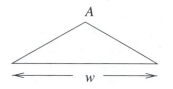

Figure 5.8: Tree constructed in the basis case of Theorem 5.12

We can break w up as $w_1 w_2 \cdots w_k$, where:

1. If X_i is a terminal, then $w_i = X_i$; i.e., w_i consists of only this one terminal from the production.

2. If X_i is a variable, then w_i is a string that was previously inferred to be in the language of X_i. That is, this inference about w_i took at most n of the $n+1$ steps of the inference that w is in the language of A. It cannot take all $n+1$ steps, because the final step, using production $A \to X_1 X_2 \cdots X_k$, is surely not part of the inference about w_i. Consequently, we may apply the inductive hypothesis to w_i and X_i, and conclude that there is a parse tree with yield w_i and root X_i.

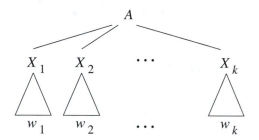

Figure 5.9: Tree used in the inductive part of the proof of Theorem 5.12

We then construct a tree with root A and yield w, as suggested in Fig. 5.9. There is a root labeled A, whose children are $X_1, X_2, \ldots, X_k$. This choice is valid, since $A \to X_1 X_2 \cdots X_k$ is a production of G.

The node for each X_i is made the root of a subtree with yield w_i. In case (1), where X_i is a terminal, this subtree is a trivial tree with a single node labeled X_i. That is, the subtree consists of only this child of the root. Since $w_i = X_i$ in case (1), we meet the condition that the yield of the subtree is w_i.

In case (2), X_i is a variable. Then, we invoke the inductive hypothesis to claim that there is some tree with root X_i and yield w_i. This tree is attached to the node for X_i in Fig. 5.9.

The tree so constructed has root A. Its yield is the yields of the subtrees, concatenated from left to right. That string is $w_1 w_2 \cdots w_k$, which is w.   □

5.2.5   From Trees to Derivations

We shall now show how to construct a leftmost derivation from a parse tree. The method for constructing a rightmost derivation uses the same ideas, and we shall not explore the rightmost-derivation case. In order to understand how derivations may be constructed, we need first to see how one derivation of a string from a variable can be embedded within another derivation. An example should illustrate the point.

Example 5.13: Let us again consider the expression grammar of Fig. 5.2. It is easy to check that there is a derivation

$$E \Rightarrow I \Rightarrow Ib \Rightarrow ab$$

As a result, for any strings α and β, it is also true that

$$\alpha E \beta \Rightarrow \alpha I \beta \Rightarrow \alpha Ib\beta \Rightarrow \alpha ab\beta$$

The justification is that we can make the same replacements of production bodies for heads in the context of α and β as we can in isolation.[1]

For instance, if we have a derivation that begins $E \Rightarrow E + E \Rightarrow E + (E)$, we could apply the derivation of ab from the second E by treating "$E + ($" as α and "$)$" as β. This derivation would then continue

$$E + (E) \Rightarrow E + (I) \Rightarrow E + (Ib) \Rightarrow E + (ab)$$

□

We are now able to prove a theorem that lets us convert a parse tree to a leftmost derivation. The proof is an induction on the *height* of the tree, which is the maximum length of a path that starts at the root, and proceeds downward through descendants, to a leaf. For instance, the height of the tree in Fig. 5.6 is 7. The longest root-to-leaf path in this tree goes to the leaf labeled b. Note that path lengths conventionally count the edges, not the nodes, so a path consisting of a single node is of length 0.

Theorem 5.14: Let $G = (V, T, P, S)$ be a CFG, and suppose there is a parse tree with root labeled by variable A and with yield w, where w is in T^*. Then there is a leftmost derivation $A \underset{lm}{\overset{*}{\Rightarrow}} w$ in grammar G.

PROOF: We perform an induction on the height of the tree.

---

[1] In fact, it is this property of being able to make a string-for-variable substitution regardless of context that gave rise originally to the term "context-free." There is a more powerful classes of grammars, called "context-sensitive," where replacements are permitted only if certain strings appear to the left and/or right. Context-sensitive grammars do not play a major role in practice today.

BASIS: The basis is height 1, the least that a parse tree with a yield of terminals can be. In this case, the tree must look like Fig. 5.8, with a root labeled A and children that read w, left-to-right. Since this tree is a parse tree, $A \to w$ must be a production. Thus, $A \underset{lm}{\Rightarrow} w$ is a one-step, leftmost derivation of w from A.

INDUCTION: If the height of the tree is n, where $n > 1$, it must look like Fig 5.9. That is, there is a root labeled A, with children labeled $X_1, X_2, \ldots, X_k$ from the left. The X's may be either terminals or variables.

1. If X_i is a terminal, define w_i to be the string consisting of X_i alone.

2. If X_i is a variable, then it must be the root of some subtree with a yield of terminals, which we shall call w_i. Note that in this case, the subtree is of height less than n, so the inductive hypothesis applies to it. That is, there is a leftmost derivation $X_i \underset{lm}{\overset{*}{\Rightarrow}} w_i$.

Note that $w = w_1 w_2 \cdots w_k$.

We construct a leftmost derivation of w as follows. We begin with the step $A \underset{lm}{\Rightarrow} X_1 X_2 \cdots X_k$. Then, for each $i = 1, 2, \ldots, k$, in order, we show that

$$A \underset{lm}{\overset{*}{\Rightarrow}} w_1 w_2 \cdots w_i X_{i+1} X_{i+2} \cdots X_k$$

This proof is actually another induction, this time on i. For the basis, $i = 0$, we already know that $A \underset{lm}{\Rightarrow} X_1 X_2 \cdots X_k$. For the induction, assume that

$$A \underset{lm}{\overset{*}{\Rightarrow}} w_1 w_2 \cdots w_{i-1} X_i X_{i+1} \cdots X_k$$

a) If X_i is a terminal, do nothing. However, we shall subsequently think of X_i as the terminal string w_i. Thus, we already have

$$A \underset{lm}{\overset{*}{\Rightarrow}} w_1 w_2 \cdots w_i X_{i+1} X_{i+2} \cdots X_k$$

b) If X_i is a variable, continue with a derivation of w_i from X_i, in the context of the derivation being constructed. That is, if this derivation is

$$X_i \underset{lm}{\Rightarrow} \alpha_1 \underset{lm}{\Rightarrow} \alpha_2 \cdots \underset{lm}{\Rightarrow} w_i$$

we proceed with

$$w_1 w_2 \cdots w_{i-1} X_i X_{i+1} \cdots X_k \underset{lm}{\Rightarrow}$$
$$w_1 w_2 \cdots w_{i-1} \alpha_1 X_{i+1} \cdots X_k \underset{lm}{\Rightarrow}$$
$$w_1 w_2 \cdots w_{i-1} \alpha_2 X_{i+1} \cdots X_k \underset{lm}{\Rightarrow}$$
$$\cdots$$
$$w_1 w_2 \cdots w_i X_{i+1} X_{i+2} \cdots X_k$$

The result is a derivation $A \stackrel{*}{\underset{lm}{\Rightarrow}} w_1 w_2 \cdots w_i X_{i+1} \cdots X_k$.

When $i = k$, the result is a leftmost derivation of w from A. $\square$

Example 5.15 : Let us construct the leftmost derivation for the tree of Fig. 5.6. We shall show only the final step, where we construct the derivation from the entire tree from derivations that correspond to the subtrees of the root. That is, we shall assume that by recursive application of the technique in Theorem 5.14, we have deduced that the subtree rooted at the first child of the root has leftmost derivation $E \underset{lm}{\Rightarrow} I \underset{lm}{\Rightarrow} a$, while the subtree rooted at the third child of the root has leftmost derivation

$$E \underset{lm}{\Rightarrow} (E) \underset{lm}{\Rightarrow} (E+E) \underset{lm}{\Rightarrow} (I+E) \underset{lm}{\Rightarrow} (a+E) \underset{lm}{\Rightarrow}$$

$$(a+I) \underset{lm}{\Rightarrow} (a+I0) \underset{lm}{\Rightarrow} (a+I00) \underset{lm}{\Rightarrow} (a+b00)$$

To build a leftmost derivation for the entire tree, we start with the step at the root: $A \underset{lm}{\Rightarrow} E * E$. Then, we replace the first E according to its derivation, following each step by $*E$ to account for the larger context in which that derivation is used. The leftmost derivation so far is thus

$$E \underset{lm}{\Rightarrow} E * E \underset{lm}{\Rightarrow} I * E \underset{lm}{\Rightarrow} a * E$$

The $*$ in the production used at the root requires no derivation, so the above leftmost derivation also accounts for the first two children of the root. We complete the leftmost derivation by using the derivation of $E \stackrel{*}{\underset{lm}{\Rightarrow}} (a+b00)$, in a context where it is preceded by $a*$ and followed by the empty string. This derivation actually appeared in Example 5.6; it is:

$$E \underset{lm}{\Rightarrow} E * E \underset{lm}{\Rightarrow} I * E \underset{lm}{\Rightarrow} a * E \underset{lm}{\Rightarrow}$$

$$a * (E) \underset{lm}{\Rightarrow} a * (E+E) \underset{lm}{\Rightarrow} a * (I+E) \underset{lm}{\Rightarrow} a * (a+E) \underset{lm}{\Rightarrow}$$

$$a * (a+I) \underset{lm}{\Rightarrow} a * (a+I0) \underset{lm}{\Rightarrow} a * (a+I00) \underset{lm}{\Rightarrow} a * (a+b00)$$

$\square$

A similar theorem lets us convert a tree to a rightmost derivation. The construction of a rightmost derivation from a tree is almost the same as the construction of a leftmost derivation. However, after starting with the step $A \underset{rm}{\Rightarrow} X_1 X_2 \cdots X_k$, we expand X_k first, using a rightmost derivation, then expand X_{k-1}, and so on, down to X_1. Thus, we shall state without further proof:

Theorem 5.16 : Let $G = (V, T, P, S)$ be a CFG, and suppose there is a parse tree with root labeled by variable A and with yield w, where w is in T^*. Then there is a rightmost derivation $A \stackrel{*}{\underset{rm}{\Rightarrow}} w$ in grammar G. $\square$

5.2.6   From Derivations to Recursive Inferences

We now complete the loop suggested by Fig. 5.7 by showing that whenever there is a derivation $A \overset{*}{\Rightarrow} w$ for some CFG, then the fact that w is in the language of A is discovered in the recursive inference procedure. Before giving the theorem and proof, let us observe something important about derivations.

Suppose that we have a derivation $A \Rightarrow X_1 X_2 \cdots X_k \overset{*}{\Rightarrow} w$. Then we can break w into pieces $w = w_1 w_2 \cdots w_k$ such that $X_i \overset{*}{\Rightarrow} w_i$. Note that if X_i is a terminal, then $w_i = X_i$, and the derivation is zero steps. The proof of this observation is not hard. You can show by induction on the number of steps of the derivation, that if $X_1 X_2 \cdots X_k \overset{*}{\Rightarrow} \alpha$, then all the positions of α that come from expansion of X_i are to the left of all the positions that come from expansion of X_j, if $i < j$.

If X_i is a variable, we can obtain the derivation of $X_i \overset{*}{\Rightarrow} w_i$ by starting with the derivation $A \overset{*}{\Rightarrow} w$, and stripping away:

a) All the positions of the sentential forms that are either to the left or right of the positions that are derived from X_i.

b) All the steps that are not relevant to the derivation of w_i from X_i, and

An example should make this process clear.

Example 5.17: Using the expression grammar of Fig. 5.2, consider the derivation

$$E \Rightarrow E * E \Rightarrow E * E + E \Rightarrow I * E + E \Rightarrow I * I + E \Rightarrow$$

$$I * I + I \Rightarrow a * I + I \Rightarrow a * b + I \Rightarrow a * b + a$$

Consider the third sentential form, $E * E + E$, and the middle E in this form.[2]

Starting from $E * E + E$, we may follow the steps of the above derivation, but strip away whatever positions are derived from the $E*$ to the left of the central E or derived from the $+E$ to its right. The steps of the derivation then become E, E, I, I, I, b, b. That is, the next step does not change the central E, the step after that changes it to I, the next two steps leave it as I, the next changes it to b, and the final step does not change what is derived from the central E.

If we take only the steps that change what comes from the central E, the sequence of strings E, E, I, I, I, b, b becomes the derivation $E \Rightarrow I \Rightarrow b$. That derivation correctly describes how the central E evolves during the complete derivation.   □

Theorem 5.18: Let $G = (V, T, P, S)$ be a CFG, and suppose there is a derivation $A \overset{*}{\underset{G}{\Rightarrow}} w$, where w is in T^*. Then the recursive inference procedure applied to G determines that w is in the language of variable A.

---

[2] Our discussion of finding subderivations from larger derivations assumed we were concerned with a variable in the second sentential form of some derivation. However, the idea applies to a variable in any step of a derivation.

PROOF: The proof is an induction on the length of the derivation $A \overset{*}{\Rightarrow} w$.

BASIS: If the derivation is one-step, then $A \rightarrow w$ must be a production. Since w consists of terminals only, the fact that w is in the language of A will be discovered in the basis part of the recursive inference procedure.

INDUCTION: Suppose the derivation takes $n + 1$ steps, and assume that for any derivation of n or fewer steps, the statement holds. Write the derivation as $A \Rightarrow X_1 X_2 \cdots X_k \overset{*}{\Rightarrow} w$. Then, as discussed prior to the theorem, we can break w as $w = w_1 w_2 \cdots w_k$, where:

a) If X_i is a terminal, then $w_i = X_i$.

b) If X_i is a variable, then $X_i \overset{*}{\Rightarrow} w_i$. Since the first step of the derivation $A \overset{*}{\Rightarrow} w$ is surely not part of the derivation $X_i \overset{*}{\Rightarrow} w_i$, we know that this derivation is of n or fewer steps. Thus, the inductive hypothesis applies to it, and we know that w_i is inferred to be in the language of X_i.

Now, we have a production $A \rightarrow X_1 X_2 \cdots X_k$, with w_i either equal to X_i or known to be in the language of X_i. In the next round of the recursive inference procedure, we shall discover that $w_1 w_2 \cdots w_k$ is in the language of A. Since $w_1 w_2 \cdots w_k = w$, we have shown that w is inferred to be in the language of A. $\square$

5.2.7 Exercises for Section 5.2

Exercise 5.2.1: For the grammar and each of the strings in Exercise 5.1.2, give parse trees.

! **Exercise 5.2.2:** Suppose that G is a CFG without any productions that have ϵ as the right side. If w is in $L(G)$, the length of w is n, and w has a derivation of m steps, show that w has a parse tree with $n + m$ nodes.

! **Exercise 5.2.3:** Suppose all is as in Exercise 5.2.2, but G may have some productions with ϵ as the right side. Show that a parse tree for w may have as many as $n + 2m - 1$ nodes, but no more.

! **Exercise 5.2.4:** In Section 5.2.6 we mentioned that if $X_1 X_2 \cdots X_k \overset{*}{\Rightarrow} \alpha$, then all the positions of α that come from expansion of X_i are to the left of all the positions that come from expansion of X_j, if $i < j$. Prove this fact. *Hint*: Perform an induction on the number of steps in the derivation.

5.3 Applications of Context-Free Grammars

Context-free grammars were originally conceived by N. Chomsky as a way to describe natural languages. That promise has not been fulfilled. However, as uses for recursively defined concepts in Computer Science have multiplied, so has the need for CFG's as a way to describe instances of these concepts. We shall sketch two of these uses, one old and one new.

1. Grammars are used to describe programming languages. More importantly, there is a mechanical way of turning the language description as a CFG into a parser, the component of the compiler that discovers the structure of the source program and represents that structure by a parse tree. This application is one of the earliest uses of CFG's; in fact it is one of the first ways in which theoretical ideas in Computer Science found their way into practice.

2. The development of XML (Extensible Markup Language) is widely predicted to facilitate electronic commerce by allowing participants to share conventions regarding the format of orders, product descriptions, and many other kinds of documents. An essential part of XML is the *Document Type Definition* (DTD), which is essentially a context-free grammar that describes the allowable tags and the ways in which these tags may be nested. Tags are the familiar keywords with triangular brackets that you may know from HTML, e.g., `<EM>` and `</EM>` to surround text that needs to be emphasized. However, XML tags deal not with the formatting of text, but with the meaning of text. For instance, one could surround a sequences of characters that was intended to be interpreted as a phone number by `<PHONE>` and `</PHONE>`.

5.3.1   Parsers

Many aspects of a programming language have a structure that may be described by regular expressions. For instance, we discussed in Example 3.9 how identifiers could be represented by regular expressions. However, there are also some very important aspects of typical programming languages that cannot be represented by regular expressions alone. The following are two examples.

Example 5.19: Typical languages use parentheses and/or brackets in a nested and balanced fashion. That is, we must be able to match some left parenthesis against a right parenthesis that appears immediately to its right, remove both of them, and repeat. If we eventually eliminate all the parentheses, then the string was balanced, and if we cannot match parentheses in this way, then it is unbalanced. Examples of strings of balanced parentheses are (()), ()(), (()()), and ϵ, while)(and (() are not.

A grammar $G_{bal} = (\{B\}, \{(,)\}, P, B)$ generates all and only the strings of balanced parentheses, where P consists of the productions:

$$B \rightarrow BB \mid (B) \mid \epsilon$$

The first production, $B \rightarrow BB$, says that the concatenation of two strings of balanced parentheses is balanced. That assertion makes sense, because we can match the parentheses in the two strings independently. The second production, $B \rightarrow (B)$, says that if we place a pair of parentheses around a balanced string, then the result is balanced. Again, this rule makes sense, because if we match the parentheses in the inner string, then they are all eliminated and we are then allowed to match the first and last parentheses, which have become adjacent. The third production, $B \to \epsilon$ is the basis; it says that the empty string is balanced.

The above informal arguments should convince us that G_{bal} generates all strings of balanced parentheses. We need a proof of the converse — that every string of balanced parentheses is generated by this grammar. However, a proof by induction on the length of the balanced string is not hard and is left as an exercise.

We mentioned that the set of strings of balanced parentheses is not a regular language, and we shall now prove that fact. If $L(G_{bal})$ were regular, then there would be a constant n for this language from the pumping lemma for regular languages. Consider the balanced string $w = (^n)^n$, that is, n left parentheses followed by n matching right parentheses. If we break $w = xyz$ according to the pumping lemma, then y consists of only left parentheses, and therefore xz has more right parentheses than left. This string is not balanced, contradicting the assumption that the language of balanced parentheses is regular. $\square$

Programming languages consist of more than parentheses, of course, but parentheses are an essential part of arithmetic or conditional expressions. The grammar of Fig. 5.2 is more typical of the structure of arithmetic expressions, although we used only two operators, plus and times, and we included the detailed structure of identifiers, which would more likely be handled by the lexical-analyzer portion of the compiler, as we mentioned in Section 3.3.2. However, the language described in Fig. 5.2 is not regular either. For instance, according to this grammar, $(^n a)^n$ is a legal expression. We can use the pumping lemma to show that if the language were regular, then a string with some of the left parentheses removed and the a and all right parentheses intact would also be a legal expression, which it is not.

There are numerous aspects of a typical programming language that behave like balanced parentheses. There will usually be parentheses themselves, in expressions of all types. Beginnings and endings of code blocks, such as **begin** and **end** in Pascal, or the curly braces $\{\dots\}$ of C, are examples. That is, whatever curly braces appear in a C program must form a balanced sequence, with $\{$ in place of the left parenthesis and $\}$ in place of the right parenthesis.

There is a related pattern that appears occasionally, where "parentheses" can be balanced with the exception that there can be unbalanced left parentheses. An example is the treatment of **if** and **else** in C. An if-clause can appear unbalanced by any else-clause, or it may be balanced by a matching else-clause. A grammar that generates the possible sequences of **if** and **else** (represented by i and e, respectively) is:

$$S \to \epsilon \mid SS \mid iS \mid iSe$$

For instance, *ieie*, *iie*, and *iei* are possible sequences of **if**'s and **else**'s, and each of these strings is generated by the above grammar. Some examples of illegal sequences, not generated by the grammar, are *ei* and *ieeii*.

A simple test (whose correctness we leave as an exercise), for whether a sequence of i's and e's is generated by the grammar is to consider each e, in turn from the left. Look for the first i to the left of the e being considered. If there is none, the string fails the test and is not in the language. If there is such an i, delete this i and the e being considered. Then, if there are no more e's the string passes the test and is in the language. If there are more e's, proceed to consider the next one.

Example 5.20 : Consider the string *iee*. The first e is matched with the i to its left. They are removed, leaving the string e. Since there are more e's we consider the next. However, there is no i to its left, so the test fails; *iee* is not in the language. Note that this conclusion is valid, since you cannot have more **else**'s than **if**'s in a C program.

For another example, consider *iieie*. Matching the first e with the i to its left leaves *iie*. Matching the remaining e with the i to its left leaves i. Now there are no more e's, so the test succeeds. This conclusion also makes sense, because the sequence *iieie* corresponds to a C program whose structure is like that of Fig. 5.10. In fact, the matching algorithm also tells us (and the C compiler) which **if** matches any given **else**. That knowledge is essential if the compiler is to create the control-flow logic intended by the programmer.   □

```
if (Condition) {
    ...
    if (Condition) Statement;
    else Statement;
    ...
    if (Condition) Statement;
    else Statement;
    ...
}
```

Figure 5.10: An if-else structure; the two **else**'s match their previous **if**'s, and the first **if** is unmatched

5.3.2   The YACC Parser-Generator

The generation of a parser (function that creates parse trees from source programs) has been institutionalized in the YACC command that appears in all UNIX systems. The input to YACC is a CFG, in a notation that differs only in details from the one we have used here. Associated with each production is an *action*, which is a fragment of C code that is performed whenever a node of the parse tree that (with its children) corresponds to this production is created. Typically, the action is code to construct that node, although in some YACC applications the tree is not actually constructed, and the action does something else, such as emit a piece of object code.

Example 5.21: In Fig. 5.11 is a sample of a CFG in the YACC notation. The grammar is the same as that of Fig. 5.2. We have elided the actions, just showing their (required) curly braces and their position in the YACC input.

```
Exp : Id            {...}
    | Exp '+' Exp    {...}
    | Exp '*' Exp    {...}
    | '(' Exp ')'    {...}
    ;
Id  : 'a'            {...}
    | 'b'            {...}
    | Id 'a'         {...}
    | Id 'b'         {...}
    | Id '0'         {...}
    | Id '1'         {...}
    ;
```

Figure 5.11: An example of a grammar in the YACC notation

Notice the following correspondences between the YACC notation for grammars and ours:

- The colon is used as the production symbol, our $\rightarrow$.

- All the productions with a given head are grouped together, and their bodies are separated by the vertical bar. We also allow this convention, as an option.

- The list of bodies for a given head ends with a semicolon. we have not used a terminating symbol.

- Terminals are quoted with single quotes. Several characters can appear within a single pair of quotes. Although we have not shown it, YACC allows its user to define symbolic terminals as well. The occurrence of these terminals in the source program are detected by the lexical analyzer and signaled, through the return-value of the lexical analyzer, to the parser.

- Unquoted strings of letters and digits are variable names. We have taken advantage of this capability to give our two variables more descriptive names — Exp and Id — although E and I could have been used.

□

5.3.3   Markup Languages

We shall next consider a family of "languages" called *markup* languages. The "strings" in these languages are documents with certain marks (called *tags*) in them. Tags tell us something about the semantics of various strings within the document.

The markup language with which you are probably most familiar is HTML (HyperText Markup Language). This language has two major functions: creating links between documents and describing the format ("look") of the a document. We shall offer only a simplified view of the structure of HTML, but the following examples should suggest both its structure and how a CFG could be used both to describe the legal HTML documents and to guide the processing (i.e., the display on a monitor or printer) of a document.

Example 5.22: Figure 5.12(a) shows a piece of text, comprising a list of items, and Fig. 5.12(b) shows its expression in HTML. Notice from Fig. 5.12(b) that HTML consists of ordinary text interspersed with tags. Matching tags are of the form <x> and </x> for some string x.[3] For instance, we see the matching tags <EM> and </EM>, which indicate that the text between them should be emphasized, that is, put in italics or another appropriate font. We also see the matching tags <OL> and </OL>, indicating an ordered list, i.e., an enumeration of list items.

The things I *hate*:

1. Moldy bread.

2. People who drive too slow in the fast lane.

(a) The text as viewed

```
<P>The things I <EM>hate</EM>:
<OL>
<LI>Moldy bread.
<LI>People who drive too slow
in the fast lane.
</OL>
```

(b) The HTML source

Figure 5.12: An HTML document and its printed version

We also see two examples of unmatched tags: <P> and <LI>, which introduce paragraphs and list items, respectively. HTML allows, indeed encourages, that

---

[3]Sometimes the introducing tag <x> has more information in it than just the name x for the tag. However, we shall not consider that possibility in examples.

these tags be matched by </P> and </LI> at the ends of paragraphs and list items, but it does not require the matching. We have therefore left the matching tags off, to provide some complexity to the sample HTML grammar we shall develop. □

There are a number of classes of strings that are associated with an HTML document. We shall not try to list them all, but here are the ones essential to the understanding of text like that of Example 5.22. For each class, we shall introduce a variable with a descriptive name.

1. *Text* is any string of characters that can be literally interpreted; i.e., it has no tags. An example of a *Text* element in Fig 5.12(a) is "Moldy bread."

2. *Char* is any string consisting of a single character that is legal in HTML text. Note that blanks are included as characters.

3. *Doc* represents documents, which are sequences of "elements." We define elements next, and that definition is mutually recursive with the definition of a *Doc*.

4. *Element* is either a *Text* string, or a pair of matching tags and the document between them, or an unmatched tag followed by a document.

5. *ListItem* is the <LI> tag followed by a document, which is a single list item.

6. *List* is a sequence of zero or more list items.

1.	*Char*	→	$a \mid A \mid \cdots$
2.	*Text*	→	$\epsilon \mid$ *Char Text*
3.	*Doc*	→	$\epsilon \mid$ *Element Doc*
4.	*Element*	→	*Text* $\mid$ <EM> *Doc* </EM> $\mid$ <P> *Doc* $\mid$ <OL> *List* </OL> $\mid \cdots$
5.	*ListItem*	→	<LI> *Doc*
6.	*List*	→	$\epsilon \mid$ *ListItem List*

Figure 5.13: Part of an HTML grammar

Figure 5.13 is a CFG that describes as much of the structure of the HTML language as we have covered. In line (1) it is suggested that a character can be "a" or "A" or many other possible characters that are part of the HTML character set. Line (2) says, using two productions, that *Text* can be either the empty string, or any legal character followed by more text. Put another way, *Text* is zero or more characters. Note that < and > are not legal characters, although they can be represented by the sequences < and >, respectively. Thus, we cannot accidentally get a tag into *Text*.

Line (3) says that a document is a sequence of zero or more "elements." An element in turn, we learn at line (4), is either text, an emphasized document, a paragraph-beginning followed by a document, or a list. We have also suggested that there are other productions for *Element*, corresponding to the other kinds of tags that appear in HTML. Then, in line (5) we find that a list item is the <LI> tag followed by any document, and line (6) tells us that a list is a sequence of zero or more list elements.

Some aspects of HTML do not require the power of context-free grammars; regular expressions are adequate. For example, lines (1) and (2) of Fig. 5.13 simply say that *Text* represents the same language as does the regular expression $(\mathbf{a} + \mathbf{A} + \cdots)^*$. However, some aspects of HTML *do* require the power of CFG's. For instance, each pair of tags that are a corresponding beginning and ending pair, e.g., <EM> and </EM>, are like balanced parentheses, which we already know are not regular.

5.3.4   XML and Document-Type Definitions

The fact that HTML is described by a grammar is not in itself remarkable. Essentially all programming languages can be described by their own CFG's, so it would be more surprising if we could *not* so describe HTML. However, when we look at another important markup language, XML (eXtensible Markup Language), we find that the CFG's play a more vital role, as part of the process of using that language.

The purpose of XML is not to describe the formatting of the document; that is the job for HTML. Rather, XML tries to describe the "semantics" of the text. For example, text like "12 Maple St." looks like an address, but is it? In XML, tags would surround a phrase that represented an address; for example:

```
<ADDR>12 Maple St.</ADDR>
```

However, it is not immediately obvious that <ADDR> means the address of a building. For instance, if the document were about memory allocation, we might expect that the <ADDR> tag would refer to a memory address. To make clear what the different kinds of tags are, and what structures may appear between matching pairs of these tags, people with a common interest are expected to develop standards in the form of a DTD (Document-Type Definition).

A DTD is essentially a context-free grammar, with its own notation for describing the variables and productions. In the next example, we shall show a simple DTD and introduce some of the language used for describing DTD's. The DTD language itself has a context-free grammar, but it is not that grammar we are interested in describing. Rather, the language for describing DTD's is essentially a CFG notation, and we want to see how CFG's are expressed in this language.

The form of a DTD is

```
<!DOCTYPE name-of-DTD [
    list of element definitions
]>
```

An element definition, in turn, has the form

```
<!ELEMENT element-name (description of the element)>
```

Element descriptions are essentially regular expressions. The basis of these expressions are:

1. Other element names, representing the fact that elements of one type can appear within elements of another type, just as in HTML we might find emphasized text within a list.

2. The special term \#PCDATA, standing for any text that does not involve XML tags. This term plays the role of variable $Text$ in Example 5.22.

The allowed operators are:

1. | standing for union, as in the UNIX regular-expression notation discussed in Section 3.3.1.

2. A comma, denoting concatenation.

3. Three variants of the closure operator, as in Section 3.3.1. These are *, the usual operator meaning "zero or more occurrences of," +, meaning "one or more occurrences of," and ?, meaning "zero or one occurrence of."

Parentheses may group operators to their arguments; otherwise, the usual precedence of regular-expression operators applies.

Example 5.23: Let us imagine that computer vendors get together to create a standard DTD that they can use to publish, on the Web, descriptions of the various PC's that they currently sell. Each description of a PC will have a model number, and details about the features of the model, e.g., the amount of RAM, number and size of disks, and so on. Figure 5.14 shows a hypothetical, very simple, DTD for personal computers.

```
<!DOCTYPE PcSpecs [
    <!ELEMENT PCS (PC*)>
    <!ELEMENT PC (MODEL, PRICE, PROCESSOR, RAM, DISK+)>
    <!ELEMENT MODEL (\#PCDATA)>
    <!ELEMENT PRICE (\#PCDATA)>
    <!ELEMENT PROCESSOR (MANF, MODEL, SPEED)>
    <!ELEMENT MANF (\#PCDATA)>
    <!ELEMENT MODEL (\#PCDATA)>
    <!ELEMENT SPEED (\#PCDATA)>
    <!ELEMENT RAM (\#PCDATA)>
    <!ELEMENT DISK (HARDDISK | CD | DVD)>
    <!ELEMENT HARDDISK (MANF, MODEL, SIZE)
    <!ELEMENT SIZE (\#PCDATA)>
    <!ELEMENT CD (SPEED)>
    <!ELEMENT DVD (SPEED)>
]>
```

Figure 5.14: A DTD for personal computers

The name of the DTD is `PcSpecs`. The first element, which is like the start symbol of a CFG, is `PCS` (list of PC specifications). Its definition, `PC*`, says that a `PCS` is zero or more `PC` entries.

We then see the definition of a `PC` element. It consists of the concatenation of five things. The first four are other elements, corresponding to the model, price, processor type, and RAM of the PC. Each of these must appear once, in that order, since the comma represents concatenation. The last constituent, `DISK+`, tells us that there will be one or more disk entries for a PC.

Many of the constituents are simply text; `MODEL`, `PRICE`, and `RAM` are of this type. However, `PROCESSOR` has more structure. We see from its definition that it consists of a manufacturer, model, and speed, in that order; each of these elements is simple text.

A `DISK` entry is the most complex. First, a disk is either a hard disk, CD, or DVD, as indicated by the rule for element `DISK`, which is the OR of three other elements. Hard disks, in turn, have a structure in which the manufacturer, model, and size are specified, while CD's and DVD's are represented only by their speed.

Figure 5.15 is an example of an XML document that conforms to the DTD of Fig. 5.14. Notice that each element is represented in the document by a tag with the name of that element and a matching tag at the end, with an extra slash, just as in HTML. Thus, in Fig. 5.15 we see at the outermost level the tag `<PCS>...</PCS>`. Inside these tags appears a list of entries, one for each PC sold by this manufacturer; we have only shown one such entry explicitly.

Within the illustrated `<PC>` entry, we can easily see that the model number

```
<PCS>
    <PC>
        <MODEL>4560</MODEL>
        <PRICE>$2295</PRICE>
        <PROCESSOR>
            <MANF>Intel</MANF>
            <MODEL>Pentium</MODEL>
            <SPEED>800MHz</SPEED>
        </PROCESSOR>
        <RAM>256</RAM>
        <DISK><HARDDISK>
            <MANF>Maxtor</MANF>
            <MODEL>Diamond</MODEL>
            <SIZE>30.5Gb</SIZE>
        </HARDDISK></DISK>
        <DISK><CD>
            <SPEED>32x</SPEED>
        </CD></DISK>
    </PC>
    <PC>
        . . .
    </PC>
</PCS>
```

Figure 5.15: Part of a document obeying the structure of the DTD in Fig. 5.14

is 4560, the price is $2295, and it has an 800MHz Intel Pentium processor. It has 256Mb of RAM, a 30.5Gb Maxtor Diamond hard disk, and a 32x CD-ROM reader. What is important is not that we can read these facts, but that a program could read the document, and guided by the grammar in the DTD of Fig. 5.14 that it has also read, could interpret the numbers and names in Fig. 5.15 properly. □

You may have noticed that the rules for the elements in DTD's like Fig. 5.14 are not quite like productions of context-free grammars. Many of the rules are of the correct form. For instance,

```
<!ELEMENT PROCESSOR (MANF, MODEL, SPEED)>
```

Is analogous to the production

$$Processor \rightarrow Manf\ Model\ Speed$$

However, the rule

```
<!ELEMENT DISK (HARDDISK | CD | DVD)>
```

does not have a definition for DISK that is like a production body. In this case, the extension is simple: we may interpret this rule as three productions, with the vertical bar playing the same role as it does in our shorthand for productions having a common head. Thus, this rule is equivalent to the three productions

$$Disk \rightarrow HardDisk \mid Cd \mid Dvd$$

The most difficult case is

```
<!ELEMENT PC (MODEL, PRICE, PROCESSOR, RAM, DISK+)>
```

where the "body" has a closure operator within it. The solution is to replace DISK+ by a new variable, say $Disks$, that generates, via a pair of productions, one or more instances of the variable $Disk$. The equivalent productions are thus:

$$Pc \rightarrow Model\ Price\ Processor\ Ram\ Disks$$
$$Disks \rightarrow Disk \mid DiskDisks$$

There is a general technique for converting a CFG with regular expressions as production bodies to an ordinary CFG. We shall give the idea informally; you may wish to formalize both the meaning of CFG's with regular-expression productions and a proof that the extension yields no new languages beyond the CFL's. We show, inductively, how to convert a production with a regular-expression body to a collection of equivalent ordinary productions. The induction is on the size of the expression in the body.

BASIS: If the body is the concatenation of elements, then the production is already in the legal form for CFG's, so we do nothing.

INDUCTION: Otherwise, there are five cases, depending on the final operator used.

1. The production is of the form $A \rightarrow E_1, E_2$, where E_1 and E_2 are expressions permitted in the DTD language. This is the concatenation case. Introduce two new variables, B and C, that appear nowhere else in the grammar. Replace $A \rightarrow E_1, E_2$ by the productions

$$A \rightarrow BC$$
$$B \rightarrow E_1$$
$$C \rightarrow E_2$$

   The first production, $A \rightarrow BC$, is legal for CFG's. The last two may or may not be legal. However, their bodies are shorter than the body of the original production, so we may inductively convert them to CFG form.

2. The production is of the form $A \rightarrow E_1 \mid E_2$. For this union operator, replace this production by the pair of productions:

$$A \rightarrow E_1$$
$$A \rightarrow E_2$$

Again, these productions may or may not be legal CFG productions, but their bodies are shorter than the body of the original. We may therefore apply the rules recursively and eventually convert these new productions to CFG form.

3. The production is of the form $A \rightarrow (E_1)^*$. Introduce a new variable B that appears nowhere else, and replace this production by:

$$A \rightarrow BA$$
$$A \rightarrow \epsilon$$
$$B \rightarrow E_1$$

4. The production is of the form $A \rightarrow (E_1)^+$. Introduce a new variable B that appears nowhere else, and replace this production by:

$$A \rightarrow BA$$
$$A \rightarrow B$$
$$B \rightarrow E_1$$

5. The production is of the form $A \rightarrow (E_1)?$. Replace this production by:

$$A \rightarrow \epsilon$$
$$A \rightarrow E_1$$

Example 5.24: Let us consider how to convert the DTD rule

```
<!ELEMENT PC (MODEL, PRICE, PROCESSOR, RAM, DISK+)>
```

to legal CFG productions. First, we can view the body of this rule as the concatenation of two expressions, the first of which is MODEL, PRICE, PROCESSOR, RAM and the second of which is DISK+. If we create variables for these two subexpressions, say A and B, respectively, then we can use the productions:

$$Pc \rightarrow AB$$
$$A \rightarrow Model\ Price\ Processor\ Ram$$
$$B \rightarrow Disk^+$$

Only the last of these is not in legal form. We introduce another variable C and the productions:

$$B \rightarrow CB \mid C$$
$$C \rightarrow Disk$$

In this special case, because the expression that A derives is just a concatenation of variables, and $Disk$ is a single variable, we actually have no need for the variables A or C. We could use the following productions instead:

$$Pc \rightarrow Model \; Price \; Processor \; Ram \; B$$
$$B \rightarrow Disk \; B \mid Disk$$

□

5.3.5   Exercises for Section 5.3

Exercise 5.3.1: Prove that if a string of parentheses is balanced, in the sense given in Example 5.19, then it is generated by the grammar $B \rightarrow BB \mid (B) \mid \epsilon$. *Hint*: Perform an induction on the length of the string.

* **Exercise 5.3.2:** Consider the set of all strings of balanced parentheses of two types, round and square. An example of where these strings come from is as follows. If we take expressions in C, which use round parentheses for grouping and for arguments of function calls, and use square brackets for array indexes, and drop out everything but the parentheses, we get all strings of balanced parentheses of these two types. For example,

```
f(a[i]*(b[i][j],c[g(x)]),d[i])
```

becomes the balanced-parenthesis string `([](([][][()])[])`. Design a grammar for all and only the strings of round and square parentheses that are balanced.

! **Exercise 5.3.3:** In Section 5.3.1, we considered the grammar

$$S \rightarrow \epsilon \mid SS \mid iS \mid iSe$$

and claimed that we could test for membership in its language L by repeatedly doing the following, starting with a string w. The string w changes during repetitions.

1. If the current string begins with e, fail; w is not in L.

2. If the string currently has no e's (it may have i's), succeed; w is in L.

3. Otherwise, delete the first e and the i immediately to its left. Then repeat these three steps on the new string.

Prove that this process correctly identifies the strings in L.

Exercise 5.3.4: Add the following forms to the HTML grammar of Fig. 5.13:

* a) A list item must be ended by a closing tag `</LI>`.

  b) An element can be an unordered list, as well as an ordered list. Unordered lists are surrounded by the tag `<UL>` and its closing `</UL>`.

! c) An element can be a table. Tables are surrounded by `<TABLE>` and its closer `</TABLE>`. Inside these tags are one or more rows, each of which is surrounded by `<TR>` and `</TR>`. The first row is the header, with one or more fields, each introduced by the `<TH>` tag (we'll assume these are not closed, although they should be). Subsequent rows have their fields introduced by the `<TD>` tag.

```
<!DOCTYPE CourseSpecs [
    <!ELEMENT COURSES (COURSE+)>
    <!ELEMENT COURSE (CNAME, PROF, STUDENT*, TA?)>
    <!ELEMENT CNAME (\#PCDATA)>
    <!ELEMENT STUDENT (\#PCDATA)>
    <!ELEMENT TA (\#PCDATA)>
]>
```

Figure 5.16: A DTD for courses

Exercise 5.3.5: Convert the DTD of Fig. 5.16 to a context-free grammar.

5.4 Ambiguity in Grammars and Languages

As we have seen, applications of CFG's often rely on the grammar to provide the structure of files. For instance, we saw in Section 5.3 how grammars can be used to put structure on programs and documents. The tacit assumption was that a grammar uniquely determines a structure for each string in its language. However, we shall see that not every grammar does provide unique structures.

When a grammar fails to provide unique structures, it is sometimes possible to redesign the grammar to make the structure unique for each string in the language. Unfortunately, sometimes we cannot do so. That is, there are some CFL's that are "inherently ambiguous"; every grammar for the language puts more than one structure on some strings in the language.

5.4.1 Ambiguous Grammars

Let us return to our running example: the expression grammar of Fig. 5.2. This grammar lets us generate expressions with any sequence of $*$ and $+$ operators, and the productions $E \rightarrow E + E \mid E * E$ allows us to generate these expressions in any order we choose.

Example 5.25 : For instance, consider the sentential form $E + E * E$. It has two derivations from E:

1. $E \Rightarrow E + E \Rightarrow E + E * E$

2. $E \Rightarrow E * E \Rightarrow E + E * E$

Notice that in derivation (1), the second E is replaced by $E * E$, while in derivation (2), the first E is replaced by $E + E$. Figure 5.17 shows the two parse trees, which we should note are distinct trees.

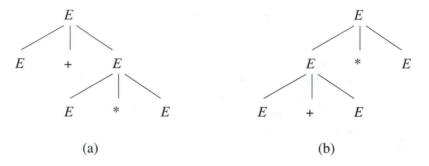

(a)   (b)

Figure 5.17: Two parse trees with the same yield

The difference between these two derivations is significant. As far as the structure of the expressions is concerned, derivation (1) says that the second and third expressions are multiplied, and the result is added to the first expression, while derivation (2) adds the first two expressions and multiplies the result by the third. In more concrete terms, the first derivation suggests that $1 + 2 * 3$ should be grouped $1 + (2 * 3) = 7$, while the second derivation suggests the same expression should be grouped $(1 + 2) * 3 = 9$. Obviously, the first of these, and not the second, matches our notion of correct grouping of arithmetic expressions.

Since the grammar of Fig. 5.2 gives two different structures to any string of terminals that is derived by replacing the three expressions in $E + E * E$ by identifiers, we see that this grammar is not a good one for providing unique structure. In particular, while it can give strings the correct grouping as arithmetic expressions, it also gives them incorrect groupings. To use this expression grammar in a compiler, we would have to modify it to provide only the correct groupings. □

On the other hand, the mere existence of different derivations for a string (as opposed to different parse trees) does not imply a defect in the grammar. The following is an example.

Example 5.26 : Using the same expression grammar, we find that the string $a + b$ has many different derivations. Two examples are:

1. $E \Rightarrow E + E \Rightarrow I + E \Rightarrow a + E \Rightarrow a + I \Rightarrow a + b$

2. $E \Rightarrow E + E \Rightarrow E + I \Rightarrow I + I \Rightarrow I + b \Rightarrow a + b$

However, there is no real difference between the structures provided by these derivations; they each say that a and b are identifiers, and that their values are to be added. In fact, both of these derivations produce the same parse tree if the construction of Theorems 5.18 and 5.12 are applied. □

The two examples above suggest that it is not a multiplicity of derivations that cause ambiguity, but rather the existence of two or more parse trees. Thus, we say a CFG $G = (V, T, P, S)$ is *ambiguous* if there is at least one string w in T^* for which we can find two different parse trees, each with root labeled S and yield w. If each string has at most one parse tree in the grammar, then the grammar is *unambiguous*.

For instance, Example 5.25 almost demonstrated the ambiguity of the grammar of Fig. 5.2. We have only to show that the trees of Fig. 5.17 can be completed to have terminal yields. Figure 5.18 is an example of that completion.

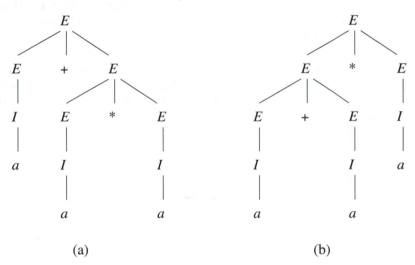

(a)   (b)

Figure 5.18: Trees with yield $a + a * a$, demonstrating the ambiguity of our expression grammar

5.4.2 Removing Ambiguity From Grammars

In an ideal world, we would be able to give you an algorithm to remove ambiguity from CFG's, much as we were able to show an algorithm in Section 4.4 to remove unnecessary states of a finite automaton. However, the surprising fact is, as we shall show in Section 9.5.2, that there is no algorithm whatsoever that can even tell us whether a CFG is ambiguous in the first place. Moreover, we

---

Ambiguity Resolution in YACC

If the expression grammar we have been using is ambiguous, we might wonder whether the sample YACC program of Fig. 5.11 is realistic. True, the underlying grammar is ambiguous, but much of the power of the YACC parser-generator comes from providing the user with simple mechanisms for resolving most of the common causes of ambiguity. For the expression grammar, it is sufficient to insist that:

a) * takes precedence over +. That is, *'s must be grouped before adjacent +'s on either side. This rule tells us to use derivation (1) in Example 5.25, rather than derivation (2).

b) Both * and + are left-associative. That is, group sequences of expressions, all of which are connected by *, from the left, and do the same for sequences connected by +.

YACC allows us to state the precedence of operators by listing them in order, from lowest to highest precedence. Technically, the precedence of an operator applies to the use of any production of which that operator is the rightmost terminal in the body. We can also declare operators to be left- or right-associative with the keywords %left and %right. For instance, to declare that + and * were both left associative, with * taking precedence over +, we would put ahead of the grammar of Fig, 5.11 the statements:

```
%left '+'
%left '*'
```

---

shall see in Section 5.4.4 that there are context-free languages that have nothing but ambiguous CFG's; for these languages, removal of ambiguity is impossible.

Fortunately, the situation in practice is not so grim. For the sorts of constructs that appear in common programming languages, there are well-known techniques for eliminating ambiguity. The problem with the expression grammar of Fig. 5.2 is typical, and we shall explore the elimination of its ambiguity as an important illustration.

First, let us note that there are two causes of ambiguity in the grammar of Fig. 5.2:

1. The precedence of operators is not respected. While Fig. 5.17(a) properly groups the * before the + operator, Fig 5.17(b) is also a valid parse tree and groups the + ahead of the *. We need to force only the structure of Fig. 5.17(a) to be legal in an unambiguous grammar.

2. A sequence of identical operators can group either from the left or from the right. For example, if the $*$'s in Fig. 5.17 were replaced by $+$'s, we would see two different parse trees for the string $E + E + E$. Since addition and multiplication are associative, it doesn't matter whether we group from the left or the right, but to eliminate ambiguity, we must pick one. The conventional approach is to insist on grouping from the left, so the structure of Fig. 5.17(b) is the only correct grouping of two $+$-signs.

The solution to the problem of enforcing precedence is to introduce several different variables, each of which represents those expressions that share a level of "binding strength." Specifically:

1. A *factor* is an expression that cannot be broken apart by any adjacent operator, either a $*$ or a $+$. The only factors in our expression language are:

   (a) Identifiers. It is not possible to separate the letters of an identifier by attaching an operator.

   (b) Any parenthesized expression, no matter what appears inside the parentheses. It is the purpose of parentheses to prevent what is inside from becoming the operand of any operator outside the parentheses.

2. A *term* is an expression that cannot be broken by the $+$ operator. In our example, where $+$ and $*$ are the only operators, a term is a product of one or more factors. For instance, the term $a * b$ can be "broken" if we use left associativity and place $a1*$ to its left. That is, $a1 * a * b$ is grouped $(a1 * a) * b$, which breaks apart the $a * b$. However, placing an additive term, such as $a1+$, to its left or $+a1$ to its right cannot break $a * b$. The proper grouping of $a1 + a * b$ is $a1 + (a * b)$, and the proper grouping of $a * b + a1$ is $(a * b) + a1$.

3. An *expression* will henceforth refer to any possible expression, including those that can be broken by either an adjacent $*$ or an adjacent $+$. Thus, an expression for our example is a sum of one or more terms.

$$
\begin{aligned}
I &\rightarrow a \mid b \mid Ia \mid Ib \mid I0 \mid I1 \\
F &\rightarrow I \mid (E) \\
T &\rightarrow F \mid T * F \\
E &\rightarrow T \mid E + T
\end{aligned}
$$

Figure 5.19: An unambiguous expression grammar

Example 5.27 : Figure 5.19 shows an unambiguous grammar that generates the same language as the grammar of Fig. 5.2. Think of F, T, and E as the variables whose languages are the factors, terms, and expressions, as defined above. For instance, this grammar allows only one parse tree for the string $a + a * a$; it is shown in Fig. 5.20.

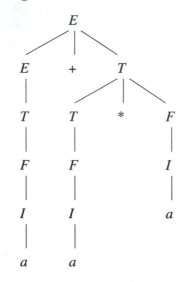

Figure 5.20: The sole parse tree for $a + a * a$

The fact that this grammar is unambiguous may be far from obvious. Here are the key observations that explain why no string in the language can have two different parse trees.

- An string derived from T, a term, must be a sequence of one or more factors, connected by $*$'s. A factor, as we have defined it, and as follows from the productions for F in Fig. 5.19, is either a single identifier or any parenthesized expression.

- Because of the form of the two productions for T, the only parse tree for a sequence of factors is the one that breaks $f_1 * f_2 * \cdots * f_n$, for $n > 1$ into a term $f_1 * f_2 * \cdots * f_{n-1}$ and a factor f_n. The reason is that F cannot derive an expression like $f_{n-1} * f_n$ without introducing parentheses around them. Thus, it is not possible that when using the production $T \to T * F$, the F derives anything but the last of the factors. That is, the parse tree for a term can only look like Fig. 5.21.

- Likewise, an expression is a sequence of terms connected by $+$. When we use the production $E \to E + T$ to derive $t_1 + t_2 + \cdots + t_n$, the T must derive only t_n, and the E in the body derives $t_1 + t_2 + \cdots + t_{n-1}$. The reason, again, is that T cannot derive the sum of two or more terms without putting parentheses around them.

□

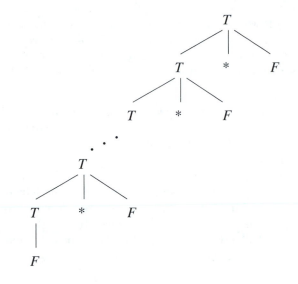

Figure 5.21: The form of all parse trees for a term

5.4.3 Leftmost Derivations as a Way to Express Ambiguity

While derivations are not necessarily unique, even if the grammar is unambiguous, it turns out that, in an unambiguous grammar, leftmost derivations will be unique, and rightmost derivations will be unique. We shall consider leftmost derivations only, and state the result for rightmost derivations.

Example 5.28: As an example, notice the two parse trees of Fig. 5.18 that each yield $E + E * E$. If we construct leftmost derivations from them we get the following leftmost derivations from trees (a) and (b), respectively:

a) $E \underset{lm}{\Rightarrow} E+E \underset{lm}{\Rightarrow} I+E \underset{lm}{\Rightarrow} a+E \underset{lm}{\Rightarrow} a+E*E \underset{lm}{\Rightarrow} a+I*E \underset{lm}{\Rightarrow} a+a*E \underset{lm}{\Rightarrow}$
$a+a*I \underset{lm}{\Rightarrow} a+a*a$

b) $E \underset{lm}{\Rightarrow} E*E \underset{lm}{\Rightarrow} E+E*E \underset{lm}{\Rightarrow} I+E*E \underset{lm}{\Rightarrow} a+E*E \underset{lm}{\Rightarrow} a+I*E \underset{lm}{\Rightarrow}$
$a+a*E \underset{lm}{\Rightarrow} a+a*I \underset{lm}{\Rightarrow} a+a*a$

Note that these two leftmost derivations differ. This example does not prove the theorem, but demonstrates how the differences in the trees force different steps to be taken in the leftmost derivation. □

Theorem 5.29: For each grammar $G = (V, T, P, S)$ and string w in T^*, w has two distinct parse trees if and only if w has two distinct leftmost derivations from S.

PROOF: (Only-if) If we examine the construction of a leftmost derivation from a parse tree in the proof of Theorem 5.14, we see that wherever the two parse trees first have a node at which different productions are used, the leftmost derivations constructed will also use different productions and thus be different derivations.

(If) While we have not previously given a direct construction of a parse tree from a leftmost derivation, the idea is not hard. Start constructing a tree with only the root, labeled S. Examine the derivation one step at a time. At each step, a variable will be replaced, and this variable will correspond to the leftmost node in the tree being constructed that has no children but that has a variable as its label. From the production used at this step of the leftmost derivation, determine what the children of this node should be. If there are two distinct derivations, then at the first step where the derivations differ, the nodes being constructed will get different lists of children, and this difference guarantees that the parse trees are distinct.   □

5.4.4   Inherent Ambiguity

A context-free language L is said to be *inherently ambiguous* if all its grammars are ambiguous. If even one grammar for L is unambiguous, then L is an unambiguous language. We saw, for example, that the language of expressions generated by the grammar of Fig. 5.2 is actually unambiguous. Even though that grammar is ambiguous, there is another grammar for the same language that is unambiguous — the grammar of Fig. 5.19.

We shall not prove that there are inherently ambiguous languages. Rather we shall discuss one example of a language that can be proved inherently ambiguous, and we shall explain intuitively why every grammar for the language must be ambiguous. The language L in question is:

$$L = \{a^n b^n c^m d^m \mid n \geq 1, m \geq 1\} \cup \{a^n b^m c^m d^n \mid n \geq 1, m \geq 1\}$$

That is, L consists of strings in $\mathbf{a^+ b^+ c^+ d^+}$ such that either:

1. There are as many a's as b's and as many c's as d's, or

2. There are as many a's as d's and as many b's as c's.

L is a context-free language. The obvious grammar for L is shown in Fig. 5.22. It uses separate sets of productions to generate the two kinds of strings in L.

This grammar is ambiguous. For example, the string $aabbccdd$ has the two leftmost derivations:

1. $S \underset{lm}{\Rightarrow} AB \underset{lm}{\Rightarrow} aAbB \underset{lm}{\Rightarrow} aabbB \underset{lm}{\Rightarrow} aabbcBd \underset{lm}{\Rightarrow} aabbccdd$

2. $S \underset{lm}{\Rightarrow} C \underset{lm}{\Rightarrow} aCd \underset{lm}{\Rightarrow} aaDdd \underset{lm}{\Rightarrow} aabDcdd \underset{lm}{\Rightarrow} aabbccdd$

$$
\begin{array}{rcl}
S & \rightarrow & AB \mid C \\
A & \rightarrow & aAb \mid ab \\
B & \rightarrow & cBd \mid cd \\
C & \rightarrow & aCd \mid aDd \\
D & \rightarrow & bDc \mid bc
\end{array}
$$

Figure 5.22: A grammar for an inherently ambiguous language

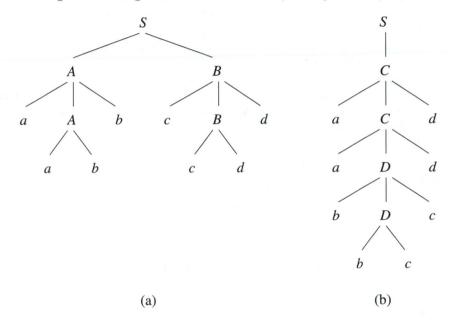

(a)   (b)

Figure 5.23: Two parse trees for *aabbccdd*

and the two parse trees shown in Fig. 5.23.

The proof that all grammars for L must be ambiguous is complex. However, the essence is as follows. We need to argue that all but a finite number of the strings whose counts of the four symbols a, b, c, and d, are all equal must be generated in two different ways: one in which the a's and b are generated to be equal and the c's and d's are generated to be equal, and a second way, where the a's and d's are generated to be equal and likewise the b's and c's.

For instance, the only way to generate strings where the a's and b's have the same number is with a variable like A in the grammar of Fig. 5.22. There are variations, of course, but these variations do not change the basic picture. For instance:

- Some small strings can be avoided, say by changing the basis production $A \rightarrow ab$ to $A \rightarrow aaabbb$, for instance.

- We could arrange that A shares its job with some other variables, e.g., by using variables A_1 and A_2, with A_1 generating the odd numbers of a's and A_2 generating the even numbers, as: $A_1 \rightarrow aA_2b \mid ab;\ A_2 \rightarrow aA_1b \mid ab$.

- We could also arrange that the numbers of a's and b's generated by A are not exactly equal, but off by some finite number. For instance, we could start with a production like $S \rightarrow AbB$ and then use $A \rightarrow aAb \mid a$ to generate one more a than b's.

However, we cannot avoid some mechanism for generating a's in a way that matches the count of b's.

Likewise, we can argue that there must be a variable like B that generates matching c's and d's. Also, variables that play the roles of C (generate matching a's and d's) and D (generate matching b's and c's) must be available in the grammar. The argument, when formalized, proves that no matter what modifications we make to the basic grammar, it will generate at least *some* of the strings of the form $a^n b^n c^n d^n$ in the two ways that the grammar of Fig. 5.22 does.

5.4.5   Exercises for Section 5.4

* **Exercise 5.4.1:** Consider the grammar

$$S \rightarrow \ \mid aS \mid aSbS \mid \epsilon$$

This grammar is ambiguous. Show in particular that the string aab has two:

a) Parse trees.

b) Leftmost derivations.

c) Rightmost derivations.

! **Exercise 5.4.2:** Prove that the grammar of Exercise 5.4.1 generates all and only the strings of a's and b's such that every prefix has at least as many a's as b's.

*! **Exercise 5.4.3:** Find an unambiguous grammar for the language of Exercise 5.4.1.

!! **Exercise 5.4.4:** Some strings of a's and b's have a unique parse tree in the grammar of Exercise 5.4.1. Give an efficient test to tell whether a given string is one of these. The test "try all parse trees to see how many yield the given string" is not adequately efficient.

! **Exercise 5.4.5:** This question concerns the grammar from Exercise 5.1.2, which we reproduce here:

$$
\begin{aligned}
S &\rightarrow A1B \\
A &\rightarrow 0A \mid \epsilon \\
B &\rightarrow 0B \mid 1B \mid \epsilon
\end{aligned}
$$

a) Show that this grammar is unambiguous.

b) Find a grammar for the same language that *is* ambiguous, and demonstrate its ambiguity.

*! **Exercise 5.4.6:** Is your grammar from Exercise 5.1.5 unambiguous? If not, redesign it to be unambiguous.

Exercise 5.4.7: The following grammar generates *prefix* expressions with operands x and y and binary operators $+$, $-$, and $*$:

$$
E \rightarrow +EE \mid * EE \mid - EE \mid x \mid y
$$

a) Find leftmost and rightmost derivations, and a derivation tree for the string +*-xyxy.

! b) Prove that this grammar is unambiguous.

5.5 Summary of Chapter 5

✦ *Context-Free Grammars*: A CFG is a way of describing languages by recursive rules called productions. A CFG consists of a set of variables, a set of terminal symbols, and a start variable, as well as the productions. Each production consists of a head variable and a body consisting of a string of zero or more variables and/or terminals.

✦ *Derivations and Languages*: Beginning with the start symbol, we derive terminal strings by repeatedly replacing a variable by the body of some production with that variable in the head. The language of the CFG is the set of terminal strings we can so derive; it is called a context-free language.

✦ *Leftmost and Rightmost Derivations*: If we always replace the leftmost (resp. rightmost) variable in a string, then the resulting derivation is a leftmost (resp. rightmost) derivation. Every string in the language of a CFG has at least one leftmost and at least one rightmost derivation.

✦ *Sentential Forms*: Any step in a derivation is a string of variables and/or terminals. We call such a string a sentential form. If the derivation is leftmost (resp. rightmost), then the string is a left- (resp. right-) sentential form.

✦ *Parse Trees*: A parse tree is a tree that shows the essentials of a derivation. Interion nodes are labeled by variables, and leaves are labeled by terminals or ϵ. For each internal node, there must be a production such that the head of the production is the label of the node, and the labels of its children, read from left to right, form the body of that production.

✦ *Equivalence of Parse Trees and Derivations*: A terminal string is in the language of a grammar if and only if it is the yield of at least one parse tree. Thus, the existence of leftmost derivations, rightmost derivations, and parse trees are equivalent conditions that each define exactly the strings in the language of a CFG.

✦ *Ambiguous Grammars*: For some CFG's, it is possible to find a terminal string with more than one parse tree, or equivalently, more than one leftmost derivation or more than one rightmost derivation. Such a grammar is called ambiguous.

✦ *Eliminating Ambiguity*: For many useful grammars, such as those that describe the structure of programs in a typical programming language, it is possible to find an unambiguous grammar that generates the same language. Unfortunately, the unambiguous grammar is frequently more complex than the simplest ambiguous grammar for the language. There are also some context-free languages, usually quite contrived, that are inherently ambiguous, meaning that every grammar for that language is ambiguous.

✦ *Parsers*: The context-free grammar is an essential concept for the implementation of compilers and other programming-language processors. Tools such as YACC take a CFG as input and produce a parser, the component of a compiler that deduces the structure of the program being compiled.

✦ *Document Type Definitions*: The emerging XML standard for sharing information through Web documents has a notation, called the DTD, for describing the structure of such documents, through the nesting of semantic tags within the document. The DTD is in essence a context-free grammar whose language is a class of related documents.

5.6   References for Chapter 5

The context-free grammar was first proposed as a description method for natural languages by Chomsky [4]. A similar idea was used shortly thereafter to describe computer languages — Fortran by Backus [2] and Algol by Naur [7]. As a result, CFG's are sometimes referred to as "Backus-Naur form grammars."

Ambiguity in grammars was identified as a problem by Cantor [3] and Floyd [5] at about the same time. Inherent ambiguity was first addressed by Gross [6].

For applications of CFG's in compilers, see [1]. DTD's are defined in the standards document for XML [8].

1. A. V. Aho, R. Sethi, and J. D. Ullman, *Compilers: Principles, Techniques, and Tools*, Addison-Wesley, Reading MA, 1986.

2. J. W. Backus, "The syntax and semantics of the proposed international algebraic language of the Zurich ACM-GAMM conference," *Proc. Intl. Conf. on Information Processing* (1959), UNESCO, pp. 125–132.

3. D. C. Cantor, "On the ambiguity problem of Backus systems," *J. ACM* **9**:4 (1962), pp. 477–479.

4. N. Chomsky, "Three models for the description of language," *IRE Trans. on Information Theory* **2**:3 (1956), pp. 113–124.

5. R. W. Floyd, "On ambiguity in phrase-structure languages," *Comm. ACM* **5**:10 (1962), pp. 526–534.

6. M. Gross, "Inherent ambiguity of minimal linear grammars," *Information and Control* **7**:3 (1964), pp. 366–368.

7. P. Naur et al., "Report on the algorithmic language ALGOL 60," *Comm. ACM* **3**:5 (1960), pp. 299–314. See also *Comm. ACM* **6**:1 (1963), pp. 1–17.

8. World-Wide-Web Consortium, `http://www.w3.org/TR/REC-xml` (1998).

Chapter 6

Pushdown Automata

The context-free languages have a type of automaton that defines them. This automaton, called a "pushdown automaton," is an extension of the nondeterministic finite automaton with ϵ-transitions, which is one of the ways to define the regular languages. The pushdown automaton is essentially and ϵ-NFA with the addition of a stack. The stack can be read, pushed, and popped only at the top, just like the "stack" data structure.

In this chapter, we define two different versions of the pushdown automaton: one that accepts by entering an accepting state, like finite automata do, and another version that accepts by emptying its stack, regardless of the state it is in. We show that these two variations accept exactly the context-free languages; that is, grammars can be converted to equivalent pushdown automata, and vice-versa. We also consider briefly the subclass of pushdown automata that is deterministic. These accept all the regular languages, but only a proper subset of the CFL's. Since they resemble closely the mechanics of the parser in a typical compiler, it is important to observe what language constructs can and cannot be recognized by deterministic pushdown automata.

6.1 Definition of the Pushdown Automaton

In this section we introduce the pushdown automaton, first informally, then as a formal construct.

6.1.1 Informal Introduction

The pushdown automaton is in essence a nondeterministic finite automaton with ϵ-transitions permitted and one additional capability: a stack on which it can store a string of "stack symbols." The presence of a stack means that, unlike the finite automaton, the pushdown automaton can "remember" an infinite amount of information. However, unlike a general-purpose computer, which also has the ability to remember arbitrarily large amounts of information, the pushdown automaton can only access the information on its stack in a first-in-first-out way.

As a result, there are languages that could be recognized by some computer program, but are not recognizable by any pushdown automaton. In fact, pushdown automata recognize all and only the context-free languages. While there are many languages that *are* context-free, including some we have seen that are not regular languages, there are also some simple-to-describe languages that are not context-free, as we shall see in Section 7.2. An example of a non-context-free language is $\{0^n1^n2^n \mid n \geq 1\}$, the set of strings consisting of equal groups of 0's, 1's, and 2's.

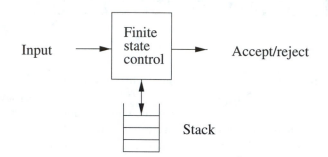

Figure 6.1: A pushdown automaton is essentially a finite automaton with a stack data structure

We can view the pushdown automaton informally as the device suggested in Fig. 6.1. A "finite-state control" reads inputs, one symbol at a time. The pushdown automaton is allowed to observe the symbol at the top of the stack and to base its transition on its current state, the input symbol, and the symbol at the top of stack. Alternatively, it may make a "spontaneous" transition, using ϵ as its input instead of an input symbol. In one transition, the pushdown automaton:

1. Consumes from the input the symbol that it uses in the transition. If ϵ is used for the input, then no input symbol is consumed.

2. Goes to a new state, which may or may not be the same as the previous state.

3. Replaces the symbol at the top of the stack by any string. The string could be ϵ, which corresponds to a pop of the stack. It could be the same symbol that appeared at the top of the stack previously; i.e., no change to the stack is made. It could also replace the top stack symbol by one other symbol, which in effect changes the top of the stack but does not push or pop it. Finally, the top stack symbol could be replaced by two or more symbols, which has the effect of (possibly) changing the top stack symbol, and then pushing one or more new symbols onto the stack.

Example 6.1 : Let us consider the language

$$L_{wwr} = \{ww^R \mid w \text{ is in } (0+1)^*\}$$

This language, often referred to as "w-w-reversed," is the even-length palindromes over alphabet $\{0, 1\}$. It is a CFL, generated by the grammar of Fig. 5.1, with the productions $P \rightarrow 0$ and $P \rightarrow 1$ omitted.

We can design an informal pushdown automaton accepting L_{wwr}, as follows.[1]

1. Start in a state q_0 that represents a "guess" that we have not yet seen the middle; i.e., we have not seen the end of the string w that is to be followed by its own reverse. While in state q_0, we read symbols and store them on the stack, by pushing a copy of each input symbol onto the stack, in turn.

2. At any time, we may guess that we have seen the middle, i.e., the end of w. At this time, w will be on the stack, with the right end of w at the top and the left end at the bottom. We signify this choice by spontaneously going to state q_1. Since the automaton is nondeterministic, we actually make both guesses: we guess we have seen the end of w, but we also stay in state q_0 and continue to read inputs and store them on the stack.

3. Once in state q_1, we compare input symbols with the symbol at the top of the stack. If they match, we consume the input symbol, pop the stack, and proceed. If they do not match, we have guessed wrong; our guessed w was not followed by w^R. This branch dies, although other branches of the nondeterministic automaton may survive and eventually lead to acceptance.

4. If we empty the stack, then we have indeed seen some input w followed by w^R. We accept the input that was read up to this point.

□

6.1.2 The Formal Definition of Pushdown Automata

Our formal notation for a *pushdown automaton* (PDA) involves seven components. We write the specification of a PDA P as follows:

$$P = (Q, \Sigma, \Gamma, \delta, q_0, Z_0, F)$$

The components have the following meanings:

Q: A finite set of *states*, like the states of a finite automaton.

---

[1] We could also design a pushdown automaton for L_{pal}, which is the language whose grammar appeared in Fig. 5.1. However, L_{wwr} is slightly simpler and will allow us to focus on the important ideas regarding pushdown automata.

No "Mixing and Matching"

There may be several pairs that are options for a PDA in some situation. For instance, suppose $\delta(q, a, X) = \{(p, YZ), (r, \epsilon)\}$. When making a move of the PDA, we have to chose one pair in its entirety; we cannot pick a state from one and a stack-replacement string from another. Thus, in state q, with X on the top of the stack, reading input a, we could go to state p and replace X by YZ, or we could go to state r and pop X. However, we cannot go to state p and pop X, and we cannot go to state r and replace X by YZ.

Σ: A finite set of *input symbols*, also analogous to the corresponding component of a finite automaton.

Γ: A finite *stack alphabet*. This component, which has no finite-automaton analog, is the set of symbols that we are allowed to push onto the stack.

δ: The *transition function*. As for a finite automaton, δ governs the behavior of the automaton. Formally, δ takes as argument a triple $\delta(q, a, X)$, where:

  1. q is a state in Q.

  2. a is either an input symbol in Σ or $a = \epsilon$, the empty string, which is assumed not to be an input symbol.

  3. X is a stack symbol, that is, a member of Γ.

  The output of δ is a finite set of pairs (p, γ), where p is the new state, and γ is the string of stack symbols that replaces X at the top of the stack. For instance, if $\gamma = \epsilon$, then the stack is popped, if $\gamma = X$, then the stack is unchanged, and if $\gamma = YZ$, then X is replaced by Z, and Y is pushed onto the stack.

q_0: The *start state*. The PDA is in this state before making any transitions.

Z_0: The *start symbol*. Initially, the PDA's stack consists of one instance of this symbol, and nothing else.

F: The set of *accepting states*, or *final states*.

Example 6.2: Let us design a PDA P to accept the language L_{wwr} of Example 6.1. First, there are a few details not present in that example that we need to understand in order to manage the stack properly. We shall use a stack symbol Z_0 to mark the bottom of the stack. We need to have this symbol present so that, after we pop w off the stack and realize that we have seen ww^R on the input, we still have something on the stack to permit us to make a transition to the accepting state, q_2. Thus, our PDA for L_{wwr} can be described as

$$P = (\{q_0, q_1, q_2\}, \{0, 1\}, \{0, 1, Z_0\}, \delta, q_0, Z_0, \{q_2\})$$

where δ is defined by the following rules:

1. $\delta(q_0, 0, Z_0) = \{(q_0, 0Z_0)\}$ and $\delta(q_0, 1, Z_0) = \{(q_0, 1Z_0)\}$. One of these rules applies initially, when we are in state q_0 and we see the start symbol Z_0 at the top of the stack. We read the first input, and push it onto the stack, leaving Z_0 below to mark the bottom.

2. $\delta(q_0, 0, 0) = \{(q_0, 00)\}$, $\delta(q_0, 0, 1) = \{(q_0, 01)\}$, $\delta(q_0, 1, 0) = \{(q_0, 10)\}$, and $\delta(q_0, 1, 1) = \{(q_0, 11)\}$. These four, similar rules allow us to stay in state q_0 and read inputs, pushing each onto the top of the stack and leaving the previous top stack symbol alone.

3. $\delta(q_0, \epsilon, Z_0) = \{(q_1, Z_0)\}$, $\delta(q_0, \epsilon, 0) = \{(q_1, 0)\}$, and $\delta(q_0, \epsilon, 1) = \{(q_1, 1)\}$. These three rules allow P to go from state q_0 to state q_1 spontaneously (on ϵ input), leaving intact whatever symbol is at the top of the stack.

4. $\delta(q_1, 0, 0) = \{(q_1, \epsilon)\}$, and $\delta(q_1, 1, 1) = \{(q_1, \epsilon)\}$. Now, in state q_1 we can match input symbols against the top symbols on the stack, and pop when the symbols match.

5. $\delta(q_1, \epsilon, Z_0) = \{(q_2, Z_0)\}$. Finally, if we expose the bottom-of-stack marker Z_0 and we are in state q_1, then we have found an input of the form ww^R. We go to state q_2 and accept.

□

6.1.3 A Graphical Notation for PDA's

The list of δ facts, as in Example 6.2, is not too easy to follow. Sometimes, a diagram, generalizing the transition diagram of a finite automaton, will make aspects of the behavior of a given PDA clearer. We shall therefore introduce and subsequently use a *transition diagram* for PDA's in which:

a) The nodes correspond to the states of the PDA.

b) An arrow labeled *Start* indicates the start state, and doubly circled states are accepting, as for finite automata.

c) The arcs correspond to transitions of the PDA in the following sense. An arc labeled $a, X/\alpha$ from state q to state p means that $\delta(q, a, X)$ contains the pair (p, α), perhaps among other pairs. That is, the arc label tells what input is used, and also gives the old and new tops of the stack.

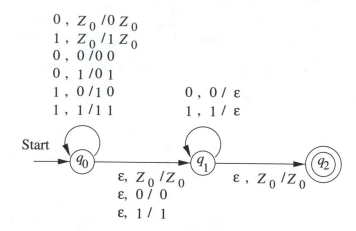

Figure 6.2: Representing a PDA as a generalized transition diagram

The only thing that the diagram does not tell us is which stack symbol is the start symbol. Conventionally, it is Z_0, unless we indicate otherwise.

Example 6.3: The PDA of Example 6.2 is represented by the diagram shown in Fig. 6.2. □

6.1.4 Instantaneous Descriptions of a PDA

To this point, we have only an informal notion of how a PDA "computes." Intuitively, the PDA goes from configuration to configuration, in response to input symbols (or sometimes ϵ), but unlike the finite automaton, where the state is the only thing that we need to know about the automaton, the PDA's configuration involves both the state and the contents of the stack. Being arbitrarily large, the stack is often the more important part of the total configuration of the PDA at any time. It is also useful to represent as part of the configuration the portion of the input that remains.

Thus, we shall represent the configuration of a PDA by a triple (q, w, γ), where

1. q is the state,

2. w is the remaining input, and

3. γ is the stack contents.

Conventionally, we show the top of the stack at the left end of γ and the bottom at the right end. Such a triple is called an *instantaneous description*, or ID, of the pushdown automaton.

For finite automata, the $\hat{\delta}$ notation was sufficient to represent sequences of instantaneous descriptions through which a finite automaton moved, since the ID for a finite automaton is just its state. However, for PDA's we need a notation that describes changes in the state, the input, and stack. Thus, we adopt the "turnstile" notation for connecting pairs of ID's that represent one or many moves of a PDA.

Let $P = (Q, \Sigma, \Gamma, \delta, q_0, Z_0, F)$ be a PDA. Define $\vdash_P$, or just $\vdash$ when P is understood, as follows. Suppose $\delta(q, a, X)$ contains (p, α). Then for all strings w in Σ^* and β in Γ^*:

$$(q, aw, X\beta) \vdash (p, w, \alpha\beta)$$

This move reflects the idea that, by consuming a (which may be ϵ) from the input and replacing X on top of the stack by α, we can go from state q to state p. Note that what remains on the input, w, and what is below the top of the stack, β, do not influence the action of the PDA; they are merely carried along, perhaps to influence events later.

We also use the symbol $\overset{*}{\vdash}$, or $\overset{*}{\vdash}$ when the PDA P is understood, to represent zero or more moves of the PDA. That is:

BASIS: $I \overset{*}{\vdash} I$ for any ID I.

INDUCTION: $I \overset{*}{\vdash} J$ if there exists some ID K such that $I \vdash K$ and $K \overset{*}{\vdash} J$.

That is, $I \overset{*}{\vdash} J$ if there is a sequence of ID's $K_1, K_2, \ldots, K_n$ such that $I = K_1$, $J = K_n$, and for all $i = 1, 2, \ldots, n-1$, we have $K_i \vdash K_{i+1}$.

Example 6.4: Let us consider the action of the PDA of Example 6.2 on the input 1111. Since q_0 is the start state and Z_0 is the start symbol, the initial ID is $(q_0, 1111, Z_0)$. On this input, the PDA has an opportunity to guess wrongly several times. The entire sequence of ID's that the PDA can reach from the initial ID $(q_0, 1111, Z_0)$ is shown in Fig. 6.3. Arrows represent the $\vdash$ relation.

From the initial ID, there are two choices of move. The first guesses that the middle has not been seen and leads to ID $(q_0, 111, 1Z_0)$. In effect, a 1 has been removed from the input and pushed onto the stack.

The second choice from the initial ID guesses that the middle has been reached. Without consuming input, the PDA goes to state q_1, leading to the ID $(q_1, 1111, Z_0)$. Since the PDA may accept if it is in state q_1 and sees Z_0 on top of its stack, the PDA goes from there to ID $(q_2, 1111, Z_0)$. That ID is not exactly an accepting ID, since the input has not been completely consumed. Had the input been ϵ rather than 1111, the same sequence of moves would have led to ID (q_2, ϵ, Z_0), which would show that ϵ is accepted.

The PDA may also guess that it has seen the middle after reading one 1, that is, when it is in the ID $(q_0, 111, 1Z_0)$. That guess also leads to failure, since the entire input cannot be consumed. The correct guess, that the middle is reached after reading two 1's, gives us the sequence of ID's $(q_0, 1111, Z_0) \vdash (q_0, 111, 1Z_0) \vdash (q_0, 11, 11Z_0) \vdash (q_1, 11, 11Z_0) \vdash (q_1, 1, 1Z_0) \vdash (q_1, \epsilon, Z_0) \vdash (q_2, \epsilon, Z_0)$. $\square$

There are three important principles about ID's and their transitions that we shall need in order to reason about PDA's:

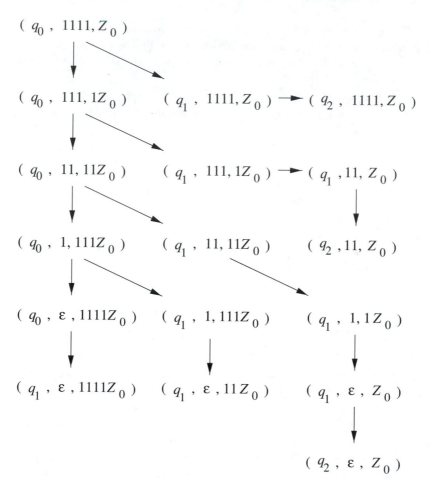

Figure 6.3: ID's of the PDA of Example 6.2 on input 1111

1. If a sequence of ID's (*computation*) is legal for a PDA P, then the computation formed by adding the same additional input string to the end of the input (second component) in each ID is also legal.

2. If a computation is legal for a PDA P, then the computation formed by adding the same additional stack symbols below the stack in each ID is also legal.

3. If a computation is legal for a PDA P, and some tail of the input is not consumed, then we can remove this tail from the input in each ID, and the resulting computation will still be legal.

Intuitively, data that P never looks at cannot affect its computation. We formalize points (1) and (2) in a single theorem.

Notational Conventions for PDA's

We shall continue using conventions regarding the use of symbols that we introduced for finite automata and grammars. In carrying over the notation, it is useful to realize that the stack symbols play a role analogous to the union of the terminals and variables in a CFG. Thus:

1. Symbols of the input alphabet will be represented by lower-case letters near the beginning of the alphabet, e.g., a, b.

2. States will be represented by q and p, typically, or other letters that are nearby in alphabetical order.

3. Strings of input symbols will be represented by lower-case letters near the end of the alphabet, e.g., w or z.

4. Stack symbols will be represented by capital letters near the end of the alphabet, e.g., X or Y.

5. Strings of stack symbols will be represented by Greek letters, e.g., α or γ.

Theorem 6.5: If $P = (Q, \Sigma, \Gamma, \delta, q_0, Z_0, F)$ is a PDA, and $(q, x, \alpha) \overset{*}{\underset{P}{\vdash}} (p, y, \beta)$, then for any strings w in Σ^* and γ in Γ^*, it is also true that

$$(q, xw, \alpha\gamma) \overset{*}{\underset{P}{\vdash}} (p, yw, \beta\gamma)$$

Note that if $\gamma = \epsilon$, then we have a formal statement of principle (1) above, and if $w = \epsilon$, then we have the second principle.

PROOF: The proof is actually a very simple induction on the number of steps in the sequence of ID's that take $(q, xw, \alpha\gamma)$ to $(p, yw, \beta\gamma)$. Each of the moves in the sequence $(q, x, \alpha) \overset{*}{\underset{P}{\vdash}} (p, y, \beta)$ is justified by the transitions of P without using w and/or γ in any way. Therefore, each move is still justified when these strings are sitting on the input and stack. □

Incidentally, note that the converse of this theorem is false. There are things that a PDA might be able to do by popping its stack, using some symbols of γ, and then replacing them on the stack, that it couldn't do if it never looked at γ. However, as principle (3) states, we can remove unused input, since it is not possible for a PDA to consume input symbols and then restore those symbols to the input. We state principle (3) formally as:

ID's for Finite Automata?

One might wonder why we did not introduce for finite automata a notation like the ID's we use for PDA's. Although a FA has no stack, we could use a pair (q, w), where q is the state and w the remaining input, as the ID of a finite automaton.

   While we could have done so, we would not glean any more information from reachability among ID's than we obtain from the $\hat{\delta}$ notation. That is, for any finite automaton, we could show that $\hat{\delta}(q, w) = p$ if and only if $(q, wx) \overset{*}{\vdash} (p, x)$ for all strings x. The fact that x can be anything we wish without influencing the behavior of the FA is a theorem analogous to Theorems 6.5 and 6.6.

Theorem 6.6: If $P = (Q, \Sigma, \Gamma, \delta, q_0, Z_0, F)$ is a PDA, and

$$(q, xw, \alpha) \overset{*}{\underset{P}{\vdash}} (p, yw, \beta)$$

then it is also true that $(q, x, \alpha) \overset{*}{\underset{P}{\vdash}} (p, y, \beta)$.   □

6.1.5 Exercises for Section 6.1

Exercise 6.1.1: Suppose the PDA $P = (\{q, p\}, \{0, 1\}, \{Z_0, X\}, \delta, q, Z_0, \{p\})$ has the following transition function:

1. $\delta(q, 0, Z_0) = \{(q, X Z_0)\}$.

2. $\delta(q, 0, X) = \{(q, XX)\}$.

3. $\delta(q, 1, X) = \{(q, X)\}$.

4. $\delta(q, \epsilon, X) = \{(p, \epsilon)\}$.

5. $\delta(p, \epsilon, X) = \{(p, \epsilon)\}$.

6. $\delta(p, 1, X) = \{(p, XX)\}$.

7. $\delta(p, 1, Z_0) = \{(p, \epsilon)\}$.

Starting from the initial ID (q, w, Z_0), show all the reachable ID's when the input w is:

* a) 01.

  b) 0011.

  c) 010.

6.2 The Languages of a PDA

We have assumed that a PDA accepts its input by consuming it and entering an accepting state. We call this approach "acceptance by final state." There is a second approach to defining the language of a PDA that has important applications. We may also define for any PDA the language "accepted by empty stack," that is, the set of strings that cause the PDA to empty its stack, starting from the initial ID.

These two methods are equivalent, in the sense that a language L has a PDA that accepts it by final state if and only if L has a PDA that accepts it by empty stack. However, for a given PDA P, the languages that P accepts by final state and by empty stack are usually different. We shall show in this section how to convert a PDA accepting L by final state into another PDA that accepts L by empty stack, and vice-versa.

6.2.1 Acceptance by Final State

Let $P = (Q, \Sigma, \Gamma, \delta, q_0, Z_0, F)$ be a PDA. Then $L(P)$, the *language accepted by P by final state*, is

$$\{w \mid (q_0, w, Z_0) \overset{*}{\underset{P}{\vdash}} (q, \epsilon, \alpha)\}$$

for some state q in F and any stack string α. That is, starting in the initial ID with w waiting on the input, P consumes w from the input and enters an accepting state. The contents of the stack at that time is irrelevant.

Example 6.7: We have claimed that the PDA of Example 6.2 accepts the language L_{wwr}, the language of strings in $\{0, 1\}^*$ that have the form ww^R. Let us see why that statement is true. The proof is an if-and-only-if statement: the PDA P of Example 6.2 accepts string x by final state if and only if x is of the form ww^R.

(If) This part is easy; we have only to show the accepting computation of P. If $x = ww^R$, then observe that

$$(q_0, ww^R, Z_0) \overset{*}{\vdash} (q_0, w^R, w^R Z_0) \vdash (q_1, w^R, w^R Z_0) \overset{*}{\vdash} (q_1, \epsilon, Z_0) \vdash (q_2, \epsilon, Z_0)$$

That is, one option the PDA has is to read w from its input and store it on its stack, in reverse. Next, it goes spontaneously to state q_1 and matches w^R on the input with the same string on its stack, and finally goes spontaneously to state q_2.

(Only-if) This part is harder. First, observe that the only way to enter accepting state q_2 is to be in state q_1 and have Z_0 at the top of the stack. Also, any accepting computation of P will start in state q_0, make one transition to q_1, and never return to q_0. Thus, it is sufficient to find the conditions on x such that $(q_0, x, Z_0) \overset{*}{\vdash} (q_1, \epsilon, Z_0)$; these will be exactly the strings x that P accepts by final state. We shall show by induction on $|x|$ the slightly more general statement:

- If $(q_0, x, \alpha) \overset{*}{\vdash} (q_1, \epsilon, \alpha)$, then x is of the form ww^R.

BASIS: If $x = \epsilon$, then x is of the form ww^R (with $w = \epsilon$). Thus, the conclusion is true, so the statement is true. Note we do not have to argue that the hypothesis $(q_0, \epsilon, \alpha) \overset{*}{\vdash} (q_1, \epsilon, \alpha)$ is true, although it is.

INDUCTION: Suppose $x = a_1 a_2 \cdots a_n$ for some $n > 0$. There are two moves that P can make from ID (q_0, x, α):

1. $(q_0, x, \alpha) \vdash (q_1, x, \alpha)$. Now P can only pop the stack when it is in state q_1. P must pop the stack with every input symbol it reads, and $|x| > 0$. Thus, if $(q_1, x, \alpha) \overset{*}{\vdash} (q_1, \epsilon, \beta)$, then β will be shorter than α and cannot be equal to α.

2. $(q_0, a_1 a_2 \cdots a_n, \alpha) \vdash (q_0, a_2 \cdots a_n, a_1 \alpha)$. Now the only way a sequence of moves can end in (q_1, ϵ, α) is if the last move is a pop:

$$(q_1, a_n, a_1 \alpha) \vdash (q_1, \epsilon, \alpha)$$

In that case, it must be that $a_1 = a_n$. We also know that

$$(q_0, a_2 \cdots a_n, a_1 \alpha) \overset{*}{\vdash} (q_1, a_n, a_1 \alpha)$$

By Theorem 6.6, we can remove the symbol a_n from the end of the input, since it is not used. Thus,

$$(q_0, a_2 \cdots a_{n-1}, a_1 \alpha) \overset{*}{\vdash} (q_1, \epsilon, a_1 \alpha)$$

Since the input for this sequence is shorter than n, we may apply the inductive hypothesis and conclude that $a_2 \cdots a_{n-1}$ is of the form yy^R for some y. Since $x = a_1 yy^R a_n$, and we know $a_1 = a_n$, we conclude that x is of the form ww^R; specifically $w = a_1 y$.

The above is the heart of the proof that the only way to accept x is for x to be equal to ww^R for some w. Thus, we have the "only-if" part of the proof, which, with the "if" part proved earlier, tells us that P accepts exactly those strings in L_{wwr}.   □

6.2.2   Acceptance by Empty Stack

For each PDA $P = (Q, \Sigma, \Gamma, \delta, q_0, Z_0, F)$, we also define

$$N(P) = \{w \mid (q_0, w, Z_0) \overset{*}{\vdash} (q, \epsilon, \epsilon)\}$$

for any state q. That is, $N(P)$ is the set of inputs w that P can consume and at the same time empty its stack.[2]

---

[2]The N in $N(P)$ stands for "null stack," a synonym for "empty stack."

Example 6.8: The PDA P of Example 6.2 never empties its stack, so $N(P) = \emptyset$. However, a small modification will allow P to accept L_{wwr} by empty stack as well as by final state. Instead of the transition $\delta(q_1, \epsilon, Z_0) = \{(q_2, Z_0)\}$, use $\delta(q_1, \epsilon, Z_0) = \{(q_2, \epsilon)\}$. Now, P pops the last symbol off its stack as it accepts, and $L(P) = N(P) = L_{wwr}$.   □

Since the set of accepting states is irrelevant, we shall sometimes leave off the last (seventh) component from the specification of a PDA P, if all we care about is the language that P accepts by empty stack. Thus, we would write P as a six-tuple $(Q, \Sigma, \Gamma, \delta, q_0, Z_0)$.

6.2.3   From Empty Stack to Final State

We shall show that the classes of languages that are $L(P)$ for some PDA P is the same as the class of languages that are $N(P)$ for some PDA P. This class is also exactly the context-free languages, as we shall see in Section 6.3. Our first construction shows how to take a PDA P_N that accepts a language L by empty stack and construct a PDA P_F that accepts L by final state.

Theorem 6.9: If $L = N(P_N)$ for some PDA $P_N = (Q, \Sigma, \Gamma, \delta_N, q_0, Z_0)$, then there is a PDA P_F such that $L = L(P_F)$.

PROOF: The idea behind the proof is in Fig. 6.4. We use a new symbol X_0, which must not be a symbol of Γ; X_0 is both the start symbol of P_F and a marker on the bottom of the stack that lets us know when P_N has reached an empty stack. That is, if P_F sees X_0 on top of its stack, then it knows that P_N would empty its stack on the same input.

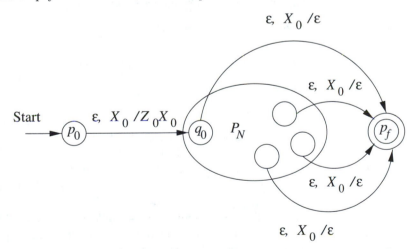

Figure 6.4: P_F simulates P_N and accepts if P_N empties its stack

We also need a new start state, p_0, whose sole function is to push Z_0, the start symbol of P_N, onto the top of the stack and enter state q_0, the start state of P_N. Then, P_F simulates P_N, until the stack of P_N is empty, which P_F detects because it sees X_0 on the top of the stack. Finally, we need another new state, p_f, which is the accepting state of P_F; this PDA transfers to state p_f whenever it discovers that P_N would have emptied its stack.

The specification of P_F is as follows:

$$P_F = (Q \cup \{p_0, p_f\}, \Sigma, \Gamma \cup \{X_0\}, \delta_F, p_0, X_0, \{p_f\})$$

where δ_F is defined by:

1. $\delta_F(p_0, \epsilon, X_0) = \{(q_0, Z_0 X_0)\}$. In its start state, P_F makes a spontaneous transition to the start state of P_N, pushing its start symbol Z_0 onto the stack.

2. For all states q in Q, inputs a in Σ or $a = \epsilon$, and stack symbols Y in Γ, $\delta_F(q, a, Y)$ contains all the pairs in $\delta_N(q, a, Y)$.

3. In addition to rule (2), $\delta_F(q, \epsilon, X_0)$ contains (p_f, ϵ) for every state q in Q.

We must show that w is in $L(P_F)$ if and only if w is in $N(P_N)$.

(If) We are given that $(q_0, w, Z_0) \underset{P_N}{\overset{*}{\vdash}} (q, \epsilon, \epsilon)$ for some state q. Theorem 6.5 lets us insert X_0 at the bottom of the stack and conclude $(q_0, w, Z_0 X_0) \underset{P_N}{\overset{*}{\vdash}} (q, \epsilon, X_0)$. Since by rule (2) above, P_F has all the moves of P_N, we may also conclude that $(q_0, w, Z_0 X_0) \underset{P_F}{\overset{*}{\vdash}} (q, \epsilon, X_0)$. If we put this sequence of moves together with the initial and final moves from rules (1) and (3) above, we get:

$$(p_0, w, X_0) \underset{P_F}{\vdash} (q_0, w, Z_0 X_0) \underset{P_F}{\overset{*}{\vdash}} (q, \epsilon, X_0) \underset{P_F}{\vdash} (p_f, \epsilon, \epsilon) \qquad (6.1)$$

Thus, P_F accepts w by final state.

(Only-if) The converse requires only that we observe the additional transitions of rules (1) and (3) give us very limited ways to accept w by final state. We must use rule (3) at the last step, and we can only use that rule if the stack of P_F contains only X_0. No X_0's ever appear on the stack except at the bottommost position. Further, rule (1) is only used at the first step, and it *must* be used at the first step.

Thus, any computation of P_F that accepts w must look like sequence (6.1). Moreover, the middle of the computation — all but the first and last steps — must also be a computation of P_N with X_0 below the stack. The reason is that, except for the first and last steps, P_F cannot use any transition that is not also a transition of P_N, and X_0 cannot be exposed or the computation would end at the next step. We conclude that $(q_0, w, Z_0) \underset{P_N}{\overset{*}{\vdash}} (q, \epsilon, \epsilon)$. That is, w is in $N(P_N)$.
□

Example 6.10: Let us design a PDA that processes sequences of if's and else's in a C program, where i stands for if and e stands for else. Recall from Section 5.3.1 that there is a problem whenever the number of else's in any prefix exceeds the number of if's, because then we cannot match each else against its previous if. Thus, we shall use a stack symbol Z to count the difference between the number of i's seen so far and the number of e's. This simple, one-state PDA, is suggested by the transition diagram of Fig. 6.5.

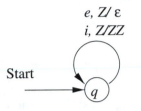

Figure 6.5: A PDA that accepts the if/else errors by empty stack

We shall push another Z whenever we see an i and pop a Z whenever we see an e. Since we start with one Z on the stack, we actually follow the rule that if the stack is Z^n, then there have been $n - 1$ more i's than e's. In particular, if the stack is empty, than we have seen one more e than i, and the input read so far has just become illegal for the first time. It is these strings that our PDA accepts by empty stack. The formal specification of P_N is:

$$P_N = (\{q\}, \{i, e\}, \{Z\}, \delta_N, q, Z)$$

where δ_N is defined by:

1. $\delta_N(q, i, Z) = \{(q, ZZ)\}$. This rule pushes a Z when we see an i.

2. $\delta_N(q, e, Z) = \{(q, \epsilon)\}$. This rule pops a Z when we see an e.

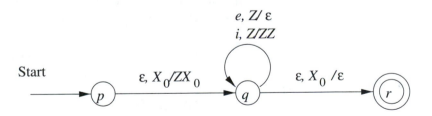

Figure 6.6: Construction of a PDA accepting by final state from the PDA of Fig. 6.5

Now, let us construct from P_N a PDA P_F that accepts the same language by final state; the transition diagram for P_F is shown in Fig. 6.6.[3] We introduce

---

[3]Do not be concerned that we are using new states p and q here, while the construction in Theorem 6.9 used p_0 and p_f. Names of states are arbitrary, of course.

a new start state p and an accepting state r. We shall use X_0 as the bottom-of stack marker. P_F is formally defined:

$$P_F = (\{p, q, r\}, \{i, e\}, \{Z, X_0\}, \delta_F, p, X_0, \{r\})$$

where δ_F consists of:

1. $\delta_F(p, \epsilon, X_0) = \{(q, ZX_0)\}$. This rule starts P_F simulating P_N, with X_0 as a bottom-of-stack-marker.

2. $\delta_F(q, i, Z) = \{(q, ZZ)\}$. This rule pushes a Z when we see an i; it simulates P_N.

3. $\delta_F(q, e, Z) = \{(q, \epsilon)\}$. This rule pops a Z when we see an e; it also simulates P_N.

4. $\delta_F(q, \epsilon, X_0) = \{(r, \epsilon, \epsilon)\}$. That is, P_F accepts when the simulated P_N would have emptied its stack.

□

6.2.4 From Final State to Empty Stack

Now, let us go in the opposite direction: take a PDA P_F that accepts a language L by final state and construct another PDA P_N that accepts L by empty stack. The construction is simple and is suggested in Fig. 6.7. From each accepting state of P_F, add a transition on ϵ to a new state p. When in state p, P_N pops its stack and does not consume any input. Thus, whenever P_F enters an accepting state after consuming input w, P_N will empty its stack after consuming w.

To avoid simulating a situation where P_F accidentally empties its stack without accepting, P_N must also use a marker X_0 on the bottom of its stack. The marker is P_N's start symbol, and like the construction of Theorem 6.9, P_N must start in a new state p_0, whose sole function is to push the start symbol of P_F on the stack and go to the start state of P_F. The construction is sketched in Fig. 6.7, and we give it formally in the next theorem.

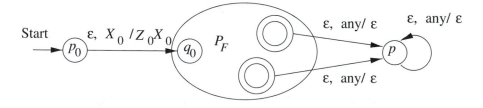

Figure 6.7: P_N simulates P_F and empties its stack when and only when P_N enters an accepting state

Theorem 6.11: Let L be $L(P_F)$ for some PDA $P_F = (Q, \Sigma, \Gamma, \delta_F, q_0, Z_0, F)$. Then there is a PDA P_N such that $L = N(P_N)$.

PROOF: The construction is as suggested in Fig. 6.7. Let

$$P_N = (Q \cup \{p_0, p\}, \Sigma, \Gamma \cup \{X_0\}, \delta_N, p_0, X_0)$$

where δ_N is defined by:

1. $\delta_N(p_0, \epsilon, X_0) = \{(q_0, Z_0 X_0)\}$. We start by pushing the start symbol of P_F onto the stack and going to the start state of P_F.

2. For all states q in Q, input symbols a in Σ or $a = \epsilon$, and Y in Γ, $\delta_N(q, a, Y)$ contains every pair that is in $\delta_F(q, a, Y)$. That is, P_N simulates P_F.

3. For all accepting states q in F and stack symbols Y in Γ or $Y = X_0$, $\delta_N(q, \epsilon, Y)$ contains (p, ϵ). By this rule, whenever P_F accepts, P_N can start emptying its stack without consuming any more input.

4. For all stack symbols Y in Γ or $Y = X_0$, $\delta_N(p, \epsilon, Y) = \{(p, \epsilon)\}$. Once in state p, which only occurs when P_F has accepted, P_N pops every symbol on its stack, until the stack is empty. No further input is consumed.

Now, we must prove that w is in $N(P_N)$ if and only if w is in $L(P_F)$. The ideas are similar to the proof for Theorem 6.9. The 'if' part is a direct simulation, and the 'only-if' part requires that we examine the limited number of things that the constructed PDA P_N can do.

(If) Suppose $(q_0, w, Z_0) \overset{*}{\underset{P_F}{\vdash}} (q, \epsilon, \alpha)$ for some accepting state q and stack string α. Using the fact that every transition of P_F is a move of P_N, and invoking Theorem 6.5 to allow us to keep X_0 below the symbols of Γ on the stack, we know that $(q_0, w, Z_0 X_0) \overset{*}{\underset{P_N}{\vdash}} (q, \epsilon, \alpha X_0)$. Then P_N can do the following:

$$(p_0, w, X_0) \underset{P_N}{\vdash} (q_0, w, Z_0 X_0) \overset{*}{\underset{P_N}{\vdash}} (q, \epsilon, \alpha X_0) \overset{*}{\underset{P_N}{\vdash}} (p, \epsilon, \epsilon)$$

The first move is by rule (1) of the construction of P_N, while the last sequence of moves is by rules (3) and (4). Thus, w is accepted by P_N, by empty stack.

(Only-if) The only way P_N can empty its stack is by entering state p, since X_0 is sitting at the bottom of stack and X_0 is not a symbol on which P_F has any moves. The only way P_N can enter state p is if the simulated P_F enters an accepting state. The first move of P_N is surely the move given in rule (1). Thus, every accepting computation of P_N looks like

$$(p_0, w, X_0) \underset{P_N}{\vdash} (q_0, w, Z_0 X_0) \overset{*}{\underset{P_N}{\vdash}} (q, \epsilon, \alpha X_0) \overset{*}{\underset{P_N}{\vdash}} (p, \epsilon, \epsilon)$$

where q is an accepting state of P_F.

Moreover, between ID's $(q_0, w, Z_0 X_0)$ and $(q, \epsilon, \alpha X_0)$, all the moves are moves of P_F. In particular, X_0 was never the top stack symbol prior to reaching ID $(q, \epsilon, \alpha X_0)$.[4] Thus, we conclude that the same computation can occur in P_F, without the X_0 on the stack; that is, $(q_0, w, Z_0) \overset{*}{\underset{P_F}{\vdash}} (q, \epsilon, \alpha)$. Now we see that P_F accepts w by final state, so w is in $L(P_F)$. $\square$

---

[4]Although α could be ϵ, in which case P_F has emptied its stack at the same time it accepts.

6.2.5   Exercises for Section 6.2

Exercise 6.2.1 : Design a PDA to accept each of the following languages. You may accept either by final state or by empty stack, whichever is more convenient.

* a) $\{0^n1^n \mid n \geq 1\}$.

  b) The set of all strings of 0's and 1's such that no prefix has more 1's than 0's.

  c) The set of all strings of 0's and 1's with an equal number of 0's and 1's.

! **Exercise 6.2.2 :** Design a PDA to accept each of the following languages.

* a) $\{a^ib^jc^k \mid i = j \text{ or } j = k\}$. Note that this language is different from that of Exercise 5.1.1(b).

  b) The set of all strings with twice as many 0's as 1's.

!! **Exercise 6.2.3 :** Design a PDA to accept each of the following languages.

  a) $\{a^ib^jc^k \mid i \neq j \text{ or } j \neq k\}$.

  b) The set of all strings of a's and b's that are *not* of the form ww, that is, not equal to any string repeated.

*! **Exercise 6.2.4 :** Let P be a PDA with empty-stack language $L = N(P)$, and suppose that ϵ is not in L. Describe how you would modify P so that it accepts $L \cup \{\epsilon\}$ by empty stack.

Exercise 6.2.5 : PDA $P = (\{q_0, q_1, q_2, q_3, f\}, \{a, b\}, \{Z_0, A, B\}, \delta, q_0, Z_0, \{f\})$ has the following rules defining δ:

$$\delta(q_0, a, Z_0) = (q_1, AAZ_0) \quad \delta(q_0, b, Z_0) = (q_2, BZ_0) \quad \delta(q_0, \epsilon, Z_0) = (f, \epsilon)$$
$$\delta(q_1, a, A) = (q_1, AAA) \quad \delta(q_1, b, A) = (q_1, \epsilon) \quad \delta(q_1, \epsilon, Z_0) = (q_0, Z_0)$$
$$\delta(q_2, a, B) = (q_3, \epsilon) \quad \delta(q_2, b, B) = (q_2, BB) \quad \delta(q_2, \epsilon, Z_0) = (q_0, Z_0)$$
$$\delta(q_3, \epsilon, B) = (q_2, \epsilon) \quad \delta(q_3, \epsilon, Z_0) = (q_1, AZ_0)$$

Note that, since each of the sets above has only one choice of move, we have omitted the set brackets from each of the rules.

* a) Give an execution trace (sequence of ID's) showing that string bab is in $L(P)$.

  b) Give and execution trace showing that abb is in $L(P)$.

  c) Give the contents of the stack after P has read b^7a^4 from its input.

! d) Informally describe $L(P)$.

Exercise 6.2.6 : Consider the PDA P from Exercise 6.1.1.

   a) Convert P to another PDA P_1 that accepts by empty stack the same language that P accepts by final state; i.e., $N(P_1) = L(P)$.

   b) Find a PDA P_2 such that $L(P_2) = N(P)$; i.e., P_2 accepts by final state what P accepts by empty stack.

! **Exercise 6.2.7:** Show that if P is a PDA, then there is a PDA P_2 with only two stack symbols, such that $L(P_2) = L(P)$. *Hint*: Binary-code the stack alphabet of P.

*! **Exercise 6.2.8:** A PDA is called *restricted* if on any transition it can increase the height of the stack by at most one symbol. That is, for any rule $\delta(q, a, Z)$ contains (p, γ), it must be that $|\gamma| \leq 2$. Show that if P is a PDA, then there is a restricted PDA P_3 such that $L(P) = L(P_3)$.

6.3 Equivalence of PDA's and CFG's

Now, we shall demonstrate that the languages defined by PDA's are exactly the context-free languages. The plan of attack is suggested by Fig. 6.8. The goal is to prove that the following three classes of languages:

  1. The context-free languages, i.e., the languages defined by CFG's.

  2. The languages that are accepted by final state by some PDA.

  3. The languages that are accepted by empty stack by some PDA.

are all the same class. We have already shown that (2) and (3) are the same. It turns out to be easiest next to show that (1) and (3) are the same, thus implying the equivalence of all three.

Figure 6.8: Organization of constructions showing equivalence of three ways of defining the CFL's

6.3.1 From Grammars to Pushdown Automata

Given a CFG G, we construct a PDA that simulates the leftmost derivations of G. Any left-sentential form that is not a terminal string can be written as $xA\alpha$, where A is the leftmost variable, x is whatever terminals appear to its left, and α is the string of terminals and variables that appear to the right of A.

We call $A\alpha$ the *tail* of this left-sentential form. If a left-sentential form consists of terminals only, then its tail is ϵ.

The idea behind the construction of a PDA from a grammar is to have the PDA simulate the sequence of left-sentential forms that the grammar uses to generate a given terminal string w. The tail of each sentential form $xA\alpha$ appears on the stack, with A at the top. At that time, x will be "represented" by our having consumed x from the input, leaving whatever of w follows its prefix x. That is, if $w = xy$, then y will remain on the input.

Suppose the PDA is in an ID $(q, y, A\alpha)$, representing left-sentential form $xA\alpha$. It guesses the production to use to expand A, say $A \to \beta$. The move of the PDA is to replace A on the top of the stack by β, entering ID $(q, y, \beta\alpha)$. Note that there is only one state, q, for this PDA.

Now $(q, y, \beta\alpha)$ may not be a representation of the next left-sentential form, because β may have a prefix of terminals. In fact, β may have no variables at all, and α may have a prefix of terminals. Whatever terminals appear at the beginning of $\beta\alpha$ need to be removed, to expose the next variable at the top of the stack. These terminals are compared against the next input symbols, to make sure our guesses at the leftmost derivation of input string w are correct; if not, this branch of the PDA dies.

If we succeed in this way to guess a leftmost derivation of w, then we shall eventually reach the left-sentential form w. At that point, all the symbols on the stack have either been expanded (if they are variables) or matched against the input (if they are terminals). The stack is empty, and we accept by empty stack.

The above informal construction can be made precise as follows. Let $G = (V, T, Q, S)$ be a CFG. Construct the PDA P that accepts $L(G)$ by empty stack as follows:

$$P = (\{q\}, T, V \cup T, \delta, q, S)$$

where transition function δ is defined by:

1. For each variable A,

$$\delta(q, \epsilon, A) = \{(q, \beta) \mid A \to \beta \text{ is a production of } P\}$$

2. For each terminal a, $\delta(q, a, a) = \{(q, \epsilon)\}$.

Example 6.12: Let us convert the expression grammar of Fig. 5.2 to a PDA. Recall this grammar is:

$$
\begin{aligned}
I &\to a \mid b \mid Ia \mid Ib \mid I0 \mid I1 \\
E &\to I \mid E * E \mid E + E \mid (E)
\end{aligned}
$$

The set of terminals for the PDA is $\{a, b, 0, 1, (,), +, *\}$. These eight symbols and the symbols I and E form the stack alphabet. The transition function for the PDA is:

a) $\delta(q, \epsilon, I) = \{(q, a),\ (q, b),\ (q, Ia),\ (q, Ib),\ (q, I0),\ (q, I1)\}$.

b) $\delta(q, \epsilon, E) = \{(q, I),\ (q, E + E),\ (q, E * E),\ (q, (E))\}$.

c) $\delta(q, a, a) = \{(q, \epsilon)\}$; $\delta(q, b, b) = \{(q, \epsilon)\}$; $\delta(q, 0, 0) = \{(q, \epsilon)\}$; $\delta(q, 1, 1) = \{(q, \epsilon)\}$; $\delta(q, (, () = \{(q, \epsilon)\}$; $\delta(q,),)) = \{(q, \epsilon)\}$; $\delta(q, +, +) = \{(q, \epsilon)\}$; $\delta(q, *, *) = \{(q, \epsilon)\}$.

Note that (a) and (b) come from rule (1), while the eight transitions of (c) come from rule (2). Also, δ is empty except as defined by (a) through (c). □

Theorem 6.13: If PDA P is constructed from CFG G by the construction above, then $N(P) = L(G)$.

PROOF: We shall prove that w is in $N(P)$ if and only if w is in $L(G)$.

(If) Suppose w is in $L(G)$. Then w has a leftmost derivation

$$S = \gamma_1 \underset{lm}{\Rightarrow} \gamma_2 \underset{lm}{\Rightarrow} \cdots \underset{lm}{\Rightarrow} \gamma_n = w$$

We show by induction on i that $(q, w, S) \overset{*}{\underset{P}{\vdash}} (q, y_i, \alpha_i)$, where y_i and α_i are a representation of the left-sentential form γ_i. That is, let α_i be the tail of γ_i, and let $\gamma_i = x_i \alpha_i$. Then y_i is that string such that $x_i y_i = w$; i.e., it is what remains when x_i is removed from the input.

BASIS: For $i = 1$, $\gamma_1 = S$. Thus, $x_1 = \epsilon$, and $y_1 = w$. Since $(q, w, S) \overset{*}{\vdash} (q, w, S)$ by 0 moves, the basis is proved.

INDUCTION: Now we consider the case of the second and subsequent left-sentential forms. We assume

$$(q, w, S) \overset{*}{\vdash} (q, y_i, \alpha_i)$$

and prove $(q, w, S) \overset{*}{\vdash} (q, y_{i+1}, \alpha_{i+1})$. Since α_i is a tail, it begins with a variable A. Moreover, the step of the derivation $\gamma_i \Rightarrow \gamma_{i+1}$ involves replacing A by one of its production bodies, say β. Rule (1) of the construction of P lets us replace A at the top of the stack by β, and rule (2) then allows us to match any terminals on top of the stack with the next input symbols. As a result, we reach the ID $(q, y_{i+1}, \alpha_{i+1})$, which represents the next left-sentential form γ_{i+1}.

To complete the proof, we note that $\alpha_n = \epsilon$, since the tail of γ_n (which is w) is empty. Thus, $(q, w, S) \overset{*}{\vdash} (q, \epsilon, \epsilon)$, which proves that P accepts w by empty stack.

(Only-if) We need to prove something more general: that if P executes a sequence of moves that has the net effect of popping a variable A from the top of its stack, without ever going below A on the stack, then A derives, in G, whatever input string was consumed from the input during this process. Precisely:

- If $(q, x, A) \overset{*}{\underset{P}{\vdash}} (q, \epsilon, \epsilon)$, then $A \overset{*}{\underset{G}{\Rightarrow}} x$.

The proof is an induction on the number of moves taken by P.

BASIS: One move. The only possibility is that $A \to \epsilon$ is a production of G, and this production is used in a rule of type (1) by the PDA P. In this case, $x = \epsilon$, and we know that $A \Rightarrow \epsilon$.

INDUCTION: Suppose P takes n moves, where $n > 1$. The first move must be of type (1), where A is replaced by one of its production bodies on the top of the stack. The reason is that a rule of type (2) can only be used when there is a terminal on top of the stack. Suppose the production used is $A \to Y_1 Y_2 \cdots Y_k$, where each Y_i is either a terminal or variable.

The next $n - 1$ moves of P must consume x from the input and have the net effect of popping each of Y_1, Y_2, and so on from the stack, one at a time. We can break x into $x_1 x_2 \cdots x_k$, where x_1 is the portion of the input consumed until Y_1 is popped off the stack (i.e., the stack first is as short as $k - 1$ symbols). Then x_2 is the next portion of the input that is consumed while popping Y_2 off the stack, and so on.

Figure 6.9 suggests how the input x is broken up, and the corresponding effects on the stack. There, we suggest that β was BaC, so x is divided into three parts $x_1 x_2 x_3$, where $x_2 = a$. Note that in general, if Y_i is a terminal, then x_i must be that terminal.

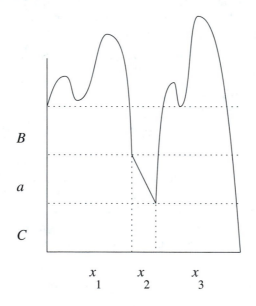

Figure 6.9: The PDA P consumes x and pops BaC from its stack

Formally, we can conclude that $(q, x_i x_{i+1} \cdots x_k, Y_i) \overset{*}{\vdash} (q, x_{i+1} \cdots x_k, \epsilon)$ for all $i = 1, 2, \ldots, k$. Moreover, none of these sequences can be more than $n - 1$ moves, so the inductive hypothesis applies if Y_i is a variable. That is, we may conclude $Y_i \overset{*}{\Rightarrow} x_i$.

If Y_i is a terminal, then there must be only one move involved, and it matches the one symbol of x_i against Y_i, which are the same. Again, we can conclude

$Y_i \overset{*}{\Rightarrow} x_i$; this time, zero steps are used. Now we have the derivation

$$A \Rightarrow Y_1 Y_2 \cdots Y_k \overset{*}{\Rightarrow} x_1 Y_2 \cdots Y_k \overset{*}{\Rightarrow} \cdots \overset{*}{\Rightarrow} x_1 x_2 \cdots x_k$$

That is, $A \overset{*}{\Rightarrow} x$.

To complete the proof, we let $A = S$ and $x = w$. Since we are given that w is in $N(P)$, we know that $(q, w, S) \overset{*}{\vdash} (q, \epsilon, \epsilon)$. By what we have just proved inductively, we have $S \overset{*}{\Rightarrow} w$; i.e., w is in $L(G)$. □

6.3.2 From PDA's to Grammars

Now, we complete the proofs of equivalence by showing that for every PDA P, we can find a CFG G whose language is the same language that P accepts by empty stack. The idea behind the proof is to recognize that the fundamental event in the history of a PDA's processing of a given input is the net popping of one symbol off the stack, while consuming some input. A PDA may change state as it pops stack symbols, so we should also note the state that it enters when it finally pops a level off its stack.

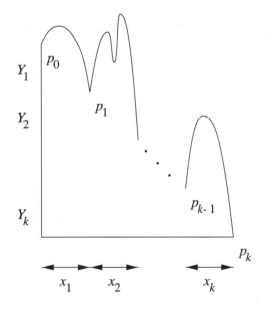

Figure 6.10: A PDA makes a sequence of moves that have the net effect of popping a symbol off the stack

Figure 6.10 suggests how we pop a sequence of symbols $Y_1, Y_2, \ldots Y_k$ off the stack. Some input x_1 is read while Y_1 is popped. We should emphasize that this "pop" is the net effect of (possibly) many moves. For example, the first move may change Y_1 to some other symbol Z. The next move may replace Z by UV, later moves have the effect of popping U, and then other moves pop V.

The net effect is that Y_1 has been replaced by nothing; i.e., it has been popped, and all the input symbols consumed so far constitute x_1.

We also show in Fig. 6.10 the net change of state. We suppose that the PDA starts out in state p_0, with Y_1 at the top of the stack. After all the moves whose net effect is to pop Y_1, the PDA is in state p_1. It then proceeds to (net) pop Y_2, while reading input string x_2 and winding up, perhaps after many moves, in state p_2 with Y_2 off the stack. The computation proceeds until each of the symbols on the stack is removed.

Our construction of an equivalent grammar uses variables each of which represents an "event" consisting of:

1. The net popping of some symbol X from the stack, and

2. A change in state from some p at the beginning to q when X has finally been replaced by ϵ on the stack.

We represent such a variable by the composite symbol $[pXq]$. Remember that this sequence of characters is our way of describing *one* variable; it is not five grammar symbols. The formal construction is given by the next theorem.

Theorem 6.14: Let $P = (Q, \Sigma, \Gamma, \delta, q_0, Z_0)$ be a PDA. Then there is a context-free grammar G such that $L(G) = N(P)$.

PROOF: We shall construct $G = (V, \Sigma, R, S)$, where the set of variables V consists of:

1. The special symbol S, which is the start symbol, and

2. All symbols of the form $[pXq]$, where p and q are states in Q, and X is a stack symbol, in Γ.

The productions of G are as follows:

a) For all states p, G has the production $S \rightarrow [q_0 Z_0 p]$. Recall our intuition that a symbol like $[q_0 Z_0 p]$ is intended to generate all those strings w that cause P to pop Z_0 from its stack while going from state q_0 to state p. That is, $(q_0, w, Z_0) \overset{*}{\vdash} (p, \epsilon, \epsilon)$. If so, then these productions say that start symbol S will generate all strings w that cause P to empty its stack, after starting in its initial ID.

b) Let $\delta(q, a, X)$ contain the pair $(r, Y_1 Y_2 \cdots Y_k)$, where:

    1. a is either a symbol in Σ or $a = \epsilon$.

    2. k can be any number, including 0, in which case the pair is (r, ϵ).

Then for all lists of states $r_1, r_2, \ldots, r_k$, G has the production

$$[qXr_k] \rightarrow a[rY_1 r_1][r_1 Y_2 r_2] \cdots [r_{k-1} Y_k r_k]$$

This production says that one way to pop X and go from state q to state r_k is to read a (which may be ϵ), then use some input to pop Y_1 off the stack while going from state r to state r_1, then read some more input that pops Y_2 off the stack and goes from state r_1 to r_2, and so on.

We shall now prove that the informal interpretation of the variables $[qXp]$ is correct:

- $[qXp] \overset{*}{\Rightarrow} w$ if and only if $(q, w, X) \overset{*}{\vdash} (p, \epsilon, \epsilon)$.

(If) Suppose $(q, w, X) \overset{*}{\vdash} (p, \epsilon, \epsilon)$. We shall show $[qXp] \overset{*}{\Rightarrow} w$ by induction on the number of moves made by the PDA.

BASIS: One step. Then (p, ϵ) must be in $\delta(q, w, X)$, and w is either a single symbol or ϵ. By the construction of G, $[qXp] \to w$ is a production, so $[qXp] \Rightarrow w$.

INDUCTION: Suppose the sequence $(q, w, X) \overset{*}{\vdash} (p, \epsilon, \epsilon)$ takes n steps, and $n > 1$. The first move must look like

$$(q, w, X) \vdash (r_0, x, Y_1 Y_2 \cdots Y_k) \overset{*}{\vdash} (p, \epsilon, \epsilon)$$

where $w = ax$ for some a that is either ϵ or a symbol in Σ. It follows that the pair $(r_0, Y_1 Y_2 \cdots Y_k)$ must be in $\delta(q, a, X)$. Further, by the construction of G, there is a production $[qXr_k] \to a[r_0 Y_1 r_1][r_1 Y_2 r_2] \cdots [r_{k-1} Y_k r_k]$, where:

1. $r_k = p$, and

2. $r_1, r_2, \ldots, r_{k-1}$ are any states in Q.

In particular, we may observe, as was suggested in Fig. 6.10, that each of the symbols $Y_1, Y_2, \ldots, Y_k$ gets popped off the stack in turn, and we may choose p_i to be the state of the PDA when Y_i is popped, for $i = 1, 2, \ldots, k-1$. Let $x = w_1 w_2 \cdots w_k$, where w_i is the input consumed while Y_i is popped off the stack. Then we know that $(r_{i-1}, w_i, Y_i) \overset{*}{\vdash} (r_i, \epsilon, \epsilon)$.

As none of these sequences of moves can take as many as n moves, the inductive hypothesis applies to them. We conclude that $[r_{i-1} Y_i r_i] \overset{*}{\Rightarrow} w_i$. We may put these derivations together with the first production used to conclude:

$$
\begin{aligned}
[qXr_k] &\Rightarrow a[r_0 Y_1 r_1][r_1 Y_1 r_2] \cdots [r_{k-1} Y_k r_k] \overset{*}{\Rightarrow} \\
&aw_1 [r_1 Y_2 r_2][r_2 Y_3 r_3] \cdots [r_{k-1} Y_k r_k] \overset{*}{\Rightarrow} \\
&aw_1 w_2 [r_2 Y_3 r_3] \cdots [r_{k-1} Y_k r_k] \overset{*}{\Rightarrow} \\
&\cdots \\
&aw_1 w_2 \cdots w_k = w
\end{aligned}
$$

where $r_k = p$.

(Only-if) The proof is an induction on the number of steps in the derivation.

BASIS: One step. Then $[qXp] \to w$ must be a production. The only way for this production to exist is if there is a transition of P in which X is popped and state q becomes state p. That is, (p, ϵ) must be in $\delta(q, a, X)$, and $a = w$. But then $(q, w, X) \vdash (p, \epsilon, \epsilon)$.

INDUCTION: Suppose $[qXp] \overset{*}{\Rightarrow} w$ by n steps, where $n > 1$. Consider the first sentential form explicitly, which must look like

$$[qXr_k] \Rightarrow a[r_0 Y_1 r_1][r_1 Y_2 r_2] \cdots [r_{k-1} Y_k r_k] \overset{*}{\Rightarrow} w$$

where $r_k = p$. This production must come from the fact that $(r_0, Y_1 Y_2 \cdots Y_k)$ is in $\delta(q, a, X)$.

We can break w into $w = a w_1 w_2 \cdots w_k$ such that $[r_{i-1} Y_i r_i] \overset{*}{\Rightarrow} w_i$ for all $i = 1, 2, \ldots, r_k$. By the inductive hypothesis, we know that for all i,

$$(r_{i-1}, w_i, Y_i) \overset{*}{\vdash} (r_i, \epsilon, \epsilon)$$

If we use Theorem 6.5 to put the correct strings beyond w_i on the input and below Y_i on the stack, we also know that

$$(r_{i-1}, w_i w_{i+1} \cdots w_k, Y_i Y_{i+1} \cdots Y_k) \overset{*}{\vdash} (r_i, w_{i+1} \cdots w_k, Y_{i+1} \cdots Y_k)$$

If we put all these sequences together, we see that

$$(q, a w_1 w_2 \cdots w_k, X) \vdash (r_0, w_1 w_2 \cdots w_k, Y_1 Y_2 \cdots Y_k) \overset{*}{\vdash}$$
$$(r_1, w_2 w_3 \cdots w_k, Y_2 Y_3 \cdots Y_k) \overset{*}{\vdash} (r_2, w_3 \cdots w_k, Y_3 \cdots Y_k) \overset{*}{\vdash} \cdots \overset{*}{\vdash} (r_k, \epsilon, \epsilon)$$

Since $r_k = p$, we have shown that $(q, w, X) \overset{*}{\vdash} (p, \epsilon, \epsilon)$.

We complete the proof as follows. $S \overset{*}{\Rightarrow} w$ if and only if $[q_0 Z_0 p] \overset{*}{\Rightarrow} w$ for some p, because of the way the rules for start symbol S are constructed. We just proved that $[q_0 Z_0 p] \overset{*}{\Rightarrow} w$ if and only if $(q, w, Z_0) \overset{*}{\vdash} (p, \epsilon, \epsilon)$, i.e., if and only if P accepts x by empty stack. Thus, $L(G) = N(P)$. □

Example 6.15 : Let us convert the PDA $P_N = (\{q\}, \{i, e\}, \{Z\}, \delta_N, q, Z)$ from Example 6.10 to a grammar. Recall that P_N accepts all strings that violate, for the first time, the rule that every e (else) must correspond to some preceding i (if). Since P_N has only one state and one stack symbol, the construction is particularly simple. There are only two variables in the grammar G:

a) S, the start symbol, which is in every grammar constructed by the method of Theorem 6.14, and

b) $[qZq]$, the only triple that can be assembled from the states and stack symbols of P_N.

The productions of grammar G are as follows:

1. The only production for S is $S \rightarrow [qZq]$. However, if there were n states of the PDA, then there would be n productions of this type, since the last state could be any of the n states. The first state would have to be the start state, and the stack symbol would have to be the start symbol, as in our production above.

2. From the fact that $\delta_N(q, i, Z)$ contains (q, ZZ), we get the production $[qZq] \rightarrow i[qZq][qZq]$. Again, for this simple example, there is only one production. However, if there were n states, then this one rule would produce n^2 productions, since the middle two states of the body could be any one state p, and the last states of the head and body could also be any one state. That is, if p and r were any two states of the PDA, then production $[qZp] \rightarrow i[qZr][rZp]$ would be produced.

3. From the fact that $\delta_N(q, e, Z)$ contains (q, ϵ), we have production

$$[qZq] \rightarrow e$$

   Notice that in this case, the list of stack symbols by which Z is replaced is empty, so the only symbol in the body is the input symbol that caused the move.

We may, for convenience, replace the triple $[qZq]$ by some less complex symbol, say A. If we do, then the complete grammar consists of the productions:

$$S \rightarrow A$$
$$A \rightarrow iAA \mid e$$

In fact, if we notice that A and S derive exactly the same strings, we may identify them as one, and write the complete grammar as

$$G = (\{S\}, \{i, e\}, \{S \rightarrow iSS \mid e\}, S)$$

$\square$

6.3.3 Exercises for Section 6.3

* **Exercise 6.3.1:** Convert the grammar

$$
\begin{aligned}
S &\rightarrow & 0S1 \mid A \\
A &\rightarrow & 1A0 \mid S \mid \epsilon
\end{aligned}
$$

to a PDA that accepts the same language by empty stack.

Exercise 6.3.2: Convert the grammar

$$
\begin{aligned}
S &\rightarrow & aAA \\
A &\rightarrow & aS \mid bS \mid a
\end{aligned}
$$

to a PDA that accepts the same language by empty stack.

* **Exercise 6.3.3:** Convert the PDA $P = (\{p, q\}, \{0, 1\}, \{X, Z_0\}, \delta, q, Z_0)$ to a CFG, if δ is given by:

   1. $\delta(q, 1, Z_0) = \{(q, X Z_0)\}$.

   2. $\delta(q, 1, X) = \{(q, XX)\}$.

   3. $\delta(q, 0, X) = \{(p, X)\}$.

   4. $\delta(q, \epsilon, X) = \{(q, \epsilon)\}$.

   5. $\delta(p, 1, X) = \{(p, \epsilon)\}$.

   6. $\delta(p, 0, Z_0) = \{(q, Z_0)\}$.

Exercise 6.3.4: Convert the PDA of Exercise 6.1.1 to a context-free grammar.

Exercise 6.3.5: Below are some context-free languages. For each, devise a PDA that accepts the language by empty stack. You may, if you wish, first construct a grammar for the language, and then convert to a PDA.

   a) $\{a^n b^m c^{2(n+m)} \mid n \geq 0,\ m \geq 0\}$.

   b) $\{a^i b^j c^k \mid i = 2j \text{ or } j = 2k\}$.

   ! c) $\{0^n 1^m \mid n \leq m \leq 2n\}$.

*! **Exercise 6.3.6:** Show that if P is a PDA, then there is a one-state PDA P_1 such that $N(P_1) = N(P)$.

! **Exercise 6.3.7:** Suppose we have a PDA with s states, t stack symbols, and no rule in which a replacement stack string has length greater than u. Give a tight upper bound on the number of variables in the CFG that we construct for this PDA by the method of Section 6.3.2.

6.4   Deterministic Pushdown Automata

While PDA's are by definition allowed to be nondeterministic, the deterministic subcase is quite important. In particular, parsers generally behave like deterministic PDA's, so the class of languages that can be accepted by these automata is interesting for the insights it gives us into what constructs are suitable for use in programming languages. In this section, we shall define deterministic PDA's and investigate some of the things they can and cannot do.

6.4.1 Definition of a Deterministic PDA

Intuitively, a PDA is deterministic if there is never a choice of move in any situation. These choices are of two kinds. If $\delta(q, a, X)$ contains more than one pair, then surely the PDA is nondeterministic because we can choose among these pairs when deciding on the next move. However, even if $\delta(q, a, X)$ is always a singleton, we could still have a choice between using a real input symbol, or making a move on ϵ. Thus, we define a PDA $P = (Q, \Sigma, \Gamma, \delta, q_0, Z_0, F)$ to be *deterministic* (a deterministic PDA or DPDA), if and only if the following conditions are met:

1. $\delta(q, a, X)$ has at most one member for any q in Q, a in Σ or $a = \epsilon$, and X in Γ.

2. If $\delta(q, a, X)$ is nonempty, for some a in Σ, then $\delta(q, \epsilon, X)$ must be empty.

Example 6.16: It turns out that the language L_{wwr} of Example 6.2 is a CFL that has no DPDA. However, by putting a "center-marker" c in the middle, we can make the language recognizable by a DPDA. That is, we can recognize the language $L_{wcwr} = \{wcw^R \mid w$ is in $(\mathbf{0} + \mathbf{1})^*\}$ by a deterministic PDA.

The strategy of the DPDA is to store 0's and 1's on its stack, until it sees the center marker c. it then goes to another state, in which it matches input symbols against stack symbols and pops the stack if they match. If it ever finds a nonmatch, it dies; its input cannot be of the form wcw^R. If it succeeds in popping its stack down to the initial symbol, which marks the bottom of the stack, then it accepts its input.

The idea is very much like the PDA that we saw in Fig. 6.2. However, that PDA is nondeterministic, because in state q_0 it always has the choice of pushing the next input symbol onto the stack or making a transition on ϵ to state q_1; i.e., it has to guess when it has reached the middle. The DPDA for L_{wcwr} is shown as a transition diagram in Fig. 6.11.

This PDA is clearly deterministic. It never has a choice of move in the same state, using the same input and stack symbol. As for choices between using a real input symbol or ϵ, the only ϵ-transition it makes is from q_1 to q_2 with Z_0 at the top of the stack. However, in state q_1, there are no other moves when Z_0 is at the stack top. □

6.4.2 Regular Languages and Deterministic PDA's

The DPDA's accept a class of languages that is between the regular languages and the CFL's. We shall first prove that the DPDA languages include all the regular languages.

Theorem 6.17: If L is a regular language, then $L = L(P)$ for some DPDA P.

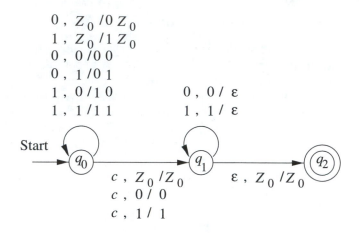

Figure 6.11: A deterministic PDA accepting L_{wcwr}

PROOF: Essentially, a DPDA can simulate a deterministic finite automaton. The PDA keeps some stack symbol Z_0 on its stack, because a PDA has to have a stack, but really the PDA ignores its stack and just uses its state. Formally, let $A = (Q, \Sigma, \delta_A, q_0, F)$ be a DFA. Construct DPDA

$$P = (Q, \Sigma, \{Z_0\}, \delta_P, q_0, Z_0, F)$$

by defining $\delta_P(q, a, Z_0) = \{(p, Z_0)\}$ for all states p and q in Q, such that $\delta_A(q, a) = p$.

We claim that $(q_0, w, Z_0) \overset{*}{\underset{P}{\vdash}} (p, \epsilon, Z_0)$ if and only if $\hat{\delta}_A(q_0, w) = p$. That is, P simulates A using its state. The proofs in both directions are easy inductions on $|w|$, and we leave them for the reader to complete. Since both A and P accept by entering one of the states of F, we conclude that their languages are the same. $\square$

If we want the DPDA to accept by empty stack, then we find that our language-recognizing capability is rather limited. Say that a language L has the *prefix property* if there are no two different strings x and y in L such that x is a prefix of y.

Example 6.18 : The language L_{wcwr} of Example 6.16 has the prefix property. That is, it is not possible for there to be two strings wcw^R and xcx^R, one of which is a prefix of the other, unless they are the same string. To see why, suppose wcw^R is a prefix of xcx^R, and $w \neq x$. Then w must be shorter than x. Therefore, the c in wcw^R comes in a position where xcx^R has a 0 or 1; it is a position in the first x. That point contradicts the assumption that wcw^R is a prefix of xcx^R.

On the other hand, there are some very simple languages that do not have the prefix property. Consider $\{0\}^*$, i.e., the set of all strings of 0's. Clearly, there are pairs of strings in this language one of which is a prefix of the other, so this language does not have the prefix property. In fact, of *any* two strings, one is a prefix of the other, although that condition is stronger than we need to establish that the prefix property does not hold. □

Note that the language $\{0\}^*$ is a regular language. Thus, it is not even true that every regular language is $N(P)$ for some DPDA P. We leave as an exercise the following relationship:

Theorem 6.19: A language L is $N(P)$ for some DPDA P if and only if L has the prefix property and L is $L(P')$ for some DPDA P'. □

6.4.3 DPDA's and Context-Free Languages

We have already seen that a DPDA can accept languages like L_{wcwr} that are not regular. To see this language is not regular, suppose it were, and use the pumping lemma. If n is the constant of the pumping lemma, then consider the string $w = 0^n c 0^n$, which is in L_{wcwr}. However, when we "pump" this string, it is the first group of 0's whose length must change, so we get in L_{wcwr} strings that have the "center" marker not in the center. Since these strings are not in L_{wcwr}, we have a contradiction and conclude that L_{wcwr} is not regular.

On the other hand, there are CFL's like L_{wwr} that cannot be $L(P)$ for any DPDA P. A formal proof is complex, but the intuition is transparent. If P is a DPDA accepting L_{wwr}, then given a sequence of 0's, it must store them on the stack, or do something equivalent to count an arbitrary number of 0's. For instance, it could store one X for every two 0's it sees, and use the state to remember whether the number was even or odd.

Suppose P has seen n 0's and then sees 110^n. It must verify that there were n 0's after the 11, and to do so it must pop its stack.[5] Now, P has seen $0^n 110^n$. If it sees an identical string next, it must accept, because the complete input is of the form ww^R, with $w = 0^n 110^n$. However, if it sees $0^m 110^m$ for some $m \neq n$, P must *not* accept. Since its stack is empty, it cannot remember what arbitrary integer n was, and must fail to recognize L_{wwr} correctly. Our conclusion is that:

- The languages accepted by DPDA's by final state properly include the regular languages, but are properly included in the CFL's.

6.4.4 DPDA's and Ambiguous Grammars

We can refine the power of the DPDA's by noting that the languages they accept all have unambiguous grammars. Unfortunately, the DPDA languages are not

---

[5]This statement is the intuitive part that requires a (hard) formal proof; could there be some other way for P to compare equal blocks of 0's?

exactly equal to the subset of the CFL's that are not inherently ambiguous. For instance, L_{wwr} has an unambiguous grammar

$$S \rightarrow 0S0 \mid 1S1 \mid \epsilon$$

even though it is not a DPDA language. The following theorems refine the bullet point above.

Theorem 6.20 : If $L = N(P)$ for some DPDA P, then L has an unambiguous context-free grammar.

PROOF: We claim that the construction of Theorem 6.14 yields an unambiguous CFG G when the PDA to which it is applied is deterministic. First recall from Theorem 5.29 that it is sufficient to show that the grammar has unique leftmost derivations in order to prove that G is unambiguous.

Suppose P accepts string w by empty stack. Then it does so by a unique sequence of moves, because it is deterministic, and cannot move once its stack is empty. Knowing this sequence of moves, we can determine the one choice of production in a leftmost derivation whereby G derives w. There can never by a choice of which rule of P motivated the production to use. However, a rule of P, say $\delta(q, a, X) = \{(r, Y_1 Y_2 \cdots Y_k)\}$ might cause many productions of G, with different states in the positions that reflect the states of P after popping each of $Y_1, Y_2, \ldots, Y_{k-1}$. Because P is deterministic, only one of these sequences of choices will be consistent with what P actually does, and therefore, only one of these productions will actually lead to derivation of w.   □

However, we can prove more: even those languages that DPDA's accept by final state have unambiguous grammars. Since we only know how to construct grammars directly from PDA's that accept by empty stack, we need to change the language involved to have the prefix property, and then modify the resulting grammar to generate the original language. We do so by use of an "endmarker" symbol.

Theorem 6.21 : If $L = L(P)$ for some DPDA P, then L has an unambiguous CFG.

PROOF: let \$ be an "endmarker" symbol that does not appear in the strings of L, and let $L' = L\$$. That is, the strings of L' are the strings of L, each followed by the symbol \$. Then L' surely has the prefix property, and by Theorem 6.19, $L' = M(P')$ for some DPDA P'.[6] By Theorem 6.20, there is an unambiguous grammar G' generating the language $N(P')$, which is L'.

Now, construct from G' a grammar G such that $L(G) = L$. To do so, we have only to get rid of the endmarker \$ from strings. Thus, treat \$ as a variable

---

[6]The proof of Theorem 6.19 appears in Exercise 6.4.3, but we can easily see how to construct P' from P. Add a new state q that P' enters whenever P is in an accepting state and the next input is \$. In state q, P' pops all symbols off its stack. Also, P' needs its own bottom-of-stack marker to avoid accidentally emptying its stack as it simulates P.

of G, and introduce production $\$ \to \epsilon$; otherwise, the productions of G' and G are the same. Since $L(G') = L'$, it follows that $L(G) = L$.

We claim that G is unambiguous. In proof, the leftmost derivations in G are exactly the same as the leftmost derivations in G', except that the derivations in G have a final step in which $\$$ is replaced by ϵ. Thus, if a terminal w string had two leftmost derivations in G, then $w\$$ would have two leftmost derivations in G'. Since we know G' is unambiguous, so is G. $\square$

6.4.5 Exercises for Section 6.4

Exercise 6.4.1: For each of the following PDA's, tell whether or not it is deterministic. Either show that it meets the definition of a DPDA or find a rule or rules that violate it.

a) The PDA of Example 6.2.

* b) The PDA of Exercise 6.1.1.

c) The PDA of Exercise 6.3.3.

Exercise 6.4.2: Give deterministic pushdown automata to accept the following languages:

a) $\{0^n 1^m \mid n \le m\}$.

b) $\{0^n 1^m \mid n \ge m\}$.

c) $\{0^n 1^m 0^n \mid n \text{ and } m \text{ are arbitrary}\}$.

Exercise 6.4.3: We can prove Theorem 6.19 in three parts:

* a) Show that if $L = N(P)$ for some DPDA P, then L has the prefix property.

! b) Show that if $L = N(P)$ for some DPDA P, then there exists a DPDA P' such that $L = L(P')$.

*! c) Show that if L has the prefix property and is $L(P')$ for some DPDA P', then there exists a DPDA P such that $L = N(P)$.

!! **Exercise 6.4.4:** Show that the language

$$L = \{0^n 1^n \mid n \ge 1\} \cup \{0^n 1^{2n} \mid n \ge 1\}$$

is a context-free language that is not accepted by any DPDA. *Hint*: Show that there must be two strings of the form $0^n 1^n$ for different values of n, say n_1 and n_2 that cause a hypothetical DPDA for L to enter the same ID after reading both strings. Intuitively, the DPDA must erase from its stack almost everything it placed there on reading the 0's, in order to check that it has seen the same number of 1's. Thus, the DPDA cannot tell whether or not to accept next after seeing n_1 1's or after seeing n_2 1's.

6.5   Summary of Chapter 6

✦ *Pushdown Automata*: A PDA is a nondeterministic finite automaton coupled with a stack that can be used to store a string of arbitrary length. The stack can be read and modified only at its top.

✦ *Moves of a Pushdown Automata*: A PDA chooses its next move based on its current state, the next input symbol, and the symbol at the top of its stack. It may also choose to make a move independent of the input symbol and without consuming that symbol from the input. Being nondeterministic, the PDA may have some finite number of choices of move; each is a new state and a string of stack symbols with which to replace the symbol currently on top of the stack.

✦ *Acceptance by Pushdown Automata*: There are two ways in which we may allow the PDA to signal acceptance. One is by entering an accepting state; the other by emptying its stack. These methods are equivalent, in the sense that any language accepted by one method is accepted (by some other PDA) by the other method.

✦ *Instantaneous Descriptions*: We use an ID consisting of the state, remaining input, and stack contents to describe the "current condition" of a PDA. A transition function ⊢ between ID's represents single moves of a PDA.

✦ *Pushdown Automata and Grammars*: The languages accepted by PDA's either by final state or by empty stack, are exactly the context-free languages.

✦ *Deterministic Pushdown Automata*: A PDA is deterministic if it never has a choice of move for a given state, input symbol (including ϵ), and stack symbol. Also, it never has a choice between making a move using a true input and a move using ϵ input.

✦ *Acceptance by Deterministic Pushdown Automata*: The two modes of acceptance — final state and empty stack — are not the same for DPDA's. Rather, the languages accepted by empty stack are exactly those of the languages accepted by final state that have the prefix property: no string in the language is a prefix of another word in the language.

✦ *The Languages Accepted by DPDA's*: All the regular languages are accepted (by final state) by DPDA's, and there are nonregular languages accepted by DPDA's. The DPDA languages are context-free languages, and in fact are languages that have unambiguous CFG's. Thus, the DPDA languages lie strictly between the regular languages and the context-free languages.

6.6 References for Chapter 6

The idea of the pushdown automaton is attributed independently to Oettinger [4] and Schutzenberger [5]. The equivalence between pushdown automata and context-free languages was also the result of independent discoveries; it appears in a 1961 MIT technical report by N. Chomsky but was first published by Evey [1].

The deterministic PDA was first introduced by Fischer [2] and Schutzenberger [5]. It gained significance later as a model for parsers. Notably, [3] introduces the "LR(k) grammars," a subclass of CFG's that generate exactly the DPDA languages. The LR(k) grammars, in turn, form the basis for YACC, the parser-generating tool discussed in Section 5.3.2.

1. J. Evey, "Application of pushdown store machines," *Proc. Fall Joint Computer Conference* (1963), AFIPS Press, Montvale, NJ, pp. 215–227.

2. P. C. Fischer, "On computability by certain classes of restricted Turing machines," *Proc. Fourth Annl. Symposium on Switching Circuit Theory and Logical Design* (1963), pp. 23–32.

3. D. E. Knuth, "On the translation of languages from left to right," *Information and Control* **8**:6 (1965), pp. 607–639.

4. A. G. Oettinger, "Automatic syntactic analysis and the pushdown store," *Proc. Symposia on Applied Math.* **12** (1961), American Mathematical Society, Providence, RI.

5. M. P. Schutzenberger, "On context-free languages and pushdown automata," *Information and Control* **6**:3 (1963), pp. 246–264.

Chapter 7

Properties of Context-Free Languages

We shall complete our study of context-free languages by learning some of their properties. Our first task is to simplify context-free grammars; these simplifications make it easier to prove facts about CFL's, since we can claim that if a language is a CFL, then it has a grammar in some special form.

We then prove a "pumping lemma" for CFL's. This theorem is in the same spirit as Theorem 4.1 for regular languages, but can be used to prove a language not to be context-free. Next, we consider the sorts of properties that we studied in Chapter 4 for the regular languages: closure properties and decision properties. We shall see that some, but not all, of the closure properties that the regular languages have are also possessed by the CFL's. Likewise, some questions about CFL's can be decided by algorithms that generalize the tests we developed for regular languages, but there are also certain questions about CFL's that we cannot answer.

7.1 Normal Forms for Context-Free Grammars

The goal of this section is to show that every CFL (without ϵ) is generated by a CFG in which all productions are of the form $A \rightarrow BC$ or $A \rightarrow a$, where A, B, and C are variables, and a is a terminal. This form is called *Chomsky Normal Form*. To get there, we need to make a number of preliminary simplifications, which are themselves useful in various ways:

1. We must eliminate *useless symbols*, those variables or terminals that do not appear in any derivation of a terminal string from the start symbol.

2. We must eliminate ϵ-*productions*, those of the form $A \rightarrow \epsilon$ for some variable A.

3. We must eliminate *unit productions*, those of the form $A \to B$ for variables A and B.

7.1.1 Eliminating Useless Symbols

We say a symbol X is *useful* for a grammar $G = (V, T, P, S)$ if there is some derivation of the form $S \stackrel{*}{\Rightarrow} \alpha X \beta \stackrel{*}{\Rightarrow} w$, where w is in T^*. Note that X may be in either V or T, and the sentential form $\alpha X \beta$ might be the first or last in the derivation. If X is not useful, we say it is *useless*. Evidently, omitting useless symbols from a grammar will not change the language generated, so we may as well detect and eliminate all useless symbols.

Our approach to eliminating useless symbols begins by identifying the two things a symbol has to be able to do to be useful:

1. We say X is *generating* if $X \stackrel{*}{\Rightarrow} w$ for some terminal string w. Note that every terminal is generating, since w can be that terminal itself, which is derived by zero steps.

2. We say X is *reachable* if there is a derivation $S \stackrel{*}{\Rightarrow} \alpha X \beta$ for some α and β.

Surely a symbol that is useful will be both generating and reachable. If we eliminate the symbols that are not generating first, and then eliminate from the remaining grammar those symbols that are not reachable, we shall, as will be proved, have only the useful symbols left.

Example 7.1: Consider the grammar:

$$S \to AB \mid a$$
$$A \to b$$

All symbols but B are generating; a and b generate themselves; S generates a, and A generates b. If we eliminate B, we must eliminate the production $S \to AB$, leaving the grammar:

$$S \to a$$
$$A \to b$$

Now, we find that only S and a are reachable from S. Eliminating A and b leaves only the production $S \to a$. That production by itself is a grammar whose language is $\{a\}$, just as is the language of the original grammar.

Note that if we start by checking for reachability first, we find that all symbols of the grammar

$$S \to AB \mid a$$
$$A \to b$$

are reachable. If we then eliminate the symbol B because it is not generating, we are left with a grammar that still has useless symbols, in particular, A and b. □

Theorem 7.2: Let $G = (V, T, P, S)$ be a CFG, and assume that $L(G) \neq \emptyset$; i.e., G generates at least one string. Let $G_1 = (V_1, T_1, P_1, S)$ be the grammar we obtain by the following steps:

1. First eliminate nongenerating symbols and all productions involving one or more of those symbols. Let $G_2 = (V_2, T_2, P_2, S)$ be this new grammar. Note that S must be generating, since we assume $L(G)$ has at least one string, so S has not been eliminated.

2. Second, eliminate all symbols that are not reachable in the grammar G_2.

Then G_1 has no useless symbols, and $L(G_1) = L(G)$.

PROOF: Suppose X is a symbol that remains; i.e., X is in $V_1 \cup T_1$. We know that $X \overset{*}{\underset{G}{\Rightarrow}} w$ for some w in T^*. Moreover, every symbol used in the derivation of w from X is also generating. Thus, $X \overset{*}{\underset{G_2}{\Rightarrow}} w$.

Since X was not eliminated in the second step, we also know that there are α and β such that $S \overset{*}{\underset{G_2}{\Rightarrow}} \alpha X \beta$. Further, every symbol used in this derivation is reachable, so $S \overset{*}{\underset{G_1}{\Rightarrow}} \alpha X \beta$.

We know that every symbol in $\alpha X \beta$ is reachable, and we also know that all these symbols are in $V_2 \cup T_2$, so each of them is generating in G_2. The derivation of some terminal string, say $\alpha X \beta \overset{*}{\underset{G_2}{\Rightarrow}} xwy$, involves only symbols that are reachable from S, because they are reached by symbols in $\alpha X \beta$. Thus, this derivation is also a derivation of G_1; that is,

$$S \overset{*}{\underset{G_1}{\Rightarrow}} \alpha X \beta \overset{*}{\underset{G_1}{\Rightarrow}} xwy$$

We conclude that X is useful in G_1. Since X is an arbitrary symbol of G_1, we conclude that G_1 has no useless symbols.

The last detail is that we must show $L(G_1) = L(G)$. As usual, to show two sets the same, we show each is contained in the other.

$L(G_1) \subseteq L(G)$: Since we have only eliminated symbols and productions from G to get G_1, it follows that $L(G_1) \subseteq L(G)$.

$L(G) \subseteq L(G_1)$: We must prove that if w is in $L(G)$, then w is in $L(G_1)$. If w is in $L(G)$, then $S \overset{*}{\underset{G}{\Rightarrow}} w$. Each symbol in this derivation is evidently both reachable and generating, so it is also a derivation of G_1. That is, $S \overset{*}{\underset{G_1}{\Rightarrow}} w$, and thus w is in $L(G_1)$. □

7.1.2   Computing the Generating and Reachable Symbols

Two points remain. How do we compute the set of generating symbols of a grammar, and how do we compute the set of reachable symbols of a grammar? For both problems, the algorithm we use tries its best to discover symbols of these types. We shall show that if the proper inductive constructions of these sets fails to discover a symbol to be generating or reachable, respectively, then the symbol is not of these types.

Let $G = (V, T, P, S)$ be a grammar. To compute the generating symbols of G, we perform the following induction.

BASIS: Every symbol of T is obviously generating; it generates itself.

INDUCTION: Suppose there is a production $A \rightarrow \alpha$, and every symbol of α is already known to be generating. Then A is generating. Note that this rule includes the case where $\alpha = \epsilon$; all variables that have ϵ as a production body are surely generating.

Example 7.3: Consider the grammar of Example 7.1. By the basis, a and b are generating. For the induction, we can use the production $A \rightarrow b$ to conclude that A is generating, and we can use the production $S \rightarrow a$ to conclude that S is generating. At that point, the induction is finished. We cannot use the production $S \rightarrow AB$, because B has not been established to be generating. Thus, the set of generating symbols is $\{a, b, A, S\}$. $\square$

Theorem 7.4: The algorithm above finds all and only the generating symbols of G.

PROOF: For one direction, it is an easy induction on the order in which symbols are added to the set of generating symbols that each symbol added really is generating. We leave to the reader this part of the proof.

For the other direction, suppose X is a generating symbol, say $X \overset{*}{\underset{G}{\Rightarrow}} w$. We prove by induction on the length of this derivation that X is found to be generating.

BASIS: Zero steps. Then X is a terminal, and X is found in the basis.

INDUCTION: If the derivation takes n steps for $n > 0$, then X is a variable. Let the derivation be $X \Rightarrow \alpha \overset{*}{\Rightarrow} w$; that is, the first production used is $X \rightarrow \alpha$. Each symbol of α derives some terminal string that is a part of w, and that derivation must take fewer than n steps. By the inductive hypothesis, each symbol of α is found to be generating. The inductive part of the algorithm allows us to use production $X \rightarrow \alpha$ to infer that X is generating. $\square$

Now, let us consider the inductive algorithm whereby we find the set of reachable symbols for the grammar $G = (V, T, P, S)$. Again, we can show that by trying our best to discover reachable symbols, any symbol we do not add to the reachable set is really not reachable.

BASIS: S is surely reachable.

INDUCTION: Suppose we have discovered that some variable A is reachable. Then for all productions with A in the head, all the symbols of the bodies of those productions are also reachable.

Example 7.5: Again start with the grammar of Example 7.1. By the basis, S is reachable. Since S has production bodies AB and a, we conclude that A, B, and a are reachable. B has no productions, but A has $A \rightarrow b$. We therefore conclude that b is reachable. Now, no more symbols can be added to the reachable set, which is $\{S, A, B, a, b\}$.   □

Theorem 7.6: The algorithm above finds all and only the reachable symbols of G.

PROOF: This proof is another pair of simple inductions akin to Theorem 7.4. We leave these arguments as an exercise.   □

7.1.3 Eliminating ϵ-Productions

Now, we shall show that ϵ-productions, while a convenience in many grammar-design problems, are not essential. Of course without a production that has an ϵ body, it is impossible to generate the empty string as a member of the language. Thus, what we actually prove is that if language L has a CFG, then $L - \{\epsilon\}$ has a CFG without ϵ-productions. If ϵ is not in L, then L itself is $L - \{\epsilon\}$, so L has a CFG with out ϵ-productions.

Our strategy is to begin by discovering which variables are "nullable." A variable A is *nullable* if $A \overset{*}{\Rightarrow} \epsilon$. If A is nullable, then whenever A appears in a production body, say $B \rightarrow CAD$, A might (or might not) derive ϵ. We make two versions of the production, one without A in the body ($B \rightarrow CD$), which corresponds to the case where A would have been used to derive ϵ, and the other with A still present ($B \rightarrow CAD$). However, if we use the version with A present, then we cannot allow A to derive ϵ. That proves not to be a problem, since we shall simply eliminate all productions with ϵ bodies, thus preventing any variable from deriving ϵ.

Let $G = (V, T, P, S)$ be a CFG. We can find all the nullable symbols of G by the following iterative algorithm. We shall then show that there are no nullable symbols except what the algorithm finds.

BASIS: If $A \rightarrow \epsilon$ is a production of G, then A is nullable.

INDUCTION: If there is a production $B \rightarrow C_1 C_2 \cdots C_k$, where each C_i is nullable, then B is nullable. Note that each C_i must be a variable to be nullable, so we only have to consider productions with all-variable bodies.

Theorem 7.7: In any grammar G, the only nullable symbols are the variables found by the algorithm above.

PROOF: For the "if" direction of the implied "A is nullable if and only if the algorithm identifies A as nullable," we simply observe that, by an easy induction on the order in which nullable symbols are discovered, that the each such symbol truly derives ϵ. For the "only-if" part, we can perform an induction on the length of the shortest derivation $A \overset{*}{\Rightarrow} \epsilon$.

BASIS: One step. Then $A \to \epsilon$ must be a production, and A is discovered in the basis part of the algorithm.

INDUCTION: Suppose $A \overset{*}{\Rightarrow} \epsilon$ by n steps, where $n > 1$. The first step must look like $A \Rightarrow C_1 C_2 \cdots C_k \overset{*}{\Rightarrow} \epsilon$, where each C_i derives ϵ by a sequence of fewer than n steps. By the inductive hypothesis, each C_i is discovered by the algorithm to be nullable. Thus, by the inductive step, A, thanks to the production $A \to C_1 C_2 \cdots C_k$, is found to be nullable. □

Now we give the construction of a grammar without ϵ-productions. Let $G = (V, T, P, S)$ be a CFG. Determine all the nullable symbols of G. We construct a new grammar $G_1 = (V, T, P_1, S)$, whose set of productions P_1 is determined as follows.

For each production $A \to X_1 X_2 \cdots X_k$ of P, where $k \geq 1$, suppose that m of the k X_i's are nullable symbols. The new grammar G_1 will have 2^m versions of this production, where the nullable X_i's, in all possible combinations are present or absent. There is one exception: if $m = k$, i.e., all symbols are nullable, then we do not include the case where all X_i's are absent. Also, note that if a production of the form $A \to \epsilon$ is in P, we do not place this production in P_1.

Example 7.8 : Consider the grammar

$$S \to AB$$
$$A \to aAA \mid \epsilon$$
$$B \to bBB \mid \epsilon$$

First, let us find the nullable symbols. A and B are directly nullable because they have productions with ϵ as the body. Then, we find that S is nullable, because the production $S \to AB$ has a body consisting of nullable symbols only. Thus, all three variables are nullable.

Now, let us construct the productions of grammar G_1. First consider $S \to AB$. All symbols of the body are nullable, so there are four ways we could choose present or absent for A and B, independently. However, we are not allowed to choose to make all symbols absent, so there are only three productions:

$$S \to AB \mid A \mid B$$

Next, consider production $A \to aAA$. The second and third positions hold nullable symbols, so again there are four choices of present/absent. In this case, all four choices are allowable, since the nonnullable symbol a will be present in any case. Our four choices yield productions:

$$A \to aAA \mid aA \mid aA \mid a$$

Note that the two middle choices happen to yield the same production, since it doesn't matter which of the A's we eliminate if we decide to eliminate one of them. Thus, the final grammar G_1 will only have three productions for A.

Similarly, the production B yields for G_1:

$$B \to bBB \mid bB \mid b$$

The two ϵ-productions of G yield nothing for G_1. Thus, the following productions:

$$S \to AB \mid A \mid B$$
$$A \to aAA \mid aA \mid a$$
$$B \to bBB \mid bB \mid b$$

constitute G_1. $\square$

We conclude our study of the elimination of ϵ-productions by proving that the construction given above does not change the language, except that ϵ is no longer present if it was in the language of G. Since the construction obviously eliminates ϵ-productions, we shall have a complete proof of the claim that for every CFG G, there is a grammar G_1 with no ϵ-productions, such that

$$L(G_1) = L(G) - \{\epsilon\}$$

Theorem 7.9: If the grammar G_1 is constructed from G by the above construction for eliminating ϵ-productions, then $L(G_1) = L(G) - \{\epsilon\}$.

PROOF: We must show that if $w \neq \epsilon$, then w is in $L(G_1)$ if and only if w is in $L(G)$. As is often the case, we find it easier to prove a more general statement. In this case, we need to talk about the terminal strings that each variable generates, even though we only care what the start symbol S generates. Thus, we shall prove:

- $A \underset{G_1}{\overset{*}{\Rightarrow}} w$ if and only if $A \underset{G}{\overset{*}{\Rightarrow}} w$ and $w \neq \epsilon$.

In each case, the proof is an induction on the length of the derivation.

(Only-if) Suppose that $A \underset{G_1}{\overset{*}{\Rightarrow}} w$. Then surely $w \neq \epsilon$, because G_1 has no ϵ-productions. We must show by induction on the length of the derivation that $A \underset{G}{\overset{*}{\Rightarrow}} w$.

BASIS: One step. Then there is a production $A \to w$ in G_1. The construction of G_1 tells us that there is some production $A \to \alpha$ of G, such that α is w, with zero or more nullable variables interspersed. Then in G, $A \underset{G}{\Rightarrow} \alpha \underset{G}{\overset{*}{\Rightarrow}} w$, where the steps after the first, if any, derive ϵ from whatever variables there are in α.

INDUCTION: Suppose the derivation takes $n > 1$ steps. Then the derivation looks like $A \underset{G_1}{\Rightarrow} X_1 X_2 \cdots X_k \underset{G_1}{\overset{*}{\Rightarrow}} w$. The first production used must come from a production $A \to Y_1 Y_2 \cdots Y_m$, where the Y's are the X's, in order, with zero or more additional, nullable variables interspersed. Also, we can break w into $w_1 w_2 \cdots w_k$, where $X_i \underset{G_1}{\overset{*}{\Rightarrow}} w_i$ for $i = 1, 2, \ldots, k$. If X_i is a terminal, then $w_i = X_i$, and if X_i is a variable, then the derivation $X_i \underset{G_1}{\overset{*}{\Rightarrow}} w_i$ takes fewer than n steps. By the inductive hypothesis, we can conclude $X_i \underset{G}{\overset{*}{\Rightarrow}} w_i$.

Now, we construct a corresponding derivation in G as follows:

$$A \underset{G}{\Rightarrow} Y_1 Y_2 \cdots Y_m \underset{G}{\overset{*}{\Rightarrow}} X_1 X_2 \cdots X_k \underset{G}{\overset{*}{\Rightarrow}} w_1 w_2 \cdots w_k = w$$

The first step is application of the production $A \to Y_1 Y_2 \cdots Y_k$ that we know exists in G. The next group of steps represents the derivation of ϵ from each of the Y_j's that is not one of the X_i's. The final group of steps represents the derivations of the w_i's from the X_i's, which we know exist by the inductive hypothesis.

(If) Suppose $A \underset{G}{\overset{*}{\Rightarrow}} w$ and $w \neq \epsilon$. We show by induction on the length n of the derivation, that $A \underset{G_1}{\overset{*}{\Rightarrow}} w$.

BASIS: One step. Then $A \to w$ is a production of G. Since $w \neq \epsilon$, this production is also a production of G_1, and $A \underset{G_1}{\overset{*}{\Rightarrow}} w$.

INDUCTION: Suppose the derivation takes $n > 1$ steps. Then the derivation looks like $A \underset{G}{\Rightarrow} Y_1 Y_2 \cdots Y_m \underset{G}{\overset{*}{\Rightarrow}} w$. We can break $w = w_1 w_2 \cdots w_m$, such that $Y_i \underset{G}{\overset{*}{\Rightarrow}} w_i$ for $i = 1, 2, \ldots, m$. Let $X_1, X_2, \ldots, X_k$ be those of the Y_j's, in order, such that $w_j \neq \epsilon$. We must have $k \geq 1$, since $w \neq \epsilon$. Thus, $A \to X_1 X_2 \cdots X_k$ is a production of G_1.

We claim that $X_1 X_2 \cdots X_k \underset{G}{\overset{*}{\Rightarrow}} w$, since the only Y_j's that are not present among the X's were used to derive ϵ, and thus do not contribute to the derivation of w. Since each of the derivations $Y_j \underset{G}{\overset{*}{\Rightarrow}} w_j$ takes fewer than n steps, we may apply the inductive hypothesis and conclude that, if $w_j \neq \epsilon$, then $Y_j \underset{G_1}{\overset{*}{\Rightarrow}} w_j$. Thus, $A \underset{G_1}{\Rightarrow} X_1 X_2 \cdots X_k \underset{G_1}{\overset{*}{\Rightarrow}} w$.

Now, we complete the proof as follows. We know w is in $L(G_1)$ if and only if $S \underset{G_1}{\overset{*}{\Rightarrow}} w$. Letting $A = S$ in the above, we know that w is in $L(G_1)$ if and only if $S \underset{G}{\overset{*}{\Rightarrow}} w$ and $w \neq \epsilon$. That is, w is in $L(G_1)$ if and only if w is in $L(G)$ and $w \neq \epsilon$. □

7.1.4 Eliminating Unit Productions

A *unit production* is a production of the form $A \to B$, where both A and B are variables. These productions can be useful. For instance, in Example 5.27, we saw how using unit productions $E \to T$ and $T \to F$ allowed us to create an unambiguous grammar for simple arithmetic expressions:

$$
\begin{aligned}
I &\to a \mid b \mid Ia \mid Ib \mid I0 \mid I1 \\
F &\to I \mid (E) \\
T &\to F \mid T * F \\
E &\to T \mid E + T
\end{aligned}
$$

However, unit productions can complicate certain proofs, and they also introduce extra steps into derivations that technically need not be there. For instance, we could expand the T in production $E \to T$ in both possible ways, replacing it by the two productions $E \to F \mid T * F$. That change still doesn't eliminate unit productions, because we have introduced unit production $E \to F$ that was not previously part of the grammar. Further expanding $E \to F$ by the two productions for F gives us $E \to I \mid (E) \mid T * F$. We still have a unit production; it is $E \to I$. But if we further expand this I in all six possible ways, we get

$$E \to a \mid b \mid Ia \mid Ib \mid I0 \mid I1 \mid (E) \mid T * F$$

Now the unit production for E is gone. Note that $E \to a$ is *not* a unit production, since the lone symbol in the body is a terminal, rather than a variable as is required for unit productions.

The technique suggested above — expand unit productions until they disappear — often works. However, it can fail if there is a cycle of unit productions, such as $A \to B$, $B \to C$, and $C \to A$. The technique that is guaranteed to work involves first finding all those pairs of variables A and B such that $A \overset{*}{\Rightarrow} B$ using a sequence of unit productions only. Note that it is possible for $A \overset{*}{\Rightarrow} B$ to be true even though no unit productions are involved. For instance, we might have productions $A \to BC$ and $C \to \epsilon$.

Once we have determined all such pairs, we can replace any sequence of derivation steps in which $A \Rightarrow B_1 \Rightarrow B_2 \Rightarrow \cdots \Rightarrow B_n \Rightarrow \alpha$ by a production that uses the nonunit production $B_n \to \alpha$ directly from A; that is, $A \to \alpha$. To begin, here is the inductive construction of the pairs (A, B) such that $A \overset{*}{\Rightarrow} B$ using only unit productions. Call such a pair a *unit pair*.

BASIS: (A, A) is a unit pair for any variable A. That is, $A \overset{*}{\Rightarrow} A$ by zero steps.

INDUCTION: Suppose we have determined that (A, B) is a unit pair, and $B \to C$ is a production, where C is a variable. Then (A, C) is a unit pair.

Example 7.10 : Consider the expression grammar of Example 5.27, which we reproduced above. The basis gives us the unit pairs (E, E), (T, T), (F, F), and (I, I). For the inductive step, we can make the following inferences:

1. (E, E) and the production $E \to T$ gives us unit pair (E, T).

2. (E, T) and the production $T \to F$ gives us unit pair (E, F).

3. (E, F) and the production $F \to I$ gives us unit pair (E, I).

4. (T, T) and the production $T \to F$ gives us unit pair (T, F).

5. (T, F) and the production $F \to I$ gives us unit pair (T, I).

6. (F, F) and the production $F \to I$ gives us unit pair (F, I).

There are no more pairs that can be inferred, and in fact these ten pairs represent all the derivations that use nothing but unit productions. $\square$

The pattern of development should by now be familiar. There is an easy proof that our proposed algorithm does get all the pairs we want. We then use the knowledge of those pairs to remove unit productions from a grammar and show that the language of the two grammars is the same.

Theorem 7.11: The algorithm above finds exactly the unit pairs for a CFG G.

PROOF: In one direction, it is an easy induction on the order in which the pairs are discovered, that if (A, B) is found to be a unit pair, then $A \overset{*}{\underset{G}{\Rightarrow}} B$ using only unit productions. We leave this part of the proof to you.

In the other direction, suppose that $A \overset{*}{\underset{G}{\Rightarrow}} B$ using unit productions only. We can show by induction on the length of the derivation that the pair (A, B) will be found.

BASIS: Zero steps. Then $A = B$, and the pair (A, B) is added in the basis.

INDUCTION: Suppose $A \overset{*}{\Rightarrow} B$ using n steps, for some $n > 0$, each step being the application of a unit production. Then the derivation looks like

$$A \overset{*}{\Rightarrow} C \Rightarrow B$$

The derivation $A \overset{*}{\Rightarrow} C$ takes $n - 1$ steps, so by the inductive hypothesis, we discover the pair (A, C). Then the inductive part of the algorithm combines the pair (A, C) with the production $C \to B$ to infer the pair (A, B). $\square$

To eliminate unit productions, we proceed as follows. Given a CFG $G = (V, T, P, S)$, construct CFG $G_1 = (V, T, P_1, S)$:

1. Find all the unit pairs of G.

2. For each unit pair (A, B), add to P_1 all the productions $A \to \alpha$, where $B \to \alpha$ is a nonunit production in P. Note that $A = B$ is possible; in that way, P_1 contains all the nonunit productions in P.

Example 7.12: Let us continue with Example 7.10, which performed step (1) of the construction above for the expression grammar of Example 5.27. Figure 7.1 summarizes step (2) of the algorithm, where we create the new set of productions by using the first member of a pair as the head and all the nonunit bodies for the second member of the pair as the production bodies.

The final step is to eliminate the unit productions from the grammar of Fig. 7.1. The resulting grammar:

Pair	Productions
(E, E)	$E \to E + T$
(E, T)	$E \to T * F$
(E, F)	$E \to (E)$
(E, I)	$E \to a \mid b \mid Ia \mid Ib \mid I0 \mid I1$
(T, T)	$T \to T * F$
(T, F)	$T \to (E)$
(T, I)	$T \to a \mid b \mid Ia \mid Ib \mid I0 \mid I1$
(F, F)	$F \to (E)$
(F, I)	$F \to a \mid b \mid Ia \mid Ib \mid I0 \mid I1$
(I, I)	$I \to a \mid b \mid Ia \mid Ib \mid I0 \mid I1$

Figure 7.1: Grammar constructed by step (2) of the unit-production-elimination algorithm

$$E \to E + T \mid T * F \mid (E) \mid a \mid b \mid Ia \mid Ib \mid I0 \mid I1$$
$$T \to T * F \mid (E) \mid a \mid b \mid Ia \mid Ib \mid I0 \mid I1$$
$$F \to (E) \mid a \mid b \mid Ia \mid Ib \mid I0 \mid I1$$
$$I \to a \mid b \mid Ia \mid Ib \mid I0 \mid I1$$

has no unit productions, yet generates the same set of expressions as the grammar of Fig. 5.19. □

Theorem 7.13: If grammar G_1 is constructed from grammar G by the algorithm described above for eliminating unit productions, then $L(G_1) = L(G)$.

PROOF: We show that w is in $L(G)$ if and only if w is in $L(G_1)$.

(If) Suppose $S \stackrel{*}{\underset{G_1}{\Rightarrow}} w$. Since every production of G_1 is equivalent to a sequence of zero or more unit productions of G followed by a nonunit production of G, we know that $\alpha \underset{G_1}{\Rightarrow} \beta$ implies $\alpha \stackrel{*}{\underset{G}{\Rightarrow}} \beta$. That is, every step of a derivation in G_1 can be replaced by one or more derivation steps in G. If we put these sequences of steps together, we conclude that $S \stackrel{*}{\underset{G}{\Rightarrow}} w$.

(Only-if) Suppose now that w is in $L(G)$. Then by the equivalences in Section 5.2, we know that w has a leftmost derivation, i.e., $S \underset{lm}{\Rightarrow} w$. Whenever a unit production is used in a leftmost derivation, the variable of the body becomes the leftmost variable, and so is immediately replaced. Thus, the leftmost derivation in grammar G can be broken into a sequence of steps in which zero or more unit productions are followed by a nonunit production. Note that any nonunit production that is not preceded by a unit production is a "step" by itself. Each of these steps can be performed by one production of G_1, because the construction of G_1 created exactly the productions that reflect zero or more unit productions followed by a nonunit production. Thus, $S \stackrel{*}{\underset{G_1}{\Rightarrow}} w$. □

We can now summarize the various simplifications described so far. We want to convert any CFG G into an equivalent CFG that has no useless symbols, ϵ-productions, or unit productions. Some care must be taken in the order of application of the constructions. A safe order is:

1. Eliminate ϵ-productions.

2. Eliminate unit productions.

3. Eliminate useless symbols.

You should notice that, just as in Section 7.1.1, where we had to order the two steps properly or the result might have useless symbols, we must order the three steps above as shown, or the result might still have some of the features we thought we were eliminating.

Theorem 7.14: If G is a CFG generating a language that contains at least one string other than ϵ, then there is another CFG G_1 such that $L(G_1) = L(G) - \{\epsilon\}$, and G_1 has no ϵ-productions, unit productions, or useless symbols.

PROOF: Start by eliminating the ϵ-productions by the method of Section 7.1.3. If we then eliminate unit productions by the method of Section 7.1.4, we do not introduce any ϵ-productions, since the bodies of the new productions are each identical to some body of an old production. Finally, we eliminate useless symbols by the method of Section 7.1.1. As this transformation only eliminates productions and symbols, never introducing a new production, the resulting grammar will still be devoid of ϵ-productions and unit productions.   □

7.1.5   Chomsky Normal Form

We complete our study of grammatical simplifications by showing that every nonempty CFL without ϵ has a grammar G in which all productions are in one of two simple forms, either:

1. $A \rightarrow BC$, where A, B, and C, are each variables, or

2. $A \rightarrow a$, where A is a variable and a is a terminal.

Further, G has no useless symbols. Such a grammar is said to be in *Chomsky Normal Form*, or CNF.[1]

To put a grammar in CNF, start with one that satisfies the restrictions of Theorem 7.14; that is, the grammar has no ϵ-productions, unit productions, or useless symbols. Every production of such a grammar is either of the form $A \rightarrow a$, which is already in a form allowed by CNF, or it has a body of length 2 or more. Our tasks are to:

---

[1]N. Chomsky is the linguist who first proposed context-free grammars as a way to describe natural languages, and who proved that every CFG could be converted to this form. Interestingly, CNF does not appear to have important uses in natural linguistics, although we shall see it has several other uses, such as an efficient test for membership of a string in a context-free language (Section 7.4.4).

a) Arrange that all bodies of length 2 or more consist only of variables.

b) Break bodies of length 3 or more into a cascade of productions, each with a body consisting of two variables.

The construction for (a) is as follows. For every terminal a that appears in a body of length 2 or more, create a new variable, say A. This variable has only one production, $A \rightarrow a$. Now, we use A in place of a everywhere a appears in a body of length 2 or more. At this point, every production has a body that is either a single terminal or at least two variables and no terminals.

For step (b), we must break those productions $A \rightarrow B_1 B_2 \cdots B_k$, for $k \geq 3$, into a group of productions with two variables in each body. We introduce $k - 2$ new variables, $C_1, C_2, \ldots, C_{k-2}$. The original production is replaced by the $k - 1$ productions

$$A \rightarrow B_1 C_1, \quad C_1 \rightarrow B_2 C_2, \ldots, C_{k-3} \rightarrow B_{k-2} C_{k-2}, \quad C_{k-2} \rightarrow B_{k-1} B_k$$

Example 7.15: Let us convert the grammar of Example 7.12 to CNF. For part (a), notice that there are eight terminals, a, b, 0, 1, +, *, (, and), each of which appears in a body that is not a single terminal. Thus, we must introduce eight new variables, corresponding to these terminals, and eight productions in which the new variable is replaced by its terminal. Using the obvious initials as the new variables, we introduce:

$$
\begin{array}{cccc}
A \rightarrow a & B \rightarrow b & Z \rightarrow 0 & O \rightarrow 1 \\
P \rightarrow + & M \rightarrow * & L \rightarrow (& R \rightarrow)
\end{array}
$$

If we introduce these productions, and replace every terminal in a body that is other than a single terminal by the corresponding variable, we get the grammar shown in Fig. 7.2.

$$
\begin{array}{rcl}
E & \rightarrow & EPT \mid TMF \mid LER \mid a \mid b \mid IA \mid IB \mid IZ \mid IO \\
T & \rightarrow & TMF \mid LER \mid a \mid b \mid IA \mid IB \mid IZ \mid IO \\
F & \rightarrow & LER \mid a \mid b \mid IA \mid IB \mid IZ \mid IO \\
I & \rightarrow & a \mid b \mid IA \mid IB \mid IZ \mid IO \\
A & \rightarrow & a \\
B & \rightarrow & b \\
Z & \rightarrow & 0 \\
O & \rightarrow & 1 \\
P & \rightarrow & + \\
M & \rightarrow & * \\
L & \rightarrow & (\\
R & \rightarrow &)
\end{array}
$$

Figure 7.2: Making all bodies either a single terminal or several variables

Now, all productions are in Chomsky Normal Form except for those with the bodies of length 3: EPT, TMF, and LER. Some of these bodies appear in more than one production, but we can deal with each body once, introducing one extra variable for each. For EPT, we introduce new variable C_1, and replace the one production, $E \to EPT$, where it appears, by $E \to EC_1$ and $C_1 \to PT$.

For TMF we introduce new variable C_2. The two productions that use this body, $E \to TMF$ and $T \to TMF$, are replaced by $E \to TC_2$, $T \to TC_2$, and $C_2 \to MF$. Then, for LER we introduce new variable C_3 and replace the three productions that use it, $E \to LER$, $T \to LER$, and $F \to LER$, by $E \to LC_3$, $T \to LC_3$, $F \to LC_3$, and $C_3 \to ER$. The final grammar, which is in CNF, is shown in Fig. 7.3.   □

$$
\begin{aligned}
E &\to EC_3 \mid TC_2 \mid LC_3 \mid a \mid b \mid IA \mid IB \mid IZ \mid IO \\
T &\to TC_2 \mid LC_3 \mid a \mid b \mid IA \mid IB \mid IZ \mid IO \\
F &\to LC_3 \mid a \mid b \mid IA \mid IB \mid IZ \mid IO \\
I &\to a \mid b \mid IA \mid IB \mid IZ \mid IO \\
A &\to a \\
B &\to b \\
Z &\to 0 \\
O &\to 1 \\
P &\to + \\
M &\to * \\
L &\to (\\
R &\to) \\
C_1 &\to PT \\
C_2 &\to MF \\
C_3 &\to ER
\end{aligned}
$$

Figure 7.3: Making all bodies either a single terminal or two variables

Theorem 7.16: If G is a CFG whose language contains at least one string other than ϵ, then there is a grammar G_1 in Chomsky Normal Form, such that $L(G_1) = L(G) - \{\epsilon\}$.

PROOF: By Theorem 7.14, we can find CFG G_2 such that $L(G_2) = L(G) - \{\epsilon\}$, and such that G_2 has no useless symbols, ϵ-productions, or unit productions. The construction that converts G_2 to CNF grammar G_1 changes the productions in such a way that each production of G_1 can be simulated by one or more productions of G_2. Conversely, the introduced variables of G_2 each have only one production, so they can only be used in the manner intended. More formally, we prove that w is in $L(G_2)$ if and only if w is in $L(G_1)$.

(Only-if) If w has a derivation in G_2, it is easy to replace each production used, say $A \to X_1 X_2 \cdots X_k$, by a sequence of productions of G_1. That is, one step in the derivation in G_2 becomes one or more steps in the derivation of w using the productions of G_1. First, if any X_i is a terminal, we know G_1 has a corresponding variable B_i and a production $B_i \to X_i$. Then, if $k > 2$, G_1 has productions $A \to B_1 C_1$, $C_1 \to B_2 C_2$, and so on, where B_i is either the introduced variable for terminal X_i or X_i itself, if X_i is a variable. These productions simulate in G_1 one step of a derivation of G_2 that uses $A \to X_1 X_2 \cdots X_k$. We conclude that there is a derivation of w in G_1, so w is in $L(G_1)$.

(If) Suppose w is in $L(G_1)$. Then there is a parse tree in G_1, with S at the root and yield w. We convert this tree to a parse tree of G_2 that also has root S and yield w.

First, we "undo" part (b) of the CNF construction. That is, suppose there is a node labeled A, with two children labeled B_1 and C_1, where C_1 is one of the variables introduced in part (b). Then this portion of the parse tree must look like Fig. 7.4(a). That is, because these introduced variables each have only one production, there is only one way that they can appear, and all the variables introduced to handle the production $A \to B_1 B_2 \cdots B_k$ must appear together, as shown.

Any such cluster of nodes in the parse tree may be replaced by the production that they represent. The parse-tree transformation is suggested by Fig. 7.4(b).

The resulting parse tree is still not necessarily a parse tree of G_2. The reason is that step (a) in the CNF construction introduced other variables that derive single terminals. However, we can identify these in the current parse tree and replace a node labeled by such a variable A and its one child labeled a, by a single node labeled a. Now, every interior node of the parse tree forms a production of G_2. Since w is the yield of a parse tree in G_2, we conclude that w is in $L(G_2)$. □

7.1.6 Exercises for Section 7.1

* **Exercise 7.1.1 :** Find a grammar equivalent to

$$
\begin{aligned}
S &\to AB \mid CA \\
A &\to a \\
B &\to BC \mid AB \\
C &\to aB \mid b
\end{aligned}
$$

with no useless symbols.

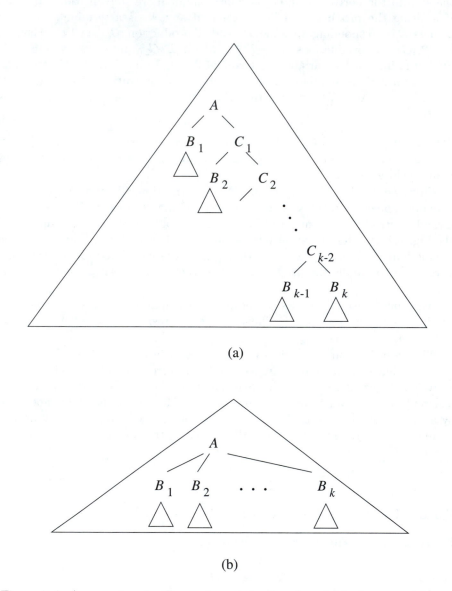

Figure 7.4: A parse tree in G_1 must use introduced variables in a special way

Greibach Normal Form

There is another interesting normal form for grammars that we shall not prove. Every nonempty language without ϵ is $L(G)$ for some grammar G each of whose productions are of the form $A \to a\alpha$, where a is a terminal and α is a string of zero or more variables. Converting a grammar to this form is complex, even if we simplify the task by, say, starting with a Chomsky-Normal-Form grammar. Roughly, we expand the first variable of each production, until we get a terminal. However, because there can be cycles, where we never reach a terminal, it is necessary to "short-circuit" the process, creating a production that introduces a terminal as the first symbol of the body and has variables following it to generate all the sequences of variables that might have been generated on the way to generation of that terminal.

This form, called *Greibach Normal Form*, after Sheila Greibach, who first gave a way to construct such grammars, has several interesting consequences. Since each use of a production introduces exactly one terminal into a sentential form, a string of length n has a derivation of exactly n steps. Also, if we apply the PDA construction of Theorem 6.13 to a Greibach-Normal-Form grammar, then we get a PDA with no ϵ-rules, thus showing that it is always possible to eliminate such transitions of a PDA.

---

* Exercise 7.1.2 : Begin with the grammar:

$$
\begin{aligned}
S &\to ASB \mid \epsilon \\
A &\to aAS \mid a \\
B &\to SbS \mid A \mid bb
\end{aligned}
$$

a) Are there any useless symbols? Eliminate them if so.

b) Eliminate ϵ-productions.

c) Eliminate unit productions.

d) Put the grammar into Chomsky normal form.

Exercise 7.1.3 : Repeat Exercise 7.1.2 for the following grammar:

$$
\begin{aligned}
S &\to 0A0 \mid 1B1 \mid BB \\
A &\to C \\
B &\to S \mid A \\
C &\to S \mid \epsilon
\end{aligned}
$$

Exercise 7.1.4 : Repeat Exercise 7.1.2 for the following grammar:

$$
\begin{aligned}
S &\rightarrow AAA \mid B \\
A &\rightarrow aA \mid B \\
B &\rightarrow \epsilon
\end{aligned}
$$

Exercise 7.1.5: Repeat Exercise 7.1.2 for the following grammar:

$$
\begin{aligned}
S &\rightarrow aAa \mid bBb \mid \epsilon \\
A &\rightarrow C \mid a \\
B &\rightarrow C \mid b \\
C &\rightarrow CDE \mid \epsilon \\
D &\rightarrow A \mid B \mid ab
\end{aligned}
$$

Exercise 7.1.6: Design a CNF grammar for the set of strings of balanced parentheses. You need not start from any particular non-CNF grammar.

!! **Exercise 7.1.7:** Suppose G is a CFG with p productions, and no production body longer than n. Show that if $A \overset{*}{\underset{G}{\Rightarrow}} \epsilon$, then there is a derivation of ϵ from A of no more than $(n^p - 1)/(n - 1)$ steps. How close can you actually come to this bound?

! **Exercise 7.1.8:** Suppose we have a grammar G with n productions, none of them ϵ-productions, and we we convert this grammar to CNF.

a) Show that the CNF grammar has at most $O(n^2)$ productions.

b) Show that it is possible for the CNF grammar to have a number of productions proportional to n^2. *Hint*: Consider the construction that eliminates unit productions.

Exercise 7.1.9: Provide the inductive proofs needed to complete the following theorems:

a) The part of Theorem 7.4 where we show that discovered symbols really are generating.

b) Both directions of Theorem 7.6, where we show the correctness of the algorithm in Section 7.1.2 for detecting the reachable symbols.

c) The part of Theorem 7.11 where we show that all pairs discovered really are unit pairs.

*! **Exercise 7.1.10:** Is it possible to find, for every context-free language, a grammar such that all its productions are either of the form $A \rightarrow BCD$ (i.e., a body consisting of three variables), or $A \rightarrow a$ (i.e., a body consisting of a single terminal)? Give either a proof or a counterexample.

Exercise 7.1.11: In this exercise, we shall show that for every context-free language L containing at least one string other than ϵ, there is a CFG in Greibach normal form that generates $L - \{\epsilon\}$. Recall that a Greibach normal form (GNF) grammar is one where every production body starts with a terminal. The construction will be done using a series of lemmas and constructions.

a) Suppose that a CFG G has a production $A \to \alpha B \beta$, and all the productions for B are $B \to \gamma_1 \mid \gamma_2 \mid \cdots \mid \gamma_n$. Then if we replace $A \to \alpha B \beta$ by all the productions we get by substituting some body of a B-production for B, that is, $A \to \alpha \gamma_1 \beta \mid \alpha \gamma_2 \beta \mid \cdots \mid \alpha \gamma_n \beta$, the resulting grammar generates the same language as G.

In what follows, assume that the grammar G for L is in Chomsky Normal Form, and that the variables are called $A_1, A_2, \ldots, A_k$.

*! b) Show that, by repeatedly using the transformation of part (a), we can convert G to an equivalent grammar in which every production body for A_i either starts with a terminal or starts with A_j, for some $j \geq i$. In either case, all symbols after the first in any production body are variables.

! c) Suppose G_1 is the grammar that we get by performing step (b) on G. Suppose that A_i is any variable, and let $A \to A_i \alpha_1 \mid \cdots \mid A_i \alpha_m$ be all the A_i-productions that have a body beginning with A_i. Let

$$A_i \to \beta_1 \mid \cdots \mid \beta_p$$

be all the other A_i-productions. Note that each β_j must start with either a terminal or a variable with index higher than j. Introduce a new variable B_i, and replace the first group of m productions by

$$A_i \to \beta_1 B_i \mid \cdots \mid \beta_p B_i$$
$$B_i \to \alpha_1 B_i \mid \alpha_1 \mid \cdots \mid \alpha_m B_i \mid \alpha_m$$

Prove that the resulting grammar generates the same language as G and G_1.

*! d) Let G_2 be the grammar that results from step (c). Note that all the A_i productions have bodies that begin with either a terminal or an A_j for $j > i$. Also, all the B_i productions have bodies that begin with either a terminal or some A_j. Prove that G_2 has an equivalent grammar in GNF. *Hint*: First fix the productions for A_k, then A_{k-1}, and so on, down to A_1, using part (a). Then fix the B_i productions in any order, again using part (a).

Exercise 7.1.12 : Use the construction of Exercise 7.1.11 to convert the grammar

$$
\begin{aligned}
S &\to AA \mid 0 \\
A &\to SS \mid 1
\end{aligned}
$$

to GNF.

7.2   The Pumping Lemma for Context-Free Languages

Now, we shall develop a tool for showing that certain languages are not context-free. The theorem, called the "pumping lemma for context-free languages," says that in any sufficiently long string in a CFL, it is possible to find at most two short, nearby substrings, that we can "pump" in tandem. That is, we may repeat both of the strings i times, for any integer i, and the resulting string will still be in the language.

We may contrast this theorem with the analogous pumping lemma for regular languages, Theorem 4.1, which says we can always find one small string to pump. The difference is seen when we consider a language like $L = \{0^n 1^n \mid n \geq 1\}$. We can show it is not regular, by fixing n and pumping a substring of 0's, thus getting a string with more 0's than 1's. However, the CFL pumping lemma states only that we can find two small strings, so we might be forced to use a string of 0's and a string of 1's, thus generating only strings in L when we "pump." That outcome is fortunate, because L is a CFL, and thus we should not be able to use the CFL pumping lemma to construct strings not in L.

7.2.1   The Size of Parse Trees

Our first step in deriving a pumping lemma for CFL's is to examine the shape and size of parse trees. One of the uses of CNF is to turn parse trees into binary trees. These trees have some convenient properties, one of which we exploit here.

Theorem 7.17: Suppose we have a parse tree according to a Chomsky-Normal-Form grammar $G = (V, T, P, S)$, and suppose that the yield of the tree is a terminal string w. If the length of the longest path is n, then $|w| \leq 2^{n-1}$.

PROOF: The proof is a simple induction on n.

BASIS: $n = 1$. Recall that the length of a path in a tree is the number of edges, i.e., one less than the number of nodes. Thus, a tree with a maximum path length of 1 consists of only a root and one leaf labeled by a terminal. String w is this terminal, so $|w| = 1$. Since $2^{n-1} = 2^0 = 1$ in this case, we have proved the basis.

INDUCTION: Suppose the longest path has length n, and $n > 1$. The root of the tree uses a production, which must be of the form $A \to BC$, since $n > 1$; i.e., we could not start the tree using a production with a terminal. No path in the subtrees rooted at B and C can have length greater than $n - 1$, since these paths exclude the edge from the root to its child labeled B or C. Thus, by the inductive hypothesis, these two subtrees each have yields of length at most 2^{n-2}. The yield of the entire tree is the concatenation of these two yields, and therefore has length at most $2^{n-2} + 2^{n-2} = 2^{n-1}$. Thus, the inductive step is proved. $\square$

7.2.2 Statement of the Pumping Lemma

The pumping lemma for CFL's is quite similar to the pumping lemma for regular languages, but we break each string z in the CFL L into five parts, and we pump the second and fourth, in tandem.

Theorem 7.18: (The pumping lemma for context-free languages) Let L be a CFL. Then there exists a constant n such that if z is any string in L such that $|z|$ is at least n, then we can write $z = uvwxy$, subject to the following conditions:

1. $|vwx| \leq n$. That is, the middle portion is not too long.

2. $vx \neq \epsilon$. Since v and x are the pieces to be "pumped," this condition says that at least one of the strings we pump must not be empty.

3. For all $i \geq 0$, uv^iwx^iy is in L. That is, the two strings v and x may be "pumped" any number of times, including 0, and the resulting string will still be a member of L.

PROOF: Our first step is to find a Chomsky-Normal-Form grammar G for L. Technically, we cannot find such a grammar if L is the CFL $\emptyset$ or $\{\epsilon\}$. However, if $L = \emptyset$ then the statement of the theorem, which talks about a string z in L surely cannot be violated, since there is no such z in $\emptyset$. Also, the CNF grammar G will actually generate $L - \{\epsilon\}$, but that is again not of importance, since we shall surely pick $n > 0$, in which case z cannot be ϵ anyway.

Now, starting with a CNF grammar $G = (V, T, P, S)$ such that $L(G) = L - \{\epsilon\}$, let G have m variables. Choose $n = 2^m$. Next, suppose that z in L is of length at least n. By Theorem 7.17, any parse tree whose longest path is of length m or less must have a yield of length $2^{m-1} = n/2$ or less. Such a parse tree cannot have yield z, because z is too long. Thus, any parse tree with yield z has a path of length at least $m + 1$.

Figure 7.5 suggests the longest path in the tree for z, where k is at least m and the path is of length $k+1$. Since $k \geq m$, there are at least $m+1$ occurrences of variables $A_0, A_1, \ldots, A_k$ on the path. As there are only m different variables in V, at least two of the last $m + 1$ variables on the path (that is, A_{k-m} through A_k, inclusive) must be the same variable. Suppose $A_i = A_j$, where $k - m \leq i < j \leq k$.

Then it is possible to divide the tree as shown in Fig. 7.6. String w is the yield of the subtree rooted at A_j. Strings v and x are the strings to the left and right, respectively, of w in the yield of the larger subtree rooted at A_i. Note that, since there are no unit productions, v and x could not both be ϵ, although one could be. Finally, u and y are those portions of z that are to the left and right, respectively, of the subtree rooted at A_i.

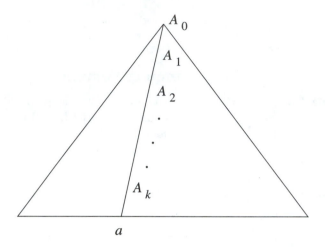

Figure 7.5: Every sufficiently long string in L must have a long path in its parse tree

If $A_i = A_j = A$, then we can construct new parse trees from the original tree, as suggested in Fig. 7.7(a). First, we may replace the subtree rooted at A_i, which has yield vwx, by the subtree rooted at A_j, which has yield w. The reason we can do so is that both of these trees have root labeled A. The resulting tree is suggested in Fig. 7.7(b); it has yield uwy and corresponds to the case $i = 0$ in the pattern of strings uv^iwx^iy.

Another option is suggested by Fig. 7.7(c). There, we have replaced the subtree rooted at A_j by the entire subtree rooted at A_i. Again, the justification is that we are substituting one tree with root labeled A for another tree with the same root label. The yield of this tree is uv^2wx^2y. Were we to then replace the subtree of Fig. 7.7(c) with yield w by the larger subtree with yield vwx, we would have a tree with yield uv^3wx^3y, and so on, for any exponent i. Thus, there are parse trees in G for all strings of the form uv^iwx^iy, and almost proved the pumping lemma.

The remaining detail is condition (1), which says that $|vwx| \leq n$. However, we picked A_i to be close to the bottom of the tree; that is, $k - i \leq m$. Thus, the longest path in the subtree rooted at A_i is no greater than $m + 1$. By Theorem 7.17, the subtree rooted at A_i has a yield whose length is no greater than $2^m = n$. □

7.2.3 Applications of the Pumping Lemma for CFL's

Notice that, like the earlier pumping lemma for regular languages, we use the CFl pumping lemma as an "adversary game, as follows."

1. We pick a language L that we want to show is not a CFL.

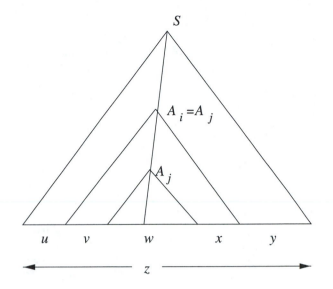

Figure 7.6: Dividing the string w so it can be pumped

2. Our "adversary" gets to pick n, which we do not know, and we therefore must plan for any possible n.

3. We get to pick z, and may use n as a parameter when we do so.

4. Our adversary gets to break z into $uvwxy$, subject only to the constraints that $|vwx| \leq n$ and $vx \neq \epsilon$.

5. We "win" the game, if we can, by picking i and showing that uv^iwx^iy is not in L.

We shall now see some examples of languages that we can prove, using the pumping lemma, not to be context-free. Our first example shows that, while context-free languages can match two groups of symbols for equality or inequality, they cannot match three such groups.

Example 7.19: Let L be the language $\{0^n1^n2^n \mid n \geq 1\}$. That is, L consists of all strings in $0^+1^+2^+$ with an equal number of each symbol, e.g., 012, 001122, and so on. Suppose L were context-free. Then there is an integer n given to us by the pumping lemma.[2] Let us pick $z = 0^n1^n2^n$.

Suppose the "adversary" breaks z as $z = uvwxy$, where $|vwx| \leq n$ and v and x are not both ϵ. Then we know that vwx cannot involve both 0's and 2's, since the last 0 and the first 2 are separated by $n+1$ positions. We shall prove that L contains some string known not to be in L, thus contradicting the assumption that L is a CFL. The cases are as follows:

---

[2] Remember that this n is the constant provided by the pumping lemma, and it has nothing to do with the local variable n used in the definition of L itself.

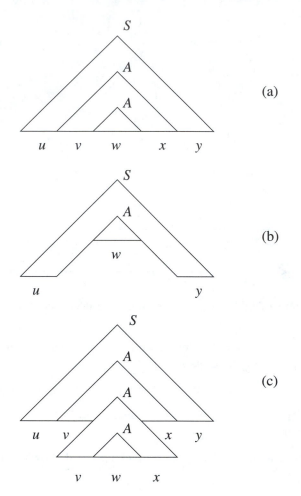

Figure 7.7: Pumping strings v and x zero times and pumping them twice

1. vwx has no 2's. Then vx consists of only 0's and 1's, and has at least one of these symbols. Then uwy, which would have to be in L by the pumping lemma, has n 2's, but has fewer than n 0's or fewer than n 1's, or both. It therefore does not belong in L, and we conclude L is not a CFL in this case.

2. vwx has no 0's. Similarly, uwy has n 0's, but fewer 1's or fewer 2's. It therefore is not in L.

Whichever case holds, we conclude that L has a string we know not to be in L. This contradiction allows us to conclude that our assumption was wrong; L is *not* a CFL. □

Another thing that CFL's cannot do is match two pairs of equal numbers of symbols, provided that the pairs interleave. The idea is made precise in the following example of a proof of non-context-freeness using the pumping lemma.

Example 7.20: Let L be the language $\{0^i1^j2^i3^j \mid i \geq 1 \text{ and } j \geq 1\}$. If L is context-free, let n be the constant for L, and pick $z = 0^n1^n2^n3^n$. We may write $z = uvwxy$ subject to the usual constraints $|vwx| \leq n$ and $vx \neq \epsilon$. Then vwx is either contained in the substring of one symbol, or it straddles two adjacent symbols.

If vwx consists of only one symbol, then uwy has n of three different symbols and fewer than n of the fourth symbol. Thus, it cannot be in L. If vwx straddles two symbols, say the 1's and 2's, then uwy is missing either some 1's or some 2's, or both. Suppose it is missing 1's. As there are n 3's, this string cannot be in L. Similarly, if it is missing 2's, then as it has n 0's, uwy cannot be in L. We have contradicted the assumption that L is a CFL and conclude that it is not. $\square$

As a final example, we shall show that CFL's cannot match two strings of arbitrary length, if the strings are chosen from an alphabet of more than one symbol. An implication of this observation, incidentally, is that grammars are not a suitable mechanism for enforcing certain "semantic" constraints in programming languages, such as the common requirement that an identifier be declared before use. In practice, another mechanism, such as a "symbol table" is used to record declared identifiers, and we do not try to design a parser that, by itself, checks for "definition prior to use."

Example 7.21: Let $L = \{ww \mid w \text{ is in } \{0,1\}^*\}$. That is, L consists of repeating strings, such as ϵ, 0101, 00100010, or 110110. If L is context-free, then let n be its pumping-lemma constant. Consider the string $z = 0^n1^n0^n1^n$. This string is 0^n1^n repeated, so z is in L.

Following the pattern of the previous examples, we can break $z = uvwxy$, such that $|vwx| \leq n$ and $vx \neq \epsilon$. We shall show that uwy is not in L, and thus show L not to be a context-free language, by contradiction.

First, observe that, since $|vwx| \leq n$, $|uwy| \geq 3n$. Thus, if uwy is some repeating string, say tt, then t is of length at least $3n/2$. There are several cases to consider, depending where vwx is within z.

1. Suppose vwx is within the first n 0's. In particular, let vx consist of k 0's, where $k > 0$. Then uwy begins with $0^{n-k}1^n$. Since $|uwy| = 4n - k$, we know that if $uwy = tt$, then $|t| = 2n - k/2$. Thus, t does not end until after the first block of 1's; i.e., t ends in 0. But uwy ends in 1, and so it cannot equal tt.

2. Suppose vwx straddles the first block of 0's and the first block of 1's. It may be that vx consists only of 0's, if $x = \epsilon$. Then, the argument that uwy is not of the form tt is the same as case (1). If vx has at least one

1, then we note that t, which is of length at least $3n/2$, must end in 1^n, because uwy ends in 1^n. However, there is no block of n 1's except the final block, so t cannot repeat in uwy.

3. If vwx is contained in the first block of 1's, then the argument that uwy is not in L is like the second part of case (2).

4. Suppose vwx straddles the first block of 1's and the second block of 0's. If vx actually has no 0's, then the argument is the same as if vwx were contained in the first block of 1's. If vx has at least one 0, then uwy starts with a block of n 0's, and so does t if $uvw = tt$. However, there is no other block of n 0's in uwy for the second copy of t. We conclude in this case too, that uwy is not in L.

5. In the other cases, where vwy is in the second half of z, the argument is symmetric to the cases where vwx is contained in the first half of z.

Thus, in no case is uwy in L, and we conclude that L is not context-free.   □

7.2.4   Exercises for Section 7.2

Exercise 7.2.1: Use the CFL pumping lemma to show each of these languages not to be context-free:

* a) $\{a^i b^j c^k \mid i < j < k\}$.

  b) $\{a^n b^n c^i \mid i \leq n\}$.

  c) $\{0^p \mid p$ is a prime$\}$. *Hint*: Adapt the same ideas used in Example 4.3, which showed this language not to be regular.

*! d) $\{0^i 1^j \mid j = i^2\}$.

! e) $\{a^n b^n c^i \mid n \leq i \leq 2n\}$.

! f) $\{ww^R w \mid w$ is a string of 0's and 1's$\}$. That is, the set of strings consisting of some string w followed by the same string in reverse, and then the string w again, such as 001100001.

! **Exercise 7.2.2:** When we try to apply the pumping lemma to a CFL, the "adversary wins," and we cannot complete the proof. Show what goes wrong when we choose L to be one of the following languages:

  a) $\{00, 11\}$.

* b) $\{0^n 1^n \mid n \geq 1\}$.

* c) The set of palindromes over alphabet $\{0, 1\}$.

! **Exercise 7.2.3:** There is a stronger version of the CFL pumping lemma known as *Ogden's lemma*. It differs from the pumping lemma we proved by allowing us to focus on any n "distinguished" positions of a string z and guaranteeing that the strings to be pumped have between 1 and n distinguished positions. The advantage of this ability is that a language may have strings consisting of two parts, one of which can be pumped without producing strings not in the language, while the other *does* produce strings outside the language when pumped. Without being able to insist that the pumping take place in the latter part, we cannot complete a proof of non-context-freeness. The formal statement of Ogden's lemma is: If L is a CFL, then there is a constant n, such that if z is any string of length at least n in L, in which we select at least n positions to be *distinguished*, then we can write $z = uvwxy$, such that:

1. vwx has at most n distinguished positions.

2. vx has at least one distinguished position.

3. For all i, $uv^i wx^i y$ is in L.

Prove Ogden's lemma. *Hint:* The proof is really the same as that of the pumping lemma of Theorem 7.18 if we pretend that the nondistinguished positions of z are not present as we select a long path in the parse tree for z.

* **Exercise 7.2.4:** Use Ogden's lemma (Exercise 7.2.3 to simplify the proof in Example 7.21 that $L = \{ww \mid w \text{ is in } \{0,1\}^*\}$ is not a CFL. *Hint:* Make only one group of n consecutive symbols distinguished in the chosen string z.

Exercise 7.2.5: Use Ogden's lemma (Exercise 7.2.3) to show the following languages are not CFL's:

! a) $\{0^i 1^j 0^k \mid j = \max(i, k)\}$.

!! b) $\{a^n b^n c^i \mid i \neq n\}$. *Hint:* If n is the constant for Ogden's lemma, consider the string $z = a^n b^n c^{n!}$.

7.3 Closure Properties of Context-Free Languages

We shall now consider some of the operations on context-free languages that are guaranteed to produce a CFL. Many of these closure properties will parallel the theorems we had for regular languages in Section 4.2. However, there are some differences.

First, we introduce an operation called substitution, in which we replace each symbol in the strings of one language by an entire language. This operation, a generalization of the homomorphism that we studied in Section 4.2.3, is useful in proving some other closure properties of CFL's, such as the regular-expression operations: union, concatenation, and closure. We show that CFL's are closed under homomorphisms and inverse homomorphisms. Unlike the regular languages, the CFL's are not closed under intersection or difference. However, the intersection or difference of a CFL and a regular language is always a CFL.

7.3.1   Substitutions

Let Σ be an alphabet, and suppose that for every symbol a in Σ, we choose a language L_a. These chosen languages can be over any alphabets, not necessarily Σ and not necessarily the same. This choice of languages defines a function s (a *substitution*) on Σ, and we shall refer to L_a as $s(a)$ for each symbol a.

If $w = a_1 a_2 \cdots a_n$ is a string in Σ^*, then $s(w)$ is the language of all strings $x_1 x_2 \cdots x_n$ such that string x_i is in the language $s(a_i)$, for $i = 1, 2, \ldots, n$. Put another way, $s(w)$ is the concatenation of the languages $s(a_1)s(a_2) \cdots s(a_n)$. We can further extend the definition of s to apply to languages: $s(L)$ is the union of $s(w)$ for all strings w in L.

Example 7.22: Suppose $s(0) = \{a^n b^n \mid n \geq 1\}$ and $s(1) = \{aa, bb\}$. That is, s is a substitution on alphabet $\Sigma = \{0, 1\}$. Language $s(0)$ is the set of strings with one or more a's followed by an equal number of b's, while $s(1)$ is the finite language consisting of the two strings aa and bb.

Let $w = 01$. Then $s(w)$ is the concatenation of the languages $s(0)s(1)$. To be exact, $s(w)$ consists of all strings of the forms $a^n b^n aa$ and $a^n b^{n+2}$, where $n \geq 1$.

Now, suppose $L = L(0^*)$, that is, the set of all strings of 0's. Then $s(L) = \big(s(0)\big)^*$. This language is the set of all strings of the form

$$a^{n_1} b^{n_1} a^{n_2} b^{n_2} \cdots a^{n_k} b^{n_k}$$

for some $k \geq 0$ and any sequence of choices of positive integers $n_1, n_2, \ldots, n_k$. It includes strings such as ϵ, $aabbaaabbb$, and $abaabbabab$. $\square$

Theorem 7.23: If L is a context-free language over alphabet Σ, and s is a substitution on Σ such that $s(a)$ is a CFL for each a in Σ, then $s(L)$ is a CFL.

PROOF: The essential idea is that we may take a CFG for L and replace each terminal a by the start symbol of a CFG for language $s(a)$. The result is a single CFG that generates $s(L)$. However, there are a few details that must be gotten right to make this idea work.

More formally, start with grammars for each of the relevant languages, say $G = (V, \Sigma, P, S)$ for L and $G_a = (V_a, T_a, P_a, S_a)$ for each a in Σ. Since we can choose any names we wish for variables, let us make sure that the sets of variables are disjoint; that is, there is no symbol A that is in two or more of V and any of the V_a's. The purpose of this choice of names is to make sure that when we combine the productions of the various grammars into one set of productions, we cannot get accidental mixing of the productions from two grammars and thus have derivations that do not resemble the derivations in any of the given grammars.

We construct a new grammar $G' = (V', T', P', S)$ for $s(L)$, as follows:

- V' is the union of V and all the V_a's for a in Σ.

- T' is the union of all the T_a's for a in Σ.

- P' consists of:

    1. All productions in any P_a, for a in Σ.
    2. The productions of P, but with each terminal a in their bodies replaced by S_a everywhere a occurs.

Thus, all parse trees in grammar G' start out like parse trees in G, but instead of generating a yield in Σ^*, there is a frontier in the tree where all nodes have labels that are S_a for some a in Σ. Then, dangling from each such node is a parse tree of G_a, whose yield is a terminal string that is in the language $s(a)$. The typical parse tree is suggested in Fig. 7.8.

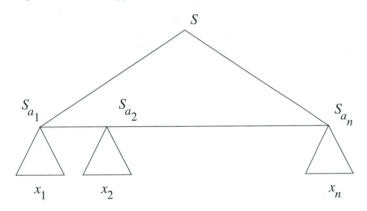

Figure 7.8: A parse tree in G' begins with a parse tree in G and finishes with many parse trees, each in one of the grammars G_a

Now, we must prove that this construction works, in the sense that G' generates the language $s(L)$. Formally:

- A string w is in $L(G')$ if and only if w is in $s(L)$.

(If) Suppose w is in $s(L)$. Then there is some string $x = a_1 a_2 \cdots a_n$ in L, and strings x_i in $s(a_i)$ for $i = 1, 2, \ldots, n$, such that $w = x_1 x_2 \cdots x_n$. Then the portion of G' that comes from the productions of G with S_a substituted for each a will generate a string that looks like x, but with S_a in place of each a. This string is $S_{a_1} S_{a_2} \cdots S_{a_n}$. This part of the derivation of w is suggested by the upper triangle in Fig. 7.8.

Since the productions of each G_a are also productions of G', the derivation of x_i from S_{a_i} is also a derivation in G'. The parse trees for these derivations are suggested by the lower triangles in Fig. 7.8. Since the yield of this parse tree of G' is $x_1 x_2 \cdots x_n = w$, we conclude that w is in $L(G')$.

(Only-if) Now suppose w is in $L(G')$. We claim that the parse tree for w must look like the tree of Fig. 7.8. The reason is that the variables of each of the grammars G and G_a for a in Σ are disjoint. Thus, the top of the tree, starting from variable S, must use only productions of G until some symbol S_a is derived, and below that S_a only productions of grammar G_a may be used. As a result, whenever w has a parse tree T, we can identify a string $a_1 a_2 \cdots a_n$ in $L(G)$, and strings x_i in language $s(a_i)$, such that

1. $w = x_1 x_2 \cdots x_n$, and

2. The string $S_{a_1} S_{a_2} \cdots S_{a_n}$ is the yield of a tree that is formed from T by deleting some subtrees (as suggested by Fig. 7.8).

But the string $x_1 x_2 \cdots x_n$ is in $s(L)$, since it is formed by substituting strings x_i for each of the a_i's. Thus, we conclude w is in $s(L)$. □

7.3.2 Applications of the Substitution Theorem

There are several familiar closure properties, which we studied for regular languages, that we can show for CFL's using Theorem 7.23. We shall list them all in one theorem.

Theorem 7.24: The context-free languages are closed under the following operations:

1. Union.

2. Concatenation.

3. Closure (*), and positive closure ($^+$).

4. Homomorphism.

PROOF: Each requires only that we set up the proper substitution. The proofs below each involve substitution of context-free languages into other context-free languages, and therefore produce CFL's by Theorem 7.23.

1. *Union:* Let L_1 and L_2 be CFL's. Then $L_1 \cup L_2$ is the language $s(L)$, where L is the language $\{1, 2\}$, and s is the substitution defined by $s(1) = L_1$ and $s(2) = L_2$.

2. *Concatenation:* Again let L_1 and L_2 be CFL's. Then $L_1 L_2$ is the language $s(L)$, where L is the language $\{12\}$, and s is the same substitution as in case (1).

3. *Closure and positive closure:* If L_1 is a CFL, L is the language $\{1\}^*$, and s is the substitution $s(1) = L_1$, then $L_1^* = s(L)$. Similarly, if L is instead the language $\{1\}^+$, then $L_1^+ = s(L)$.

4. Suppose L is a CFL over alphabet Σ, and h is a homomorphism on Σ. Let s be the substitution that replaces each symbol a in Σ by the language consisting of the one string that is $h(a)$. That is, $s(a) = \{h(a)\}$, for all a in Σ. Then $h(L) = s(L)$.

□

7.3.3 Reversal

The CFL's are also closed under reversal. We cannot use the substitution theorem, but there is a simple construction using grammars.

Theorem 7.25: If L is a CFL, then so is L^R.

PROOF: Let $L = L(G)$ for some CFL $G = (V, T, P, S)$. Construct $G^R = (V, T, P^R, S)$, where P^R is the "reverse" of each production in P. That is, if $A \rightarrow \alpha$ is a production of G, then $A \rightarrow \alpha^R$ is a production of G^R. It is an easy induction on the lengths of derivations in G and G^R to show that $L(G^R) = L^R$. Essentially, all the sentential forms of G^R are reverses of sentential forms of G, and vice-versa. We leave the formal proof as an exercise. □

7.3.4 Intersection With a Regular Language

The CFL's are not closed under intersection. Here is a simple example that proves they are not.

Example 7.26: We learned in Example 7.19 that the language

$$L = \{0^n 1^n 2^n \mid n \geq 1\}$$

is not a context-free language. However, the following two languages *are* context-free:

$$L_1 = \{0^n 1^n 2^i \mid n \geq 1, i \geq 1\}$$
$$L_2 = \{0^i 1^n 2^n \mid n \geq 1, i \geq 1\}$$

A grammar for L_1 is:

$$S \rightarrow AB$$
$$A \rightarrow 0A1 \mid 01$$
$$B \rightarrow 2B \mid 2$$

In this grammar, A generates all strings of the form $0^n 1^n$, and B generates all strings of 2's. A grammar for L_2 is:

$$S \rightarrow AB$$
$$A \rightarrow 0A \mid 0$$
$$B \rightarrow 1B2 \mid 12$$

It works similarly, but with A generating any string of 0's, and B generating matching strings of 1's and 2's.

However, $L = L_1 \cap L_2$. To see why, observe that L_1 requires that there be the same number of 0's and 1's, while L_2 requires the numbers of 1's and 2's to be equal. A string in both languages must have equal numbers of all three symbols and thus be in L.

If the CFL's were closed under intersection, then we could prove the false statement that L is context-free. We conclude by contradiction that the CFL's are not closed under intersection. □

On the other hand, there is a weaker claim we can make about intersection. The context-free languages are closed under the operation of "intersection with a regular language." The formal statement and proof is in the next theorem.

Theorem 7.27: If L is a CFL and R is a regular language, then $L \cap R$ is a CFL.

PROOF: This proof requires the pushdown-automaton representation of CFL's, as well as the finite-automaton representation of regular languages, and generalizes the proof of Theorem 4.8, where we ran two finite automata "in parallel" to get the intersection of their languages. Here, we run a finite automaton "in parallel" with a PDA, and the result is another PDA, as suggested in Fig. 7.9.

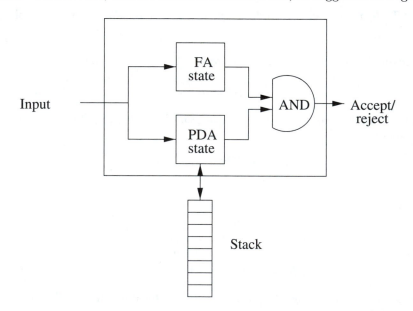

Figure 7.9: A PDA and a FA can run in parallel to create a new PDA

Formally, let
$$P = (Q_P, \Sigma, \Gamma, \delta_P, q_P, Z_0, F_P)$$

be a PDA that accepts L by final state, and let

$$A = (Q_A, \Sigma, \delta_A, q_A, F_A)$$

be a DFA for R. Construct PDA

$$P' = (Q_P \times Q_A, \Sigma, \Gamma, \delta, (q_P, q_A), Z_0, F_P \times F_A)$$

where $\delta\big((q, p), a, X\big)$ is defined to be the set of all pairs $\big((r, s), \gamma\big)$ such that:

1. $s = \hat{\delta}_A(p, a)$, and

2. Pair (r, γ) is in $\delta_P(q, a, X)$.

That is, for each move of PDA P, we can make the same move in PDA P', and in addition, we carry along the state of the DFA A in a second component of the state of P'. Note that a may be a symbol of Σ, or $a = \epsilon$. In the former case, $\hat{\delta}(p, a) = \delta_A(p)$, while if $a = \epsilon$, then $\hat{\delta}(p, a) = p$; i.e., A does not change state while P makes moves on ϵ input.

It is an easy induction on the numbers of moves made by the PDA's that $(q_P, w, Z_0) \overset{*}{\underset{P}{\vdash}} (q, \epsilon, \gamma)$ if and only if $\big((q_P, q_A), w, Z_0\big) \overset{*}{\underset{P'}{\vdash}} \big((q, p), \epsilon, \gamma\big)$, where $p = \hat{\delta}(p_A, w)$. We leave these inductions as exercises. Since (q, p) is an accepting state of P' if and only if q is an accepting state of P, and p is an accepting state of A, we conclude that P' accepts w if and only if both P and A do; i.e., w is in $L \cap R$. □

Example 7.28: In Fig. 6.6 we designed a PDA called F to accept by final state the set of strings of i's and e's that represent minimal violations of the rule regarding how if's and else's may appear in C programs. Call this language L. The PDA F was defined by

$$P_F = (\{p, q, r\}, \{i, e\}, \{Z, X_0\}, \delta_F, p, X_0, \{r\})$$

where δ_F consists of the rules:

1. $\delta_F(p, \epsilon, X_0) = \{(q, ZX_0)\}$.

2. $\delta_F(q, i, Z) = \{(q, ZZ)\}$.

3. $\delta_F(q, e, Z) = \{(q, \epsilon)\}$.

4. $\delta_F(q, \epsilon, X_0) = \{(r, \epsilon, \epsilon)\}$.

Now, let us introduce a finite automaton

$$A = (\{s, t\}, \{i, e\}, \delta_A, s, \{s, t\})$$

that accepts the strings in the language of $\mathbf{i}^* \mathbf{e}^*$, that is, all strings of i's followed by e's. Call this language R. Transition function δ_A is given by the rules:

a) $\delta_A(s, i) = s$.

b) $\delta_A(s, e) = t$.

c) $\delta_A(t, e) = t$.

Strictly speaking, A is not a DFA, as assumed in Theorem 7.27, because it is missing a dead state for the case that we see input i when in state t. However, the same construction works even for an NFA, since the PDA that we construct is allowed to be nondeterministic. In this case, the constructed PDA is actually deterministic, although it will "die" on certain sequences of input.

We shall construct a PDA

$$P = (\{p, q, r\} \times \{s, t\}, \{i, e\}, \{Z, X_0\}, \delta, (p, s), X_0, \{r\} \times \{s, t\})$$

The transitions of δ are listed below and indexed by the rule of PDA F (a number from 1 to 4) and the rule of DFA A (a letter a, b, or c) that gives rise to the rule. In the case that the PDA F makes an ϵ-transition, there is no rule of A used. Note that we construct these rules in a "lazy" way, starting with the state of P that is the start states of F and A, and constructing rules for other states only if we discover that P can enter that pair of states.

1: $\delta\big((p, s), \epsilon, X_0\big) = \{((q, s), ZX_0)\}$.

2a: $\delta\big((q, s), i, Z\big) = \{((q, s), ZZ)\}$.

3b: $\delta\big((q, s), e, Z\big) = \{((q, t), \epsilon)\}$.

4: $\delta\big((q, s), \epsilon, X_0\big) = \{((r, s), \epsilon)\}$. Note: one can prove that this rule is never exercised. The reason is that it is impossible to pop the stack without seeing an e, and as soon as P sees an e the second component of its state becomes t.

3c: $\delta\big((q, t), e, Z\big) = \{((q, t), \epsilon)\}$.

4: $\delta\big((q, t), \epsilon, X_0\big) = \{((r, t), \epsilon)\}$.

The language $L \cap R$ is the set of strings with some number of i's followed by one more e, that is, $\{i^n e^{n+1} \mid n \geq 0\}$. This set is exactly those if-else violations that consist of a block of if's followed by a block of else's. The language is evidently a CFL, generated by the grammar with productions $S \to iSe \mid e$.

Note that the PDA P accepts this language $L \cap R$. After pushing Z onto the stack, it pushes more Z's onto the stack in response to inputs i, staying in state (q, s). As soon as it sees and e, it goes to state (q, t) and starts popping the stack. It dies if it sees an i until X_0 is exposed on the stack. At that point, it spontaneously transitions to state (r, t) and accepts. $\square$

Since we know that the CFL's are not closed under intersection, but are closed under intersection with a regular language, we also know about the set-difference and complementation operations on CFL's. We summarize these properties in one theorem.

Theorem 7.29: The following are true about a CFL's L, L_1, and L_2, and a regular language R.

1. $L - R$ is a context-free language.

2. $\overline{L}$ is not necessarily a context-free language.

3. $L_1 - L_2$ is not necessarily context-free.

PROOF: For (1), note that $L - R = L \cap \overline{R}$. If R is regular, so is $\overline{R}$ regular by Theorem 4.5. Then $L - R$ is a CFL by Theorem 7.27.

For (2), suppose that $\overline{L}$ is always context-free when L is. Then since

$$L_1 \cap L_2 = \overline{\overline{L_1} \cup \overline{L_2}}$$

and the CFL's are closed under union, it would follow that the CFL's are closed under intersection. However, we know they are not from Example 7.26.

Lastly, let us prove (3). We know Σ^* is a CFL for every alphabet Σ; designing a grammar or PDA for this regular language is easy. Thus, if $L_1 - L_2$ were always a CFL when L_1 and L_2 are, it would follow that $\Sigma^* - L$ was always a CFL when L is. However, $\Sigma^* - L$ is $\overline{L}$ when we pick the proper alphabet Σ. Thus, we would contradict (2) and we have proved by contradiction that $L_1 - L_2$ is not necessarily a CFL. $\square$

7.3.5 Inverse Homomorphism

Let us review from Section 4.2.4 the operation called "inverse homomorphism." If h is a homomorphism, and L is any language, then $h^{-1}(L)$ is the set of strings w such that $h(w)$ is in L. The proof that regular languages are closed under inverse homomorphism was suggested in Fig. 4.6. There, we showed how to design a finite automaton that processes its input symbols a by applying a homomorphism h to it, and simulating another finite automaton on the sequence of inputs $h(a)$.

We can prove this closure property of CFL's in much the same way, by using PDA's instead of finite automata. However, there is one problem that we face with PDA's that did not arise when we were dealing with finite automata. The action of a finite automaton on a sequence of inputs is a state transition, and thus looks, as far as the constructed automaton is concerned, just like a move that a finite automaton might make on a single input symbol.

When the automaton is a PDA, in contrast, a sequence of moves might not look like a move on one input symbol. In particular, in n moves, the PDA can pop n symbols off its stack, while one move can only pop one symbol. Thus, the construction for PDA's that is analogous to Fig. 4.6 is somewhat more complex; it is sketched in Fig. 7.10. The key additional idea is that after input a is read, $h(a)$ is placed in a "buffer." The symbols of $h(a)$ are used one at a time, and fed to the PDA being simulated. Only when the buffer is empty does the constructed PDA read another of its input symbols and apply the homomorphism to it. We shall formalize this construction in the next theorem.

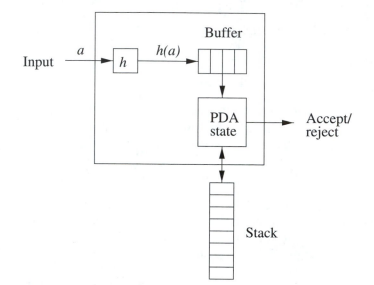

Figure 7.10: Constructing a PDA to accept the inverse homomorphism of what a given PDA accepts

Theorem 7.30: Let L be a CFL and h a homomorphism. Then $h^{-1}(L)$ is a CFL.

PROOF: Suppose h applies to symbols of alphabet Σ and produces strings in T^*. We also assume that L is a language over alphabet T. As suggested above, we start with a PDA $P = (Q, T, \Gamma, \delta, q_0, Z_0, F)$ that accepts L by final state. We construct a new PDA

$$P' = (Q', \Sigma, \delta', (q_0, \epsilon), Z_0, F \times \{\epsilon\}) \tag{7.1}$$

where:

1. Q' is the set of pairs (q, x) such that:

   (a) q is a state in Q, and

   (b) x is a suffix (not necessarily proper) of some string $h(a)$ for some input symbol a in Σ.

That is, the first component of the state of P' is the state of P, and the second component is the buffer. We assume that the buffer will periodically be loaded with a string $h(a)$, and then allowed to shrink from the front, as we use its symbols to feed the simulated PDA P. Note that since Σ is finite, and $h(a)$ is finite for all a, there are only a finite number of states for P'.

2. δ' is defined by the following rules:

   (a) $\delta'\big((q, \epsilon), a, X\big) = \{\big((q, h(a)), X\big)\}$ for all symbols a in Σ, all states q in Q, and stack symbols X in Γ. Note that a cannot be ϵ here. When the buffer is empty, P' can consume its next input symbol a and place $h(a)$ in the buffer.

   (b) If $\delta(q, b, X)$ contains (p, γ), where b is in T or $b = \epsilon$, then

   $$\delta'\big((q, bx), \epsilon, X\big)$$

   contains $\big((p, x), \gamma\big)$. That is, P' always has the option of simulating a move of P, using the front of its buffer. If b is a symbol in T, then the buffer must not be empty, but if $b = \epsilon$, then the buffer can be empty.

3. Note that, as defined in (7.1), the start state of P' is (q_0, ϵ); i.e., P' starts in the start state of P with an empty buffer.

4. Likewise, the accepting states of P', as per (7.1), are those states (q, ϵ) such that q is an accepting state of P.

The following statement characterizes the relationship between P' and P:

- $(q_0, h(w), Z_0) \overset{*}{\underset{P}{\vdash}} (p, \epsilon, \gamma)$ if and only if $\big((q_0, \epsilon), w, Z_0\big) \overset{*}{\underset{P'}{\vdash}} \big((p, \epsilon), \epsilon, \gamma\big)$.

The proofs in both directions are inductions on the number of moves made by the two automata. In the "if" portion, one needs to observe that once the buffer of P' is nonempty, it cannot read another input symbol and must simulate P, until the buffer has become empty (although when the buffer is empty, it may still simulate P). We leave further details as an exercise.

Once we accept this relationship between P' and P, we note that P accepts $h(w)$ if and only if P' accepts w, because of the way the accepting states of P' are defined. Thus, $L(P') = h^{-1}\big(L(P)\big)$. $\square$

7.3.6 Exercises for Section 7.3

Exercise 7.3.1: Show that the CFL's are closed under the following operations:

* a) *init*, defined in Exercise 4.2.6(c). *Hint:* Start with a CNF grammar for the language L.

*! b) The operation L/a, defined in Exercise 4.2.2. *Hint*: Again, start with a CNF grammar for L.

!! c) *cycle*, defined in Exercise 4.2.11. *Hint*: Try a PDA-based construction.

Exercise 7.3.2: Consider the following two languages:

$$L_1 = \{a^n b^{2n} c^m \mid n, m \geq 0\}$$
$$L_2 = \{a^n b^m c^{2m} \mid n, m \geq 0\}$$

a) Show that each of these languages is context-free by giving grammars for each.

! b) Is $L_1 \cap L_2$ a CFL? Justify your answer.

!! **Exercise 7.3.3:** Show that the CFL's are *not* closed under the following operations:

* a) *min*, as defined in Exercise 4.2.6(a).

b) *max*, as defined in Exercise 4.2.6(b).

c) *half*, as defined in Exercise 4.2.8.

d) *alt*, as defined in Exercise 4.2.7.

Exercise 7.3.4: The *shuffle* of two strings w and x is the set of all strings that one can get by interleaving the positions of w and x in any way. More precisely, *shuffle*(w, x) is the set of strings z such that

1. Each position of z can be assigned to w or x, but not both.

2. The positions of z assigned to w form w when read from left to right.

3. The positions of z assigned to x form x when read from left to right.

For example, if $w = 01$ and $x = 110$, then *shuffle*$(01, 110)$ is the set of strings $\{01110, 01101, 10110, 10101, 11010, 11001\}$. To illustrate the necessary reasoning, the third string, 10110, is justified by assigning the second and fifth positions to 01 and positions one, three, and four to 110. The first string, 01110 has three justifications. Assign the first position and either the second, third, or fourth to 01, and the other three to 110. We can also define the shuffle of languages, *shuffle*(L_1, L_2) to the the union over all pairs of strings, w from L_1 and x from L_2, of *shuffle*(w, x).

a) What is *shuffle*$(00, 111)$?

* b) What is *shuffle*(L_1, L_2) if $L_1 = L(0^*)$ and $L_2 = \{0^n 1^n \mid n \geq 0\}$.

*! c) Show that if L_1 and L_2 are both regular languages, then so is

$$shuffle(L_1, L_2)$$

Hint: Start with DFA's for L_1 and L_2.

! d) Show that if L is a CFL and R is a regular language, then $shuffle(L, R)$ is a CFL. *Hint*: start with a PDA for L and a DFA for R.

!! e) Give a counterexample to show that if L_1 and L_2 are both CFL's, then $shuffle(L_1, L_2)$ need not be a CFL.

*!! **Exercise 7.3.5**: A string y is said to be a *permutation* of the string x if the symbols of y can be reordered to make x. For instance, the permutations of string $x = 011$ are 110, 101, and 011. If L is a language, then $perm(L)$ is the set of strings that are permutations of strings in L. For example, if $L = \{0^n 1^n \mid n \geq 0\}$, then $perm(L)$ is the set of strings with equal numbers of 0's and 1's.

   a) Give an example of a regular language L over alphabet $\{0, 1\}$ such that $perm(L)$ is not regular. Justify your answer. *Hint*: Try to find a regular language whose permutations are all strings with an equal number of 0's and 1's.

   b) Give an example of a regular language L over alphabet $\{0, 1, 2\}$ such that $perm(L)$ is not context-free.

   c) Prove that for every regular language L over a two-symbol alphabet, $perm(L)$ is context-free.

Exercise 7.3.6: Give the formal proof of Theorem 7.25: that the CFL's are closed under reversal.

Exercise 7.3.7: Complete the proof of Theorem 7.27 by showing that

$$(q_P, w, Z_0) \stackrel{*}{\underset{P}{\vdash}} (q, \epsilon, \gamma)$$

if and only if $((q_P, q_A), w, Z_0) \stackrel{*}{\underset{P'}{\vdash}} ((q, p), \epsilon, \gamma)$ and $p = \hat{\delta}(p_A, w)$.

7.4 Decision Properties of CFL's

Now, let us consider what kinds of questions we can answer about context-free languages. In analogy with Section 4.3 about decision properties of the regular languages, our starting point for a question is always some representation of a CFL — either a grammar or a PDA. Since we know from Section 6.3 that we can convert between grammars and PDA's, we may assume we are given either representation of a CFL, whichever is more convenient.

We shall discover that very little can be decided about a CFL; the major tests we are able to make are whether the language is empty and whether a given string is in the language. We thus close the section with a brief discussion of the kinds of problems that we shall later show (in Chapter 9) are "undecidable," i.e., they have no algorithm. We begin this section with some observations about the complexity of converting between the grammar and PDA notations for a language. These calculations enter into any question of how efficiently we can decide a property of CFL's with a given representation.

7.4.1   Complexity of Converting Among CFG's and PDA's

Before proceeding to the algorithms for deciding questions about CFL's, let us consider the complexity of converting from one representation to another. The running time of the conversion is a component of the cost of the decision algorithm whenever the language is given in a form other than the one for which the algorithm is designed.

In what follows, we shall let n be the length of the entire representation of a PDA or CFG. Using this parameter as the representation of the size of the grammar or automaton is "coarse," in the sense that some algorithms have a running time that could be described more precisely in terms of more specific parameters, such as the number of variables of a grammar or the sum of the lengths of the stack strings that appear in the transition function of a PDA.

However, the total-length measure is sufficient to distinguish the most important issues: is an algorithm linear in the length (i.e., does it take little more time than it takes to read its input), is it exponential in the length (i.e., you can perform the conversion only for rather small examples), or is it some nonlinear polynomial (i.e., you can run the algorithm, even for large examples, but the time is often quite significant).

There are several conversions we have seen so far that are linear in the size of the input. Since they take linear time, the representation that they produce as output is not only produced quickly, but it is of size comparable to the input size. These conversions are:

1. Converting a CFG to a PDA, by the algorithm of Theorem 6.13.

2. Converting a PDA that accepts by final state to a PDA that accepts by empty stack, using the construction of Theorem 6.11.

3. Converting a PDA that accepts by empty stack to a PDA that accepts by final state, using the construction of Theorem 6.9.

On the other hand, the running time of the conversion from a PDA to a grammar (Theorem 6.14) is much more complex. First, note that n, the total length of the input, is surely an upper bound on the number of states and stack symbols, so there cannot be more than n^3 variables of the form $[pXq]$ constructed for the grammar. However, the running time of the conversion can be exponential, if there is a transition of the PDA that puts a large number of symbols on the stack. Note that one rule could place almost n symbols on the stack.

If we review the construction of grammar productions from a rule like "$\delta(q, a, X)$ contains $(r_0, Y_1 Y_2 \cdots Y_k)$," we note that it gives rise to a collection of productions of the form $[qXr_k] \rightarrow [r_0 Y_1 r_1][r_1 Y_2 r_2] \cdots [r_{k-1} Y_k r_k]$ for all lists of states $r_1, r_2, \ldots, r_k$. As k could be close to n, and there could be close to n states, the total number of productions grows as n^n. We cannot carry out such a construction for reasonably sized PDA's if the PDA has even one long stack string to write.

Fortunately, this worst case never has to occur. As was suggested by Exercise 6.2.8, we can break the pushing of a long string of stack symbols into a sequence of at most n steps that each pushes one symbol. That is, if $\delta(q, a, X)$ contains $(r_0, Y_1 Y_2 \cdots Y_k)$, we may introduce new states $p_2, p_3, \ldots, p_{k-1}$. Then, we replace $(r_0, Y_1 Y_2 \cdots Y_k)$ in $\delta(q, a, X)$ by $(p_{k-1}, Y_{k-1} Y_k)$, and introduce the new transitions

$$\delta(p_{k-1}, Y_{k-1}) = \{(p_{k-2}, Y_{k-2} Y_{k-1})\}, \; \delta(p_{k-2}, Y_{k-2}) = \{(p_{k-3}, Y_{k-3} Y_{k-2})\}$$

and so on, down to $\delta(p_2, Y_2) = \{(r_0, Y_1 Y_2)\}$.

Now, no transition has more than two stack symbols. We have added at most n new states, and the total length of all the transition rules of δ has grown by at most a constant factor; i.e., it is still $O(n)$. There are $O(n)$ transition rules, and each generates $O(n^2)$ productions, since there are only two states that need to be chosen in the productions that come from each rule. Thus, the constructed grammar has length $O(n^3)$ and can be constructed in cubic time. We summarize this informal analysis in the theorem below.

Theorem 7.31: There is an $O(n^3)$ algorithm that takes a PDA P whose representation has length n and produces a CFG of length at most $O(n^3)$. This CFG generates the same language as P accepts by empty stack. Optionally, we can cause G to generate the language that P accepts by final state. $\square$

7.4.2 Running Time of Conversion to Chomsky Normal Form

As decision algorithms may depend on first putting a CFG into Chomsky Normal Form, we should also look at the running time of the various algorithms that we used to convert an arbitrary grammar to a CNF grammar. Most of the steps preserve, up to a constant factor, the length of the grammar's description; that is, starting with a grammar of length n they produce another grammar of length $O(n)$. The good news is summarized in the following list of observations:

1. Using the proper algorithm (See Section 7.4.3), detecting the reachable and generating symbols of a grammar can be done in $O(n)$ time. Eliminating the resulting useless symbols takes $O(n)$ time and does not increase the size of the grammar.

2. Constructing the unit pairs and eliminating unit productions, as in Section 7.1.4, takes $O(n^2)$ time and the resulting grammar has length $O(n^2)$.

3. The replacement of terminals by variables in production bodies, as in Section 7.1.5 (Chomsky Normal Form), takes $O(n)$ time and results in a grammar whose length is $O(n)$.

4. The breaking of production bodies of length 3 or more into bodies of length 2, as carried out in Section 7.1.5 also takes $O(n)$ time and results in a grammar of length $O(n)$.

The bad news concerns the construction of Section 7.1.3, where we eliminate ϵ-productions. If we have a production body of length k, we could construct from that one production $2^k - 1$ productions for the new grammar. Since k could be proportional to n, this part of the construction could take $O(2^n)$ time and result in a grammar whose length is $O(2^n)$.

To avoid this exponential blowup, we need only to bound the length of production bodies. The trick of Section 7.1.5 can be applied to any production body, not just to one without terminals. Thus, we recommend, as a preliminary step before eliminating ϵ-productions, the breaking of all long production bodies into a sequence of productions with bodies of length 2. This step takes $O(n)$ time and grows the grammar only linearly. The construction of Section 7.1.3, to eliminate ϵ-productions, will work on bodies of length at most 2 in such a way that the running time is $O(n)$ and the resulting grammar has length $O(n)$.

With this modification to the overall CNF construction, the only step that is not linear is the elimination of unit productions. As that step is $O(n^2)$, we conclude the following:

Theorem 7.32 : Given a grammar G of length n, we can find an equivalent Chomsky-Normal-Form grammar for G in time $O(n^2)$; the resulting grammar has length $O(n^2)$. $\Box$

7.4.3 Testing Emptiness of CFL's

We have already seen the algorithm for testing whether a CFL L is empty. Given a grammar G for the language L, use the algorithm of Section 7.1.2 to decide whether the start symbol S of G is generating, i.e., whether S derives at least one string. L is empty if and only if S is not generating.

Because of the importance of this test, we shall consider in detail how much time it takes to find all the generating symbols of a grammar G. Suppose the length of G is n. Then there could be on the order of n variables, and each pass of the inductive discovery of generating variables could take $O(n)$ time to examine all the productions of G. If only one new generating variable is discovered on each pass, then there could be $O(n)$ passes. Thus, a naive implementation of the generating-symbols test is $O(n^2)$.

However, there is a more careful algorithm that sets up a data structure in advance to make our discovery of generating symbols take $O(n)$ time only. The data structure, suggested in Fig. 7.11, starts with an array indexed by the variables, as shown on the left, which tells whether or not we have established that the variable is generating. In Fig. 7.11, the array suggests that we have discovered B is generating, but we do not know whether or not A is generating. At the end of the algorithm, each question mark will become "no," since any variable not discovered by the algorithm to be generating is in fact nongenerating.

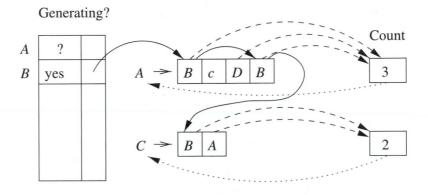

Figure 7.11: Data structure for the linear-time emptiness test

The productions are preprocessed by setting up several kinds of useful links. First, for each variable there is a chain of all the positions in which that variable appears. For instance, the chain for variable B is suggested by the solid lines. For each production, there is a count of the number of positions holding variables whose ability to generate a terminal string has not yet been taken into account. The dashed lines suggest links from the productions to their counts. The counts shown in Fig. 7.11 suggests that we have not yet taken any of the variables into account, even though we just established that B is generating.

Suppose that we have discovered that B is generating. We go down the list of positions of the bodies holding B. For each such position, we decrement the count for that production by 1; there is now one fewer position we need to find generating in order to conclude that the variable at the head is also generating.

If a count reaches 0, then we know the head variable is generating. A link, suggested by the dotted lines, gets us to the variable, and we may put that variable on a queue of generating variables whose consequences need to be explored (as we just did for variable B). This queue is not shown.

We must argue that this algorithm takes $O(n)$ time. The important points are as follows:

- Since there are at most n variables in a grammar of size n, creation and initialization of the array takes $O(n)$ time.

- There are at most n productions, and their total length is at most n, so initialization of the links and counts suggested in Fig. 7.11 can be done in $O(n)$ time.

- When we discover a production has count 0 (i.e., all positions of its body are generating), the work involved can be put into two categories:

Other Uses for the Linear Emptiness Test

The same data structure and accounting trick that we used in Section 7.4.3 to test whether a variable is generating can be used to make some of the other tests of Section 7.1 linear-time. Two important examples are:

1. Which symbols are reachable?

2. Which symbols are nullable?

---

1. Work done for that production: discovering the count is 0, finding which variable, say A, is at the head, checking whether it is already known to be generating, and putting it on the queue if not. All these steps are $O(1)$ for each production, and so at most $O(n)$ work of this type is done in total.

2. Work done when visiting the positions of the production bodies that have the head variable A. This work is proportional to the number of positions with A. Therefore, the aggregate amount of work done processing all generating symbols is proportional to the sum of the lengths of the production bodies, and that is $O(n)$.

We conclude that the total work done by this algorithm is $O(n)$.

7.4.4   Testing Membership in a CFL

We can also decide membership of a string w in a CFL L. There are several inefficient ways to make the test; they take time that is exponential in $|w|$, assuming a grammar or PDA for the language L is given and its size is treated as a constant, independent of w. For instance, start by converting whatever representation of L we are given into a CNF grammar for L. As the parse trees of a Chomsky-Normal-Form grammar are binary trees, if w is of length n then there will be exactly $2n - 1$ nodes labeled by variables in the tree (that result has an easy, inductive proof, which we leave to you). The number of possible trees and node-labelings is thus "only" exponential in n, so in principle we can list them all and check to see if any of them yields w.

There is a much more efficient technique based on the idea of "dynamic programming," which may also be known to you as a "table-filling algorithm" or "tabulation." This algorithm, known as the *CYK Algorithm*,[3] starts with a CNF grammar $G = (V, T, P, S)$ for a language L. The input to the algorithm is a string $w = a_1 a_2 \cdots a_n$ in T^*. In $O(n^3)$ time, the algorithm constructs a table

---

[3]It is named after three people, each of whom independently discovered essentially the same idea: J. Cocke, D. Younger, and T. Kasami.

that tells whether w is in L. Note that when computing this running time, the grammar itself is considered fixed, and its size contributes only a constant factor to the running time, which is measured in terms of the length of the string w whose membership in L is being tested.

In the CYK algorithm, we construct a triangular table, as suggested in Fig. 7.12. The horizontal axis corresponds to the positions of the string $w = a_1 a_2 \cdots a_n$, which we have supposed has length 5. The table entry X_{ij} is the set of variables A such that $A \overset{*}{\Rightarrow} a_i a_{i+1} \cdots a_j$. Note in particular, that we are interested in whether S is in the set X_{1n}, because that is the same as saying $S \overset{*}{\Rightarrow} w$, i.e., w is in L.

X_{15}

X_{14} X_{25}

X_{13} X_{24} X_{35}

X_{12} X_{23} X_{34} X_{45}

X_{11} X_{22} X_{33} X_{44} X_{55}

a_1 a_2 a_3 a_4 a_5

Figure 7.12: The table constructed by the CYK algorithm

To fill the table, we work row-by-row, upwards. Notice that each row corresponds to one length of substrings; the bottom row is for strings of length 1, the second-from-bottom row for strings of length 2, and so on, until the top row corresponds to the one substring of length n, which is w itself. It takes $O(n)$ time to compute any one entry of the table, by a method we shall discuss next. Since there are $n(n + 1)/2$ table entries, the whole table-construction process takes $O(n^3)$ time. Here is the algorithm for computing the X_{ij}'s:

BASIS: We compute the first row as follows. Since the string beginning and ending at position i is just the terminal a_i, and the grammar is in CNF, the only way to derive the string a_i is to use a production of the form $A \rightarrow a_i$. Thus, X_{ii} is the set of variables A such that $A \rightarrow a_i$ is a production of G.

INDUCTION: Suppose we want to compute X_{ij}, which is in row $j - i + 1$, and we have computed all the X's in the rows below. That is, we know about all strings shorter than $a_i a_{i+1} \cdots a_j$, and in particular we know about all proper prefixes and proper suffixes of that string. As $j - i > 0$ may be assumed (since the case $i = j$ is the basis), we know that any derivation $A \overset{*}{\Rightarrow} a_i a_{i+1} \cdots a_j$ must start out with some step $A \Rightarrow BC$. Then, B derives some prefix of $a_i a_{i+1} \cdots a_j$, say $B \overset{*}{\Rightarrow} a_i a_{i+1} \cdots a_k$, for some $k < j$. Also, C must then derive the remainder of $a_i a_{i+1} \cdots a_j$, that is, $C \overset{*}{\Rightarrow} a_{k+1} a_{k+2} \cdots a_j$.

We conclude that in order for A to be in X_{ij}, we must find variables B and C, and integer k such that:

1. $i \leq k < j$.

2. B is in X_{ik}.

3. C is in $X_{k+1,j}$.

4. $A \to BC$ is a production of G.

Finding such variables A requires us to compare at most n pairs of previously computed sets: $(X_{ii}, X_{i+1,j})$, $(X_{i,i+1}, X_{i+2,j})$, and so on, until $(X_{i,j-1}, X_{jj})$. The pattern, in which we go up the column below X_{ij} at the same time we go down the diagonal, is suggested by Fig. 7.13.

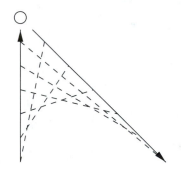

Figure 7.13: Computation of X_{ij} requires matching the column below with the diagonal to the right

Theorem 7.33 : The algorithm described above correctly computes X_{ij} for all i and j; thus w is in $L(G)$ if and only if S is in X_{1n}. Moreover, the running time of the algorithm is $O(n^3)$.

PROOF: The reason the algorithm finds the correct sets of variables was explained as we introduced the basis and inductive parts of the algorithm. For the running time, note that there are $O(n^2)$ entries to compute, and each involves comparing and computing with n pairs of entries. It is important to remember that, although there can be many variables in each set X_{ij}, the grammar G is fixed and the number of its variables does not depend on n, the length of the string w whose membership is being tested. Thus, the time to compare two entries X_{ik} and $X_{k+1,j}$, and find variables to go into X_{ij} is $O(1)$. As there are at most n such pairs for each X_{ij}, the total work is $O(n^3)$.   □

Example 7.34: The following are the productions of a CNF grammar G:

$$
\begin{aligned}
S &\rightarrow AB \mid BC \\
A &\rightarrow BA \mid a \\
B &\rightarrow CC \mid b \\
C &\rightarrow AB \mid a
\end{aligned}
$$

We shall test for membership in $L(G)$ the string *baaba*. Figure 7.14 shows the table filled in for this string.

$\{S,A,C\}$

$\quad - \qquad \{S,A,C\}$

$\quad - \qquad \{B\} \qquad \{B\}$

$\{S,A\} \qquad \{B\} \qquad \{S,C\} \qquad \{S,A\}$

$\{B\} \qquad \{A,C\} \qquad \{A,C\} \qquad \{B\} \qquad \{A,C\}$

$\qquad b \qquad\quad a \qquad\quad a \qquad\quad b \qquad\quad a$

Figure 7.14: The table for string *baaba* constructed by the CYK algorithm

To construct the first (lowest) row, we use the basis rule. We have only to consider which variables have a production body a (those variables are A and C) and which variables have body b (only B does). Thus, above those positions holding a we see the entry $\{A, C\}$, and above the positions holding b we see $\{B\}$. That is, $X_{11} = X_{44} = \{B\}$, and $X_{22} = X_{33} = X_{55} = \{A, C\}$.

In the second row we see the values of X_{12}, X_{23}, X_{34}, and X_{45}. For instance, let us see how X_{12} is computed. There is only one way to break the string from positions 1 to 2, which is *ba*, into two nonempty substrings. The first must be position 1 and the second must be position 2. In order for a variable to generate *ba*, it must have a body whose first variable is in $X_{11} = \{B\}$ (i.e., it generates the b) and whose second variable is in $X_{22} = \{A, C\}$ (i.e., it generates the a). This body can only be BA or BC. If we inspect the grammar, we find that the productions $A \rightarrow BA$ and $S \rightarrow BC$ are the only ones with these bodies. Thus, the two heads, A and S, constitute X_{12}.

For a more complex example, consider the computation of X_{24}. We can break the string *aab* that occupies positions 2 through 4 by ending the first string after position 2 or position 3. That is, we may choose $k = 2$ or $k = 3$ in the definition of X_{24}. Thus, we must consider all bodies in $X_{22}X_{34} \cup X_{23}X_{44}$. This set of strings is $\{A, C\}\{S, C\} \cup \{B\}\{B\} = \{AS, AC, CS, CC, BB\}$. Of the

five strings in this set, only CC is a body, and its head is B. Thus, $X_{24} = \{B\}$.
□

7.4.5 Preview of Undecidable CFL Problems

In the next chapters we shall develop a remarkable theory that lets us prove
formally that there are problems we cannot solve by any algorithm that can
run on a computer. We shall use it to show that a number of simple-to-state
questions about grammars and CFL's have no algorithm; they are called "undecidable problems." For now, we shall have to content ourselves with a list
of the most significant undecidable questions about context-free grammars and
languages. The following are undecidable:

1. Is a given CFG G ambiguous?

2. Is a given CFL inherently ambiguous?

3. Is the intersection of two CFL's empty?

4. Are two CFL's the same?

5. Is a given CFL equal to Σ^*, where Σ is the alphabet of this language?

   Notice that the flavor of question (1), about ambiguity, is somewhat different
from the others, in that it is a question about a grammar, not a language. All
the other questions assume that the language is represented by a grammar or
PDA, but the question is about the language(s) defined by the grammar or
PDA. For instance, in contrast to question (1), the second question asks, given
a grammar G (or a PDA, for that matter), does there exist some equivalent
grammar G' that is unambiguous. If G is itself unambiguous, then the answer
is surely "yes," but if G is ambiguous, there could still be some other grammar
G' for the same language that is unambiguous, as we learned about expression
grammars in Example 5.27.

7.4.6 Exercises for Section 7.4

Exercise 7.4.1: Give algorithms to decide the following:

* a) Is $L(G)$ finite, for a given CFG G? *Hint*: Use the pumping lemma.

! b) Does $L(G)$ contain at least 100 strings, for a given CFG G?

!! c) Given a CFG G and one of its variables A, is there any sentential form
   in which A is the first symbol. *Note*: Remember that it is possible for A
   to appear first in the middle of some sentential form but then for all the
   symbols to its left to derive ϵ.

Exercise 7.4.2: Use the technique described in Section 7.4.3 to develop linear-
time algorithms for the following questions about CFG's:

a) Which symbols appear in some sentential form?

b) Which symbols are nullable (derive ϵ)?

Exercise 7.4.3: Using the grammar G of Example 7.34, use the CYK algorithm to determine whether each of the following strings is in $L(G)$:

* a) *ababa.*

b) *baaab.*

c) *aabab.*

* **Exercise 7.4.4:** Show that in any CNF grammar, all parse trees for strings of length n have $2n - 1$ interior nodes (i.e., $2n - 1$ nodes with variables for labels).

! **Exercise 7.4.5:** Modify the CYK algorithm so can report the number of distinct parse trees for the given input, rather than just reporting membership in the language.

7.5 Summary of Chapter 7

✦ *Eliminating Useless Symbols*: A variable can be eliminated from a CFG unless it derives some string of terminals and also appears in at least one string derived from the start symbol. To correctly eliminate such useless symbols, we must first test whether a variable derives a terminal string, and eliminate those that do not, along with all their productions. Only then do we eliminate variables that are not derivable from the start symbol.

✦ *Eliminating ϵ- and Unit-productions*: Given a CFG, we can find another CFG that generates the same language, except for string ϵ, yet has no ϵ-productions (those with body ϵ) or unit productions (those with a single variable as the body).

✦ *Chomsky Normal Form*: Given a CFG that derives at least one nonempty string, we can find another CFG that generates the same language, except for ϵ, and is in Chomsky Normal Form: there are no useless symbols, and every production body consists of either two variables or one terminal.

✦ *The Pumping Lemma*: In any CFL, it is possible to find, in any sufficiently long string of the language, a short substring such that the two ends of that substring can be "pumped" in tandem; i.e., each can be repeated any desired number of times. The strings being pumped are not both ϵ. This lemma, and a more powerful version called Ogden's lemma mentioned in Exercise 7.2.3, allow us to prove many languages not to be context-free.

✦ *Operations That Preserve Context-Free Languages*: The CFL's are closed under substitution, union, concatenation, closure (star), reversal, and inverse homomorphisms. CFL's are not closed under intersection or complementation, but the intersection of a CFL and a regular language is always a CFL.

✦ *Testing Emptiness of a CFL*: Given a CFG, there is an algorithm to tell whether it generates any strings at all. A careful implementation allows this test to be conducted in time that is proportional to the size of the grammar itself.

✦ *Testing Membership in a CFL*: The Cocke-Younger-Kasami algorithm tells whether a given string is in a given context-free language. For a fixed CFL, this test takes time $O(n^3)$, if n is the length of the string being tested.

7.6   References for Chapter 7

Chomsky normal form comes from [2]. Greibach normal form is from [4], although the construction outlined in Exercise 7.1.11 is due to M. C. Paull.

Many of the fundamental properties of context-free languages come from [1]. These ideas include the pumping lemma, basic closure properties, and tests for simple questions such as emptiness and finiteness of a CFL. In addition [6] is the source for the nonclosure under intersection and complementation, and [3] provides additional closure results, including closure of the CFL's under inverse homomorphism. Ogden's lemma comes from [5].

The CYK algorithm has three known independent sources. J. Cocke's work was circulated privately and never published. T. Kasami's rendition of essentially the same algorithm appeared only in an internal US-Air-Force memorandum. However, the work of D. Younger was published conventionally [7].

1. Y. Bar-Hillel, M. Perles, and E. Shamir, "On formal properties of simple phrase-structure grammars," *Z. Phonetik. Sprachwiss. Kommunikationsforsch.* **14** (1961), pp. 143–172.

2. N. Chomsky, "On certain formal properties of grammars," *Information and Control* **2**:2 (1959), pp. 137–167.

3. S. Ginsburg and G. Rose, "Operations which preserve definability in languages," *J. ACM* **10**:2 (1963), pp. 175–195.

4. S. A. Greibach, "A new normal-form theorem for context-free phrase structure grammars," *J. ACM* **12**:1 (1965), pp. 42–52.

5. W. Ogden, "A helpful result for proving inherent ambiguity," *Mathematical Systems Theory* **2**:3 (1969), pp. 31–42.

6. S. Scheinberg, "Note on the boolean properties of context-free languages," *Information and Control* **3**:4 (1960), pp. 372–375.

7. D. H. Younger, "Recognition and parsing of context-free languages in time n^3," *Information and Control* **10**:2 (1967), pp. 189–208.

Chapter 8

Introduction to Turing Machines

In this chapter we change our direction significantly. Until now, we have been interested primarily in simple classes of languages and the ways that they can be used for relatively constrainted problems, such as analyzing protocols, searching text, or parsing programs. Now, we shall start looking at the question of what languages can be defined by any computational device whatsoever. This question is tantamount to the question of what computers can do, since recognizing the strings in a language is a formal way of expressing any problem, and solving a problem is a reasonable surrogate for what it is that computers do.

We begin with an informal argument, using an assumed knowledge of C programming, to show that there are specific problems we cannot solve using a computer. These problems are called "undecidable." We then introduce a venerable formalism for computers, called the Turing machine. While a Turing machine looks nothing like a PC, and would be grossly inefficient should some startup company decide to manufacture and sell them, the Turing machine long has been recognized as an accurate model for what any physical computing device is capable of doing.

In Chapter 9, we use the Turing machine to develop a theory of "undecidable" problems, that is, problems that no computer can solve. We show that a number of problems that are easy to express are in fact undecidable. An example is telling whether a given grammar is ambiguous, and we shall see many others.

8.1 Problems That Computers Cannot Solve

The purpose of this section is to provide an informal, C-programming-based introduction to the proof of a specific problem that computers cannot solve. The particular problem we discuss is whether the first thing a C program prints is `hello, world`. Although we might imagine that simulation of the program would allow us to tell what the program does, we must in reality contend with programs that take an unimaginably long time before making any output at all. This problem — not knowing when, if ever, something will occur — is the ultimate cause of our inability to tell what a program does. However, proving formally that there is no program to do a stated task is quite tricky, and we need to develop some formal mechanics. In this section, we give the intuition behind the formal proofs.

8.1.1 Programs that Print "Hello, World"

In Fig. 8.1 is the first C program met by students who read Kernighan and Ritchie's classic book.[1] It is rather easy to discover that this program prints `hello, world` and terminates. This program is so transparent that it has become a common practice to introduce languages by showing how to write a program to print `hello, world` in those languages.

```
main()
{
    printf("hello, world\n");
}
```

Figure 8.1: Kernighan and Ritchie's hello-world program

However, there are other programs that also print `hello, world`; yet the fact that they do so is far from obvious. Figure 8.2 shows another program that might print `hello, world`. It takes an input n, and looks for positive integer solutions to the equation $x^n + y^n = z^n$. If it finds one, it prints `hello, world`. If it never finds integers x, y, and z to satisfy the equation, then it continues searching forever, and never prints `hello, world`.

To understand what this program does, first observe that `exp` is an auxiliary function to compute exponentials. The main program needs to search through triples (x, y, z) in an order such that we are sure we get to every triple of positive integers eventually. To organize the search properly, we use a fourth variable, `total`, that starts at 3 and, in the while-loop, is increased one unit at a time, eventually reaching any finite integer. Inside the while-loop, we divide `total` into three positive integers x, y, and z, by first allowing x to range from 1 to `total-2`, and within that for-loop allowing y to range from 1 up to one less than what x has not already taken from `total`. What remains, which must be between 1 and `total-2`, is given to z.

In the innermost loop, the triple (x, y, z) is tested to see if $x^n + y^n = z^n$. If so, the program prints `hello, world`, and if not, it prints nothing.

---

[1] B. W. Kernighan and D. M. Ritchie, *The C Programming Language*, 1978, Prentice-Hall, Englewood Cliffs, NJ.

```
int exp(int i, n)
/* computes i to the power n */
{
    int ans, j;
    ans = 1;
    for (j=1; j<=n; j++) ans *= i;
    return(ans);
}

main ()
{
    int n, total, x, y, z;
    scanf("%d", &n);
    total = 3;
    while (1) {
        for (x=1; x<=total-2; x++)
            for (y=1; y<=total-x-1; y++) {
                z = total - x - y;
                if (exp(x,n) + exp(y,n) == exp(z,n))
                    printf("hello, world\n");
            }
        total++;
    }
}
```

Figure 8.2: Fermat's last theorem expressed as a hello-world program

If the value of n that the program reads is 2, then it will eventually find combinations of integers such as $total = 12$, $x = 3$, $y = 4$, and $z = 5$, for which $x^n + y^n = z^n$. Thus, for input 2, the program *does* print hello, world.

However, for any integer $n > 2$, the program will never find a triple of positive integers to satisfy $x^n + y^n = z^n$, and thus will fail to print hello, world. Interestingly, until a few years ago, it was not known whether or not this program would print hello, world for some large integer n. The claim that it would not, i.e., that there are no integer solutions to the equation $x^n + y^n = z^n$ if $n > 2$, was made by Fermat 300 years ago, but no proof was found until quite recently. This statement is often referred to as "Fermat's last theorem."

Let us define the *hello-world problem* to be: determine whether a given C program, with a given input, prints hello, world as the first 12 characters that it prints. In what follows, we often use, as a shorthand, the statement about a program that it prints hello, world to mean that it prints hello, world as the first 12 characters that it prints.

It seems likely that, if it takes mathematicians 300 years to resolve a question

---

Why Undecidable Problems Must Exist

While it is tricky to prove that a specific problem, such as the "hello-world problem" discussed here, must be undecidable, it is quite easy to see why almost all problems must be undecidable by any system that involves programming. Recall that a "problem" is really membership of a string in a language. The number of different languages over any alphabet of more than one symbol is not countable. That is, there is no way to assign integers to the languages such that every language has an integer, and every integer is assigned to one language.

On the other hand programs, being finite strings over a finite alphabet (typically a subset of the ASCII alphabet), *are* countable. That is, we can order them by length, and for programs of the same length, order them lexicographically. Thus, we can speak of the first program, the second program, and in general, the ith program for any integer i.

As a result, we know there are infinitely fewer programs than there are problems. If we picked a language at random, almost certainly it would be an undecidable problem. The only reason that most problems *appear* to be decidable is that we rarely are interested in random problems. Rather, we tend to look at fairly simple, well-structured problems, and indeed these are often decidable. However, even among the problems we are interested in and can state clearly and succinctly, we find many that are undecidable; the hello-world problem is a case in point.

---

about a single, 22-line program, then the general problem of telling whether a given program, on a given input, prints `hello, world` must be hard indeed. In fact, any of the problems that mathematicians have not yet been able to resolve can be turned into a question of the form "does this program, with this input, print `hello, world`? Thus, it would be remarkable indeed if we could write a program that could examine any program P and input I for P, and tell whether P, run with I as its input, would print `hello, world`. We shall prove that no such program exists.

8.1.2   The Hypothetical "Hello, World" Tester

The proof of impossibility of making the hello-world test is a proof by contradiction. That is, we assume there is a program, call it H, that takes as input a program P and an input I, and tells whether P with input I prints `hello, world`. Figure 8.3 is a representation of what H does. In particular, the only output H makes is either to print the three characters `yes` or to print the two characters `no`. It always does one or the other.

If a problem has an algorithm like H, that always tells correctly whether an instance of the problem has answer "yes" or "no," then the problem is said to

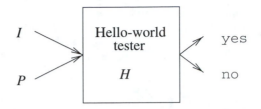

Figure 8.3: A hypothetical program H that is a hello-world detector

be "decidable." Otherwise, the problem is "undecidable." Our goal is to prove that H doesn't exist; i.e., the hello-world problem is undecidable.

In order to prove that statement by contradiction, we are going to make several changes to H, eventually constructing a related program called H_2 that we show does not exist. Since the changes to H are simple transformations that can be done to any C program, the only questionable statement is the existence of H, so it is that assumption we have contradicted.

To simplify our discussion, we shall make a few assumptions about C programs. These assumptions make H's job easier, not harder, so if we can show a "hello-world tester" for these restricted programs does not exist, then surely there is no such tester that could work for a broader class of programs. Our assumptions are:

1. All output is character-based, e.g., we are not using a graphics package or any other facility to make output that is not in the form of characters.

2. All character-based output is performed using `printf`, rather than `put-char()` or another character-based output function.

We now assume that the program H exists. Our first modification is to change the output `no`, which is the response that H makes when its input program P does not print `hello, world` as its first output in response to input I. As soon as H prints "n," we know it will eventually follow with the "o."[2] Thus, we can modify any `printf` statement in H that prints "n" to instead print `hello, world`. Another `printf` statement that prints an "o" but not the "n" is omitted. As a result, the new program, which we call H_1, behaves like H, except it prints `hello, world` exactly when H would print `no`. H_1 is suggested by Fig. 8.4.

Our next transformation on the program is a bit trickier; it is essentially the insight that allowed Alan Turing to prove his undecidability result about Turing machines. Since we are really interested in programs that take other programs as input and tell something about them, we shall restrict H_1 so it:

a) Takes only input P, not P and I.

---

[2] Most likely, the program would put `no` in one `printf`, but it could print the "n" in one `printf` and the "o" in another.

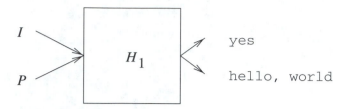

Figure 8.4: H_1 behaves like H, but it says `hello, world` instead of `no`

b) Asks what P would do if its input were its own code, i.e., what would H_1 do on inputs P as program and P as input I as well?

The modifications we must perform on H_1 to produce the program H_2 suggested in Fig. 8.5 are as follows:

1. H_2 first reads the entire input P and stores it in an array A, which it "malloc's" for the purpose.[3]

2. H_2 then simulates H_1, but whenever H_1 would read input from P or I, H_2 reads from the stored copy in A. To keep track of how much of P and I H_1 has read, H_2 can maintain two cursors that mark positions in A.

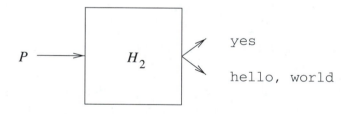

Figure 8.5: H_2 behaves like H_1, but uses its input P as both P and I

We are now ready to prove H_2 cannot exist. Thus, H_1 does not exist, and likewise, H does not exist. The heart of the argument is to envision what H_2 does when given itself as input. This situation is suggested in Fig. 8.6. Recall that H_2, given any program P as input, makes output `yes` if P prints `hello, world` when given itself as input. Also, H_2 prints `hello, world` if P, given itself as input, does not print `hello, world` as its first output.

Suppose that the H_2 represented by the box in Fig. 8.6 makes the output `yes`. Then the H_2 in the box is saying about its input H_2 that H_2, given itself

---

[3]The UNIX `malloc` system function allocates a block of memory of a size specified in the call to `malloc`. This function is used when the amount of storage needed cannot be determined until the program is run, as would be the case if an input of arbitrary length were read. Typically, `malloc` would be called several times, as more and more input is read and progressively more space is needed.

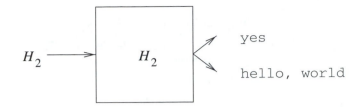

Figure 8.6: What does H_2 do when given itself as input?

as input, prints `hello, world` as its first output. But we just supposed that the first output H_2 makes in this situation is `yes` rather than `hello, world`.

Thus, it appears that in Fig. 8.6 the output of the box is `hello, world`, since it must be one or the other. But if H_2, given itself as input, prints `hello, world` first, then the output of the box in Fig. 8.6 must be `yes`. Whichever output we suppose H_2 makes, we can argue that it makes the other output.

This situation is paradoxical, and we conclude that H_2 cannot exist. As a result, we have contradicted the assumption that H exists. That is, we have proved that no program H can tell whether or not a given program P with input I prints `hello, world` as its first output.

8.1.3 Reducing One Problem to Another

Now, we have one problem — does a given program with given input print `hello, world` as the first thing it prints? — that we know no computer program can solve. A problem that cannot be solved by computer is called *undecidable*. We shall give the formal definition of "undecidable" in Section 9.3, but for the moment, let us use the term informally. Suppose we want to determine whether or not some other problem is solvable by a computer. We can try to write a program to solve it, but if we cannot figure out how to do so, then we might try a proof that there is no such program.

Perhaps we could prove this new problem undecidable by a technique similar to what we did for the hello-world problem: assume there is a program to solve it and develop a paradoxical program that must do two contradictory things, like the program H_2. However, once we have one problem that we know is undecidable, we no longer have to prove the existence of a paradoxical situation. It is sufficient to show that if we could solve the new problem, then we could use that solution to solve a problem we already know is undecidable. The strategy is suggested in Fig. 8.7; the technique is called the *reduction* of P_1 to P_2.

Suppose that we know problem P_1 is undecidable, and P_2 is a new problem that we would like to prove is undecidable as well. We suppose that there is a program represented in Fig. 8.7 by the diamond labeled "decide"; this program prints `yes` or `no`, depending on whether its input instance of problem P_2 is or is not in the language of that problem.[4]

---

[4]Recall that a problem is really a language. When we talked of the problem of deciding

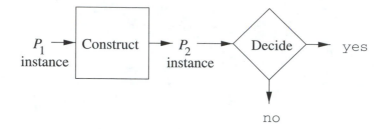

Figure 8.7: If we could solve problem P_2, then we could use its solution to solve problem P_1

In order to make a proof that problem P_2 is undecidable, we have to invent a construction, represented by the square box in Fig. 8.7, that converts instances of P_1 to instances of P_2 that have the same answer. That is, any string in the language P_1 is converted to some string in the language P_2, and any string over the alphabet of P_1 that is *not* in the language P_1 is converted to a string that is not in the language P_2. Once we have this construction, we can solve P_1 as follows:

1. Given an instance of P_1, that is, given a string w that may or may not be in the language P_1, apply the construction algorithm to produce a string x.

2. Test whether x is in P_2, and give the same answer about w and P_1.

If w is in P_1, then x is in P_2, so this algorithm says **yes**. If w is not in P_1, then x is not in P_2, and the algorithm says **no**. Either way, it says the truth about w. Since we assumed that no algorithm to decide membership of a string in P_1 exists, we have a proof by contradiction that the hypothesized decision algorithm for P_2 does not exist; i.e., P_2 is undecidable.

Example 8.1 : Let us use this methodology to show that the question "does program Q, given input y, ever call function `foo`" is undecidable. Note that Q may not have a function `foo`, in which case the problem is easy, but the hard cases are when Q has a function `foo` but may or may not reach a call to `foo` with input y. Since we only know one undecidable problem, the role of P_1 in Fig. 8.7 will be played by the hello-world problem. P_2 will be the *calls-foo problem* just mentioned. We suppose there is a program that solves the calls-foo problem. Our job is to design an algorithm that converts the hello-world problem into the calls-foo problem.

That is, given program Q and its input y, we must construct a program R and an input z such that R, with input z, calls `foo` if and only if Q with input y prints `hello, world`. The construction is not hard:

---

whether a given program and input results in `hello, world` as the first output, we were really talking about strings consisting of a C source program followed by whatever input file(s) the program reads. This set of strings is a language over the alphabet of ASCII characters.

Can a Computer Really Do All That?

If we examine a program such as Fig. 8.2, we might ask whether it really searches for counterexamples to Fermat's last theorem. After all, integers are only 32 bits long in the typical computer, and if the smallest counterexample involved integers in the billions, there would be an overflow error before the solution was found. In fact, one could argue that a computer with 128 megabytes of main memory and a 30 gigabyte disk, has "only" $256^{30128000000}$ states, and is thus a finite automaton.

However, treating computers as finite automata (or treating brains as finite automata, which is where the FA idea originated), is unproductive. The number of states involved is so large, and the limits so unclear, that you don't draw any useful conclusions. In fact, there is every reason to believe that, if we wanted to, we could expand the set of states of a computer arbitrarily.

For instance, we can represent integers as linked lists of digits, of arbitrary length. If we run out of memory, the program can print a request for a human to dismount its disk, store it, and replace it by an empty disk. As time goes on, the computer could print requests to swap among as many disks as the computer needs. This program would be far more complex than that of Fig. 8.2, but not beyond our capabilities to write. Similar tricks would allow any other program to avoid finite limitations on the size of memory or on the size of integers or other data items.

---

1. If Q has a function called `foo`, rename it and all calls to that function. Clearly the new program Q_1 does exactly what Q does.

2. Add to Q_1 a function `foo`. This function does nothing, and is not called. The resulting program is Q_2.

3. Modify Q_2 to remember the first 12 characters that it prints, storing them in a global array A. Let the resulting program be Q_3.

4. Modify Q_3 so that whenever it executes any output statement, it then checks in the array A to see if it has written 12 characters or more, and if so, whether `hello, world` are the first 12 characters. In that case, call the new function `foo` that was added in item (2). The resulting program is R, and input z is the same as y.

Suppose that Q with input y prints `hello, world` as its first output. Then R as constructed will call `foo`. However, if Q with input y does not print `hello, world` as its first output, then R will never call `foo`. If we can decide whether R with input z calls `foo`, then we also know whether Q with input y (remember $y = z$) prints `hello, world`. Since we know that no algorithm to

The Direction of a Reduction Is Important

It is a common mistake to try to prove a problem P_2 undecidable by reducing P_2 to some known undecidable problem P_1; i.e., showing the statement "if P_1 is decidable, then P_2 is decidable." That statement, although surely true, is useless, since its hypothesis "P_1 is decidable" is false.

The only way to prove a new problem P_2 to be undecidable is to reduce a known undecidable problem P_1 to P_2. That way, we prove the statement "if P_2 is decidable, then P_1 is decidable." The contrapositive of that statement is "if P_1 is undecidable, then P_2 is undecidable." Since we know that P_1 undecidable, we can deduce that P_2 is undecidable.

decide the hello-world problem exists, and all four steps of the construction of R from Q could be carried out by a program that edited the code of programs, our assumption that there was a calls-foo tester is wrong. No such program exists, and the calls-foo problem is undecidable. $\square$

8.1.4 Exercises for Section 8.1

Exercise 8.1.1: Give reductions from the hello-world problem to each of the problems below. Use the informal style of this section for describing plausible program transformations, and do not worry about the real limits such as maximum file size or memory size that real computers impose.

*! a) Given a program and an input, does the program eventually halt; i.e., does the program not loop forever on the input?

  b) Given a program and an input, does the program ever produce *any* output?

 ! c) Given two programs and an input, do the programs produce the same output for the given input?

8.2 The Turing Machine

The purpose of the theory of undecidable problems is not only to establish the existence of such problems — an intellectually exciting idea in its own right — but to provide guidance to programmers about what they might or might not be able to accomplish through programming. The theory also has great pragmatic impact when we discuss, as we shall in Chapter 10, problems that although decidable, require large amounts of time to solve them. These problems, called "intractable problems," tend to present greater difficulty to the programmer and system designer than do the undecidable problems. The reason is that, while undecidable problems are usually quite obviously so, and their solutions are rarely attempted in practice, the intractable problems are faced every day. Moreover, they often yield to small modifications in the requirements or to heuristic solutions. Thus, the designer is faced quite frequently with having to decide whether or not a problem is in the intractable class, and what to do about it, if so.

We need tools that will allow us to prove everyday questions undecidable or intractable. The technology introduced in Section 8.1 is useful for questions that deal with programs, but it does not translate easily to problems in unrelated domains. For example, we would have great difficulty reducing the hello-world problem to the question of whether a grammar is ambiguous.

As a result, we need to rebuild our theory of undecidability, based not on programs in C or another language, but based on a very simple model of a computer, called the Turing machine. This device is essentially a finite automaton that has a single tape of infinite length on which it may read and write data. One advantage of the Turing machine over programs as representation of what can be computed is that the Turing machine is sufficiently simple that we can represent its configuration precisely, using a simple notation much like the ID's of a PDA. In comparison, while C programs have a state, involving all the variables in whatever sequence of function calls have been made, the notation for describing these states is far too complex to allow us to make understandable, formal proofs.

Using the Turing machine notation, we shall prove undecidable certain problems that appear unrelated to programming. For instance, we shall show in Section 9.4 that "Post's Correspondence Problem," a simple question involving two lists of strings, is undecidable, and this problem makes it easy to show questions about grammars, such as ambiguity, to be undecidable. Likewise, when we introduce intractable problems we shall find that certain questions, seemingly having little to do with computation (e.g., satisfiability of boolean formulas), are intractable.

8.2.1 The Quest to Decide All Mathematical Questions

At the turn of the 20th century, the mathematician D. Hilbert asked whether it was possible to find an algorithm for determining the truth or falsehood of any mathematical proposition. In particular, he asked if there was a way to determine whether any formula in the first-order predicate calculus, applied to integers, was true. Since the first-order predicate calculus of integers is sufficiently powerful to express statements like "this grammar is ambiguous," or "this program prints `hello, world`," had Hilbert been successful, these problems would have algorithms that we now know do not exist.

However, in 1931, K. Gödel published his famous incompleteness theorem. He constructed a formula in the predicate calculus applied to integers, which asserted that the formula itself could be neither proved nor disproved within the predicate calculus. Gödel's technique resembles the construction of the self-contradictory program H_2 in Section 8.1.2, but deals with functions on the integers, rather than with C programs.

The predicate calculus was not the only notion that mathematicians had for "any possible computation." In fact predicate calculus, being declarative rather than computational, had to compete with a variety of notations, including the "partial-recursive functions," a rather programming-language-like notation, and other similar notations. In 1936, A. M. Turing proposed the Turing machine as a model of "any possible computation." This model is computer-like, rather than program-like, even though true electronic, or even electromechanical computers were several years in the future (and Turing himself was involved in the construction of such a machine during World War II).

Interestingly, all the serious proposals for a model of computation have the same power; that is, they compute the same functions or recognize the same languages. The unprovable assumption that any general way to compute will allow us to compute only the partial-recursive functions (or equivalently, what Turing machines or modern-day computers can compute) is known as *Church's hypothesis* (after the logician A. Church) or the *Church-Turing thesis*.

8.2.2   Notation for the Turing Machine

We may visualize a Turing machine as in Fig. 8.8. The machine consists of a *finite control*, which can be in any of a finite set of states. There is a *tape* divided into squares or *cells*; each cell can hold any one of a finite number of symbols.

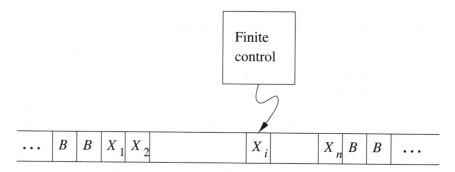

Figure 8.8: A Turing machine

Initially, the *input*, which is a finite-length string of symbols chosen from the *input alphabet*, is placed on the tape. All other tape cells, extending infinitely to the left and right, initially hold a special symbol called the *blank*. The blank is a *tape symbol*, but not an input symbol, and there may be other tape symbols besides the input symbols and the blank, as well.

There is a *tape head* that is always positioned at one of the tape cells. The Turing machine is said to be *scanning* that cell. Initially, the tape head is at the leftmost cell that holds the input.

A *move* of the Turing machine is a function of the state of the finite control and the tape symbol scanned. In one move, the Turing machine will:

1. Change state. The next state optionally may be the same as the current state.

2. Write a tape symbol in the cell scanned. This tape symbol replaces whatever symbol was in that cell. Optionally, the symbol written may be the same as the symbol currently there.

3. Move the tape head left or right. In our formalism we require a move, and do not allow the head to remain stationary. This restriction does not constrain what a Turing machine can compute, since any sequence of moves with a stationary head could be condensed, along with the next tape-head move, into a single state change, a new tape symbol, and a move left or right.

The formal notation we shall use for a *Turing machine* (TM) is similar to that used for finite automata or PDA's. We describe a TM by the 7-tuple

$$M = (Q, \Sigma, \Gamma, \delta, q_0, B, F)$$

whose components have the following meanings:

Q: The finite set of *states* of the finite control.

Σ: The finite set of *input symbols*.

Γ: The complete set of *tape symbols*; Σ is always a subset of Γ.

δ: The *transition function*. The arguments of $\delta(q, X)$ are a state q and a tape symbol X. The value of $\delta(q, X)$, if it is defined, is a triple (p, Y, D), where:

1. p is the next state, in Q.

2. Y is the symbol, in Γ, written in the cell being scanned, replacing whatever symbol was there.

3. D is a *direction*, either L or R, standing for "left" or "right," respectively, and telling us the direction in which the head moves.

q_0: The *start state*, a member of Q, in which the finite control is found initially.

B: The *blank* symbol. This symbol is in Γ but not in Σ; i.e., it is not an input symbol. The blank appears initially in all but the finite number of initial cells that hold input symbols.

F: The set of *final* or *accepting* states, a subset of Q.

8.2.3 Instantaneous Descriptions for Turing Machines

In order to describe formally what a Turing machine does, we need to develop a notation for configurations or *instantaneous descriptions* (ID's), like the notation we developed for PDA's. Since a TM, in principle, has an infinitely long tape, we might imagine that it is impossible to describe the configurations of a TM succinctly. However, after any finite number of moves, the TM can have visited only a finite number of cells, even though the number of cells visited can eventually grow beyond any finite limit. Thus, in every ID, there is an infinite prefix and an infinite suffix of cells that have never been visited. These cells must all hold either blanks or one of the finite number of input symbols. We thus show in an ID only the cells between the leftmost and the rightmost non-blanks. Under special conditions, when the head is scanning one of the leading or trailing blanks, a finite number of blanks to the left or right of the nonblank portion of the tape must also be included in the ID.

In addition to representing the tape, we must represent the finite control and the tape-head position. To do so, we embed the state in the tape, and place it immediately to the left of the cell scanned. To disambiguate the tape-plus-state string, we have to make sure that we do not use as a state any symbol that is also a tape symbol. However, it is easy to change the names of the states so they have nothing in common with the tape symbols, since the operation of the TM does not depend on what the states are called. Thus, we shall use the string $X_1 X_2 \cdots X_{i-1} q X_i X_{i+1} \cdots X_n$ to represent an ID in which

1. q is the state of the Turing machine.

2. The tape head is scanning the ith symbol from the left.

3. $X_1 X_2 \cdots X_n$ is the portion of the tape between the leftmost and the right-most nonblank. As an exception, if the head is to the left of the leftmost nonblank or to the right of the rightmost nonblank, then some prefix or suffix of $X_1 X_2 \cdots X_n$ will be blank, and i will be 1 or n, respectively.

We describe moves of a Turing machine $M = (Q, \Sigma, \Gamma, \delta, q_0, B, F)$ by the $\vdash_M$ notation that was used for PDA's. When the TM M is understood, we shall use just $\vdash$ to reflect moves. As usual, $\overset{*}{\underset{M}{\vdash}}$, or just $\overset{*}{\vdash}$, will be used to indicate zero, one, or more moves of the TM M.

Suppose $\delta(q, X_i) = (p, Y, L)$; i.e., the next move is leftward. Then

$$X_1 X_2 \cdots X_{i-1} q X_i X_{i+1} \cdots X_n \underset{M}{\vdash} X_1 X_2 \cdots X_{i-2} p X_{i-1} Y X_{i+1} \cdots X_n$$

Notice how this move reflects the change to state p and the fact that the tape head is now positioned at cell $i - 1$. There are two important exceptions:

1. If $i = 1$, then M moves to the blank to the left of X_1. In that case,

$$X_1 X_2 \cdots X_{i-1} q X_i X_{i+1} \cdots X_n \underset{M}{\vdash} pBY X_2 \cdots X_n$$

2. If $i = n$ and $Y = B$, then the symbol B written over X_n joins the infinite sequence of trailing blanks and does not appear in the next ID. Thus,

$$X_1 X_2 \cdots X_{n-1} q X_n \underset{M}{\vdash} X_1 X_2 \cdots X_{n-2} p X_{n-1}$$

Now, suppose $\delta(q, X_i) = (p, Y, R)$; i.e., the next move is rightward. Then

$$X_1 X_2 \cdots X_{i-1} q X_i X_{i+1} \cdots X_n \underset{M}{\vdash} X_1 X_2 \cdots X_{i-1} Y p X_{i+1} \cdots X_n$$

Here, the move reflects the fact that the head has moved to cell $i + 1$. Again there are two important exceptions:

1. If $i = n$, then the $i + 1$st cell holds a blank, and that cell was not part of the previous ID. Thus, we instead have

$$X_1 X_2 \cdots X_{n-1} q X_n \underset{M}{\vdash} X_1 X_2 \cdots X_{n-1} Y p B$$

2. If $i = 1$ and $Y = B$, then the symbol B written over X_1 joins the infinite sequence of leading blanks and does not appear in the next ID. Thus,

$$q X_1 X_2 \cdots X_n \underset{M}{\vdash} p X_2 \cdots X_{n-1}$$

Example 8.2 : Let us design a Turing machine and see how it behaves on a typical input. The TM we construct will accept the language $\{0^n 1^n \mid n \geq 1\}$. Initially, it is given a finite sequence of 0's and 1's on its tape, preceded and followed by an infinity of blanks. Alternately, the TM will change a 0 to an X and then a 1 to a Y, until all 0's and 1's have been matched.

In more detail, starting at the left end of the input, it repeatedly changes a 0 to an X and moves to the right over whatever 0's and Y's it sees, until it comes to a 1. It changes the 1 to a Y, and moves left, over Y's and 0's, until it finds an X. At that point, it looks for a 0 immediately to the right, and if it finds one, changes it to X and repeats the process, changing a matching 1 to a Y.

If the nonblank input is not in $\mathbf{0^* 1^*}$, then the TM will eventually fail to have a next move and will die without accepting. However, if it finishes changing all the 0's to X's on the same round it changes the last 1 to a Y, then it has found its input to be of the form $0^n 1^n$ and accepts. The formal specification of the TM M is

$$M = (\{q_0, q_1, q_2, q_3, q_4\}, \{0, 1\}, \{0, 1, X, Y, B\}, \delta, q_0, B, \{q_4\})$$

where δ is given by the table in Fig. 8.9.

As M performs its computation, the portion of the tape, where M's tape head has visited, will always be a sequence of symbols described by the regular expression $\mathbf{X^* 0^* Y^* 1^*}$. That is, there will be some 0's that have been changed

State	Symbol				
	0	1	X	Y	B
q_0	(q_1, X, R)	$-$	$-$	(q_3, Y, R)	$-$
q_1	$(q_1, 0, R)$	(q_2, Y, L)	$-$	(q_1, Y, R)	$-$
q_2	$(q_2, 0, L)$	$-$	(q_0, X, R)	(q_2, Y, L)	$-$
q_3	$-$	$-$	$-$	(q_3, Y, R)	(q_4, B, R)
q_4	$-$	$-$	$-$	$-$	$-$

Figure 8.9: A Turing machine to accept $\{0^n 1^n \mid n \geq 1\}$

to X's, followed by some 0's that have not yet been changed to X's. Then there are some 1's that were changed to Y's, and 1's that have not yet been changed to Y's. There may or may not be some 0's and 1's following.

State q_0 is the initial state, and M also enters state q_0 every time it returns to the leftmost remaining 0. If M is in state q_0 and scanning a 0, the rule in the upper-left corner of Fig. 8.9 tells it to go to state q_1, change the 0 to an X, and move right. Once in state q_1, M keeps moving right over all 0's and Y's that it finds on the tape, remaining in state q_1. If M sees an X or a B, it dies. However, if M sees a 1 when in state q_1, it changes that 1 to a Y, enters state q_2, and starts moving left.

In state q_2, M moves left over 0's and Y's, remaining in state q_2. When M reaches the rightmost X, which marks the right end of the block of 0's that have already been changed to X, M returns to state q_0 and moves right. There are two cases:

1. If M now sees a 0, then it repeats the matching cycle we have just described.

2. If M sees a Y, then it has changed all the 0's to X's. If all the 1's have been changed to Y's, then the input was of the form $0^n 1^n$, and M should accept. Thus, M enters state q_3, and starts moving right, over Y's. If the first symbol other than a Y that M sees is a blank, then indeed there were an equal number of 0's and 1's, so M enters state q_4 and accepts. On the other hand, if M encounters another 1, then there are too many 1's, so M dies without accepting. If it encounters a 0, then the input was of the wrong form, and M also dies.

Here is an example of an accepting computation by M. Its input is 0011. Initially, M is in state q_0, scanning the first 0, i.e., M's initial ID is $q_0 0011$. The entire sequence of moves of M is:

$$q_0 0011 \vdash X q_1 011 \vdash X 0 q_1 11 \vdash X q_2 0 Y 1 \vdash q_2 X 0 Y 1 \vdash$$
$$X q_0 0 Y 1 \vdash X X q_1 Y 1 \vdash X X Y q_1 1 \vdash X X q_2 Y Y \vdash X q_2 X Y Y \vdash$$
$$X X q_0 Y Y \vdash X X Y q_3 Y \vdash X X Y Y q_3 B \vdash X X Y Y B q_4 B$$

For another example, consider what M does on the input 0010, which is not in the language accepted.

$$q_0 0010 \vdash X q_1 010 \vdash X 0 q_1 10 \vdash X q_2 0 Y 0 \vdash q_2 X 0 Y 0 \vdash$$
$$X q_0 0 Y 0 \vdash X X q_1 Y 0 \vdash X X Y q_1 0 \vdash X X Y 0 q_1 B$$

The behavior of M on 0010 resembles the behavior on 0011, until in ID $XXYq_1 0$ M scans the final 0 for the first time. M must move right, staying in state q_1, which takes it to the ID $XXY0q_1 B$. However, in state q_1 M has no move on tape symbol B; thus M dies and does not accept its input. $\square$

8.2.4 Transition Diagrams for Turing Machines

We can represent the transitions of a Turing machine pictorially, much as we did for the PDA. A *transition diagram* consists of a set of nodes corresponding to the states of the TM. An arc from state q to state p is labeled by one or more items of the form X/YD, where X and Y are tape symbols, and D is a direction, either L or R. That is, whenever $\delta(q, X) = (p, Y, D)$, we find the label X/YD on the arc from q to p. However, in our diagrams, the direction D is represented pictorially by $\leftarrow$ for "left" and $\rightarrow$ for "right."

As for other kinds of transition diagrams, we represent the start state by the word "Start" and an arrow entering that state. Accepting states are indicated by double circles. Thus, the only information about the TM one cannot read directly from the diagram is the symbol used for the blank. We shall assume that symbol is B unless we state otherwise.

Example 8.3: Figure 8.10 shows the transition diagram for the Turing machine of Example 8.2, whose transition function was given in Fig. 8.9. $\square$

Example 8.4: While today we find it most convenient to think of Turing machines as recognizers of languages, or equivalently, solvers of problems, Turing's original view of his machine was as a computer of integer-valued functions. In his scheme, integers were represented in unary, as blocks of a single character, and the machine computed by changing the lengths of the blocks or by constructing new blocks elsewhere on the tape. In this simple example, we shall show how a Turing machine might compute the function $\dotdiv$, which is called *monus* or *proper subtraction* and is defined by $m \dotdiv n = \max(m - n, 0)$. That is, $m \dotdiv n$ is $m - n$ if $m \geq n$ and 0 if $m < n$.

A TM that performs this operation is specified by

$$M = (\{q_0, q_1, \ldots, q_6\}, \{0, 1\}, \{0, 1, B\}, \delta, q_0, B)$$

Note that, since this TM is not used to accept inputs, we have omitted the seventh component, which is the set of accepting states. M will start with a tape consisting of $0^m 10^n$ surrounded by blanks. M halts with $0^{m \dotdiv n}$ on its tape, surrounded by blanks.

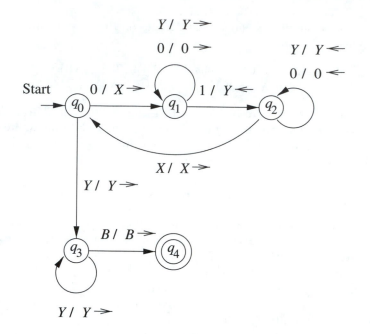

Figure 8.10: Transition diagram for a TM that accepts strings of the form 0^n1^n

M repeatedly finds its leftmost remaining 0 and replaces it by a blank. It then searches right, looking for a 1. After finding a 1, it continues right, until it comes to a 0, which it replaces by a 1. M then returns left, seeking the leftmost 0, which it identifies when it first meets a blank and then moves one cell to the right. The repetition ends if either:

1. Searching right for a 0, M encounters a blank. Then the n 0's in 0^m10^n have all been changed to 1's, and $m + 1$ of the m 0's have been changed to B. M replaces the $n + 1$ 1's by one 0 and n B's, leaving $m - n$ 0's on the tape. Since $m \geq n$ in this case, $m - n = m \dotminus n$.

2. Beginning the cycle, M cannot find a 0 to change to a blank, because the first m 0's already have been changed to B. Then $n \geq m$, so $m \dotminus n = 0$. M replaces all remaining 1's and 0's by B and ends with a completely blank tape.

Figure 8.11 gives the rules of the transition function δ, and we have also represented δ as a transition diagram in Fig. 8.12. The following is a summary of the role played by each of the seven states:

q_0: This state begins the cycle, and also breaks the cycle when appropriate. If M is scanning a 0, the cycle must repeat. The 0 is replaced by B, the head moves right, and state q_1 is entered. On the other hand, if M is

| | Symbol | | |
State	0	1	B
q_0	(q_1, B, R)	(q_5, B, R)	$-$
q_1	$(q_1, 0, R)$	$(q_2, 1, R)$	$-$
q_2	$(q_3, 1, L)$	$(q_2, 1, R)$	(q_4, B, L)
q_3	$(q_3, 0, L)$	$(q_3, 1, L)$	(q_0, B, R)
q_4	$(q_4, 0, L)$	(q_4, B, L)	$(q_6, 0, R)$
q_5	(q_5, B, R)	(q_5, B, R)	(q_6, B, R)
q_6	$-$	$-$	$-$

Figure 8.11: A Turing machine that computes the proper-subtraction function

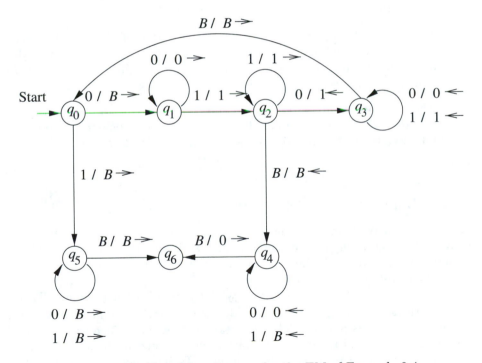

Figure 8.12: Transition diagram for the TM of Example 8.4

scanning B, then all possible matches between the two groups of 0's on the tape have been made, and M goes to state q_5 to make the tape blank.

q_1: In this state, M searches right, through the initial block of 0's, looking for the leftmost 1. When found, M goes to state q_2.

q_2: M moves right, skipping over 1's, until it finds a 0. It changes that 0 to a 1, turns leftward, and enters state q_3. However, it is also possible that there are no more 0's left after the block of 1's. In that case, M in state q_2 encounters a blank. We have case (1) described above, where n 0's in the second block of 0's have been used to cancel n of the m 0's in the first block, and the subtraction is complete. M enters state q_4, whose purpose is to convert the 1's on the tape to blanks.

q_3: M moves left, skipping over 0's and 1's, until it finds a blank. When it finds B, it moves right and returns to state q_0, beginning the cycle again.

q_4: Here, the subtraction is complete, but one unmatched 0 in the first block was incorrectly changed to a B. M therefore moves left, changing 1's to B's, until it encounters a B on the tape. It changes that B back to 0, and enters state q_6, wherein M halts.

q_5: State q_5 is entered from q_0 when it is found that all 0's in the first block have been changed to B. In this case, described in (2) above, the result of the proper subtraction is 0. M changes all remaining 0's and 1's to B and enters state q_6.

q_6: The sole purpose of this state is to allow M to halt when it has finished its task. If the subtraction had been a subroutine of some more complex function, then q_6 would initiate the next step of that larger computation.

$\square$

8.2.5 The Language of a Turing Machine

We have intuitively suggested the way that a Turing machine accepts a language. The input string is placed on the tape, and the tape head begins at the leftmost input symbol. If the TM eventually enters an accepting state, then the input is accepted, and otherwise not.

More formally, let $M = (Q, \Sigma, \Gamma, \delta, q_0, B, F)$ be a Turing machine. Then $L(M)$ is the set of strings w in Σ^* such that $q_0 w \overset{*}{\vdash} \alpha p \beta$ for some state p in F and any tape strings α and β. This definition was assumed when we discussed the Turing machine of Example 8.2, which accepts strings of the form $0^n 1^n$.

The set of languages we can accept using a Turing machine is often called the *recursively enumerable languages* or RE languages, The term "recursively enumerable" comes from computational formalisms that predate the Turing machine but that define the same class of languages or arithmetic functions. We discuss the origins of the term as an aside (box) in Section 9.2.1.

Notational Conventions for Turing Machines

The symbols we normally use for Turing machines resemble those for the other kinds of automata we have seen.

1. Lower-case letters at the beginning of the alphabet stand for input symbols.

2. Capital letters, typically near the end of the alphabet, are used for tape symbols that may or may not be input symbols. However, B is generally used for the blank symbol.

3. Lower-case letters near the end of the alphabet are strings of input symbols.

4. Greek letters are strings of tape symbols.

5. Letters such as q, p, and nearby letters are states.

8.2.6 Turing Machines and Halting

There is another notion of "acceptance" that is commonly used for Turing machines: acceptance by halting. We say a TM *halts* if it enters a state q, scanning a tape symbol X, and there is no move in this situation; i.e., $\delta(q, X)$ is undefined.

Example 8.5: The Turing machine M of Example 8.4 was not designed to accept a language; rather we viewed it as computing an arithmetic function. Note, however, that M halts on all strings of 0's and 1's, since no matter what string M finds on its tape, it will eventually cancel its second group of 0's, if it can find such a group, against its first group of 0's, and thus must reach state q_6 and halt. $\square$

We can always assume that a TM halts if it accepts. That is, without changing language accepted, we can make $\delta(q, X)$ undefined whenever q is an accepting state. In general, without otherwise stating so:

- We assume that a TM always halts when it is in an accepting state.

Unfortunately, it is not always possible to require that a TM halts even if it does not accept. Those languages with Turing machines that do halt eventually, regardless of whether or not they accept, are called *recursive*, and we shall consider their important properties starting in Section 9.2.1. Turing machines that always halt, regardless of whether or not they accept, are a good model of an "algorithm." If an algorithm to solve a given problem exists, then we say the problem is "decidable," so TM's that always halt figure importantly into decidability theory in Chapter 9.

8.2.7   Exercises for Section 8.2

Exercise 8.2.1: Show the ID's of the Turing machine of Fig. 8.9 if the input tape contains:

* a) 00.

  b) 000111.

  c) 00111.

! Exercise 8.2.2: Design Turing machines for the following languages:

* a) The set of strings with an equal number of 0's and 1's.

  b) $\{a^n b^n c^n \mid n \geq 1\}$.

  c) $\{ww^R \mid w$ is any string of 0's and 1's$\}$.

Exercise 8.2.3: Design a Turing machine that takes as input a number N and adds 1 to it in binary. To be precise, the tape initially contains a $ followed by N in binary. The tape head is initially scanning the $ in state q_0. Your TM should halt with N+1, in binary, on its tape, scanning the leftmost symbol of $N + 1$, in state q_f. You may destroy the $ in creating $N + 1$, if necessary. For instance, $q_0\$10011 \overset{*}{\vdash} \$q_f 10100$, and $q_0\$11111 \overset{*}{\vdash} q_f 100000$.

  a) Give the transitions of your Turing machine, and explain the purpose of each state.

  b) Show the sequence of ID's of your TM when given input $111.

*! Exercise 8.2.4: In this exercise we explore the equivalence between function computation and language recognition for Turing machines. For simplicity, we shall consider only functions from nonnegative integers to nonnegative integers, but the ideas of this problem apply to any computable functions. Here are the two central definitions:

  • Define the *graph* of a function f to be the set of all strings of the form $[x, f(x)]$, where x is a nonnegative integer in binary, and $f(x)$ is the value of function f with argument x, also written in binary.

  • A Turing machine is said to *compute* function f if, started with any nonnegative integer x on its tape, in binary, it halts (in any state) with $f(x)$, in binary, on its tape.

Answer the following, with informal, but clear constructions.

a) Show how, given a TM that computes f, you can construct a TM that accepts the graph of f as a language.

b) Show how, given a TM that accepts the graph of f, you can construct a TM that computes f.

c) A function is said to be *partial* if it may be undefined for some arguments. If we extend the ideas of this exercise to partial functions, then we do not require that the TM computing f halts if its input x is one of the integers for which $f(x)$ is not defined. Do your constructions for parts (a) and (b) work if the function f is partial? If not, explain how you could modify the construction to make it work.

Exercise 8.2.5: Consider the Turing machine

$$M = (\{q_0, q_1, q_2, q_f\}, \{0, 1\}, \{0, 1, B\}, \delta, q_0, B, \{q_f\})$$

Informally but clearly describe the language $L(M)$ if δ consists of the following sets of rules:

* a) $\delta(q_0, 0) = (q_1, 1, R)$; $\delta(q_1, 1) = (q_0, 0, R)$; $\delta(q_1, B) = (q_f, B, R)$.

b) $\delta(q_0, 0) = (q_0, B, R)$; $\delta(q_0, 1) = (q_1, B, R)$; $\delta(q_1, 1) = (q_1, B, R)$; $\delta(q_1, B) = (q_f, B, R)$.

! c) $\delta(q_0, 0) = (q_1, 1, R)$; $\delta(q_1, 1) = (q_2, 0, L)$; $\delta(q_2, 1) = (q_0, 1, R)$; $\delta(q_1, B) = (q_f, B, R)$.

8.3   Programming Techniques for Turing Machines

Our goal is to give you a sense of how a Turing machine can be used to compute in a manner not unlike that of a conventional computer. Eventually, we want to convince you that a TM is exactly as powerful as a conventional computer. In particular, we shall learn that the Turing machine can perform the sort of calculations on other Turing machines that we saw performed in Section 8.1.2 by a program that examined other programs. This "introspective" ability of both Turing machines and computer programs is what enables us to prove problems undecidable.

To make the ability of a TM clearer, we shall present a number of examples of how we might think of the tape and finite control of the Turing machine. None of these tricks extend the basic model of the TM; they are only notational conveniences. Later, we shall use them to simulate extended Turing-machine models that have additional features — for instance, more than one tape — by the basic TM model.

8.3.1 Storage in the State

We can use the finite control not only to represent a position in the "program" of the Turing machine, but to hold a finite amount of data. Figure 8.13 suggests this technique (as well as another idea: multiple tracks). There, we see the finite control consisting of not only a "control" state q, but three data elements A, B, and C. The technique requires no extension to the TM model; we merely think of the state as a tuple. In the case of Fig. 8.13, we should think of the state as $[q, A, B, C]$. Regarding states this way allows us to describe transitions in a more systematic way, often making the strategy behind the TM program more transparent.

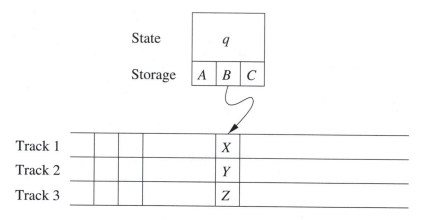

Figure 8.13: A Turing machine viewed as having finite-control storage and multiple tracks

Example 8.6: We shall design a TM

$$M = (Q, \{0, 1\}, \{0, 1, B\}, \delta, [q_0, B], \{[q_1, B]\})$$

that remembers in its finite control the first symbol (0 or 1) that it sees, and checks that it does not appear elsewhere on its input. Thus, M accepts the language $01^* + 10^*$. Accepting regular languages such as this one does not stress the ability of Turing machines, but it will serve as a simple demonstration.

The set of states Q is $\{q_0, q_1\} \times \{0, 1, B\}$. That is, the states may be thought of as pairs with two components:

a) A control portion, q_0 or q_1, that remembers what the TM is doing. Control state q_0 indicates that M has not yet read its first symbol, while q_1 indicates that it *has* read the symbol, and is checking that it does not appear elsewhere, by moving right and hoping to reach a blank cell.

b) A data portion, which remembers the first symbol seen, which must be 0 or 1. The symbol B in this component means that no symbol has been read.

The transition function δ of M is as follows:

1. $\delta([q_0, B], a) = ([q_1, a], a, R)$ for $a = 0$ or $a = 1$. Initially, q_0 is the control state, and the data portion of the state is B. The symbol scanned is copied into the second component of the state, and M moves right, entering control state q_1 as it does so.

2. $\delta([q_1, a], \bar{a}) = ([q_1, a], \bar{a}, R)$ where $\bar{a}$ is the "complement" of a, that is, 0 if $a = 1$ and 1 if $a = 0$. In state q_1, M skips over each symbol 0 or 1 that is different from the one it has stored in its state, and continues moving right.

3. $\delta([q_1, a], B) = ([q_1, B], B, R)$ for $a = 0$ or $a = 1$. If M reaches the first blank, it enters the accepting state $[q_1, B]$.

Notice that M has no definition for $\delta([q_1, a], a)$ for $a = 0$ or $a = 1$. Thus, if M encounters a second occurrence of the symbol it stored initially in its finite control, it halts without having entered the accepting state. □

8.3.2 Multiple Tracks

Another useful "trick" is to think of the tape of a Turing machine as composed of several tracks. Each track can hold one symbol, and the tape alphabet of the TM consists of tuples, with one component for each "track." Thus, for instance, the cell scanned by the tape head in Fig. 8.13 contains the symbol $[X, Y, Z]$. Like the technique of storage in the finite control, using multiple tracks does not extend what the Turing machine can do. It is simply a way to view tape symbols and to imagine that they have a useful structure.

Example 8.7 : A common use of multiple tracks is to treat one track as holding the data and a second track as holding a mark. We can check off each symbol as we "use" it, or we can keep track of a small number of positions within the data by marking only those positions. Examples 8.2 and 8.4 were two instances of this technique, but in neither example did we think explicitly of the tape as if it were composed of tracks. In the present example, we shall use a second track explicitly to recognize the non-context-free language

$$L_{wcw} = \{wcw \mid w \text{ is in } (\mathbf{0} + \mathbf{1})^+\}$$

The Turing machine we shall design is:

$$M = (Q, \Sigma, \Gamma, \delta, [q_1, B], [B, B], \{[q_9, B]\})$$

where:

Q: The set of states is $\{q_1, q_2, \ldots, q_9\} \times \{0, 1\}$, that is, pairs consisting of a control state q_i and a data component 0 or 1. We again use the technique of storage in the finite control, as we allow the state to remember an input symbol 0 or 1.

Γ: The set of tape symbols is $\{B, *\} \times \{0, 1, c, B\}$. The first component, or track, can be either blank or "checked," represented by the symbols B and $*$, respectively. We use the $*$ to check off symbols of the first and second groups of 0's and 1's, eventually confirming that the string to the left of the center marker c is the same as the string to its right. The second component of the tape symbol is what we think of as the tape symbol itself. That is, we may think of the symbol $[B, X]$ as if it were the tape symbol X, for $X = 0, 1, c, B$.

Σ: The input symbols are $[B, 0]$ and $[B, 1]$, which, as just mentioned, we identify with 0 and 1, respectively.

δ: The transition function δ is defined by the following rules, in which a and b each may stand for either 0 or 1.

1. $\delta([q_1, B], [B, a]) = ([q_2, a], [*, a], R)$. In the initial state, M picks up the symbol a (which can be either 0 or 1), stores it in its finite control, goes to control state q_2, "checks off" the symbol it just scanned, and moves right. Notice that by changing the first component of the tape symbol from B to $*$, it performs the check-off.

2. $\delta([q_2, a], [B, b]) = ([q_2, a], [B, b], R)$. M moves right, looking for the symbol c. Remember that a and b can each be either 0 or 1, independently, but cannot be c.

3. $\delta([q_2, a], [B, c]) = ([q_3, a], [B, c], R)$. When M finds the c, it continues to move right, but changes to control state q_3.

4. $\delta([q_3, a], [*, b]) = ([q_3, a], [*, b], R)$. In state q_3, M continues past all checked symbols.

5. $\delta([q_3, a], [B, a]) = ([q_4, B], [*, a], L)$. If the first unchecked symbol that M finds is the same as the symbol in its finite control, it checks this symbol, because it has matched the corresponding symbol from the first block of 0's and 1's. M goes to control state q_4, dropping the symbol from its finite control, and starts moving left.

6. $\delta([q_4, B], [*, a]) = ([q_4, B], [*, a], L)$. M moves left over checked symbols.

7. $\delta([q_4, B], [B, c]) = ([q_5, B], [B, c], L)$. When M encounters the symbol c, it switches to state q_5 and continues left. In state q_5, M must make a decision, depending on whether or not the symbol immediately to the left of the c is checked or unchecked. If checked, then we have already considered the entire first block of 0's and 1's — those to the left of the c. We must make sure that all the 0's and 1's to the right of the c are also checked, and accept if no unchecked symbols remain to the right of the c. If the symbol immediately to the left of the c is unchecked, we find the leftmost unchecked symbol, pick it up, and start the cycle that began in state q_1.

8. $\delta([q_5, B], [B, a]) = ([q_6, B], [B, a], L)$. This branch covers the case where the symbol to the left of c is unchecked. M goes to state q_6 and continues left, looking for a checked symbol.

9. $\delta([q_6, B], [B, a]) = ([q_6, B], [B, a], L)$. As long as symbols are unchecked, M remains in state q_6 and proceeds left.

10. $\delta([q_6, B], [*, a]) = ([q_1, B], [*, a], R)$. When the checked symbol is found, M enters state q_1 and moves right to pick up the first unchecked symbol.

11. $\delta([q_5, B], [*, a]) = ([q_7, B], [*, a], R)$. Now, let us pick up the branch from state q_5 where we have just moved left from the c and find a checked symbol. We start moving right again, entering state q_7.

12. $\delta([q_7, B], [B, c]) = ([q_8, B], [B, c], R)$. In state q_7 we shall surely see the c. We enter state q_8 as we do so, and proceed right.

13. $\delta([q_8, B], [*, a]) = ([q_8, B], [*, a], R)$. M moves right in state q_8, skipping over any checked 0's or 1's that it finds.

14. $\delta([q_8, B], [B, B]) = ([q_9, B], [B, B], R)$. If M reaches a blank cell is state q_8 without encountering any unchecked 0 or 1, then M accepts. If M first finds an unchecked 0 or 1, then the blocks before and after the c do not match, and M halts without accepting.

$\square$

8.3.3 Subroutines

As with programs in general, it helps to think of Turing machines as built from a collection of interacting components, or "subroutines." A Turing-machine subroutine is a set of states that perform some useful process. This set of states includes a start state and another state that temporarily has no moves, and that serves as the "return" state to pass control to whatever other set of states called the subroutine. The "call" of a subroutine occurs whenever there is a transition to its initial state. Since the TM has no mechanism for remembering a "return address," that is, a state to go to after it finishes, should our design of a TM call for one subroutine to be called from several states, we can make copies of the subroutine, using a new set of states for each copy. The "calls" are made to the start states of different copies of the subroutine, and each copy "returns" to a different state.

Example 8.8: We shall design a TM to implement the function "multiplication." That is, our TM will start with $0^m 10^n$ on its tape, and will end with 0^{mn} on the tape. An outline of the strategy is:

1. The tape will, in general, have one nonblank string of the form $0^i 10^n 10^{kn}$ for some k.

2. In one basic step, we change a 0 in the first group to B and add n 0's to the last group, giving us a string of the form $0^{i-1}10^n10^{(k+1)n}$.

3. As a result, we copy the group of n 0's to the end m times, once each time we change a 0 in the first group to B. When the first group of 0's is completely changed to blanks, there will be mn 0's in the last group.

4. The final step is to change the leading 10^n1 to blanks, and we are done.

The heart of this algorithm is a subroutine, which we call Copy. This subroutine implements step (2) above, copying the block of n 0's to the end. More precisely, Copy converts an ID of the form $0^{m-k}1q_10^n10^{(k-1)n}$ to ID $0^{m-k}1q_50^n10^{kn}$. Figure 8.14 shows the transitions of subroutine Copy. This subroutine marks the first 0 with an X, moves right in state q_2 until it finds a blank, copies the 0 there, and moves left in state q_3 to find the marker X. It repeats this cycle until in state q_1 it finds a 1 instead of a 0. At that point, it uses state q_4 to change the X's back to 0's, and ends in state q_5.

The complete multiplication Turing machine starts in state q_0. The first thing it does is go, in several steps, from ID $q_00^m10^n$ to ID $0^{m-1}1q_10^n1$. The transitions needed are shown in the portion of Fig. 8.15 to the left of the subroutine call; these transitions involve states q_0 and q_6 only.

Then, to the right of the subroutine call in Fig. 8.15 we see states q_7 through q_{12}. The purpose of states q_7, q_8, and q_9 is to take control after Copy has just copied a block of n 0's, and is in ID $0^{m-k}1q_50^n10^{kn}$. Eventually, these states bring us to state $q_00^{m-k}10^n10^{kn}$. At that point, the cycle starts again, and Copy is called to copy the block of n 0's again.

As an exception, in state q_8 the TM may find that all m 0's have been changed to blanks (i.e., $k = m$). In that case, a transition to state q_{10} occurs. This state, with the help of state q_{11}, changes the leading 10^n1 to blanks and enters the halting state q_{12}. At this point, the TM is in ID $q_{12}0^{mn}$, and its job is done. □

8.3.4 Exercises for Section 8.3

! **Exercise 8.3.1:** Redesign your Turing machines from Exercise 8.2.2 to take advantage of the programming techniques discussed in Section 8.3.

! **Exercise 8.3.2:** A common operation in Turing-machine programs involves "shifting over." Ideally, we would like to create an extra cell at the current head position, in which we could store some character. However, we cannot edit the tape in this way. Rather, we need to move the contents of each of the cells to the right of the current head position one cell right, and then find our way back to the current head position. Show how to perform this operation. *Hint*: Leave a special symbol to mark the position to which the head must return.

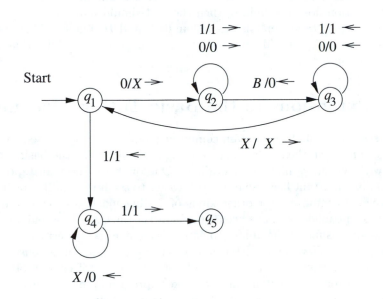

Figure 8.14: The subroutine Copy

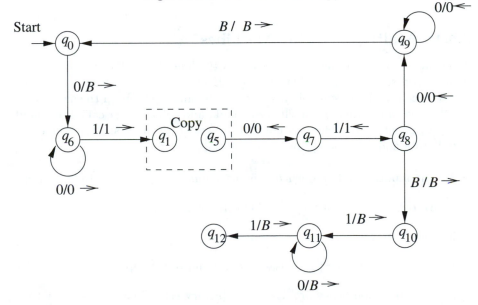

Figure 8.15: The complete multiplication program uses the subroutine Copy

* **Exercise 8.3.3:** Design a subroutine to move a TM head from its current position to the right, skipping over all 0's, until reaching a 1 or a blank. If the current position does not hold 0, then the TM should halt. You may assume that there are no tape symbols other than 0, 1, and B (blank). Then, use this subroutine to design a TM that accepts all strings of 0's and 1's that do not have two 1's in a row.

8.4   Extensions to the Basic Turing Machine

In this section we shall see certain computer models that are related to Turing machines and have the same language-recognizing power as the basic model of a TM with which we have been working. One of these, the multitape Turing machine, is important because it is much easier to see how a multitape TM can simulate real computers (or other kinds of Turing machines), compared with the single-tape model we have been studying. Yet the extra tapes add no power to the model, as far as the ability to accept languages is concerned.

We then consider the nondeterministic Turing machine, an extension of the basic model that is allowed to make any of a finite set of choices of move in a given situation. This extension also makes "programming" Turing machines easier in some circumstances, but adds no language-defining power to the basic model.

8.4.1   Multitape Turing Machines

A multitape TM is as suggested by Fig. 8.16. The device has a finite control (state), and some finite number of tapes. Each tape is divided into cells, and each cell can hold any symbol of the finite tape alphabet. As in the single-tape TM, the set of tape symbols includes a blank, and has a subset called the input symbols, of which the blank is not a member. The set of states includes an initial state and some accepting states. Initially:

1. The input, a finite sequence of input symbols, is placed on the first tape.

2. All other cells of all the tapes hold the blank.

3. The finite control is in the initial state.

4. The head of the first tape is at the left end of the input.

5. All other tape heads are at some arbitrary cell. Since tapes other than the first tape are completely blank, it does not matter where the head is placed initially; all cells of these tapes "look" the same.

A move of the multitape TM depends on the state and the symbol scanned by each of the tape heads. In one move, the multitape TM does the following:

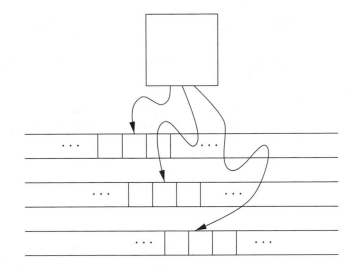

Figure 8.16: A multitape Turing machine

1. The control enters a new state, which could be the same as the previous state.

2. On each tape, a new tape symbol is written on the cell scanned. Any of these symbols may be the same as the symbol previously there.

3. Each of the tape heads makes a move, which can be either left, right, or stationary. The heads move independently, so different heads may move in different directions, and some may not move at all.

We shall not give the formal notation of transition rules, whose form is a straightforward generalization of the notation for the one-tape TM, except that directions are now indicated by a choice of L, R, or S. For the one-tape machine, we did not allow the head to remain stationary, so the S option was not present. You should be able to imagine an appropriate notation for instantaneous descriptions of the configuration of a multitape TM; we shall not give this notation formally. Multitape Turing machines, like one-tape TM's, accept by entering an accepting state.

8.4.2 Equivalence of One-Tape and Multitape TM's

Recall that the recursively enumerable languages are defined to be those accepted by a one-tape TM. Surely, multitape TM's accept all the recursively enumerable languages, since a one-tape TM *is* a multitape TM. However, are there languages that are not recursively enumerable, yet are accepted by multitape TM's? The answer is "no," and we prove this fact by showing how to simulate a multitape TM by a one-tape TM.

Theorem 8.9 : Every language accepted by a multitape TM is recursively enumerable.

PROOF: The proof is suggested by Fig. 8.17. Suppose language L is accepted by a k-tape TM M. We simulate M with a one-tape TM N whose tape we think of as having $2k$ tracks. Half these tracks hold the tapes of M, and the other half of the tracks each hold only a single marker that indicates where the head for the corresponding tape of M is currently located. Figure 8.17 assumes $k = 2$. The second and fourth tracks hold the contents of the first and second tapes of M, track 1 holds the position of the head of tape 1, and track 3 holds the position of the second tape head.

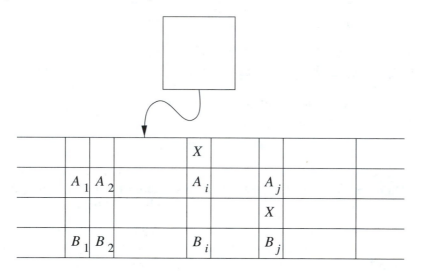

Figure 8.17: Simulation of a two-tape Turing machine by a one-tape Turing machine

To simulate a move of M, N's head must visit the k head markers. So that N not get lost, it must remember how many head markers are to its left at all times; that count is stored as a component of N's finite control. After visiting each head marker and storing the scanned symbol in a component of its finite control, N knows what tape symbols are being scanned by each of M's heads. N also knows the state of M, which it stores in N's own finite control. Thus, N knows what move M will make.

N now revisits each of the head markers on its tape, changes the symbol in the track representing the corresponding tapes of M, and moves the head markers left or right, if necessary. Finally, N changes the state of M as recorded in its own finite control. At this point, N has simulated one move of M.

We select as N's accepting states all those states that record M's state as one of the accepting states of M. Thus, whenever the simulated M accepts, N also accepts, and N does not accept otherwise. □

A Reminder About Finiteness

A common fallacy is to confuse a value that is finite at any time with a set of values that is finite. The many-tapes-to-one construction may help us appreciate the difference. In that construction, we used tracks on the tape to record the positions of the tape heads. Why could we not store these positions as integers in the finite control? Carelessly, one could argue that after n moves, the TM can have tape head positions that must be within n positions of original head positions, and so the head only has to store integers up to n.

The problem is that, while the positions are finite at any time, the complete set of positions possible at any time is infinite. If the state is to represent any head position, then there must be a data component of the state that has any integer as value. This component forces the set of states to be infinite, even if only a finite number of them can be used at any finite time. The definition of a Turing machine requires that the *set* of states be finite. Thus, it is not permissible to store a tape-head position in the finite control.

8.4.3 Running Time and the Many-Tapes-to-One Construction

Let us now introduce a concept that will become quite important later: the "time complexity" or "running time" of a Turing machine. we say the *running time* of TM M on input w is the number of steps that M makes before halting. If M doesn't halt on w, then the running time of M on w is infinite. The *time complexity* of TM M is the function $T(n)$ that is the maximum, over all inputs w of length n, of the running time of M on w. For Turing machines that do not halt on all inputs, $T(n)$ may be infinite for some or even all n. However, we shall pay special attention to TM's that do halt on all inputs, and in particular, those that have a polynomial time complexity $T(n)$; Section 10.1 initiates this study.

The construction of Theorem 8.9 seems clumsy. In fact, the constructed one-tape TM may take much more running time than the multitape TM. However, the amounts of time taken by the two Turing machines are commensurate in a weak sense: the one-tape TM takes time that is no more than the square of the time taken by the other. While "squaring" is not a very strong guarantee, it does preserve polynomial running time. We shall see in Chapter 10 that:

a) The difference between polynomial time and higher growth rates in running time is really the divide between what we can solve by computer and what is in practice not solvable.

b) Despite extensive research, the running time needed to solve many problems has not been resolved closer than to within some polynomial. Thus, the question of whether we are using a one-tape or multitape TM to solve the problem is not crucial when we examine the running time needed to solve a particular problem.

The argument that the running times of the one-tape and multitape TM's are within a square of each other is as follows.

Theorem 8.10: The time taken by the one-tape TM N of Theorem 8.9 to simulate n moves of the k-tape TM M is $O(n^2)$.

PROOF: After n moves of M, the tape head markers cannot have separated by more than $2n$ cells. Thus, if M starts at the leftmost marker, it has to move no more than $2n$ cells right, to find all the head markers. It can then make an excursion leftward, changing the contents of the simulated tapes of M, and moving head markers left or right as needed. Doing so requires no more than $2n$ moves left, plus at most $2k$ moves to reverse direction and write a marker X in the cell to the right (in the case that a tape head of M moves right).

Thus, the number of moves by N needed to simulate one of the first n moves is no more than $4n + 2k$. Since k is a constant, independent of the number of moves simulated, this number of moves is $O(n)$. To simulate n moves requires no more than n times this amount, or $O(n^2)$. □

8.4.4   Nondeterministic Turing Machines

A *nondeterministic* Turing machine (*NTM*) differs from the deterministic variety we have been studying by having a transition function δ such that for each state q and tape symbol X, $\delta(q, X)$ is a set of triples

$$\{(q_1, Y_1, D_1),\ (q_2, Y_2, D_2), \dots, (q_k, Y_k, D_k)\}$$

where k is any finite integer. The NTM can choose, at each step, any of the triples to be the next move. It cannot, however, pick a state from one, a tape symbol from another, and the direction from yet another.

The language accepted by an NTM M is defined in the expected manner, in analogy with the other nondeterministic devices, such as NFA's and PDA's, that we have studied. That is, M accepts an input w if there is any sequence of choices of move that leads from the initial ID with w as input, to an ID with an accepting state. The existence of other choices that do *not* lead to an accepting state is irrelevant, as it is for the NFA or PDA.

The NTM's accept no languages not accepted by a deterministic TM (or *DTM* if we need to emphasize that it is deterministic). The proof involves showing that for every NTM M_N, we can construct a a DTM M_D that explores the ID's that M_N can reach by any sequence of its choices. If M_D finds one that has an accepting state, then M_D enters an accepting state of its own. M_D must be systematic, putting new ID's on a queue, rather than a stack, so that after some finite time M_D has simulated all sequences of up to k moves of M_N, for $k = 1, 2, \dots$.

Theorem 8.11: If M_N is a nondeterministic Turing machine, then there is a deterministic Turing machine M_D such that $L(M_N) = L(M_D)$.

PROOF: M_D will be designed as a multitape TM, sketched in Fig. 8.18. The first tape of M_D holds a sequence of ID's of M_N, including the state of M_N. One ID of M_N is marked as the "current" ID, whose successor ID's are in the process of being discovered. In Fig. 8.18, the third ID is marked by an x along with the inter-ID separator, which is the $*$. All ID's to the left of the current one have been explored and can be ignored subsequently.

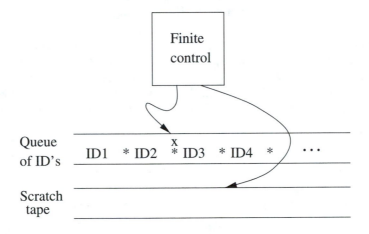

Figure 8.18: Simulation of an NTM by a DTM

To process the current ID, M_D does the following:

1. M_D examines the state and scanned symbol of the current ID. Built into the finite control of M_D is the knowledge of what choices of move M_N has for each state and symbol. If the state in the current ID is accepting, then M_D accepts and simulates M_N no further.

2. However, if the state is not accepting, and the state-symbol combination has k moves, then M_D uses its second tape to copy the ID and then make k copies of that ID at the end of the sequence of ID's on tape 1.

3. M_D modifies each of those k ID's according to a different one of the k choices of move that M_N has from its current ID.

4. M_D returns to the marked, current ID, erases the mark, and moves the mark to the next ID to the right. The cycle then repeats with step (1).

It should be clear that the simulation is accurate, in the sense that M_D will only accept if it finds that M_N can enter an accepting ID. However, we need to confirm that if M_N enters an accepting ID after a sequence of n of its own moves, then M_D will eventually make that ID the current ID and will accept.

Suppose that m is the maximum number of choices M_N has in any configuration. Then there is one initial ID of M_N, at most m ID's that M_N can reach after one move, at most m^2 ID's M_N can reach after two moves, and so on. Thus, after n moves, M_N can reach at most $1 + m + m^2 + \cdots + m^n$ ID's. This number is at most nm^n ID's.

The order in which M_D explores ID's of M_N is "breadth first"; that is, it explores all ID's reachable by 0 moves (i.e., the initial ID), then all ID's reachable by one move, then those reachable by two moves, and so on. In particular, M_D will make current, and consider the successors of, all ID's reachable by up to n moves before considering any ID's that are only reachable by more than n moves.

As a consequence, the accepting ID of M_N will be considered by M_D among the first nm^n ID's that it considers. We only care that M_D considers this ID in some finite time, and this bound is sufficient to assure us that the accepting ID is considered eventually. Thus, if M_N accepts, then so does M_D. Since we already observed that if M_D accepts it does so only because M_N accepts, we conclude that $L(M_N) = L(M_D)$. □

Notice that the constructed deterministic TM may take exponentially more time than the nondeterministic TM. It is unknown whether or not this exponential slowdown is necessary. In fact, Chapter 10 is devoted to this question and the consequences of someone discovering a better way to simulate NTM's deterministically.

8.4.5   Exercises for Section 8.4

Exercise 8.4.1: Informally but clearly describe multitape Turing machines that accept each of the languages of Exercise 8.2.2. Try to make each of your Turing machines run in time proportional to the input length.

Exercise 8.4.2: Here is the transition function of a nondeterministic TM $M = (\{q_0, q_1, q_2\}, \{0, 1\}, \{0, 1, B\}, \delta, q_0, B, \{q - 2\})$:

δ	0	1	B
q_0	$\{(q_0, 1, R)\}$	$\{(q_1, 0, R)\}$	$\emptyset$
q_1	$\{(q_1, 0, R), (q_0, 0, L)\}$	$\{(q_1, 1, R), (q_0, 1, L)\}$	$\{(q_2, B, R)\}$
q_2	$\emptyset$	$\emptyset$	$\emptyset$

Show the ID's reachable from the initial ID if the input is:

* a) 01.

  b) 001.

! **Exercise 8.4.3:** Informally but clearly describe nondeterministic Turing machines — multitape if you like — that accept the following languages. Try to take advantage of nondeterminism to avoid iteration and save time in the non-deterministic sense. That is, prefer to have your NTM branch a lot, while each branch is short.

* a) The language of all strings of 0's and 1's that have some string of length 100 that repeats, not necessarily consecutively. Formally, this language is the set of strings of 0's and 1's of the form $wxyxz$, where $|x| = 100$, and w, y, and z are of arbitrary length.

   b) The language of all strings of the form $w_1 \# w_2 \# \cdots \# w_n$, for any n, such that each w_i is a string of 0's and 1's, and for some j, w_j is the integer j in binary.

   c) The language of all strings of the same form as (b), but for at least two values of j, we have w_j equal to j in binary.

! **Exercise 8.4.4:** Consider the nondeterministic Turing machine

$$M = (\{q_0, q_1, q_2, q_f\}, \{0, 1\}, \{0, 1, B\}, \delta, q_0, B, \{q_f\})$$

Informally but clearly describe the language $L(M)$ if δ consists of the following sets of rules: $\delta(q_0, 0) = \{(q_0, 1, R), (q_1, 1, R)\}$; $\delta(q_1, 1) = \{(q_2, 0, L)\}$; $\delta(q_2, 1) = \{(q_0, 1, R)\}$; $\delta(q_1, B) = \{(q_f, B, R)\}$.

* **Exercise 8.4.5:** Consider a nondeterministic TM whose tape is infinite in both directions. At some time, the tape is completely blank, except for one cell, which holds the symbol $. The head is currently at some blank cell, and the state is q.

   a) Write transitions that will enable the NTM to enter state p, scanning the $.

   ! b) Suppose the TM were deterministic instead. How would you enable it to find the $ and enter state p?

Exercise 8.4.6: Design the following 2-tape TM to accept the language of all strings of 0's and 1's with an equal number of each. The first tape contains the input, and is scanned from left to right. The second tape is used to store the excess of 0's over 1's, or vice-versa, in the part of the input seen so far. Specify the states, transitions, and the intuitive purpose of each state.

Exercise 8.4.7: In this exercises, we shall implement a stack using a special 3-tape TM.

   1. The first tape will be used only to hold and read the input. The input alphabet consists of the symbol ↑, which we shall interpret as "pop the stack," and the symbols a and b, which are interpreted as "push an a (respectively b) onto the stack."

2. The second tape is used to store the stack.

3. The third tape is the output tape. Every time a symbol is popped from the stack, it must be written on the output tape, following all previously written symbols.

The Turing machine is required to start with an empty stack and implement the sequence of push and pop operations, as specified on the input, reading from left to right. If the input causes the TM to try to pop and empty stack, then it must halt in a special error state q_e. If the entire input leaves the stack empty at the end, then the input is accepted by going to the final state q_f. Describe the transition function of the TM informally but clearly. Also, give a summary of the purpose of each state you use.

Exercise 8.4.8: In Fig. 8.17 we saw an example of the general simulation of a k-tape TM by a one-tape TM.

* a) Suppose this technique is used to simulate a 5-tape TM that had a tape alphabet of seven symbols. How many tape symbols would the one-tape TM have?

* b) An alternative way to simulate k tapes by one is to use a $(k + 1)$st track to hold the head positions of all k tapes, while the first k tracks simulate the k tapes in the obvious manner. Note that in the $(k + 1)$st track, we must be careful to distinguish among the tape heads and to allow for the possibility that two or more heads are at the same cell. Does this method reduce the number of tape symbols needed for the one-tape TM?

c) Another way to simulate k tapes by 1 is to avoid storing the head positions altogether. Rather, a $(k + 1)$st track is used only to mark one cell of the tape. At all times, each simulated tape is positioned on its track so the head is at the marked cell. If the k-tape TM moves the head of tape i, then the simulating one-tape TM slides the entire nonblank contents of the ith track one cell in the opposite direction, so the marked cell continues to hold the cell scanned by the ith tape head of the k-tape TM. Does this method help reduce the number of tape symbols of the one-tape TM? Does it have any drawbacks compared with the other methods discussed?

! **Exercise 8.4.9:** A k-*head* Turing machine has k heads reading cells of one tape. A move of this TM depends on the state and on the symbol scanned by each head. In one move, the TM can change state, write a new symbol on the cell scanned by each head, and can move each head left, right, or keep it stationary. Since several heads may be scanning the same cell, we assume the heads are numbered 1 through k, and the symbol written by the highest numbered head scanning a given cell is the one that actually gets written there. Prove that the languages accepted by k-head Turing machines are the same as those accepted by ordinary TM's.

!! **Exercise 8.4.10:** A *two-dimensional* Turing machine has the usual finite-state control but a tape that is a two-dimensional grid of cells, infinite in all directions. The input is placed on one row of the grid, with the head at the left end of the input and the control in the start state, as usual. Acceptance is by entering a final state, also as usual. Prove that the languages accepted by two-dimensional Turing machines are the same as those accepted by ordinary TM's.

8.5 Restricted Turing Machines

We have seen seeming generalizations of the Turing machine that do not add any language-recognizing power. Now, we shall consider some examples of apparent restrictions on the TM that also give exactly the same language-recognizing power. Our first restriction is minor but useful in a number of constructions to be seen later: we replace the TM tape that is infinite in both directions by a tape that is infinite only to the right. We also forbid this restricted TM to print a blank as the replacement tape symbol. The value of these restrictions is that we can assume ID's consist of only nonblank symbols, and that they always begin at the left end of the input.

We then explore certain kinds of multitape Turing machines that are generalized pushdown automata. First, we restrict the tapes of the TM to behave like stacks. Then, we further restrict the tapes to be "counters," that is, they can only represent one integer, and the TM can only distinguish a count of 0 from any nonzero count. The impact of this discussion is that there are several very simple kinds of automata that have the full power of any computer. Moreover, undecidable problems about Turing machines, which we see in Chapter 9, apply as well to these simple machines.

8.5.1 Turing Machines With Semi-infinite Tapes

While we have allowed the tape head of a Turing machine to move either left or right from its initial position, it is only necessary that the TM's head be allowed to move within the positions at and to the right of the initial head position. In fact, we can assume the tape is *semi-infinite*, that is, there are no cells to the left of the initial head position. In the next theorem, we shall give a construction that shows a TM with a semi-infinite tape can simulate one whose tape is, like our original TM model, infinite in both directions.

The trick behind the construction is to use two tracks on the semi-infinite tape. The upper track represents the cells of the original TM that are at or to the right of the initial head position. The lower track represents the positions left of the initial position, but in reverse order. The exact arrangement is suggested in Fig. 8.19. The upper track represents cells $X_0, X_1, \ldots$, where X_0 is the initial position of the head; X_1, X_2, and so on, are the cells to its right. Cells X_{-1}, X_{-2}, and so on, represent cells to the left of the initial position. Notice the * on the leftmost cell's bottom track. This symbol serves as an endmarker and prevents the head of the semi-infinite TM from accidentally falling off the left end of the tape.

X_0	X_1	X_2	$\cdots$
*	X_{-1}	X_{-2}	$\cdots$

Figure 8.19: A semi-infinite tape can simulate a two-way infinite tape

We shall make one more restriction to our Turing machine: it never writes a blank. This simple restriction, coupled with the restriction that the tape is only semi-infinite means that the tape is at all times a prefix of nonblank symbols followed by an infinity of blanks. Further, the sequence of nonblanks always begins at the initial tape position. We shall see in Theorem 9.19, and again in Theorem 10.9, how useful it is to assume ID's have this form.

Theorem 8.12: Every language accepted by a TM M_2 is also accepted by a TM M_1 with the following restrictions:

1. M_1's head never moves left of its initial position.

2. M_1 never writes a blank.

PROOF: Condition (2) is quite easy. Create a new tape symbol B' that functions as a blank, but is not the blank B. That is:

a) If M_2 has a rule $\delta_2(q, X) = (p, B, D)$, change this rule to $\delta_2(q, X) = (p, B', D)$.

b) Then, let $\delta_2(q, B')$ be the same as $\delta_2(q, B)$, for every state q.

Condition (1) requires more effort. Let

$$M_2 = (Q_2, \Sigma, \Gamma_2, \delta_2, q_2, B, F_2)$$

be the TM M_2 as modified above, so it never writes the blank B. Construct

$$M_1 = (Q_1, \Sigma \times \{B\}, \Gamma_1, \delta_1, q_0, [B, B], F_1)$$

where:

Q_1: The states of M_1 are $\{q_0, q_1\} \cup (Q_2 \times \{U, L\})$. That is, the states of M_1 are the initial state q_0 another state q_1, and all the states of M_2 with a second data component that is either U or L (upper or lower). The second component tells us whether the upper or lower track, as in Fig. 8.19 is being scanned by M_2. Put another way, U means the head of M_2 is at or to the right of its initial position, and L means it is to the left of that position.

Γ_1: The tape symbols of M_1 are all pairs of symbols from Γ_2, that is, $\Gamma_2 \times \Gamma_2$. The input symbols of M_1 are those pairs with an input symbol of M_2 in the first component and a blank in the second component, that is, pairs of the form $[a, B]$, where a is in Σ. The blank of M_1 has blanks in both components. Additionally, for every symbol X in Γ_2, there is a pair $[X, *]$ in Γ_1. Here, $*$ is a new symbol, not in Γ_2, and serves to mark the left end of M_1's tape.

δ_1: The transitions of M_1 are as follows:

1. $\delta_1(q_0, [a, B]) = (q_1, [a, *], R)$, for any a in Σ. The first move of M_1 puts the $*$ marker in the lower track of the leftmost cell. The state becomes q_1, and the head moves right, because it cannot move left or remain stationary.

2. $\delta_1(q_1, [X, B]) = ([q_2, U], [X, B], L)$, for any X in Γ_2. In state q_1, M_1 establishes the initial conditions of M_2, by returning the head to its initial position and changing the state to $[q_2, U]$, i.e., the initial state of M_2, with attention focused on the upper track of M_1.

3. If $\delta_2(q, X) = (p, Y, D)$, then for every Z in Γ_2:

   (a) $\delta_1([q, U], [X, Z]) = ([p, U], [Y, Z], D)$ and

   (b) $\delta_1([q, L], [Z, X]) = ([p, L], [Z, Y], \overline{D})$,

   where $\overline{D}$ is the direction opposite D, that is, L if $D = R$ and R if $D = L$. If M_1 is not at its leftmost cell, then it simulates M_2 on the appropriate track — the upper track if the second component of state is U and the lower track if the second component is L. Note, however, that when working on the lower track, M_2 moves in the direction opposite that of M_2. That choice makes sense, because the left half of M_2's tape has been folded, in reverse, along the lower track of M_1's tape.

4. If $\delta_2(q, X) = (p, Y, R)$, then

$$\delta_1([q, L], [X, *]) = \delta_1([q, U], [X, *]) = ([p, U], [Y, *], R)$$

   This rule covers one case of how the left endmarker $*$ is handled. If M_2 moves right from its initial position, then regardless of whether it had previously been to the left or the right of that position (as reflected in the fact that the second component of M_1's state could be L or U), M_1 must move right and focus on the upper track. That is, M_1 will next be at the position represented by X_1 in Fig. 8.19.

5. If $\delta_2(q, X) = (p, Y, L)$, then

$$\delta_1([q, L], [X, *]) = \delta_1([q, U], [X, *]) = ([p, L], [Y, *], R)$$

   This rule is similar to the previous, but covers the case where M_2 moves left from its initial position. M_1 must move right from its endmarker, but now focuses on the lower track, i.e., the cell indicated by X_{-1} in Fig. 8.19.

F_1: The accepting states F_1 are those states in $F_2 \times \{U, L\}$, that is all states of M_1 whose first component is an accepting state of M_2. The attention of M_1 may be focused on either the upper or lower track at the time it accepts.

The proof of the theorem is now essentially complete. We may observe by induction on the number of moves made by M_2 that M_1 will mimic the ID of M_2 on its own tape, if you take the lower track, reverse it, and follow it by the upper track. Also, we note that M_1 enters one of its accepting states exactly when M_2 does. Thus, $L(M_1) = L(M_2)$.   □

8.5.2   Multistack Machines

We now consider several computing models that are based on generalizations of the pushdown automaton. First, we consider what happens when we give the PDA several stacks. We already know, from Example 8.7, that a Turing machine can accept languages that are not accepted by any PDA with one stack. It turns out that if we give the PDA two stacks, then it can accept any language that a TM can accept.

We shall then consider a class of machines called "counter machines." These machines have only the ability to store a finite number of integers ("counters"), and to make different moves depending on which if any of the counters are currently 0. The counter machine can only add or subtract one from the counter, and cannot tell two different nonzero counts from each other. In effect, a counter is like a stack on which we can place only two symbols: a bottom-of-stack marker that appears only at the bottom, and one other symbol that may be pushed and popped from the stack.

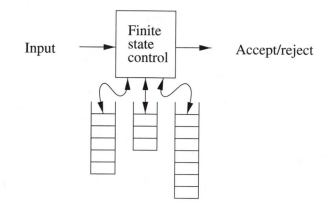

Figure 8.20: A machine with three stacks

We shall not give a formal treatment of the multistack machine, but the idea is suggested by Fig. 8.20. A k-stack machine is a deterministic PDA with k stacks. It obtains its input, like the PDA does, from an input source, rather than having the input placed on a tape or stack, as the TM does. The multistack machine has a finite control, which is in one of a finite set of states. It has a finite stack alphabet, which it uses for all its stacks. A move of the multistack machine is based on:

1. The state of the finite control.

2. The input symbol read, which is chosen from the finite input alphabet. Alternatively, the multistack machine can make a move using ϵ input, but to make the machine deterministic, there cannot be a choice of an ϵ-move or a non-ϵ-move in any situation.

3. The top stack symbol on each of its stacks.

In one move, the multistack machine can:

a) Change to a new state.

b) Replace the top symbol of each stack with a string of zero or more stack symbols. There can be (and usually is) a different replacement string for each stack.

Thus, a typical transition rule for a k-stack machine looks like:

$$\delta(q, a, X_1, X_2, \ldots, X_k) = (p, \gamma_1, \gamma_2, \ldots, \gamma_k)$$

The interpretation of this rule is that in state q, with X_i on top of the ith stack, for $i = 1, 2, \ldots, k$, the machine may consume a (either an input symbol or ϵ) from its input, go to state p, and replace X_i on top of the ith stack by string γ_i, for each $i = 1, 2, \ldots, k$. The multistack machine accepts by entering a final state.

We add one capability that simplifies input processing by this deterministic machine: we assume there is a special symbol \$, called the *endmarker*, that appears only at the end of the input and is not part of that input. The presence of the endmarker allows us to know when we have consumed all the available input. We shall see in the next theorem how the endmarker makes it easy for the multistack machine to simulate a Turing machine. Notice that the conventional TM needs no special endmarker, because the first blank serves to mark the end of the input.

Theorem 8.13: If a language L is accepted by a Turing machine, then L is accepted by a two-stack machine.

PROOF: The essential idea is that two stacks can simulate one Turing-machine tape, with one stack holding what is to the left of the head and the other stack holding what is to the right of the head, except for the infinite strings of blanks beyond the leftmost and rightmost nonblanks. In more detail, let L be $L(M)$ for some (one-tape) TM M. Our two-stack machine S will do the following:

1. S begins with a *bottom-of-stack marker* on each stack. This marker can be the start symbol for the stacks, and must not appear elsewhere on the stacks. In what follows, we shall say that a "stack is empty" when it contains only the bottom-of-stack marker.

2. Suppose that $w\$$ is on the input of S. S copies w onto its first stack, ceasing to copy when it reads the endmarker on the input.

3. S pops each symbol in turn from its first stack and pushes it onto its second stack. Now, the first stack is empty, and the second stack holds w, with the left end of w at the top.

4. S enters the (simulated) start state of M. It has an empty first stack, representing the fact that M has nothing but blanks to the left of the cell scanned by its tape head. S has a second stack holding w, representing the fact that w appears at and to the right of the cell scanned by M's head.

5. S simulates a move of M as follows.

   (a) S knows the state of M, say q, because S simulates the state of M in its own finite control.

   (b) S knows the symbol X scanned by M's tape head; it is the top of S's second stack. As an exception, if the second stack has only the bottom-of-stack marker, then M has just moved to a blank; S interprets the symbol scanned by M as the blank.

   (c) Thus, S knows the next move of M.

   (d) The next state of M is recorded in a component of S's finite control, in place of the previous state.

   (e) If M replaces X by Y and moves right, then S pushes Y onto its first stack, representing the fact that Y is now to the left of M's head. X is popped off the second stack of S. However, there are two exceptions:

      i. If the second stack has only a bottom-of-stack marker (and therefore, X is the blank), then the second stack is not changed; M has moved to yet another blank further to the right.

      ii. If Y is blank, and the first stack is empty, then that stack remains empty. The reason is that there are still only blanks to the left of M's head.

(f) If M replaces X by Y and moves left, S pops the top of the first stack, say Z, then replaces X by ZY on the second stack. This change reflects the fact that what used to be one position left of the head is now at the head. As an exception, if Z is the bottom-of-stack marker, then M must push BY onto the second stack and not pop the first stack.

6. S accepts if the new state of M is accepting. Otherwise, S simulates another move of M in the same way.

□

8.5.3 Counter Machines

A *counter machine* may be thought of in one of two ways:

1. The counter machine has the same structure as the multistack machine (Fig. 8.20), but in place of each stack is a counter. Counters hold any nonnegative integer, but we can only distinguish between zero and nonzero counters. That is, the move of the counter machine depends on its state, input symbol, and which, if any, of the counters are zero. In one move, the counter machine can:

   (a) Change state.

   (b) Add or subtract 1 from any of its counters, independently. However, a counter is not allowed to become negative, so it cannot subtract 1 from a counter that is currently 0.

2. A counter machine may also be regarded as a restricted multistack machine. The restrictions are as follows:

   (a) There are only two stack symbols, which we shall refer to as Z_0 (the *bottom-of-stack marker*), and X.

   (b) Z_0 is initially on each stack.

   (c) We may replace Z_0 only by a string of the form $X^i Z_0$, for some $i \geq 0$.

   (d) We may replace X only by X^i for some $i \geq 0$. That is, Z_0 appears only on the bottom of each stack, and all other stack symbols, if any, are X.

We shall use definition (1) for counter machines, but the two definitions clearly define machines of equivalent power. The reason is that stack $X^i Z_0$ can be identified with the count i. In definition (2), we can tell count 0 from other counts, because for count 0 we see Z_0 on top of the stack, and otherwise we see X. However, we cannot distinguish two positive counts, since both have X on top of the stack.

8.5.4   The Power of Counter Machines

There are a few observations about the languages accepted by counter machines that are obvious but worth stating:

- Every language accepted by a counter machine is recursively enumerable. The reason is that a counter machine is a special case of a stack machine, and a stack machine is a special case of a multitape Turing machine, which accepts only recursively enumerable languages by Theorem 8.9.

- Every language accepted by a one-counter machine is a CFL. Note that a counter, in point-of-view (2), is a stack, so a one-counter machine is a special case of a one-stack machine, i.e., a PDA. In fact, the languages of one-counter machines are accepted by deterministic PDA's, although the proof is surprisingly complex. The difficulty in the proof stems from the fact that the multistack and counter machines have an endmarker $ at the end of their input. A nondeterministic PDA can guess that it has seen the last input symbol and is about to see the $; thus it is clear that a nondeterministic PDA without the endmarker can simulate a DPDA with the endmarker. However, the hard proof, which we shall not attack, is to show that a DPDA without the endmarker can simulate a DPDA *with* the endmarker.

The surprising result about counter machines is that two counters are enough to simulate a Turing machine and therefore to accept every recursively enumerable language. It is this result we address now, first showing that three counters are enough, and then simulating three counters by two counters.

Theorem 8.14: Every recursively enumerable language is accepted by a three-counter machine.

PROOF: Begin with Theorem 8.13, which says that every recursively enumerable language is accepted by a two-stack machine. We then need to show how to simulate a stack with counters. Suppose there are $r - 1$ tape symbols used by the stack machine. We may identify the symbols with the digits 1 through $r - 1$, and think of a stack $X_1 X_2 \cdots X_n$ as an integer in base r. That is, this stack (whose top is at the left end, as usual) is represented by the integer $X_n r^{n-1} + X_{n-1} r^{n-2} + \cdots + X_2 r + X_1$.

We use two counters to hold the integers that represent each of the two stacks. The third counter is used to adjust the other two counters. In particular, we need the third counter when we either divide or multiply a count by r.

The operations on a stack can be broken into three kinds: pop the top symbol, change the top symbol, and push a symbol onto the stack. A move of the two-stack machine may involve several of these operations; in particular, replacing the top stack symbol X by a string of symbols must be broken down into replacing X and then pushing additional symbols onto the stack. We perform these operations on a stack that is represented by a count i, as follows.

Note that it is possible to use the finite control of the multistack machine to do each of the operations that requires counting up to r or less.

1. To pop the stack, we must replace i by i/r, throwing away any remainder, which is X_1. Starting with the third counter at 0, we repeatedly reduce the count i by r, and increase the third counter by 1. When the counter that originally held i reaches 0, we stop. Then, we repeatedly increase the original counter by 1 and decrease the third counter by 1, until the third counter becomes 0 again. At this time, the counter that used to hold i holds i/r.

2. To change X to Y on the top of a stack that is represented by count i, we increment or decrement i by a small amount, surely no more than r. If $Y > X$, as digits, increment i by $Y - X$; if $Y < X$ then decrement i by $X - Y$.

3. To push X onto a stack that initially holds i, we need to replace i by $ir + X$. We first multiply by r. To do so, repeatedly decrement the count i by 1 and increase the third counter (which starts from 0, as always), by r. When the original counter becomes 0, we have ir on the third counter. Copy the third counter to the original counter and make the third counter 0 again, as we did in item (1). Finally, we increment the original counter by X.

To complete the construction, we must initialize the counters to simulate the stacks in their initial condition: holding only the start symbol of the two-stack machine. This step is accomplished by incrementing the two counters involved to some small integer, whichever integer from 1 to $r - 1$ corresponds to the start symbol. $\Box$

Theorem 8.15: Every recursively enumerable language is accepted by a two-counter machine.

PROOF: With the previous theorem, we only have to show how to simulate three counters with two counters. The idea is to represent the three counters, say i, j, and k, by a single integer. The integer we choose is $m = 2^i 3^j 5^k$. One counter will hold this number, while the other is used to help multiply or divide m by one of the first three primes: 2, 3, and 5. To simulate the three-counter machine, we need to perform the following operations:

1. Increment i, j, and/or k. To increment i by 1, we multiply m by 2. We already saw in the proof of Theorem 8.14 how to multiply a count by any constant r, using a second counter. Likewise, we increment j by multiplying m by 3, and we increment k by multiplying m by 5.

2. Tell which, if any, of i, j, and k are 0. To tell if $i = 0$, we must determine whether m is divisible by 2. Copy m into the second counter, using the state of the counter machine to remember whether we have decremented

---

Choice of Constants in the 3-to-2 Counter Construction

Notice how important it is in the proof of Theorem 8.15 2, 3, and 5 are distinct primes. If we had chosen, say $m = 2^i 3^j 4^k$, then $m = 12$ could represent either $i = 0$, $j = 1$, and $k = 1$, or it could represent $i = 2$, $j = 1$, and $k = 0$. Thus, we could not tell whether i or k was 0, and thus could not simulate the 3-counter machine reliably.

---

m an even or odd number of times. If we have decremented m and odd number of times when it becomes 0, then $i = 0$. We then restore m by copying the second counter to the first. Similarly, we test if $j = 0$ by determining whether m is divisible by 3, and we test if $k = 0$ by determining whether m is divisible by 5.

3. Decrement i, j, and/or k. To do so, we divide m by 2, 3, or 5, respectively. The proof of Theorem 8.14 tells us how to perform the division by any constant, using an extra counter. Since the 3-counter machine cannot decrease a count below 0, it is an error, and the simulating 2-counter machine halts without accepting, if m is not evenly divisible by the constant by which we are dividing.

□

8.5.5   Exercises for Section 8.5

Exercise 8.5.1 : Informally but clearly describe counter machines that accept the following languages. In each case, use as few counters as possible, but not more than two counters.

* a) $\{0^n 1^m \mid n \geq m \geq 1\}$.

b) $\{0^n 1^m \mid 1 \leq m \leq n\}$.

*! c) $\{a^i b^j c^k \mid i = j \text{ or } i = k\}$.

!! d) $\{a^i b^j c^k \mid i = j \text{ or } i = k \text{ or } j = k\}$.

!! **Exercise 8.5.2 :** The purpose of this exercise is to show that a one-stack machine with an endmarker on the input has no more power than a deterministic PDA. $L\$$ is the concatenation of language L with the language containing only the one string $\$$; that is, $L\$$ is the set of all strings $w\$$ such that w is in L. Show that if $L\$$ is a language accepted by a DPDA, where $\$$ is the endmarker symbol, not appearing in any string of L, then L is also accepted by some DPDA. *Hint:*

This question is really one of showing that the DPDA languages are closed under the operation L/a defined in Exercise 4.2.2. You must modify the DPDA P for $L\$$ by replacing each of its stack symbols X by all possible pairs (X, S), where S is a set of states. If P has stack $X_1 X_2 \cdots X_n$, then the constructed DPDA for L has stack $(X_1, S_1)(X_2, S_2) \cdots (X_n, S_n)$, where each S_i is the set of states q such that P, started in ID $(q, a, X_i X_{i+1} \cdots X_n)$ will accept.

8.6 Turing Machines and Computers

Now, let us compare the Turing machine and the common sort of computer that we use daily. While these models appear rather different, they can accept exactly the same languages — the recursively enumerable languages. Since the notion of "a common computer" is not well defined mathematically, the arguments in this section are necessarily informal. We must appeal to your intuition about what computers can do, especially when the numbers involved exceed normal limits that are built into the architecture of these machines (e.g., 32-bit address spaces). The claims of this section can be divided into two parts:

1. A computer can simulate a Turing machine.

2. A Turing machine can simulate a computer, and can do so in an amount of time that is at most some polynomial in the number of steps taken by the computer.

8.6.1 Simulating a Turing Machine by Computer

Let us first examine how a computer can simulate a Turing machine. Given a particular TM M, we must write a program that acts like M. One aspect of M is its finite control. Since there are only a finite number of states and a finite number of transition rules, our program can encode states as character strings and use a table of transitions, which it looks up to determine each move. Likewise, the tape symbols can be encoded as character strings of a fixed length, since there are only a finite number of tape symbols.

A serious question arises when we consider how our program is to simulate the Turing-machine tape. This tape can grow infinitely long, but the computer's memory — main memory, disk, and other storage devices — are finite. Can we simulate an infinite tape with a fixed amount of memory?

If there is no opportunity to replace storage devices, then in fact we cannot; a computer would then be a finite automaton, and the only languages it could accept would we regular. However, common computers have swappable storage devices, perhaps a "Zip" disk, for example. In fact, the typical hard disk is removable and can be replaced by an empty, but otherwise identical disk.

Since there is no obvious limit on how many disks we could use, let us assume that as many disks as the computer needs is available. We can thus arrange that the disks are placed in two stacks, as suggested by Fig. 8.21. One stack holds the data in cells of the Turing-machine tape that are located significantly to the left of the tape head, and the other stack holds data significantly to the right of the tape head. The further down the stacks, the further away from the tape head the data is.

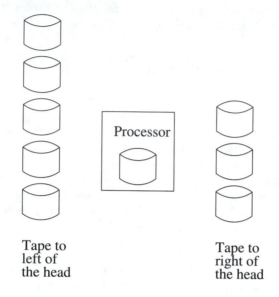

Tape to   Tape to
left of   right of
the head   the head

Figure 8.21: Simulating a Turing machine with a common computer

If the tape head of the TM moves sufficiently far to the left that it reaches cells that are not represented by the disk currently mounted in the computer, then it prints a message "swap left." The currently mounted disk is removed by a human operator and placed on the top of the right stack. The disk on top of the left stack is mounted in the computer, and computation resumes.

Similarly, if the TM's tape head reaches cells so far to the right that these cells are not represented by the mounted disk, then a "swap right" message is printed. The human operator moves the currently mounted disk to the top of the left stack, and mounts the disk on top of the right stack in the computer. If either stack is empty when the computer asks that a disk from that stack be mounted, then the TM has entered an all-blank region of the tape. In that case, the human operator must go to the store and buy a fresh disk to mount.

8.6.2 Simulating a Computer by a Turing Machine

We also need to consider the opposite comparison: are there things a common computer can do that a Turing machine cannot. An important subordinate question is whether the computer can do certain things much faster than a Turing machine. In this section, we argue that a TM can simulate a computer, and in Section 8.6.3 we argue that the simulation can be done sufficiently fast that "only" a polynomial separates the running times of the computer and TM

The Problem of Very Large Tape Alphabets

The argument of Section 8.6.1 becomes questionable if the number of tape symbols is so large that the code for one tape symbol doesn't fit on a disk. There would have to be very many tape symbols indeed, since a 30 gigabyte disk, for instance, can represent any of $2^{240000000000}$ symbols. Likewise, the number of states could be so large that we could not represent the state using the entire disk.

One resolution of this problem begins by limiting the number of tape symbols a TM uses. We can always encode an arbitrary tape alphabet in binary. Thus, any TM M can be simulated by another TM M' that uses only tape symbols 0, 1, and B. However, M' needs many states, since to simulate a move of M, the TM M' must scan its tape and remember, in its finite control, all the bits that tell it what symbol M is scanning. In this manner, we are left with very large state sets, and the PC that simulates M' may have to mount and dismount several disks when deciding what the state of M' is and what the next move of M' should be. No one ever thinks about computers performing tasks of this nature, so the typical operating system has no support for a program of this type. However, if we wished, we could program the raw computer and give it this capability.

Fortunately, the question of how to simulate a TM with a huge number of states or tape symbols can be finessed. We shall see in Section 9.2.3 that one can design a TM that is in effect a "stored program" TM. This TM, called "universal," takes the transition function of any TM, encoded in binary on its tape, and simulates that TM. The universal TM has quite reasonable numbers of states and tape symbols. By simulating the universal TM, a common computer can be programmed to accept any recursively enumerable language that we wish, without having to resort to simulation of numbers of states that stress the limits of what can be stored on a disk.

---

on a given problem. Again, let us remind the reader that there are important reasons to think of all running times that lie within a polynomial of one another to be similar, while exponential differences in running time are "too much." We take up the theory of polynomial versus exponential running times in Chapter 10.

To begin our study of how a TM simulates a computer, let us give a realistic but informal model of how a typical computer operates.

a) First, we shall suppose that the storage of a computer consists of an indefinitely long sequence of *words*, each with an *address*. In a real computer, words might be 32 or 64 bits long, but we shall not put a limit on the length of a given word. Addresses will be assumed to be integers 0, 1,

2, and so on. In a real computer, individual bytes would be numbered by consecutive integers, so words would have addresses that are multiples of 4 or 8, but this difference is unimportant. Also, in a real computer, there would be a limit on the number of words in "memory," but since we want to account for the content of an arbitrary number of disks or other storage devices, we shall assume there is no limit to the number of words.

b) We assume that the program of the computer is stored in some of the words of memory. These words each represent a simple instruction, as in the machine or assembly language of a typical computer. Examples are instructions that move data from one word to another or that add one word to another. We assume that "indirect addressing" is permitted, so one instruction could refer to another word and use the contents of that word as the address of the word to which the operation is applied. This capability, found in all modern computers, is needed to perform array accesses, to follow links in a list, or to do pointer operations in general.

c) We assume that each instruction involves a limited (finite) number of words, and that each instruction changes the value of at most one word.

d) A typical computer has *registers*, which are memory words with especially fast access. Often, operations such as addition are restricted to occur in registers. We shall not make any such restrictions, but will allow any operation to be performed on any word. The relative speed of operations on different words will not be taken into account, nor need it be if we are only comparing the language-recognizing abilities of computers and Turing machines. Even if we are interested in running time to within a polynomial, the relative speeds of different word accesses is unimportant, since those differences are "only" a constant factor.

Figure 8.22 suggests how the Turing machine would be designed to simulate a computer. This TM uses several tapes, but it could be converted to a one-tape TM using the construction of Section 8.4.1. The first tape represents the entire memory of the computer. We have used a code in which addresses of memory words, in numerical order, alternate with the contents of those memory words. Both addresses and contents are written in binary. The marker symbols * and # are used to make it easy to find the ends of addresses and contents, and to tell whether a binary string is an address or contents. Another marker, $, indicates the beginning of the sequence of addresses and contents.

The second tape is the "instruction counter." This tape holds one integer in binary, which represents one of the memory locations on tape 1. The value stored in this location will be interpreted as the next computer instruction to be executed.

The third tape holds a "memory address" or the contents of that address after the address has been located on tape 1. To execute an instruction, the TM must find the contents of one or more memory addresses that hold data

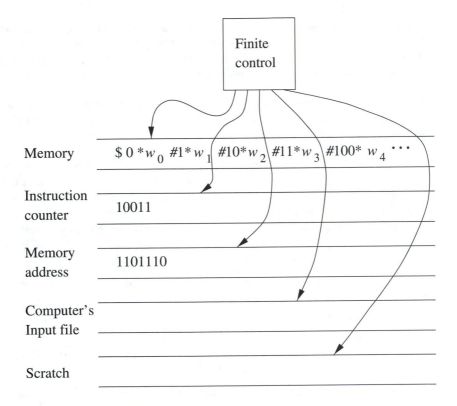

Figure 8.22: A Turing machine that simulates a typical computer

involved in the computation. First, the desired address is copied onto tape 3 and compared with the addresses on tape 1, until a match is found. The contents of this address is copied onto the third tape and moved to wherever it is needed, typically to one of the low-numbered addresses that represent the registers of the computer.

Our TM will simulate the *instruction cycle* of the computer, as follows.

1. Search the first tape for an address that matches the instruction number on tape 2. We start at the $ on the first tape, and move right, comparing each address with the contents of tape 2. The comparison of addresses on the two tapes is easy, since we need only move the tape heads right, in tandem, checking that the symbols scanned are always the same.

2. When the instruction address is found, examine its value. Let us assume that when a word is an instruction, its first few bits represent the action to be taken (e.g., copy, add, branch), and the remaining bits code an address or addresses that are involved in the action.

3. If the instruction requires the value of some address, then that address will be part of the instruction. Copy that address onto the third tape, and

mark the position of the instruction, using a second track of the first tape (not shown in Fig. 8.22), so we can find our way back to the instruction, if necessary. Now, search for the memory address on the first tape, and copy its value onto tape 3, the tape that holds the memory address.

4. Execute the instruction, or the part of the instruction involving this value. We cannot go into all the possible machine instructions. However, a sample of the kinds of things we might do with the new value are:

   (a) Copy it to some other address. We get the second address from the instruction, find this address by putting it on tape 3 and searching for the address on tape 1, as discussed previously. When we find the second address, we copy the value into the space reserved for the value of that address. If more space is needed for the new value, or the new value uses less space than the old value, change the available space by *shifting over*. That is:

      i. Copy, onto a scratch tape the entire nonblank tape to the right of where the new value goes.

      ii. Write the new value, using the correct amount of space for that value.

      iii. Recopy the scratch tape onto tape 1, immediately to the right of the new value.

   As a special case, the address may not yet appear on the first tape, because it has not been used by the computer previously. In this case, we find the place on the first tape where it belongs, shift-over to make adequate room, and store both the address and the new value there.

   (b) Add the value just found to the value of some other address. Go back to the instruction to locate the other address. find this address on tape 1. Perform a binary addition of the value of that address and the value stored on tape 3. By scanning the two values from their right ends, a TM can perform a ripple-carry addition with little difficulty. Should more space be needed for the result, use the shifting-over technique to create space on tape 1.

   (c) The instruction is a "jump," that is, a directive to take the next instruction from the address that is the value now stored on tape 3. Simply copy tape 3 to tape 2 and begin the instruction cycle again.

5. After performing the instruction, and determining that the instruction is not a jump, add 1 to the instruction counter on tape 2 and begin the instruction cycle again.

There are many other details of how the TM simulates a typical computer. We have suggested in Fig. 8.22 a fourth tape holding the simulated input to the computer, since the computer must read its input (the word whose membership in a language it is testing) from a file. The TM can read from this tape instead.

A scratch tape is also shown. Simulation of some computer instructions might make effective use of a scratch tape or tapes to compute arithmetic operations such as multiplication.

Finally, we assume that the computer makes an output that tells whether or not its input is accepted. To translate this action into terms that the Turing machine can execute, we shall suppose that there is an "accept" instruction of the computer, perhaps corresponding to a function call by the computer to put yes on an output file. When the TM simulates the execution of this computer instruction, it enters an accepting state of its own and halts.

While the above discussion is far from a complete, formal proof that a TM can simulate a typical computer, it should provide you with enough detail to convince you that a TM is a valid representation for what a computer can do. Thus, in the future, we shall use only the Turing machine as the formal representation of what can be computed by any kind of computing device.

8.6.3 Comparing the Running Times of Computers and Turing Machines

We now must address the issue of running time for the Turing machine that simulates a computer. As we have suggested previously:

- The issue of running time is important because we shall use the TM not only to examine the question of what can be computed at all, but what can be computed with enough efficiency that a problem's computer-based solution can be used in practice.

- The dividing line between the *tractable* — that which can be solved efficiently — from the *intractable* — problems that can be solved, but not fast enough for the solution to be usable — is generally held to be between what can be computed in polynomial time and what requires more than any polynomial running time.

- Thus, we need to assure ourselves that if a problem can be solved in polynomial time on a typical computer, then it can be solved in polynomial time by a Turing machine, and conversely. Because of this polynomial equivalence, our conclusions about what a Turing machine can or cannot do with adequate efficiency apply equally well to a computer.

Recall that in Section 8.4.3 we determined that the difference in running time between one-tape and multitape TM's was polynomial — quadratic, in particular. Thus, it is sufficient to show that anything the computer can do, the multitape TM described in Section 8.6.2 can do in an amount of time that is polynomial in the amount of time the computer takes. We then know that the same holds for a one-tape TM.

Before giving the proof that the Turing machine described above can simulate n steps of a computer in $O(n^3)$ time, we need to confront the issue of multiplication as a computer instruction. The problem is that we have not put a limit on the number of bits that one computer word can hold. If, say, the computer were to start with a word holding integer 2, and were to multiply that word by itself for n consecutive steps, then the word would hold the number 2^{2^n}. This number requires $2^n + 1$ bits to represent, so the time the Turing machine takes to simulate these n instructions would be exponential in n, at least.

One approach is to insist that words retain a fixed maximum length, say 64 bits. Then, multiplications (or other operations) that produced a word too long would cause the computer to halt, and the Turing machine would not have to simulate it any further. We shall take a more liberal stance: the computer may use words that grow to any length, but one computer instruction can only produce a word that is one bit longer than the longer of its arguments.

Example 8.16 : Under the above restriction, addition is allowed, since the result can only be one bit longer than the maximum length of the addends. Multiplication is not allowed, since two m-bit words can have a product of length $2m$. However, we can simulate a multiplication of m-bit integers by a sequence of m additions, interspersed with shifts of the multiplicand one bit left (which is another operation that only increases the length of the word by 1). Thus, we can still multiply arbitrarily long words, but the time taken by the computer is proportional to the square of the length of the operands. $\Box$

Assuming one-bit maximum growth per computer instruction executed, we can prove our polynomial relationship between the two running times. The idea of the proof is to notice that after n instructions have been executed, the number of words mentioned on the memory tape of the TM is $O(n)$, and each computer word requires $O(n)$ Turing-machine cells to represent it. Thus, the tape is $O(n^2)$ cells long, and the TM can locate the finite number of words needed by one computer instruction in $O(n^2)$ time.

There is, however, one additional requirement that must be placed on the instructions. Even if the instruction does not produce a long word as a result, it could take a great deal of time to compute the result. We therefore make the additional assumption that the instruction itself, applied to words of length up to k, can be performed in $O(k^2)$ steps by a multitape Turing machine. Surely the typical computer operations, such as addition, shifting, and comparison of values, can be done in $O(k)$ steps of a multitape TM, so we are being overly liberal in what we allow a computer to do in one instruction.

Theorem 8.17 : If a computer:

1. Has only instructions that increase the maximum word length by at most 1, and

2. Has only instructions that a multitape TM can perform on words of length k in $O(k^2)$ steps or less,

then the Turing machine described in Section 8.6.2 can simulate n steps of the computer in $O(n^3)$ of its own steps.

PROOF: Begin by noticing that the first (memory) tape of the TM in Fig. 8.22 starts with only the computer's program. That program may be long, but it is fixed and of constant length, independent of n, the number of instruction steps the computer executes. Thus, there is some constant c that is the largest of the computer's words and addresses appearing in the program. There is also a constant d that is the number of words occupied by the program.

Thus, after executing n steps, the computer cannot have created any words longer than $c + n$, and therefore, it cannot have created or used any addresses that are longer than $c+n$ bits either. Each instruction creates at most one new address that gets a value, so the total number of addresses after n instructions have been executed is at most $d + n$. Since each address-word combination requires at most $2(c + n) + 2$ bits, including the address, the contents, and two marker symbols to separate them, the total number of TM tape cells occupied after n instructions have been simulated is at most $2(d + n)(c + n + 1)$. As c and d are constants, this number of cells is $O(n^2)$.

We now know that each of the fixed number of lookups of addresses involved in one computer instruction can be done in $O(n^2)$ time. Since words are $O(n)$ in length, our second assumption tells us that the instructions themselves can each be carried out by a TM in $O(n^2)$ time. The only significant, remaining cost of an instruction is the time it takes the TM to create more space on its tape to hold a new or expanded word. However, shifting-over involves copying at most $O(n^2)$ data from tape 1 to the scratch tape and back again. Thus, shifting-over also requires only $O(n^2)$ time per computer instruction.

We conclude that the TM simulates one step of the computer in $O(n^2)$ of its own steps. Thus, as we claimed in the theorem statement, n steps of the computer can be simulated in $O(n^3)$ steps of the Turing machine. $\square$

As a final observation, we now see that cubing the number of steps lets a multitape TM simulate a computer. We also know from Section 8.4.3 that a one-tape TM can simulate a multitape TM by squaring the number of steps, at most. Thus:

Theorem 8.18: A computer of the type described in Theorem 8.17 can be simulated for n steps by a one-tape Turing machine, using at most $O(n^6)$ steps of the Turing machine. $\square$

8.7 Summary of Chapter 8

✦ *The Turing Machine*: The TM is an abstract computing machine with the power of both real computers and of other mathematical definitions of what can be computed. The TM consists of a finite-state control and an infinite tape divided into cells. Each cell holds one of a finite number of tape symbols, and one cell is the current position of the tape head. The TM makes moves based on its current state and the tape symbol at the cell scanned by the tape head. In one move, it changes state, overwrites the scanned cell with some tape symbol, and moves the head one cell left or right.

✦ *Acceptance by a Turing Machine*: The TM starts with its input, a finite-length string of tape symbols, on its tape, and the rest of the tape containing the blank symbol on each cell. The blank is one of the tape symbols, and the input is chosen from a subset of the tape symbols, not including blank, called the input symbols. The TM accepts its input if it ever enters an accepting state.

✦ *Recursively Enumerable Languages*: The languages accepted by TM's are called recursively enumerable (RE) languages. Thus, the RE languages are those languages that can be recognized or accepted by any sort of computing device.

✦ *Instantaneous Descriptions of a TM*: We can describe the current configuration of a TM by a finite-length string that includes all the tape cells from the leftmost to the rightmost nonblank. The state and the position of the head are shown by placing the state within the sequence of tape symbols, just to the left of the cell scanned.

✦ *Storage in the Finite Control*: Sometimes, it helps to design a TM for a particular language if we imagine that the state has two or more components. One component is the control component, and functions as a state normally does. The other components hold data that the TM needs to remember.

✦ *Multiple Tracks*: It also helps frequently if we think of the tape symbols as vectors with a fixed number of components. We may visualize each component as a separate track of the tape.

✦ *Multitape Turing Machines*: An extended TM model has some fixed number of tapes greater than one. A move of this TM is based on the state and on the vector of symbols scanned by the head on each of the tapes. In a move, the multitape TM changes state, overwrites symbols on the cells scanned by each of its tape heads, and moves any or all of its tape heads one cell in either direction. Although able to recognize certain languages faster than the conventional one-tape TM, the multitape TM cannot recognize any language that is not RE.

✦ *Nondeterministic Turing Machines*: The NTM has a finite number of choices of next move (state, new symbol, and head move) for each state and symbol scanned. It accepts an input if any sequence of choices leads to an ID with an accepting state. Although seemingly more powerful than the deterministic TM, the NTM is not able to recognize any language that is not RE.

✦ *Semi-infinite-Tape Turing Machines*: We can restrict a TM to have a tape that is infinite only to the right, with no cells to the left of the initial head position. Such a TM can accept any RE language.

✦ *Multistack Machines*: We can restrict the tapes of a multitape TM to behave like a stack. The input is on a separate tape, which is read once from left-to-right, mimicking the input mode for a finite automaton or PDA. A one-stack machine is really a DPDA, while a machine with two stacks can accept any RE language.

✦ *Counter Machines*: We may further restrict the stacks of a multistack machine to have only one symbol other than a bottom-marker. Thus, each stack functions as a counter, allowing us to store a nonnegative integer, and to test whether the integer stored is 0, but nothing more. A machine with two counters is sufficient to accept any RE language.

✦ *Simulating a Real Computer by a Turing Machine*: It is possible, in principle, to simulate a TM by a real computer if we accept that there is a potentially infinite supply of a removable storage device such as a disk, to simulate the nonblank portion of the TM tape. Since the physical resources to make disks are not infinite, this argument is questionable. However, since the limits on how much storage exists in the universe are unknown and undoubtedly vast, the assumption of an infinite resource, as in the TM tape, is realistic in practice and generally accepted.

✦ *Simulating a Computer by a Turing Machine*: A TM can simulate the storage and control of a real computer by using one tape to store all the locations and their contents: registers, main memory, disks, and other storage devices. Thus, we can be confident that something not doable by a TM cannot be done by a real computer.

8.8 References for Chapter 8

The Turing machine is taken from [8]. At about the same time there were several less machine-like proposals for characterizing what can be computed, including the work of Church [1], Kleene [5], and Post [7]. All these were preceded by the work of Gödel [3], which in effect showed that there was no way for a computer to answer all mathematical questions.

The study of multitape Turing machines, especially the matter of how their running time compares with that of the one-tape model initiated with Hartmanis and Stearns [4]. The examination of multistack and counter machines comes from [6], although the construction given here is from [2].

The approach in Section 8.1 of using "hello, world" as a surrogate for acceptance or halting by a Turing machine appeared in unpublished notes of S. Rudich.

1. A. Church, "An undecidable problem in elementary number theory," *American J. Math.* **58** (1936), pp. 345–363.

2. P. C. Fischer, "Turing machines with restricted memory access," *Information and Control* **9**:4 (1966), pp. 364–379.

3. K. Gödel, "Uber formal unentscheidbare satze der Principia Mathematica und verwander systeme," *Monatschefte fur Mathematik und Physik* **38** (1931), pp. 173–198.

4. J. Hartmanis and R. E. Stearns, "On the computational complexity of algorithms," *Transactions of the AMS* **117** (1965), pp. 285–306.

5. S. C. Kleene, "General recursive functions of natural numbers," *Mathematische Annalen* **112** (1936), pp. 727–742.

6. M. L. Minsky, "Recursive unsolvability of Post's problem of 'tag' and other topics in the theory of Turing machines," *Annals of Mathematics* **74**:3 (1961), pp. 437–455.

7. E. Post, "Finite combinatory processes-formulation," *J. Symbolic Logic* **1** (1936), pp. 103–105.

8. A. M. Turing, "On computable numbers with an application to the Entscheidungsproblem," *Proc. London Math. Society* **2**:42 (1936), pp. 230–265. See also *ibid.* **2**:43, pp. 544–546.

Chapter 9

Undecidability

This chapter begins by repeating, in the context of Turing machines, the argument of Section 8.1, which was a plausibility argument for the existence of problems that could not be solved by computer. The problem with the latter "proof" was that we were forced to ignore the real limitations that every implementation of C (or any other programming language) has on any real computer. Yet these limitations, such as the size of the address space, are not fundamental limits. Rather, as the years progress we expect computers will grow indefinitely in measures such as address-space size, main-memory size, and others.

By focusing on the Turing machine, where these limitations do not exist, we are better able to capture the essential idea of what some computing device will be capable of doing, if not today, then at some time in the future. In this chapter, we shall give a formal proof of the existence of a problem about Turing machines that no Turing machine can solve. Since we know from Section 8.6 that Turing machines can simulate real computers, even those without the limits that we know exist today, we shall have a rigorous argument that the following problem:

- Does this Turing machine accept (the code for) itself as input?

cannot be solved by a computer, no matter how generously we relax those practical limits.

We then divide problems that can be solved by a Turing machine into two classes: those that have an *algorithm* (i.e., a Turing machine that halts whether or not it accepts its input), and those that are only solved by Turing machines that may run forever on inputs they do not accept. The latter form of acceptance is problematic, since no matter how long the TM runs, we cannot know whether the input is accepted or not. Thus, we shall concentrate on techniques for showing problems to be "undecidable," i.e., to have no algorithm, regardless of whether or not they are accepted by a Turing machine that fails to halt on some inputs.

We prove undecidable the following problem:

- Does this Turing machine accept this input?

Then, we exploit this undecidability result to exhibit a number of other un-decidable problems. For instance, we show that all nontrivial problems about the language accepted by a Turing machine are undecidable, as are a number of problems that have nothing at all to do with Turing machines, programs, or computers.

9.1   A Language That Is Not Recursively Enumerable

Recall that a language L is *recursively enumerable* (abbreviated RE) if $L = L(M)$ for some TM M. Also, we shall in Section 9.2 introduce "recursive" or "decidable" languages that are not only recursively enumerable, but are accepted by a TM that always halts, regardless of whether or not it accepts.

Our long-range goal is to prove undecidable the language consisting of pairs (M, w) such that:

1. M is a Turing machine (suitably coded, in binary) with input alphabet $\{0, 1\}$,

2. w is a string of 0's and 1's, and

3. M accepts input w.

If this problem with inputs restricted to the binary alphabet is undecidable, then surely the more general problem, where TM's may have any alphabet, is undecidable.

Our first step is to set this question up as a true question about membership in a particular language. Thus, we must give a coding for Turing machines that uses only 0's and 1's, regardless of how many states the TM has. Once we have this coding, we can treat any binary string as if it were a Turing machine. If the string is not a well-formed representation of some TM, we may think of it as representing a TM with no moves. Thus, we may think of every binary string as some TM.

An intermediate goal, and the subject of this section, involves the language L_d, the "diagonalization language," which consists of all those strings w such that the TM represented by w does not accept the input w. We shall show that L_d has no Turing machine at all that accepts it. Remember that showing there is no Turing machine at all for a language is showing something stronger than that the language is undecidable (i.e., that it has no algorithm, or TM that always halts).

The language L_d plays a role analogous to the hypothetical program H_2 of Section 8.1.2, which prints `hello, world` whenever its input does *not* print `hello, world` when given itself as input. More precisely, just as H_2 cannot exist because its response when given itself as input is paradoxical, L_d cannot be accepted by a Turing machine, because if it were, then that Turing machine would have to disagree with itself when given a code for itself as input.

9.1.1   Enumerating the Binary Strings

In what follows, we shall need to assign integers to all the binary strings so that each string corresponds to one integer, and each integer corresponds to one string. If w is a binary string, treat $1w$ as a binary integer i. Then we shall call w the ith string. That is, ϵ is the first string, 0 is the second, 1 the third, 00 the fourth, 01 the fifth, and so on. Equivalently, strings are ordered by length, and strings of equal length are ordered lexicographically. Hereafter, we shall refer to the ith string as w_i.

9.1.2   Codes for Turing Machines

Our next goal is to devise a binary code for Turing machines so that each TM with input alphabet $\{0, 1\}$ may be thought of as a binary string. Since we just saw how to enumerate the binary strings, we shall then have an identification of the Turing machines with the integers, and we can talk about "the ith Turing machine, M_i." To represent a TM $M = (Q, \{0, 1\}, \Gamma, \delta, q_1, B, F)$ as a binary string, we must first assign integers to the states, tape symbols, and directions L and R.

- We shall assume the states are $q_1, q_2, \ldots, q_k$ for some k. The start state will always be q_1, and q_2 will be the only accepting state. Note that, since we may assume the TM halts whenever it enters an accepting state, there is never any need for more than one accepting state.

- We shall assume the tape symbols are $X_1, X_2, \ldots, X_m$ for some m. X_1 always will be the symbol 0, X_2 will be 1, and X_3 will be B, the blank. However, other tape symbols can be assigned to the remaining integers arbitrarily.

- We shall refer to direction L as D_1 and direction R as D_2.

Since each TM M can have integers assigned to its states and tape symbols in many different orders, there will be more than one encoding of the typical TM. However, that fact is unimportant in what follows, since we shall show that no encoding can represent a TM M such that $L(M) = L_d$.

Once we have established an integer to represent each state, symbol, and direction, we can encode the transition function δ. Suppose one transition rule is $\delta(q_i, X_j) = (q_k, X_l, D_m)$, for some integers i, j, k, l, and m. We shall code this rule by the string $0^i 1 0^j 1 0^k 1 0^l 1 0^m$. Notice that, since all of i, j, k, l, and m are at least one, there are no occurrences of two or more consecutive 1's within the code for a single transition.

A code for the entire TM M consists of all the codes for the transitions, in some order, separated by pairs of 1's:

$$C_1 11 C_2 11 \cdots C_{n-1} 11 C_n$$

where each of the C's is the code for one transition of M.

Example 9.1 : Let the TM in question be

$$M = (\{q_1, q_2, q_3\}, \{0, 1\}, \{0, 1, B\}, \delta, q_1, B, \{q_2\})$$

where δ consists of the rules:

$$\delta(q_1, 1) = (q_3, 0, R)$$
$$\delta(q_3, 0) = (q_1, 1, R)$$
$$\delta(q_3, 1) = (q_2, 0, R)$$
$$\delta(q_3, B) = (q_3, 1, L)$$

The codes for each of these rules, respectively, are:

0100100010100

0001010100100

00010010010100

0001000100010010

For example, the first rule can be written as $\delta(q_1, X_2) = (q_3, X_1, D_2)$, since $1 = X_2$, $0 = X_1$, and $R = D_2$. Thus, its code is $0^1 10^2 10^3 10^1 10^2$, as was indicated above. A code for M is:

0100100010100110001010100100110001001001010011000100010010

Note that there are many other possible codes for M. In particular, the codes for the four transitions may be listed in any of 4! orders, giving us 24 codes for M.   □

In Section 9.2.3, we shall have need to code pairs consisting of a TM and a string, (M, w). For this pair we use the code for M followed by 111, followed by w. Note that, since no valid code for a TM contains three 1's in a row, we can be sure that the first occurrence of 111 separates the code for M from w. For instance, if M were the TM of Example 9.1, and w were 1011, then the code for (M, w) would be the string shown at the end of Example 9.1 followed by 1111011.

9.1.3   The Diagonalization Language

In Section 9.1.2 we coded Turing machines so there is now a concrete notion of M_i, the "ith Turing machine": that TM M whose code is w_i, the ith binary string. Many integers do not correspond to any TM at all. For instance, 11001 does not begin with 0, and 0010111010010100 has three consecutive consecutive 1's. If w_i is not a valid TM code, we shall take M_i to be the TM with one state and no transitions. That is, for these values of i, M_i is a Turing machine that immediately halts on any input. Thus, $L(M_i)$ is $\emptyset$ if w_i fails to be a valid TM code.

Now, we can make a vital definition.

- The language L_d, the *diagonalization language*, is the set of strings w_i such that w_i is not in $L(M_i)$.

That is, L_d consists of all strings w such that the TM M whose code is w does not accept when given w as input.

The reason L_d is called a "diagonalization" language can be seen if we consider Fig. 9.1. This table tells for all i and j, whether the TM M_i accepts input string w_j; 1 means "yes it does" and 0 means "no it doesn't."[1] We may think of the ith row as the *characteristic vector* for the language $L(M_i)$; that is, the 1's in this row indicate the strings that are members of this language.

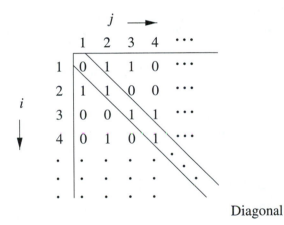

Figure 9.1: The table that represents acceptance of strings by Turing machines

The diagonal values tell whether M_i accepts w_i. To construct L_d, we complement the diagonal. For instance, if Fig. 9.1 were the correct table, then the complemented diagonal would begin $1, 0, 0, 0, \ldots$. Thus, L_d would contain $w_1 = \epsilon$, not contain w_2 through w_4, which are 0, 1, and 00, and so on.

The trick of complementing the diagonal to construct the characteristic vector of a language that cannot be the language that appears in any row, is called *diagonalization*. It works because the complement of the diagonal is itself a characteristic vector describing membership in some language, namely

---

[1]You should note that the actual table does not look anything like the one suggested by the figure. Since all low integers fail to represent a valid TM code, and thus represent the trivial TM that makes no moves, the top rows of the table are in fact solid 0's.

L_d. This characteristic vector disagrees in some column with every row of the table suggested by Fig. 9.1. Thus, the complement of the diagonal cannot be the characteristic vector of any Turing machine.

9.1.4   Proof that L_d is not Recursively Enumerable

Following the above intuition about characteristic vectors and the diagonal, we shall now prove formally a fundamental result about Turing machines: there is no Turing machine that accepts the language L_d.

Theorem 9.2: L_d is not a recursively enumerable language. That is, there is no Turing machine that accepts L_d.

PROOF: Suppose L_d were $L(M)$ for some TM M. Since L_d is a language over alphabet $\{0, 1\}$, M would be in the list of Turing machines we have constructed, since it includes all TM's with input alphabet $\{0, 1\}$. Thus, there is at least one code for M, say i; that is, $M = M_i$.

Now, ask if w_i is in L_d.

- If w_i is in L_d, then M_i accepts w_i. But then, by definition of L_d, w_i is not in L_d, because L_d contains only those w_j such that M_j does *not* accept w_j.

- Similarly, if w_i is not in L_d, then M_i does not accept w_i, Thus, by definition of L_d, w_i *is* in L_d.

Since w_i can neither be in L_d nor fail to be in L_d, we conclude that there is a contradiction of our assumption that M exists. That is, L_d is not a recursively enumerable language.   □

9.1.5   Exercises for Section 9.1

Exercise 9.1.1: What strings are:

* a) w_{37}?

  b) w_{100}?

Exercise 9.1.2: Write one of the possible codes for the Turing machine of Fig. 8.9.

! **Exercise 9.1.3:** Here are two definitions of languages that are similar to the definition of L_d, yet different from that language. For each, show that the language is not accepted by a Turing machine, using a diagonalization-type argument. Note that you cannot develop an argument based on the diagonal itself, but must find another infinite sequence of points in the matrix suggested by Fig. 9.1.

* a) The set of all w_i such that w_i is not accepted by M_{2i}.

b) The set of all w_i such that w_{2i} is not accepted by M_i.

! Exercise 9.1.4: We have considered only Turing machines that have input alphabet $\{0, 1\}$. Suppose that we wanted to assign an integer to all Turing machines, regardless of their input alphabet. That is not quite possible because, while the names of the states or noninput tape symbols are arbitrary, the particular input symbols matter. For instance, the languages $\{0^n 1^n \mid n \geq 1\}$ and $\{a^n b^n \mid n \geq 1\}$, while similar in some sense, are *not* the same language, and they are accepted by different TM's. However, suppose that we have an infinite set of symbols, $\{a_1, a_2, \ldots\}$ from which all TM input alphabets are chosen. Show how we could assign an integer to all TM's that had a finite subset of these symbols as its input alphabet.

9.2 An Undecidable Problem That is RE

Now, we have seen a problem — the diagonalization language L_d — that has no Turing machine to accept it. Our next goal is to refine the structure of the recursively enumerable (RE) languages (those that are accepted by TM's) into two classes. One class, which corresponds to what we commonly think of as an algorithm, has a TM that not only recognizes the language, but it tells us when it has decided the input string is not in the language. Such a Turing machine always halts eventually, regardless of whether or not it reaches an accepting state.

The second class of languages consists of those RE languages that are not accepted by any Turing machine with the guarantee of halting. These languages are accepted in an inconvenient way: if the input is in the language, we'll eventually know that, but if the input is not in the language, then the Turing machine may run forever, and we shall never be sure the input won't be accepted eventually. An example of this type of language, as we shall see, is the set of coded pairs (M, w) such that TM M accepts input w.

9.2.1 Recursive Languages

We call a language L *recursive* if $L = L(M)$ for some Turing machine M such that:

1. If w is in L, then M accepts (and therefore halts).

2. If w is not in L, then M eventually halts, although it never enters an accepting state.

A TM of this type corresponds to our informal notion of an "algorithm," a well-defined sequence of steps that always finishes and produces an answer. If we think of the language L as a "problem," as will be the case frequently, then problem L is called *decidable* if it is a recursive language, and it is called *undecidable* if it is not a recursive language.

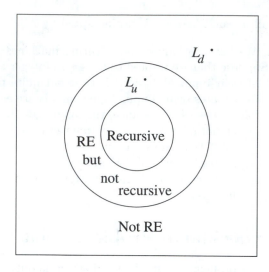

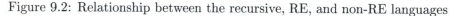

Figure 9.2: Relationship between the recursive, RE, and non-RE languages

The existence or nonexistence of an algorithm to solve a problem is often of more importance than the existence of some TM to solve the problem. As mentioned above, the Turing machines that are not guaranteed to halt may not give us enough information ever to conclude that a string is not in the language, so there is a sense in which they have not "solved the problem." Thus, dividing problems or languages between the decidable — those that are solved by an algorithm — and those that are undecidable is often more important than the division between the recursively enumerable languages (those that have TM's of some sort) and the non-recursively-enumerable languages (which have no TM at all). Figure 9.2 suggests the relationship among three classes of languages:

1. The recursive languages.

2. The languages that are recursively enumerable but not recursive.

3. The non-recursively-enumerable (*non-RE*) languages.

We have positioned the non-RE language L_d properly, and we also show the language L_u, or "universal language," that we shall prove shortly not to be recursive, although it is RE.

9.2.2   Complements of Recursive and RE languages

A powerful tool in proving languages to belong in the second ring of Fig. 9.2 (i.e., to be RE, but not recursive) is consideration of the complement of the language. We shall show that the recursive languages are closed under complementation. Thus, if a language L is RE, but $\overline{L}$, the complement of L, is not RE, then we

---

Why "Recursive"?

Programmers today are familiar with recursive functions. Yet these recursive functions don't seem to have anything to with Turing machines that always halt. Worse, the opposite — nonrecursive or undecidable — refers to languages that cannot be recognized by any algorithm, yet we are accustomed to thinking of "nonrecursive" as referring to computations that are so simple there is no need for recursive function calls.

    The term "recursive," as a synonym for "decidable," goes back to Mathematics as it existed prior to computers. Then, formalisms for computation based on recursion (but not iteration or loops) were commonly used as a notion of computation. These notations, which we shall not cover here, had some of the flavor of computation in functional programming languages such as LISP or ML. In that sense, to say a problem was "recursive" had the positive sense of "it is sufficiently simple that I can write a recursive function to solve it, and the function always finishes." That is exactly the meaning carried by the term today, in connection with Turing machines.

    The term "recursively enumerable" harks back to the same family of concepts. A function could list all the members of a language, in some order; that is, it could "enumerate" them. The languages that can have their members listed in some order are the same as the languages that are accepted by some TM, although that TM might run forever on inputs that it does not accept.

---

know L cannot be recursive. For if L were recursive, then $\overline{L}$ would also be recursive and thus surely RE. We now prove this important closure property of the recursive languages.

Theorem 9.3: If L is a recursive language, so is $\overline{L}$.

PROOF: Let $L = L(M)$ for some TM M that always halts. We construct a TM $\overline{M}$ such that $\overline{L} = L(\overline{M})$ by the construction suggested in Fig. 9.3. That is, $\overline{M}$ behaves just like M. However, M is modified as follows to create $\overline{M}$:

1. The accepting states of M are made nonaccepting states of $\overline{M}$ with no transitions; i.e., in these states $\overline{M}$ will halt without accepting.

2. $\overline{M}$ has a new accepting state r; there are no transitions from r.

3. For each combination of a nonaccepting state of M and a tape symbol of M such that M has no transition (i.e., M halts without accepting), add a transition to the accepting state r.

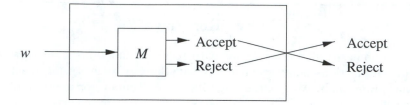

Figure 9.3: Construction of a TM accepting the complement of a recursive language

Since M is guaranteed to halt, we know that $\overline{M}$ is also guaranteed to halt. Moreover, $\overline{M}$ accepts exactly those strings that M does not accept. Thus $\overline{M}$ accepts $\overline{L}$. □

There is another important fact about complements of languages that further restricts where in the diagram of Fig. 9.2 a language and its complement can fall. We state this restriction in the next theorem.

Theorem 9.4: If both a language L and its complement are RE, then L is recursive. Note that then by Theorem 9.3, $\overline{L}$ is recursive as well.

PROOF: The proof is suggested by Fig. 9.4. Let $L = L(M_1)$ and $\overline{L} = L(M_2)$. Both M_1 and M_2 are simulated in parallel by a TM M. We can make M a two-tape TM, and then convert it to a one-tape TM, to make the simulation easy and obvious. One tape of M simulates the tape of M_1, while the other tape of M simulates the tape of M_2. The states of M_1 and M_2 are each components of the state of M.

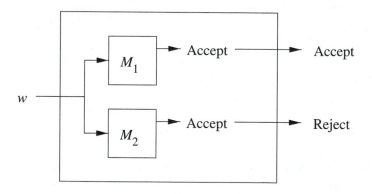

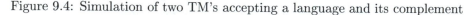

Figure 9.4: Simulation of two TM's accepting a language and its complement

If input w to M is in L, then M_1 will eventually accept. If so, M accepts and halts. If w is not in L, then it is in $\overline{L}$, so M_2 will eventually accept. When M_2 accepts, M halts without accepting. Thus, on all inputs, M halts, and

$L(M)$ is exactly L. Since M always halts, and $L(M) = L$, we conclude that L is recursive. □

We may summarize Theorems 9.3 and 9.4 as follows. Of the nine possible ways to place a language L and its complement $\overline{L}$ in the diagram of Fig. 9.2, only the following four are possible:

1. Both L and $\overline{L}$ are recursive; i.e., both are in the inner ring.

2. Neither L nor $\overline{L}$ is RE; i.e., both are in the outer ring.

3. L is RE but not recursive, and $\overline{L}$ is not RE; i.e., one is in the middle ring and the other is in the outer ring.

4. $\overline{L}$ is RE but not recursive, and L is not RE; i.e., the same as (3), but with L and $\overline{L}$ swapped.

In proof of the above, Theorem 9.3 eliminates the possibility that one language (L or $\overline{L}$) is recursive and the other is in either of the other two classes. Theorem 9.4 eliminates the possibility that both are RE but not recursive.

Example 9.5: As an example, consider the language L_d, which we know is not RE. Thus, $\overline{L_d}$ could not be recursive. It is, however, possible that $\overline{L_d}$ could be either non-RE or RE-but-not-recursive. It is in fact the latter.

$\overline{L_d}$ is the set of strings w_i such that M_i accepts w_i. This language is similar to the universal language L_u consisting of all pairs (M, w) such that M accepts w, which we shall show in Section 9.2.3 is RE. The same argument can be used to show $\overline{L_d}$ is RE. □

9.2.3 The Universal Language

We already discussed informally in Section 8.6.2 how a Turing machine could be used to simulate a computer that had been loaded with an arbitrary program. That is to say, a single TM can be used as a "stored program computer," taking its program as well as its data from one or more tapes on which input is placed. In this section, we shall repeat the idea with the additional formality that comes with talking about the Turing machine as our representation of a stored program.

We define L_u, the *universal language*, to be the set of binary strings that encode, in the notation of Section 9.1.2, a pair (M, w), where M is a TM with the binary input alphabet, and w is a string in $(\mathbf{0} + \mathbf{1})^*$, such that w is in $L(M)$. That is, L_u is the set of strings representing a TM and an input accepted by that TM. We shall show that there is a TM U, often called the *universal Turing machine*, such that $L_u = L(U)$. Since the input to U is a binary string, U is in fact some M_j in the list of binary-input Turing machines we developed in Section 9.1.2.

It is easiest to describe U as a multitape Turing machine, in the spirit of Fig. 8.22. In the case of U, the transitions of M are stored initially on the first tape, along with the string w. A second tape will be used to hold the simulated tape of M, using the same format as for the code of M. That is, tape symbol X_i of M will be represented by 0^i, and tape symbols will be separated by single 1's. The third tape of U holds the state of M, with state q_i represented by i 0's. A sketch of U is in Fig. 9.5.

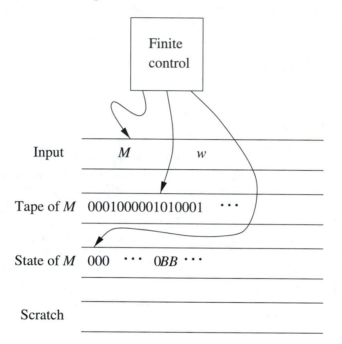

Figure 9.5: Organization of a universal Turing machine

The operation of U can be summarized as follows:

1. Examine the input to make sure that the code for M is a legitimate code for some TM. If not, U halts without accepting. Since invalid codes are assumed to represent the TM with no moves, and such a TM accepts no inputs, this action is correct.

2. Initialize the second tape to contain the input w, in its encoded form. That is, for each 0 of w, place 10 on the second tape, and for each 1 of w, place 100 there. Note that the blanks on the simulated tape of M, which are represented by 1000, will not actually appear on that tape; all cells beyond those used for w will hold the blank of U. However, U knows that, should it look for a simulated symbol of M and find its own blank, it must replace that blank by the sequence 1000 to simulate the blank of M.

A More Efficient Universal TM

A efficient simulation of M by U, one that would not require us to shift symbols on the tape, would have U first determine the number of tape symbols M used. If there are between $2^{k-1} + 1$ and 2^k symbols, U could use a k-bit binary code to represent the different tape symbols uniquely. Tape cells of M could be simulated by k of U's tape cells. To make things even easier, the given transitions of M could be rewritten by U to use the fixed-length binary code instead of the variable-length unary code we introduced.

---

3. Place 0, the start state of M, on the third tape, and move the head of U's second tape to the first simulated cell.

4. To simulate a move of M, U searches on its first tape for a transition $0^i 10^j 10^k 10^l 10^m$, such that 0^i is the state on tape 3, and 0^j is the tape symbol of M that begins at the position on tape 2 scanned by U. This transition is the one M would next make. U should:

   (a) Change the contents of tape 3 to 0^k; that is, simulate the state change of M. To do so, U first changes all the 0's on tape 3 to blanks, and then copies 0^k from tape 1 to tape 3.

   (b) Replace 0^j on tape 2 by 0^l; that is, change the tape symbol of M. If more or less space is needed (i.e., $i \neq l$), use the scratch tape and the shifting-over technique of Section 8.6.2 to manage the spacing.

   (c) Move the head on tape 2 to the position of the next 1 to the left or right, respectively, depending on whether $m = 1$ (move left) or $m = 2$ (move right). Thus, U simulates the move of M to the left or to the right.

5. If M has no transition that matches the simulated state and tape symbol, then in (4), no transition will be found. Thus, M halts in the simulated configuration, and U must do likewise.

6. If M enters its accepting state, then U accepts.

In this manner, U simulates M on w. U accepts the coded pair (M, w) if and only if M accepts w.

9.2.4 Undecidability of the Universal Language

We can now exhibit a problem that is RE but not recursive; it is the language L_u. Knowing that L_u is undecidable (i.e., not a recursive language) is in many ways more valuable than our previous discovery that L_d is not RE. The reason

The Halting Problem

One often hears of the *halting problem* for Turing machines as a problem similar to L_u — one that is RE but not recursive. In fact, the original Turing machine of A. M. Turing accepted by halting, not by final state. We could define $H(M)$ for TM M to be the set of inputs w such that M halts given input w, regardless of whether or not M accepts w. Then, the *halting problem* is the set of pairs (M, w) such that w is in $H(M)$. This problem/language is another example of one that is RE but not recursive.

is that the reduction of L_u to another problem P can be used to show there is no algorithm to solve P, regardless of whether or not P is RE. However, reduction of L_d to P is only possible if P is not RE, so L_d cannot be used to show undecidability for those problems that are RE but not recursive. On the other hand, if we want to show a problem not to be RE, then only L_d can be used; L_u is useless since it *is* RE.

Theorem 9.6: L_u is RE but not recursive.

PROOF: We just proved in Section 9.2.3 that L_u is RE. Suppose L_u were recursive. Then by Theorem 9.3, $\overline{L_u}$, the complement of L_u, would also be recursive. However, if we have a TM M to accept $\overline{L_u}$, then we can construct a TM to accept L_d (by a method explained below). Since we already know that L_d is not RE, we have a contradiction of our assumption that L_u is recursive.

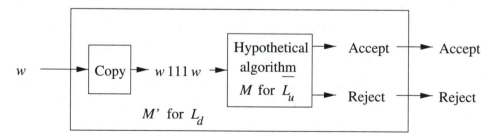

Figure 9.6: Reduction of L_d to $\overline{L_u}$

Suppose $L(M) = \overline{L_u}$. As suggested by Fig. 9.6, we can modify TM M into a TM M' that accepts L_d as follows.

1. Given string w on its input, M' changes the input to $w111w$. You may, as an exercise, write a TM program to do this step on a single tape. However, an easy argument that it can be done is to use a second tape to copy w, and then convert the two-tape TM to a one-tape TM.

2. M' simulates M on the new input. If w is w_i in our enumeration, then M' determines whether M_i accepts w_i. Since M accepts $\overline{L_u}$, it will accept if and only if M_i does not accept w_i; i.e., w_i is in L_d.

Thus, M' accepts w if and only if w is in L_d. Since we know M' cannot exist by Theorem 9.2, we conclude that L_u is not recursive. □

9.2.5 Exercises for Section 9.2

Exercise 9.2.1: Show that the halting problem, the set of (M, w) pairs such that M halts (with or without accepting) when given input w is RE but not recursive. (See the box on "The Halting Problem" in Section 9.2.4.)

Exercise 9.2.2: In the box "Why 'Recursive'?" in Section 9.2.1 we suggested that there was a notion of "recursive function" that competed with the Turing machine as a model for what can be computed. In this exercise, we shall explore an example of the recursive-function notation. A *recursive function* is a function F defined by a finite set of rules. Each rule specifies the value of the function F for certain arguments; the specification can use variables, nonnegative-integer constants, the successor (add one) function, the function F itself, and expressions built from these by composition of functions. For example, *Ackermann's function* is defined by the rules:

1. $A(0, y) = 1$ for any $y \geq 0$.

2. $A(1, 0) = 2$.

3. $A(x, 0) = x + 2$ for $x \geq 2$.

4. $A(x + 1, y + 1) = A\big(A(x, y + 1), y\big)$ for any $x \geq 0$ and $y \geq 0$.

Answer the following:

* a) Evaluate $A(2, 1)$.

! b) What function of x is $A(x, 2)$?

! c) Evaluate $A(4, 3)$.

Exercise 9.2.3: Informally describe multitape Turing machines that *enumerate* the following sets of integers, in the sense that started with blank tapes, it prints on one of its tapes $10^{i_1} 10^{i_2} 1 \cdots$ to represent the set $\{i_1, i_2, \ldots\}$.

* a) The set of all perfect squares $\{1, 4, 9, \ldots\}$.

b) The set of all primes $\{2, 3, 5, 7, 11, \ldots\}$.

!! c) The set of all i such that M_i accepts w_i. *Hint*: It is not possible to generate all these i's in numerical order. The reason is that this language, which is $\overline{L_d}$, is RE but not recursive. In fact, a definition of the RE-but-not-recursive languages is that they can be enumerated, but not in numerical order. The "trick" to enumerating them at all is that we have to simulate all M_i's on w_i, but we cannot allow any M_i to run forever, since it would preclude trying any other M_j for $j \neq i$ as soon as we encountered some M_i that does not halt on w_i. Thus, we need to operate in rounds, where in the kth round we try only a limited set of M_i's, and we do so for only a limited number of steps. Thus, each round can be completed in finite time. As long as for each TM M_i and for each number of steps s there is some round such that M_i will be simulated for at least s steps, then we shall eventually discover each M_i that accepts w_i and enumerate i.

* **Exercise 9.2.4:** Let $L_1, L_2, \ldots, L_k$ be a collection of languages over alphabet Σ such that:

1. For all $i \neq j$, $L_i \cap L_j = \emptyset$; i.e., no string is in two of the languages.

2. $L_1 \cup L_2 \cup \cdots \cup L_k = \Sigma^*$; i.e., every string is in one of the languages.

3. Each of the languages L_i, for $i = 1, 2, \ldots, k$ is recursively enumerable.

Prove that each of the languages is therefore recursive.

*! **Exercise 9.2.5:** Let L be recursively enumerable and let $\overline{L}$ be non-RE. Consider the language

$$L = \{0w \mid w \text{ is in } L\} \cup \{1w \mid w \text{ is not in } L\}$$

Can you say for certain whether L or its complement are recursive, RE, or non-RE? Justify your answer.

! **Exercise 9.2.6:** We have not discussed closure properties of the recursive languages or the RE languages, other than our discussion of complementation in Section 9.2.2. Tell whether the recursive languages and/or the RE languages are closed under the following operations. You may give informal, but clear, constructions to show closure.

* a) Union.

  b) Intersection.

  c) Concatenation.

  d) Kleene closure (star).

* e) Homomorphism.

  f) Inverse homomorphism.

9.3 Undecidable Problems About Turing Machines

We shall now use the languages L_u and L_d, whose status regarding decidability and recursive enumerability we know, to exhibit other undecidable or non-RE languages. The reduction technique will be exploited in each of these proofs. Our first undecidable problems are all about Turing machines. In fact, our discussion in this section culminates with the proof of "Rice's theorem," which says that any nontrivial property of Turing machines that depends only on the language the TM accepts must be undecidable. Section 9.4 will let us investigate some undecidable problems that do not involve Turing machines or their languages.

9.3.1 Reductions

We introduced the notion of a reduction in Section 8.1.3. In general, if we have an algorithm to convert instances of a problem P_1 to instances of a problem P_2 that have the same answer, then we say that P_1 *reduces to* P_2. We can use this proof to show that P_2 is at least as hard as P_1. Thus, if P_1 is not recursive, then P_2 cannot be recursive. If P_2 is non-RE, then P_1 cannot be RE. As we mentioned in Section 8.1.3, you must be careful to reduce a known hard problem to one you wish to prove to be at least as hard, never the opposite.

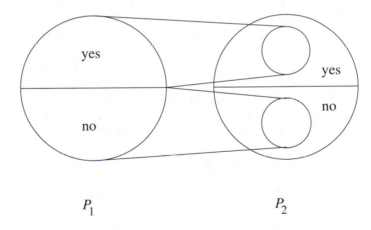

Figure 9.7: Reductions turn positive instances into positive, and negative to negative

As suggested in Fig. 9.7, a reduction must turn any instance of P_1 that has a "yes" answer into an instance of P_2 with a "yes" answer, and every instance of P_1 with a "no" answer must be turned into an instance of P_2 with a "no" answer. Note that it is not essential that every instance of P_2 be the target of one or more instances of P_1, and in fact it is quite common that only a small fraction of P_2 is a target of the reduction.

Formally, a reduction from P_1 to P_2 is a Turing machine that takes an instance of P_1 written on its tape and halts with an instance of P_2 on its tape. In practice, we shall generally describe reductions as if they were computer programs that take an instance of P_1 as input and produce an instance of P_2 as output. The equivalence of Turing machines and computer programs allows us to describe the reduction by either means. The importance of reductions is emphasized by the following theorem, of which we shall see numerous applications.

Theorem 9.7: If there is a reduction from P_1 to P_2, then:

a) If P_1 is undecidable then so is P_2.

b) If P_1 is non-RE, then so is P_2.

PROOF: First suppose P_1 is undecidable. If it is possible to decide P_2, then we can combine the reduction from P_1 to P_2 with the algorithm that decides P_2 to construct an algorithm that decides P_1. The idea was suggested in Fig. 8.7. In more detail, suppose we are given an instance w of P_1. Apply to w the algorithm that converts w into an instance x of P_2. Then apply the algorithm that decides to P_2 to x. If that algorithm says "yes," then x is in P_2. Because we reduced P_1 to P_2, we know the answer to w for P_1 is "yes"; i.e., w is in P_1. Likewise, if x is not in P_2 then w is not in P_1, and whatever answer we give to the question "is x in P_2?" is also the correct answer to "is w in P_1?"

We have thus contradicted the assumption that P_1 is undecidable. Our conclusion is that if P_1 is undecidable, then P_2 is also undecidable.

Now, consider part (b). Assume that P_1 is non-RE, but P_2 is RE. Now, we have an algorithm to reduce P_1 to P_2, but we have only a procedure to recognize P_2; that is, there is a TM that says "yes" if its input is in P_2 but may not halt if its input is not in P_2. As for part (a), starting with an instance w of P_1, convert it by the reduction algorithm to an instance x of P_2. Then apply the TM for P_2 to x. If x is accepted, then accept w.

This procedure describes a TM (which may not halt) whose language is P_1. If w is in P_1, then x is in P_2, so this TM will accept w. If w is not in P_1, then x is not in P_2. Then, the TM may or may not halt, but will surely not accept w. Since we assumed no TM for P_1 exists, we have shown by contradiction that no TM for P_2 exists either; i.e., if P_1 is non-RE, then P_2 is non-RE. □

9.3.2 Turing Machines That Accept the Empty Language

As an example of reductions involving Turing machines, let us investigate two languages called L_e and L_{ne}. Each consists of binary strings. If w is a binary string, then it represents some TM, M_i, in the enumeration of Section 9.1.2.

If $L(M_i) = \emptyset$, that is, M_i does not accept any input, then w is in L_e. Thus, L_e is the language consisting of all those encoded TM's whose language is empty. On the other hand, if $L(M_i)$ is not the empty language, then w is in L_{ne}. Thus, L_{ne} is the language of all codes for Turing machines that accept at least one input string.

In what follows, it is convenient to regard strings as the Turing machines they represent. Thus, we may define the two languages just mentioned as:

- $L_e = \{M \mid L(M) = \emptyset\}$

- $L_{ne} = \{M \mid L(M) \neq \emptyset\}$

Notice that L_e and L_{ne} are both languages over the binary alphabet $\{0, 1\}$, and that they are complements of one another. We shall see that L_{ne} is the "easier" of the two languages; it is RE but not recursive. On the other hand, L_e is non-RE.

Theorem 9.8: L_{ne} is recursively enumerable.

PROOF: We have only to exhibit a TM that accepts L_{ne}. It is easiest to describe a nondeterministic TM M, whose plan is shown in Fig. 9.8. By Theorem 8.11, M can be converted to a deterministic TM.

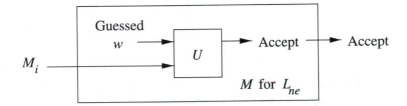

Figure 9.8: Construction of a NTM to accept L_{ne}

The operation of M is as follows.

1. M takes as input a TM code M_i.

2. Using its nondeterministic capability, M guesses an input w that M_i might accept.

3. M tests whether M_i accepts w. For this part, M can simulate the universal TM U that accepts L_u.

4. If M_i accepts w, then M accepts its own input, which is M_i.

In this manner, if M_i accepts even one string, M will guess that string (among all others, of course), and accept M_i. However, if $L(M_i) = \emptyset$, then no guess w leads to acceptance by M_i, so M does not accept M_i. Thus, $L(M) = L_{ne}$. □

Our next step is to prove that L_{ne} is not recursive. To do so, we reduce L_u to L_{ne}. That is, we shall describe an algorithm that transforms an input (M, w) into an output M', the code for another Turing machine, such that w is in $L(M)$ if and only if $L(M')$ is not empty. That is, M accepts w if and only if M' accepts at least one string. The trick is to have M' ignore its input, and instead simulate M on input w. If M accepts, then M' accepts its own input; thus acceptance of w by M is tantamount to $L(M')$ being nonempty. If L_{ne} were recursive, then we would have an algorithm to tell whether or not M accepts w: construct M' and see whether $L(M') = \emptyset$.

Theorem 9.9: L_{ne} is not recursive.

PROOF: We shall follow the outline of the proof given above. We must design an algorithm that converts an input that is a binary-coded pair (M, w) into a TM M' such that $L(M') \neq \emptyset$ if and only if M accepts input w. The construction of M' is sketched in Fig. 9.9. As we shall see, if M does not accept w, then M' accepts none of its inputs; i.e., $L(M') = \emptyset$. However, if M accepts w, then M' accepts every input, and thus $L(M')$ surely is not $\emptyset$.

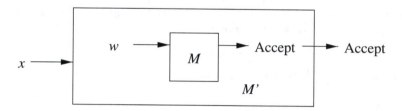

Figure 9.9: Plan of the TM M' constructed from (M, w) in Theorem 9.9; M' accepts arbitrary input if and only if M accepts w

M' is designed to do the following:

1. M' ignores its own input x. Rather, it replaces its input by the string that represents TM M and input string w. Since M' is designed for a specific pair (M, w), which has some length n, we may construct M' to have a sequence of states $q_0, q_1, \ldots, q_n$, where q_0 is the start state.

   (a) In state q_i, for $i = 0, 1, \ldots, n - 1$, M' writes the $(i + 1)st$ bit of the code for (M, w), goes to state q_{i+1}, and moves right.

   (b) In state q_n, M' moves right, if necessary, replacing any nonblanks (which would be the tail of x, if that input to M' is longer than n) by blanks.

2. When M' reaches a blank in state q_n, it uses a similar collection of states to reposition its head at the left end of the tape.

3. Now, using additional states, M' simulates a universal TM U on its present tape.

4. If U accepts, then M' accepts. If U never accepts, then M' never accepts either.

The description of M' above should be sufficient to convince you that you could design a Turing machine that would transform the code for M and the string w into the code for M'. That is, there is an algorithm to perform the reduction of L_u to L_{ne}. We also see that if M accepts w, then M' accepts whatever input x was originally on its tape. The fact that x was ignored is irrelevant; the definition of acceptance by a TM says that whatever was placed on the tape, before commencing operation, is what the TM accepts. Thus, if M accepts w, then the code for M' is in L_{ne}.

Conversely, if M does not accept w, then M' never accepts, no matter what its input is. Hence, in this case the code for M' is not in L_{ne}. We have successfully reduced L_u to L_{ne} by the algorithm that constructs M' from M and w; we may conclude that, since L_u is not recursive, neither is L_{ne}. The existence of this reduction is sufficient to complete the proof. However, to illustrate the impact of the reduction, we shall take this argument one step further. If L_{ne} were recursive, then we could develop an algorithm for L_u as follows:

1. Convert (M, w) to the TM M' as above.

2. Use the hypothetical algorithm for L_{ne} to tell whether or not $L(M') = \emptyset$. If so, say M does not accept w; if $L(M') \neq \emptyset$, say M does accept w.

Since we know by Theorem 9.6 that no such algorithm for L_u exists, we have contradicted the assumption that L_{ne} is recursive, and conclude that L_{ne} is not recursive. □

Now, we know the status of L_e. If L_e were RE, then by Theorem 9.4, both it and L_{ne} would be recursive. Since L_{ne} is not recursive by Theorem 9.9, we conclude that:

Theorem 9.10: L_e is not RE. □

9.3.3 Rice's Theorem and Properties of the RE Languages

The fact that languages like L_e and L_{ne} are undecidable is actually a special case of a far more general theorem: all nontrivial properties of the RE languages are undecidable, in the sense that it is impossible to recognize by a Turing machine those binary strings that are codes for a TM whose language has the property. An example of a property of the RE languages is "the language is context free." It is undecidable whether a given TM accepts a context-free language, as a special case of the general principle that all nontrivial properties of the RE languages are undecidable.

A *property* of the RE languages is simply a set of RE languages. Thus, the property of being context-free is formally the set of all CFL's. The property of being empty is the set $\{\emptyset\}$ consisting of only the empty language.

Why Problems and Their Complements are Different

Our intuition tells us that a problem and its complement are really the same problem. To solve one, we can use an algorithm for the other, and at the last step, complement the output: say "yes" instead of "no," and vice-versa. That instinct is exactly right, as long as the problem and its complement are recursive.

However, as we discussed in Section 9.2.2, there are two other possibilities. First, neither the problem nor its complement are even RE. Then, neither can be solved by any kind of TM at all, so in a sense the two are again similar. However, the interesting case, typified by L_e and L_{ne}, is when one is RE and the other is non-RE.

For the language that is RE, we can design a TM that takes an input w and searches for a reason why w is in the language. Thus, for L_{ne}, given a TM M as input, we set our TM looking for strings that the TM M accepts, and as soon as we find one, we accept M. If M is a TM with an empty language, we never know for certain that M is not in L_{ne}, but we never accept M, and that is the correct response by the TM.

On the other hand, for the complement problem L_e, which is not RE, there is no way ever to accept all its strings. Suppose we are given a string M that is a TM whose language is empty. We can test inputs to the TM M, and we may never find one that M accepts, yet we can never be sure that there isn't some input we've not yet tested, that this TM accepts. Thus, M can never be accepted, even if it should be.

A property is *trivial* if it is either empty (i.e., satisfied by no language at all), or is all RE languages. Otherwise, it is *nontrivial*.

- Note that the empty property, $\emptyset$, is different from the property of being an empty language, $\{\emptyset\}$.

We cannot recognize a set of languages as the languages themselves. The reason is that the typical language, being infinite, cannot be written down as a finite-length string that could be input to a TM. Rather, we must recognize the Turing machines that accept those languages; the TM code itself is finite, even if the language it accepts is infinite. Thus, if $\mathcal{P}$ is a property of the RE languages, the language $L_{\mathcal{P}}$ is the set of codes for Turing machines M_i such that $L(M_i)$ is a language in $\mathcal{P}$. When we talk about the decidability of a property $\mathcal{P}$, we mean the decidability of the language $L_{\mathcal{P}}$.

Theorem 9.11: (Rice's Theorem) Every nontrivial property of the RE languages is undecidable.

PROOF: Let $\mathcal{P}$ be a nontrivial property of the RE languages. Assume to begin that $\emptyset$, the empty language, is not in $\mathcal{P}$; we shall return later to the opposite case. Since $\mathcal{P}$ is nontrivial, there must be some nonempty language L that is in $\mathcal{P}$. Let M_L be a TM accepting L.

We shall reduce L_u to $L_{\mathcal{P}}$, thus proving that $L_{\mathcal{P}}$ is undecidable, since L_u is undecidable. The algorithm to perform the reduction takes as input a pair (M, w) and produces a TM M'. The design of M' is suggested by Fig. 9.10; $L(M')$ is $\emptyset$ if M does not accept w, and $L(M') = L$ if M accepts w.

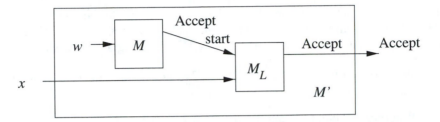

Figure 9.10: Construction of M' for the proof of Rice's Theorem

M' is a two-tape TM. One tape is used to simulate M on w. Remember that the algorithm performing the reduction is given M and w as input, and can use this input in designing the transitions of M'. Thus, the simulation of M on w is "built into" M'; the latter TM does not have to read the transitions of M on a tape of its own.

The other tape of M' is used to simulate M_L on the input x to M', if necessary. Again, the transitions of M_L are known to the reduction algorithm and may be "built into" the transitions of M'. The TM M' is constructed to do the following:

1. Simulate M on input w. Note that w is not the input to M'; rather, M' writes M and w onto one of its tapes and simulates the universal TM U on that pair, as in the proof of Theorem 9.8.

2. If M does not accept w, then M' does nothing else. M' never accepts its own input, x, so $L(M') = \emptyset$. Since we assume $\emptyset$ is not in property $\mathcal{P}$, that means the code for M' is not in $L_{\mathcal{P}}$.

3. If M accepts w, then M' begins simulating M_L on its own input x. Thus, M' will accept exactly the language L. Since L is in $\mathcal{P}$, the code for M' is in $L_{\mathcal{P}}$.

You should observe that constructing M' from M and w can be carried out by an algorithm. Since this algorithm turns (M, w) into an M' that is in $L_{\mathcal{P}}$ if and only if (M, w) is in L_u, this algorithm is a reduction of L_u to $L_{\mathcal{P}}$, and proves that the property $\mathcal{P}$ is undecidable.

We are not quite done. We need to consider the case where $\emptyset$ *is* in $\mathcal{P}$. If so, consider the complement property $\overline{\mathcal{P}}$, the set of RE languages that do not have property $\mathcal{P}$. By the foregoing, $\overline{\mathcal{P}}$ is undecidable. However, since every TM accepts an RE language, $\overline{L_\mathcal{P}}$, the set of (codes for) Turing machines that do not accept a language in $\mathcal{P}$ is the same as $L_{\overline{\mathcal{P}}}$, the set of TM's that accept a language in $\overline{\mathcal{P}}$. Suppose $L_\mathcal{P}$ were decidable. Then so would be $L_{\overline{\mathcal{P}}}$, because the complement of a recursive language is recursive (Theorem 9.3). □

9.3.4   Problems about Turing-Machine Specifications

All problems about Turing machines that involve only the language that the TM accepts are undecidable, by Theorem 9.11. Some of these problems are interesting in their own right. For instance, the following are undecidable:

1. Whether the language accepted by a TM is empty (which we knew from Theorems 9.9 and 9.3).

2. Whether the language accepted by a TM is finite.

3. Whether the language accepted by a TM is a regular language.

4. Whether the language accepted by a TM is a context-free language.

   However, Rice's Theorem does not imply that everything about a TM is undecidable. For instance, questions that ask about the states of the TM, rather than about the language it accepts, could be decidable.

Example 9.12: It is decidable whether a TM has five states. The algorithm to decide this question simply looks at the code for the TM and counts the number of states that appear in any of its transitions.

As another example, it is decidable whether there exists some input such that the TM makes at least five moves. The algorithm becomes obvious when we remember that if a TM makes five moves, then it does so looking only at the nine cells of its tape surrounding its initial head position. Thus, we may simulate the TM for five moves on any of the finite number of tapes consisting of five or fewer input symbols, preceded and followed by blanks. If any of these simulations fails to reach a halting situation, then we conclude that the TM makes at least five moves on some input. □

9.3.5   Exercises for Section 9.3

* **Exercise 9.3.1:** Show that the set of Turing-machine codes for TM's that accept all inputs that are palindromes (possibly along with some other inputs) is undecidable.

Exercise 9.3.2: The Big Computer Corp. has decided to bolster its sagging market share by manufacturing a high-tech version of the Turing machine, called BWTM, that is equipped with *bells* and *whistles*. The BWTM is basically the same as your ordinary Turing machine, except that each state of the machine is labeled either a "bell-state" or a "whistle-state." Whenever the BWTM enters a new state, it either rings the bell or blows the whistle, depending on which type of state it has just entered. Prove that it is undecidable whether a given BWTM M, on given input w, ever blows the whistle.

Exercise 9.3.3: Show that the language of codes for TM's M that, when started with blank tape, eventually write a 1 somewhere on the tape is undecidable.

! **Exercise 9.3.4:** We know by Rice's theorem that none of the following problems are decidable. However, are they recursively enumerable, or non-RE?

  a) Does $L(M)$ contain at least two strings?

  b) Is $L(M)$ infinite?

  c) Is $L(M)$ a context-free language?

  * d) Is $L(M) = (L(M))^R$?

! **Exercise 9.3.5:** let L be the language consisting of pairs of TM codes plus an integer, (M_1, M_2, k), such that $L(M_1) \cap L(M_2)$ contains at least k strings. Show that L is RE, but not recursive.

Exercise 9.3.6: Show that the following questions are decidable:

  * a) The set of codes for TM's M such that, when started with blank tape will eventually write some nonblank symbol on its tape. *Hint*: If M has m states, consider the first $m + 1$ transitions that it makes.

  ! b) The set of codes for TM's that never make a move left.

  ! c) The set of pairs (M, w) such that TM M, started with input w, never scans any tape cell more than once.

! **Exercise 9.3.7:** Show that the following problems are not recursively enumerable:

  * a) The set of pairs (M, w) such that TM M, started with input w, does not halt.

  b) The set of pairs (M_1, M_2) such that $L(M_1) \cap L(M_2) = \emptyset$.

  c) The set of triples (M_1, M_2, M_3) such that $L(M_1) = L(M_2)L(M_3)$; i.e., the language of the first is the concatenation of the languages of the other two TM's.

!! **Exercise 9.3.8:** Tell whether each of the following are recursive, RE-but-not-recursive, or non-RE.

  * a) The set of all TM codes for TM's that halt on every input.

  b) The set of all TM codes for TM's that halt on no input.

  c) The set of all TM codes for TM's that halt on at least one input.

  * d) The set of all TM codes for TM's that fail to halt on at least one input.

9.4   Post's Correspondence Problem

In this section, we begin reducing undecidable questions about Turing machines to undecidable questions about "real" things, that is, common matters that have nothing to do with the abstraction of the Turing machine. We begin with a problem called "Post's Correspondence Problem" (*PCP*), which is still abstract, but it involves strings rather than Turing machines. Our goal is to prove this problem about strings to be undecidable, and then use its undecidability to prove other problems undecidable by reducing PCP to those.

We shall prove PCP undecidable by reducing L_u to PCP. To facilitate the proof, we introduce a "modified" PCP, and reduce the modified problem to the original PCP. Then, we reduce L_u to the modified PCP. The chain of reductions is suggested by Fig. 9.11. Since the original L_u is known to be undecidable, we conclude that PCP is undecidable.

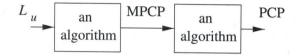

Figure 9.11: Reductions proving the undecidability of Post's Correspondence Problem

9.4.1   Definition of Post's Correspondence Problem

An instance of *Post's Correspondence Problem* (PCP) consists of two lists of strings over some alphabet Σ; the two lists must be of equal length. We generally refer to the A and B lists, and write $A = w_1, w_2, \ldots, w_k$ and $B = x_1, x_2, \ldots, x_k$, for some integer k. For each i, the pair (w_i, x_i) is said to be a *corresponding* pair.

We say this instance of PCP *has a solution*, if there is a sequence of one or more integers $i_1, i_2, \ldots, i_m$ that, when interpreted as indexes for strings in the A and B lists, yield the same string. That is, $w_{i_1} w_{i_2} \cdots w_{i_m} = x_{i_1} x_{i_2} \cdots x_{i_m}$. We say the sequence $i_1, i_2, \ldots, i_m$ is a *solution* to this instance of PCP, if so. The Post's correspondence problem is:

- Given an instance of PCP, tell whether this instance has a solution.

Example 9.13 : Let $\Sigma = \{0, 1\}$, and let the A and B lists be as defined in Fig. 9.12. In this case, PCP has a solution. For instance, let $m = 4$, $i_1 = 2$, $i_2 = 1$, $i_3 = 1$, and $i_4 = 3$; i.e., the solution is the list $2, 1, 1, 3$. We verify that this list is a solution by concatenating the corresponding strings in order for the two lists. That is, $w_2 w_1 w_1 w_3 = x_2 x_1 x_1 x_3 = 101111110$. Note this solution is not unique. For instance, $2, 1, 1, 3, 2, 1, 1, 3$ is another solution.   □

	List A	List B
i	w_i	x_i
1	1	111
2	10111	10
3	10	0

Figure 9.12: An instance of PCP

PCP as a Language

Since we are discussing the problem of deciding whether a given instance of PCP has a solution, we need to express this problem as a language. As PCP allows instances to have arbitrary alphabets, the language PCP is really a set of strings over some fixed alphabet, which codes instances of PCP, much as we coded Turing machines that have arbitrary sets of states and tape symbols, in Section 9.1.2. For example, if a PCP instance has an alphabet with up to 2^k symbols, we can use distinct k-bit binary codes for each of the symbols.

Since each PCP instance has a finite alphabet, we can find some k for each instance. We can then code all instances in a 3-symbol alphabet consisting of 0, 1, and a "comma" symbol to separate strings. We begin the code by writing k in binary, followed by a comma. Then follow each of the pairs of strings, with strings separated by commas and their symbols coded in a k-bit binary code.

Example 9.14: Here is an example where there is no solution. Again we let $\Sigma = \{0, 1\}$, but now the instance is the two lists given in Fig. 9.13.

Suppose that the PCP instance of Fig. 9.13 has a solution, say $i_1, i_2, \ldots, i_m$, for some $m \geq 1$. We claim $i_1 = 1$. For if $i_1 = 2$, then a string beginning with $w_2 = 011$ would have to equal a string that begins with $x_2 = 11$. But that equality is impossible, since the first symbols of these two strings are 0 and 1, respectively. Similarly, it is not possible that $i_1 = 3$, since then a string beginning with $w_3 = 101$ would have to equal a string beginning with $x_3 = 011$.

If $i_1 = 1$, then the two corresponding strings from lists A and B would have to begin:

$$A:\ 10\cdots$$
$$B:\ 101\cdots$$

Now, let us see what i_2 could be.

1. If $i_2 = 1$, then we have a problem, since no string beginning with $w_1 w_1 =$

	List A	List B
i	w_i	x_i
1	10	101
2	011	11
3	101	011

Figure 9.13: Another PCP instance

1010 can match a string that begins with $x_1 x_1 = 101101$; they must disagree at the fourth position.

2. If $i_2 = 2$, we again have a problem, because no string that begins with $w_1 w_2 = 10011$ can match a string that begins with $x_1 x_2 = 10111$; they must differ at the third position.

3. Only $i_2 = 3$ is possible.

If we choose $i_2 = 3$, then the corresponding strings formed from list of integers i_1, i_3 are:

$$A: 10101 \cdots$$
$$B: 101011 \cdots$$

There is nothing about these strings that immediately suggests we cannot extend list $1, 3$ to a solution. However, we can argue that it is not possible to do so. The reason is that we are in the same condition we were in after choosing $i_1 = 1$. The string from the B list is the same as the string from the A list except that in the B list there is an extra 1 at the end. Thus, we are forced to choose $i_3 = 3$, $i_4 = 3$, and so on, to avoid creating a mismatch. We can never allow the A string to catch up to the B string, and thus can never reach a solution.   □

9.4.2   The "Modified" PCP

It is easier to reduce L_u to PCP if we first introduce an intermediate version of PCP, which we call the *Modified Post's Correspondence Problem*, or MPCP. In the modified PCP, there is the additional requirement on a solution that the first pair on the A and B lists must be the first pair in the solution. More formally, an instance of MPCP is two lists $A = w_1, w_2, \ldots, w_k$ and $B = x_1, x_2, \ldots, x_k$, and a solution is a list of 0 or more integers $i_1, i_2, \ldots, i_m$ such that

$$w_1 w_{i_1} w_{i_2} \cdots w_{i_m} = x_1 x_{i_1} x_{i_2} \cdots x_{i_m}$$

Notice that the pair (w_1, x_1) is forced to be at the beginning of the two strings, even though the index 1 is not mentioned at the front of the list that

---

Partial Solutions

In Example 9.14 we used a technique for analyzing PCP instances that comes up frequently. We considered what the possible *partial solutions* were, that is, sequences of indexes $i_1, i_2, \ldots, i_r$ such that one of $w_{i_1} w_{i_2} \cdots w_{i_r}$ and $x_{i_1} x_{i_2} \cdots x_{i_r}$ is a prefix of the other, although the two strings are not equal. Notice that if a sequence of integers is a solution, then every prefix of that sequence must be a partial solution. Thus, understanding what the partial solutions are allows us to argue about what solutions there might be.

Note, however, that because PCP is undecidable, there is no algorithm to compute all the partial solutions. There can be an infinite number of them, and worse, there is no upper bound on how different the lengths of the strings $w_{i_1} w_{i_2} \cdots w_{i_r}$ and $x_{i_1} x_{i_2} \cdots x_{i_r}$ can be, even though the partial solution leads to a solution.

---

is the solution. Also, unlike PCP, where the solution has to have at least one integer on the solution list, in MPCP, the empty list could be a solution if $w_1 = x_1$ (but those instances are rather uninteresting and will not figure in our use of MPCP).

Example 9.15 : The lists of Fig. 9.12 may be regarded as an instance of MPCP. However, as an instance of MPCP it has no solution. In proof, observe that any partial solution has to begin with index 1, so the two strings of a solution would begin:

$$A: 1 \cdots$$
$$B: 111 \cdots$$

The next integer could not be 2 or 3, since both w_2 and w_3 begin with 10 and thus would produce a mismatch at the third position. Thus, the next index would have to be 1, yielding:

$$A: 11 \cdots$$
$$B: 111111 \cdots$$

We can argue this way indefinitely. Only another 1 in the solution can avoid a mismatch, but if we can only pick index 1, the B string remains three times as long as the A string, and the two strings can never become equal. □

An important step in showing PCP is undecidable is reducing MPCP to PCP. Later, we show MPCP is undecidable by reducing L_u to MPCP. At that point, we will have a proof that PCP is undecidable as well; if it were decidable, then we could decide MPCP, and thus L_u.

Given an instance of MPCP with alphabet Σ, we construct an instance of PCP as follows. First, we introduce a new symbol $*$ that, in the PCP instance, goes between every symbol in the strings of the MPCP instance. However, in the strings of the A list, the $*$'s follow the symbols of Σ, and in the B list, the $*$'s precede the symbols of Σ. The one exception is a new pair that is based on the first pair of the MPCP instance; this pair has an extra $*$ at the beginning of w_1, so it can be used to start the PCP solution. A final pair $(*, *\$)$ is added to the PCP instance. This pair serves as the last in a PCP solution that mimics a solution to the MPCP instance.

Now, let us formalize the above construction. We are given an instance of MPCP with lists $A = w_1, w_2, \ldots, w_k$ and $B = x_1, x_2, \ldots, x_k$. We assume $*$ and $\$$ are symbols not present in the alphabet Σ of this MPCP instance. We construct a PCP instance $C = y_0, y_1, \ldots, y_{k+1}$ and $D = z_0, z_1, \ldots, z_{k+1}$, as follows:

1. For $i = 1, 2, \ldots, k$, let y_i be w_i with a $*$ after each symbol of w_i, and let z_i be x_i with a $*$ before each symbol of x_i.

2. $y_0 = *y_1$, and $z_0 = z_1$. That is, the 0th pair looks like pair 1, except that there is an extra $*$ at the beginning of the string from the first list. Note that the 0th pair will be the only pair in the PCP instance where both strings begin with the same symbol, so any solution to this PCP instance will have to begin with index 0.

3. $y_{k+1} = \$$ and $z_{k+1} = *\$$.

Example 9.16: Suppose Fig. 9.12 is an MPCP instance. Then the instance of PCP constructed by the above steps is shown in Fig. 9.14. $\square$

i	List C y_i	List D z_i
0	*1*	*1*1*1
1	1*	*1*1*1
2	1*0*1*1*1*	*1*0
3	1*0*	*0
4	$	*$

Figure 9.14: Constructing an instance of PCP from an MPCP instance

Theorem 9.17: MPCP reduces to PCP.

PROOF: The construction given above is the heart of the proof. First, suppose that $i_1, i_2, \ldots, i_m$ is a solution to the given MPCP instance with lists A and B. Then we know $w_1 w_{i_1} w_{i_2} \cdots w_{i_m} = x_1 x_{i_1} x_{i_2} \cdots x_{i_m}$. If we were to replace the

w's by y's and the x's by z's, we would have two strings that were almost the same: $y_1 y_{i_1} y_{i_2} \cdots y_{i_m}$ and $z_1 z_{i_1} z_{i_2} \cdots z_{i_m}$. The difference is that the first string would be missing a $*$ at the beginning, and the second would be missing a $*$ at the end. That is,

$$*y_1 y_{i_1} y_{i_2} \cdots y_{i_m} = z_1 z_{i_1} z_{i_2} \cdots z_{i_m} *$$

However, $y_0 = *y_1$, and $z_0 = z_1$, so we can fix the initial $*$ by replacing the first index by 0. We then have:

$$y_0 y_{i_1} y_{i_2} \cdots y_{i_m} = z_0 z_{i_1} z_{i_2} \cdots z_{i_m} *$$

We can take care of the final $*$ by appending the index $k+1$. Since $y_{k+1} = \$$, and $z_{k+1} = *\$$, we have:

$$y_0 y_{i_1} y_{i_2} \cdots y_{i_m} y_{k+1} = z_0 z_{i_1} z_{i_2} \cdots z_{i_m} z_{k+1}$$

We have thus shown that $0, i_1, i_2, \ldots, i_m, k+1$ is a solution to the instance of PCP.

Now, we must show the converse, that if the constructed instance of PCP has a solution, then the original MPCP instance has a solution as well. We observe that a solution to the PCP instance must begin with index 0 and end with index $k+1$, since only the 0th pair has strings y_0 and z_0 that begin with the same symbol, and only the $(k+1)$st pair has strings that end with the same symbol. Thus, the PCP solution can be written $0, i_1, i_2, \ldots, i_m, i_{k+1}$.

We claim that $i_1, i_2, \ldots, i_m$ is a solution to the MPCP instance. The reason is that if we remove the $*$'s and the final $\$$ from the string $y_0 y_{i_1} y_{i_2} \cdots y_{i_m} y_{k+1}$ we get the string $w_1 w_{i_1} w_{i_2} \cdots w_{i_m}$. Also, if we remove the $*$'s and $\$$ from the string $z_0 z_{i_1} z_{i_2} \cdots z_{i_m} z_{k_1}$ we get $x_1 x_{i_1} x_{i_2} \cdots x_{i_m}$. We know that

$$y_0 y_{i_1} y_{i_2} \cdots y_{i_m} y_{k+1} = z_0 z_{i_1} z_{i_2} \cdots z_{i_m} z_{k+1}$$

so it follows that

$$w_1 w_{i_1} w_{i_2} \cdots w_{i_m} = x_1 x_{i_1} x_{i_2} \cdots x_{i_m}$$

Thus, a solution to the PCP instance implies a solution to the MPCP instance.

We now see that the construction described prior to this theorem is an algorithm that converts an instance of MPCP with a solution to an instance of PCP with a solution, and also converts an instance of MPCP with no solution to an instance of PCP with no solution. Thus, there is a reduction of MPCP to PCP, which confirms that if PCP were decidable, MPCP would also be decidable. $\square$

9.4.3 Completion of the Proof of PCP Undecidability

We now complete the chain of reductions of Fig. 9.11 by reducing L_u to MPCP. That is, given a pair (M, w), we construct an instance (A, B) of MPCP such that TM M accepts input w if and only if (A, B) has a solution.

The essential idea is that MPCP instance (A, B) simulates, in its partial solutions, the computation of M on input w. That is, partial solutions will consist of strings that are prefixes of the sequence of ID's of M: $\#\alpha_1\#\alpha_2\#\alpha_3\#\cdots$, where α_1 is the initial ID of M with input w, and $\alpha_i \vdash \alpha_{i+1}$ for all i. The string from the B list will always be one ID ahead of the string from the A list, unless M enters an accepting state. In that case, there will be pairs to use that will allow the A list to "catch up" to the B list and eventually produce a solution. However, without entering an accepting state, there is no way that these pairs can be used, and no solution exists.

To simplify the construction of an MPCP instance, we shall invoke Theorem 8.12, which says that we may assume our TM never prints a blank, and never moves left from its initial head position. In that case, an ID of the Turing machine will always be a string of the form $\alpha q\beta$, where α and β are strings of nonblank tape symbols, and q is a state. However, we shall allow β to be empty if the head is at the blank immediately to the right of α, rather than placing a blank to the right of the state. Thus, the symbols of α and β will correspond exactly to the contents of the cells that held the input, plus any cells to the right that the head has previously visited.

Let $M = (Q, \Sigma, \Gamma, \delta, q_0, B, F)$ be a TM satisfying Theorem 8.12, and let w in Σ^* be an input string. We construct an instance of MPCP as follows. To understand the motivation behind our choice of pairs, remember that the goal is for the first list to be one ID behind the second list, unless M accepts.

1. The first pair is:

List A	List B
$\#$	$\#q_0w\#$

   This, pair, which must start any solution according to the rules of MPCP, begins the simulation of M on input w. Notice that initially, the B list is a complete ID ahead of the A list.

2. Tape symbols and the separator $\#$ can be appended to both lists. The pairs

List A	List B	
X	X	for each X in Γ
$\#$	$\#$	

   allow symbols not involving the state to be "copied." In effect, choice of these pairs lets us extend the A string to match the B string, and at the same time copy parts of the previous ID to the end of the B string. So doing helps to form the next ID in the sequence of moves of M, at the end of the B string.

3. To simulate a move of M, we have certain pairs that reflect those moves. For all q in $Q - F$ (i.e., q is a nonaccepting state), p in Q, and X, Y, and Z in Γ we have:

List A	List B	
qX	Yp	if $\delta(q, X) = (p, Y, R)$
ZqX	pZY	if $\delta(q, X) = (p, Y, L)$; Z is any tape symbol
$q\#$	$Yp\#$	if $\delta(q, B) = (p, Y, R)$
$Zq\#$	$pZY\#$	if $\delta(q, B) = (p, Y, L)$; Z is any tape symbol

Like the pairs of (2), these pairs help extend the B string to add the next ID, by extending the A string to match the B string. However, these pairs use the state to determine the change in the current ID that is needed to produce the next ID. These changes — a new state, tape symbol, and head move — are reflected in the ID being constructed at the end of the B string.

4. If the ID at the end of the B string has an accepting state, then we need to allow the partial solution to become a complete solution. We do so by extending with "ID's" that are not really ID's of M, but represent what would happen if the accepting state were allowed to consume all the tape symbols to either side of it. Thus, if q is an accepting state, then for all tape symbols X and Y, there are pairs:

List A	List B
XqY	q
Xq	q
qY	q

5. Finally, once the accepting state has consumed all tape symbols, it stands alone as the last ID on the B string. That is, the *remainder* of the two strings (the suffix of the B string that must be appended to the A string to match the B string) is $q\#$. We use the final pair:

List A	List B
$q\#\#$	$\#$

to complete the solution.

In what follows, we refer to the five kinds of pairs generated above as the pairs from rule (1), rule (2), and so on.

Example 9.18: Let us convert the TM

$$M = (\{q_1, q_2, a_3\}, \{0, 1\}, \{0, 1, B\}, \delta, q_1, B, \{q_3\})$$

where δ is given by:

q_i	$\delta(q_i, 0)$	$\delta(q_i, 1)$	$\delta(q_i, B)$
q_1	$(q_2, 1, R)$	$(q_2, 0, L)$	$(q_2, 1, L)$
q_2	$(q_3, 0, L)$	$(q_1, 0, R)$	$(q_2, 0, R)$
q_3	—	—	—

and input string $w = 01$ to an instance of MPCP. To simplify, notice that M never writes a blank, so we shall never have B in an ID. Thus, we shall omit all the pairs that involve B. The entire list of pairs is in Fig. 9.15, along with explanations about where each pair comes from.

Rule	List A	List B	Source
(1)	#	$\#q_1 01\#$	
(2)	0	0	
	1	1	
	#	#	
(3)	$q_1 0$	$1q_2$	from $\delta(q_1, 0) = (q_2, 1, R)$
	$0q_1 1$	$q_2 00$	from $\delta(q_1, 1) = (q_2, 0, L)$
	$1q_1 1$	$q_2 10$	from $\delta(q_1, 1) = (q_2, 0, L)$
	$0q_1 \#$	$q_2 01\#$	from $\delta(q_1, B) = (q_2, 1, L)$
	$1q_1 \#$	$q_2 11\#$	from $\delta(q_1, B) = (q_2, 1, L)$
	$0q_2 0$	$q_3 00\#$	from $\delta(q_2, 0) = (q_3, 0, L)$
	$1q_2 0$	$q_3 10\#$	from $\delta(q_2, 0) = (q_3, 0, L)$
	$q_2 1$	$0q_1$	from $\delta(q_2, 1) = (q_1, 0, R)$
	$q_2 \#$	$0q_2 \#$	from $\delta(q_2, B) = (q_2, 0, R)$
(4)	$0q_3 0$	q_3	
	$0q_3 1$	q_3	
	$1q_3 0$	q_3	
	$1q_3 1$	q_3	
	$0q_3$	q_3	
	$1q_3$	q_3	
	$q_3 0$	q_3	
	$q_3 1$	q_3	
(5)	$q_3 \#\#$	#	

Figure 9.15: MPCP instance constructed from TM M of Example 9.18

Note that M accepts the input 01 by the sequence of moves

$$q_1 01 \vdash 1q_2 1 \vdash 10q_1 \vdash 1q_2 01 \vdash q_3 101$$

Let us see the sequence of partial solutions that mimics this computation of M and eventually leads to a solution. We must start with the first pair, as required in any solution to MPCP:

$$A: \#$$
$$B: \#q_1 01\#$$

The only way to extend the partial solution is for the string from the A list to be a prefix of the remainder, $q_1 01\#$. Thus, we must next choose the pair $(q_1 0, 1q_2)$, which is one of those move-simulating pairs that we got from rule (3). The partial solution is thus:

$$A: \#q_1 0$$
$$B: \#q_1 01\#1q_2$$

We may now further extend the partial solution using the "copying" pairs from rule (2), until we get to the state in the second ID. The partial solution is then:

$$A: \#q_1 01\#1$$
$$B: \#q_1 01\#1q_2 1\#1$$

At this point, we can use another of the rule-(3) pairs to simulate a move; the appropriate pair is $(q_2 1, 0q_1)$, and the resulting partial solution is:

$$A: \#q_1 01\#1q_2 1$$
$$B: \#q_1 01\#1q_2 1\#10q_1$$

We now could use rule-(2) pairs to "copy" the next three symbols: $\#$, 1, and 0. However, to go that far would be a mistake, since the next move of M moves the head left, and the 0 just before the state is needed in the next rule-(3) pair. Thus, we only "copy" the next two symbols, leaving partial solution:

$$A: \#q_1 01\#1q_2 1\#1$$
$$B: \#q_1 01\#1q_2 1\#10q_1 \#1$$

The appropriate rule-(3) pair to use is $(0q_1 \#, q_2 01\#)$, which gives us the partial solution:

$$A: \#q_1 01\#1q_2 1\#10q_1 \#$$
$$B: \#q_1 01\#1q_2 1\#10q_1 \#1q_2 01\#$$

Now, we may use another rule-(3) pair, $(1q_2 0, q_3 10)$, which leads to acceptance:

$$A: \#q_1 01\#1q_2 1\#10q_1 \#1q_2 0$$
$$B: \#q_1 01\#1q_2 1\#10q_1 \#1q_2 01\#q_3 10$$

At this point, we use pairs from rule (4) to eliminate all but q_3 from the ID. We also need pairs from rule (2) to copy symbols as necessary. The continuation of the partial solution is:

$$A: \#q_1 01\#1q_2 1\#10q_1 \#1q_2 01\#q_3 101\#q_3 01\#q_3 1\#$$
$$B: \#q_1 01\#1q_2 1\#10q_1 \#1q_2 01\#q_3 101\#q_3 01\#q_3 1\#q_3 \#$$

With only q_3 left in the ID, we can use the pair $(q_3 \#\#, \#)$ from rule (5) to finish the solution:

A: $\#q_101\#1q_21\#10q_1\#1q_201\#q_3101\#q_301\#q_31\#q_3\#\#$
B: $\#q_101\#1q_21\#10q_1\#1q_201\#q_3101\#q_301\#q_31\#q_3\#\#$

□

Theorem 9.19 : Post's Correspondence Problem is undecidable.

PROOF: We have almost completed the chain of reductions suggested by Fig. 9.11. The reduction of MPCP to PCP was shown in Theorem 9.17. The construction of this section shows how to reduce L_u to MPCP. Thus, we complete the proof of undecidability of PCP by proving that the construction is correct, that is:

- M accepts w if and only if the constructed MPCP instance has a solution.

(Only if) Example 9.18 gives the fundamental idea. If w is in $L(M)$, then we can start with the pair from rule (1), and simulate the computation of M on w. We use a pair from rule (3) to copy the state from each ID and simulate one move of M, and we use the pairs from rule (2) to copy tape symbols and the marker $\#$ as needed. If M reaches an accepting state, then the pairs from rule (4) and a final use of the pair from rule (5) allow the A string to catch up to the B string and form a solution.

(If) We need to argue that if the MPCP instance has a solution, it could only be because M accepts w. First, because we are dealing with MPCP, any solution must begin with the first pair, so a partial solution begins

$$A: \#$$
$$B: \#q_0w\#$$

As long as there is no accepting state in the partial solution, the pairs from rules (4) and (5) are useless. States and one or two of their surrounding tape symbols in an ID can only be handled by the pairs of rule (3), and all other tape symbols and $\#$ must be handled by pairs from rule (2). Thus, unless M reaches an accepting state, all partial solutions have the form

$$A: x$$
$$B: xy$$

where x is a sequence of ID's of M representing a computation of M on input w, possibly followed by $\#$ and the beginning of the next ID α. The remainder y is the completion of α, another $\#$, and the beginning of the ID that follows α, up to the point that x ended within α itself.

In particular, as long as M does not enter an accepting state, the partial solution is not a solution; the B string is longer than the A string. Thus, if there is a solution, M must at some point enter an accepting state; i.e., M accepts w.   □

9.4.4 Exercises for Section 9.4

Exercise 9.4.1: Tell whether each of the following instances of PCP has a solution. Each is presented as two lists A and B, and the ith strings on the two lists correspond for each $i = 1, 2, \ldots$.

* a) $A = (01, 001, 10); B = (011, 10, 00)$.

  b) $A = (01, 001, 10); B = (011, 01, 00)$.

  c) $A = (ab, a, bc, c); B = (bc, ab, ca, a)$.

! **Exercise 9.4.2:** We showed that PCP was undecidable, but we assumed that the alphabet Σ could be arbitrary. Show that PCP is undecidable even if we limit the alphabet to $\Sigma = \{0, 1\}$ by reducing PCP to this special case of PCP.

*! **Exercise 9.4.3:** Suppose we limited PCP to a one-symbol alphabet, say $\Sigma = \{0\}$. Would this restricted case of PCP still be undecidable?

! **Exercise 9.4.4:** A *Post tag system* consists of a set of pairs of strings chosen from some finite alphabet Σ and a start string. If (w, x) is a pair, and y is any string over Σ, we say that $wy \vdash yx$. That is, on one move, we can remove some prefix w of the "current" string wy and instead add at the end the second component of a string x with which w is paired. Define $\overset{*}{\vdash}$ to mean zero or more steps of $\vdash$, just as for derivations in a context-free grammar. Show that it is undecidable, given a set of pairs P and a start string z, whether $z \overset{*}{\vdash} \epsilon$. *Hint*: For each TM M and input w, let z be the initial ID of M with input w, followed by a separator symbol #. Select the pairs P such that any ID of M must eventually become the ID that follows by one move of M. If M enters an accepting state, arrange that the current string can eventually be erased, i.e., reduced to ϵ.

9.5 Other Undecidable Problems

Now, we shall consider a variety of other problems that we can prove undecidable. The principal technique is reducing PCP to the problem we wish to prove undecidable.

9.5.1 Problems About Programs

Our first observation is that we can write a program, in any conventional language, that takes as input an instance of PCP and searches for solutions some systematic manner, e.g., in order of the *length* (number of pairs) of potential solutions. Since PCP allows arbitrary alphabets, we should encode the symbols of its alphabet in binary or some other fixed alphabet, as discussed in the box on "PCP as a Language" in Section 9.4.1.

We can have our program do any particular thing we want, e.g., halt or print `hello, world`, when and if it finds a solution. Otherwise, the program will never perform that particular action. Thus, it is undecidable whether a program prints `hello, world`, whether it halts, whether it calls a particular function, rings the console bell, or makes any other nontrivial action. In fact, there is an analog of Rice's Theorem for programs: any nontrivial property that involves what the program does (rather than a lexical or syntactic property of the program itself) must be undecidable.

9.5.2   Undecidability of Ambiguity for CFG's

Programs are sufficiently like Turing machines that the observations of Section 9.5.1 are unsurprising. Now, we shall see how to reduce PCP to a problem that looks nothing like a question about computers: the question of whether a given context-free grammar is ambiguous.

The key idea is to consider strings that represent a list of indexes (integers), in reverse, and the corresponding strings according to one of the lists of a PCP instance. These strings can be generated by a grammar. The similar set of strings for the other list in the PCP instance can also be generated by a grammar. If we take the union of these grammars in the obvious way, then there is a string generated through the productions of each original grammar if and only if there is a solution to this PCP instance. Thus, there is a solution if and only if there is ambiguity in the grammar for the union.

Let us now make these ideas more precise. Let the PCP instance consist of lists $A = w_1, w_2, \ldots, w_k$ and $B = x_1, x_2, \ldots, x_k$. For list A we shall construct a CFG with A as the only variable. The terminals are all the symbols of the alphabet Σ used for this PCP instance, plus a distinct set of *index symbols* $a_1, a_2, \ldots, a_k$ that represent the choices of pairs of strings in a solution to the PCP instance. That is, the index symbol a_i represents the choice of w_i from the A list or x_i from the B list. The productions for the CFG for the A list are:

$$A \quad \to \quad w_1 A a_1 \mid w_2 A a_2 \mid \cdots \mid w_k A a_k \mid$$
$$w_1 a_1 \mid w_2 a_2 \mid \cdots \mid w_k a_k$$

We shall call this grammar G_A and its language L_A. In the future, we shall refer to a language like L_A as *the language for the list* A.

Notice that the terminal strings derived by G_A are all those of the form $w_{i_1} w_{i_2} \cdots w_{i_m} a_{i_m} \cdots a_{i_2} a_{i_1}$ for some $m \geq 1$ and list of integers $i_1, i_2, \ldots, i_m$; each integer is in the range 1 to k. The sentential forms of G_A all have a single A between the strings (the w's) and the index symbols (the a's), until we use one of the last group of k productions, none of which have an A in the body. Thus, parse trees look like the one suggested in Fig. 9.16.

Observe also that any terminal string derivable from A in G_A has a unique derivation. The index symbols at the end of the string determine uniquely which production must be used at each step. That is, only two production bodies end with a given index symbol a_i: $A \to w_i A a_i$ and $A \to w_i a_i$. We must

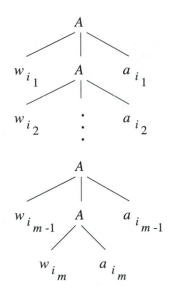

Figure 9.16: The form of parse trees in the grammar G_A

use the first of these if the derivation step is not the last, and we must use the second production if it is the last step.

Now, let us consider the other part of the given PCP instance, the list $B = x_1, x_2, \ldots, x_k$. For this list we develop another grammar G_B:

$$B \quad \rightarrow \quad x_1 B a_1 \mid x_2 B a_2 \mid \cdots \mid x_k B a_k \mid$$
$$x_1 a_1 \mid x_2 a_2 \mid \cdots \mid x_k a_k$$

The language of this grammar will be referred to as L_B. The same observations that we made for G_A apply also to G_B. In particular, a terminal string in L_B has a unique derivation, which can be determined by the index symbols in the tail of the string.

Finally, we combine the languages and grammars of the two lists to form a grammar G_{AB} for the entire PCP instance. G_{AB} consists of:

1. Variables A, B, and S; the latter is the start symbol.

2. Productions $S \rightarrow A \mid B$.

3. All the productions of G_A.

4. All the productions of G_B.

We claim that G_{AB} is ambiguous if and only if the instance (A, B) of PCP has a solution; that argument is the core of the next theorem.

Theorem 9.20: It is undecidable whether a CFG is ambiguous.

PROOF: We have already given most of the reduction of PCP to the question of whether a CFG is ambiguous; that reduction proves the problem of CFG ambiguity to be undecidable, since PCP is undecidable. We have only to show that the above construction is correct; that is:

- G_{AB} is ambiguous if and only if instance (A, B) of PCP has a solution.

(If) Suppose $i_1, i_2, \ldots, i_m$ is a solution to this instance of PCP. Consider the two derivations in G_{AB}:

$$S \Rightarrow A \Rightarrow w_{i_1} A a_{i_1} \Rightarrow w_{i_1} w_{i_2} A a_{i_2} a_{i_1} \Rightarrow \cdots \Rightarrow$$
$$w_{i_1} w_{i_2} \cdots w_{i_{m-1}} A a_{i_{m-1}} \cdots a_{i_2} a_{i_1} \Rightarrow w_{i_1} w_{i_2} \cdots w_{i_m} a_{i_m} \cdots a_{i_2} a_{i_1}$$

$$S \Rightarrow B \Rightarrow x_{i_1} B a_{i_1} \Rightarrow x_{i_1} x_{i_2} B a_{i_2} a_{i_1} \Rightarrow \cdots \Rightarrow$$
$$x_{i_1} x_{i_2} \cdots x_{i_{m-1}} B a_{i_{m-1}} \cdots a_{i_2} a_{i_1} \Rightarrow x_{i_1} x_{i_2} \cdots x_{i_m} a_{i_m} \cdots a_{i_2} a_{i_1}$$

Since $i_1, i_2, \ldots, i_m$ is a solution, we know that $w_{i_1} w_{i_2} \cdots w_{i_m} = x_{i_1} x_{i_2} \cdots x_{i_m}$. Thus, these two derivations are derivations of the same terminal string. Since the derivations themselves are clearly two distinct, leftmost derivations of the same terminal string, we conclude that G_{AB} is ambiguous.

(Only if) We already observed that a given terminal string cannot have more than one derivation in G_A and not more than one in G_B. So the only way that a terminal string could have two leftmost derivations in G_{AB} is if one of them begins $S \Rightarrow A$ and continues with a derivation in G_A, while the other begins $S \Rightarrow B$ and continues with a derivation of the same string in G_B.

The string with two derivations has a tail of indexes $a_{i_m} \cdots a_{i_2} a_{i_1}$, for some $m \geq 1$. This tail must be a solution to the PCP instance, because what precedes the tail in the string with two derivations is both $w_{i_1} w_{i_2} \cdots w_{i_m}$ and $x_{i_1} x_{i_2} \cdots x_{i_m}$. $\Box$

9.5.3   The Complement of a List Language

Having context-free languages like L_A for the list A lets us show a number of problems about CFL's to be undecidable. More undecidability facts for CFL's can be obtained by considering the complement language $\overline{L_A}$. Notice that the language $\overline{L_A}$ consists of all strings over the alphabet $\Sigma \cup \{a_1, a_2, \ldots, a_k\}$ that are not in L_A, where Σ is the alphabet of some instance of PCP, and the a_i's are distinct symbols representing the indexes of pairs in that PCP instance.

The interesting members of $\overline{L_A}$ are those strings consisting of a prefix in Σ^* that is the concatenation of some strings from the A list, followed by a suffix of index symbols that does *not* match the strings from A. However, there are also many strings in $\overline{L_A}$ that are simply of the wrong form: they are not in the language of regular expression $\Sigma^*(a_1 + a_2 + \cdots + a_k)^*$.

We claim that $\overline{L_A}$ is a CFL. Unlike L_A, it is not very easy to design a grammar for $\overline{L_A}$, but we can design a PDA, in fact a deterministic PDA, for $\overline{L_A}$. The construction is in the next theorem.

Theorem 9.21: If L_A is the language for list A, then $\overline{L_A}$ is a context-free language.

PROOF: Let Σ be the alphabet of the strings on list $A = w_1, w_2, \ldots, w_k$, and let I be the set of index symbols: $I = \{a_1, a_2, \ldots, a_k\}$. The DPDA P we design to accept $\overline{L_A}$ works as follows.

1. As long as P sees symbols in Σ, it stores them on its stack. Since all strings in Σ^* are in $\overline{L_A}$, P accepts as it goes.

2. As soon as a P sees an index symbol in I, say a_i, it pops its stack to see if the top symbols form w_i^R, that is, the reverse of the corresponding string.

   (a) If not, then the input seen so far, and any continuation of this input is in $\overline{L_A}$. Thus, P goes to an accepting state in which it consumes all future inputs without changing its stack.

   (b) If w_i^R was popped from the stack, but the bottom-of-stack marker is not yet exposed on the stack, then P accepts, but remembers, in its state that it is looking for symbols in I only, and may yet see a string in L_A (which P will *not* accept). P repeats step (2) as long as the question of whether the input is in L_A is unresolved.

   (c) If w_i^R was popped from the stack, and the bottom-of-stack marker is exposed, then P has seen an input in L_A. P does not accept this input. However, since any input continuation cannot be in L_A, P goes to a state where it accepts all future inputs, leaving the stack unchanged.

3. If, after seeing one or more symbols of I, P sees another symbol of Σ, then the input is not of the correct form to be in L_A. Thus, P goes to a state in which it accepts this and all future inputs, without changing its stack.

□

We can use L_A, L_B and their complements in various ways to show undecidability results about context-free languages. The next theorem summarizes some of these facts.

Theorem 9.22: Let G_1 and G_2 be context-free grammars, and let R be a regular expression. Then the following are undecidable:

a) Is $L(G_1) \cap L(G_2) = \emptyset$?

b) Is $L(G_1) = L(G_2)$?

c) Is $L(G_1) = L(R)$?

d) Is $L(G_1) = T^*$ for some alphabet T?

e) Is $L(G_1) \subseteq L(G_2)$?

f) Is $L(R) \subseteq L(G_1)$?

PROOF: Each of the proofs is a reduction from PCP. We show how to take an instance (A, B) of PCP and convert it to a question about CFG's and/or regular expressions that has answer "yes" if and only if the instance of PCP has a solution. In some cases, we reduce PCP to the question as stated in the theorem; in other cases we reduce it to the complement. It doesn't matter, since if we show the complement of a problem to be undecidable, it is not possible that the problem itself is decidable, since the recursive languages are closed under complementation (Theorem 9.3).

We shall refer to the alphabet of the strings for this instance as Σ and the alphabet of index symbols as I. Our reductions depend on the fact that L_A, L_B, $\overline{L_A}$, and $\overline{L_B}$ all have CFG's. We construct these CFG's either directly, as in Section 9.5.2, or by the construction of a PDA for the complement languages given in Theorem 9.21 coupled with the conversion from a PDA to a CFG by Theorem 6.14.

a) Let $L(G_1) = L_A$ and $L(G_2) = L_B$. Then $L(G_1) \cap L(G_2)$ is the set of solutions to this instance of PCP. The intersection is empty if and only if there is no solution. Note that, technically, we have reduced PCP to the language of pairs of CFG's whose intersection is nonempty; i.e., we have shown the problem "is the intersection of two CFG's nonempty" to be undecidable. However, as mentioned in the introduction to the proof, showing the complement of a problem to be undecidable is tantamount to showing the problem itself undecidable.

b) Since CFG's are closed under union, we can construct a CFG G_1 for $\overline{L_A} \cup \overline{L_B}$. Since $(\Sigma \cup I)^*$ is a regular set, we surely may construct for it a CFG G_2. Now $\overline{L_A} \cup \overline{L_B} = \overline{L_A \cap L_B}$. Thus, $L(G_1)$ is missing only those strings that represent solutions to the instance of PCP. $L(G_2)$ is missing no strings in $(\Sigma \cup I)^*$. Thus, their languages are equal if and only if the PCP instance has no solution.

c) The argument is the same as for (b), but we let R be the regular expression $(\Sigma \cup I)^*$.

d) The argument of (c) suffices, since $\Sigma \cup I$ is the only alphabet of which $\overline{L_A} \cup \overline{L_B}$ could possibly be the closure.

e) Let G_1 be a CFG for $(\Sigma \cup I)^*$ and let G_2 be a CFG for $\overline{L_A} \cup \overline{L_B}$. Then $L(G_1) \subseteq L(G_2)$ if and only if $\overline{L_A} \cup \overline{L_B} = (\Sigma \cup I)^*$, i.e., if and only if the PCP instance has no solution.

f) The argument is the same as (f), but let R be the regular expression $(\Sigma \cup I)^*$, and let $L(G_1)$ be $\overline{L_A} \cup \overline{L_B}$.

$\square$

9.5.4 Exercises for Section 9.5

* **Exercise 9.5.1:** Let L be the set of (codes for) context-free grammars G such that $L(G)$ contains at least one palindrome. Show that L is undecidable. *Hint*: Reduce PCP to L by constructing, from each instance of PCP a grammar whose language contains a palindrome if and only if the PCP instance has a solution.

! **Exercise 9.5.2:** Show that the language $\overline{L_A} \cup \overline{L_B}$ is a regular language if and only if it is the set of all strings over its alphabet; i.e., if and only if the instance (A, B) of PCP has no solution. Thus, prove that it is undecidable whether or not a CFG generates a regular language. *Hint*: Suppose there is a solution to PCP; say the string wx is missing from $\overline{L_A} \cup \overline{L_B}$, where w is a string from the alphabet Σ of this PCP instance, and x is the reverse of the corresponding string of index symbols. Define a homomorphism $h(0) = w$ and $h(1) = x$. Then what is $h^{-1}(\overline{L_A} \cup \overline{L_B})$? Use the fact that regular sets are closed under inverse homomorphism, complementation, and the pumping lemma for regular sets to show that $\overline{L_A} \cup \overline{L_B}$ is not regular.

!! **Exercise 9.5.3:** It is undecidable whether the complement of a CFL is also a CFL. Exercise 9.5.2 can be used to show it is undecidable whether the complement of a CFL is regular, but that is not the same thing. To prove our initial claim, we need to define a different language that represents the nonsolutions to an instance (A, B) of PCP. Let L_{AB} be the set of strings of the form $w\#x\#y\#z$ such that:

1. w and x are strings over the alphabet Σ of the PCP instance.

2. y and z are strings over the index alphabet I for this instance.

3. $\#$ is a symbol in neither Σ nor I.

4. $w \neq x^R$.

5. $y \neq z^R$.

6. x^R is *not* what the index string y generates according to list B.

7. w is not what the index string z^R generates according to the list A.

Notice that L_{AB} consists of all strings in $\Sigma^*\#\Sigma^*\#I^*\#I^*$ unless the instance (A, B) has a solution, but L_{AB} is a CFL regardless. Prove that $\overline{L_{AB}}$ is a CFL if and only if there is no solution. *Hint*: Use the inverse homomorphism trick from Exercise 9.5.2 and use Ogden's lemma to force equality in the lengths of certain substrings as in the hint to Exercise 7.2.5(b).

9.6   Summary of Chapter 9

✦ *Recursive and Recursively Enumerable Languages*: The languages accepted by Turing machines are called recursively enumerable (RE), and
the subset of RE languages that are accepted by a TM that always halts
are called recursive.

✦ *Complements of Recursive and RE Languages*: The recursive languages
are closed under complementation, and if a language and its complement
are both RE, then both languages are actually recursive. Thus, the complement of an RE-but-not-recursive language can never be RE.

✦ *Decidability and Undecidability*: "Decidable" is a synonym for "recursive," although we tend to refer to languages as "recursive" and problems (which are languages interpreted as a question) as "decidable." If
a language is not recursive, then we call the problem expressed by that
language "undecidable."

✦ *The Language L_d*: This language is the set of strings of 0's and 1's that,
when interpreted as a TM, are *not* in the language of that TM. The
language L_d is a good example of a language that is not RE; i.e., no
Turing machine accepts it.

✦ *The Universal Language*: The language L_u consists of strings that are
interpreted as a TM followed by an input for that TM. The string is in
L_u if the TM accepts that input. L_u is a good example of a language that
is RE but not recursive.

✦ *Rice's Theorem*: Any nontrivial property of the languages accepted by
Turing machines is undecidable. For instance, the set of codes for Turing
machines whose language is empty is undecidable by Rice's theorem. In
fact, this language is not RE, although its complement — the set of codes
for TM's that accept at least one string — is RE but not recursive.

✦ *Post's Correspondence Problem*: This question asks, given two lists of the
same number of strings, whether we can pick a sequence of corresponding
strings from the two lists and form the same string by concatenation. PCP
is an important example of an undecidable problem. PCP is a good choice
for reducing to other problems and thereby proving them undecidable.

✦ *Undecidable Context-Free-Language Problems*: By reduction from PCP,
we can show a number of questions about CFL's or their grammars to be
undecidable. For instance, it is undecidable whether a CFG is ambiguous,
whether one CFL is contained in another, or whether the intersection of
two CFL's is empty.

9.7 References for Chapter 9

The undecidability of the universal language is essentially the result of Turing [9], although there it was expressed in terms of computation of arithmetic functions and halting, rather than languages and acceptance by final state. Rice's theorem is from [8].

The undecidability of Post's Correspondence problem was shown in [7], although the proof used here was devised by R. W. Floyd, in unpublished notes. The undecidability of Post tag systems (defined in Exercise 9.4.4) is from [6].

The fundamental papers on undecidability of questions about context-free languages are [1] and [5]. However, the fact that it is undecidable whether a CFG is ambiguous was discovered independently by Cantor [2], Floyd [4], and Chomsky and Schutzenberger [3].

1. Y. Bar-Hillel, M. Perles, and E. Shamir, "On formal properties of simple phrase-structure grammars," *Z. Phonetik. Sprachwiss. Kommunikationsforsch.* **14** (1961), pp. 143–172.

2. D. C. Cantor, "On the ambiguity problem in Backus systems," *J. ACM* **9**:4 (1962), pp. 477–479.

3. N. Chomsky and M. P. Schutzenberger, "The algebraic theory of context-free languages," *Computer Programming and Formal Systems* (1963), North Holland, Amsterdam, pp. 118–161.

4. R. W. Floyd, "On ambiguity in phrase structure languages," *Communications of the ACM* **5**:10 (1962), pp. 526–534.

5. S. Ginsburg and G. F. Rose, "Some recursively unsolvable problems in ALGOL-like languages," *J. ACM* **10**:1 (1963), pp. 29–47.

6. M. L. Minsky, "Recursive unsolvability of Post's problem of 'tag' and other topics in the theory of Turing machines," *Annals of Mathematics* **74**:3 (1961), pp. 437–455.

7. E. Post, "A variant of a recursively unsolvable problem," *Bulletin of the AMS* **52** (1946), pp. 264–268.

8. H. G. Rice, "Classes of recursively enumerable sets and their decision problems," *Transactions of the AMS* **89** (1953), pp. 25–59.

9. A. M. Turing, "On computable numbers with an application to the Entscheidungsproblem," *Proc. London Math. Society* **2**:42 (1936), pp. 230–265.

Chapter 10

Intractable Problems

We now bring our discussion of what can or cannot be computed down to the level of efficient versus inefficient computation. We focus on problems that are decidable, and ask which of them can be computed by Turing machines that run in an amount of time that is polynomial in the size of the input. You should review in Section 8.6.3 two important points:

- The problems solvable in polynomial time on a typical computer are exactly the same as the problems solvable in polynomial time on a Turing machine.

- Experience has shown that the dividing line between problems that can be solved in polynomial time and those that require exponential time or more is quite fundamental. Practical problems requiring polynomial time are almost always solvable in an amount of time that we can tolerate, while those that require exponential time generally cannot be solved except for small instances.

In this chapter we introduce the theory of "intractability," that is, techniques for showing problems not to be solvable in polynomial time. We start with a particular problem — the question of whether a boolean expression can be *satisfied*, that is, made true for some assignment of the truth values TRUE and FALSE to its variables. This problem plays the role for intractable problems that L_u or PCP played for undecidable problems. That is, we begin with "Cook's Theorem," which implies that the satisfiability of boolean formulas cannot be decided in polynomial time. We then show how to reduce this problem to many other problems, which are therefore shown intractable as well.

Since we are dealing with whether problems can be solved in polynomial time, our notion of a reduction must change. It is no longer sufficient that there be an algorithm to transform instances of one problem to instances of another. The algorithm itself must take at most polynomial time, or the reduction does not let us conclude that the target problem is intractable, even if the source

413

problem is. Thus, we introduce the notion of "polynomial-time reductions" in the first section.

There is another important distinction between the kinds of conclusions we drew in the theory of undecidability and those that intractability theory lets us draw. The proofs of undecidability that we gave in Chapter 9 are incontrovertible; they depend on nothing but the definition of a Turing machine and common mathematics. In contrast, the results on intractable problems that we give here are all predicated on an unproved, but strongly believed, assumption, often referred to as the assumption $\mathcal{P} \neq \mathcal{NP}$.

That is, we assume the class of problems that can be solved by nondeterministic TM's operating in polynomial time includes at least some problems that cannot be solved by deterministic TM's operating in polynomial time (even if we allow a higher degree polynomial for the deterministic TM). There are literally thousands of problems that *appear* to be in this category, since they can be solved easily by a polynomial time NTM, yet no polynomial-time DTM (or computer program, which is the same thing) is known for their solution. Moreover, an important consequence of intractability theory is that either all these problems have polynomial-time deterministic solutions, which have eluded us for centuries, or none do; i.e., they really require exponential time.

10.1   The Classes $\mathcal{P}$ and $\mathcal{NP}$

In this section, we introduce the basic concepts of intractability theory: the classes $\mathcal{P}$ and $\mathcal{NP}$ of problems solvable in polynomial time by deterministic and nondeterministic TM's, respectively, and the technique of polynomial-time reduction. We also define the notion of "NP-completeness," a property that certain problems in $\mathcal{NP}$ have; they are at least as hard (to within a polynomial in time) as any problem in $\mathcal{NP}$.

10.1.1   Problems Solvable in Polynomial Time

A Turing machine M is said to be of *time complexity $T(n)$* [or to have "running time $T(n)$"] if whenever M is given an input w of length n, M halts after making at most $T(n)$ moves, regardless of whether or not M accepts. This definition applies to any function $T(n)$, such as $T(n) = 50n^2$ or $T(n) = 3^n + 5n^4$; we shall be interested predominantly in the case where $T(n)$ is a polynomial in n. We say a language L is in class $\mathcal{P}$ if there is some polynomial $T(n)$ such that $L = L(M)$ for some deterministic TM M of time complexity $T(n)$.

10.1.2   An Example: Kruskal's Algorithm

You are probably familiar with many problems that have efficient solutions; perhaps you studied some in a course on data structures and algorithms. These problems are generally in $\mathcal{P}$. We shall consider one such problem: finding a minimum-weight spanning tree (*MWST*) for a graph.

Is There Anything Between Polynomials and Exponentials?

In the introductory discussion, and subsequently, we shall often act as if all programs either ran in polynomial time [time $O(n^k)$ for some integer k] or in exponential time [time $O(2^{cn})$ for some constant $c > 0$], or more. In practice, the known algorithms for common problems generally do fall into one of these two categories. However, there are running times that lie between the polynomials and the exponentials. In all that we say about exponentials, we really mean "any running time that is bigger than all the polynomials."

An example of a function between the polynomials and exponentials is $n^{\log_2 n}$. This function grows faster than any polynomial in n, since $\log n$ eventually (for large n) becomes bigger than any constant k. On the other hand, $n^{\log_2 n} = 2^{(\log_2 n)^2}$; if you don't see why, take logarithms of both sides. This function grows more slowly that 2^{cn} for any $c > 0$. That is, no matter how small the positive constant c is, eventually cn becomes bigger than $(\log_2 n)^2$.

Informally, we think of graphs as diagrams such as that of Fig. 10.1. There are nodes, which are numbered 1–4 in this example graph, and there are edges between some pairs of nodes. Each edge has a *weight*, which is an integer. A *spanning tree* is a subset of the edges such that all nodes are connected through these edges, yet there are no cycles. An example of a spanning tree appears in Fig. 10.1; it is the three edges drawn with heavy lines. A *minimum-weight spanning tree* has the least possible total edge weight of all spanning trees.

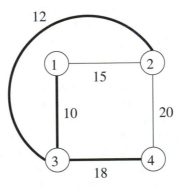

Figure 10.1: A graph; its minimum-weight spanning tree is indicated by heavy lines

There is a well-known "greedy" algorithm, called *Kruskal's Algorithm*,[1] for finding a MWST. Here is an informal outline of the key ideas:

1. Maintain for each node the *connected component* in which the node appears, using whatever edges of the tree have been selected so far. Initially, no edges are selected, so every node is in its a connected component by itself.

2. Consider the lowest-weight edge that has not yet been considered; break ties any way you like. If this edge connects two nodes that are currently in different connected components then:

   (a) Select that edge for the spanning tree, and

   (b) Merge the two connected components involved, by changing the component number of all nodes in one of the two components to be the same as the component number of the other.

   If, on the other hand, the selected edge connects two nodes of the same component, then this edge does not belong in the spanning tree; it would create a cycle.

3. Continue considering edges until either all edges have been considered, or the number of edges selected for the spanning tree is one less than the number of nodes. Note that in the latter case, all nodes must be in one connected component, and we can stop considering edges.

Example 10.1 : In the graph of Fig. 10.1, we first consider the edge $(1,3)$, because it has the lowest weight, 10. Since 1 and 3 are initially in different components, we accept this edge, and make 1 and 3 have the same component number, say "component 1." The next edge in order of weights is $(2,3)$, with weight 12. Since 2 and 3 are in different components, we accept this edge and merge node 2 into "component 1." The third edge is $(1,2)$, with weight 15. However, 1 and 2 are now in the same component, so we reject this edge and proceed to the fourth edge, $(3,4)$. Since 4 is not in "component 1," we accept this edge. Now, we have three edges for the spanning tree of a 4-node graph, and so may stop. □

It is possible to implement this algorithm (using a computer, not a Turing machine) on a graph with m nodes and e edges in time $O(m + e \log e)$. A simpler, easier to follow implementation proceeds in e rounds. A table gives the current component of each node. We pick the lowest-weight remaining edge in $O(e)$ time, and find the components of the two nodes connected by the edges in $O(m)$ time. If they are in different components, merge all nodes with those numbers in $O(m)$ time, by scanning the table of nodes. The total time taken

---

[1] J. B. Kruskal Jr., "On the shortest spanning subtree of a graph and the traveling salesman problem," *Proc. AMS* **7**:1 (1956), pp. 48–50.

by this algorithm is $O\big(e(e+m)\big)$. This running time is polynomial in the "size" of the input, which we might informally take to be the sum of e and m.

When we translate the above ideas to Turing machines, we face several issues:

- When we study of algorithms, we encounter "problems" that ask for outputs in a variety of forms, such as the list of edges in a MWST. When we deal with Turing machines, we may only think of problems as languages, and the only output is **yes** or **no**, i.e., accept or reject. For instance, the MWST tree problem could be couched as: "given this graph G and limit W, does G have a spanning tree of weight W or less?" That problem may seem easier to answer than the MWST problem with which we are familiar, since we don't even learn what the spanning tree is. However, in the theory of intractability, we generally want to argue that a problem is hard, not easy, and the fact that a yes-no version of a problem is hard implies that a more standard version, where a full answer must be computed, is also hard.

- While we might think informally of the "size" of a graph as the number of its nodes or edges, the input to a TM is a string over a finite alphabet. Thus, problem elements such as nodes and edges must be encoded suitably. The effect of this requirement is that inputs to Turing machines are generally slightly longer than the intuitive "size" of the input. However, there are two reasons why the difference is not significant:

  1. The difference between the size as a TM input string and as an informal problem input is never more than a small factor, usually the logarithm of the input size. Thus, what can be done in polynomial time using one measure can be done in polynomial time using the other measure.

  2. The length of a string representing the input is actually a more accurate measure of the number of bytes a real computer has to read to get its input. For instance, if a node is represented by an integer, then the number of bytes needed to represent that integer is proportional to the logarithm of the integer's size, and it is not "1 byte for any node" as we might imagine in an informal accounting for input size.

Example 10.2: Let us consider a possible code for the graphs and weight limits that could be the input to the MWST problem. The code has five symbols, 0, 1, the left and right parentheses, and the comma.

1. Assign integers 1 through m to the nodes.

2. Begin the code with the value of m in binary and the weight limit W in binary, separated by a comma.

3. If there is an edge between nodes i and j with weight w, place (i, j, w) in the code. The integers i, j, and w are coded in binary. The order of i and j within an edge, and the order of the edges within the code are immaterial.

Thus, one of the possible codes for the graph of Fig. 10.1 with limit $W = 40$ is

$$100, 101000(1, 10, 1111)(1, 11, 1010)(10, 11, 1100)(10, 100, 10100)(11, 100, 10010)$$

□

If we represent inputs to the MWST problem as in Example 10.2, then an input of length n can represent at most $O(n/\log n)$ edges. It is possible that m, the number of nodes, could be exponential in n, if there are very few edges. However, unless the number of edges, e, is at least $m - 1$, the graph cannot be connected and therefore will have no MWST, regardless of its edges. Consequently, if the number of nodes is not at least some fraction of $n/\log n$, there is no need to run Kruskal's algorithm at all; we simply say "no; there is no spanning tree of that weight."

Thus, if we have an upper bound on the running time of Kruskal's algorithm as a function of m and e, such as the upper bound $O(e(m+e))$ developed above, we can conservatively replace both m and e by n and say that the running time, as a function of the input length n is $O(n(n + n))$, or $O(n^2)$. In fact, a better implementation of Kruskal's algorithm takes time $O(n \log n)$, but we need not concern ourselves with that improvement here.

Of course, we are using a Turing machine as our model of computation, while the algorithm we described was intended to be implemented in a programming language with useful data structures such as arrays and pointers. However, we claim that in $O(n^2)$ steps we can implement the version of Kruskal's algorithm described above on a multitape TM. The extra tapes are used for several jobs:

1. One tape can be used to store the nodes and their current component numbers. The length of this table is $O(n)$.

2. A tape can be used, as we scan the edges on the input tape, to hold the currently least edge-weight found, among those edges that have not been marked "used." We could use a second track of the input tape to mark those edges that were selected as the edge of least remaining weight in some previous round of the algorithm. Scanning for the lowest-weight, unmarked edge takes $O(n)$ time, since each edge is considered only once, and comparisons of weight can be done by a linear, right-to-left scan of the binary numbers.

3. When an edge is selected in a round, place its two nodes on a tape. Search the table of nodes and components to find the components of these two nodes. This task takes $O(n)$ time.

4. A tape can be used to hold the two components, i and j, being merged when an edge is found to connect two previously unconnected components. We then scan the table of nodes and components, and each node found to be in component i has its component number changed to j. This scan also takes $O(n)$ time.

You should thus be able to complete the argument that says one round can be executed in $O(n)$ time on a multitape TM. Since the number of rounds, e, is at most n, we conclude that $O(n^2)$ time suffices on a multitape TM. Now, remember Theorem 8.10, which says that whatever a multitape TM can do in s steps, a single-tape TM can do in $O(s^2)$ steps. Thus, if the multitape TM takes $O(n^2)$ steps, then we can construct a single-tape TM to do the same thing in $O\big((n^2)^2\big) = O(n^4)$ steps. Our conclusion is that the yes-no version of the MWST problem, "does graph G have a MWST of total weight W or less," is in $\mathcal{P}$.

10.1.3 Nondeterministic Polynomial Time

A fundamental class of problems in the study of intractability is those problems that can be solved by a nondeterministic TM that runs in polynomial time. Formally, we say a language L is in the class $\mathcal{NP}$ (nondeterministic polynomial) if there is a nondeterministic TM M and a polynomial time complexity $T(n)$ such that $L = L(M)$, and when M is given an input of length n, there are no sequences of more than $T(n)$ moves of M.

Our first observation is that, since every deterministic TM is a nondeterministic TM that happens never to have a choice of moves, $\mathcal{P} \subseteq \mathcal{NP}$. However, it appears that $\mathcal{NP}$ contains many problems not in $\mathcal{P}$. The intuitive reason is that a NTM running in polynomial time has the ability to guess an exponential number of possible solutions to a problem and check each one in polynomial time, "in parallel." However:

- It is one of the deepest open questions of Mathematics whether $\mathcal{P} = \mathcal{NP}$, i.e., whether in fact everything that can be done in polynomial time by a NTM can in fact be done by a DTM in polynomial time, perhaps with a higher-degree polynomial.

10.1.4 An $\mathcal{NP}$ Example: The Traveling Salesman Problem

To get a feel for the power of $\mathcal{NP}$, we shall consider an example of a problem that appears to be in $\mathcal{NP}$ but not in $\mathcal{P}$: the *Traveling Salesman Problem* (*TSP*). The input to TSP is the same as to MWST, a graph with integer weights on the edges such as that of Fig. 10.1, and a weight limit W. The question asked is whether the graph has a "Hamilton circuit" of total weight at most W. A *Hamilton circuit* is a set of edges that connect the nodes into a single cycle,

---

A Variant of Nondeterministic Acceptance

Notice that we have required of our NTM that it halt in polynomial time along all branches, regardless of whether or not it accepts. We could just as well have put the polynomial time bound $T(n)$ on only those branches that lead to acceptance; i.e., we could have defined $\mathcal{NP}$ as those languages that are accepted by a NTM such that if it accepts, does so by at least one sequence of at most $T(n)$ moves, for some polynomial $T(n)$.

However, we would get the same class of languages had we done so. For if we know that M accepts within $T(n)$ moves if it accepts at all, then we could modify M to count up to $T(n)$ on a separate track of its tape and halt without accepting if it exceeds count $T(n)$. The modified M might take $O(T^2(n))$ steps, but $T^2(n)$ is a polynomial if $T(n)$ is.

In fact, we could also have defined $\mathcal{P}$ through acceptance by TM's that accept within time $T(n)$, for some polynomial $T(n)$. These TM's might not halt if they do not accept. However, by the same construction as for NTM's, we could modify the DTM to count to $T(n)$ and halt if the limit is exceeded. The DTM would run in $O(T^2(n))$ time.

---

with each node appearing exactly once. Note that the number of edges on a Hamilton circuit must equal the number of nodes in the graph.

Example 10.3: The graph of Fig 10.1 actually has only one Hamilton circuit: the cycle $(1,2,4,3,1)$. The total weight of this cycle is $15 + 20 + 18 + 10 = 63$. Thus, if W is 63 or more, the answer is "yes," and if $W < 63$ the answer is "no."

However, the TSP on four-node graphs is deceptively simple, since there can never be more than two different Hamilton circuits once we account for the different nodes at which the same cycle can start, and for the direction in which we traverse the cycle. In m-node graphs, the number of distinct cycles grows as $O(m!)$, the factorial of m, which is more than 2^{cm} for any constant c. □

It appears that all ways to solve the TSP involve trying essentially all cycles and computing their total weight. By being clever, we can eliminate some obviously bad choices. But it seems that no matter what we do, we must examine an exponential number of cycles before we can conclude that there is none with the desired weight limit W, or to find one if we are unlucky in the order in which we consider the cycles.

On the other hand, if we had a nondeterministic computer, we could guess a permutation of the nodes, and compute the total weight for the cycle of nodes in that order. If there were a real computer that was nondeterministic, no branch would use more than $O(n)$ steps if the input was of length n. On a multitape NTM, we can guess a permutation in $O(n^2)$ steps and check its total weight in a similar amount of time. Thus, a single-tape NTM can solve the TSP in $O(n^4)$ time at most. We conclude that the TSP is in $\mathcal{NP}$.

10.1.5 Polynomial-Time Reductions

Our principal methodology for proving that a problem P_2 cannot be solved in polynomial time (i.e., P_2 is not in $\mathcal{P}$) is the reduction of a problem P_1, which is known not to be in $\mathcal{P}$, to P_2.[2] The approach was suggested in Fig. 8.7, which we reproduce here as Fig. 10.2.

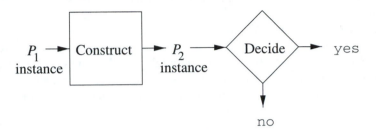

Figure 10.2: Reprise of the picture of a reduction

Suppose we want to prove the statement "if P_2 is in $\mathcal{P}$, then so is P_1." Since we claim that P_1 is *not* in $\mathcal{P}$, we could then claim that P_2 is not in $\mathcal{P}$ either. However, the mere existence of the algorithm labeled "Construct" in Fig. 10.2 is not sufficient to prove the desired statement.

For instance, suppose that when given an instance of P_1 of length m, the algorithm produced an output string of length 2^m, which it fed to the hypothetical polynomial-time algorithm for P_2. If that decision algorithm ran in, say, time $O(n^k)$, then on an input of length 2^m it would run in time $O(2^{km})$, which is exponential in m. Thus, the decision algorithm for P_1 takes, when given an input of length m, time that is exponential in m. These facts are entirely consistent with the situation where P_2 is in $\mathcal{P}$ and P_1 is not in $\mathcal{P}$.

Even if the algorithm that constructs a P_2 instance from a P_1 instance always produces an instance that is polynomial in the size of its input, we can fail to reach our desired conclusion. For instance, suppose that the instance of P_2 constructed is of the same size, m, as the P_1 instance, but the construction algorithm itself takes time that is exponential in m, say $O(2^m)$. Now, a decision algorithm for P_2 that takes polynomial time $O(n^k)$ on input of length n only implies that there is a decision algorithm for P_1 that takes time $O(2^m + m^k)$ on input of length m. This running time bound takes into account the fact that we have to perform the translation to P_2 as well as solve the resulting P_2 instance. Again it would be possible for P_1 to be in $\mathcal{P}$ and P_2 not.

---

[2]That statement is a slight lie. In practice, we only *assume* P_1 is not in $\mathcal{P}$, using the very strong evidence that P_1 is "NP-complete," a concept we discuss in Section 10.1.6. We then prove that P_2 is also "NP-complete," and thus suggest just as strongly that P_1 is not in $\mathcal{P}$.

The correct restriction to place on the translation from P_1 to P_2 is that it requires time that is polynomial in the length of its input. Note that if the translation takes time $O(m^j)$ on input of length m, then the output instance of P_2 cannot be longer than the number of steps taken, i.e., it is at most cm^j for some constant c. Now, we can prove that if P_2 is in $\mathcal{P}$, then so is P_1.

For the proof, suppose that we can decide membership in P_2 of a string of length n in time $O(n^k)$. Then we can decide membership in P_1 of a string of length m in time $O\big(m^j + (cm^j)^k\big)$ time; the term m^j accounts for the time to do the translation, and the term $(cm^j)^k$ accounts for the time to decide the resulting instance of P_2. Simplifying the expression, we see that P_1 can be solved in time $O(m^j + cm^{jk})$. Since c, j, and k are all constants, this time is polynomial in m, and we conclude P_1 is in $\mathcal{P}$.

Thus, in the theory of intractability we shall use *polynomial-time reductions* only. A reduction from P_1 to P_2 is polynomial-time if it takes time that is some polynomial in the length of the P_1 instance. Note that as a consequence, the P_2 instance will be of a length that is polynomial in the length of the P_1 instance.

10.1.6   NP-Complete Problems

We shall next meet the family of problems that are the best-known candidates for being in $\mathcal{NP}$ but not in $\mathcal{P}$. Let L be a language (problem) in $\mathcal{NP}$. We say L is *NP-complete* if the following statements are true about L:

1. L is in $\mathcal{NP}$.

2. For every language L' in $\mathcal{NP}$ there is a polynomial-time reduction of L' to L.

An example of an NP-complete problem, as we shall see, is the Traveling Salesman Problem, which we introduced in Section 10.1.4. Since it appears that $\mathcal{P} \neq \mathcal{NP}$, and in particular, all the NP-complete problems are in $\mathcal{NP} - \mathcal{P}$, we generally view a proof of NP-completeness for a problem as a proof that the problem is not in $\mathcal{P}$.

We shall prove our first problem, called SAT (for boolean satisfiability) to be NP-complete by showing that the language of every polynomial-time NTM has a polynomial-time reduction to SAT. However, once we have some NP-complete problems, we can prove a new problem to be NP-complete by reducing some known NP-complete problem to it, using a polynomial-time reduction. The following theorem shows why such a reduction proves the target problem to be NP-complete.

Theorem 10.4: If P_1 is NP-complete, and there is a polynomial-time reduction of P_1 to P_2, then P_2 is NP-complete.

PROOF: We need to show that every language L in $\mathcal{NP}$ polynomial-time reduces to P_2. We know that there is a polynomial-time reduction of L to P_1;

NP-Hard Problems

Some problems L are so hard that although we can prove condition (2) of the definition of NP-completeness (every language in $\mathcal{NP}$ reduces to L in polynomial time), we cannot prove condition (1): that L is in $\mathcal{NP}$. If so, we call L *NP-hard*. We have previously used the informal term "intractable" to refer to problems that appeared to require exponential time. It is generally acceptable to use "intractable" to mean "NP-hard," although in principle there might be some problems that require exponential time even though they are not NP-hard in the formal sense.

A proof that L is NP-hard is sufficient to show that L is very likely to require exponential time, or worse. However, if L is not in $\mathcal{NP}$, then its apparent difficulty does not support the argument that all NP-complete problems are difficult. That is, it could turn out that $\mathcal{P} = \mathcal{NP}$, and yet L still requires exponential time.

---

this reduction takes some polynomial time $p(n)$. Thus, a string w in L of length n is converted to a string x in P_1 of length at most $p(n)$.

We also know that there is a polynomial-time reduction of P_1 to P_2; let this reduction take polynomial time $q(m)$. Then this reduction transforms x to some string y in P_2, taking time at most $q\big(p(n)\big)$. Thus, the transformation of w to y takes time at most $p(n) + q\big(p(n)\big)$, which is a polynomial. We conclude that L is polynomial-time reducible to P_2. Since L could be any language in $\mathcal{NP}$, we have shown that all of $\mathcal{NP}$ polynomial-time reduces to P_2; i.e., P_2 is NP-complete. □

There is one more important theorem to be proven about NP-complete problems: if any one of them is in $\mathcal{P}$, then all of $\mathcal{NP}$ is in $\mathcal{P}$. Since we believe strongly that there are many problems in $\mathcal{NP}$ that are *not* in $\mathcal{P}$, we thus consider a proof that a problem is NP-complete to be tantamount to a proof that in has no polynomial-time algorithm, and thus has no good computer solution.

Theorem 10.5: If some NP-complete problem P is in $\mathcal{P}$, then $\mathcal{P} = \mathcal{NP}$.

PROOF: Suppose P is both NP-complete and in $\mathcal{P}$. Then all languages L in $\mathcal{NP}$ reduce in polynomial-time to P. If P is in $\mathcal{P}$, then L is in $\mathcal{P}$, as we discussed in Section 10.1.5. □

10.1.7 Exercises for Section 10.1

Exercise 10.1.1: Suppose we make the following changes to the weights of the edges in Fig. 10.1. What would the resulting MWST be?

* a) Change the weight 10 on edge $(1, 3)$ to 25.

Other Notions of NP-completeness

The goal of the study of NP-completeness is really Theorem 10.5, that is, the identification of problems P for which their presence in the class $\mathcal{P}$ implies $\mathcal{P} = \mathcal{NP}$. The definition of "NP-complete" we have used, which is often called *Karp-completeness* because it was first used in a fundamental paper on the subject by R. Karp, is adequate to capture every problem that we have reason to believe satisfies Theorem 10.5. However, there are other, broader notions of NP-completeness that also allow us to claim Theorem 10.5.

For instance, S. Cook, in his original paper on the subject, defined a problem P to be "NP-complete" if, given an *oracle* for the problem P, i.e., a mechanism that in one unit of time would answer any question about membership of a given string in P, it was possible to recognize any language in $\mathcal{NP}$ in polynomial time. This type of NP-completeness is called *Cook-completeness*. In a sense, Karp-completeness is the special case where you ask only one question of the oracle. However, Cook completeness also allows complementation of the answer; e.g., you might ask the oracle a question and then answer the opposite of what the oracle says. A consequence of Cook's definition is that the complements of NP-complete problems would also be NP-complete. Using the more restricted notion of Karp-completeness, as we do, we are able to make an important distinction between the NP-complete problems (in the Karp sense) and their complements, in Section 11.1.

---

b) Instead, change the weight on edge $(2, 4)$ to 16.

Exercise 10.1.2: If we modify the graph of Fig. 10.1 by adding an edge of weight 19 between nodes 1 and 4, what is the minimum-weight Hamilton circuit?

*! **Exercise 10.1.3:** Suppose that there is an NP-complete problem that has a deterministic solution that takes time $O(n^{\log_2 n})$. Note that this function lies between the polynomials and the exponentials, and is in neither class of functions. What could we say about the running time of any problem in $\mathcal{NP}$?

!! **Exercise 10.1.4:** Consider the graphs whose nodes are grid points in an n-dimensional cube of side m, that is, the nodes are vectors $(i_1, i_2, \ldots, i_n)$, where each i_j is in the range 1 to m. There is an edge between two nodes if and only if they differ by one in exactly one dimension. For instance, the case $n = 2$ and $m = 2$ is a square, $n = 3$ and $m = 2$ is a cube, and $n = 2$ and $m = 3$ is the graph shown in Fig. 10.3. Some of these graphs have a Hamilton circuit, and some do not. For instance, the square obviously does, and the cube does too, although it

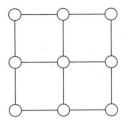

Figure 10.3: A graph with $n = 2$; $m = 3$

may not be obvious; one is $(0,0,0)$, $(0,0,1)$, $(0,1,1)$, $(0,1,0)$, $(1,1,0)$, $(1,1,1)$, $(1,0,1)$, $(1,0,0)$, and back to $(0,0,0)$. Figure 10.3 has no Hamilton circuit.

a) Prove that Fig. 10.3 has no Hamilton circuit. *Hint*: Consider what happens when a hypothetical Hamilton circuit passes through the central node. Where can in come from, and where can it go to, without cutting off one piece of the graph from the Hamilton circuit?

b) For what values of n and m is there a Hamilton circuit?

! **Exercise 10.1.5:** Suppose we have an encoding of context-free grammars using some finite alphabet. Consider the following two languages:

1. $L_1 = \{(G, A, B) \mid G$ is a (coded) CFG, A and B are (coded) variables of G, and the sets of terminal strings derived from A and B are the same$\}$.

2. $L_2 = \{(G_1, G_2) \mid G_1$ and G_2 are (coded) CFG's, and $L(G_1) = L(G_2)\}$.

Answer the following:

* a) Show that L_1 is polynomial-time reducible to L_2.

b) Show that L_2 is polynomial-time reducible to L_1.

* c) What do (a) and (b) say about whether or not L_1 and L_2 are NP-complete?

Exercise 10.1.6: As classes of languages, $\mathcal{P}$ and $\mathcal{NP}$ each have certain closure properties. Show that $\mathcal{P}$ is closed under each of the following operations:

a) Reversal.

* b) Union.

*! c) Concatenation.

! d) Closure (star).

e) Inverse homomorphism.

* f) Complementation.

Exercise 10.1.7: $\mathcal{NP}$ is also closed under each of the operations listed for $\mathcal{P}$ in Exercise 10.1.6, with the (presumed) exception of (f) complementation. It is not known whether or not $\mathcal{NP}$ is closed under complementation, an issue we discuss further in Section 11.1. Prove that each of Exercise 10.1.6(a) through (e) hold for $\mathcal{NP}$.

10.2   An NP-Complete Problem

We now introduce you to the first NP-complete problem. This problem — whether a boolean expression is satisfiable — is proved NP-complete by explicitly reducing the language of any nondeterministic, polynomial-time TM to the satisfiability problem.

10.2.1   The Satisfiability Problem

The *boolean expressions* are built from:

  1. Variables whose values are boolean; i.e., they either have the value 1 (true) or 0 (false).

  2. Binary operators $\wedge$ and $\vee$, standing for the logical AND and OR of two expressions.

  3. Unary operator $\neg$ standing for logical negation.

  4. Parentheses to group operators and operands, if necessary to alter the default precedence of operators: $\neg$ highest, then $\wedge$, and finally $\vee$.

Example 10.6: An example of a boolean expression is $x \wedge \neg(y \vee z)$. The subexpression $y \vee z$ is true whenever either variable y or variable z has the value true, but the subexpression is false whenever both y and z are false. The larger subexpression $\neg(y \vee z)$ is true exactly when $y \vee z$ is false, that is, when both y and z are false. If either y or z or both are true, then $\neg(y \vee z)$ is false.

Finally, consider the entire expression. Since it is the logical AND of two subexpressions, it is true exactly when both subexpressions are true. That is, $x \wedge \neg(y \vee z)$ is true exactly when x is true, y is false, and z is false. □

A *truth assignment* for a given boolean expression E assigns either true or false to each of the variables mentioned in E. The *value* of expression E given a truth assignment T, denoted $E(T)$, is the result of evaluating E with each variable x replaced by the value $T(x)$ (true or false) that T assigns to x.

A truth assignment T *satisfies* boolean expression E if $E(T) = 1$; i.e., the truth assignment T makes expression E true. A boolean expression E is said to be *satisfiable* if there exists at least one truth assignment T that satisfies E.

Example 10.7 : The expression $x \wedge \neg(y \vee z)$ of Example 10.6 is satisfiable. We saw that the truth assignment T defined by $T(x) = 1$, $T(y) = 0$, and $T(z) = 0$ satisfies this expression, because it makes the value of the expression true (1). We also observed that T is the *only* satisfying assignment for this expression, since the other seven combinations of values for the three variables give the expression the value false (0).

For another example, consider the expression $E = x \wedge (\neg x \vee y) \wedge \neg y$. We claim that E is not satisfiable. Since there are only two variables, the number of truth assignments is $2^2 = 4$, so it is easy for you to try all four assignments and verify that E has value 0 for all of them. However, we can also argue as follows. E is true only if all three terms connected by $\wedge$ are true. That means x must be true (because of the first term) and y must be false (because of the last term). But under that truth assignment, the middle term $\neg x \vee y$ is false. Thus, E cannot be made true and is in fact unsatisfiable.

We have seen an example where an expression has exactly one satisfying assignment and an example where it has none. There are also many examples where an expression has more than one satisfying assignment. For a simple example, consider $F = x \vee \neg y$. The value of F is 1 for three assignments:

1. $T_1(x) = 1$; $T_1(y) = 1$.

2. $T_2(x) = 1$; $T_2(y) = 0$.

3. $T_3(x) = 0$; $T_3(y) = 0$.

F has value 0 only for the fourth assignment, where $x = 0$ and $y = 1$. Thus, F is satisfiable. $\square$

The *satisfiability problem* is:

- Given a boolean expression, is it satisfiable?

We shall generally refer to the satisfiability problem as *SAT*. Stated as a language, the problem SAT is the set of (coded) boolean expressions that are satisfiable. Strings that either are not valid codes for a boolean expression or that are codes for an unsatisfiable boolean expression are not in SAT.

10.2.2 Representing SAT Instances

The symbols in a boolean expression are $\wedge$, $\vee$, $\neg$, the left and right parentheses, and symbols representing variables. The satisfiability of an expression does not depend on the names of the variables, only on whether two occurrences of variables are the same variable or different variables. Thus, we may assume that the variables are $x_1, x_2, \ldots$, although in examples we shall continue to use variable names like y or z, as well as x's. We shall also assume that variables are renamed so we use the lowest possible subscripts for the variables. For instance, we would not use x_5 unless we also used x_1 through x_4 in the same expression.

Since there are an infinite number of symbols that could in principle, appear in a boolean expression, we have a familiar problem of having to devise a code with a fixed, finite alphabet to represent expressions with arbitrarily large numbers of variables. Only then can we talk about SAT as a "problem," that is, as a language over a fixed alphabet consisting of the codes for those boolean expressions that are satisfiable. The code we shall use is as follows:

1. The symbols $\wedge$, $\vee$, $\neg$, (, and) are represented by themselves.

2. The variable x_i is represented by the symbol x followed by 0's and 1's that represent i in binary.

Thus, the alphabet for the SAT problem/language has only eight symbols. All instances of SAT are strings in this fixed, finite alphabet.

Example 10.8: Consider the expression $x \wedge \neg(y \vee z)$ from Example 10.6. Our first step in coding it is to replace the variables by subscripted x's. Since there are three variables, we must use x_1, x_2, and x_3. We have freedom regarding which of x, y, and z is replaced by each of the x_i's, and to be specific, let $x = x_1$, $y = x_2$, and $z = x_3$. Then the expression becomes $x_1 \wedge \neg(x_2 \vee x_3)$. The code for this expression is:

$$x1 \wedge \neg(x10 \vee x11)$$

$\square$

Notice that the length of a coded boolean expression is approximately the same as the number of positions in the expression, counting each variable occurrence as 1. The reason for the difference is that if the expression has m positions, it can have $O(m)$ variables, so variables may take $O(\log m)$ symbols to code. Thus, an expression whose length is m positions can have a code as long as $n = O(m \log m)$ symbols.

However, the difference between m and $m \log m$ is surely limited by a polynomial. Thus, as long as we only deal with the issue of whether or not a problem can be solved in time that is polynomial in its input length, there is no need to distinguish between the length of an expression's code and the number of positions in the expression itself.

10.2.3   NP-Completeness of the SAT Problem

We now prove "Cook's Theorem," the fact that SAT is NP-complete. To prove a problem is NP-complete, we need first to show that it is in $\mathcal{NP}$. Then, we must show that every language in $\mathcal{NP}$ reduces to the problem in question. In general, we show the second part by offering a polynomial-time reduction from some other NP-complete problem, and then invoking Theorem 10.5. But right now, we don't know any NP-complete problems to reduce to SAT. Thus, the only strategy available is to reduce absolutely every problem in $\mathcal{NP}$ to SAT.

Theorem 10.9: (Cook's Theorem) SAT is NP-complete.

PROOF: The first part of the proof is showing that SAT is in $\mathcal{NP}$. This part is easy:

1. Use the nondeterministic ability of an NTM to guess a truth assignment T for the given expression E. If the encoded E is of length n, then $O(n)$ time suffices on a multitape NTM. Note that this NTM has many choices of move, and may have as many as 2^n different ID's reached at the end of the guessing process, where each branch represents the guess of a different truth assignment.

2. Evaluate E for the truth assignment T. If $E(T) = 1$, then accept. Note that this part is deterministic. The fact that other branches of the NTM may not lead to acceptance has no bearing on the outcome, since if even one satisfying truth assignment is found, the NTM accepts.

The evaluation can be done easily in $O(n^2)$ time on a multitape NTM. Thus, the entire recognition of SAT by the multitape NTM takes $O(n^2)$ time. Converting to a single-tape NTM may square the amount of time, so $O(n^4)$ time suffices on a single-tape NTM.

Now, we must prove the hard part: that if L is any language in $\mathcal{NP}$, then there is a polynomial-time reduction of L to SAT. We may assume that there is some single-tape NTM M and a polynomial $p(n)$ such that M takes no more than $p(n)$ steps on an input of length n, along any branch. Further, the restrictions of Theorem 8.12, which we proved for DTM's, can be proved in the same way for NTM's. Thus, we may assume that M never writes a blank, and never moves its head left of its initial head position.

Thus, if M accepts an input w, and $|w| = n$, then there is a sequence of moves of M such that:

1. α_0 is the initial ID of M with input w.

2. $\alpha_0 \vdash \alpha_1 \vdash \cdots \vdash \alpha_k$, where $k \leq p(n)$.

3. α_k is an ID with an accepting state.

4. Each α_i consists of nonblanks only (except if α_i ends in a state and a blank), and extends from the initial head position — the leftmost input symbol — to the right.

Our strategy can be summarized as follows.

a) Each α_i can be written as a sequence of symbols $X_{i0}X_{i1} \cdots X_{i,p(n)}$. One of these symbols is a state, and the others are tape symbols. As always, we assume that the states and tape symbols are disjoint, so we can tell which X_{ij} is the state, and therefore tell where the tape head is. Note that there is no reason to represent symbols to the right of the first $p(n)$ symbols on the tape [which with the state makes an ID of length $p(n)+1$], because they cannot influence a move of M if M is guaranteed to halt after $p(n)$ moves or less.

b) To describe the sequence of ID's in terms of boolean variables, we create variable y_{ijA} to represent the proposition that $X_{ij} = A$. Here, i and j are each integers in the range 0 to $p(n)$, and A is either a tape symbol or a state.

c) We express the condition that the sequence of ID's represents acceptance of an input w by writing a boolean expression that is satisfiable if and only if M accepts w by a sequence of at most $p(n)$ moves. The satisfying assignment will be the one that "tells the truth" about the ID's; that is, y_{ijA} will be true if and only if $X_{ij} = A$. To make sure that the polynomial-time reduction of $L(M)$ to SAT is correct, we write this expression so that it says the computation:

   i. *Starts right.* That is, the initial ID is $q_0 w$ followed by blanks.

   ii. *Next move is right* (i.e., the move correctly follows the rules of the TM). That is, each subsequent ID follows from the previous by one of the possible legal moves of M.

   iii. *Finishes right.* That is, there is some ID that is an accepting state.

There are a few details that must be introduced before we can make the construction of our boolean expression precise.

- First, we have specified ID's to end when the infinite tail of blanks begin. However, it is more convenient when simulating a polynomial-time computation to think of all ID's as having the same length, $p(n) + 1$. Thus, a tail of blanks may be present in an ID.

- Second, it is convenient to assume that all computations continue for exactly $p(n)$ moves [and therefore have $p(n) + 1$ ID's], even if acceptance occurs earlier. We therefore allow each ID with an accepting state to be its own successor. That is, if α has an accepting state, we allow a "move" $\alpha \vdash \alpha$. Thus, we can assume that if there is an accepting computation, then $\alpha_{p(n)}$ will have an accepting ID, and that is all we have to check for the condition "finishes right."

Figure 10.4 suggests what a polynomial-time computation of M looks like. The rows correspond to the sequence of ID's, and the columns are the cells of the tape that can be used in the computation. Notice that the number of squares in Fig. 10.4 is $(p(n) + 1)^2$. Also, the number of variables that represent each square is finite, depending only on M; it is the sum of the number of states and tape symbols of M.

Let us now give an algorithm to construct from M and w a boolean expression $E_{M,w}$. The overall form of $E_{M,w}$ is $S \wedge N \wedge F$, where S, N, and F are expressions that say M starts, moves, and finishes right.

ID	0	1	...				...	p(n)
α_0	X_{00}	X_{01}						$X_{0,p(n)}$
α_1	X_{10}	X_{11}						$X_{1,p(n)}$
α_i				$X_{i,j-1}$	$X_{i,j}$	$X_{i,j+1}$		
α_{i+1}				$X_{i+1,j-1}$	$X_{i+1,j}$	$X_{i+1,j+1}$		
$\alpha_{p(n)}$	$X_{p(n),0}$	$X_{p(n),1}$						$X_{p(n),p(n)}$

Figure 10.4: Constructing the array of cell/ID facts

Starts Right

X_{00} must be the start state q_0 of M, X_{01} through X_{0n} must be w (where n is the length of w), and the remaining X_{0j}, must be the blank, B. That is, if $w = a_1 a_2 \cdots a_n$, then:

$$S = y_{00q_0} \wedge y_{01a_1} \wedge y_{02a_2} \wedge \cdots \wedge y_{0na_n} \wedge y_{0,n+1,B} \wedge y_{0,n+2,B} \wedge \cdots \wedge y_{0,p(n),B}$$

Surely, given the encoding of M and given w, we can write S in $O(p(n))$ time on a second tape of a multitape TM.

Finishes Right

Since we assume that an accepting ID repeats forever, acceptance by M is the same as finding an accepting state in $\alpha_{p(n)}$. Remember that we assume M is an NTM that, if it accepts, does so within $p(n)$ steps. Thus, F is the OR of expressions F_j, for $j = 0, 1, \ldots, p(n)$, where F_j says that $X_{p(n),j}$ is an accepting state. That is, F_j is $y_{p(n),j,a_1} \vee y_{p(n),j,a_2} \vee \cdots \vee y_{p(n),j,a_k}$, where $a_1, a_2, \ldots, a_k$ are all the accepting states of M. Then,

$$F = F_0 \vee F_1 \vee \cdots \vee F_{p(n)}$$

Notice that each F_i uses a constant number of symbols, that depends on M, but not on the length n of its input w. Thus, F has length $O(n)$. More importantly, the time to write F, given an encoding of M and the input w is polynomial in n; actually, F can be written in $O(p(n))$ time on a multitape TM.

Next Move is Right

Assuring that the moves of M are correct is by far the most complicated part. The expression N will be the AND of expressions N_i, for $i = 0, 1, \ldots, p(n) - 1$, and each N_i will be designed to assure that ID α_{i+1} is one of the ID's that M allows to follow α_i. To begin the explanation of how to write N_i, observe symbol $X_{i+1,j}$ in Fig. 10.4. We can always determine $X_{i+1,j}$ from:

1. The three symbols above it: $X_{i,j-1}$, X_{ij}, and $X_{i,j+1}$, and

2. If one of these symbols is the state of α_i, then the particular choice of move by the NTM M.

We shall write N_i as the $\wedge$ of expressions $A_{ij} \vee B_{ij}$, where $j = 0, 1, \ldots, p(n)$.

- Expression A_{ij} says that:

  a) The state of α_i is at position j (i.e., X_{ij} is the state), and

  b) There is a choice of move of M, where X_{ij} is the state and $X_{i,j+1}$ is the symbol scanned, such that this move transforms the sequence of symbols $X_{i,j-1}X_{ij}X_{i,j+1}$ into $X_{i+1,j-1}X_{i+1,j}X_{i+1,j+1}$. Note that if X_{ij} is an accepting state, there is the "choice" of making no move at all, so all subsequent ID's are the same as the one that first led to acceptance.

- Expression B_{ij} says that:

  a) The state of α_i is sufficiently far away from X_{ij} that it cannot influence $X_{i+1,j}$ (i.e., neither $X_{i,j-1}$, X_{ij}, nor $X_{i,j+1}$ is a state).

  b) $X_{i+1,j} = X_{ij}$.

B_{ij} is the easier to write. Let $q_1, q_2, \ldots, q_m$ be the states of M, and let $Z_1, Z_2, \ldots, Z_r$ be the tape symbols. Then:

$$
\begin{aligned}
B_{ij} \;=\; & (y_{i,j-1,Z_1} \vee y_{i,j-1,Z_2} \vee \cdots \vee y_{i,j-1,Z_r}) \;\wedge \\
& (y_{i,j,Z_1} \vee y_{i,j,Z_2} \vee \cdots \vee y_{i,j,Z_r}) \;\wedge \\
& (y_{i,j+1,Z_1} \vee y_{i,j+1,Z_2} \vee \cdots \vee y_{i,j+1,Z_r}) \;\wedge \\
& (y_{i,j,Z_1} \wedge y_{i+1,j,Z_1}) \vee (y_{i,j,Z_2} \wedge y_{i+1,j,Z_2}) \vee \cdots \vee (y_{i,j,Z_r} \wedge y_{i+1,j,Z_r})
\end{aligned}
$$

The first line of B_{ij} says that $X_{i,j-1}$ is one of the tape symbols; the second line says X_{ij} is one of the tape symbols, and the third line says the same about $X_{i,j+1}$. The final line says that $X_{ij} = X_{i+1,j}$ by enumerating all the possible tape symbols Z and saying that either both are Z_1, or both are Z_2, and so on.

There are two important special cases: either $j = 0$ or $j = p(n)$. In one case there are no variables $y_{i,j-1,Z}$, and in the other, no variables $y_{i,j+1,Z}$. However, we know the head never moves to the left of its initial position, and we know it will not have time to get more than $p(n)$ cells to the right of where it started. Thus, we may eliminate certain terms from B_{i0} and $B_{i,p(n)}$; we leave you to make the simplification.

Now, let us consider the expressions A_{ij}. These expressions reflect all possible relationships among the 2×3 rectangle of symbols in the array of Fig. 10.4: $X_{i,j-1}$, X_{ij}, $X_{i,j+1}$, $X_{i+1,j-1}$, $X_{i+1,j}$, and $X_{i+1,j+1}$. An assignment of symbols to each of these six variables is *valid* if:

1. X_{ij} is a state, but $X_{i,j-1}$ and $X_{i,j+1}$ are tape symbols.

2. Exactly one of $X_{i+1,j-1}$, $X_{i+1,j}$, and $X_{i+1,j+1}$ is a state.

3. There is a move of M that explains how $X_{i,j-1}X_{ij}X_{i,j+1}$ becomes

$$X_{i+1,j-1}X_{i+1,j}X_{i+1,j+1}$$

There are thus a finite number of assignments of symbols to the six variables that are valid. Let A_{ij} be the OR of terms, one term for each set of six variables that form a valid assignment.

For instance, suppose that one move of M comes from the fact that $\delta(q, A)$ contains (p, C, L). Let D be some tape symbol of M. Then one valid assignment is $X_{i,j-1}X_{ij}X_{i,j+1} = DqA$ and $X_{i+1,j-1}X_{i+1,j}X_{i+1,j+1} = pDC$. Notice how this assignment reflects the change in ID that is caused by making this move of M. The term that reflects this possibility is

$$y_{i,j-1,D} \wedge y_{i,j,q} \wedge y_{i,j+1,A} \wedge y_{i+1,j-1,p} \wedge y_{i+1,j,D} \wedge y_{i+1,j+1,C}$$

If, instead, $\delta(q, A)$ contains (p, C, R) (i.e., the move is the same, but the head moves right), then the corresponding valid assignment is $X_{i,j-1}X_{ij}X_{i,j+1} = DqA$ and $X_{i+1,j-1}X_{i+1,j}X_{i+1,j+1} = DCp$. The term for this valid assignment is

$$y_{i,j-1,D} \wedge y_{i,j,q} \wedge y_{i,j+1,A} \wedge y_{i+1,j-1,D} \wedge y_{i+1,j,C} \wedge y_{i+1,j+1,p}$$

A_{ij} is the OR of all valid terms. In the special cases $j = 0$ and $j = p(n)$, we must make certain modifications to reflect the nonexistence of the variables y_{ijZ} for $j < 0$ or $j > p(n)$, as we did for A_{ij}. Finally,

$$N_i = (A_{i0} \vee B_{i0}) \wedge (A_{i1} \vee B_{i1}) \wedge \cdots \wedge (A_{i,p(n)} \vee B_{i,p(n)})$$

and then

$$N = N_0 \wedge N_1 \wedge \cdots \wedge N_{p(n)-1}$$

Although A_{ij} and B_{ij} can be very large if M has many states and/or tape symbols, their size is actually a constant as far as the length of input w is concerned; that is, their size is independent of n, the length of w. Thus, the length of N_i is $O(p(n))$, and the length of N is $O(p^2(n))$. More importantly, we can write N on a tape of a multitape TM in an amount of time that is proportional to its length, and that amount of time is polynomial in n, the length of w.

Conclusion of the Proof of Cook's Theorem

Although we have described the construction of the expression

$$E_{M,w} = S \wedge N \wedge F$$

as a function of both M and w, the fact is that only the "starts right" part S that depends on w, and it does so in a simple way (w is on the tape of the initial ID). The other parts, N and F, depend on M and on n, the length of w, only.

Thus, for any NTM M that runs in some polynomial time $p(n)$, we can devise an algorithm that takes an input w of length n, and produces $E_{M,w}$. The running time of this algorithm on a multitape, deterministic TM is $O(p^2(n))$, and that multitape TM can be converted to a single-tape TM that runs in time $O(p^4(n))$. The output of this algorithm is a boolean expression $E_{M,w}$ that is satisfiable if and only if M accepts w within $p(n)$ moves. $\square$

To emphasize the importance of Cook's Theorem 10.9, let us see how Theorem 10.5 applies to it. Suppose SAT had a deterministic TM that recognized its instances in polynomial time, say time $q(n)$. Then every language accepted by an NTM M that accepted within polynomial time $p(n)$ would be accepted in deterministic polynomial time by the DTM whose operation is suggested by Fig. 10.5. The input w to M is converted to a boolean expression $E_{M,w}$. This expression is fed to the SAT tester, and whatever this tester answers about $E_{M,w}$, our algorithm answers about w.

10.2.4   Exercises for Section 10.2

Exercise 10.2.1: How many satisfying truth assignments do the following boolean expressions have? Which are in SAT?

* a) $x \wedge (y \vee \neg x) \wedge (z \vee \neg y)$.

  b) $(x \vee y) \wedge \big(\neg(x \vee z) \vee (\neg z \wedge \neg y)\big)$.

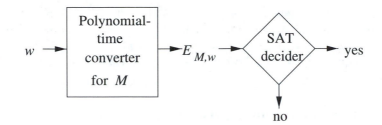

Figure 10.5: If SAT is in $\mathcal{P}$, then every language in $\mathcal{NP}$ could be shown to be in $\mathcal{P}$ by a DTM designed in this manner

! **Exercise 10.2.2:** Suppose G is a graph of four nodes: 1, 2, 3, and 4. Let x_{ij}, for $1 \le i < j \le 4$ be a propositional variable that we interpret as saying "there is an edge between nodes i and j. Any graph on these four nodes can be represented by a truth assignment. For instance, the graph of Fig. 10.1 is represented by making x_{14} false and the other five variables true. For any property of the graph that involves only the existence or nonexistence of edges, we can express that property as a boolean expression that is true if and only if the truth assignment to the variables describes a graph that has the property. Write expressions for the following properties:

* a) G has a Hamilton circuit.

  b) G is connected.

  c) G contains a clique of size 3, that is, a set of three nodes such that there is an edge between every two of them (i.e., a triangle in the graph).

  d) G contains at least one isolated node, that is, a node with no edges.

10.3   A Restricted Satisfiability Problem

Our plan is to demonstrate a wide variety of problems, such as the TSP problem mentioned in Section 10.1.4, to be NP-complete. In principle, we do so by finding polynomial-time reductions from the problem SAT to each problem of interest. However, there is an important intermediate problem, called "3SAT," that is much easier than SAT to reduce to typical problems. 3SAT is still a problem about satisfiability of boolean expressions, but these expressions have a very regular form: they are the AND of "clauses," each of which is the OR of exactly three variables or negated variables.

In this section we introduce some important terminology about boolean expressions. We then reduce satisfiability for any expression to satisfiability for expressions in the normal form for the 3SAT problem. It is interesting to observe that, while every boolean expression E has an equivalent expression F in the normal form of 3SAT, the size of F may be exponential in the size of

E. Thus, our polynomial-time reduction of SAT to 3SAT must be more subtle than simple boolean-algebra manipulation. We need to convert each expression E in SAT to another expression F in the normal form for 3SAT. Yet F is not necessarily equivalent to E. We can be sure only that F is satisfiable if and only if E is.

10.3.1   Normal Forms for Boolean Expressions

The following are three essential definitions:

- A *literal* is either a variable, or a negated variable. Examples are x and $\neg y$. To save space, we shall often use an overbar $\overline{y}$ in place of a literal such as $\neg y$.

- A *clause* is the logical OR of one or more literals. Examples are x, $x \vee y$, and $x \vee \overline{y} \vee z$.

- A boolean expression is said to be in *conjunctive normal form*[3] or *CNF*, if it is the AND of clauses.

To further compress the expressions we write, we shall adopt the alternative notation in which $\vee$ is treated as a sum, using the $+$ operator, and $\wedge$ is treated as a product. For products, we normally use juxtaposition, i.e., no operator, just as we do for concatenation in regular expressions. It is also then natural to refer to a clause as a "sum of literals" and a CNF expression as a "product of clauses."

Example 10.10 : The expression $(x \vee \neg y) \wedge (\neg x \vee z)$ will be written in our compressed notation as $(x + \overline{y})(\overline{x} + z)$. It is in conjunctive normal form, since it is the AND (product) of the clauses $(x + \overline{y})$ and $(\overline{x} + z)$.
  Expression $(x + y\overline{z})(x + y + z)(\overline{y} + \overline{z})$ is not in CNF. It is the AND of three subexpressions, $(x + y\overline{z})$, $(x + y + z)$, and $(\overline{y} + \overline{z})$. The last two are clauses, but the first is not; it is the sum of a literal and a product of two literals.
  Expression xyz is in CNF. Remember that a clause can have only one literal. Thus, our expression is the product of three clauses, (x), (y), and (z).   □

An expression is said to be in *k-conjunctive normal form* (*k-CNF*) if it is the product of clauses, each of which is the sum of exactly k distinct literals. For instance, $(x + \overline{y})(y + \overline{z})(z + \overline{x})$ is in 2-CNF, because each of its clauses has exactly two literals.
  All of these restrictions on boolean expressions give rise to their own problems about satisfiability for expressions that meet the restriction. Thus, we shall speak of the following problems:

- CSAT is the problem: given a boolean expression in CNF, is it satisfiable?

---

[3] "Conjunction" is a fancy term for logical OR.

Handling Bad Input

Each of the problems we have discussed — SAT, CSAT, 3SAT, and so on — are languages over a fixed, 8-symbol alphabet, whose strings we sometimes may interpret as boolean expressions. A string that is not interpretable as an expression cannot be in the language SAT. Likewise, when we consider expressions of restricted form, a string that is a well-formed boolean expression, but not an expression of the required form, is never in the language. Thus, an algorithm that decides the CSAT problem, for example, will say "no" if it is given a boolean expression that is satisfiable, but not in CNF.

- kSAT is the problem: given a boolean expression in k-CNF, is it satisfiable?

We shall see that CSAT, 3SAT, and kSAT for all k higher than 3 are NP-complete. However, there are linear-time algorithms for 1SAT and 2SAT.

10.3.2 Converting Expressions to CNF

Two boolean expressions are said to be *equivalent* if they have the same result on any truth assignment to their variables. If two expressions are equivalent, then surely either both are satisfiable or neither is. Thus, converting arbitrary expressions to equivalent CNF expressions is a promising approach to developing a polynomial-time reduction from SAT to CSAT. That reduction would show CSAT to be NP-complete.

However, things are not quite so simple. While we can convert any expression to CNF, the conversion can take more than polynomial time. In particular, it may exponentiate the length of the expression, and thus surely take exponential time to generate the output.

Fortunately, conversion of an arbitrary boolean expression to an expression in CNF is only one way that we might reduce SAT to CSAT, and thus prove CSAT is NP-complete. All we *have* to do is take a SAT instance E and convert it to a CSAT instance F such that F is satisfiable if and only if E is. It is not necessary that E and F be equivalent. It is not even necessary for E and F to have the same set of variables, and in fact, generally F will have a superset of the variables of E.

The reduction of SAT to CSAT will consist of two parts. First, we push all $\neg$'s down the expression tree so that the only negations are of variables; i.e., the boolean expression becomes an AND and OR of literals. This transformation produces an equivalent expression and takes time that is at most quadratic in the size of the expression. On a conventional computer, with a carefully designed data structure, it takes only linear time.

Expression	Rule
$\neg\big((\neg(x+y))(\overline{x}+y)\big)$	start
$\neg(\neg(x+y)) + \neg(\overline{x}+y)$	(1)
$x+y+\neg(\overline{x}+y)$	(3)
$x+y+(\neg(\overline{x}))\overline{y}$	(2)
$x+y+x\overline{y}$	(3)

Figure 10.6: Pushing $\neg$'s down the expression tree so they appear only in literals

The second step is to write an expression that is the AND and OR of literals as a product of clauses; i.e., to put it in CNF. By introducing new variables, we are able to perform this transformation in time that is a polynomial in the size of the given expression. The new expression F will not be equivalent to the old expression E, in general. However, F will be satisfiable if and only if E is. More specifically, if T is a truth assignment that makes E true, then there is an *extension* of T, say S, that makes F true; we say S is an extension of T if S assigns the same value as T to each variable that T assigns, but S may also assign a value to variables that T does not mention.

Our first step is to push $\neg$'s below $\wedge$'s and $\vee$'s. The rules we need are:

1. $\neg(E \wedge F) \Rightarrow \neg(E) \vee \neg(F)$. This rule, one of *DeMorgan's laws*, allows us to push $\neg$ below $\wedge$. Note that as a side-effect, the $\wedge$ is changed to an $\vee$.

2. $\neg(E \vee F) \Rightarrow \neg(E) \wedge \neg(F)$. The other "DeMorgan's law" pushes $\neg$ below $\vee$. The $\vee$ is changed to $\wedge$ as a side-effect.

3. $\neg(\neg(E)) \Rightarrow E$. This *law of double negation* cancels a pair of $\neg$'s that apply to the same expression.

Example 10.11 : Consider the expression $E = \neg\big((\neg(x+y))(\overline{x}+y)\big)$. Notice that we have used a mixture of our two notations, with the $\neg$ operator used explicitly when the expression to be negated is more than a single variable. Figure 10.6 shows the steps in which expression E has all its $\neg$'s pushed down until they become parts of literals.

The final expression is equivalent to the original and is and OR-and-AND expression of literals. It may be further simplified to the expression $x + y$, but that simplification is not essential to our claim that every expression can be rewritten so the $\neg$'s appear only in literals.   □

Theorem 10.12 : Every boolean expression E is equivalent to an expression F in which the only negations occur in literals; i.e., they apply directly to variables. Moreover, the length of F is linear in the number of symbols of E, and F can be constructed from E in polynomial time.

PROOF: The proof is an induction on the number of operators ($\land$, $\lor$, and $\neg$) in E. We show that there is an equivalent expression F with $\neg$'s only in literals. Additionally, if E has $n \geq 1$ operators, then F has no more than $2n - 1$ operators.

Since F need not have more than one pair of parentheses per operator, and the number of variables in an expression cannot exceed the number of operators by more than one, we conclude that the length of F is linearly proportional to the length of E. More importantly, we shall see that, because the construction of F is quite simple, the time it takes to construct F is proportional to its length, and therefore proportional to the length of E.

BASIS: If E has one operator, it must be of the form $\neg x$, $x \lor y$, or $x \land y$, for variables x and y. In each case, E is already in the required form, so $F = E$ serves. Note that since E and F each have one operator, the relationship "F has at most twice the number of operators of E, minus 1" holds.

INDUCTION: Suppose the statement is true for all expressions with fewer operators than E. If the highest operator of E is not $\neg$, then E must be of the form $E_1 \lor E_2$ or $E_1 \land E_2$. In either case, the inductive hypothesis applies to E_1 and E_2; it says that there are equivalent expressions F_1 and F_2, respectively, in which all $\neg$'s occur in literals only. Then $F = F_1 \lor F_2$ or $F = (F_1) \land (F_2)$ serves as a suitable equivalent for E. Let E_1 and E_2 have a and b operators, respectively. Then E has $a + b + 1$ operators. By the inductive hypothesis, F_1 and F_2 have at most $2a - 1$ and $2b - 1$ operators, respectively. Thus, F has at most $2a + 2b - 1$ operators, which is no more than $2(a + b + 1) - 1$, or twice the number of operators of E, minus 1.

Now, consider the case where E is of the form $\neg E_1$. There are three cases, depending on what the top operator of E_1 is. Note that E_1 must have an operator, or E is really a basis case.

1. $E_1 = \neg E_2$. Then by the law of double negation, $E = \neg(\neg E_2)$ is equivalent to E_2. Since E_2 has fewer operators than E, the inductive hypothesis applies. We can find an equivalent F for E_2 in which the only $\neg$'s are in literals. F serves for E as well. Since the number of operators of F is at most twice the number in E_2 minus 1, it is surely no more than twice the number of operators in E minus 1.

2. $E_1 = E_2 \lor E_3$. By DeMorgan's law, $E = \neg(E_2 \lor E_3)$ is equivalent to $\left(\neg(E_2)\right) \land \left(\neg(E_3)\right)$. Both $\neg(E_2)$ and $\neg(E_3)$ have fewer operators than E, so by the inductive hypothesis they have equivalents F_2 and F_3 that have $\neg$'s only in literals. Then $F = (F_2) \land (F_3)$ serves as such an equivalent for E. We also claim that the number of operators in F is not too great. Let E_2 and E_3 have a and b operators respectively. Then E has $a + b + 2$ operators. Since $\neg(E_2)$ and $\neg(E_3)$ have $a + 1$ and $b + 1$ operators, respectively, and F_2 and F_3 are constructed from these expressions, by the inductive hypothesis we know that F_2 and F_3 have at most $2(a + 1) - 1$ and $2(b + 1) - 1$ operators, respectively. Thus, F has $2a + 2b + 3$ operators

---

Descriptions of Algorithms

While formally, the running time of a reduction is the time it takes to execute on a single-tape Turing machine, these algorithms are needlessly complex. We know that the sets of problems that can be solved on conventional computers, on multitape TM's and on single tape TM's in some polynomial time are the same, although the degrees of the polynomials may differ. Thus, as we describe some fairly sophisticated algorithms that are needed to reduce one NP-complete problem to another, let us agree that times will be measured by efficient implementations on a conventional computer. That understanding will allow us to avoid details regarding manipulation of tapes and will let us emphasize the important algorithmic ideas.

---

at most. This number is exactly twice the number of operators of E, minus 1.

3. $E_1 = E_2 \wedge E_3$. This argument, using the second of DeMorgan's laws, is essentially the same as (2).

$\square$

10.3.3   NP-Completeness of CSAT

Now, we need to take an expression E that is the AND and OR of literals and convert it to CNF. As we mentioned, in order to produce in polynomial time an expression F from E that is satisfiable if and only if E is satisfiable, we must forgo an equivalence-preserving transformation, and introduce some new variables for F that do not appear in E. We shall introduce this "trick" in the proof of the theorem that CSAT is NP-complete, and then give an example of the trick to make the construction clearer.

Theorem 10.13: CSAT is NP-complete.

PROOF: We show how to reduce SAT to CSAT in polynomial time. First, use the method of Theorem 10.12 to convert a given instance of SAT to an expression E whose ¬'s are only in literals. We then show how to convert E to a CNF expression F in polynomial time and show that F is satisfiable if and only if E is. The construction of F is by an induction on the length of E. The particular property that F has is somewhat more than we need. Precisely, we show by induction on the number of symbol occurrences ("length") E that:

- There is a constant c such that if E is a boolean expression of length n with ¬'s appearing only in literals, then there is an expression F such that:

   a) F is in CNF, and consists of at most n clauses.

   b) F is constructible from E in time at most $c|E|^2$.

   c) A truth assignment T for E makes E true if and only if there exists an extension S of T that makes F true.

BASIS: If E consists of one or two symbols, then it is a literal. A literal is a clause, so E is already in CNF.

INDUCTION: Assume that every expression shorter than E can be converted to a product of clauses, and that this conversion takes at most cn^2 time on an expression of length n. There are two cases, depending on the top-level operator of E.

Case 1: $E = E_1 \wedge E_2$. By the inductive hypothesis, there are expressions F_1 and F_2 derived from E_1 and E_2, respectively, in CNF. All and only the satisfying assignments for E_1 can be extended to a satisfying assignment for F_1, and similarly for E_2 and F_2. Without loss of generality, we may assume that the variables of F_1 and F_2 are disjoint, except for those variables that appear in E; i.e., if we have to introduce variables into F_1 and/or F_2, use distinct variables.

   Let $F = F_1 \wedge F_2$. Evidently $F_1 \wedge F_2$ is a CNF expression if F_1 and F_2 are. We must show that a truth assignment T for E can be extended to a satisfying assignment for F if and only if T satisfies E.

(If) Suppose T satisfies E. Let T_1 be T restricted so it applies only to the variables that appear in E_1, and let T_2 be the same for E_2. Then by the inductive hypothesis, T_1 and T_2 can be extended to an assignments S_1 and S_2 that satisfy F_1 and F_2, respectively. Let S agree with S_1 and S_2 on each of the variables they define. Note that, since the only variables F_1 and F_2 have in common are the variables of E, and S_1 and S_2 must agree on those variables if both are defined, it is always possible to construct S. But S is then an extension of T that satisfies F.

(Only if) Conversely, suppose that T has an extension S that satisfies F. Let T_1 (resp., T_2) be T restricted to the variables of E_1 (resp., E_2). Let S restricted to the variables of F_1 (resp., F_2) be S_1 (resp., S_2). Then S_1 is an extension of T_1, and S_2 is an extension of T_2. Because F is the AND of F_1 and F_2, it must be that S_1 satisfies F_1, and S_2 satisfies F_2. By the inductive hypothesis, T_1 (resp., T_2) must satisfy E_1 (resp., E_2). Thus, T satisfies E.

Case 2: $E = E_1 \vee E_2$. As in case 1, we invoke the inductive hypothesis to assert that there are CNF expressions F_1 and F_2 with the properties:

1. A truth assignment for E_1 (resp., E_2) satisfies E_1 (resp., E_2), if and only if it can be extended to a satisfying assignment for F_1 (resp., F_2).

2. The variables of F_1 and F_2 are disjoint, except for those variables that appear in E.

3. F_1 and F_2 are in CNF.

We cannot simply take the OR of F_1 and F_2 to construct the desired F, because the resulting expression would not be in CNF. However, a more complicated construction, which takes advantage of the fact that we only want to preserve satisfiability, rather than equivalence, will work. Suppose

$$F_1 = g_1 \wedge g_2 \wedge \cdots \wedge g_p$$

and $F_2 = h_1 \wedge h_2 \wedge \cdots \wedge h_q$, where the g's and h's are clauses. Introduce a new variable y, and let

$$F = (y + g_1) \wedge (y + g_2) \wedge \cdots \wedge (y + g_p) \wedge (\overline{y} + h_1) \wedge (\overline{y} + h_2) \wedge \cdots \wedge (\overline{y} + h_q)$$

We must prove that a truth assignment T for E satisfies E if and only if T can be extended to a truth assignment S that satisfies F.

(If) Assume T satisfies E. As in Case 1, let T_1 (resp., T_2) be T restricted to the variables of E_1 (resp., E_2). Since $E = E_1 \vee E_2$, either T satisfies E_1 or T satisfies E_2. Let us assume T satisfies E_1. Then T_1, which is T restricted to the variables of E_1, can be extended to S_1, which satisfies F_1. Construct an extension S for T, as follows; S will satisfy the expression F defined above:

1. For all variables x in F_1, $S(x) = S_1(x)$.

2. $S(y) = 0$. This choice makes all the clauses of F that are derived from F_2 true.

3. For all variables x that are in F_2 but not in F_1, $S(x)$ can be either 0 or 1, arbitrarily.

Then S makes all the clauses derived from the g's true because of rule 1. S makes all the clauses derived from the h's true by rule 2 — the truth assignment for y. Thus, S satisfies F.

If T does not satisfy E_1, but satisfies E_2, then the argument is the same, except $S(y) = 1$ in rule 2. Also, $S(x)$ must agree with $S_2(x)$ whenever $S_2(x)$ is defined, but $S(x)$ for variables appearing only in S_1 is arbitrary. We conclude that S satisfies F in this case also.

(Only if) Suppose that truth assignment T for E is extended to truth assignment S for F, and S satisfies F. There are two cases, depending on what truth-value is assigned to y. First suppose that $S(y) = 0$. Then all the clauses of F derived from the h's are true. However, y is no help for the clauses of the form $(y + g_i)$ that are derived from the g's, which means that S must make true each of the g_i's themselves; in essence, S makes F_1 true.

More precisely, let S_1 be S restricted to the variables of F_1. Then S_1 satisfies F_1. By the inductive hypothesis, T_1, which is T restricted to the variables of E_1, must satisfy E_1. The reason is that S_1 is an extension of T_1. Since T_1 satisfies F_1, T must satisfy E, which is $E_1 \vee E_2$.

We must also consider the case that $S(y) = 1$, but this case is symmetric to what we have just seen, and we leave it to the reader. We conclude that T satisfies E whenever S satisfies F.

Now, we must show that the time to construct F from E is at most quadratic, in n, the length of E. Regardless of which case applies, the splitting apart of E into E_1 and E_2, and construction of F from F_1 and F_2 each take time that is linear in the size of E. Let dn be an upper bound on the time to construct E_1 and E_2 from E plus the time to construct F from F_1 and F_2, in either case 1 or case 2. Then there is a recurrence equation for $T(n)$, the time to construct F from any E of length n; its form is:

$$T(1) = T(2) \leq e \text{ for some constant } e$$
$$T(n) \leq dn + c\max_{0 < i < n-1}\bigl(T(i) + T(n-1-i)\bigr) \text{ for } n \geq 3$$

Where c is a constant as yet to be determined, such that we can show $T(n) \leq cn^2$. The basis rule for $T(1)$ and $T(2)$ simply says that if E is a single symbol or a pair of symbols, then we need no recursion because E can only be a single literal, and the entire process takes some amount of time e. The recursive rule uses the fact that if E is composed of subexpressions E_1 and E_2 connected by an operator $\wedge$ or $\vee$, and E_1 is of length i, then E_2 is of length $n - i - 1$. Moreover, the entire conversion of E to F consists of the two simple steps — changing E to E_1 and E_2 and changing F_1 and F_2 to F — that we know take time at most dn, plus the two recursive conversions of E_1 to F_1 and E_2 to F_2.

We need to show by induction on n that there is a constant c such that for all n, $T(n) \leq cn^2$.

BASIS: For $n = 1$, we just need to pick c at least as large as e.

INDUCTION: Assume the statement for lengths less than n. Then $T(i) \leq ci^2$ and $T(n - i - 1) \leq c(n - i - 1)^2$. Thus,

$$T(i) + T(n - i - 1) \leq n^2 - 2i(n - i) - 2(n - i) + 1 \tag{10.1}$$

Since $n \geq 3$, and $0 < i < n - 1$, $2i(n - i)$ is at least n, and $2(n - i)$ is at least 2. Thus, the right side of (10.1) is less than $n^2 - n$, for any i in the allowed range. The recursive rule in the definition of $T(n)$ thus says $T(n) \leq dn + cn^2 - cn$. If we pick $c \geq d$, we may infer that $T(n) \leq cn^2$ holds for n, which concludes the induction. Thus, the construction of F from E takes time $O(n^2)$. $\square$

Example 10.14: Let us show how the construction of Theorem 10.13 applies to a simple expression: $E = x\bar{y} + \bar{x}(y + z)$. Figure 10.7 shows the parse of this expression. Attached to each node is the CNF expression constructed for the expression represented by that node.

The leaves correspond to the literals, and for each literal, the CNF expression is one clause consisting of that literal alone. For instance, we see that the leaf labeled $\bar{y}$ has an associated CNF expression $(\bar{y})$. The parentheses are

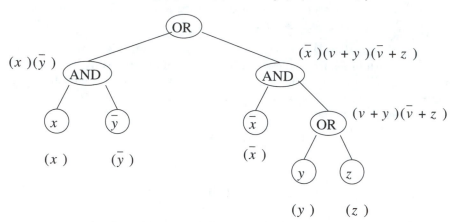

Figure 10.7: Transforming a boolean expression into CNF

unnecessary, but we put them in CNF expressions to help remind you that we are talking about a product of clauses.

For an AND node, the construction of a CNF expression is simply to take the product (AND) of all the clauses for the two subexpressions. Thus, for instance, the node for the subexpression $\bar{x}(y+z)$ has an associated CNF expression that is the product of the one clause for $\bar{x}$, namely $(\bar{x})$, and the two clauses for $y+z$, namely $(v+y)(\bar{v}+z)$.[4]

For an OR node, we must introduce a new variable. We add it to all the clauses for the left operand, and we add its negation to the clauses for the right operand. For instance, consider the root node in Fig. 10.7. It is the OR of expressions $x\bar{y}$ and $\bar{x}(y+z)$, whose CNF expressions have been determined to be $(x)(\bar{y})$ and $(\bar{x})(v+y)(\bar{v}+z)$, respectively. We introduce a new variable u, which is added without negation to the first group of clauses and negated in the second group. The result is

$$F = (u+x)(u+\bar{y})(\bar{u}+\bar{x})(\bar{u}+v+y)(\bar{u}+\bar{v}+z)$$

Theorem 10.13 tells us that any truth assignment T that satisfies E can be extended to a truth assignment S that satisfies F. For instance, the assignment $T(x) = 0$, $T(y) = 1$, and $T(z) = 1$ satisfies E. We can extend T to S by adding $S(u) = 1$ and $S(v) = 0$ to the required $S(x) = 0$, $S(y) = 1$, and $S(z) = 1$ that we get from T. You may check that S satisfies F.

Notice that in choosing S, we were required to pick $S(u) = 1$, because T makes only the second part of E, that is $\bar{x}(y+z)$, true. Thus, we need $S(u) = 1$

---

[4]In this special case, where the subexpression $y+z$ is already a clause, we did not have to perform the general construction for the OR of expressions, and could have produced $(y+z)$ as the product of clauses equivalent to $y+z$. However, in this example, we stick to the general rules.

to make true the clauses $(u + x)(u + \bar{y})$, which come from the first part of E. However, we could pick either value for v, because in the subexpression $y + z$, both sides of the OR are true according to T. $\square$

10.3.4 NP-Completeness of 3SAT

Now, we show an even smaller class of boolean expressions with an NP-complete satisfiability problem. Recall the problem 3SAT is:

- Given a boolean expression E that is the product of clauses, each of which is the sum of three distinct literals, is E satisfiable?

Although the 3-CNF expressions are a small fraction of the CNF expressions, they are complex enough to make their satisfiability test NP-complete, as the next theorem shows.

Theorem 10.15: 3SAT is NP-complete.

PROOF: Evidently 3SAT is in $\mathcal{NP}$, since SAT is in $\mathcal{NP}$. To prove NP-completeness, we shall reduce CSAT to 3SAT. The reduction is as follows. Given a CNF expression $E = e_1 \wedge e_2 \wedge \cdots \wedge e_k$, we replace each clause e_i as follows, to create a new expression F. The time taken to construct F is linear in the length of E, and we shall see that a truth assignment satisfies E if and only if it can be extended to a satisfying truth assignment for F.

1. If e_i is a single literal, say (x),[5] Introduce two new variables u and v. Replace (x) by the four clauses $(x+u+v)(x+u+\bar{v})(x+\bar{u}+v)(x+\bar{u}+\bar{v})$. Since u and v appear in all combinations, the only way to satisfy all four clauses is to make x true. Thus, all and only the satisfying assignments for E can be extended to a satisfying assignment for F.

2. Suppose e_i is the sum of two literals, $(x+y)$. Introduce a new variable z, and replace e_i by the product of two clauses $(x+y+z)(x+y+\bar{z})$. As in case 1, the only way to satisfy both clauses is to satisfy $(x+y)$.

3. If e_i is the sum of three literals, it is already in the form required for 3-CNF, so we leave e_i in the expression F being constructed.

4. Suppose $e_i = (x_1 + x_2 + \cdots + x_m)$ for some $m \geq 4$. Introduce new variables $y_1, y_2, \ldots, y_{m-3}$ and replace e_i by the product of clauses

$$(x_1 + x_2 + y_1)(x_3 + \bar{y_1} + y_2)(x_4 + \bar{y_2} + y_3) \cdots \qquad (10.2)$$
$$(x_{m-2} + \bar{y_{m-4}} + y_{m-3})(x_{m-1} + x_m + \bar{y_{m-3}})$$

An assignment T that satisfies E must make at least one literal of e_i true; say it makes x_j true (recall x_j could be a variable or a negated variable).

---

[5] For convenience, we shall talk of literals as if they were unnegated variables, like x. However, the constructions apply equally well if some or all of the literals are negated, like $\bar{x}$.

Then, if we make $y_1, y_2, \ldots, y_{j-1}$ false and make $y_j, y_{j+1}, \ldots, y_{m-3}$ true, we satisfy all the clauses of (10.2). Thus, T may be extended to satisfy these clauses. Conversely, if T makes all the x's false, it is not possible to extend T to make (10.2) true. The reason is that there are $m - 2$ clauses, and each of the $m - 3$ y's can only make one clause true, regardless of whether it is true or false.

We have thus shown how to reduce each instance E of CSAT to an instance F of 3SAT, such that F is satisfiable if and only if E is satisfiable. The construction evidently requires time that is linear in the length of E, because none of the four cases above expand a clause by more than a factor $32/3$ (that is the ratio of symbol counts in case 1), and it is easy to calculate the needed symbols of F in time proportional to the number of those symbols. Since CSAT is NP-complete, it follows that 3-SAT is likewise NP-complete. $\square$

10.3.5   Exercises for Section 10.3

Exercise 10.3.1: Put the following boolean expressions into 3-CNF:

* a) $xy + \bar{x}z$.

  b) $wxyz + u + v$.

  c) $wxy + \bar{x}uv$.

Exercise 10.3.2: The problem *4TA-SAT* is defined as follows: Given a boolean expression E, does E have at least four satisfying truth assignments. Show that 4TA-SAT is NP-complete.

Exercise 10.3.3: In this exercise, we shall define a family of 3-CNF expressions. The expression E_n has n variables, $x_1, x_2, \ldots, x_n$. For each set of three distinct integers between 1 and n, E_n has clauses $(x_1 + x_2 + x_3)$ and $(\bar{x_1} + \bar{x_2} + \bar{x_3})$. Is E_n satisfiable for:

*! a) $n = 4$?

!! b) $n = 5$?

! **Exercise 10.3.4:** Give a polynomial-time algorithm to solve the problem 2SAT, i.e., satisfiability for CNF boolean expressions with only two literals per clause. *Hint:* If one of two literals in a clause is false, the other is forced to be true. Start with an assumption about the truth of one variable, and chase down all the consequences for other variables.

10.4   Additional NP-Complete Problems

We shall now give you a small sample of the process whereby one NP-complete problem leads to proofs that other problems are also NP-complete. This process of discovering new NP-complete problems has two important effects:

- When we discover a problem to be NP-complete, it tells us that there is little chance an efficient algorithm can be developed to solve it. We are encouraged to look for heuristics, partial solutions, approximations, or other ways to avoid attacking the problem head-on. Moreover, we can do so with confidence that we are not just "missing the trick."

- Each time we add a new NP-complete problem P to the list, we re-enforce the idea that *all* NP-complete problems require exponential time. The effort that has undoubtedly gone into finding a polynomial-time algorithm for problem P was, unknowingly, effort devoted to showing $\mathcal{P} = \mathcal{NP}$. It is the accumulated weight of the unsuccessful attempts by many skilled scientists and mathematicians to show something that is tantamount to $\mathcal{P} = \mathcal{NP}$ that ultimately convinces us that it is very unlikely that $\mathcal{P} = \mathcal{NP}$, but rather that *all* the NP-complete problems require exponential time.

In this section, we meet several NP-complete problems involving graphs. These problems are among those graph problems most commonly used in the solution to questions of practical importance. We shall talk about the Traveling Salesman problem (TSP), which we met earlier in Section 10.1.4. We shall show that a simpler, and also important version, called the Hamilton-Circuit problem (HC), is NP-complete, thus showing that the more general TSP is NP complete. We introduce several other problems involving "covering," of graphs, such as the "node-cover problem," which asks us to find the smallest set of nodes that "cover" all the edges, in the sense that at least one end of every edge is in the selected set.

10.4.1   Describing NP-complete Problems

As we introduce new NP-complete problems, we shall use a stylized form of definition, as follows:

1. The *name* of the problem, and usually an abbreviation, like 3SAT or TSP.

2. The *input* to the problem: what is represented, and how.

3. The *output* desired: under what circumstances should the output be "yes"?

4. The problem from which a reduction is made to prove the problem NP-complete.

Example 10.16: Here is how the description of the problem 3SAT and its proof of NP-completeness might look:

PROBLEM: Satisfiability for 3-CNF expressions (3SAT).

INPUT: A boolean expression in 3-CNF.

OUTPUT: "Yes" if and only if the expression is satisfiable.

REDUCTION FROM: CSAT. □

10.4.2   The Problem of Independent Sets

Let G be an undirected graph. We say a subset I of the nodes of G is an *independent set* if no two nodes of I are connected by an edge of G. An independent set is *maximal* if it is as large (has as many nodes) as any independent set for the same graph.

Example 10.17: In the graph of Fig. 10.1 (See Section 10.1.2), $\{1, 4\}$ is a maximal independent set. It is the only set of size two that is independent, because there is an edge between any other pair of nodes. Thus, no set of size three or more is independent; for instance, $\{1, 2, 4\}$ is not independent because there is an edge between 1 and 2. Thus, $\{1, 4\}$ is a maximal independent set. In fact, it is the only maximal independent set for this graph, although in general a graph may have many maximal independent sets. As another example, $\{1\}$ is an independent set for this graph, but not maximal. □

In combinatorial optimization, the maximal-independent-set problem is usually stated as: given a graph, find a maximal independent set. However, as with all problems in the theory of intractable problems, we need to state our problem in yes/no terms. Thus, we need to introduce a lower bound into the statement of the problem, and we phrase the question as whether a given graph has an independent set at least as large as the bound. The formal definition of the maximal-independent-set problem is:

PROBLEM: Independent Set (IS).

INPUT: A graph G and a lower bound k, which must be between 1 and the number of nodes of G.

OUTPUT: "Yes" if and only if G has an independent set of k nodes.

REDUCTION FROM: 3SAT.

We must prove IS to be NP-complete by a polynomial-time reduction from 3SAT, as promised. That reduction is in the next theorem.

Theorem 10.18: The independent-set problem is NP-complete.

PROOF: First, it is easy to see that IS is in $\mathcal{NP}$. Given a graph G and a bound k, guess k nodes and check that they are independent.

Now, let us show how to perform the reduction of 3SAT to IS. Let $E = (e_1)(e_2)\cdots(e_m)$ be a 3-CNF expression. We construct from E a graph G with $3m$ nodes, which we shall give the names $[i, j]$, where $1 \le i \le m$ and $j = 1, 2,$ or 3. The node $[i, j]$ represents the jth literal in the clause e_i. Figure 10.8 is an example of a graph G, based on the 3-CNF expression

$$(x_1 + x_2 + x_3)(\overline{x_1} + x_2 + x_4)(\overline{x_2} + x_3 + x_5)(\overline{x_3} + \overline{x_4} + \overline{x_5})$$

The columns represent the clauses; we shall explain shortly why the edges are as they are.

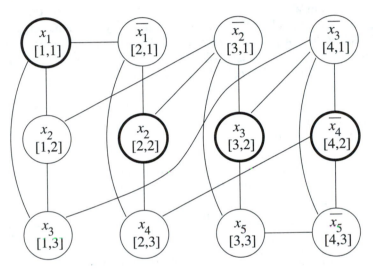

Figure 10.8: Construction of an independent set from a satisfiable boolean expression in 3-CNF

The "trick" behind the construction of G is to use edges to force any independent set with m nodes to represent a way to satisfy the expression E. There are two key ideas.

1. We want to make sure that only one node corresponding to a given clause can be chosen. We do so by putting edges between all pairs of nodes in a column, i.e., we create the edges $([i, 1], [i, 2])$, $([i, 1], [i, 3])$, and $([i, 2], [i, 3])$, for all i, as in Fig. 10.8.

2. We must prevent nodes from being chosen for the independent set if they represent literals that are complementary. Thus, if there are two nodes $[i_1, j_1]$ and $[i_2, j_2]$, such that one of them represents a variable x, and the other represents $\overline{x}$, we place an edge between these two nodes. Thus, it is not possible to choose both of these nodes for an independent set.

Are Yes-No Problems Easier?

We might worry that a yes/no version of a problem is easier than the optimization version. For instance, it might be hard to find a largest independent set, but given a small bound k, it might be easy to verify that there is an independent set of size k. While true, it is also the case that we *might* be given a constant k that is exactly largest size for which an independent set exists. If so, then solving the yes/no version requires us to find a maximal independent set.

In fact, for all the common problems that are NP-complete, their yes/no versions and optimization versions are equivalent in complexity, at least to within a polynomial. Typically, as in the case of IS, if we had a polynomial-time algorithm to *find* maximal independent sets, then we could solve the yes/no problem by finding a maximal independent set, and seeing if it was at least as large as the limit k. Since we shall show the yes/no version is NP-complete, the optimization version must be intractable as well.

The comparison can also be made the other way. Suppose we had a polynomial-time algorithm for the yes/no problem IS. If the graph has n nodes, the size of the maximal independent set is between 1 and n. By running IS with all bounds between 1 and n, we can surely find the size of a maximal independent set (although not necessarily the set itself) in n times the amount of time it takes to solve IS once. In fact, by using binary search, we need only a $\log_2 n$ a factor in the running time.

The bound k for the graph G constructed by these two rules is m.

It is not hard to see how graph G and bound k can be constructed from expression E in time that is proportional to the square of the length of E, so the conversion of E to G is a polynomial-time reduction. We must show that it correctly reduces 3SAT to IS. That is:

- E is satisfiable if and only if G has an independent set of size m.

(If) First, observe that an independent set may not include two nodes from the same clause, $[i, j_1]$ and $[i, j_2]$ for some $j_1 \neq j_2$. The reason is that there are edges between each pair of such nodes, as we observe from the columns in Fig. 10.8. Thus, if there is an independent set of size m, this set must include exactly one node from each clause.

Moreover, the independent set may not include nodes that correspond to both a variable x and its negation $\bar{x}$. The reason is that all pairs of such nodes also have an edge between them. Thus, the independent set I of size m yields a satisfying truth assignment T for E as follows. If a node corresponding to a variable x is in I, then make $T(x) = 1$; if a node corresponding to a negated variable $\overline{x}$ is in I, then choose $T(x) = 0$. If there is no node in I that corresponds to either x or $\overline{x}$, then pick $T(x)$ arbitrarily. Note that item (2) above explains why there cannot be a contradiction, with nodes corresponding to both x and $\overline{x}$ in I.

We claim that T satisfies E. The reason is that each clause of E has the node corresponding to one of its literals in I, and T is chosen so that literal is made true by T. Thus, when an independent set of size m exists, E is satisfiable.

(Only if) Now suppose E is satisfied by some truth assignment, say T. Since T makes each clause of E true, we can identify one literal from each clause that T makes true. For some clauses, we may have a choice of two or three of the literals, and if so, pick one of them arbitrarily. Construct a set of m nodes I by picking the node corresponding to the selected literal from each clause.

We claim I is an independent set. The edges between nodes that come from the same clause (the columns in Fig. 10.8) cannot have both ends in I, because we pick only one node from each clause. An edge connecting a variable and its negation cannot have both ends in I, because we selected for I only nodes that correspond to literals made true by the truth assignment T. Of course T will make one of x and $\overline{x}$ true, but never both. We conclude that if E is satisfiable, then G has an independent set of size m.

Thus, there is a polynomial time reduction from 3SAT to IS. Since 3SAT is known to be NP-complete, so is IS by Theorem 10.5.   □

Example 10.19: Let us see how the construction of Theorem 10.18 works for the case where

$$E = (x_1 + x_2 + x_3)(\overline{x_1} + x_2 + x_4)(\overline{x_2} + x_3 + x_5)(\overline{x_3} + \overline{x_4} + \overline{x_5})$$

We already saw the graph obtained from this expression in Fig. 10.8. The nodes are in four columns corresponding to the four clauses. We have shown for each node not only its name (a pair of integers), but the literal to which it corresponds. Notice how there are edges between each pair of nodes in a column, which corresponds to the literals of one clause. There are also edges between each pair of nodes that corresponds to a variable and its complement. for instance, the node $[3, 1]$, which corresponds to $\overline{x_2}$, has edges to the two nodes, $[1, 2]$ and $[2, 2]$, each of which corresponds to an occurrence of x_2.

We have selected, by boldface outline, a set I of four nodes, one from each column. These evidently form an independent set. Since their four literals are x_1, x_2, x_3, and $\overline{x_4}$, we can construct from them a truth assignment T that has $T(x_1) = 1$, $T(x_2) = 1$, $T(x_3) = 1$, and $T(x_4) = 0$. There must also be an assignment for x_5, but we may pick that arbitrarily, say $T(x_5) = 0$. Now T satisfies E, and the set of nodes I indicates a literal from each clause that is made true by T.   □

What are Independent Sets Good For?

It is not the purpose of this book to cover applications of the problems we prove NP-complete. However, the selection of problems in Section 10.4 was taken from a fundamental paper on NP-completeness by R. Karp, where he examined the most important problems from the field of Operations Research and showed a good number of them to be NP-complete. Thus, there is ample evidence available of "real" problems that are solved using these abstract problems.

As an example, we could use a good algorithm for finding large independent sets to schedule final exams. Let the nodes of the graph be the classes, and place an edge between two nodes if one or more students are taking both those classes, and therefore their finals could not be scheduled for the same time. If we find a maximal independent set, then we can schedule all those classes for finals at the same time, sure that no student will have a conflict.

10.4.3 The Node-Cover Problem

Another important class of combinatorial optimization problems involve "covering" of a graph. For instance, an *edge covering* is a set of edges such that every node in the graph is an end of at least one edge in the set. An edge covering is *minimal* if it has as few edges as any edge covering for the same graph. The problem of deciding whether a graph has an edge covering with k edges is NP-complete, although we shall not prove it here.

We *shall* prove NP-complete the problem of *node covering*. A node cover of a graph is a set of nodes such that each edge has at least one of its ends at a node of the set. A node cover is *minimal* if it has as few nodes as any node cover for the given graph.

Node covers and independent sets are closely related. In fact, the complement of an independent set is a node cover, and vice-versa. Thus, if we state the yes/no version of the node-cover problem (NC) properly, a reduction from IS is very simple.

PROBLEM: The Node-Cover Problem (NC).

INPUT: A graph G and an upper limit k, which must be between 0 and one less than the number of nodes of G.

OUTPUT: "Yes" if and only if G has a node cover with k or fewer nodes.

REDUCTION FROM: Independent Set.

Theorem 10.20: The node-cover problem is NP-complete.

PROOF: Evidently, NC is in $\mathcal{NP}$. Guess a set of k nodes, and check that each edge of G has at least one end in the set.

To complete the proof, we shall reduce IS to NC. The idea, which is suggested by Fig. 10.8, is that the complement of an independent set is a node cover. For instance, the set of nodes that do *not* have boldface outlines in Fig. 10.8 form a node cover. Since the boldface nodes are in fact a maximal independent set, the other nodes form a minimal node cover.

The reduction is as follows. Let G with lower limit k be an instance of the independent-set problem. if G has n nodes, let G with upper limit $n - k$ be the instance of the node-cover problem we construct. Evidently this transformation can be accomplished in linear time. We claim that

- G has an independent set of size k if and only if G has a node cover of size $n - k$.

(If) Let N be the set of nodes of G, and let C be the node cover of size $n - k$. We claim that $N - C$ is an independent set. Suppose not; that is, there is a pair of nodes v and w in $N - C$ that has an edge between them in G. Then since neither v nor w is in C, the edge (v, w) in G is not covered by the alleged node cover C. We have proved by contradiction that $N - C$ is an independent set. Evidently, this set has k nodes, so this direction of the proof is complete.

(Only if) Suppose I is an independent set of k nodes. We claim that $N - I$ is a node cover of with $n - k$ nodes. Again, we proceed by contradiction. If there is some edge (v, w) not covered by $N - I$, then both v and w are in I, yet are connected by an edge, which contradicts the definition of an independent set. $\square$

10.4.4 The Directed Hamilton-Circuit Problem

We would like to show NP-complete the Traveling Salesman Problem (TSP), because this problem is one of great interest in combinatorics. The best known proof of its NP-completeness is actually a proof that a simpler problem, called the "Hamilton-Circuit Problem" (HC) is NP-complete. The *Hamilton-Circuit Problem* can be described as follows:

PROBLEM: Hamilton-Circuit Problem.

INPUT: An undirected graph G.

OUTPUT: "Yes" if and only if G has a *Hamilton circuit*, that is, a cycle that passes through each node of G exactly once.

Notice that the HC problem is a special case of the TSP, in which all the weights on the edges are 1. Thus, a polynomial-time reduction of HC to TSP is very simple: just add a weight of 1 to the specification of each edge in the graph.

The proof of NP-completeness for HC is very hard. Our approach is to introduce a more constrained version of HC, in which the edges have directions (i.e., they are directed edges, or arcs), and the Hamilton circuit is required to follow arcs in the proper direction. We reduce 3SAT to this directed version of the HC problem, then reduce it to the standard, or undirected, version of HC. Formally:

PROBLEM: The Directed Hamilton-Circuit Problem (DHC).

INPUT: A directed Graph G.

OUTPUT: "Yes" if and only if there is a directed cycle in G that passes through each node exactly once.

REDUCTION FROM: 3SAT.

Theorem 10.21: The Directed Hamilton-Circuit Problem is NP-complete.

PROOF: The proof that DHC is in $\mathcal{NP}$ is easy; guess a cycle and check that all the arcs it needs are present in the graph. We must reduce 3SAT to DHC, and this reduction requires the construction of a complicated graph, with "gadgets," or specialized subgraphs, representing each variable and each clause of the 3SAT instance.

To begin the construction of a DHC instance from a 3-CNF boolean expression, let the expression be $E = e_1 \wedge e_2 \wedge \cdots \wedge e_k$, where each e_i is a clause, the sum of three literals, say $e_i = (\alpha_{i1} + \alpha_{i2} + \alpha_{i3})$. Let $x_1, x_2, \ldots, x_n$ be the variables of E. For each clause and for each variable, we construct a "gadget," suggested in Fig. 10.9.

For each variable x_i we construct a subgraph H_i with the structure shown in Fig. 10.9(a). Here, m_i is the larger of the number of occurrences of x_i and the number of occurrences of $\overline{x_i}$ in E. In the two columns of nodes, the b's and the c's, there are arcs between b_{ij} and c_{ij} in both directions. Also, each of the b's has an arc to the c below it; i.e., b_{ij} has an arc to $c_{i,j+1}$, as long as $j < m_i$. Likewise, c_{ij} has an arc to $b_{i,j+1}$, for $j < m_i$. Finally, there is a head node a_i with arcs to both b_{i0} and c_{i0}, and a foot node d_i, with arcs from b_{im_i} and c_{im_i}.

Figure 10.9(b) outlines the structure of the entire graph. Each hexagon represents one of the gadgets for a variable, with the structure of Fig. 10.9(a). The foot node of one gadget has an arc to the head node of the next gadget, in a cycle.

Suppose we had a directed Hamilton circuit for the graph of Fig. 10.9(b). We may as well suppose the cycle starts at a_1. If it next goes to b_{10}, we claim it must then go to c_{10}, for if not, then c_{10} could never appear on the cycle. In proof, note that if the cycle goes from a_1 to b_{10} to c_{11}, then as both predecessors of c_{10} (that is, a_0 and b_{10}) are already on the cycle, the cycle can never include c_{10}.

Thus, if the cycle begins a_1, b_{10}, then it must continue down the "ladder," alternating between the sides, as

$$a_1, b_{10}, c_{10}, b_{11}, c_{11}, \ldots, b_{1m_1}, c_{1m_1}, d_1$$

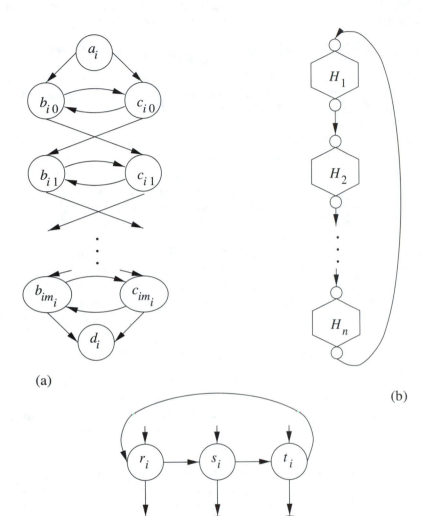

(a)

(b)

(c)

Figure 10.9: Constructions used in the proof that the Hamilton-circuit problem is NP-complete

If the cycle begins with a_1, c_{10}, then the ladder is descended in an order where the c at a level precedes the b as:

$$a_1, c_{10}, b_{10}, c_{11}, b_{11}, \ldots, c_{1m_1}, b_{1m_1}, d_1$$

A crucial point in the proof is that we can treat the first order, where descent is from c's to lower b's as if the variable corresponding to the gadget is made true, while the order in which descent is from b's to the lower c's corresponds to making that variable false.

After traversing the gadget H_1, the cycle must go to a_2, where there is another choice: go to b_{20} or c_{20} next. However, as we argued for H_1, once we make a choice of whether to go left or right from a_2, the path through H_2 is fixed. In general, when we enter each H_i we have a choice of going left or right, but no other choices if we are not to render a node *inaccessible* (i.e., the node cannot appear on a directed Hamilton circuit, because all of its predecessors have appeared already).

In what follows, it helps to think of making the choice of going from a_i to b_{i0} as making variable x_i true, while choosing to go from a_i to c_{i0} is tantamount to making x_i false. Thus, the graph of Fig. 10.9(b) has exactly 2^n directed Hamilton circuits, corresponding to the 2^n truth assignments to n variables.

However, Fig. 10.9(b) is only the skeleton of the graph that we generate for 3-CNF expression E. For each clause e_j, we introduce another subgraph I_j, shown in Fig. 10.9(c). Gadget I_j has the property that if a cycle enters at r_j, it must leave at u_j; if it enters at s_j it must leave at v_j, and if it enters at t_j it must leave at w_j. The argument we shall offer is that if the cycle, once it reaches I_j, does anything but leave by the node below the one in which it entered, then one or more nodes are inaccessible — they can never appear on the cycle. By symmetry, we can consider only the case where r_j is the first node of I_j on the cycle. There are three cases:

1. The next two vertices on the cycle are s_j and t_j. If the cycle then goes to w_j and leaves, v_j is inaccessible. If the cycle goes to w_j and v_j and then leaves, u_j is inaccessible. Thus, the cycle must leave at u_j, having traversed all six nodes of the gadget.

2. The next two vertices after r_j are s_j and v_j. If the cycle does not next go to u_j, then u_j becomes inaccessible. If after u_j, the cycle next goes to w_j, then t_j can never appear on the cycle. The argument is the 'reverse" of the inaccessibility argument. Now, t_j can be reached from outside, but if the cycle later includes t_j, there will be no next node possible, because both successors of t_j appeared earlier on the cycle. Thus, in this case also, the cycle leaves by u_j. Note, however, that t_j and w_j are left untraversed; they will have to appear later on the cycle, which is possible.

3. The circuit goes from r_j directly to u_j. If the cycle then goes to w_j, then t_j cannot appear on the cycle because its successors have both appeared previously, as we argued in case (2). Thus, in this case, the cycle must

leave directly by u_j, leaving the other four nodes to be added to the cycle later.

To complete the construction of the graph G for expression E, we connect the I_j's to the H_i's as follows: Suppose the first literal in clause e_j is x_i, an unnegated variable. Pick some node c_{ip}, for p in the range 0 to $m_i - 1$, that has not yet been used for the purpose of connecting to one of the I gadgets. Introduce arcs from c_{ip} to r_j and from u_j to $b_{i,p+1}$. If the first literal of clause e_j is $\overline{x_i}$, a negated literal, then find an unused b_{ip}. Connect b_{ip} to r_j and connect u_j to $c_{i,p+1}$.

For the second and third literals of e_j, we make the same additions to the graph, with one exception. For the second literal, we use nodes s_j and v_j, and for the third literal we use nodes t_j and w_j. Thus, each I_j has three connections to the H gadgets that represent the variables involved in the clause e_j. The connection comes from a c-node and returns to the b-node below if the literal is unnegated, and it comes from a b-node, returning to the c-node below, if the literal is negated. We claim that:

- The graph G so constructed has a directed Hamilton circuit if and only if the expression E is satisfiable.

(If) Suppose there is a satisfying truth assignment T for E. Construct a directed Hamilton circuit as follows.

1. Begin with the path that traverses only the H's [i.e., the graph of Fig. 10.9(b)] according to the truth assignment T. That is, the cycle goes from a_i to b_{i0} if $T(x_i) = 1$, and it goes from a_i to c_{i0} if $T(x_i) = 0$.

2. However, if the cycle constructed so far follows an arc from b_{ip} to $c_{i,p+1}$, and b_{ip} has another arc to one of the I_j's that has not yet been included in the cycle, introduce a "detour" in the cycle that includes all six nodes of I_j on the cycle, returning to $c_{i,p+1}$. The arc $b_{ip} \to c_{i,p+1}$ will no longer be on the cycle, but the nodes at its ends remain on the cycle.

3. Likewise, if the cycle has an arc from c_{ip} to $b_{i,p+1}$, and c_{ip} has another arc out that goes to an I_j that has not yet been incorporated into the cycle, modify the cycle to "detour" through all six nodes of I_j.

The fact that T satisfies E assures us that the original path constructed by step (1) will include at least one arc that, in step (2) or (3), allows us to include the gadget I_j for each clause e_j. Thus, all the I_j's get included in the cycle, which becomes a directed Hamilton circuit.

(Only if) Now, suppose that the graph G has a directed Hamilton circuit. we must show that E is satisfiable. First, recall two important points from the analysis we have done so far:

1. If a Hamilton circuit enters some I_j at r_j, s_j, or t_j, then it must leave at u_j, v_j, or w_j, respectively.

2. Thus, if we view the Hamilton circuit as moving through the cycle of H gadgets, as in Fig. 10.9(b), the excursions that the path makes to some I_j can be viewed as if the cycle followed an arc that was "in parallel" with one of the arcs $b_{ip} \to c_{i,p+1}$ or $c_{ip} \to b_{i,p+1}$.

If we ignore the excursions to the I_j's, then the Hamilton circuit must be one of the 2^n cycles that are possible using the H_i's only — those that make choices to move from each a_i to either b_{i0} or c_{i0}. Each of these choices corresponds to a truth assignment for the variables of E. If one of these choices yields a Hamilton circuit including the I_j's, then this truth assignment must satisfy E.

The reason is that if the cycle goes from a_i to b_{i0}, then we can only make an excursion to I_j if the jth clause has x_i as one of its three literals. If the cycle goes from a_i to c_{i0}, then we can only make an excursion to I_j if the jth clause has $\overline{x_i}$ as a literal. Thus, the fact that all I_j gadgets can be included implies that the truth assignment makes at least one of the three literals of each clause true; i.e., E is satisfiable.   □

Example 10.22: Let us give a very simple example of the construction of Theorem 10.21, based on the 3-CNF expression $E = (x_1 + x_2 + x_3)(\overline{x_1} + \overline{x_2} + x_3)$. The constructed graph is shown in Fig. 10.10. Arcs that connect H-type gadgets to I-type gadgets are shown dotted, to improve readability, but there is no other distinction between dotted and solid arcs.

For instance, at the top left, we see the gadget for x_1. Since x_1 appears once negated and once unnegated, the "ladder" needs only one step, so there are two rows of b's and c's. At the bottom left, we see the gadget for x_3, which appears twice unnegated and does not appear negated. Thus, we need two different $c_{3p} \to b_{3,p+1}$ arcs that we can use to attach the gadgets for I_1 and I_2 to represent uses of x_3 in these clauses. That is why the gadget for x_3 needs three b-c rows.

Let us consider the gadget I_2, which corresponds to the clause $(\overline{x_1} + \overline{x_2} + x_3)$. For the first literal, $\overline{x_1}$, we attach b_{10} to r_2 and we attach u_2 to c_{11}. For the second literal, $\overline{x_2}$, we do the same with b_{20}, s_2, v_2, and c_{21}. The third literal, being unnegated, is attached to a c and the b below; that is, we attach c_{31} to t_2 and w_2 to b_{32}.

One of several satisfying truth assignments is $x_1 = 1$; $x_2 = 0$, and $x_3 = 0$. For this assignment, the first clause is satisfied by its first literal x_1, while the second clause is satisfied by the second literal, $\overline{x_2}$. For this truth assignment, we can devise a Hamilton circuit in which the arcs $a_1 \to b_{10}$, $a_2 \to c_{20}$, and $a_3 \to c_{30}$ are present. The cycle covers the first clause by detouring from H_1 to I_1; i.e., it uses the arc $c_{10} \to r_1$, traverses all the nodes of I_1, and returns to b_{11}. The second clause is covered by the detour from H_2 to I_2 starting with the arc $b_{20} \to s_2$, traversing all of I_2, and returning to c_{21}. The entire hamilton cycle is shown with thicker lines (solid or dotted) and very large arrows, in Fig. 10.10. □

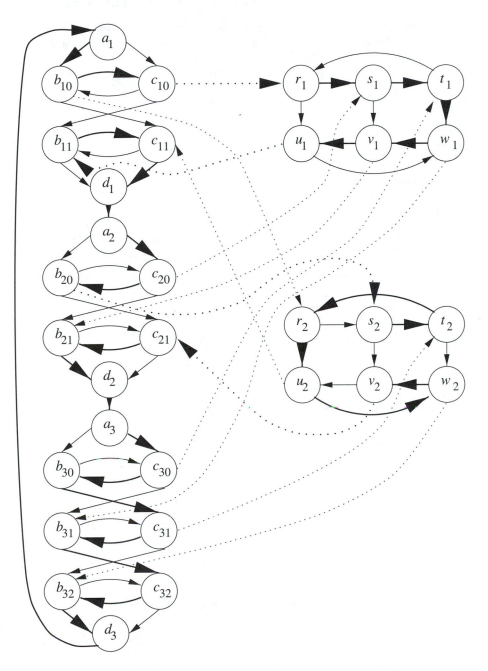

Figure 10.10: Example of the Hamilton-circuit construction

10.4.5 Undirected Hamilton Circuits and the TSP

The proofs that the undirected Hamilton-circuit problem and the Traveling Salesman problem are also NP-complete are relatively easy. We already saw in Section 10.1.4 that TSP is in $\mathcal{NP}$. HC is a special case of TSP, so it is also in $\mathcal{NP}$. We must perform the reductions of DHC to HC and HC to TSP.

PROBLEM: Undirected Hamilton-Circuit Problem.

INPUT: An undirected graph G.

OUTPUT: "Yes" if and only if G has a Hamilton circuit.

REDUCTION FROM: DHC.

Theorem 10.23: HC is NP-complete.

PROOF: We reduce DHC to HC, as follows. Suppose we are given a directed graph G_d. The undirected graph we construct will be called G_u. For every node v of G_d, there are three nodes v_0, v_1, and v_2 in G_u. The edges of G_u are:

1. For all nodes v of G_d, there are edges $(v^{(0)}, v^{(1)})$ and $(v^{(1)}, v^{(2)})$ in G_u.

2. If there is an arc $v \to w$ in G_d, then there is an edge $(v^{(2)}, w^{(0)})$ in G_u.

Figure 10.11 suggests the pattern of edges, including the edge for an arc $v \to w$.

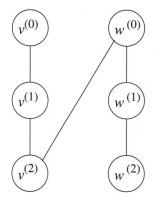

Figure 10.11: Arcs in G_d are replaced by edges in G_u that go from rank 2 to rank 0

Clearly the construction of G_u from G_d can be performed in polynomial time. We must show that

- G_u has a Hamilton circuit if and only if G_d has a directed Hamilton circuit.

(If) Suppose $v_1, v_2, \ldots, v_n, v_1$ is a directed Hamilton circuit. Then surely

$$v_1^{(0)}, v_1^{(1)}, v_1^{(2)}, v_2^{(0)}, v_2^{(1)}, v_2^{(2)}, v_3^{(0)}, \ldots, v_n^{(0)}, v_n^{(1)}, v_n^{(2)}, v_1^{(0)}$$

is an undirected Hamilton circuit in G_u. That is, we go down each column, and then jump to the top of the next column to follow an arc of G_d.

(Only if) Observe that each node $v^{(1)}$ of G_u has only two edges, and therefore must appear in a Hamilton circuit with one of $v^{(0)}$ and $v^{(2)}$ its immediate predecessor, and the other its immediate successor. Thus, a Hamilton circuit in G_u must have superscripts on its nodes that vary in the pattern $0, 1, 2, 0, 1, 2, \ldots$ or its opposite, $2, 1, 0, 2, 1, 0, \ldots$. Since these patterns correspond to traversing a cycle in the two different directions, we may as well assume the pattern is $0, 1, 2, 0, 1, 2, \ldots$. Thus, if we look at the edges of the cycle that go from a node with superscript 2 to one with superscript 0, we know that these edges are arcs of G_d, and that each is followed in the direction in which the arc points. Thus, an undirected Hamilton circuit in G_u yields a directed Hamilton circuit in G_d. □

PROBLEM: Traveling Salesman Problem.

INPUT: An undirected graph G with integer weights on the edges, and a limit k.

OUTPUT: "Yes" if and only if there is a Hamilton circuit of G, such that the sum of the weights on the edges of the cycle is less than or equal to k.

REDUCTION FROM: HC.

Theorem 10.24: The Traveling Salesman Problem is NP-complete.

PROOF: The reduction from HC is as follows. Given a graph G, construct a weighted graph G' whose nodes and edges are the same as the edges of G, with a weight of 1 on each edge, and a limit k that is equal to the number of nodes n of G. Then a Hamilton circuit of weight n exists in G' if and only if there is a Hamilton circuit in G. □

10.4.6   Summary of NP-Complete Problems

Figure 10.12 indicates all the reductions we have made in this chapter. Notice that we have suggested reductions from all the specific problems, like TSP, to SAT. What happened was that we reduced the language of every polynomial-time, nondeterministic Turing machine to SAT in Theorem 10.9. Without mentioning it explicitly, these TM's included at least one that solves TSP, one that solves IS, and so on. Thus, all the NP-complete problems are polynomial-time reducible to one another, and are, in effect, different faces of the same problem.

All of $\mathcal{NP}$

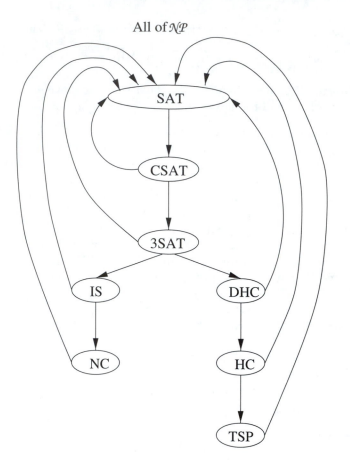

Figure 10.12: Reductions among NP-complete problems

10.4.7   Exercises for Section 10.4

* **Exercise 10.4.1:** A *k-clique* in a graph G is a set of k nodes of G such that there is an edge between every two nodes in the clique. Thus, a 2-clique is just a pair of nodes connected by an edge, and a 3-clique is a triangle. The problem CLIQUE is: given a graph G and a constant k, does G have a k-clique?

   a) What is the largest k for which the graph G of Fig. 10.1 satisfies CLIQUE?

   b) How many edges does a k-clique have, as a function of k?

   c) Prove that CLIQUE is NP-complete by reducing the node-cover problem to CLIQUE.

*! **Exercise 10.4.2:** The *coloring problem* is: given a graph G and an integer k, is G "k-colorable"; that is, can we assign one of k colors to each node of G in such a way that no edge has both of its ends colored with the same color. For

example, the graph of Fig. 10.1 is 3-colorable, since we can assign nodes 1 and 4 the color red, 2 green, and 3 blue. In general, if a graph has a k-clique, then it can be no less than k-colorable, although it might require many more than k colors.

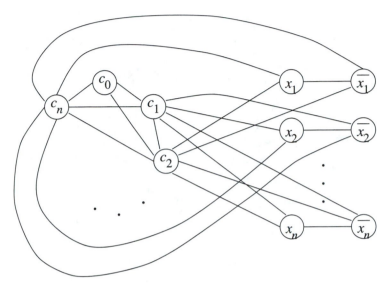

Figure 10.13: Part of the construction showing the coloring problem to be NP-complete

In this exercise, we shall give part of a construction to show that the coloring problem is NP-complete; you must fill in the rest. The reduction is from 3SAT. Suppose that we have a 3-CNF expression with n variables. The reduction converts this expression into a graph, part of which is shown in Fig. 10.13. There are, as seen on the left, $n + 1$ nodes $c_0, c_1, \ldots, c_n$ that form an $(n + 1)$-clique. Thus, each of these nodes must be colored with a different color. We should think of the color assigned to c_j as "the color c_j."

Also, for each variable x_i, there are two nodes, which we may think of as x_i and $\overline{x_i}$. These two are connected by an edge, so they cannot get the same color. Moreover, each of the nodes for x_i are connected to c_j for all j other than 0 and i. As a result, one of x_i and $\overline{x_i}$ must be colored c_0, and the other is colored c_i. Think of the one colored c_0 as true and the other as false. Thus, the coloring chosen corresponds to a truth assignment.

To complete the construction, you need to design a portion of the graph for each clause of the expression. It should be possible to complete the coloring of the graph using only the colors c_0 through c_n if and only if each clause is made true by the truth assignment corresponding to the choice of colors. Thus, the constructed graph is $(n + 1)$-colorable if and only if the given expression is satisfiable.

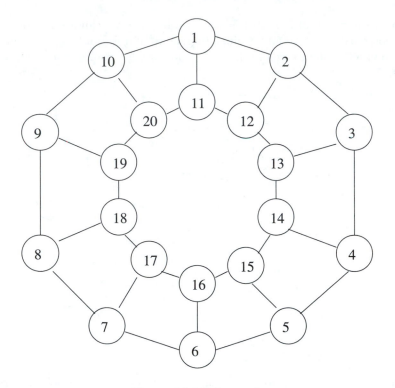

Figure 10.14: A graph

! **Exercise 10.4.3:** A graph does not have to be too large before NP-complete questions about it become very hard to solve by hand. Consider the graph of Fig. 10.14.

* a) Does this graph have a Hamilton circuit?

  b) What is the largest independent set?

  c) What is the smallest node cover?

  d) What is the smallest edge cover (see Exercise 10.4.4(c))?

  e) Is the graph 2-colorable?

Exercise 10.4.4: Show the following problems to be NP-complete:

  a) The *subgraph-isomorphism problem*: given graphs G_1 and G_2, does G_1 contain a copy of G_2 as a subgraph? That is, can we find a subset of the nodes of G_1 that, together with the edges among them in G_1, forms an exact copy of G_2 when we choose the correspondence between nodes of G_2 and nodes of the subgraph of G_1 properly? *Hint:* Consider a reduction from the clique problem of Exercise 10.4.1.

! b) The *edge-cover problem*: given a graph G and an integer k, does G have an "edge cover" of k edges, that is, a set of k edges such that every node of G is an end of at least one edge in the edge cover.

! c) The *linear integer programming problem*: given a set of linear constraints of the form $\sum_{i=1}^{n} a_i x_i \leq c$ or $\sum_{i=1}^{n} a_i x_i \geq c$, where the a's and c are integer constants and $x_1, x_2, \ldots, x_n$ are variables, does there exist an assignment of integers to each of the variables that makes all the constraints true?

! d) The *dominating-set problem*: given a graph G and an integer k, does there exist a subset S of k nodes of G such that each node is either in S or adjacent to a node of S?

e) The *firehouse problem*: given a graph G, a distance d, and a budget f of "firehouses," is it possible to choose f nodes of G such that no node is of distance (number of edges that must be traversed) greater than d from some firehouse?

*! f) The *half-clique problem*: Given a graph G with an even number of vertices, does there exist a clique of G (see Exercise 10.4.1) consisting of exactly half the nodes of G? *Hint*: Reduce CLIQUE to the half-clique problem. You must figure out how to add nodes to adjust the size of the largest clique.

!! g) The *unit-execution-time-scheduling problem*: given k "tasks"

$$T_1, T_2, \ldots, T_k$$

a number of "processors" p, a 'time limit t, and some "precedence constraints" of the form $T_i < T_j$ between pairs of tasks, does there exist a *schedule* of the tasks, such that:

1. Each task is assigned to one time unit between 1 and t,

2. At most p tasks are assigned to any one time unit, and

3. The precedence constraints are respected; that is, if $T_i < T_j$ is a constraint, then T_i is assigned to an earlier time unit than T_j?

!! h) The *exact-cover problem*: given a set S and a set of subsets $S_1, S_2, \ldots, S_n$ of S, is there a set of sets $T \subseteq \{S_1, S_2, \ldots, S_n\}$ such that each element x of S is in exactly one member of T?

!! i) The *knapsack problem*: given a list of k integers $i_1, i_2, \ldots, i_k$, can we partition them into two sets whose sums are the same? *Note*: This problem appears superficially to be in $\mathcal{P}$, since you might assume that the integers themselves are small. Indeed, if the values of the integers are limited to some polynomial in the number of integers k, then there is a polynomial-time algorithm. However, in a list of k integers represented in binary, having total length n, we can have certain integers whose values are almost exponential in n.

Exercise 10.4.5: A *Hamilton path* in a graph G is an ordering of all the nodes $n_1, n_2, \ldots, n_k$ such that there is an edge from n_i to n_{i+1}, for all $i = 1, 2, \ldots, k-1$. A *directed Hamilton path* is the same for a directed graph; there must be an arc from each n_i to n_{i_1}. Notice that the Hamilton path requirement is just slightly weaker than the Hamilton-circuit condition. If we also required an edge or arc from n_k to n_1, then it would be exactly the Hamilton-circuit condition. The (directed) Hamilton-path problem is: given a (directed) graph, does it have at least one (directed) Hamilton path?

* a) Prove that the directed Hamilton-path problem in NP-complete. *Hint*: Perform a reduction from DHC. Pick any node, and split it into two, such that these two nodes must be the endpoints of a directed Hamilton path, and such a path exists if and only if the original graph has a directed Hamilton circuit.

 b) Show that the (undirected) Hamilton-path problem is NP-complete. *Hint*: Adapt the construction of Theorem 10.23.

*! c) Show that the following problem is NP-complete: given a graph G and an integer k, does G have a spanning tree with at most k leaf vertices? *Hint*: Perform a reduction from the Hamilton-path problem.

! d) Show that the following problem is NP-complete: given a graph G and an integer d, does G have a spanning tree with no node of degree greater than d? (The *degree* of a node n in the spanning tree is the number of edges of the tree that have n as an end.)

10.5 Summary of Chapter 10

✦ *The Classes $\mathcal{P}$ and $\mathcal{NP}$*: $\mathcal{P}$ consists of all those languages or problems accepted by some Turing machine that runs in some polynomial amount of time, as a function of its input length. $\mathcal{NP}$ is the class of languages or problems that are accepted by nondeterministic TM's with a polynomial bound on the time taken along any sequence of nondeterministic choices.

✦ *The $\mathcal{P} = \mathcal{NP}$ Question*: It is unknown whether or not $\mathcal{P}$ and $\mathcal{NP}$ are really the same classes of languages, although we suspect strongly that there are languages in $\mathcal{NP}$ that are not in $\mathcal{P}$.

✦ *Polynomial-Time Reductions*: If we can transform instances of one problem in polynomial time into instances of a second problem that has the same answer — yes or no — then we say the first problem is polynomial-time reducible to the second.

✦ *NP-Complete Problems*: A language is NP-complete if it is in $\mathcal{NP}$, and there is a polynomial-time reduction from each language in $\mathcal{NP}$ to the language in question. We believe strongly that none of the NP-complete problems are in $\mathcal{P}$, and the fact that no one has ever found a polynomial-time algorithm for any of the thousands of known NP-complete problems is mutually re-enforcing evidence that none are in $\mathcal{P}$.

✦ *NP-Complete Satisfiability Problems*: Cook's theorem showed the first NP-complete problem — whether a boolean expression is satisfiable — by reducing all problems in $\mathcal{NP}$ to the SAT problem in polynomial time. In addition, the problem remains NP-complete even if the expression is restricted to consist of a product of clauses, each of which consists of only three literals — the problem 3SAT.

✦ *Other NP-Complete Problems*: There is a vast collection of known NP-complete problems; each is proved NP-complete by a polynomial-time reduction from some previously known NP-complete problem. We have given reductions that show the following problems NP-complete: independent set, node cover, directed and undirected versions of the Hamilton circuit problem, and the traveling-salesman problem.

10.6 References for Chapter 10

The concept of NP-completeness as evidence that the problem could not be solved in polynomial time, as well as the proof that SAT, CSAT, and 3SAT are NP-complete, comes from Cook [3]. A follow-on paper by Karp [6] is generally accorded equal importance, because that paper showed that NP-completeness was not just an isolated phenomenon, but rather applied to very many of the hard combinatorial problems that people in Operations Research and other disciplines had been studying for years. Each of the problems proved NP-complete in Section 10.4 are from that paper: independent set, node cover, Hamilton circuit, and TSP. In addition, we can find there the solutions to several of the problems mentioned in the exercises: clique, edge cover, knapsack, coloring, and exact-cover.

The book by Garey and Johnson [4] summarizes a great deal about what is known concerning which problems are NP-complete, and special cases that are polynomial-time. In [5] are articles about approximating the solution to an NP-complete problem in polynomial time.

Several other contributions to the theory of NP-completeness should be acknowledged. The study of classes of languages defined by the running time of Turing machines began with Hartmanis and Stearns [8]. Cobham [2] was the first to isolate the concept of the class $\mathcal{P}$, as opposed to algorithms that had a particular polynomial running time, such as $O(n^2)$. Levin [7] was an independent, although somewhat later, discovery of the NP-completeness idea.

NP-completeness of linear integer programming [Exercise 10.4.4(c)] appears in [1] and also in unpublished notes of J. Gathen and M. Sieveking. NP-completeness of unit-execution-time scheduling [Exercise 10.4.4(d)] is from [9].

1. I. Borosh and L. B. Treybig, "Bounds on positive integral solutions of linear Diophantine equations," *Proceedings of the AMS* **55** (1976), pp. 299–304.

2. A Cobham, "The intrinsic computational difficulty of functions," *Proc. 1964 Congress for Logic, Mathematics, and the Philosophy of Science,* North Holland, Amsterdam, pp. 24–30.

3. S. C. Cook, "The complexity of theorem-proving procedures," *Third ACM Symposium on Theory of Computing* (1971), ACM, New York, pp. 151–158.

4. M. R. Garey and D. S. Johnson, *Computers and Intractability: a Guide to the Theory of NP-Completeness*, H. Freeman, New York, 1979.

5. D. S. Hochbaum (ed.), *Approximation Algorithms for NP-Hard Problems*, PWS Publishing Co., 1996.

6. R. M. Karp, "Reducibility among combinatorial problems," in *Complexity of Computer Computations* (R. E. Miller, ed.), Plenum Press, New York, pp. 85–104.

7. L. A. Levin, "Universal sorting problems," *Problemi Peredachi Informatsii* **9**:3 (1973), pp. 265–266.

8. J. Hartmanis and R. E. Stearns, "On the computational complexity of algorithms," *Transactions of the AMS* **117** (1965), pp. 285–306.

9. J. D. Ullman, "NP-complete scheduling problems," *J. Computer and System Sciences* **10**:3 (1975), pp. 384–393.

Chapter 11

Additional Classes of Problems

The story of intractable problems does not begin and end with $\mathcal{NP}$. There are many other classes of problems that appear to be intractable, or are interesting for some other reason. Several questions involving these classes, like the $\mathcal{P} = \mathcal{NP}$ question, remain unresolved.

We shall begin by looking at a class that is closely related to $\mathcal{P}$ and $\mathcal{NP}$: the class of complements of $\mathcal{NP}$ languages, often called "co-$\mathcal{NP}$." If $\mathcal{P} = \mathcal{NP}$, then co-$\mathcal{NP}$ is equal to both, since $\mathcal{P}$ is closed under complementation. However, it is likely that co-$\mathcal{NP}$ is different from both these classes, and in fact likely that no NP-complete problem is in co-$\mathcal{NP}$.

Then, we consider the class $\mathcal{PS}$, which is all the problems that can be solved by a Turing machine using an amount of tape that is polynomial in the length of its input. These TM's are allowed to use an exponential amount of time, as long as they stay within a limited region of the tape. In contrast to the situation for polynomial time, we can prove that nondeterminism doesn't increase the power of the TM when the limitation is polynomial space. However, even though $\mathcal{PS}$ clearly includes all of $\mathcal{NP}$, we do not know whether $\mathcal{PS}$ is equal to $\mathcal{NP}$, or even whether it is equal to $\mathcal{P}$. We expect that neither equality is true, however, and we give a problem that is complete for $\mathcal{PS}$ and appears not to be in $\mathcal{NP}$.

Then, we turn to randomized algorithms, and two classes of languages that lie between $\mathcal{P}$ and $\mathcal{NP}$. One is the class $\mathcal{RP}$ of "random polynomial" languages. These languages have an algorithm that runs in polynomial time, using some "coin flipping" or (in practice) a random-number generator. The algorithm either confirms membership of the input in the language, or says "I don't know." Moreover, if the input is in the language, then there is some probability greater than 0 that the algorithm will report success, so repeated application of the algorithm will, with probability approaching 1, confirm membership.

The second class, called $\mathcal{ZPP}$ (zero-error, probabilistic polynomial), also involves randomization. However, algorithms for languages in this class either

469

say "yes" the input is in the language, or "no" it is not. The expected running time of the algorithm is polynomial. However, there might be runs of the algorithm that take more time than would be allowed by any polynomial bound.

To tie these concepts together, we consider the important issue of primality testing. Many cryptographic systems today rely on both:

1. The ability to discover large primes quickly (in order to allow communication between machines in a way that is not subject to interception by an outsider) and

2. The assumption that it takes exponential time to factor integers, if time is measured as a function of the length n of the integer written in binary.

We shall see that testing primes is both in $\mathcal{NP}$ and co-$\mathcal{NP}$, and therefore it is unlikely that we can prove primality testing to be NP-complete. That is unfortunate, because proofs of NP-completeness are the most common arguments that a problem most likely requires exponential time. We shall also see that primality testing is in the class $\mathcal{RP}$. This situation is both good news and bad news. It is good, because in practice, cryptographic systems that require primes really do use an algorithm in the $\mathcal{RP}$ class to find them. It is bad because it provides further weight to the assumption that we shall not be able to prove primality testing to be NP-complete.

11.1 Complements of Languages in $\mathcal{NP}$

The class of languages $\mathcal{P}$ is closed under complementation (see Exercise 10.1.6). For a simple argument why, let L be in $\mathcal{P}$ and let M be a TM for L. Modify M as follows, to accept $\overline{L}$. Introduce a new accepting state q and have the new TM transition to q whenever M halts in a state that is not accepting. Make the former accepting states of M be nonaccepting. Then the modified TM accepts $\overline{L}$, and runs in the same amount of time that M does, with the possible addition of one move. Thus, $\overline{L}$ is in $\mathcal{P}$ if L is.

It is not known whether $\mathcal{NP}$ is closed under complementation. It appears not, however, and in particular we expect that whenever a language L is NP-complete, then its complement is not in $\mathcal{NP}$.

11.1.1 The Class of Languages Co-$\mathcal{NP}$

Co-$\mathcal{NP}$ is the set of languages whose complements are in $\mathcal{NP}$. We observed at the beginning of Section 11.1 that every language in $\mathcal{P}$ has its complement also in $\mathcal{P}$, and therefore in $\mathcal{NP}$. On the other hand, we believe that none of the NP-complete problems have their complements in $\mathcal{NP}$, and therefore no NP-complete problem is in co-$\mathcal{NP}$. Likewise, we believe the complements of NP-complete problems, which are by definition in co-$\mathcal{NP}$, are not in $\mathcal{NP}$. Figure 11.1 shows the way we believe the classes $\mathcal{P}$, $\mathcal{NP}$, and co-$\mathcal{NP}$ relate.

However, we should bear in mind that, should $\mathcal{P}$ turn out to equal $\mathcal{NP}$, then all three classes are actually the same.

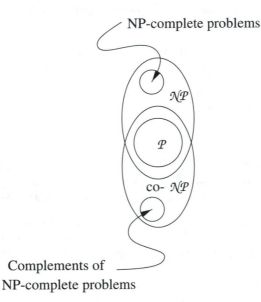

NP-complete problems

Complements of
NP-complete problems

Figure 11.1: Suspected relationship between co-$\mathcal{NP}$ and other classes of languages

Example 11.1 : Consider the complement of the language SAT, which is surely a member of co-$\mathcal{NP}$. We shall refer to this complement as *USAT* (unsatisfiable). The strings in USAT include all those that code boolean expressions that are not satisfiable. However, also in USAT are those strings that do not code valid boolean expressions, because surely none of those strings are in SAT. We believe that USAT is not in $\mathcal{NP}$, but there is no proof.

Another example of a problem we suspect is in co-$\mathcal{NP}$ but not in $\mathcal{NP}$ is TAUT, the set of all (coded) boolean expressions that are *tautologies*; i.e., they are true for every truth assignment. Note that an expression E is a tautology if and only if $\neg E$ is unsatisfiable. Thus, TAUT and USAT are related in that whenever boolean expression E is in TAUT, $\neg E$ is in USAT, and vice-versa. However, USAT also contains strings that do not represent valid expressions, while all strings in TAUT are valid expressions. □

11.1.2 NP-Complete Problems and Co-$\mathcal{NP}$

Let us assume that $\mathcal{P} \neq \mathcal{NP}$. It is still possible that the situation regarding co-$\mathcal{NP}$ is not exactly as suggested by Fig. 11.1, because we could have $\mathcal{NP}$ and co-$\mathcal{NP}$ equal, but larger than $\mathcal{P}$. That is, we might discover that problems like USAT and TAUT can be solved in nondeterministic polynomial time (i.e., they are in $\mathcal{NP}$), and yet not be able to solve them in deterministic polynomial time. However, the fact that we have not been able to find even one NP-complete problem whose complement is in $\mathcal{NP}$ is strong evidence that $\mathcal{NP} \neq$ co-$\mathcal{NP}$, as we prove in the next theorem.

Theorem 11.2: $\mathcal{NP} =$ co-$\mathcal{NP}$ if and only if there is some NP-complete problem whose complement is in $\mathcal{NP}$.

PROOF: (Only if) Should $\mathcal{NP}$ and co-$\mathcal{NP}$ be the same, then surely every NP-complete problem L, being in $\mathcal{NP}$, is also in co-$\mathcal{NP}$. But the complement of a problem in co-$\mathcal{NP}$ is in $\mathcal{NP}$, so the complement of L is in $\mathcal{NP}$.

(If) Suppose P is an NP-complete problem whose complement $\overline{P}$ is in $\mathcal{NP}$. Then for every language L in $\mathcal{NP}$, there is a polynomial-time reduction of L to P. The same reduction also is a polynomial-time reduction of $\overline{L}$ to $\overline{P}$. We prove that $\mathcal{NP} =$ co-$\mathcal{NP}$ by proving containment in both directions.

$\mathcal{NP} \subseteq$ co-$\mathcal{NP}$: Suppose L is in $\mathcal{NP}$. Then $\overline{L}$ is in co-$\mathcal{NP}$. Combine the polynomial-time reduction of $\overline{L}$ to $\overline{P}$ with the assumed nondeterministic, polynomial-time algorithm for $\overline{P}$ to yield a nondeterministic, polynomial-time algorithm for $\overline{L}$. Hence, for any L in $\mathcal{NP}$, $\overline{L}$ is also in $\mathcal{NP}$. Therefore L, being the complement of a language in $\mathcal{NP}$, is in co-$\mathcal{NP}$. This observation tells us that $\mathcal{NP} \subseteq$ co-$\mathcal{NP}$.

co-$\mathcal{NP} \subseteq \mathcal{NP}$: Suppose L is in co-$\mathcal{NP}$. Then there is a polynomial-time reduction of $\overline{L}$ to P, since P is NP-complete, and L is in $\mathcal{NP}$. This reduction is also a reduction of L to $\overline{P}$. Since $\overline{P}$ is in $\mathcal{NP}$, we combine the reduction with the nondeterministic, polynomial-time algorithm for $\overline{P}$ to show that L is in $\mathcal{NP}$. $\square$

11.1.3   Exercises for Section 11.1

! **Exercise 11.1.1:** Below are some problems. For each, tell whether it is in $\mathcal{NP}$ and whether it is in co-$\mathcal{NP}$. Describe the complement of each problem. If either the problem or its complement is NP-complete, prove that as well.

* a) The problem TRUE-SAT: given a boolean expression E that is true when all the variables are made true, is there some other truth assignment besides all-true that makes E true?

  b) The problem FALSE-SAT: given a boolean expression E that is false when all its variables are made false, is there some other truth assignment besides all-false that makes E false?

  c) The problem DOUBLE-SAT: given a boolean expression E, are there at least two truth assignments that make E true?

  d) The problem NEAR-TAUT: given a boolean expression E, is there at most one truth assignment that makes E false?

! **Exercise 11.1.2:** Suppose there were a function f that is a one-one function from n-bit integers to n-bit integers, such that:

1. $f(x)$ can be computed in polynomial time.

2. $f^{-1}(x)$ cannot be computed in polynomial time.

Show that the language consisting of pairs of integers (x, y) such that

$$f^{-1}(x) < y$$

would then be in $(\mathcal{NP} \cap \text{co-}\mathcal{NP}) - \mathcal{P}$.

11.2 Problems Solvable in Polynomial Space

Now, let us look at a class of problems that includes all of $\mathcal{NP}$, and appears to include more, although we cannot be certain it does. This class is defined by allowing a Turing machine to use an amount of space that is polynomial in the size of its input, no matter how much time it uses. Initially, we shall distinguish between the languages accepted by deterministic and nondeterministic TM's with a polynomial space bound, but we shall soon see that these two classes of languages are the same.

There are complete problems P for polynomial space, in the sense that all problems in this class are reducible in polynomial *time* to P. Thus, if P is in $\mathcal{P}$ or in $\mathcal{NP}$, then all languages with polynomial-space-bounded TM's are in $\mathcal{P}$ or $\mathcal{NP}$, respectively. We shall offer one example of such a problem: "quantified boolean formulas."

11.2.1 Polynomial-Space Turing Machines

A polynomial-space-bounded Turing machine is suggested by Fig. 11.2. There is some polynomial $p(n)$ such that when given input w of length n, the TM never visits more than $p(n)$ cells of its tape. By Theorem 8.12, we may assume that the tape is semi-infinite, and the TM never moves left from the beginning of its input.

Define the class of languages $\mathcal{PS}$ (*polynomial space*) to include all and only the languages that are $L(M)$ for some polynomial-space-bounded, deterministic Turing machine M. Also, define the class $\mathcal{NPS}$ (*nondeterministic polynomial space*) to consist of those languages that are $L(M)$ for some nondeterministic, polynomial-space-bounded TM M. Evidently $\mathcal{PS} \subseteq \mathcal{NPS}$, since every deterministic TM is technically nondeterministic also. However, we shall prove the surprising result that $\mathcal{PS} = \mathcal{NPS}$.[1]

---

[1] You may see this class written as PSPACE in other works on the subject. However, we prefer to use the script $\mathcal{PS}$ to denote the class of problems solved in deterministic (or nondeterministic) polynomial time, as we shall drop the use of $\mathcal{NPS}$ once the equivalence $\mathcal{PS} = \mathcal{NPS}$ has been proved.

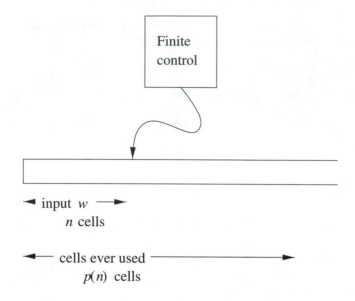

Figure 11.2: A TM that uses polynomial space

11.2.2 Relationship of $\mathcal{PS}$ and $\mathcal{NPS}$ to Previously Defined Classes

To start, the relationships $\mathcal{P} \subseteq \mathcal{PS}$ and $\mathcal{NP} \subseteq \mathcal{NPS}$ should be obvious. The reason is that if a TM makes only a polynomial number of moves, then it uses no more than a polynomial number of cells; in particular, it cannot visit more cells than one plus the number of moves it makes. Once we prove $\mathcal{PS} = \mathcal{NPS}$, we shall see that in fact the three classes form a chain of containment: $\mathcal{P} \subseteq \mathcal{NP} \subseteq \mathcal{PS}$.

An essential property of polynomial-space-bounded TM's is that they can make only an exponential number of moves before they must repeat an ID. We need this fact to prove other interesting facts about $\mathcal{PS}$, and also to show that $\mathcal{PS}$ contains only recursive languages; i.e., languages with algorithms. Note that there is nothing in the definition of $\mathcal{PS}$ or $\mathcal{NPS}$ that requires the TM to halt. It is possible that the TM cycles forever, without leaving a polynomial-sized region of its tape.

Theorem 11.3: If M is a polynomial-space-bounded TM (deterministic or nondeterministic), and $p(n)$ is its polynomial space bound, then there is a constant c such that if M accepts its input w of length n, it does so within $c^{1+p(n)}$ moves.

PROOF: The essential idea is that M must repeat an ID before making more than $c^{1+p(n)}$ moves. If M repeats an ID and then accepts, there must be a shorter sequence of ID's leading to acceptance. That is, if $\alpha \overset{*}{\vdash} \beta \vdash \beta \overset{*}{\vdash} \gamma$, where α is the initial ID, β is the repeated ID, and γ is the accepting ID, then $\alpha \overset{*}{\vdash} \beta \overset{*}{\vdash} \gamma$ is a shorter sequence of ID's leading to acceptance.

The argument that c must exist exploits the fact that there are a limited number of ID's if the space used by the TM is limited. In particular, let t be the number of tape symbols of M, and let s be the number of states of M. Then the number of different ID's of M when only $p(n)$ tape cells are used is at most $sp(n)t^{p(n)}$. That is, we can choose one of the s states, place the head at any of $p(n)$ tape positions, and fill the $p(n)$ cells with any of $t^{p(n)}$ sequences of tape symbols.

Pick $c = s + t$. Then consider the binomial expansion of $(t + s)^{1+p(n)}$, which is

$$t^{1+p(n)} + \left(1 + p(n)\right)st^{p(n)} + \cdots$$

Notice that the second term is at least as large as $sp(n)t^{p(n)}$, which proves that $c^{1+p(n)}$ is at least equal to the number of possible ID's of M. We conclude the proof by observing that if M accepts w of length n, then it does so by a sequence of moves that does not repeat an ID. Therefore, M accepts by a sequence of moves that is no longer than the number of distinct ID's, which is $c^{1+p(n)}$. $\quad\Box$

We can use Theorem 11.3 to convert any polynomial-space-bounded TM into an equivalent one that always halts after making at most an exponential number of moves. The essential point is that, since we know the TM accepts within an exponential number of moves, we can count how many moves have been made, and we can cause the TM to halt if it has made enough moves without accepting.

Theorem 11.4: If L is a language in $\mathcal{PS}$ (respectively $\mathcal{NPS}$), then L is accepted by a polynomial-space-bounded deterministic (respectively nondeterministic) TM that halts after making at most $c^{q(n)}$ moves, for some polynomial $q(n)$ and constant $c > 1$.

PROOF: We'll prove the statement for deterministic TM's; the same argument applies to NTM's. We know L is accepted by a TM M_1 that has a polynomial space bound $p(n)$. Then by Theorem 11.3, if M_1 accepts w it does so in at most $c^{1+p(|w|)}$ steps.

Design a new TM M_2 that has two tapes. On the first tape, M_2 simulates M_1, and on the second tape, M_2 counts in base c up to $c^{1+p(|w|)}$. If M_2 reaches this count, it halts without accepting. M_2 thus uses $1 + p(|w|)$ cells on the second tape. We also assumed that M_1 uses no more than $p(|w|)$ cells on its tape, so M_2 uses no more than $p(|w|)$ cells on its first tape as well.

If we convert M_2 to a one-tape TM M_3, we can be sure that M_3 uses no more than $1 + p(n)$ cells of tape, on any input of length n. Although M_3 may use the square of the running time of M_2, that time is not more than $O\left(c^{2p(n)}\right)$.[2]

---

[2] In fact, the general rule from Theorem 8.10 is not the strongest claim we can make. Because only $1 + p(n)$ cells are used by any tape, the simulated tape heads in the many-tapes-to-one construction can get only $1 + p(n)$ apart. Thus, $c^{1+p(n)}$ moves of the multitape TM M_2 can be simulated in $O\left(p(n)c^{p(n)}\right)$ steps, which is less than the claimed $O\left(c^{2p(n)}\right)$.

As M_3 makes no more than $dc^{2p(n)}$ moves for some constant d, we may pick $q(n) = 2p(n) + \log_c d$. Then M_3 makes at most $c^{q(n)}$ steps. Since M_2 always halts, M_3 always halts. Since M_1 accepts L, so do M_2 and M_3. Thus, M_3 satisfies the statement of the theorem. $\square$

11.2.3 Deterministic and Nondeterministic Polynomial Space

Since the comparison between $\mathcal{P}$ and $\mathcal{NP}$ seems so difficult, it is surprising that the same comparison between $\mathcal{PS}$ and $\mathcal{NPS}$ is easy: they are the same classes of languages. The proof involves simulating a nondeterministic TM that has a polynomial space bound $p(n)$ by a deterministic TM with polynomial space bound $O\big(p^2(n)\big)$.

The heart of the proof is a deterministic, recursive test for whether a NTM N can move from ID I to ID J in at most m moves. A DTM D systematically tries all middle ID's K to check whether I can become K in $m/2$ moves, and then K can become J in $m/2$ moves. That is, imagine there is a recursive function $reach(I, J, m)$ that decides if $I \overset{*}{\vdash} J$ by at most m moves.

Think of the tape of D as a stack, where the arguments of the recursive calls to $reach$ are placed. That is, in one *stack frame* D holds $[I, J, m]$. A sketch of the algorithm executed by $reach$ is shown in Fig. 11.3.

```
BOOLEAN FUNCTION reach(I,J,m)
    ID: I,J; INT: m;
    BEGIN
        IF (m == 1) THEN /* basis */ BEGIN
                test if I == J or I can become J after one move;
                RETURN TRUE if so, FALSE if not;
        END;
        ELSE /* inductive part */ BEGIN
            FOR each possible ID K DO
                    IF (reach(I,K,m/2) AND reach(K,J,m/2)) THEN
                            RETURN TRUE;
                RETURN FALSE;
        END;
    END;
```

Figure 11.3: The recursive function *reach* tests whether one ID can become another within a stated number of moves

It is important to observe that, although *reach* calls itself twice, it makes those calls in sequence, and therefore, only one of the calls is active at a time. That is, if we start with a stack frame $[I_1, J_1, m]$, then at any time there is only one call $[I_2, J_2, m/2]$, one call $[I_3, J_3, m/4]$, another $[I_4, J_4, m/8]$, and so on, until at some point the third argument becomes 1. At that point, *reach* can apply the basis step, and needs no more recursive calls. It tests if $I = J$ or $I \vdash J$, returning TRUE if either holds and FALSE if neither does. Figure 11.4 suggests what the stack of the DTM D looks like when there are as many active calls to *reach* as possible, given an initial move count of m.

I_1 J_1 m	I_2 J_2 $m/2$	I_3 J_3 $m/4$	I_4 J_4 $m/8$	$\cdots$

Figure 11.4: Tape of a DTM simulating a NTM by recursive calls to *reach*

While it may appear that many calls to *reach* are possible, and the tape of Fig. 11.4 can become very long, we shall show that it cannot become "too long." That is, if started with a move count of m, there can only be $\log_2 m$ stack frames on the tape at any one time. Since Theorem 11.4 assures us that the NTM N cannot make more than $c^{p(n)}$ moves, m does not have to start with a number greater than that. Thus, the number of stack frames is at most $\log_2 c^{p(n)}$, which is $O(p(n))$. We now have the essentials behind the proof of the following theorem.

Theorem 11.5: *(Savitch's Theorem)* $\mathcal{PS} = \mathcal{NPS}$.

PROOF: It is obvious that $\mathcal{PS} \subseteq \mathcal{NPS}$, since every DTM is technically a NTM as well. Thus, we need only to show that $\mathcal{NPS} \subseteq \mathcal{PS}$; that is, if L is accepted by some NTM N with space bound $p(n)$, for some polynomial $p(n)$, then L is also accepted by some DTM D with polynomial space bound $q(n)$, for some other polynomial $q(n)$. In fact, we shall show that $q(n)$ can be chosen to be on the order of the square of $p(n)$.

First, we may assume by Theorem 11.3 that if N accepts, it does so within $c^{1+p(n)}$ steps for some constant c. Given input w of length n, D discovers what N does with input w by repeatedly placing the triple $[I_0, J, m]$ on its tape and calling *reach* with these arguments, where:

1. I_0 is the initial ID of N with input w.

2. J is any accepting ID that uses at most $p(n)$ tape cells; the different J's are enumerated systematically by D, using a scratch tape.

3. $m = \log_2 c^{1+p(n)}$.

We argued above that there will never be more than $\log_2 m$ recursive calls that are active at the same time, i.e., one with third argument m, one with $m/2$, one with $m/4$, and so on, down to 1. Thus, there are no more than $\log_2 m$ stack frames on the stack, and $\log_2 m$ is $O(p(n))$.

Further, the stack frames themselves take $O(p(n))$ space. The reason is that the two ID's each require only $1 + p(n)$ cells to write down, and if we write m

in binary, it requires $= \log_2 c^{1+p(n)}$ cells, which is $O\big(p(n)\big)$. Thus, the entire stack frame, consisting of two ID's and an integer, takes $O\big(p(n)\big)$ space.

Since D can have $O\big(p(n)\big)$ stack frames at most, the total amount of space used is $O\big(p^2(n)\big)$. This amount of space is a polynomial if $p(n)$ is polynomial, so we conclude that L has a DTM that is polynomial-space bounded. $\square$

In summary, we can extend what we know about complexity classes to include the polynomial-space classes. The complete diagram is shown in Fig. 11.5.

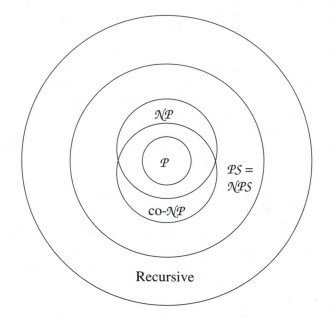

Figure 11.5: Known relationships among classes of languages

11.3 A Problem That Is Complete for $\mathcal{PS}$

In this section, we shall introduce a problem called "quantified boolean formulas" and show that it is complete for $\mathcal{PS}$.

11.3.1 PS-Completeness

We define a problem P to be *complete for $\mathcal{PS}$* (PS-complete) if:

1. P is in $\mathcal{PS}$.

2. All languages L in $\mathcal{PS}$ are polynomial-time reducible to P.

Notice that, although we are thinking about polynomial space, not time, the requirement for PS-completeness is similar to the requirement for NP-completeness: the reduction must be performed in polynomial time. The reason is that we want to know that, should some PS-complete problem turn out to be in $\mathcal{P}$, then $\mathcal{P} = \mathcal{PS}$, and also if some PS-complete problem is in $\mathcal{NP}$, then $\mathcal{NP} = \mathcal{PS}$. If the reduction were only in polynomial space, then the size of the output might be exponential in the size of the input, and therefore we could not draw the conclusions of the following theorem. However, since we focus on polynomial-time reductions, we get the desired relationships.

Theorem 11.6: Suppose P is a PS-complete problem. Then:

a) If P is in $\mathcal{P}$, then $\mathcal{P} = \mathcal{PS}$.

b) If P is in $\mathcal{NP}$, then $\mathcal{NP} = \mathcal{PS}$.

PROOF: Let us prove (a). For any L in $\mathcal{PS}$, we know there is a polynomial-time reduction of L to P. Let this reduction take time $q(n)$. Also, suppose P is in $\mathcal{P}$, and therefore has a polynomial-time algorithm; say this algorithm runs in time $p(n)$.

Given a string w, whose membership in L we wish to test, we can use the reduction to convert it to a string x that is in P if and only if w is in L. Since the reduction takes time $q(|w|)$, the string x cannot be longer than $q(|w|)$. We may test membership of x in P in time $p(|x|)$, which is $p(q(|w|))$, a polynomial in $|w|$. We conclude that there is a polynomial-time algorithm for L.

Therefore, every language L in $\mathcal{PS}$ is in $\mathcal{P}$. Since containment of $\mathcal{P}$ in $\mathcal{PS}$ is obvious, we conclude that if P is in $\mathcal{P}$, then $\mathcal{P} = \mathcal{PS}$. The proof for (b), where P is in $\mathcal{NP}$, is quite similar, and we shall leave it to the reader. $\square$

11.3.2   Quantified Boolean Formulas

We are going to exhibit a problem P that is complete for $\mathcal{PS}$. But first, we need to learn the terms in which this problem, called "quantified boolean formulas" or QBF, is defined.

Roughly, a quantified boolean formula is a boolean expression with the addition of the operators $\forall$ ("for all") and $\exists$ ("there exists"). The expression $(\forall x)(E)$ means that E is true when all occurrences of x in E are replaced by 1 (true), and also true when all occurrences of x are replaced by 0 (false). The expression $(\exists x)(E)$ means that E is true either when all occurrences of x are replaced by 1 or when all occurrences of x are replaced by 0, or both.

To simplify our description, we shall assume that no QBF contains two or more *quantifications* ($\forall$ or $\exists$) of the same variable x. This restriction is not essential, and corresponds roughly to disallowing two different functions in a program from using the same local variable.[3] Formally, the *quantified boolean*

---

[3] We can always rename one of two distinct uses of the same variable name, either in programs or in quantified boolean formulas. For programs, there is no reason to avoid reuse of the same local name, but in QBF's we find it convenient to assume there is no reuse.

formulas are defined as follows:

1. 0 (false) , 1 (true), and any variable are QBF's.

2. If E and F are QBF's then so are (E), $\neg(E)$, $(E) \wedge (F)$, and $(E) \vee (F)$, representing a parenthesized E, the negation of E, the AND of E and F, and the OR of E and F, respectively. Parentheses may be removed if they are redundant, using the usual precedence rules: NOT, then AND, then OR (lowest). We shall also tend to use the "arithmetic" style of representing AND and OR, where AND is represented by juxtaposition (no operator) and OR is represented by $+$. That is, we often use $(E)(F)$ in place of $(E) \wedge (F)$ and use $(E) + (F)$ in place of $(E) \vee (F)$.

3. If F is a QBF that does not include a quantification of the variable x, then $(\forall x)(E)$ and $(\exists x)(E)$ are QBF's. We say that the *scope* of x is the expression E. Intuitively, x is only defined within E, much as the scope of a variable in a program has a scope that is the function in which it is declared. Parentheses around E (but not around the quantification) can be removed if there is no ambiguity. However, to avoid an excess of nested parentheses, we shall write a chain of quantifiers such as

$$(\forall x)\Big((\exists y)\big((\forall z)(E)\big)\Big)$$

with only the one pair of parentheses around E, rather than one pair for each quantifier on the chain, i.e., as $(\forall x)(\exists y)(\forall z)(E)$.

Example 11.7: Here is an example of a QBF:

$$(\forall x)\big((\exists y)(xy) + (\forall z)(\neg x + z)\big) \tag{11.1}$$

Starting with the variables x and y, we connect them with AND and then apply the quantifier $(\exists y)$ to make the subexpression $(\exists y)(xy)$. Similarly, we construct the boolean expression $\neg x + z$ and apply the quantifier $(\forall z)$ to make the subexpression $(\forall z)(\neg x + z)$. Then, we combine these two expressions with an OR; no parentheses are necessary, because $+$ (OR) has lowest precedence. Finally, we apply the $(\forall x)$ quantifier to this expression to produce the QBF stated. $\square$

11.3.3   Evaluating Quantified Boolean Formulas

We have yet to define formally what the meaning of a QBF is. However, if we read $\forall$ as "for all" and $\exists$ as "exists," we can get the intuitive idea. The QBF asserts that for all x (i.e., $x = 0$ or $x = 1$), either there exists y such that both x and y are true, or for all z, $\neg x + z$ is true. This statement happens to be true. To see why, note that if $x = 1$, then we can pick $y = 1$ and make xy true. if $x = 0$, then $\neg x + z$ is true for both values of z.

If a variable x is in the scope of some quantifier of x, then that use of x is said to be *bound*. Otherwise, an occurrence of x is *free*.

Example 11.8 : Each use of a variable in the QBF of Equation (11.1) is bound, because it is in the scope of the quantifier for that variable. For instance, the scope of the variable y, quantified in $(\exists y)(xy)$, is the expression xy. Thus, the occurrence of y there is bound. The use of x in xy is bound to the quantifier $(\forall x)$ whose scope is the entire expression. □

The value of a QBF that has no free variables is either 0 or 1 (i.e., false or true, respectively). We can compute the value of such a QBF by induction on the length n of the expression.

BASIS: If the expression is of length 1, it can only be a constant 0 or 1, because any variable would be free. The value of that expression is itself.

INDUCTION: Suppose we are given an expression with no free variables and length $n > 1$, and we can evaluate any expression of shorter length, as long as that expression has no free variables. There are six possible forms such a QBF can have:

1. The expression is of the form (E). Then E is of length $n - 2$ and can be evaluated to be either 0 or 1. The value of (E) is the same.

2. The expression is of the form $\neg E$. Then E is of length $n - 1$ and can be evaluated. If $E = 1$, then $\neg E = 0$, and vice versa.

3. The expression is of the form EF. Then both E and F are shorter than n, and so can be evaluated. The value of EF is 1 if both E and F have the value 1, and $EF = 0$ if either is 0.

4. The expression is of the form $E + F$. Then both E and F are shorter than n, and so can be evaluated. The value of $E + F$ is 1 if either E or F has the value 1, and $E + F = 0$ if both are 0.

5. If the expression is of the form $(\forall x)(E)$, first replace all occurrences of x in E by 0 to get the expression E_0, and also replace each occurrence of x in E by 1, to get the expression E_1. Observe that E_0 and E_1 both:

   (a) Have no free variables, because any occurrence of a free variable in E_0 or E_1 could not be x, and therefore would be some variable that is also free in E.

   (b) Have length $n - 6$, and thus are shorter than n.

   Evaluate E_0 and E_1. If both have value 1, then $(\forall x)(E)$ has value 1; otherwise it has the value 0. Note how this rule reflects the "for all x" interpretation of $(\forall x)$.

6. If the given expression is $(\exists x)(E)$, then proceed as in (5), constructing E_0 and E_1, and evaluating them. If either E_0 or E_1 has value 1, then $(\exists x)(E)$ has value 1; otherwise it has value 0. Note that this rule reflects the "exists x" interpretation of $(\exists x)$.

Example 11.9: Let us evaluate the QBF of Equation (11.1). It is of the form $(\forall x)(E)$, so we must first evaluate E_0, which is:

$$(\exists y)(0y) + (\forall z)(\neg 0 + z) \tag{11.2}$$

The value of this expression depends on the values of the two expressions connected by the OR: $(\exists y)(0y)$ and $(\forall z)(\neg 0 + z)$; E_0 has value 1 if either of those expressions does. To evaluate $(\exists y)(0y)$, we must substitute $y = 0$ and $y = 1$ in subexpression $0y$, and check that at least one of them has the value 1. However, both $0 \wedge 0$ and $0 \wedge 1$ have the value 0, so $(\exists y)(0y)$ has value 0.[4]

Fortunately, $(\forall z)(\neg 0 + z)$ has value 1, as we can see by substituting both $z = 0$ and $z = 1$. Since $\neg 0 = 1$, the two expressions we must evaluate are $1 \vee 0$ and $1 \vee 1$. Since both have value 1, we know that $(\forall z)(\neg 0 + z)$ has value 1. We now conclude that E_0, which is Equation (11.2), has value 1.

We must also check that E_1, which we get by substituting $x = 1$ in Equation (11.1):

$$(\exists y)(1y) + (\forall z)(\neg 1 + z) \tag{11.3}$$

also has value 1. Expression $(\exists y)(1y)$ has value 1, as we can see by substituting $y = 1$. Thus, E_1, Equation (11.3), has value 1. We conclude that the entire expression, Equation (11.1), has value 1. □

11.3.4 PS-Completeness of the QBF Problem

We can now define the *quantified boolean formula problem*: Given a QBF with no free variables, does it have the value 1? We shall refer to this problem as QBF, while continuing also to use QBF as an abbreviation for "quantified boolean formula." The context should allow us to avoid confusion.

We shall show that the QBF problem is complete for $\mathcal{PS}$. The proof combines ideas from Theorems 10.9 and 11.5. From Theorem 10.9, we use the idea of representing a computation of a TM by logical variables each of which tells whether a certain cell has a certain value at a certain time. However, when we were dealing with polynomial time, as we were in Theorem 10.9, there were only polynomially many variables to concern us. We were thus able to generate, in polynomial time, an expression saying that the TM accepted its input. When we deal with a polynomial space bound, the number of ID's in the computation can be exponential in the input size, so we cannot, in polynomial time, write a boolean expression to say that the computation is correct. Fortunately, we are given a more powerful language to express what we need to say, and the availability of quantifiers lets us write a polynomial-length QBF that says the polynomial-space-bounded TM accepts its input.

---

[4]Notice our use of alternative notations for AND and OR, since we cannot use juxtaposition and + for expressions involving 0's and 1's without making the expressions look either like multidigit numbers or arithmetic addition. We hope the reader can accept both notations as standing for the same logical operators.

From Theorem 11.5 we use the idea of "recursive doubling" to express the idea that one ID can become another in some large number of moves. That is, to say that ID I can become ID J in m moves, we say that there exists some ID K such that I becomes K in $m/2$ moves and K becomes J in another $m/2$ moves. The language of quantified boolean formulas lets us say these things in a polynomial-length expression, even if m is exponential in the length of the input.

Before proceeding to the proof that every language in $\mathcal{PS}$ is polynomial-time reducible to QBF, we need to show that QBF is in $\mathcal{PS}$. Even this part of the PS-completeness proof requires some thought, so we isolate it as a separate theorem.

Theorem 11.10: QBF is in $\mathcal{PS}$.

PROOF: We discussed in Section 11.3.3 the recursive process for evaluating a QBF F. We can implement this algorithm using a stack, which we may store on the tape of a Turing machine, as we did in the proof of Theorem 11.5. Suppose F is of length n. Then we create a record of length $O(n)$ for F that includes F itself and space for a notation about which subexpression of F we are working on. Two examples among the six possible forms of F will make the evaluation process clear.

1. Suppose $F = F_1 + F_2$. Then we do the following:

   (a) Place F_1 in its own record to the right of the record for F.

   (b) Recursively evaluate F_1.

   (c) If the value of F_1 is 1, return the value 1 for F.

   (d) But if the value of F_1 is 0, replace its record by a record for F_2 and recursively evaluate F_2.

   (e) Return as the value of F whatever value F_2 returns.

2. Suppose $F = (\exists x)(E)$. Then do the following:

   (a) Create the expression E_0 by substituting 0 for each occurrence of x, and place E_0 in a record of its own, to the right of the record for F.

   (b) Recursively evaluate E_0.

   (c) If the value of E_0 is 1, then return 1 as the value of F.

   (d) But if the value of E_0 is 0, create E_1 by substituting 1 for x in E.

   (e) Replace the record for E_0 by a record for E_1, and recursively evaluate E_1.

   (f) Return as the value of F whatever value E_1 returns.

We shall leave to you the similar steps that will evaluate F for the cases that F is of the other four possible forms: $F_1 F_2$, $\neg E$, (E), or $(\forall x)(E)$. The basis case, were F is a constant, requires us to return that constant, and no further records are created on the tape.

In any case, we note that to the right of the record for an expression of length m will be a record for an expression of length less than m. Note that even though we often have to evaluate two different subexpressions, we do so one-at-a-time. Thus, in case (1) above, there are never records for both F_1 or any of its subexpressions and F_2 or its subexpressions on the tape at the same time. The same is true of E_0 and E_1 in case (2) above.

Therefore, if we start with an expression of length n, there can never be more than n records on the stack. Also, each record is $O(n)$ in length. Thus, the entire tape never grows longer than $O(n^2)$. We now have a construction for a polynomial-space-bounded TM that accepts QBF; its space bound is quadratic. Note that this algorithm will typically take time that is exponential in n, so it is *not* polynomial-time bounded. □

Now, we turn to the reduction from an arbitrary language L in $\mathcal{PS}$ to the problem QBF. We would like to use propositional variables y_{ijA} as we did in Theorem 10.9 to assert that the jth position in the ith ID is A. However, since there are exponentially many ID's, we could not take an input w of length n and even write down these variables in time that is polynomial in n. Instead, we exploit the availability of quantifiers to make the same set of variables represent many different ID's. The idea appears in the proof below.

Theorem 11.11: The problem QBF is PS-complete.

PROOF: Let L be in $\mathcal{PS}$, accepted by a deterministic TM M that uses $p(n)$ space at most, on input of length n. By Theorem 11.3, we know there is a constant c such that M accepts within $c^{1+p(n)}$ moves if it accepts an input of length n. We shall describe how, in polynomial time, we take an input w of length n and construct from w a QBF E that has no free variables, and has the value 1 if and only if w is in $L(M)$.

In writing E, we shall have need to introduce polynomially many *variable ID's*, which are sets of variables y_{jA} that assert the jth position of the represented ID has symbol A. We allow j to range from 0 to $p(n)$. Symbol A is either a tape symbol or state of M. Thus, the number of propositional variables in a variable ID is polynomial in n. We assume that all the propositional variables in different variable ID's are distinct; that is, no propositional variable belongs to two different variable ID's. As long as there is only a polynomial number of variable ID's, the total number of propositional variables is polynomial.

It is convenient to introduce a notation $(\exists I)$, where I is a variable ID. This quantifier stands for $(\exists x_1)(\exists x_2)\cdots(\exists x_m)$, where $x_1, x_2, \ldots, x_m$ are all the propositional variables in the variable ID I. Likewise, $(\forall I)$ stands for the $\forall$ quantifier applied to all the propositional variables in I.

The QBF we construct for w has the form:

$$(\exists I_0)(\exists I_f)(S \wedge N \wedge F)$$

where:

1. I_0 and I_f are variable ID's representing the initial and accepting ID's, respectively.

2. S is an expression that says "starts right"; i.e., I_0 is truly the initial ID of M with input w.

3. N is an expression that says "moves right"; i.e., M takes I_0 to I_f.

4. F is an expression that says "finishes right"; i.e., I_f is an accepting ID.

Note that, while the entire expression has no free variables, the variables of I_0 will appear as free variables in S, the variables of I_f appear free in F, and both groups of variables appear free in N.

Starts Right

S is the logical AND of literals; each literal is one of the variables of I_0. S has literal y_{jA} if the jth position of the initial ID with input w is A, and has literal $\overline{y_{jA}}$ if not. That is, if $w = a_1 a_2 \cdots a_n$, then $y_{0q_0}, y_{1a_1}, y_{2a_2}, \ldots, y_{na_n}$, and all y_{jB}, for $j = n+1, n+2, \ldots, p(n)$ appear without negation, and all other variables of I_0 are negated. Here, q_0 is assumed to be the initial state of M, and B is its blank.

Finishes Right

In order for I_f to be an accepting ID, it must have an accepting state. Therefore, we write F as the logical OR of those variables y_{jA}, chosen from the propositional variables of I_f, for which A is an accepting state. Position j is arbitrary.

Next Move Is Right

The expression N is constructed recursively in a way that lets us double the number of moves considered by adding only $O(p(n))$ symbols to the expression being constructed, and (more importantly) by spending only $O(p(n))$ time writing the expression. It is useful to have the shorthand $I = J$, where I and J are variable ID's, to stand for the logical AND of expressions that equate each of the corresponding variables of I and J. That is, if I consists of variables y_{jA} and J consists of variables z_{jA}, then $I = J$ is the AND of expressions $\left(y_{jA}z_{jA} + (\overline{y_{jA}})(\overline{z_{jA}})\right)$, where j ranges from 0 to $p(n)$, and A is any tape symbol or state of M.

We now construct expressions $N_i(I, J)$, for $i = 1, 2, 4, 8, \cdots$ to mean that $I \overset{*}{\vdash} J$ by i or fewer moves. In these expressions, only the propositional variables of variable ID's I and J are free; all other propositional variables are bound.

This Construction of N_{2i} Doesn't Work

Our first instinct about constructing N_{2i} from N_i might be to use a straightforward divide-and-conquer approach: if $I \overset{*}{\vdash} J$ in $2i$ or fewer moves, then there must be an ID K such that both $I \overset{*}{\vdash} K$ and $K \overset{*}{\vdash} J$ in i moves or fewer. However, if we write down the formula that expresses this idea, say $N_{2i}(I, J) = (\exists K)\bigl(N_i(I, K) \wedge N_i(K, J)\bigr)$, we wind up doubling the length of the expression as we double i. Since i must be exponential in n in order to express all possible computations of M, we would spend too much time writing down N, and N would be exponential in length.

BASIS: For $i = 1$, $N_i(I, J)$ asserts that either $I = J$, or $I \vdash J$. We just discussed how to express the condition $I = J$ above. For the condition $I \vdash J$, we refer you to the discussion in the "next move is right" portion of the proof of Theorem 10.9, where we deal with exactly the same problem of asserting that one ID follows from the previous one. The expression N_1 is the logical OR of these two expressions. Note that we can write N_1 in $O\bigl(p(n)\bigr)$ time.

INDUCTION: We construct $N_{2i}(I, J)$ from N_i. In the box "This Construction of N_{2i} Doesn't Work" we point out that the direct approach, using two copies of N_i to build N_{2i}, doesn't give us the time and space bounds we need. The correct way to write N_{2i} is to use one copy of N_i in the expression, passing both the arguments (I, K) and (K, J) to the same expression. That is, $N_{2i}(I, J)$ will use one subexpression $N_i(P, Q)$. We write $N_{2i}(I, J)$ to assert that there exists ID K such that for all ID's P and Q, either:

1. $(P, Q) \neq (I, K)$ and $(P, Q) \neq (K, J)$ or

2. $N_i(P, Q)$ is true.

Put equivalently, $N_i(I, K)$ and $N_i(K, J)$ are true, and we don't care about whether $N_i(P, Q)$ is true otherwise. The following is a QBF for $N_{2i}(I, J)$:

$$N_{2i}(I, J) \quad = \quad (\exists K)(\forall P)(\forall Q)\Bigl(N_i(P, Q) \vee$$
$$\bigl(\neg(I = P \wedge K = Q) \wedge \neg(K = P \wedge J = Q))\bigr)\Bigr)$$

Notice that we can write N_{2i} in the time it takes us to write N_i, plus $O\bigl(p(n)\bigr)$ additional work.

   To complete the construction of N, we must construct N_m for the smallest m that is a power of 2 and also at least $c^{1+p(n)}$, the maximum possible number of moves TM M can make before accepting input w of length n. The number of times we must apply the inductive step above is $\log_2(c^{1+p(n)})$, or $O\bigl(p(n)\bigr)$. Since each use of the inductive step takes time $O\bigl(p(n)\bigr)$, we conclude that N can be constructed in time $O\bigl(p^2(n)\bigr)$.

Conclusion of the Proof of Theorem 11.11

We have now shown how to transform input w into a QBF

$$(\exists I_0)(\exists I_f)(S \wedge N \wedge F)$$

in time that is polynomial in $|w|$. We have also argued why each of the expressions S, N, and F are true if and only if their free variables represent ID's I_0 and I_f that are respectively the initial and accepting ID's of a computation of M on input w, and also $I_0 \overset{*}{\vdash} I_f$. That is, this QBF has value 1 if and only if M accepts w. $\square$

11.3.5 Exercises for Section 11.3

Exercise 11.3.1: Complete the proof of Theorem 11.10 by handling the cases:

    a) $F = F_1 F_2$.

    b) $F = (\forall x)(E)$.

    c) $F = \neg(E)$.

    d) $F = (E)$.

*!! Exercise 11.3.2: Show that the following problem is PS-complete. Given regular expression E, is E equivalent to Σ^*, where Σ is the set of symbols that appear in E? *Hint:* Instead of trying to reduce QBF to this problem, it might be easier to show that any language in $\mathcal{PS}$ reduces to it. For each polynomial-space-bounded TM M, show how to take an input w for M and construct in polynomial time a regular expression that generates all strings that are *not* sequences of ID's of M leading to acceptance of w.

!! Exercise 11.3.3: The *Shannon Switching Game* is as follows. We are given a graph G with two terminal nodes s and t. There are two players, which we may call SHORT and CUT. Alternately, with SHORT playing first, each player selects a vertex of G, other than s and t, which then belongs to that player for the rest of the game. SHORT wins by selecting a set of nodes that, with s and t, form a path in G from s to t. CUT wins if all the nodes have been selected, and SHORT has not selected a path from s to t. Show that the following problem is PS-complete: given G, can SHORT win no matter what choices CUT makes?

11.4 Language Classes Based on Randomization

We now turn our attention to two classes of languages that are defined by Turing machines with the capability of using random numbers in their calculation. You are probably familiar with algorithms written in common programming languages that use a random-number generator for some useful purpose. Technically, the function `rand()` or similarly named function that returns to you what appears to be a "random" or unpredictable number in fact executes a specific algorithm that can be simulated, although it is very hard to see a "pattern" in the sequence of numbers it produces. A simple example of such a function (not used in practice) would be a process of taking the previous integer in the sequence, squaring it, and taking the middle bits of the product. Numbers produced by a complex, mechanical process such as this are called *pseudo-random* numbers.

In this section, we shall define a type of Turing machine that models the generation of random numbers and the use of those numbers in algorithms. We then define two classes of languages, $\mathcal{RP}$ and $\mathcal{ZPP}$, that use this randomness and a polynomial time bound in different ways. Interestingly, these classes appear to include little that is not in $\mathcal{P}$, but the differences are important. In particular, we shall see in Section 11.5 how some of the most essential matters regarding computer security are really questions about the relationship of these classes to $\mathcal{P}$ and $\mathcal{NP}$.

11.4.1   Quicksort: an Example of a Randomized Algorithm

You are probably familiar with the sorting algorithm called "Quicksort." The essence of the algorithm is as follows. Given a list of elements $a_1, a_2, \ldots, a_n$ to sort, we pick one of the elements, say a_1, and divide the list into those elements that are a_1 or less and those that are larger than a_1. The selected element is called the *pivot*. If we are careful with how the data is represented, we can separate the list of length n into two lists totaling n in length in time $O(n)$. Moreover, we can then recursively sort the list of low (less than or equal to the pivot) elements and sort the list of high (greater than the pivot) elements independently, and the result will be a sorted list of all n elements.

If we are lucky, the pivot will turn out to be a number in the middle of the sorted list, so the two sublists are each about $n/2$ in length. If we are lucky at each recursive stage, then after about $\log_2 n$ levels of recursion, we shall have lists of length 1, and these lists are already sorted. Thus, the total work will be $O(\log n)$ levels, each with $O(n)$ work required, or $O(n \log n)$ time overall.

However, we may not be lucky. For example, if the list happens to be sorted to begin with, then picking the first element of each list will divide the list with one element in the low sublist and all the rest in the high sublist. If that is the case, Quicksort behaves much like Selection-Sort, and takes time proportional to n^2 to sort n elements.

Thus, good implementations of Quicksort do not take mechanically any particular position on the list as the pivot. Rather, the pivot is chosen randomly from among all the elements on the list. That is, each of the n elements has probability $1/n$ of being chosen as the pivot. While we shall not show this claim here,[5] it turns out that the expected running time of Quicksort with this

---

[5] A proof and analysis of Quicksort's expected running time can be found in D. E. Knuth, *The Art of Computer Programming, Vol. III: Sorting and Searching*, Addison-Wesley, 1973.

randomization included is $O(n \log n)$. However, since by the tiniest of chances each of the pivot choices could take the largest or smallest element, the worst-case running time of Quicksort is still $O(n^2)$. Nevertheless, Quicksort is still the method of choice in many applications (it is used in the UNIX sort command, for example), since its expected running time is really quite good compared with other approaches, even with methods that are $O(n \log n)$ in the worst case.

11.4.2 A Turing-Machine Model Using Randomization

To represent abstractly the ability of a Turing machine to make random choices, much like a program that calls a random-number generator one or more times, we shall use the variant of a multitape TM suggested in Fig. 11.6. The first tape holds the input, as is conventional for a multitape TM. The second tape also begins with nonblanks in its cells. In fact, in principle, its entire tape is covered with 0's and 1's, each chosen randomly and independently with probability 1/2 of a 0 and the same probability of a 1. We shall refer to the second tape as the *random tape*. The third and subsequent tapes, if used, are initially blank and are used as "scratch tapes" by the TM if needed. We call this TM model a *randomized Turing machine*.

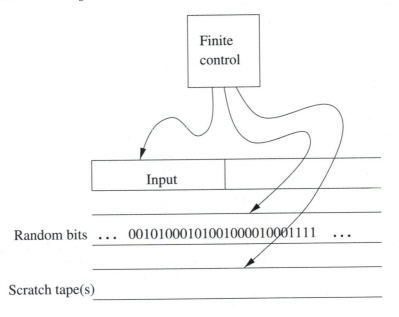

Figure 11.6: A Turing machine with the capability of using randomly "generated" numbers

Since it may not be realistic to imagine that we initialize the randomized TM by covering an infinite tape with random 0's and 1's, an equivalent view of this TM is that the second tape is initially blank. However, when the second head is scanning a blank, an internal "coin flip" occurs, and the randomized

TM immediately writes either a 0 or a 1 on the tape cell scanned and leaves it there forever without change. In that way, there is no work — certainly not infinite work — done prior to starting the randomized TM. Yet the second tape appears to be covered with random 0's and 1's, since those random bits appear wherever the randomized TM's second tape head actually looks.

Example 11.12: We can implement the randomized version of Quicksort on a randomized TM. The important step is the recursive process of taking a sublist, which we assume is stored consecutively on the input tape and delineated by markers at both ends, picking a pivot at random, and dividing the sublist into low and high sub-sublists. The randomized TM does as follows:

1. Suppose the sublist to be divided is of length m. Use about $O(\log m)$ new random bits on the second list to pick a random number between 1 and m; the mth element of the sublist becomes the pivot. Note that we may not be able to choose every integer between 1 and m with absolutely equal probability, since m not be a power of 2. However, if we take, say $\lceil 2 \log_2 m \rceil$ bits from tape 2, think of it as a number in the range 0 to about m^2, take its remainder when divided by m, and add 1, then we shall get all numbers between 1 and m with probability that is close enough to $1/m$ to make Quicksort work properly.

2. Put the pivot on tape 3.

3. Scan the sublist delineated on tape 1, copying those that are no greater than the pivot to tape 4.

4. Again scan the sublist on tape 1, copying those elements greater than the pivot to tape 5.

5. Copy tape 4 and then tape 5 to the space on tape 1 that formerly held the delineated sublist. Place a marker between the two lists.

6. If either or both of the sub-sublists have more than one element, recursively sort them by the same algorithm.

Notice that this implementation of Quicksort takes $O(n \log n)$ time, even though the computing device is a multitape TM, rather than a conventional computer. However, the point of this example is not the running time but rather the use of the random bits on the second tape to cause random behavior of the Turing machine.   □

11.4.3   The Language of a Randomized Turing Machine

We are used to a situation where every Turing machine (or FA or PDA for that matter) accepts some language, even if that language is the empty set or the set of all strings over the input alphabet. When we deal with randomized Turing machines, we need to be more careful about what it means for the TM to accept an input, and it becomes possible that a randomized TM accepts no language at all. The problem is that when we consider what a randomized TM M does in response to an input w, we need to consider M with all possible contents for the random tape. It is entirely possible that M accepts with some random strings and rejects with others; in fact, if the randomized TM is to do anything more efficiently than a deterministic TM, it is essential that different contents of the randomized tape lead to different behaviors.[6]

If we think of a randomized TM as accepting by entering a final state, as for a conventional TM, then each input w to the randomized TM M has some probability of acceptance, which is the fraction of the possible contents of the random tape that lead to acceptance. Since there are an infinite number of possible tape contents, we have to be somewhat careful computing this probability. However, any sequence of moves leading to acceptance looks at only a finite portion of the random tape, so whatever is seen there occurs with a finite probability equal to 2^{-m} if m is the number of cells of the random tape that are have been scanned and influenced at least one move of the TM. An example will illustrate the calculation in a very simple case.

Example 11.13 : Our randomized TM M has the transition function displayed in Fig. 11.7. M uses only an input tape and the random tape. It behaves in a very simple manner, never changing a symbol on either tape, and moving its heads only to the right (direction R) or keeping them stationary (direction S). Although we have not defined a formal notation for the transitions of a randomized TM, the entries in Fig. 11.7 should be understandable; each row corresponds to a state, and each column corresponds to a pair of symbols XY, where X is the symbol scanned on the input tape, and Y is the symbol scanned on the random tape. The entry in the table $qUVDE$ means that the TM enters state q, writes U on the input tape, writes V on the random tape, moves the input head in direction D, and moves the head of the random tape in direction E.

	00	01	10	11	B0	B1
$\rightarrow q_0$	$q_1 00RS$	$q_3 01SR$	$q_2 10RS$	$q_3 11SR$		
q_1	$q_1 00RS$				$q_4 B0SS$	
q_2			$q_2 10RS$		$q_4 B0SS$	
q_3	$q_3 00RR$			$q_3 11RR$	$q_4 B0SS$	$q_4 B1SS$
$*q_4$						

Figure 11.7: The transition function of a randomized Turing machine

---

[6]You should be aware that the randomized TM described in Example 11.12 is not a language-recognizing TM. Rather, it performs a transformation on its input, and the running time of the transformation, although not the outcome, depends on what was on the random tape.

Here is a summary of how M behaves on an input string w of 0's and 1's. In the start state, q_0, M looks at the first random bit, and makes one of two tests regarding w, depending on whether that random bit is 0 or 1.

If the random bit is 0, then M tests whether or not w consists of only one symbol — 0 or 1. In this case, M looks at no more random bits, but keeps its second tape head stationary. If the first bit of w is 0, then M goes to state q_1. In that state, M moves right over 0's, but dies if it sees a 1. If M reaches the first blank on the input tape while in state q_1, it goes to state q_4, the accepting state. Similarly, if the first bit of w is 1, and the first random bit is 0, then M goes to state q_2; in that state it checks if all the other bits of w are 1, and accepts if so.

Now, let us consider what M does if the first random bit is 1. It compares w with the second and subsequent random bits, accepting only if they are the same. Thus, in state q_0, scanning 1 on the second tape, M goes to state q_3. Notice that when doing so, M moves the random-tape head right, so it gets to see a new random bit, while keeping the input-tape head stationary so all of w will be compared with random bits. In state q_3, M matches the two tapes, moving both tape heads right. If it finds a mismatch at some point, it dies and fails to accept, while if it reaches the blank on the input tape, it accepts.

Now, let us compute the probability of acceptance of certain inputs. First, consider a homogeneous input, one that consists of only one symbol, such as 0^i for some $i \geq 1$. With probability $1/2$, the first random bit will be 0, and if so, then the test for homogeneity will succeed, and 0^i is surely accepted. However, also with probability $1/2$ the first random bit is 1. In that case, 0^i will be accepted if and only if random bits 2 through $i+1$ are all 0. That occurs with probability 2^{-i}. Thus, the total probability of acceptance of 0^i is

$$\frac{1}{2} + \frac{1}{2}2^{-i} = \frac{1}{2} + 2^{-(i+1)}$$

Now, consider the case of a heterogeneous input w, i.e., an input that consists of both 0's and 1's, such as 00101. This input is never accepted if the first random bit is 0. If the first random bit is 1, then its probability of acceptance is 2^{-i}, where i is the length of the input. Thus, the total probability of acceptance of a heterogeneous input of length i is $2^{-(i+1)}$. For instance, the probability of acceptance of 00101 is $1/64$. $\square$

Our conclusion is that we can compute a probability of acceptance of any given string by any given randomized TM. Whether or not the string is in the language depends on how "membership" in the language of a randomized TM is defined. We shall give two different definitions of acceptance in the next sections; each leads to a different class of languages.

11.4.4   The Class $\mathcal{RP}$

The essence of our first class of languages, called $\mathcal{RP}$, for "random polynomial," is that to be in $\mathcal{RP}$, a language L must be accepted by a randomized TM M

Nondeterminism and Randomness

There are some superficial similarities between a randomized TM and a nondeterministic TM. We could imagine that the nondeterministic choices of a NTM are governed by a tape with random bits, and every time the NTM has a choice of moves it consults the random tape and picks from among the choices with equal probability. However, if we interpret an NTM that way, then the acceptance rule is rather different from the rule for $\mathcal{RP}$. Instead, an input is rejected if its probability of acceptance is 0, and the input is accepted if its probability of acceptance is any value greater than 0, no matter how small.

---

in the following sense:

1. If w is not in L, then the probability that M accepts w is 0.

2. If w is in L, then the probability that M accepts w is at least $1/2$.

3. There is a polynomial $p(n)$ such that if input w is of length n, then all runs of M, regardless of the contents of the random tape, halt after at most $T(n)$ steps.

Notice that there are two independent issues addressed by the definition of $\mathcal{RP}$. Points (1) and (2) define a randomized Turing machine of a special type, which is sometimes called a *Monte-Carlo* algorithm. That is, regardless of running time, we may say that a randomized TM is "Monte-Carlo" if it either accepts with probability 0 or accepts with probability at least $1/2$, with nothing in between. Point (3) simply addresses the running time, which is independent of whether or not the TM is "Monte-Carlo."

Example 11.14: Consider the randomized TM of Example 11.13. It surely satisfies condition (3), since its running time is $O(n)$ regardless of the contents of the random tape. However, it does not accept any language at all, in the sense required by the definition of $\mathcal{RP}$. The reason is that, while the homogeneous inputs like 000 are accepted with probability at least $1/2$, and thus satisfy point (2), there are other inputs, like 001, that are accepted with a probability that is neither 0 nor at least $1/2$; e.g., 001 is accepted with probability $1/16$. □

Example 11.15: Let us describe, informally, a randomized TM that is both polynomial-time and Monte-Carlo, and therefore accepts a language in $\mathcal{RP}$. The input will be interpreted as a graph, and the question is whether the graph has a triangle, that is, three nodes all pairs of which are connected by edges. Inputs with a triangle are in the language; others are not.

The Monte-Carlo algorithm will repeatedly pick an edge (x, y) at random and pick a node z, other than x and y, at random as well. Each choice is determined by looking at some new random bits from the random tape. For each x, y, and z selected, the TM tests whether the input holds edges (x, z) and (y, z), and if so it declares that the input graph has a triangle.

A total of k choices of an edge and a node are made; the TM accepts if any one of them proves to be a triangle, and if not, it gives up and does not accept. If the graph has no triangle, then it is not possible that one of the k choices will prove to be a triangle, so condition (1) in the definition of $\mathcal{RP}$ is met: if the input is not in the language, the probability of acceptance is 0.

Suppose the graph has n nodes and e edges. If the graph has at least one triangle, then the probability that its three nodes will be selected on any one experiment is $(\frac{3}{e})(\frac{1}{n-2})$. That is, three of the e edges are in the triangle, and if any of these three are picked, then the probability is $1/(n-2)$ that the third node will also be selected. That probability is small, but we repeat the experiment k times. The probability that none of the k experiments will yield the triangle is:

$$ 1 - \left(1 - \frac{3}{e(n-2)}\right)^k \qquad (11.4) $$

There is a commonly used approximation that says for small x, $(1-x)^k$ is approximately e^{-kx}, where $e = 2.718\cdots$ is the base of the natural logarithms. Thus, if we pick k such that $kx = 1$, for example, e^{-kx} will be significantly less than $1/2$ and $1 - e^{-kx}$ will be significantly greater than $1/2$, about 0.63, to be more precise. Thus, we can pick $k = e(n-2)/3$ to be sure that the probability of acceptance of a graph with a triangle, as given by Equation 11.4, is at least $1/2$. Thus, the algorithm described is Monte-Carlo.

Now, we must consider the running time of the TM. Both e and n are no greater than the input length, and k was chosen to be no more than the square of the length, since it is proportional to the product of e and n. Each experiment, since it scans the input at most four times (to pick the random edge and node, and then to check the presence of two more edges), is linear in the input length. Thus, the TM halts after an amount of time that is at most cubic in the input length; i.e., the TM has a polynomial running time and therefore satisfies the third and final condition for a language to be in $\mathcal{RP}$.

We conclude that the language of graphs with a triangle is in the class $\mathcal{RP}$. Note that this language is also in $\mathcal{P}$, since one could do a systematic search of all possibilities for triangles. However, as we mentioned at the beginning of Section 11.4, it is actually hard to find examples that appear to be in $\mathcal{RP} - \mathcal{P}$.
□

11.4.5   Recognizing Languages in $\mathcal{RP}$

Suppose now that we have a polynomial-time, Monte-Carlo Turing machine M to recognize a language L. We are given a string w, and we want to know if

w is in L. If we run M on L, using coin-flips or some other random-number-generating device to simulate the creation of random bits, then we know:

1. If w is not in L, then our run will surely not lead to acceptance of w.

2. If w is in L, there is at least a 50% chance that w will be accepted.

However, if we simply take the outcome of this run to be definitive, we shall sometimes reject w when we should have accepted (a *false negative* result), although we shall never accept when we should not (a *false positive* result). Thus, we must distinguish between the randomized TM itself and the algorithm that we use to decide whether or not w is in L. We can never avoid false negatives altogether, although by repeating the test many times, we can reduce the probability of a false negative to be as small as we like.

For instance, if we want a probability of false negative of one in a billion, we may run the test thirty times. If w is in L, then the chance that all thirty tests will fail to lead to acceptance is no greater than 2^{-30}, which is less than 10^{-9}, or one in a billion. In general, if we want a probability of false negatives less than $c > 0$, we must run the test $\log_2(1/c)$ times. Since this number is a constant if c is, and since one run of the randomized TM M takes polynomial time because L is assumed to be in $\mathcal{RP}$, we know that the repeated test also takes a polynomial amount of time. The implication of these considerations is stated as a theorem, below.

Theorem 11.16: If L is in $\mathcal{RP}$, then for any constant $c > 0$, no matter how small, there is a polynomial-time randomized algorithm that renders a decision whether its given input w is in L, makes no false-positive errors, and makes false-negative errors with probability no greater than c. $\square$

11.4.6   The Class $\mathcal{ZPP}$

Our second class of languages involving randomization is called *zero-error, probabilistic, polynomial*, or $\mathcal{ZPP}$. The class is based on a randomized TM that always halts, and has an expected time to halt that is some polynomial in the length of the input. This TM accepts its input if it enters and accepting state (and therefore halts at that time), and it rejects its input if it halts without accepting. Thus, the definition of class $\mathcal{ZPP}$ is almost the same as the definition of $\mathcal{P}$, except that $\mathcal{ZPP}$ allows the behavior of the TM to involve randomness, and the expected running time, rather than the worst-case running time is measured.

A TM that always gives the correct answer, but whose running time varies depending on the values of some random bits, is sometimes called a *Las-Vegas* Turing machine or Las-Vegas algorithm. We may thus think of $\mathcal{ZPP}$ as the languages accepted by Las-Vegas Turing machines with a polynomial expected running time.

Is Fraction 1/2 Special in the Definition of $\mathcal{RP}$?

While we defined $\mathcal{RP}$ to require that the probability of accepting a string w in L should be at least 1/2, we could have defined $\mathcal{RP}$ with any constant that lies properly between 0 and 1 in place of 1/2. Theorem 11.16 says that we could, by repeating the experiment made by M the appropriate number of times, make the probability of acceptance as high as we like, up to but not including 1. Further, the same technique for decreasing the probability of nonacceptance for a string in L that we used in Section 11.4.5 will allow us to take a randomized TM with any probability greater than 0 of accepting w in L and boosting that probability to 1/2 by repeating the experiment some constant number of times.

We shall continue to require 1/2 as the probability of acceptance in the definition of $\mathcal{RP}$, but we should be aware that any nonzero probability is sufficient to use in the definition of the class $\mathcal{RP}$. On the other hand, changing the constant from 1/2 will change the language defined by a particular randomized TM. For instance, we observed in Example 11.14 how lowering the required probability to 1/16 would cause string 001 to be in the language of the randomized TM discussed there.

11.4.7 Relationship Between $\mathcal{RP}$ and $\mathcal{ZPP}$

There is a simple relationship between the two randomized classes we have defined. To state this theorem, we first need to look at the complements of the classes. It should be clear that if L is in $\mathcal{ZPP}$, then so is $\overline{L}$. The reason is that, if L is accepted by a polynomial-expected-time Las-Vegas TM M, then $\overline{L}$ is accepted by a modification of M in which we turn acceptance by M into halting without acceptance, and if M halts without accepting, we instead go to an accepting state and halt.

However, it is not obvious that $\mathcal{RP}$ is closed under complementation, because the definition of Monte-Carlo Turing machines treats acceptance and rejection asymmetrically. Thus, let us define the class co-$\mathcal{RP}$ to be the set of languages L such that $\overline{L}$ is in $\mathcal{RP}$; i.e., co-$\mathcal{RP}$ is the complements of the languages in $\mathcal{RP}$.

Theorem 11.17: $\mathcal{ZPP} = \mathcal{RP} \cap$ co-$\mathcal{RP}$.

PROOF: We first show $\mathcal{RP} \cap$ co-$\mathcal{RP} \subseteq \mathcal{ZPP}$. Suppose L is in $\mathcal{RP} \cap$ co-$\mathcal{RP}$. That is, both L and $\overline{L}$ have Monte-Carlo TM's, each with a polynomial running time. Assume that $p(n)$ is a large enough polynomial to bound the running times of both machines. We design a Las-Vegas TM M for L as follows.

1. Run the Monte-Carlo TM for L; if it accepts, then M accepts and halts.

2. If not, run the Monte-Carlo TM for $\overline{L}$. If that TM accepts, then M halts without accepting. Otherwise, M returns to step (1).

Clearly, M only accepts an input w if w is in L, and only rejects w if w is not in L. The expected running time of one round (an execution of steps 1 and 2) is $2p(n)$. Moreover, the probability that any one round will resolve the issue is at least $1/2$. If w is in L, then step (1) has a 50% chance of leading to acceptance by M, and if w is not in L, then step (2) has a 50% chance of leading to rejection by M. Thus, the expected running time of M is no more than

$$2p(n) + \frac{1}{2}2p(n) + \frac{1}{4}2p(n) + \frac{1}{8}2p(n) + \cdots = 4p(n)$$

Now, let us consider the converse: assume L is in $\mathcal{ZPP}$ and show L is in both $\mathcal{RP}$ and co-$\mathcal{RP}$. We know L is accepted by a Las-Vegas TM M_1 with an expected running time that is some polynomial $p(n)$. We construct a Monte-Carlo TM M_2 for L as follows. M_2 simulates M_1 for $2p(n)$ steps. If M_1 accepts during this time, so does M_2; otherwise M_2 rejects.

Suppose that input w of length n is not in L. Then M_1 will surely not accept w, and therefore neither will M_2. Now, suppose w is in L. M_1 will surely accept w eventually, but it might or might not accept within $2p(n)$ steps.

However, we claim that the probability M_1 accepts w within $2p(n)$ steps is at least $1/2$. Suppose the probability of acceptance of w by M_1 within time $2p(n)$ were constant $c < 1/2$. Then the expected running time of M_1 on input w is at least $(1-c)2p(n)$, since $1-c$ is the probability that M_1 will take *more* than $2p(n)$ time. However, if $c < 1/2$, then $2(1-c) > 1$, and the expected running time of M_1 on w is greater than $p(n)$. We have contradicted the assumption that M_1 has expected running time at most $p(n)$ and conclude therefore that the probability M_2 accepts is at least $1/2$. Thus, M_2 is a polynomial-time-bounded Monte-Carlo TM, proving that L is in $\mathcal{RP}$.

For the proof that L is also in co-$\mathcal{RP}$, we use essentially the same construction, but we complement the outcome of M_2. That is, to accept $\overline{L}$, we have M_2 accept when M_1 rejects within time $2p(n)$, while M_2 rejects otherwise. Now, M_2 is a polynomial-time-bounded Monte-Carlo TM for $\overline{L}$. $\square$

11.4.8 Relationships to the Classes $\mathcal{P}$ and $\mathcal{NP}$

Theorem 11.17 tells us that $\mathcal{ZPP} \subseteq \mathcal{RP}$. We can place these classes between $\mathcal{P}$ and $\mathcal{NP}$ by the following simple theorems.

Theorem 11.18: $\mathcal{P} \subseteq \mathcal{ZPP}$.

PROOF: Any deterministic, polynomial-time bounded TM is also a Las-Vegas, polynomial-time bounded TM, that happens not to use its ability to make random choices. $\square$

Theorem 11.19: $\mathcal{RP} \subseteq \mathcal{NP}$.

PROOF: Suppose we are given a polynomial-time-bounded Monte-Carlo TM M_1 for a language L. We can construct a nondeterministic TM M_2 for L with the same time bound. Whenever M_1 examines a random bit for the first time, M_2 chooses, nondeterministically, both possible values for that bit, and writes it on a tape of its own that simulates the random tape of M_1. M_2 accepts whenever M_1 accepts, and does not accept otherwise.

Suppose w is in L. Then since M_1 has at least a 50% probability of accepting w, there must be some sequence of bits on its random tape that leads to acceptance of w. M_2 will choose that sequence of bits, among others, and therefore also accepts when that choice is made. Thus, w is in $L(M_2)$. However, if w is not in L, then no sequence of random bits will make M_1 accept, and therefore no sequence of choices makes M_2 accept. Thus, w is not in $L(M_2)$. □

Figure 11.8 shows the relationship between the classes we have introduced and the other "nearby" classes.

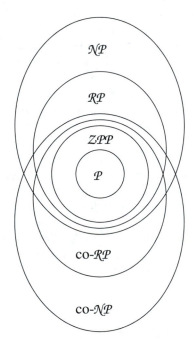

Figure 11.8: Relationship of $\mathcal{ZPP}$ and $\mathcal{RP}$ to other classes

11.5   The Complexity of Primality Testing

In this section, we shall look at a particular problem: testing whether an integer is a prime. We begin with a motivating discussion concerning the way primes and primality testing are essential ingredients in computer-security systems. We then show that the primes are in both $\mathcal{NP}$ and co-$\mathcal{NP}$. Finally, we discuss a randomized algorithm that shows the primes are in $\mathcal{RP}$ as well.

11.5.1   The Importance of Testing Primality

An integer p is *prime* if the only integers that divide p evenly are 1 and p itself. If an integer is not a prime, it is said to be *composite*. Every composite number can be written as a product of primes in a unique way, except for the order of the factors.

Example 11.20: The first few primes are 2, 3, 5, 7, 11, 13, and 17. The integer 504 is composite, and its prime factorization is $2^3 \times 3^2 \times 7$. $\square$

There are a number of techniques that enhance computer security, for which the most common methods in use today rely on the assumption that it is hard to factor numbers, that is, given a composite number, to find its prime factors. In particular, these schemes, based on what are called RSA codes (for R. Rivest, A. Shamir, and L. Adelman, the inventors of the technique), use integers of, say, 128 bits that are the product of two primes, each of about 64 bits. Here are two scenarios in which primes play an important part.

Public-Key Cryptography

You want to buy a book from an on-line bookseller. The seller asks for your credit-card number, but it is too risky to type the number into a form and have the form transmitted over phone lines or the Internet. The reason is that someone could be snooping on your line, or otherwise intercept packets as they travel over the Internet.

To avoid a snooper being able to read your card number, the seller sends your browser a key k, perhaps the 128-bit product of two primes that the seller's computer has generated just for this purpose. Your browser uses a function $y = f_k(x)$ that takes both the key k and the data x that you need to encrypt. The function f, which is part of the RSA scheme, may be generally known, including to potential snoopers, but it is believed that without knowing the factorization of k, the inverse function f_k^{-1} such that $x = f_k^{-1}(y)$ cannot be computed in time that is less than exponential in the length of k.

Thus, even if a snooper sees y and knows how f works, without first figuring out what k is and then factoring it, the snooper cannot recover x, which is in this case your credit-card number. On the other hand, the on-line seller, knowing the factorization of key k because they generated it in the first place, can easily apply f_k^{-1} and recover x from y.

Public-Key Signatures

The original scenario for which RSA codes were developed is the following. You would like to be able to "sign" email so that people could easily determine that the email was from you, and yet no one could "forge" your name to an email. For instance, you might wish to sign the message $x =$ "I promise to pay Sally Lee \$10," but you don't want Sally to be able to create the signed message herself, or for a third party to create such a signed message without your knowledge.

To support these aims, you pick a key k, whose prime factors only you know. You publish k widely, say on your Web site, so anyone can apply the function f_k to any message. If you want to sign the message x above and send it to Sally, you compute $y = f_k^{-1}(x)$ and send y to Sally instead. Sally can get f_k, your *public key*, from your Web site, and with it compute $x = f_k(y)$. Thus, she knows that you have indeed promised to pay \$10.

If you deny having sent the message y, Sally can argue before a judge that only you know the function f_k^{-1}, and it would be "impossible" for either her or any third party to have discovered that function. Thus, only you could have created y. This system relies on the likely-but-unproven assumption that it is too hard to factor numbers that are the product of two large primes.

Requirements Regarding Complexity of Primality Testing

Both scenarios above are believed to work and to be secure, in the sense that it really does take exponential time to factor the product of two large primes. The complexity theory we have studied here and in Chapter 10 enter into the study of security and cryptography in two ways:

1. The construction of public keys requires that we be able to find large primes quickly. It is a basic fact of number theory that the probability of an n-bit number being a prime is on the order of $1/n$. Thus, if we had a polynomial-time (in n, not in the value of the prime itself) way to test whether an n-bit number was prime, we could pick numbers at random, test them, and stop when we found one to be prime. That would give us a polynomial-time Las-Vegas algorithm for discovering primes, since the expected number of numbers we have to test before meeting a prime of n bits is about n. For instance, if we want 64-bit primes, we would have to test about 64 integers on the average, although by bad luck we could have to try indefinitely more than that. Unfortunately, there does not appear to be a guaranteed, polynomial-time test for primes, although there is a Monte-Carlo Algorithm that is polynomial-time, as we shall see in Section 11.5.4.

2. The security of RSA-based cryptography depends on there being no polynomial (in the number of bits of the key) way to factor in general, in particular no way to factor a number known to be the product of exactly two large primes. We would be very happy if we could show that the set of primes is an NP-complete language, or even that the set of composite numbers was NP-complete. For then, a polynomial factoring algorithm would prove $\mathcal{P} = \mathcal{NP}$, since it would yield polynomial-time

tests for both these languages. Alas, we shall see in Section 11.5.5 that both the primes and the composite numbers are in $\mathcal{NP}$. Since they are complements of each other, should either be NP-complete, it would follow that $\mathcal{NP} = \text{co-}\mathcal{NP}$, which we doubt is the case. Further, the fact that the set of primes is in $\mathcal{RP}$ means that if we could show the primes to be NP-complete then we could conclude $\mathcal{RP} = \mathcal{NP}$, another unlikely situation.

11.5.2   Introduction to Modular Arithmetic

Before looking at algorithms for recognizing the set of primes, we shall introduce some basic concepts regarding *modular arithmetic*, that is, the usual arithmetic operations executed modulo some integer, often a prime. Let p be any integer. The *integers modulo p* are $0, 1, \ldots, p-1$.

We can define addition and multiplication modulo p to apply only to this set of p integers by performing the ordinary calculation and throwing away the remainder when the result is divided by p. Addition is quite straightforward, since the sum is either less than p, in which case we have nothing additional to do, or it is between p and $2p-2$, in which case we subtract p to get an integer in the range $0, 1, \ldots, p-1$. Modular addition obeys the usual algebraic laws; it is commutative, associative, and has 0 as the identity. Subtraction is still the inverse of addition, and we can compute the modular difference $x - y$ by subtracting as usual, and adding p if the result is below 0. The negation of x, which is $-x$, is the same as $0 - x$, just as in ordinary arithmetic. Thus, $-0 = 0$, and if $x \neq 0$, then $-x$ is the same as $p - x$.

Example 11.21 : Suppose $p = 13$. Then $3 + 5 = 8$, and $7 + 10 = 4$. To see the latter, note that in ordinary arithmetic, $7 + 10 = 17$, which is not less than 13. We therefore subtract 13 to get the proper result, 4. The value of -5 modulo 13 is $13 - 5$, or 8. The difference $11 - 4$ modulo 13 is 7, while the difference $4 - 11$ is 6. To see the latter, in ordinary arithmetic, $4 - 11 = -7$, so we must add 13 to get 6.   □

Multiplication modulo p is performed by multiplying as ordinary numbers, and then taking the remainder of the result divided by p. Multiplication also satisfies the usual algebraic laws; it is commutative and associative, 1 is the identity, 0 is the annihilator, and multiplication distributes over addition. However, division by nonzero values is trickier, and even the existence of inverses for integers modulo p depends on whether or not p is a prime. In general, if x is one of the integers modulo p, that is, $0 \leq x < p$, then x^{-1}, or $1/x$ is that number y, if it exists, such that $xy = 1$ modulo p.

Example 11.22 : In Fig. 11.9 we see the multiplication table for the nonzero integers modulo the prime 7. The entry in row i and column j is the product ij modulo 7. Notice that each of the nonzero integers has an inverse; 2 and 4 are each other's inverses, so are 3 and 5, while 1 and 6 are their own inverses. That

1	2	3	4	5	6
2	4	6	1	3	5
3	6	2	5	1	4
4	1	5	2	6	3
5	3	1	6	4	2
6	5	4	3	2	1

Figure 11.9: Multiplication modulo 7

is, 2×4, 3×5, 1×1, and 6×6 are all 1. Thus, we can divide by any nonzero number x/y by computing y^{-1} and then multiplying $x \times y^{-1}$. For instance, $3/4 = 3 \times 4^{-1} = 3 \times 2 = 6$.

1	2	3	4	5
2	4	0	2	4
3	0	3	0	3
4	2	0	4	2
5	4	3	2	1

Figure 11.10: Multiplication modulo 6

Compare this situation with the multiplication table modulo 6. First, we observe that only 1 and 5 even *have* inverses; they are each their own inverse. Other numbers have no inverse. In addition, there are numbers that are not 0, but whose product is 0, such as 2 and 3. That situation never occurs for ordinary integer arithmetic, and it never happens when arithmetic is modulo a prime. □

There is another distinction between multiplication modulo a prime and modulo a composite number that turns out to be quite important for primality tests. The *degree* of a number a modulo p is the smallest positive power of a that is equal to 1. Some useful facts, which we shall not prove here are:

- If p is a prime, then $a^{p-1} = 1$ modulo p. This statement is called *Fermat's theorem*.[7]

- The degree of a modulo a prime p is always a divisor of $p - 1$.

- If p is a prime, there is always some a that has degree $p - 1$ modulo p.

---

[7]Do not confuse Fermat's theorem with "Fermat's last theorem," which asserts the nonexistence of integer solutions to $x^n + y^n = z^n$ for $n \geq 3$.

Example 11.23: Consider again the multiplication table modulo 7 in Fig. 11.9. The degree of 2 is 3, since $2^2 = 4$, and $2^3 = 1$. The degree of 3 is 6, since $3^2 = 2$, $3^3 = 6$, $3^4 = 4$, $3^5 = 5$, and $3^6 = 1$. By similar calculations, we find that 4 has degree 3, 5 has degree 6, 6 has degree 2, and 1 has degree 1. □

11.5.3 The Complexity of Modular-Arithmetic Computations

Before proceeding to the applications of modular arithmetic to primality testing, we must establish some basic facts about the running time of the essential operations. Suppose we wish to compute modulo some prime p, and the binary representation of p is n bits long; i.e., p itself is around 2^n. As always, the running time of a computation is stated in terms of n, the input length, rather than p, the "value" of the input. For instance, counting up to p takes time $O(2^n)$, so any computation that involves p steps, will *not* be polynomial-time, as a function of n.

However, we can surely add two numbers modulo p in $O(n)$ time on a typical computer or multitape TM. Recall that we simply add the binary numbers, and if the result is p or greater, then subtract p. Likewise, we can multiply two numbers in $O(n^2)$ time, either on a computer or a Turing machine. After multiplying the numbers in the ordinary way, and getting a result of at most $2n$ bits, we divide by p and take the remainder.

Raising a number x to an exponent is trickier, since that exponent may itself be exponential in n. As we shall see, an important step is raising x to the power $p - 1$. Since $p - 1$ is around 2^n, if we were to multiply x by itself $p - 2$ times, we would need $O(2^n)$ multiplications, and even though each multiplication involved only n-bit numbers and could be carried out in $O(n^2)$ time, the total time would be $O(n^2 2^n)$, which is not polynomial in n.

Fortunately, there is a "recursive-doubling" trick that lets us compute x^{p-1} (or any other power of x up to p) in time that is polynomial in n:

1. Compute the at most n exponents $x, x^2, x^4, x^8, \ldots$, until the exponent exceeds $p - 1$. Each value is an n-bit number that is computed in $O(n^2)$ time by squaring the previous value in the sequence, so the total work is $O(n^3)$.

2. Find the binary representation of $p - 1$, say $p - 1 = a_{n-1} \cdots a_1 a_0$. We can write

$$p - 1 = a_0 + 2a_1 + 4a_2 + \cdots + 2^{n-1}a_{n-1}$$

where each a_j is either 0 or 1. Therefore,

$$x^{p-1} = x^{a_0 + 2a_1 + 4a_2 + \cdots + 2^{n-1}a_{n-1}}$$

which is the product of those values x^{2^j} for which $a_j = 1$. Since we computed each of those x^{2^j}'s in step (1), and each is an n-bit number, we can compute the product of these n or fewer numbers in $O(n^3)$ time.

Thus, the entire computation of x^{p-1} takes $O(n^3)$ time.

11.5.4 Random-Polynomial Primality Testing

We shall now discuss how to use randomized computation to find large prime numbers. More precisely, we shall show that the language of composite numbers is in $\mathcal{RP}$. The method actually used to generate n-bit primes is to pick an n-bit number at random and apply the Monte-Carlo algorithm to recognize composite numbers some large number of times, say 50. If any test says that the number is composite, then we know it is not a prime. If all 50 fail to say that it is composite, there is no more than 2^{-50} probability that it really is composite. Thus, we can fairly safely say that the number is prime and base our secure operation on that fact.

We shall not give the complete algorithm here, but rather discuss an idea that works except in a very small number of cases. Recall Fermat's theorem tells us that if p is a prime, then x^{p-1} modulo p is always 1. It is also a fact that if p is a composite number, and there is any x at all for which x^{p-1} modulo p is not 1, then for at least half the values of x in the range 1 to $p-1$, we shall find $x^{p-1} \neq 1$.

Thus, we shall use as our Monte-Carlo algorithm for the composite numbers:

1. Pick an x at random in the range 1 to $p-1$.

2. Compute x^{p-1} modulo p. Note that if p is an n-bit number, then this calculation takes $O(n^3)$ time by the discussion at the end of Section 11.5.3.

3. If $x^{p-1} \neq 1$ modulo p, accept; x is composite. Otherwise, halt without accepting.

If p is prime, then $x^{p-1} = 1$, so we always halt without accepting; that is one part of the Monte-Carlo requirement, that if the input is not in the language, then we never accept. For almost all the composite numbers, at least half the values of x will have $x^{p-1} \neq 1$, so we have at least 50% chance of acceptance on any one run of this algorithm; that is the other requirement for an algorithm to be Monte-Carlo.

What we have described so far would be a demonstration that the composite numbers are in $\mathcal{RP}$, if it were not for the existence of a small number of composite numbers c that have $x^{c-1} = 1$ modulo c, for the majority of x in the range 1 to $c-1$, in particular for those x that do not share a common prime factor with c. These numbers, called *Carmichael numbers*, require us to do another, more complex test (which we do not describe here) to detect that they are composite. The smallest Carmichael number is 561. That is, one can show $x^{560} = 1$ modulo 561 for all x that are not divisible by 3, 11, or 17, even though $561 = 3 \times 11 \times 17$ is evidently composite. Thus, we shall claim, but without a complete proof, that:

Theorem 11.24: The set of composite numbers is in $\mathcal{RP}$. □

Can We Factor in Random Polynomial Time?

Notice that the algorithm of Section 11.5.4 may tell us that a number is composite, but does not tell us how to factor the composite number. It is believed that there is no way to factor numbers, even using randomness, that takes only polynomial time, or even expected polynomial time. If that assumption were incorrect, then the applications that we discussed in Section 11.5.1 would be insecure and could not be used.

11.5.5 Nondeterministic Primality Tests

Let us now take up another interesting and significant result about testing primality: that the language of primes is in $\mathcal{NP} \cap$ co-$\mathcal{NP}$. Therefore the language of composite numbers, the complement of the primes, is also in $\mathcal{NP} \cap$ co-$\mathcal{NP}$. The significance of this fact is that it is unlikely to be the case that the primes or the composite numbers are NP-complete, for if either were true then we would have the unexpected equality $\mathcal{NP} =$ co-$\mathcal{NP}$.

One part is easy: the composite numbers are obviously in $\mathcal{NP}$, so the primes are in co-$\mathcal{NP}$. We prove that fact first.

Theorem 11.25 : The set of composite numbers is in $\mathcal{NP}$.

PROOF: The nondeterministic, polynomial-time algorithm for the composite numbers is:

1. Given an n-bit number p, guess a factor f of at most n bits. Do not choose $f = 1$ or $f = p$, however. This part is nondeterministic, with all possible values of f being guessed along some sequence of choices. However, the time taken by any sequence of choices is $O(n)$.

2. Divide p by f, and check that the remainder is 0. Accept if so. This part is deterministic and can be carried out in time $O(n^2)$ on a multitape TM.

If p is composite, then it must have at least one factor f other than 1 and p. The NTM, since it guesses all possible numbers of up to n bits, will in some branch guess f. That branch leads to acceptance. Conversely, acceptance by the NTM implies that a factor of p other than 1 or p itself has been found. Thus, the NTM described accepts the language consisting of all and only the composite numbers. $\Box$

Recognizing the primes with a NTM is harder. While we were able to guess a reason (a factor) that a number is not a prime, and then check that our guess is correct, how do we "guess" a reason a number *is* a prime? The nondeterministic, polynomial-time algorithm is based on the fact (asserted but not proved) that if p is a prime, then there is a number x between 1 and $p - 1$

that has degree $p-1$. For instance, we observed in Example 11.23 that for the prime $p=7$, the numbers 3 and 5 both have degree 6.

While we could guess a number x easily, using the nondeterministic capability of a NTM, it is not immediately obvious how one then checks that x has degree $p-1$. The reason is that if we apply the definition of "degree" directly, we need to check that none of $x^2, x^3, \ldots, x^{p-2}$ are 1. To do so requires that we perform $p-3$ multiplications, and that requires time at least 2^n, if p is an n-bit number.

A better strategy is to make use of another fact that we assert but do not prove: the degree of x modulo a prime p is a divisor of $p-1$. Thus, if we knew the prime factors of $p-1$,[8] it would be sufficient to check that $x^{(p-1)/q} \neq 1$ for each prime factor q of $p-1$. If none of these powers of x is equal to 1, then the degree of x must be $p-1$. The number of these tests is $O(n)$, so we can perform them all in a polynomial-time algorithm. Of course we cannot factor $p-1$ into primes easily. However, nondeterministically we can *guess* the prime factors of $p-1$, and:

a) Check that their product is indeed $p-1$.

b) Check that each is a prime, using the nondeterministic, polynomial-time algorithm that we have been designing, recursively.

The details of the algorithm, and the proof that it is nondeterministic, polynomial-time, are in the proof of the theorem below.

Theorem 11.26 : The set of primes is in $\mathcal{NP}$.

PROOF: Given a number p of n bits, we do the following. First, if n is no more than 2 (i.e., p is 1, 2, or 3), answer the question directly; 2 and 3 are primes, while 1 is not. Otherwise:

1. Guess a list of factors $(q_1, q_2, \ldots, q_k)$, whose binary representations total at most $2n$ bits, and none of which has more than $n-1$ bits. It is permitted for the same prime to appear several times, since $p-1$ may have a factor that is a prime raised to a power greater than 1; e.g., if $p=13$, then the prime factors of $p-1=12$ are in the list $(2,2,3)$. This part is nondeterministic, but each branch takes $O(n)$ time.

2. Multiply the q's together, and verify that their product is $p-1$. This part takes no more than $O(n^2)$ time and is deterministic.

3. If their product is $p-1$, recursively verify that each is a prime, using the algorithm being described here.

---

[8]Notice that if p is a prime, then $p-1$ is *never* a prime, except in the uninteresting case $p=3$. The reason is that all primes but 2 are odd.

4. If the q's are all prime, guess a value of x and check that $x^{(p-1)/q_j} \neq 1$ for any of the q_j's. This test assures that x has degree $p-1$ modulo p, since if it did not, then its degree would have to divide at least one $(p-1)/q_j$, and we just verified that it did not. Note in justification that any x, raised to any power of its degree, must be 1. The exponentiations can be done by the efficient method described in Section 11.5.3. Thus, there are at most k exponentiations, which is surely no more than n exponentiations, and each one can be performed in $O(n^3)$ time, giving us a total time of $O(n^4)$ for this step.

Lastly, we must verify that this nondeterministic algorithm is polynomial-time. Each of the steps except the recursive step (3) takes time at most $O(n^4)$ along any nondeterministic branch. While this recursion is complicated, we can visualize the recursive calls as a tree suggested by Fig. 11.11. At the root is the prime p of n bits that we want to verify. The children of the root are the q_j's, which are the guessed factors of $p-1$ that we must also verify are primes. Below each q_j are the guessed factors of $q_j - 1$ that we must verify, and so on, until we get down to numbers of at most 2 bits, which are leaves of the tree.

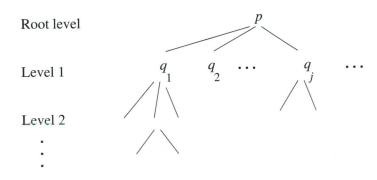

Figure 11.11: The recursive calls made by the algorithm of Theorem 11.26 form a tree of height and width at most n

Since the product of the children of any node is less than the value of the node itself, we see that the product of the values of nodes at any depth from the root is at most p. The work required at a node with value i, exclusive of work done in recursive calls, is at most $a(\log_2 i)^4$ for some constant a; the reason is that we determined this work to be on the order of the fourth power of the number of bits needed to represent that value in binary.

Thus, to get an upper bound on the work required by any one level, we must maximize the sum $\sum_j a(\log_2(i_j))^4$, subject to the constraint that the product $i_1 i_2 \cdots$ is at most p. Because the fourth power is convex, the maximum occurs when all of the value is in one of the i_j's. If $i_1 = p$, and there are no other i_j's, then the sum is $a(\log_2 p)^4$. That is at most an^4, since n is the number of bits in the binary representation of p, and therefore $\log_2 p$ is at most n.

Our conclusion is that the work required at each depth is at most $O(n^4)$. Since there are at most n levels, $O(n^5)$ work suffices in any branch of the nondeterministic test for whether p is prime. □

Now we know that both the primes and their complement are in $\mathcal{NP}$. If either were NP-complete, then by Theorem 11.2 we would have a proof that $\mathcal{NP} = \text{co-}\mathcal{NP}$.

11.5.6 Exercises for Section 11.5

Exercise 11.5.1: Compute the following modulo 13:

  a) $11 + 9$.

* b) $9 - 11$.

  c) 5×8.

* d) $5/8$.

  e) 5^8.

Exercise 11.5.2: We claimed in Section 11.5.4 that for most values of x between 1 and 560, $x^{560} = 1$ modulo 561. Pick some values of x and verify that equation. Be sure to express 560 in binary first, and then compute x^{2^j} modulo 561, for various values of j, to avoid doing 559 multiplications, as we discussed in Section 11.5.3.

Exercise 11.5.3: An integer x between 1 and $p - 1$ is said to be a *quadratic residue* modulo p if there is some integer y between 1 and $p-1$ such that $y^2 = x$.

* a) What are the quadratic residues modulo 7? You may use the table of Fig. 11.9 to help answer the question.

  b) What are the quadratic residues modulo 13?

! c) Show that if p is a prime, then the number of quadratic residues modulo p is $(p-1)/2$; i.e., exactly half the nonzero integers modulo p are quadratic residues. *Hint*: Examine your data from parts (a) and (b). Do you see a pattern explaining why every quadratic residue is the square of two different numbers? Could one integer be the square of three different numbers when p is a prime?

11.6 Summary of Chapter 11

✦ *The Class co-$\mathcal{NP}$*: A language is said to be in co-$\mathcal{NP}$ if its complement is in $\mathcal{NP}$. All languages in $\mathcal{P}$ are surely in co-$\mathcal{NP}$, but it is likely that there are some languages in $\mathcal{NP}$ that are not in co-$\mathcal{NP}$, and vice-versa. In particular, the NP-complete problems do not appear to be in co-$\mathcal{NP}$.

✦ *The Class* $\mathcal{PS}$: A language is said to be in $\mathcal{PS}$ (polynomial space) if it is accepted by a deterministic TM for which there is a polynomial $p(n)$ such that on input of length n the TM never uses more than $p(n)$ cells of its tape.

✦ *The Class* $\mathcal{NPS}$: We can also define acceptance by a nondeterministic TM whose tape-usage is limited by a polynomial function of its input length. The class of these languages is referred to as $\mathcal{NPS}$. However, Savitch's theorem tells us that $\mathcal{PS} = \mathcal{NPS}$. In particular, a NTM with space bound $p(n)$ can be simulated by a DTM using space $p^2(n)$.

✦ *Randomized Algorithms and Turing Machines*: Many algorithms use randomness productively. On a real computer, a random-number generator is used to simulate "coin-flipping." A randomized Turing machine can achieve the same random behavior if it is given an additional tape on which a sequence of random bits is written.

✦ *The Class* $\mathcal{RP}$: A language is accepted in random polynomial time if there is a polynomial-time, randomized Turing machine that has at least 50% chance of accepting its input if that input is in the language. If the input is not in the language, then this TM never accepts. Such a TM or algorithm is called "Monte-Carlo."

✦ *The Class* $\mathcal{ZPP}$: A language is in the class of zero-error, probabilistic polynomial time if it is accepted by a randomized Turing machine that always gives the correct decision regarding membership in the language; this TM must run in expected polynomial time, although the worst case may be greater than any polynomial. Such a TM or algorithm is called "Las Vegas."

✦ *Relationships Among Language Classes*: The class co-$\mathcal{RP}$ is the set of complements of languages in $\mathcal{RP}$. The following containments are known: $\mathcal{P} \subseteq \mathcal{ZPP} \subseteq (\mathcal{RP} \cap \text{co-}\mathcal{RP})$. Also, $\mathcal{RP} \subseteq \mathcal{NP}$ and therefore co-$\mathcal{RP} \subseteq$ co-$\mathcal{NP}$.

✦ *The Primes and* $\mathcal{NP}$: Both the primes and the complement of the language of primes — the composite numbers — are in $\mathcal{NP}$. These facts make it unlikely that the primes or composite numbers are NP-complete. Since there are important cryptographic schemes based on primes, such a proof would have offered strong evidence of their security.

✦ *The Primes and* $\mathcal{RP}$: The composite numbers are in $\mathcal{RP}$. The random-polynomial algorithm for testing compositeness is in common use to allow the generation of large primes, or at least large numbers that have an arbitrarily small chance of being composite.

11.7　References for Chapter 11

Paper [2] initiated the study of classes of languages defined by bounds on the amount of space used by a Turing machine. The first PS-complete problems were given by Karp [4] in his paper that explored the importance of NP-completeness. The PS-completeness of the problem of Exercise 11.3.2 — whether a regular expression is equivalent to Σ^* — is from there.

PS-completeness of quantified boolean formulas is unpublished work of L. J. Stockmeyer. PS-completeness of the Shannon switching game (Exercise 11.3.3) is from [1].

The fact that the primes are in $\mathcal{NP}$ is by Pratt [9]. The presence of the composite numbers in $\mathcal{RP}$ was first shown by Rabin [10]. Interestingly, there was published at about the same time a proof that the primes are actually in $\mathcal{P}$, provided that an unproved, but generally believed, assumption called the extended Riemann hypothesis is true [6].

Several books are available to extend your knowledge of the topics introduced in this chapter. [7] covers randomized algorithms, including the complete algorithms for primality testing. [5] is a source for the algorithms of modular arithmetic. [3] and [8] treat a number of other complexity classes not mentioned here.

1. S. Even and R. E. Tarjan, "A combinatorial problem which is complete for polynomial space," *J. ACM* **23**:4 (1976), pp. 710–719.

2. J. Hartmanis, P. M. Lewis II, and R. E. Stearns, "Hierarchies of memory limited computations," *Proc. Sixth Annual IEEE Symposium on Switching Circuit Theory and Logical Design* (1965), pp. 179–190.

3. J. E. Hopcroft and J. D. Ullman, *Introduction to Automata Theory, Languages, and Computation*, Addison-Wesley, Reading MA, 1979.

4. R. M. Karp, "Reducibility among combinatorial problems," in *Complexity of Computer Computations* (R. E. Miller, ed.), Plenum Press, New York, pp. 85–104.

5. D. E. Knuth, *The Art of Computer Programming, Vol. II: Seminumerical Algorithms*, Addison-Wesley, Reading MA, 1997 (third edition).

6. G. L. Miller, "Riemann's hypothesis and tests for primality," *J. Computer and System Sciences* **13** (1976), pp. 300–317.

7. R. Motwani and P. Raghavan, *Randomized Algorithms*, Cambridge Univ. Press, 1995.

8. C. H. Papadimitriou, *Computational Complexity*, Addison-Wesley, Reading MA, 1994.

9. V. R. Pratt, "Every prime has a succinct certificate," *SIAM J. Computing* **4**:3 (1975), pp. 214–220.

10. M. O. Rabin, "Probabilistic algorithms," in *Algorithms and Complexity: Recent Results and New Directions* (J. F. Traub, ed.), pp. 21–39, Academic Press, New York, 1976.

11. R. L. Rivest, A. Shamir, and L. Adleman, "A method for obtaining digital signatures and public-key cryptosystems," *Communications of the ACM* **21** (1978), pp. 120–126.

12. W. J. Savitch, "Relationships between deterministic and nondeterministic tape complexities," *J. Computer and System Sciences* **4**:2 (1970), pp. 177–192.

Index